JOURNALS OF GENERAL CONVENTIONS

OF THE

PROTESTANT EPISCOPAL CHURCH,

IN THE UNITED STATES, 1785--1835.

PUBLISHED BY AUTHORITY OF GENERAL CONVENTION.

EDITED BY

WILLIAM STEVENS PERRY, D. D.

VOL. I.

1785—1821.

CLAREMONT, N. H.
THE CLAREMONT MANUFACTURING COMPANY.
1874.

THE CLAREMONT MANUF'G CO.,
CLAREMONT, N. H.,
STEREOTYPERS, PRINTERS AND BINDERS.

TABLE OF CONTENTS.

JOINT COMMITTEE

ON THE RE-PUBLICATION OF THE

Early Journals of General Conventions.

THE BISHOPS of New York, Connecticut, New Jersey and Central Pennsylvania. THE REV. WILLIAM COOPER MEAD, D.D., LL.D., THE REV. WILLIAM STEVENS PERRY, D.D., MR. SAMUEL B. RUGGLES, LL.D., MR. HENRY P. BALDWIN, LL.D., MR. ENOCH R. MUDGE.

PREFACE.

The history of the various attempts to secure the re-publication of the early Journals of the General Conventions can best be learned from a report made to the Convention of 1859 by a Committee appointed to consider the practicability of reprinting the Journals from 1785 to 1853.

The Committee appointed by the House to consider the expediency and to inquire into the probable cost of reprinting the Journals of the General Convention from A.D. 1785, to A.D. 1853, inclusive, with an Index to the same, respectfully report:

The first thirty years of our legislation as an independent Church, had not passed, when, owing,—to quote the language of Bishop White,—to the "increasing difficulty of possessing sets" of these documentary annals of our Church history, the reprinting of the Journals of the General Convention from A.D. 1785, to A.D. 1814, inclusive, was imperatively required.

A few years later, and so rapidly had these documents disappeared, but one entire collection of the originals from which this reprint was made could be found, even by the venerable Presiding Bishop of the Church. At the present time, not only are the earlier editions wholly out of print, but the volume published by Bioren in Philadelphia, in accordance with the resolution of the Convention of 1814, and also many Journals of subsequent years, are rarely met with, even by the most indefatigable collector. So rare are these important documents, that it is believed by your Committee, after no little inquiry, that there are less than ten entire sets of the Journals of the General Convention in the possession of Dioceses or individuals in the land.

Efforts for the republication of these Journals, subsequent to the appearance of Bioren's edition in 1817, date back as far as the Convention of 1835. At this time, and apparently in consequence of the inability of the Secretary to procure, as directed, "ten sets of the Journals of the General Convention, from the organization of the Protestant Episcopal Church in the United States," (see p. 25, Journal of 1835,) for preservation among the archives of the Convention, the following resolution was passed by the House of Clerical and Lay Deputies:

"RESOLVED, The House of Bishops concurring, that a Joint Committee be appointed to procure, by some publishing house, the printing at its expense and for its profit, of all the Journals of the General Convention since 1785, together with all the Pastoral Letters which have been set forth by the House of Bishops."—See p. 77, Journal of 1835.

In this resolution the House of Bishops concurred, and appointed on their behalf the Right Rev. Benjamin T. Onderdonk, D.D., Bishop of New York; but owing doubtless to the pressure of business attending the close of an important and exciting Session, the names of the members of the Committee from the lower House were not designated by the Convention, and consequently no action ensued.

At the following Session in 1838, the same resolution was passed by both Houses, with this additional clause:

" . . And that the said Committee be, and hereby are, authorized to append to such edition of the Journals a suitable Index."—See p. 48, Journal of 1838.

This Committee, consisting of Bishop B. T. Onderdonk, and the Rev. Drs. Anthon and Hawks, submitted to the Convention of 1841, the following Report:

"The Joint Committee appointed by the last Convention to procure the printing of all the Journals of the General Convention, respectfully report:

" That they have not accomplished the object of their appointment, but have reason to believe that there may be action on the subject by this Convention, which will greatly facilitate the measure. The Committee therefore respectfully submit for adoption by the Convention the following resolutions:

"RESOLVED, That a Joint Committee, consisting of one Bishop, chosen by the House of Bishops, and —— Members of the House of Clerical and Lay Deputies chosen by the said House, be appointed to procure the publication by some publishing house on its own account, of a complete edition of all the Journals of the General Convention, together with the Canons and other documents which have been published with these Journals, and a complete set of the Canons, including the Constitution of this Church, as the same shall be at the adjournment of this Convention, with a copious Index or Indexes to the whole.

"RESOLVED, That the same Committee be authorized and appointed to superintend the printing of the Journals, etc., and to form the Index or Indexes and to adopt efficient means for securing the entire accuracy of the edition.

"RESOLVED, That the edition of the Journals, etc., thus published, be certified by the Committee as an edition published under the authority of the General Convention.

"RESOLVED, That as soon as arrangements conformably to the above resolutions are made with a printer, the Committee do cause proposals for the edition to be extensively circulated; and, that they be authorized and requested to adopt, in the name of this Convention, suitable measures to secure for the undertaking the general patronage of the Church.—Journal of 1841, pp. 110, 111.

"Respectfully submitted,

BENJ. T. ONDERDONK,
HENRY ANTHON,
COMMITTEE."

These resolutions, covering the whole ground of action proposed by your present Committee, were on motion of Bishop Kemper, seconded by Bishop Meade, adopted by the House of Bishops, and concurred in by the lower House; and the whole matter committed to the Bishop of New York, with the Rev. Drs. Anthon and Mead, and T. L. Ogden, Esq.—Journal of 1841, page 113.

At the session of the Convention in 1844, Bishop B. T. Onderdonk, in behalf of the Committee, reported that the Committee had not been able to accomplish the object of their appointment, and asked to be discharged. In this request both Houses concurred.—Journal of 1844, page 28.

In 1853, the House of Bishops proposed to the House of Clerical and Lay Deputies, "that the Secretaries of the two Houses be requested to prepare an Index to the whole series of Journals of the General Convention from the beginning," adding the suggestion, that this "Index, when approved by the Presiding Bishop," should "be printed in the same form as the Journal."—Journal of 1853, pp. 115, 116.

The House concurred in this resolution, with the provision that the funds in the Treasury of the Convention be sufficient to meet the cost.—Journal of 1853, page 143.

At the last meeting of the Convention, the subject was again agitated. and the Secretary was "appointed a Committee to confer with publishers about issuing a stereotype edition of all the Journals of this Convention, at the expense and for the profit of said publishers."—Journal of 1856, page 129.

This has been found impracticable.

In view, then, of this almost continuous legislation of the Convention on this subject, expressive of the deep sense of need felt throughout the Church in the matter, your Committee are convinced that the work is one that should be done, and done at once. Each unsuccessful attempt—each three years delay—but adds to the difficulty of ever securing the result desired. The Committee have therefore, in the limited time at their disposal, made such inquiries as were in their power, as to the probable cost of this republication, and have also discussed the best manner of effecting the same; and while they are convinced, both from the magnitude of the work, and the want of success of previous Committees, that this reprint would not be undertaken by any responsible publisher solely at his own risk, they feel certain that the end desired may be attained by means of subscriptions from the many individuals, libraries, and legislative bodies of our Church, to whom such documents would be peculiarly valuable and interesting.

In view of these statements, and feeling confident that a suitable publisher can be found to undertake the work upon reasonable encouragement by pledges or subscriptions from members of the Church, the Committee would respectfully offer the following preamble and resolutions:

"WHEREAS, It is the duty of the Church to make generally accessible the annals of its legislation, both for the guidance of its law-makers, and for the information of students of its history:—

"And WHEREAS, The Documentary History of the General Convention is now wholly out of print, and rarely to be met with,

"RESOLVED, That a Committee of six be appointed from this House to secure, either by subscription or otherwise, the republication of the Journals of the General Convention from A.D. 1785, to A.D. 1853, inclusive, provided that no pecuniary obligation be assumed by this Convention.

"RESOLVED, Further, that the said Committee be authorized and empowered to add to this republication suitable Historical Notes and a copious Analytical Index, and that they have full power with reference to the same.

"Respectfully submitted.

EDWARD Y. HIGBEE.
J. M. WILLEY.
WM. STEVENS PERRY.
SAMUEL B. RUGGLES.
SIMEON IDE.
M. A. DE WOLFE HOWE.

These resolutions were adopted and the Rev. Dr. Hawks, then filling the office of Historiographer of the American Church, was added to the Committee, which was continued and charged with the duty of securing the end desired. Efforts to secure the early issue of the reprint followed; and in the year 1861 the first volume of the proposed series appeared, edited by Dr. Hawks and the editor of the present edition. The attention of the public was diverted from this enterprise by the breaking out of the Civil War almost immediately after the issue of the first volume. The failure of the publisher, the apathy of subscribers and the general engrossment in other matters, caused the abandonment of the project, and fears were felt that for many years, at least, the work could not be accomplished.

A report of the Joint Committee to the Convention of 1862, detailing the hindrances to success which had arisen, will be found on pp. 266–270 of the Journal of that year. In 1865, (*vide* Journal pp. 112, 203, 206,) a further report appeared, and the work of the Committee was again commended to the attention and support of the Church. In 1865, (*vide* Journal, pp. 113, 114, 244,) the Secretary of the Joint Committee reported that the volume which had been issued, in 1861, had become out of print, and the Convention, seeking the continuance of the series, committed the conduct and progress of the work to the surviving Editor, in whose hands the plates of the first volume were placed by vote of both Houses.

In 1871, (*vide* Journal pp. 194, 195, 354, 355,) the Committee reported:

"That an effort is now on foot which, if it meets with the support it deserves, will secure the accomplishment of the end desired in the appointment of the Committee. They therefore commend to the attention and patronage of the members of the Church the proposed republication of the Journals of the first half-century of our ecclesiastical legislation, which, with the volume of documents and unpublished MSS. from the archives of the Church, which is to be issued in connection with this reprint, will place within the reach of every inquirer the facts of our history, and the opinions of those whose exertions secured, under God, our independence, and our present organization."

The work now accomplished after the failure of efforts reaching back for nearly forty years, needs but little explanation or comment. The original editions of our Journals, as collected and corrected by the venerable Bishop White, have been constantly consulted and compared with the edition issued by John Bioren in 1817 under the editorship of the same revered prelate. The text thus collated is confidently offered as authoritative, and, it is believed, few errors of the press have escaped the painstaking care which has been bestowed by the proof reader and the editor in securing this end.

Besides a complete index of the three volumes, the third volume will contain a collection of important documents illustrating the formative period of our independent Church history. These papers, selected from a mass of MS. documents in the archives of the General Convention were, in part, gathered together and arranged by the late Francis Lister Hawks, D.D. LL.D., *clarum et venerabile nomen*, and their selection was mainly made by the present editor under the advice, and with the approval of his late instructor and friend. It is with grateful memory of hours of mutual investigation and study of this portion of our Church Annals, that the editor records, in connection with the issue of this reprint, his obligations to one whose name the American Church may not wisely suffer to pass from remembrance. To the Rev. Dr. Hawks the American Church will ever owe the means for the elucidation of her colonial and her constitutional history up to the period of his too early death. And now that he has passed away from earth, it is to his sacred memory that these volumes, undertaken with his encouragement and advice, and attesting on every page his interest and care, are most affectionately and reverently inscribed.

Saint John Baptist's Day, 1874.

TRINITY RECTORY, Geneva, N. Y.

EXPLANATORY PREFACE TO THE EDITION OF 1817.

In the ensuing volume there are contained all the Journals of the General Conventions of "The Protestant Episcopal Church in the United States of America," from the beginning of its organization to the present time—including a space of thirty years.

The increasing difficulty of possessing sets of these documents, induced the House of Bishops, at the General Convention held in the month of April, 1814, with the approbation of the House of Clerical and Lay Deputies, to authorise the present publication by the Subscriber, as may be seen on their Journal of Thursday, May 19, 1814. Reference to former transactions being occasionally necessary, not only to account for existing regulations, but for the explaining of them, it must be perceived that there was great occasion for the measure adopted. It may be considered as expedient, were no other object in view than the preparing of materials which may in future interest the curiosity of the members of this Church.

As the first of the Journals refers to certain proposals, issued by sundry clergymen and laymen, assembled in the city of New York, in the month of October of the preceding year; and as the Journal states those proposals to have been acted on, without a repetition of their contents, the Subscriber finds himself called on to give the following narrative.

In pursuance of preceding correspondence, there assembled some of the Clergy of New York, of New Jersey, and of Pennsylvania, in the city of New Brunswick, New Jersey, in May, 1784; and there being a few respectable lay members of the Church attending on public business in the same city, their presence was desired. The immediate object of the meeting, was the revival of a charitable corporation which had existed before the Revolution, clothed with corporate powers, under the government of each of the said three provinces. The opportunity was improved by the

Clergy from Pennsylvania, of communicating certain measures recently adopted in that State, tending to the organizing of the Church throughout the Union. The result was, the inviting of a more general meeting in the ensuing October, at the city of New York; that being the time and place wherein, according to the charter of the above-mentioned corporation, their next meeting should be held. It was accordingly held for the revival of the corporation. And there appeared Deputies, not only from the said three States, but also from others, with the view of consulting on the existing exigency of the Church. The greater number of these Deputies were not vested with powers for the binding of their constituents; and therefore, although they called themselves a Convention, in the lax sense in which the word had before been used, yet they were not an organized body. They did not consider themselves as such; and their only act was, the issuing of a recommendation to the churches in the several States, to unite under a few articles to be considered as fundamental. These are the articles referred to, but not printed in the first Journal; and therefore are now inserted in a note to this preface.

WM. WHITE,
BISHOP OF THE PROTESTANT EPISCOPAL CHURCH
IN THE COMMONWEALTH OF PENNSYLVANIA.

THE ARTICLES REFERRED TO ARE AS FOLLOW.

I. That there shall be a General Convention of the Episcopal Church in the United States of America.

II. That the Episcopal Church in each State send Deputies to the Convention, consisting of Clergy and Laity.

III. That associated congregations in two or more States may send Deputies jointly.

IV. That the said Church shall maintain the doctrines of the Gospel as now held by the Church of England; and shall adhere to the Liturgy of the said Church, as far as shall be consistent with the American Revolution and the Constitutions of the respective States.

V. That in every State where there shall be a Bishop duly consecrated and settled, he shall be considered as a member of the Convention ex officio.

VI. That the Clergy and Laity assembled in Convention shall deliberate in one body, but shall vote separately. And the concurrence of both shall be necessary to give validity to every measure.

VII. That the first meeting of the Convention shall be at Philadelphia, the Tuesday before the Feast of St. Michael next; to which it is hoped and earnestly desired that the Episcopal churches in the respective States, will send their clerical and lay deputies, duly instructed and authorized to proceed on the necessary business herein proposed for their deliberation.

JOURNAL OF A CONVENTION

OF THE

Protestant Episcopal Church,

IN THE STATES OF

New York, New Jersey, Pennsylvania, Delaware, Maryland, Virginia, and South Carolina,

HELD IN

CHRIST CHURCH, PHILADELPHIA,

FROM

SEPTEMBER 27 TO OCTOBER 7, 1785.

LIST OF THE MEMBERS OF THE CONVENTION.

FROM THE STATE OF NEW YORK.

The Rev. Samuel Provost, A.M., Rector of Trinity Church, New York.
The Hon. James Duane, Esq.

FROM THE STATE OF NEW JERSEY.

The Rev. Abraham Beach, A.M., Rector of Christ Church, New Brunswick.
The Rev. Uzall Ogden, Rector of Christ Church, Sussex.
Patrick Dennis, Esq.

FROM THE STATE OF PENNSYLVANIA.

The Rev. William White, D.D., Rector of Christ Church and St. Peter's, Philadelphia.
The Rev. Samuel Magaw, D.D., Rector of St. Paul's Church, Philadelphia.
The Rev. Robert Blackwell, A.M, Assistant Minister of Christ Church and St. Peter's, Philadelphia.
The Rev. Joseph Hutchins, A.M., Rector of St. James's Church, Lancaster.
The Rev. John Campbell, A.M., Rector of York and Huntingdon.
Richard Peters, Esq.
Jasper Yates, Esq.
Stephen Chambers, Esq.
Samuel Powell, Esq.
Thomas Hartley, Esq.
Edward Shippen, Esq.
John Clark, Esq.
William Atlee, Esq.
Mr. Andrew Doz.
Mr. Edward Duffield.
Mr. Joseph Swift.
Mr. Nicholas Jones.
Mr. John Wood.

FROM THE STATE OF DELAWARE.

The Rev. Charles H. Wharton, Rector of Emanuel Church, New Castle.
The Hon. Thomas Duff, Esq.

James Sykes, Esq.
Mr. John Reece.
Mr. Joseph Tatlow.
Mr. Alexander Reynolds.
Mr. Robert Clay.

FROM THE STATE OF MARYLAND.

The Rev. William Smith, D.D., Principal of Washington College, and Rector of Chester Parish.
The Rev. Samuel Keene, D.D., Rector of Dorchester Parish.
The Rev. William West, D.D., Rector of St. Paul's, Baltimore Town.
The Rev. John Andrews, D.D., late Rector of St. Thomas's, Baltimore, and now Principal of the Academy of the Protestant Episcopal Church, Philadelphia.
The Rev. James Jones Wilmer, Rector of St. George's, Harford County.
Dr. Thomas Cradock.
Mr. Joseph Couden.

FROM THE STATE OF VIRGINIA.

The Rev. David Griffith, Rector of Fairfax Parish.
John Page, Esq.

FROM THE STATE OF SOUTH CAROLINA.

The Rev. Henry Purcell, D.D., Rector of St. Michael's, Charleston
The Hon. Jacob Read, Esq.
The Hon. Charles Pinckney, Esq.

JOURNAL.

TUESDAY, 27th of September, 1785.

Clerical and Lay Deputies from several of the States assembled; and judging it proper to wait the arrival of the Deputies from the other States,

Adjourned until to-morrow at 10 o'clock.

WEDNESDAY, 28th of September, 1785.

The Convention met according to adjournment; and the Rev. Dr. Keene, by desire, read prayers.

The Rev. David Griffith was unanimously chosen Secretary.

On motion, Resolved,—That a President be now chosen by ballot, and that each State have one vote; which being done, and the ballots counted, it appeared that the Rev. William White, D.D., was unanimously chosen.

Ordered, that the Deputies from the several States produce the testimonials of their appointment; which being done, and the testimonials read,

Resolved,—That the testimonials produced from the Church in the several States, viz., in New York, New Jersey, Pennsylvania, Delaware, Maryland, Virginia, and South Carolina are satisfactory.

The Resolutions of a Convention of the Protestant Episcopal Church, held in the city of New York, on the 6th and 7th days of October, 1784, were read.

Ordered, that the same lie on the table.

Adjourned to 6 o'clock this evening.

WEDNESDAY EVENING, 6 o'clock.

The Convention met, according to adjournment.

Ordered, that the proceedings of a former Convention at New York be again read; which being done, and the different articles considered,

Resolved,—That the first, second, and third articles proposed as fundamental by the said Convention, are approved of.

The fourth article being read, it was, on motion, Resolved,—That a Committee be appointed, consisting of one clerical and one lay deputy from the Church in each State, to consider of and report such alterations in the Liturgy, as shall render it consistent with the American Revolution and the Constitutions of the respective States: and such further alterations in the Liturgy as it may be advisable for this Convention to recommend to the consideration of the Church here represented.

Resolved,—That the fifth, sixth, and seventh of the aforesaid articles proposed as fundamental are approved of; the sixth article being first explained and understood, as meaning that the Deputies are to vote according to the States from which they come, and not individually.

Resolved,—That a Committee, to be composed as aforesaid, prepare and report a draft of an Ecclesiastical Constitution for the Protestant Episcopal Church in the United States of America.

A Committee was appointed accordingly: viz., the Rev. Mr. Provost and the Hon. Mr. Duane for New York; the Rev. Mr. Beach and Mr. Dennis for New Jersey; the Rev. Dr. White and Mr. Peters for Pennsylvania; the Rev. Dr. Wharton and Mr. Sykes for Delaware; the Rev. Dr. Smith and Dr. Cradock for Maryland; the Rev. Mr. Griffith and Mr. Page for Virginia; and the Rev. Dr. Purcell and the Hon. Mr. Read for South Carolina.

Resolved,—That the preparing the necessary and proposed alterations in the Liturgy be referred to the same Committee.

The Convention adjourned to 10 o'clock to-morrow morning.

THURSDAY, 29th of September, 1785.

The Convention met, according to adjournment; and the Rev. Dr. Magaw read prayers.

Resolved,—That a person be appointed to assist the Secretary, and to officiate in his stead when he shall be employed in the business of the Committee; and Mr. Clarke was appointed accordingly.

The Rev. Dr. Smith, as Chairman of the Committee for revising and altering the Liturgy, etc., reported that the Committee had made some progress in the business referred to them, but not having completed the same, desired leave to sit again; which being agreed to,

The Convention adjourned to 10 o'clock to-morrow morning.

FRIDAY, 30th of September, 1785.

The Convention met, according to adjournment; and the Rev. Mr. Provost read prayers.

On motion, Resolved,—That the Committee for revising and altering the Liturgy, etc., do also prepare and report a plan for obtaining the consecration of Bishops, together with an address to the Most Reverend the Archbishops and the Right Reverend the Bishops of the Church of England for that purpose.

The Rev. Dr. Smith from the Committee for revising, etc., reported that they had made further progress in the business referred to them, but not having finished the same, desired leave to sit again, which was agreed to.

The Convention adjourned to 9 o'clock to-morrow morning.

SATURDAY, 1st of October, 1785.

The Convention met according to adjournment; and the Rev. Dr. Smith read prayers.

The Rev. Dr. Smith from the Committee for revising, etc., reported that they had prepared a draft of the alterations to be made in the Liturgy; and that they had also prepared a draft of a general Ecclesiastical Constitution, which he was ready to report.

Ordered, that the same be now received; which being done and the Report read,

Ordered, that the said Report lie on the table for the perusal of the members.

The Rev. Dr. Smith, from the same Committee, reported, that they have had under consideration the further alterations to be proposed in the Liturgy, and were ready to report in part.

Ordered, that the Report be now received and read; which being done,

Ordered, that the Report last read lie on the table.

Ordered, that so much of the revised Liturgy as respects the American Revolution and the Constitutions of the States, be again read, and considered by paragraphs; which being done,

Ordered, that the alterations in the Liturgy to be proposed to the Church be again read, and considered by paragraphs: which being done in part,

The Convention adjourned to 6 o'clock this evening.

SATURDAY EVENING, 6 o'clock.

The Convention met, according to adjournment.

Ordered, that the Report from the Committee be resumed, and the remainder of it read and considered by paragraphs; which being done,

The Convention adjourned to 10 o'clock on Monday.

MONDAY, 3d of October, 1785.

The Convention met according to adjournment; and the Rev. Dr. West read prayers.

The Rev. Dr. Smith, from the Committee for revising, etc., reported that they had made further progress in the business referred to them, and were ready to report.

Ordered, that the Report be now received, and that the same be read and considered by paragraphs; which having been done in part,

The Convention adjourned to 6 o'clock this evening.

MONDAY EVENING, 6 o'clock.

The Convention met, according to adjournment.

Ordered, that the Report of the Committee for revising, etc., be resumed, which was accordingly done; and the Convention having made further progress therein,

Adjourned to ten o'clock to-morrow morning.

TUESDAY, 4th of October, 1785.

The Convention met, according to adjournment; and the Rev. Mr. Ogden read prayers.

Ordered, that clerks be employed to transcribe, under direction of the chairman of the Committee for revising, etc., all the alterations proposed, and other matters agreed on by the Convention.

Ordered, that the draft of an Ecclesiastical Constitution be read and considered by paragraphs, which was done; and the Convention having made some progress therein,

Adjourned to 6 o'clock this evening.

TUESDAY EVENING, 6 o'clock.

The Convention met, pursuant to adjournment.

Ordered, that the consideration of the general Ecclesiastical Constitution be resumed, and that the same be read and considered by paragraphs; which being done, and the blanks filled up, was agreed to, and is as follows, viz.:

A GENERAL ECCLESIASTICAL CONSTITUTION OF THE PROTESTANT EPISCOPAL CHURCH IN THE UNITED STATES OF AMERICA.

Whereas, in the course of Divine Providence, the Protestant Episcopal Church in the United States of America is become independent of all foreign authority, civil and ecclesiastical:

And whereas, at a meeting of Clerical and Lay Deputies of the said Church, in sundry of the said States, viz., in the States of Massachusetts, Rhode Island, Connecticut, New York, New Jersey, Pennsylvania, Delaware, and Maryland, held in the city of New York on the 6th and 7th days of October, in the year of our Lord, 1784, it was recommended to this Church in the said States represented as aforesaid, and proposed to this Church in the States not represented, that they should send Deputies to a Convention to be held in the city of Philadelphia, on the Tuesday before the Feast of St. Michael in this present year, in order to unite in a Constitution of ecclesiastical government, agreeably to certain fundamental principles, expressed in the said recommendation and proposal:

And whereas, in consequence of the said recommendation and proposal, Clerical and Lay Deputies have been duly appointed from the said Church in the States of New York, New Jersey, Pennsylvania, Delaware, Maryland, Virginia, and South Carolina:

The said Deputies being now assembled, and taking into consideration the importance of maintaining uniformity in doctrine, discipline and worship in the said Church, do hereby determine, and declare,

I. That there shall be a General Convention of the Protestant Episcopal Church in the United States of America, which shall be held in the city of Philadelphia on the third Tuesday in June, in the year of our Lord 1786, and for ever after once in three years, on the third Tuesday of June, in such place as shall be determined by the Convention; and special meetings may be held at such other times and in such place as shall be hereafter provided for; and this Church, in a majority of the States aforesaid, shall be represented before they proceed to business; except that the representation of this Church from two States shall be sufficient to adjourn; and in all business of the Convention freedom of debate shall be allowed.

II. There shall be a representation of both Clergy and Laity of the Church in each State, which shall consist of one or more Deputies, not exceeding four, of each Order; and in all questions, the said Church in each State shall have one vote; and a majority of suffrages shall be conclusive.

III. In the said Church in every State represented in this Convention, there shall be a Convention consisting of the Clergy and Lay Deputies of the congregation.

IV. "The Book of Common Prayer, and Administration of the Sacraments, and other Rites and Ceremonies of the Church, according to the use of the Church of England," shall be continued to be used by this Church, as the same is altered by this Convention, in a certain instrument of writing passed by their authority, entituled, "Alterations of the Liturgy of the Protestant Episcopal Church in the United States of America, in order to render the same conformable to the American Revolution and the Constitutions of the respective States."

V. In every State where there shall be a Bishop duly consecrated and settled, and who shall have acceded to the articles of this General Ecclesiastical Constitution, he shall be considered as a member of the Convention ex officio.

VI. The Bishop or Bishops in every State shall be chosen agreeably to such rules as shall be fixed by the respective Conventions; and every Bishop of this Church shall confine the exercise of his Episcopal office to his proper jurisdiction, unless requested to ordain or confirm by any church destitute of a Bishop.

VII. A Protestant Episcopal Church in any of the United States not now represented, may at any time hereafter be admitted, on acceding to the articles of this union.

VIII. Every clergyman, whether bishop, or presbyter, or deacon, shall be amenable to the authority of the Convention in the State to which he belongs, so far as relates to suspension or removal from office; and the Convention in each State shall institute rules for their conduct, and an equitable mode of trial.

IX. And whereas it is represented to this Convention to be the desire of the Protestant Episcopal Church in these States, that there may be further alterations of the Liturgy than such as are made necessary by the American Revolution; therefore the "Book of Common Prayer and Administration of the Sacraments and other Rites and Ceremonies of the Church, according to the use of the Church of England," as altered by an instrument of writing passed under the authority of this Convention, entituled "Alterations in the Book of Common Prayer and Administration of the Sacraments and other Rites and Ceremonies of the Church, according to the use of the Church of England, proposed and recommended to the Protestant Episcopal Church in the United States of America," shall be used in this Church when the same shall have been ratified by the

Conventions which have respectively sent Deputies to this General Convention.

X. No person shall be ordained or permitted to officiate as a minister in this Church, until he shall have subscribed the following declaration: "I do believe the Holy Scriptures of the Old and New Testament to be the word of God, and to contain all things necessary to salvation; and I do solemnly engage to conform to the doctrines and worship of the Protestant Episcopal Church, as settled and determined in the Book of Common Prayer, and Administration of the Sacraments, set forth by the General Convention of the Protestant Episcopal Church in these United States."

XI. This General Ecclesiastical Constitution, when ratified by the Church in the different States, shall be considered as fundamental, and shall be unalterable by the Convention of the Church in any State.

The Hon. Mr. Duane, from the Committee for revising, etc., reported that they had, according to order, prepared a plan for obtaining the consecration of Bishops, and a draft of an address to the Most Reverend the Archbishops and the Right Reverend the Bishops of the Church of England, and were ready to report the same.

Ordered that the plan and draft now offered be received; which being done, and the same twice read and considered by paragraphs, was ordered to be transcribed.

The Convention then adjourned to 10 o'clock to-morrow morning.

WEDNESDAY, 5th October, 1785.

The Convention met, according to adjournment; and the Rev. Mr. Provost read prayers.

Ordered, that the transcribed copy of the "Alterations in the Liturgy, to render it consistent with the American Revolution and the Constitutions of the respective States," be read and considered by paragraphs; which being done,

Resolved,—That the Liturgy shall be used in this Church as accommodated to the Revolution, agreeably to the alterations now approved of and ratified by this Convention.*

On motion, Resolved,—That the Fourth of July shall be observed by this Church for ever, as a day of thanksgiving to Almighty God for the inestimable blessings of religious and civil liberty vouchsafed to the United States of America.

On motion, Resolved,—That the first Tuesday in Novem-

* Neither these, nor the other alterations afterwards proposed, are printed in the Journal, as they will appear in the Book of Common Prayer, now in the press.-[Note in original edition.]

ber in every year for ever, shall be observed by this Church as a day of general thanksgiving to Almighty God for the fruits of the earth, and for all the other blessings of his merciful providence.

Ordered, that a Committee be appointed to prepare a Form of Prayer and Thanksgiving for the Fourth of July; and a Committee was accordingly appointed, viz., the Rev. Dr. Smith, the Rev. Dr. Magaw, the Rev. Dr. Wharton, and the Rev. Mr. Campbell.

Ordered, that the alterations in the Liturgy to be proposed to this Church, be read and considered by paragraphs; and the Convention made some progress therein.

The Rev. Dr. Smith, from the Committee to prepare a Form of Prayer and Thanksgiving for the Fourth of July, reported that they had prepared the same.

Ordered, that it be now received and read.

Ordered, that the said Report be read and considered by paragraphs; which being done,

Resolved,—That the said form of prayer be used in this Church, on the fourth of July, for ever.

Then the Convention adjourned to 6 o'clock this evening.

WEDNESDAY EVENING, 6 o'clock.

The Convention met according to adjournment.

Ordered, that the consideration of the proposed alterations in the Liturgy be resumed.

Ordered, that the same be again read and considered by paragraphs; which being done, and the alterations agreed to,

Resolved,—That the said alterations be proposed and recommended to the Protestant Episcopal Church, in the States from which there are deputies to this Convention.

Ordered, that the alterations made in the articles be again read; which being done,

Ordered that the same be read and considered by paragraphs; which being done, and some time spent thereon,

Resolved,—That the Articles, as now altered, be recommended to this Church, to be by them adopted in the next General Convention.

Ordered, that the plan for obtaining Consecration, and the address to the Archbishops and Bishops of the Church of England, be again read; which being done, the same was agreed to, and are as follow:

I. That this Convention address the Archbishops and Bishops of the Church of England, requesting them to confer the Episcopal character on such persons as shall be chosen and recommended to them for that purpose from the Conventions of this Church in the respective States.

II. That it be recommended to the said Conventions that they elect persons for this purpose.

III. That it be further recommended to the different Conventions, at their next respective sessions, to appoint committees, with powers to correspond with the English bishops, for the carrying of these resolutions into effect; and that until such committees shall be appointed, they be requested to direct any communications which they may be pleased to make on this subject, to the committee, consisting of the Rev. Dr. White, President, the Rev. Dr. Smith, the Rev. Mr. Provost, the Hon. James Duane, and Samuel Powell and Richard Peters, Esquires.

IV. That it be further recommended to the different Conventions, that they pay especial attention to the making it appear to their Lordships, that the persons who shall be sent to them for consecration are desired in the character of Bishops, as well by the Laity as by the Clergy of this Church in the said States, respectively; and that they will be received by them in that character on their return.

V. And in order to assure their Lordships of the legality of the present proposed application, that the Deputies now assembled be desired to make a respectful address to the civil rulers of the States in which they respectively reside, to certify that the said application is not contrary to the Constitutions and laws of the same.

VI. And whereas the Bishops of this Church will not be entitled to any of such temporal honors as are due to the Archbishops and Bishops of the parent Church, in quality of Lords of Parliament; and whereas the reputation and usefulness of our Bishops will considerably depend on their taking no higher titles or stile than will be due to their spiritual employments; that it be recommended to this Church, in the States here represented, to provide that their respective Bishops may be called "The Right Rev. A. B., Bishop of the Protestant Episcopal Church in C. D.," and, as Bishop, may have no other title, and may not use any such stile as is usually descriptive of temporal power and precedency.

TO THE MOST REVEREND AND RIGHT REVEREND THE ARCHBISHOPS OF CANTERBURY AND YORK, AND THE BISHOPS OF THE CHURCH OF ENGLAND.

We the Clerical and Lay Deputies of the Protestant Episcopal Church in sundry of the United States of America, think it our duty to address your Lordships on a subject deeply interesting, not only to ourselves and those whom we represent, but, as we conceive, to the common cause of Christianity.

Our forefathers, when they left the land of their nativity, did not leave the bosom of that Church over which your Lordships now preside; but, as well from a veneration for Episcopal government, as from an attachment to the admirable services of our Liturgy, continued in willing connection with their ecclesiastical superiors in England, and were subjected to many local inconveniences, rather than break the unity of the Church to which they belonged.

When it pleased the Supreme Ruler of the universe, that this part of the British empire should be free, sovereign, and independent, it became the most important concern of the members of our Communion to provide for its continuance. And while, in accomplishing of this, they kept in view that wise and liberal part of the system of the Church of England which excludes as well the claiming as the acknowledging of such spiritual subjection as may be inconsistent with the civil duties of her children; it was nevertheless their earnest desire and resolution to retain the venerable form of Episcopal government handed down to them, as they conceive, from the time of the Apostles, and endeared to them by the remembrance of the holy Bishops of the primitive Church, of the blessed Martyrs who reformed the doctrine and worship of the Church of England, and of the many great and pious Prelates who have adorned that Church in every succeeding age. But however general the desire of compleating the Orders of our Ministry, so diffused and unconnected were the members of our Communion over this extensive country, that much time and negociation were necessary for the forming a representative body of the greater number of Episcopalians in these States; and owing to the same causes, it was not until this Convention that sufficient powers could be procured for the addressing your Lordships on this subject.

The petition which we offer to your Venerable Body is,—that from a tender regard to the religious interests of thousands in this rising empire, professing the same religious principles with the Church of England, you will be pleased to confer the Episcopal character on such persons as shall be recommended by this Church in the several States here represented—full satisfaction being given of the sufficiency of the persons recommended, and of its being the intention of the general body of the Episcopalians in the said States respectively, to receive them in the quality of Bishops.

Whether this our request will meet with insurmountable impediments, from the political regulations of the kingdom in which your Lordships fill such distinguished stations, it is not for us to foresee. We have not been ascertained that any such will exist; and are humbly of opinion, that as citizens of these States, interested in their prosperity, and religiously regarding the allegiance which we owe them, it is to an ecclesiastical source only we can apply in the present exigency.

It may be of consequence to observe, that in these States there is a separation between the concerns of policy and those of religion; that, accordingly, our civil rulers cannot officially join in the present application; that, however, we are far from apprehending the opposition or even displeasure of any of those honorable personages; and finally, that in this business we are justified by the Constitutions of the States, which are the foundations and controul of all our laws. On this point we beg leave to refer to the enclosed extracts from the Constitutions of the respective States of which we are citizens, and we flatter ourselves that they must be satisfactory.

Thus, we have stated to your Lordships the nature and the grounds of our application; which we have thought it most respectful and most suitable to the magnitude of the object, to address to your Lordships for your deliberation before any person is sent over to carry them into effect. Whatever may be the event, no time will efface the remembrance of the past services of your Lordships and your predecessors. The Archbishops of Canterbury were not prevented, even by the weighty concerns of their high stations, from attending to the interests of this distant branch of the Church under their care. The Bishops of London were our Diocesans; and the uninterrupted although voluntary submission of our congregations, will remain a perpetual proof of their mild and paternal government. All the Bishops of England, with other distinguished characters, as well ecclesiastical as civil, have concurred in forming and carrying on the benevolent views of the Society for Propagating the Gospel in Foreign Parts: a Society to whom, under God, the prosperity of our Church is in an eminent degree to be ascribed. It is our earnest wish to be permitted to make, through your Lordships, this just acknowledgment to that venerable Society; a tribute of gratitude which we the rather take this opportunity of paying, as while they thought it necessary to withdraw their pecuniary assistance from our Ministers, they have endeared their past favors by a benevolent declaration, that it is far from their thoughts to alienate their affection from their brethren now under another government—with the pious wish, that their former exertions may still continue to bring forth the fruits they aimed at of pure religion and virtue. Our hearts are penetrated with the most lively gratitude by these generous sentiments; the long succession of former benefits passes in review before us; we pray that our Church may be a lasting monument of the usefulness of so worthy a body; and that her sons may never cease to be kindly affectioned to the members of that Church, the Fathers of which have so tenderly watched over her infancy.

For your Lordships in particular, we most sincerely wish and pray, that you may long continue the ornaments of the Church of England, and at last receive the reward of the righteous from the great Shepherd and Bishop of souls.

We are, with all the respect which is due to your exalted and venerable characters and stations,

Your Lordships
Most obedient and
Most humble Servants,
SIGNED BY THE CLERICAL AND LAY DEPUTIES
OF THE CONVENTION.

IN CONVENTION:
Christ Church, Philadelphia.
October 5th, 1785.

Resolved,—That a Committee be appointed to publish the Book of Common Prayer with the alterations, as well as those now ratified in order to render the Liturgy consistent with the American Revolution and the Constitutions of the respective States, as the alterations and new Offices recommended to this Church; and that the book be accompanied with a proper Preface or Address, setting forth the reason and expediency of the alterations; and that the Committee have the liberty to make verbal and grammatical corrections, but in such manner, as that nothing in form or substance be altered.

The Committee appointed were the Rev. Dr. White (President), the Rev. Dr. Smith, and the Rev. Dr. Wharton.

Ordered, that the said Committee be authorised to dispose of the copies of the Common Prayer when printed; and that after defraying all expences incurred therein, they remit the nett profits to the Treasurers of the several Corporations and Societies for the relief of the widows and children of deceased clergymen in the States represented in this Convention, the profits to be equally divided among the said societies and corporations.

Resolved,—That the same Committee be authorised to publish, with the Book of Common Prayer, such of the reading and singing Psalms, and such a Kalendar of proper lessons for the different Sundays and Holy-days throughout the year, as they may think proper.

Resolved,—That the same Committee be authorised to publish the Journal of this Convention.

Ordered, that the Journal and all the proceedings of the Convention be lodged in the hands of the President.

On motion, Resolved,—That the Rev. Dr. Wharton, having preached a Sermon last Sunday, on the Duties of the Ministerial Office, highly satisfactory to this Convention and the whole audience, be requested to publish the same.

On motion, Resolved,—That the Rev. Dr. Smith be requested to prepare and preach a Sermon suited to the solemn occasion of the present Convention on Friday next; and that the Service be then read, as proposed for future use.

On motion, Resolved,—That the thanks of this Convention be given to the President, for his able and diligent discharge of the duties of his office.

On motion, Resolved,—That the thanks of this Convention be given to the Rev. Dr. Smith for his exemplary diligence, and the great assistance he has rendered this Convention as Chairman of the Committee, in perfecting the important business in which they have been engaged.

On motion, Resolved,—That the thanks of this Convention be given to the Rev. Mr. Griffith for his ability and diligence in the discharge of his duty as Secretary.

Then the members present of the Convention signed all the acts and instruments; and afterwards adjourned, to meet on Friday, 10 o'clock, at the Academy of the Protestant Episcopal Church, in order to attend Divine Service and Sermon.

FRIDAY, 7th October, 1785.

The Convention met, according to adjournment, and attended Divine Service in Christ Church; when the Liturgy, as altered, was read by the Rev. Dr. White, and a suitable Sermon was preached by the Rev. Dr. Smith, after which the Convention adjourned, to meet this evening at 7 o'clock, at the Academy of the Protestant Episcopal Church.

FRIDAY EVENING, 7 o'clock.

The Convention met, according to adjournment.

On motion, Resolved,—That the thanks of this Convention be given to the Rev. Dr. Smith for his Sermon, preached this day before them, and that he be requested to publish the same.

Resolved,—That the President be requested to preach at the opening of the next Convention.

The Convention then adjourned.

Signed by order of the Convention:

WILLIAM WHITE, PRESIDENT.

ATTEST: DAVID GRIFFITH, Secretary.

JOURNAL OF A CONVENTION

OF THE

Protestant Episcopal Church,

IN THE STATES OF

New York, New Jersey, Pennsylvania, Delaware, Maryland, Virginia, and South Carolina,

HELD IN

CHRIST CHURCH, PHILADELPHIA,

FROM

JUNE 20 TO JUNE 26, 1786.

LIST OF THE MEMBERS OF THE CONVENTION

FROM THE STATE OF NEW YORK.

The Rev. Samuel Provost.
The Rev. Joshua Bloomer.
The Hon. John Jay.

FROM THE STATE OF NEW JERSEY.

The Rev. Abraham Beach.

The Rev. William Frazer.
The Hon. David Brearley.
James Parker, Esq.
Matthias Halsted, Esq.

FROM THE STATE OF PENNSYLVANIA.

The Rev. William White, D.D.

The Rev. Samuel Magaw, D.D.
The Rev. Robert Blackwell.

The Rev. Joseph Pilmore.
The Hon. Francis Hopkinson.
Plunket Fleeson, Esq.
Samuel Powell, Esq.

FROM THE STATE OF DELAWARE.

The Rev. Chas. H. Wharton, D.D., Rector of Emanuel Church, New Castle.
The Rev. Sydenham Thorne.
Robert Clay, Esq.
Nicholas Ridgeley, Esq.

FROM THE STATE OF MARYLAND.

The Rev. William Smith, D.D.
The Rev. William Smith, of Stepney Parish.

FROM THE STATE OF VIRGINIA.

The Rev. David Griffith.
The Hon. Cyrus Griffin.

FROM THE STATE OF SOUTH CAROLINA.

The Rev. Robert Smith.
Edward Mitchel, Esq.
The Hon. John Parker.

JOURNAL.

TUESDAY, 20th of June, 1786.

Clerical and Lay Deputies from several of the States assembled; and judging it proper to wait for a fuller Convention before they entered on business,

Adjourned to 10 o'clock to-morrow morning.

WEDNESDAY, 21st of June, 1786.

The Convention was opened with Divine Service, read by the Rev. Dr. Smith and the Rev. Mr. Griffith, and a Sermon on the occasion by the Rev. Dr. White.

Ordered, that the members present exhibit the testimonials of their respective appointments; which was done accordingly.

Adjourned to 9 o'clock to-morrow.

THURSDAY, 22d of June, 1786.

The Convention met, and proceeded to the election of a President and Secretary by ballot; when the Rev. David Griffith was duly elected President, and the Hon. Francis Hopkinson, Secretary of this Convention.

Motion made by the Rev. Robert Smith, and seconded:

That the Clergy present produce their Letters of Orders, or declare by whom they were ordained.

Whereupon the previous question was moved by the Rev. Dr. Smith, and seconded by Rev. Dr. White, viz.:

Whether this question shall now be put?—which being carried in the affirmative, the main question was then proposed, and determined in the negative.

On motion made and seconded,

Ordered, that the letter from the Archbishops and Bishops of England, to this Convention, be now read; and it was read accordingly, in the words following:

TO THE CLERICAL AND LAY DEPUTIES OF THE PROTESTANT EPISCOPAL CHURCH IN SUNDRY OF THE UNITED STATES OF AMERICA.

The Archbishop of Canterbury hath received an address, dated in Convention, Christ Church, Philadelphia, October 5, 1785, from the Clerical and Lay Deputies of the Protestant Episcopal Church in sundry of the United States of America, directed to the Archbishops and Bishops of England, and requesting them to confer the Episcopal character on such persons as shall be recommended by the Episcopal Church in the several States by them represented.

This brotherly and Christian address was communicated to the Archbishop of York, and to the Bishops, with as much dispatch as their separate and distant situations would permit, and hath been received and considered by them with that true and affectionate regard which they have always shown towards their Episcopal brethren in America.

We are now enabled to assure you, that nothing is nearer to our hearts than the wish to promote your spiritual welfare, to be instrumental in procuring for you the complete exercise of our holy religion, and the enjoyment of that Ecclesiastical Constitution which we believe to be truly apostolical, and for which you express so unreserved a veneration.

We are therefore happy to be informed, that this pious design is not likely to receive any discountenance from the civil powers under which you live; and we desire you to be persuaded, that we on our parts will use our best endeavors, which we have good reason to hope will be successful, to acquire a legal capacity of complying with the prayer of your address.

With these sentiments, we are disposed to make every allowance which candour can suggest for the difficulties of your situation, but at the same time we cannot help being afraid, that, in the proceedings of your Convention, some alterations may have been adopted or intended, which those difficulties do not seem to justify.

Those alterations are not mentioned in your address: and, as our knowledge of them is no more than what has reached us through private and less certain channels, we hope you will think it just, both to you and to ourselves, if we wait for an explanation.

For while we are anxious to give every proof, not only of our brotherly affection, but of our facility in forwarding your wishes, we cannot but be extremely cautious, lest we should be the instruments of establishing an Ecclesiastical system which will be called a branch of the Church of England, but afterwards may possibly appear to have departed from it essentially, either in doctrine or in discipline.

In the mean time, we heartily commend you to God's holy protection, and are, your affectionate brethren,

T. Cantuar.
W. Ebor.
R. London.
W. Chichester.
J. Rochester.
R. Worcester.
I. Oxford.
I. Exeter.

THO. LINCOLN.
JOHN BANGOR.
I. LITCHFIELD AND COVENTRY.
S. GLOUCESTER.
E. ST. DAVIDS.
CHR. BRISTOL.
C. BATH AND WELLS.
S. ST. ASAPH.
S. SARUM.
J. PETERBOROUGH.
JAMES ELY.

LONDON, February 24, 1786.

Resolved,—That this Convention entertain a grateful sense of the Christian affection and condescension manifested in this letter. And whereas it appears that the venerable Prelates have heard, through private channels, that the Church here represented have adopted, or intended, such alterations as would be an essential deviation from the Church of England, this Convention trust that they shall be able to give such information to those venerable Prelates, as will satisfy them that no such alterations have been adopted or intended.

Resolved,—That a Committee be now appointed, to draft an answer to the letter of the Archbishops and Bishops of England.

Resolved,—That the Rev. Dr. Smith, the Rev. Dr. White, the Rev. Dr. Wharton, James Parker and Cyrus Griffin, Esquires, be the Committee for this purpose.

A motion made by the Rev. Mr. Provost, and seconded by the Rev. Mr. Smith, of South Carolina, viz.,

That this Convention will resolve to do no act that shall imply the validity of ordinations made by Dr. Seabury.

The previous question was moved by Dr. Smith, seconded by Dr. White, viz.,

Shall this question be now put? and carried in the affirmative. The main question was then proposed and determined in the negative, as follows:

New York, Aye; New Jersey, Aye; Pennsylvania, No; Delaware, No; Maryland, No; Virginia, No; South Carolina, Aye.

On motion made by Dr. White, and seconded by Mr. Smith, of South Carolina,

Resolved unanimously,—That it be recommended to this Church in the States here represented, not to receive to the pastoral charge, within their respective limits, Clergymen professing canonical subjection to any Bishop, in any State or country, other than those Bishops who may be duly settled in the States represented in this Convention.

Adjourned to ten o'clock to-morrow.

FRIDAY, the 23d of June, 1786.

The Convention met according to adjournment.

On motion made by the Rev. Mr. Smith of South Carolina, and seconded, it was unanimously

Resolved,—That it be recommended to the Conventions of the Church, represented in this General Convention, not to admit any person as a Minister within their respective limits, who shall receive ordination from any Bishop residing in America, during the application now pending to the English Bishops for Episcopal consecration.

The Journals of the late Convention, and the proposed Constitution of the Church, were read for the first time.

Previous to a second reading, a Memorial from the Convention of the Church in the State of New Jersey was presented, and sundry communications from the Conventions in the other States were made, relative to the business of this Convention. Whereupon,

Resolved,—That the said Memorial and communications be referred to the first General Convention which shall assemble with sufficient powers to determine on the same; and that, in the mean time, they be lodged with the Secretary.

The proposed Constitution was then taken up for a second reading, and debated by paragraphs.

The Preamble, contained in three clauses or sections, was agreed to without alteration.

Sect. I. "Of the Constitution." On motion by the Rev. Mr. Smith, of South Carolina, the triennial meetings of the General Convention were changed from the third Tuesday in June to the fourth Tuesday in July.

Sect. II. After the words "of each Order," insert, "chosen by the Convention of each State."

Sect. III. Agreed to.

Sect. IV. Agreed to.

Sect. V. From the words "this general Ecclesiastical Constitution," dele the word "general," and insert the same before the word "Convention," in the next line, and the sentence will run thus—"he shall be considered as a member of the General Convention ex officio."

On motion by Dr. White, seconded by Mr. Beach. After the words "ex officio," add—"and a Bishop shall always preside in the General Convention, if any of the Episcopal Order be present."

Sect. VI. Dele the words "by the respective Conventions,"

and insert "by the Convention of that State." After the words "to ordain or confirm," insert "or perform any other act of the Episcopal office."

Sect. VII. Agreed to.

Sect. VIII. On motion by Dr. White, seconded by the Rev. Mr. Beach. After the words—"equitable mode of trial," add these words,—"And at every trial of a Bishop, there shall be one or more of the Episcopal Order present; and none but a Bishop shall pronounce sentence of deposition or degradation from the Ministry on any Clergyman, whether Bishop, or Presbyter, or Deacon."

Nicholas Ridgely, Esq., a Deputy from the State of Delaware, attended, and after producing the testimonials of his appointment, took his seat in Convention.

Adjourned to 6 o'clock in the evening.

FRIDAY EVENING.

At 6 o'clock the Convention met.

The Rev. Sydenham Thorne, a Deputy from the State of Delaware, exhibited his credentials, and took his seat in Convention.

The debates on the Constitution were renewed and continued.

Sect. IX. Instead of the words, "to be the desire," insert "to be the general desire." After the words, "therefore the," dele the whole subsequent part of the section, and in place thereof insert as follows: "Book of Common Prayer and Administration of Sacraments, and other Rites and Ceremonies, as revised and proposed to the use of the Protestant Episcopal Church, at a Convention of the said Church, in the States of New York, New Jersey, Pennsylvania, Delaware, Maryland, Virginia, and South Carolina, may be used by this Church in such of the States as have adopted, or may adopt, the same in their particular Conventions, till further provision is made in this case, by the first General Convention which shall assemble with sufficient power to ratify a Book of Common Prayer for the Church in these States."

Sect. X. Dele the whole of this section, and in place thereof insert as follows:

"No person shall be ordained until due examination had by the Bishop and two Presbyters, and exhibiting testimonials of his moral conduct for three years past, signed by the Minister and a majority of the Vestry of the Church where he last resided; or permitted to officiate as a Minister in this Church until he has exhibited his Letters of Ordination and subscribed the following declaration: 'I do believe the Holy Scriptures of the Old and New Testament to be the word of God, and to contain all things necessary to salvation: and I do solemnly engage to conform to the doctrines and worship of the Protestant Episcopal Church in these United States.'"

Sect. XI. Dele the whole, and in place thereof insert as follows:

"This Constitution of the Protestant Episcopal Church in the United States of America, when ratified by the Church in a majority of the States, assembled in General Convention, with sufficient power for the purpose of such ratification, shall be unalterable by the Convention of any particular State, which hath been represented at the time of said ratification."

From the title of the Constitution dele the word "Ecclesiastical."

The question being then put on the whole of the proposed Constitution, as now amended, the same was unanimously agreed to as follows.

A GENERAL CONSTITUTION OF THE PROTESTANT EPISCOPAL CHURCH IN THE UNITED STATES OF AMERICA.

Whereas, in the course of Divine Providence, the Protestant Episcopal Church in the United States of America is become independent of all foreign authority, civil and ecclesiastical;—

And whereas, at a meeting of Clerical and Lay Deputies of the said Church in sundry of the said States, viz., in the States of Massachusetts, Rhode Island, Connecticut, New York, New Jersey, Pennsylvania, Delaware, and Maryland, held in the city of New York on the 6th and 7th days of October, in the year of our Lord 1784, it was recommended to this Church in the said States represented as aforesaid, and proposed to this Church in the States not represented, that they should send Deputies to a Convention to be held in the city of Philadephia, on the Tuesday before the Feast of St. Michael, in the year of our Lord 1785, in order to unite in a Constitution of Ecclesiastical government, agreeably to certain fundamental principles, expressed in the said recommendation and proposal;

And whereas, in consequence of the said recommendation and proposal, Clerical and Lay Deputies have been duly appointed from the said Church in the States of New York, New Jersey, Pennsylvania, Delaware, Maryland, Virginia, and South Carolina;

The said Deputies being now assembled, and taking into consideration the importance of maintaining uniformity in doctrine, discipline and worship in the said Church, do hereby determine and declare:

I. That there shall be a General Convention of the Protestant Episcopal Church in the United States of America, which shall be held in the city of Philadelphia, on the third Tuesday in June, in the year of our Lord, 1786, and for ever after once in three years, on the fourth Tuesday in July, in such place as shall be determined by the Convention; and special meetings may be held at such other times, and in such place, as shall be hereafter provided for. And this Church, in a majority of the States aforesaid, shall be represented before they shall proceed to business, except that the representation of this Church from two States shall be sufficient to adjourn. And in all business of the Convention, freedom of debate shall be allowed.

II. There shall be a representation of both Clergy and Laity of the Church in each State, which shall consist of one or more Deputies, not exceeding four, of each Order, chosen by the Convention of each State; and in all questions the said Church in each State shall have but one vote, and a majority of suffrages shall be conclusive.

III. In the said Church, in every State represented in this Convention, there shall be a Convention consisting of the Clergy and Lay Deputies of the congregations.

IV. "The Book of Common Prayer and Administration of the Sacraments, and other Rites and Ceremonies of the Church, according to the use of the Church of England," shall be continued to be used by this Church, as the same is altered by this Convention, in a certain instrument of writing passed by their authority, entituled, "Alterations of the Liturgy of the Protestant Episcopal Church in the United States of America, in order to render the same conformable to the American Revolution and the Constitutions of the respective States."

V. In every State where there shall be a Bishop duly consecrated and settled, who shall have acceded to the articles of this Ecclesiastical Constitution, he shall be considered as a member of the General Convention ex officio; and a Bishop shall always preside in the General Convention, if any of the Episcopal Order be present.

VI. The Bishop or Bishops in every State shall be chosen agreeably to such rules as shall be fixed by the Convention of that State; and every Bishop of this Church shall confine the exercise of his Episcopal office to his proper jurisdiction, unless requested to ordain or confirm, or perform any other act of the Episcopal office, by any Church destitute of a Bishop.

VII. A Protestant Episcopal Church, in any of the United States not now represented, may at any time hereafter be admitted, on acceding to the articles of this union.

VIII. Every Clergyman, whether Bishop, or Presbyter, or Deacon, shall be amenable to the authority of the Convention in the State to which he belongs, so far as relates to suspension or removal from office; and the Convention in each State shall institute rules for their conduct, and an equitable mode of trial. And at every trial of a Bishop, there shall be one or more of the Episcopal Order present, and none but a Bishop shall pronounce sentence of deposition or degradation from the ministry on any Clergyman, whether Bishop, or Presbyter, or Deacon.

IX. And whereas it is represented to this Convention to be the general desire of the Protestant Episcopal Church in these States, that there may be further alterations of the Liturgy than such as are made necessary by the American Revolution,—therefore "The Book of Common Prayer and Administration of the Sacraments, and other Rites and Ceremonies, as revised and proposed to the use of the Protestant Episcopal Church, at a Convention of the said Church in the States of New York, New Jersey, Pennsylvania, Delaware, Maryland, Virginia, and South Carolina," may be used by the Church in such of the States as have adopted, or may adopt, the same in their particular Conventions, till further provision is made, in this case, by the first General Convention which shall assemble with sufficient power to ratify a Book of Common Prayer for the Church in these States.

X. No person shall be ordained, until due examination had by the Bishop and two Presbyters, and exhibiting testimonials of his moral conduct for three years past, signed by the Minister and a majority of the Vestry of the Church where he has last resided; or permitted to officiate as a Minister in this Church until he has exhibited his Letters of Ordination and subscribed the following declaration: "I do believe the Holy Scriptures of the Old and New Testament to be the word of God, and to contain all things necessary to our salvation; and I do solemnly engage to conform to the doctrines and worship of the Protestant Episcopal Church in these United States.

XI. The Constitution of the Protestant Episcopal Church in the United States of America, when ratified by the Church in a majority of the States assembled in General Convention, with sufficient power for the purpose of such ratification, shall be unalterable by the Convention of any particular State, which hath been represented at the time of such ratification.

Adjourned to 10 o'clock to-morrow.

SATURDAY, 24th of June, 1786.

The Convention met.

The Committee appointed for that purpose, reported an answer to the letter from the Archbishops and Bishops of England.

On motion by Mr. Halsted,

Resolved,—That it be recommended to the Conventions of this Church, in the several States represented in this Convention, that they authorise and empower their Deputies to the next General Convention, after we shall have obtained a Bishop or Bishops in our Church, to confirm and ratify a general Constitution, respecting both the doctrine and discipline of the Protestant Episcopal Church in the United States of America.

On motion, Resolved,—That the thanks of this Convention be given to the Rev. Dr. White for his Sermon at the opening of this Convention, and that he be requested to have the same printed.

Resolved,—That the thanks of this Convention be given to his Excellency John Adams, Minister Plenipotentiary of the United States at the Court of London; to the Hon. Richard Henry Lee, late President of Congress; to the Hon. John Jay, Secretary for Foreign Affairs; and to Richard Peters, Esq., for their kind attention to the concerns of this Church,—and that the President be desired to transmit the same.

Resolved,—That a Committee of Correspondence be appointed, and the following gentlemen were appointed accordingly:—The Rev. Mr. Griffith, President; Rev. Dr. Smith, Rev. Dr. White, Rev. Mr. Provost, Hon. John Jay, Hon. James Duane, Samuel Powell, Esq., and Francis Hopkinson, Esq.

Resolved,—That the Rev. Dr. White, Dr. Magaw, Mr. Blackwell, and F. Hopkinson, Esq., be a Committee for publishing the Journals of this Convention.

Adjourned, to meet at Christ Church to-morrow afternoon, immediately after Divine Service.

SUNDAY AFTERNOON, 25th of June, 1786.

The Convention met.

The Hon. Mr. Jay, a Delegate from New York, attended, and took his seat in Convention.

Some objections having been made to the draft of an answer to the letter from the Archbishops and Bishops of England, the same was recommitted.

On motion made and seconded, Mr. Jay and Mr. Hopkinson were added to this Committee.

Adjourned to 11 o'clock to-morrow.

MONDAY, 26th of June, 1786.

The Convention met.

The Committee reported a draft of an answer to the letter from the Archbishops and Bishops of England, which, being read and considered, was agreed to, and is as follows:

TO THE MOST REVEREND AND RIGHT REVEREND FATHERS IN GOD, THE ARCHBISHOPS AND BISHOPS OF THE CHURCH OF ENGLAND.

Most Worthy and Venerable Prelates:

We, the Clerical and Lay Deputies of the Protestant Episcopal Church in the States of New York, New Jersey, Pennsylvania, Delaware, Maryland, Virginia, and South Carolina, have received the friendly and affectionate letter which your Lordships did us the honour to write on the 24th day of February, and for which we request you to accept our sincere and grateful acknowledgments.

It gives us pleasure to be assured, that the success of our application will probably meet with no greater obstacles than what have arisen from doubts respecting the extent of the alterations we have made and proposed; and we are happy to learn, that as no political impediments oppose us here, those which at present exist in England may be removed.

While doubts remain of our continuing to hold the same essential articles of faith and discipline with the Church of England, we acknowledge the propriety of suspending a compliance with our request.

We are unanimous and explicit in assuring your Lordships, that we neither have departed, nor propose to depart from the doctrines of your Church. We have retained the same discipline and forms of worship, as far as was consistent with our civil Constitutions; and we have made no alterations or omissions in the Book of Common Prayer but such as that consideration prescribed, and such as were calculated to remove objections, which it appeared to us more conducive to union and general content to obviate,than to dispute. It is well known, that many great and pious men of the Church of England have long wished for a revision of the Liturgy, which it was deemed imprudent to hazard, lest it might become a precedent for repeated and improper alterations. This is with us the proper season for such a revision. We are now settling and ordering the affairs of our Church, and if wisely done, we shall have reason to promise ourselves all the advantages than can result from stability and union.

We are anxious to complete our Episcopal system, by means of the Church of England. We esteem and prefer it, and with gratitude acknowledge the patronage and favours for which, while connected, we have constantly been indebted to that Church. These considerations, added to that of agreement in faith and worship, press us to repeat our former request, and to endeavour to remove your present hesitation, by sending you our proposed Ecclesiastical Constitution and Book of Common Prayer.

These documents, we trust, will afford a full answer to every question that can arise on the subject. We consider your Lordships' letter as very candid and kind. We repose full confidence in the assurance it gives; and that confidence, together with the liberality and catholicism of your venerable body, leads us to flatter ourselves, that you will not disclaim a branch of your Church merely for having been, in your Lordships' opinion, if that should be the case, pruned rather more closely than its separation made absolutely necessary.

We have only to add, that as our Church in sundry of these States have already proceeded to the election of persons to be sent for consecration, and others may soon proceed to the same, we pray to be favoured with as speedy an answer to this our second address, as in your great goodness you were pleased to give to our former one.

We are,
With great and sincere respect,
Most worthy and venerable Prelates,
Your obedient and
Very humble servants,

In Convention:
Christ Church, Philadelphia,
June 26, 1786.

VIRGINIA	David Griffith, President.
	Cyrus Griffin.
NEW YORK . . .	Samuel Provost, Rector of Trinity Church, New York.
	Joshua Bloomer, Rector of Jamaica, Long Island.
	John Jay.
NEW JERSEY. . . .	Abraham Beach, Rector of Christ Church, New Brunswick.
	James Parker.
	Matthias Halsted.
PENNSYLVANIA .	William White, D.D., Rector of Christ Church and St. Peter's.
	Samuel Magaw, D.D., Vice Provost of the University of Pennsylvania and Rector of St. Paul's.
	Robert Blackwell, Assistant Minister of Christ Church and St. Peter's.
	Samuel Powell.
	Francis Hopkinson.
DELAWARE . . .	Sydenham Thorne, Rector of Christ Church and St. Paul's.
	Charles H. Wharton, D.D., Rector of Emanuel Church, New Castle.
	Robert Clay.
	Nicholas Ridgeley.
MARYLAND . . .	William Smith, D.D., Principal of Washington College, and Rector of Chester Parish.
	William Smith, Rector of Stepney Parish.
SOUTH CAROLINA	Robert Smith, Rector of St. Philip's Church, Charleston.
	John Parker.

A fair copy of the above being engrossed and compared at the table, the same was signed by the Members present, and delivered to the Committee of Correspondence to be forwarded to England.

Resolved,—That the Committee of Correspondence be empowered to call a General Convention whenever a majority of the said Committee shall think it necessary.

It was determined by ballot that Wilmington, in the State of Delaware, shall be the next place of meeting.

Resolved,—That the thanks of this Convention be given to the President, for his impartial and diligent discharge of the duties of his office.

Resolved,—That, the thanks of this Convention be given Francis Hopkinson, Esq., for his diligence in the discharge of his duty as Secretary.

Resolved,—That the President be requested to open the next Convention with a Sermon.

The Convention adjourned sine die.

Signed by order of the Convention,

DAVID GRIFFITH, President.

Francis Hopkinson, Secretary.

JOURNAL OF A CONVENTION

OF THE

Protestant Episcopal Church

IN THE STATES OF

New York, New Jersey, Pennsylvania, Delaware, and South Carolina,

HELD AT

WILMINGTON, STATE OF DELAWARE,

OCTOBER 10TH AND 11TH. 1786.

LIST OF THE MEMBERS OF THE CONVENTION.

FROM THE STATE OF NEW YORK.

The Rev. Samuel Provost, D.D.
The Hon. James Duane.
John Rutherford, Esq.

FROM THE STATE OF NEW JERSEY.

The Rev. Uzal Ogden.
The Rev. William Frazer.
John Cox, Esq.
Henry Waddel, Esq.
Joshua Maddox Wallace, Esq.

FROM THE STATE OF PENNSYLVANIA.

The Rev. William White, D.D., Rector of Christ Church and St. Peter's, Philadelphia.
The Rev. Samuel Magaw, D.D., Rector of St. Paul's Church, Philadelphia.
The Rev. Robert Blackwell, A.M., Assistant Minister of Christ Church and St. Peter's, Philadelphia.
The Hon. Francis Hopkinson.
Samuel Powell, Esq.
Bernard Gilpin, Esq.

FROM THE STATE OF DELAWARE.

The Rev. Chas. H. Wharton, D.D.
The Rev. Sydenham Thorne.
Isaac Grantham, Esq.
James Sykes, Esq.

FROM THE STATE OF SOUTH CAROLINA.

The Rev. Robert Smith.
John Rutledge, Jun., Esq.

FROM THE STATE OF MARYLAND.

The Rev. William Smith, D.D.

JOURNAL.

TUESDAY, October 10th, 1786.

Dr. GRIFFITH, the President, not attending, the Secretary was desired to take the Chair.

A question was then agitated, whether this meeting is to be considered as a new Convention, or an adjournment of that lately held at Philadelphia. And it was unanimously determined that this shall be considered as an adjourned Convention.

On motion, it was agreed that the Rev. Dr. Magaw be requested to preach the Convention Sermon to-morrow, in case Dr. Griffith, who was appointed to that service, should not come in time.

On motion, the letters received, since the last meeting, from the Archbishops of England, with the forms of testimonials, and Act of Parliament, enclosed and referred to, be now read, and they were read accordingly, in the words following.

TO THE COMMITTEE OF THE GENERAL CONVENTION AT PHILADELPHIA, THE REV. DR. WHITE, PRESIDENT, THE REV. DR. SMITH, THE REV. MR. PROVOST, THE HON. JAMES DUANE, SAMUEL POWEL, AND RICHARD PETERS, ESQRS.

MR. PRESIDENT AND GENTLEMEN:

Influenced by the same sentiments of fraternal regard expressed by the Archbishops and Bishops in their answer to your address, we desire you to be persuaded, that if we have not yet been able to comply with your request, the delay has proceeded from no tardiness on our part. The only cause of it has been the uncertainty in which we were left by receiving your address, unaccompanied by those communications with regard to your Liturgy, Articles and Ecclesiastical Constitution, without the knowledge of which we could not presume to apply to the Legislature for such powers as were necessary to the completion of your wishes. The Journal of your Convention, and the first part of your Liturgy, did not reach us till more than two months after our receipt of your address; and we were not in possession of the remaining part of it, and of your articles, till the last day of April. The whole of your communications was then, with as little delay as possible, taken into consideration at a meeting of the Archbishops and fifteen of the Bishops, being all who were then in London and able to attend; and it was impossible not to observe with concern, that if the essential doctrines of our common faith were retained, less respect, however, was paid to our Liturgy than its own excellence, and your declared attachment to it, had led us to expect: not to mention a variety of verbal alterations, of the necessity or propriety of which we are by no means satisfied, we saw with grief, that two of the Confessions of our Christian faith, respectable for their antiquity, have been intirely laid aside; and that even in that which is called the Apostles, Creed, an article is omitted which was thought necessary to be inserted, with a view to a particular heresy, in a very early age of the Church, and has ever since had the venerable sanction of universal reception. Nevertheless, as a proof of the sincere desire which we feel to continue in spiritual communion with the members of your Church in America, and to complete the Orders of your Ministry, and trusting that the communications which we shall make to you, on the subject of these and some other alterations, will have their desired effect, we have, even under these circumstances, prepared a Bill for conveying to us the powers necessary for this purpose. It will in a few days be presented to Parliament, and we have the best reasons to hope that it will receive the assent of the Legislature. This Bill will enable the Archbishops and Bishops to give Episcopal Consecration to the persons who shall be recommended, without requiring from them any oaths or subscriptions inconsistent with the situation in which the late Revolution has placed them; upon condition that the full satisfaction of the sufficiency of the persons recommended, which you offer to us in your address, be given to the Archbishops and Bishops. You will doubtless receive it as a mark both of our friendly disposition toward you, and of our desire to avoid all delay on this occasion, that we have taken this earliest opportunity of conveying to you this intelligence, and that we proceed (as supposing ourselves invested with that power which for your sakes we have requested) to state to you particularly the several heads, upon which that satisfaction which you offer, will be accepted, and the mode in which it may be given. The anxiety which is shewn by the Church of England to prevent the intrusion of unqualified persons into even the inferior Offices of our Ministry, confirms our own sentiments, and points it out to be our duty, very earnestly to require the most decisive proofs of the qualifications of those who may be offered for admission to that Order to which the superintendence of those offices is committed. At our several Ordinations of a Deacon and a Priest, the candidate submits himself to the examination of the Bishop as to his proficiency in learning; he gives the proper security of his soundness in the Faith by the subscriptions which are made previously necessary; he is required to bring testimonials of his virtuous conversation during the three preceding years; and that no mode of inquiry may be omitted, publick notice of his offering himself to be ordained is given in the Parish church where he resides or ministers, and the people are solemnly called upon to declare, if they know any impediment, for the which he ought not to be admitted. At the time of Ordination, too, the same solemn call is made on the congregation then present.

Examination, subscription, and testimonials are not indeed repeated at the consecration of an English bishop, because the person to be consecrated has added to the securities given at his former ordinations, that sanction which arises from his having constantly lived and exercised his ministry under the eyes and observation of his country. But the objects of our present consideration are very differently circumstanced; their sufficiency in learning, the soundness of their faith, and the purity of their manners, are not matters of notoriety here; means, therefore, must be found to satisfy the Archbishop who consecrates, and the Bishops who present them, that, in the words of our Church, "they be apt and meet for their learning and godly conversation, to exercise their ministry duly to the honour of God and the edifying of his Church, and to be wholesome examples and patterns to the flock of Christ."

With regard to the first qualification, sufficiency in good learning, we apprehend that the subjecting a person, who is to be admitted to the office of a Bishop in the Church, to that examination which is required previous to the ordination of Priests and Deacons, might lessen that reverend estimation which ought never to be separated from the Episcopal character: we therefore do not require any farther satisfaction on this point, than will be given to us by the forms of testimonials in the annexed paper, fully trusting that those who sign them will be well aware, how greatly incompetence in this respect must lessen the weight and authority of the Bishop and affect the credit of the Episcopal Church.

Under the second head, that of subscription, our desire is to require that subscription only to be repeated, which you have already been called upon to make by the Tenth Article of your Ecclesiastical Constitution: but we should forget the duty which we owe to our own Church, and act inconsistently with that sincere regard which we bear to yours, if we were not explicit in declaring, that, after the disposition we have shown to comply with the prayer of your address, we think it now incumbent upon you to use your utmost exertions also for the removal of any stumbling block of offence which may possibly prove an obstacle to the success of it. We therefore most earnestly exhort you, that previously to the time of your making such subscription, you restore to its integrity the Apostles' Creed, in which you have omitted an article, merely, as it seems, from misapprehension of the sense in which it is understood by our Church; nor can we help adding, that we hope you will think it but a decent proof of the attachment which you profess to the services of our Liturgy, to give to the other two Creeds a place in your Book of Common Prayer, even tho' the use of them should be left discretional. We should be inexcusable, too, if, at the time when you are requesting the establishment of Bishops in your Church, we did not strongly represent to you that the Eighth Article of your Ecclesiastical Constitution appears to us to be a degradation of the Clerical, and still more of the Episcopal character. We persuade ourselves, that in your ensuing Convention some alteration will be thought necessary in this article, before this reaches you; or, if not, that due attention will be given to it in consequence of our representation.

On the third and last head, which respects purity of manners, the reputation of the Church, both in England and America, and the interest of our common Christianity is so deeply concerned in it, that we feel it our indispensible duty to provide, on this subject, the most effectual securities. It is presumed, that the same previous public notice of the intention of the person to be consecrated, will be given in the Church where he resides in America, for the same reasons, and therefore nearly in the same form, with that used in England before our Ordinations. The call upon the persons present at the time of consecration, must be deemed of little use before a congregation composed of those to whom the person to be consecrated is unknown. The testimonials signed by persons living in England admit of reference and examination, and the characters of those who give them are subject to scrutiny, and in cases of criminal deceit, to punishment. In proportion as these circumstances are less applicable to testimonials from America, those testimonials must be more explicit, and supported by a greater number of signatures. We therefore think it necessary that the several persons, candidates for Episcopal consecration, should bring to us, both a testimonial from the General Convention of the Episcopal Church, with as many signatures as can be obtained, and a more particular one, from the respective Conventions in those States which recommend them. It will appear from the tenor of the Letters Testimonial used in England, a form of which is annexed, that the ministers who sign them bear testimony to the qualifications of the candidates on their own personal knowledge. Such a testimony is not to be expected from the members of the General Convention of the Episcopal Church in America on this occasion. We think it sufficient, therefore, that they declare they know no impediment, but believe the person to be consecrated is of a virtuous life and sound faith; we have sent you such a form as appears to us proper to be used for that purpose. More specific declarations must be made by the members of the Convention in each State from which the persons offered for consecration are respectively recommended; their personal knowledge of them there can be no doubt of; we trust, therefore, they will have no objection to the adoption of the form of a testimonial which is annexed, and drawn upon the same principles, and containing the same attestations of personal knowledge with that above mentioned, as required previously to our Ordinations: we trust we shall receive these testimonials signed by such a majority in each Convention that recommend, as to leave no doubt of the fitness of the candidates upon the minds of those whose consciences are concerned in the consecration of them.

Thus much we have thought it right to communicate to you, without reserve, at present, intending to give you farther information as soon as we are able. In the mean time, we pray God to direct your counsels in this very weighty matter, and are,

Mr. President and gentlemen,

Your affectionate Brethren,

J. CANTUAR.

W. EBOR.

Form of a Testimonial for Priests' Orders, in England.

To the Right Reverend Father in God, ———, by Divine permission Lord Bishop of ———.

We, whose names are hereunder written, testify, from our personal knowledge of the life and behaviour of A. B. for the space of three years last past, that he hath during that time lived piously, soberly, and honestly: Nor hath he at any time, as far as we know or believe, written, taught, or held, any thing contrary to the doctrine or discipline of the Church of England. And, moreover, we think him a person worthy to be admitted to the sacred order of Priest. In witness whereof we have hereunto set our hands. Dated the . . . day of . . . in the year of our Lord . . .

Testimony from the General Convention.

We whose names are underwritten, fully sensible how important it is that the sacred office of a Bishop should not be unworthily conferred, and firmly persuaded that it is our duty to bear our testimony on this solemn occasion without partiality or affection, do, in the presence of Almighty God, testify that A. B. is not, so far as we are informed, justly liable to evil report either for error in religion or for viciousness of life; and that we do not know or believe there is any impediment or notable crime, on account of which he ought not to be consecrated to that holy office, but that he hath led his life, for the three years last past, piously, soberly, and honestly.

Testimony from the Members of the Convention in the State from whence the person is recommended for Consecration.

We whose names are underwritten, fully sensible how important it is, that the sacred office of a Bishop should not be unworthily conferred, and firmly persuaded that it is our duty to bear testimony on this solemn occasion without partiality or affection, do, in the presence of Almighty God, testify that A. B. is not, so far as we are informed, justly liable to evil report, either for error in religion or for viciousness of life; and that we do not know or believe there is any impediment or notable crime for which he ought not to be consecrated to that holy office. We do, moreover, jointly and severally declare that, having personally known him for three years last past, we do in our consciences believe him to be of such sufficiency in good learning, such soundness in the faith, and of such virtuous and pure manners and godly conversation, that he is apt and meet to exercise the Office of a Bishop, to the honour of God and the edifying of his Church, and to be an wholesome example to the flock of Christ.

TO THE COMMITTEE OF THE GENERAL CONVENTION, ETC., ETC.

CANTERBURY, JULY 4TH, 1786.

GENTLEMEN:

The enclosed Act, being now passed, I have the satisfaction of communicating it to you. It is accompanied by a copy of a letter, and some forms of testimonials, which I sent you by the packet of last month. It is the opinion here, that no more than three Bishops should be consecrated for the United States of America, who may consecrate others at their return, if more be found necessary. But whether we can consecrate any or not, must yet depend on the answers we may receive, to what we have written.

I am your humble servant,

J. CANTUAR.

"An Act to empower the Archbishop of Canterbury, or the Archbishop of York, for the time being, to consecrate to the Office of a Bishop, Persons, being Subjects or Citizens of Countries out of His Majesty's dominions.

Whereas, by the laws of this realm, no person can be consecrated to the Office of a Bishop, without the King's licence for his election to that office, and the Royal mandate under the Great Seal for his confirmation and consecration; and whereas every person who shall be consecrated to the said office is required to take the oaths of allegiance and supremacy, and also the oath of due obedience to the Archbishop: And whereas there are divers persons, subjects or citizens of countries out of his Majesty's dominions, inhabiting and residing within the said countries, who profess the publick worship of Almighty God according to the principles of the Church of England, and who, in order to provide a regular succession of Ministers for the service of their Church, are desirous of having certain of the subjects or citizens of those countries consecrated Bishops, according to the form of consecration in the Church of England: Be it enacted by the King's most excellent Majesty, by and with the advice and consent of the Lords Spiritual and Temporal and Commons in this present Parliament assembled, and by the authority of the same, that from and after the passing of this Act, it shall and may be lawful to and for the Archbishop of Canterbury, or the Archbishop of York for the time being, together with such other Bishops as they shall call to their assistance, to consecrate persons being subjects or citizens of countries out of his Majesty's dominions, Bishops for the purposes aforesaid, without the King's licence for their election, or the Royal mandate under the great Seal for their confirmation and consecration, and without requiring them to take the oaths of allegiance and supremacy, and the oath of due obedience to the Archbishop for the time being. Provided always, that no persons shall be consecrated Bishops in the manner herein provided, until the Archbishop of Canterbury or the Archbishop of York, for the time being, shall have first applied for and obtained his Majesty's licence, by warrant under his Royal signet and sign manual, authorizing and empowering him to perform such consecration, and expressing the name or names of the persons so to be consecrated; nor until the said Archbishop has been fully ascertained of their sufficiency in good learning, of the soundness of their faith, and of the purity of their manners. Provided also, and be it hereby declared, that no person or persons consecrated to the office of a Bishop in the manner aforesaid, nor any person or persons deriving their consecration from or under any Bishop so consecrated, nor any person or persons admitted to the Order of Deacon or Priest by any Bishop or Bishops so consecrated, or by the successor or successors of any Bishop or Bishops so consecrated, shall be thereby enabled to exercise his or their respctive office or offices within his Majesty's dominions. Provided always, and be it further enacted, that a certificate of such consecration shall be given under the hand and seal of the Archbishop who consecrates, containing the name of the person so consecrated, with the addition as well of the country whereof he is a subject or citizen, as of the Church in which he is appointed Bishop, and the farther description of his not having taken the said oaths, being exempted from the obligation of so doing by virtue of this Act."

Resolved,—That a Committee be now appointed, to take into consideration the letters and papers read, and to report thereon.

Resolved,—That this Committee shall consist of a Clerical and Lay Deputy from each State.

Whereupon the following gentlemen were appointed:—

New York—The Rev. Dr. Provost, James Duane, Esq.

New Jersey—The Rev. Uzal Ogden, Henry Waddel, Esq.

Pennsylvania—The Rev. Dr. White, Samuel Powel, Esq.

Delaware—The Rev. Sydenham Thorne, Isaac Grantham, Esq.

South Carolina—The Rev. Robert Smith, John Rutledge, Esq.

From Maryland—The Rev. Dr. Smith.

The Convention then adjourned, to meet at 8 o'clock to-morrow morning.

Wednesday, October 11th, 1786.

The Convention met, and after some time adjourned to the Swedes Church, to attend Divine Service, read by the Rev. Dr. Provost, and a Sermon by the Rev. Dr. Magaw.

After Sermon, returned to the Academy Hall, and entered on business.

It was moved, and seconded, to proceed to the election of a President. The ballots being taken, it appeared that the Rev. Dr. Provost was unanimously elected President.

A question was then proposed and seconded, viz., whether this Convention hath authority to admit as members persons deriving their appointment, not from a State Convention, but from a particular parish or parishes only.

On the question being put, it was determined in the negative.

Another question was then proposed and seconded, viz., whether this Convention can, consistently with its fundamental articles, admit a State to be represented by a Clerical or Lay Deputy only. Which was also determined in the negative.

The Committee appointed last evening, to take into consideration the matters contained in the letters from the Archbishops of England, delivered in their Report; which, after mature delberation and some amendments, was agreed to, and established as an Act of this Corporation, and is in the words following, viz.:

An Act of the General Convention of Clerical and Lay Deputies of the Protestant Episcopal Church, in the States of New-York, New-Jersey, Pennsylvania, Delaware, and South Carolina, held at Wilmington, in the State of Delaware, on Wednesday, the 11th of October, 1786.

Whereas, at a General Convention of Clerical and Lay Deputies of the Protestant Episcopal Church in sundry of the United States of America, viz., New-York, New-Jersey, Pennsylvania, Delaware, Maryland, Virginia, and South Carolina, holden at the City of Philadelphia, on the Tuesday before the Feast of St. Michael, in the year of our Lord, 1785, and divers subsequent days, it was agreed and declared, that "The Book of Common Prayer and Administration of the Sacraments and other Rites and Ceremonies of the Church, according to the use of the Church of England," should be continued to be used by this Church, as the same was altered by the said Convention, in a certain instrument of writing, passed by their authority, intituled "Alterations of the Liturgy of the Protestant Episcopal Church in the United States of America, in order to render the same conformable to the American Revolution and the Constitutions of the respective States." And it was further agreed and declared, that the Book of Common Prayer and Administration of the Sacraments and other Rites and Ceremonies of the Church, according to the use of the Church of England, as altered by an instrument of writing passed under the authority of the aforesaid Convention, intituled, "Alterations in the Book of Common Prayer and Administration of the Sacraments and other Rites and Ceremonies of the Church, according to the use of the Church of England, proposed and recommended to the Protestant Episcopal Church, in the United States of America, should be used in this Church, when the same should have been ratified by the Conventions which had respectively sent deputies to the said General Convention." And thereupon the said Convention, anxious to compleat their Episcopal system by means of the Church of England, did subscribe and transmit an address to the Most Reverend and Right Reverend the Archbishops of Canterbury and York, and the Bishops of the Church of England, earnestly entreating that venerable body to confer the Episcopal character on such persons as should be recommended by this Church in the several States so represented.

And whereas, the Clerical and Lay Deputies of this Church have received the most friendly and affectionate letters, in answer to the said address, from the said Archbishops and Bishops, opening a fair prospect of the success of their said applications, but at the same time earnestly exhorting this Convention to use their utmost exertions for the removal of certain objections by them made, against some parts of the alterations in the Book of Common Prayer and Rites and Ceremonies of this Church last mentioned. In pursuance whereof, this present General Convention hath been called and is now assembled: and being sincerely desirous to give every satisfaction to their Lordships which will be consistent with the union and general content of the Church they represent, and declaring their steadfast resolution to maintain the same essential Articles of Faith and Discipline with the Church of England:

Now, therefore, the said Deputies do hereby determine and declare·

First,—That in the Creed commonly called the Apostles' Creed, these words, "He descended into Hell," shall be and continue a part of that Creed.

Secondly,—That the Nicene Creed shall also be inserted in the said Book of Common Prayer, immediately after the Apostles' Creed, prefaced with the Rubrick (or this).

And whereas,—In consequence of the objections expressed by their Lordships to the alterations in the Book of Common Prayer last mentioned, the Conventions in some of the States represented in this General Convention have suspended the ratification and use of the said Book of Common Prayer, by reason whereof it will be improper that persons to be consecrated or ordained as Bishops, Priests, or Deacons respectively, should subscribe the declaration contained in the Tenth Article of the General Ecclesiastical Constitution, without some modification:

Therefore it is hereby determined and declared,

Thirdly,—That the second clause so to be subscribed by a Bishop, Priest, or Deacon of this Church, in any of the States which have not already ratified or used the last mentioned Book of Common Prayer, shall be in the words following: "And I do solemnly engage to conform to the doctrine and worship of the Protestant Episcopal Church, according to the use of the Church of England, as the same is altered by the General Convention, in a certain instrument of writing passed by their authority, intituled, 'Alterations of the Liturgy of the Protestant Episcopal Church in the United States of America, in order to render the same conformable to the American Revolution and the Constitutions of the respective States,' until the new Book of Common Prayer, recommended by the General Convention, shall be ratified or used in the State in which I am —(Bishop, Priest, or Deacon, as the case may be)—by the authority of the Convention thereof. And I do further solemnly engage, that when the said new Book of Common Prayer shall be ratified or used by the authority of the Convention in the State for which I am consecrated a Bishop—(or ordained a Priest or Deacon)—I will conform to the doctrines and worship of the Protestant Episcopal Church, as settled and determined in the last mentioned Book of Common Prayer and Administration of the Sacraments, set forth by the General Convention of the Protestant Episcopal Church in the United States."

And it is hereby further determined and declared,

That these words in the Preface to the new proposed Book of Common Prayer, viz., "In the Creed, commonly called 'the Apostles' Creed,' one clause is omitted, as being of uncertain meaning, and"—together with the note referred to in that place, be, from henceforth, no part of the Preface to the said proposed Book of Common Prayer.

And it is hereby further determined and declared,

That the Fourth Article of Religion in the new proposed Book of Common Prayer, be altered to render it conformable to the adoption of the Nicene Creed, as follows: "Of the Creeds. The two Creeds, namely, that commonly called the Apostles' Creed and the Nicene Creed, ought to be received and believed, because they," etc., etc.

Done in General Convention, at Wilmington, in the State of Delaware, the day and year first aforesaid.

The first question taken on the Report of the Committee was, whether the words, "He descended into Hell," should be restored in the Apostles' Creed.

When, the Ayes and Nays being called for, the votes were as follow:

NEW YORK.—Dr. Provost, Aye; Mr. Duane, Aye; Mr. Rutherford, No—Divided.

NEW JERSEY.—Rev. Mr. Ogden, Aye; Rev. Mr. Frazer, Aye; Mr. Wallace, Aye; Mr. Cox, No; Mr. Waddel, Aye.—Aye.

PENNSYLVANIA.—Dr. White, Aye; Dr. Magaw, Aye; Mr. Blackwell, Aye; Mr. Hopkinson, No; Mr. Powel, No; Mr. Gilpin, No.—Divided.

DELAWARE.—Dr. Wharton, No; Rev. Mr. Thorne, Aye; Mr. Sykes, Aye; Mr. Grantham, No.—Divided.

SOUTH CAROLINA.—Rev. Mr. R. Smith, Aye; Mr. Rutledge, Aye.—Aye.

And so the words are to be restored, there being two Ayes and no Negative.

On the question, Shall the Nicene Creed be restored in the Liturgy? the same was unanimously agreed to.

Adjourned to 6 o'clock in the evening.

WEDNESDAY EVENING, 6 o'clock.

A 6 o'clock the Convention met.

On the question, Shall the Creed commonly called the Athanasian Creed, be admitted in the Liturgy of the Protestant Episcopal Church in the United States of America?

The Ayes and Nays being taken, were as follow:

NEW YORK.—Dr. Provost, No; Mr. Duane, No; Mr. Rutherford, No.—Nay.

NEW JERSEY.—Rev. Mr. Ogden, No; Rev. Mr. Frazer, No; Mr. Cox, No; Mr. Wallace, Aye; Mr. Waddel, Aye.—Divided.

PENNSYLVANIA.—Dr. White, No; Dr. Magaw, No; Rev. Mr. Blackwell, No; Mr. Hopkinson, No; Mr. Powel, No; Mr. Gilpin, No.—Nay.

DELAWARE.—Dr. Wharton, No; Rev. Mr. Thorne, Aye; Mr. Sykes, No; Mr. Grantham, No.—Divided.

SOUTH CAROLINA.—Rev. Mr. Smith, No; Mr. Rutledge, No.—Nay.

And so it was determined in the negative.

On the question, Shall the Eighth Article of the Ecclesiastical Constitution remain as proposed and published by the late Convention? it was unanimously determined in the affirmative.

Resolved,—That in the opinion of this Convention, it is proper for those gentlemen, who shall proceed from any of these States for England, for the purpose of obtaining Episcopal consecration, first to subscribe either the form directed in the Tenth Article of the proposed Ecclesiastical Constitution or else the form directed in the Act or Instrument now passed by this Convention; and that they respectively lodge their subscriptions with the Secretary, taking from him a certificate of their having so done.

Resolved,—That the Secretary be desired to transmit a copy of the proceedings of this Convention to the Standing Committees of the Protestant Episcopal Church in the States of Maryland and Virginia, with the affectionate hope of this body, that their brethren of the said States, after duly considering the principles on which these proceedings have been held, will approve and adopt the same.

It was moved and seconded, that a Committee be appointed to draft a letter from this Convention, to the Archbishops of England, in answer to their late letters.

And the following gentlemen were appointed accordingly—Dr. Smith, Dr. White, and Dr. Wharton.

This Committee retired, and after some time returned and reported a letter, which, after a few amendments, was agreed to as follows:

TO THE ARCHBISHOPS OF CANTERBURY AND YORK.

MOST WORTHY AND VENERABLE PRELATES:

In pursuance of your Graces' communications to the Standing Committee of our Church, received by the June packet, and the letter of his Grace the Archbishop of Canterbury of July the fourth, enclosing the Act of Parliament "to empower the Archbishop of Canterbury, or the Archbishop of York, for the time being, to consecrate to the office of a Bishop, persons being subjects or citizens of countries out of his Majesty's dominions," a General Convention, now sitting, have the honour of offering their unanimous and hearty thanks for the continuance of your Christian attention to this Church, and particularly for your having so speedily acquired a legal capacity of complying with the prayer of our former addresses.

We have taken into our most serious and deliberate consideration the several matters so affectionately recommended to us in those communications, and whatever could be done towards a compliance with your fatherly wishes and advice, consistently with our local circumstances, and the peace and unity of our Church, hath been agreed to, as, we trust, will appear from the enclosed Act of our Convention, which we have the honour to transmit to you, together with the Journal of our proceedings.

We are, with great and sincere respect,
Most worthy and venerable Prelates,
Your obedient and very humble servants.
(By order) SAMUEL PROVOST, PRESIDENT.

IN GENERAL CONVENTION:
At Wilmington, in the State of Delaware,
October 11, 1786.

The above letter being fairly copied, was signed by the President in behalf of the Convention.

On motion, the States were respectively called upon to know if, in their several Conventions, any person had been elected and recommended for Episcopal consecration; when it appeared that the Convention of New York had elected and recommended the Rev. Dr. Samuel Provost to that office.

The members present then proceeded to sign his testimonials in the form prescribed by the Archbishops of England for the General Convention.

The Convention of Pennsylvania had elected and recommended the Rev. Dr. William White, and his testimonials were in like manner signed by the members present.

It appeared also, that the Convention of Virginia had elected and recommended the Rev. Dr. David Griffith, and his testimonials were accordingly signed.

Resolved,—That the thanks of this Convention be given to the Rev. Dr. Magaw for his Sermon this forenoon; to the President for his impartial and judicious conduct; and to the Secretary for his attention and services.

Resolved,—That the Rev. Dr. Provost, President, Rev. Dr. Smith, Rev. Dr. White, Rev. Dr. Griffith, Hon. John Jay, Hon. James Duane, Hon. Francis Hopkinson, and Samuel Powel, Esq., be the Committee of Correspondence; and that they have power to call a General Convention of the Church, to meet at Philadelphia, whenever a majority of the said Committee shall think it necessary.

Resolved,—That the Rev. Dr. Provost be requested to preach before the Convention, at their next meeting.

Adjourned, sine die.

Signed by order of the Convention,

SAMUEL PROVOST, PRESIDENT.

FRANCIS HOPKINSON, Secretary.

JOURNAL OF A CONVENTION

OF THE

Protestant Episcopal Church

IN THE STATES OF

New-York, New-Jersey, Pennsylvania, Delaware, Maryland, Virginia, and South-Carolina,

HELD IN

CHRIST CHURCH, PHILADELPHIA.

FROM

JULY 28TH TO AUGUST 8TH, 1789.

LIST OF THE MEMBERS OF THE CONVENTION.

The Right Rev. William White, D.D., Bishop of the Protestant Episcopal Church in the State of Pennsylvania, and President of the Convention.

FROM THE STATE OF NEW-YORK.

The Rev. Abraham Beach, D.D.
The Rev. Benjamin Moore, D.D.
Mr. Moses Rogers.

FROM THE STATE OF NEW-JERSEY.

The Rev. William Frazer.
The Rev. Uzal Ogden.
The Rev. Henry Waddel.
The Rev. George H. Spieren.
John Cox, Esq.
Róbert Strettel Jones, Esq.
Samuel Ogden, Esq.

FROM THE STATE OF PENNSYLVANIA.

The Rev. Samuel Magaw, D.D.
The Rev. Robert Blackwell, D.D.
The Rev. Joseph Pilmore.
The Rev. Joseph G. J. Bend.
The Hon. Francis Hopkinson.
Samuel Powel, Esq.
Dr. Gerardus Clarkson.
Tench Coxe, Esq.

FROM THE STATE OF DELAWARE.

The Rev. Joseph Couden.
The Rev. Stephen Sykes.
James Sykes, Esq.
Thomas Duff, Esq.
Mr. Philip Reading.

FROM THE STATE OF MARYLAND.

The Rev. William Smith, D.D.
The Rev. Thomas John Claggett, D.D.
The Rev. Colin Ferguson, D.D.
The Rev. John Bisset.
Richard B. Carmichael, Esq.
Dr. William Frisby.

FROM THE STATE OF VIRGINIA.

Robert Andrews, Esq.

FROM THE STATE OF SOUTH CAROLINA.

The Rev. Robert Smith.
William Ward Burrows, Esq.
William Brisbane, Esq.

JOURNAL.

TUESDAY, July 28th, 1789.

Clerical and Lay Deputies from several of the States assembled; and judging it proper to wait the arrival of the Deputies from the other States,

Adjourned to 9 o'clock to-morrow morning.

WEDNESDAY, July 29th, 1789.

The Convention met.

The Right Rev. Dr. White, President, ex officio.

The Rev. Dr. Claggett read prayers.

The Right Rev. Dr. Provost, who was to have preached on the opening of the Convention, being absent through indisposition, the Rev. Dr. Smith preached, agreeably to request made yesterday.

The Hon. Mr. Hopkinson was unanimously chosen Secretary, but being indisposed, Mr. Tench Coxe was requested to officiate.

Ordered, that the members present produce the testimonials of their respective appointments, which being produced, were read, and deemed satisfactory.

Mr. Andrews, Lay Deputy from Virginia, informed the Convention, that the Rev. Dr. Griffith, the Clerical Delegate from the said State, was in town, but detained by sickness from the Convention.

A certificate of the consecration of the Right Rev. William White, D.D., Bishop of the Protestant Episcopal Church in the State of Pennsylvania, and the Right Rev. Samuel Provost, D.D., Bishop of said Church in the State of New York, signed by Robert Jenner, Notary Public, and dated February 4, 1787, was produced and read; also a certificate of the consecration of the Right Rev. Dr. White, signed by his Grace the Archbishop of Canterbury, and countersigned by his Grace the Archbishop of York, and the Right Rev. the Bishops of Bath and Wells and of Peterborough.

Mr. Andrews communicated to the Convention the following extract from the Minutes of the Convention of this Church in the State of Virginia.

"In Convention, May 8, 1789.

"Resolved,—That the Deputies appointed to attend the next General Convention of the Protestant Episcopal Church, be desired to notify to the next General Convention, that the Rev. Dr. Griffith, Bishop elect of the said Church in this State, has relinquished the said appointment, and that no person has been elected in his room."

A copy from the Journal of the Convention of the Protestant Episcopal Church in Virginia, held from May 6 to May 9, 1789, inclusive.

Robert Andrews,
Secretary of the Protestant Episcopal Convention in Virginia.

The Rev. Dr. Moore, Mr. Hopkinson, and Mr. Andrews, were appointed a Committee to prepare Rules of Order.

An invitation from the University of Pennsylvania to the Convention, to attend a Commencement, was presented by the Rev. Dr. Magaw, which was unanimously accepted, and the President was requested to signify the same, in writing, to the Trustees and Faculty.

Adjourned to 5 o'clock, P.M.

Wednesday, July 29th, 1789, P. M.

The Convention met.

Mr. Hopkinson remaining indisposed, the Rev. Mr. Bend was requested to officiate during his indisposition.

Ordered, that the Rev. Dr. Smith, the Rev. Dr. Moore, and Mr. Ogden, be a Committee to prepare an address to the President of the United States.

On motion, ordered, that the Letters of Consecration of the Right Rev. Dr. White and the Right Rev. Dr. Provost, and the notarial certificate thereof, be recorded. (See Appendix.)

Ordered, that the Secretary procure a book for recording the Minutes and papers of the General Convention.

Ordered, that the Rev. Dr. Smith, the Rev. Dr. Beach, and Mr. Andrews, be a Committee to prepare an address of thanks to the Most Reverend the Archbishops of Canterbury and York for their good offices in procuring the consecration of the American Bishops.

The Deputies from the several States being called upon to declare their powers, relative to the object of the following resolution of the Protestant Episcopal Church, viz.,—"Resolved, that it be recommended to the Conventions of this Church in the several States represented in this Convention, that they authorise and empower their Deputies to the next General Convention, after we shall have obtained a Bishop or Bishops in our Church, to confirm and ratify a General Constitution, respecting both the doctrine and discipline of the Protestant Episcopal Church in the United States of America,"—gave information that they came fully authorised to ratify a Book of Common Prayer, etc., for the use of the Church.

Ordered, that the Journal of the last General Convention be read, and that a copy of the Journals of the Convention be procured for each member.

Resolved,—That the thanks of this Convention be given to the Rev. Dr. Smith for his Sermon, and that he be requested to publish the same.

Adjourned to 9 o'clock to-morrow morning.

THURSDAY, July 30th, 1789.

The Convention met.

The Rev. Dr. Beach read prayers.

The Rev. Mr. Sykes, the Rev. Mr. Couden, James Sykes, and Thomas Duff, Esquires, Deputies from Delaware, produced the credentials of their appointment, which being read and approved, they took their seats in the Convention.

The aforesaid Deputies were requested to state their powers relative to the ratification of a Book of Common Prayer, etc., which were deemed sufficient.

The Hon. Mr. Hopkinson, a Deputy for Pennsylvania, took his seat in Convention.

The Committee appointed to prepare rules for the orderly conduct of the Convention, reported the same, which were adopted.

On motion, ordered, that a Committee, consisting of a Deputy from each State, be appointed to take into consideration the proposed Constitution of the Protestant Episcopal

Church, and to recommend such alterations, additions, and amendments as they shall think necessary and proper.

The Rev. Dr. Moore, Mr. Jones, the Rev. Dr. Blackwell, Mr. Sykes, the Rev. Dr. Smith, Mr. Andrews, and the Rev. Mr. Smith, were appointed accordingly.

An act of the Clergy of Massachusetts and New Hampshire, recommending the Rev. Edward Bass for consecration, was laid before the Convention by the Right Rev. Dr. White, and is as follows.

The good providence of Almighty God, the fountain of all goodness, having lately blessed the Protestant Episcopal Church in the United States of America, by supplying it with a complete and entire Ministry, and affording to many of her communion the benefit of the labours, advice, and government of the successors of the Apostles:

We, Presbyters of said Church in the States of Massachusetts and New Hampshire, deeply impressed with the most lively gratitude to the Supreme Governor of the universe, for his goodness in this respect, and with the most ardent love to his Church, and concern for the interest of her sons, that they may enjoy all the means that Christ, the great Shepherd and Bishop of souls, has instituted for leading his followers into the ways of truth and holiness, and preserving his Church in the unity of the spirit and the bond of peace; to the end that the people committed to our respective charges may enjoy the benefit and advantage of those offices, the administration of which belongs to the highest Order of the Ministry, and to encourage and promote, as far as in us lies, a union of the whole Episcopal Church in these States, and to perfect and compact this mystical body of Christ, do hereby nominate, elect and appoint, the Rev. Edward Bass, a Presbyter of said Church, and Rector of St. Paul's, in Newburyport, to be our Bishop; and we do promise and engage to receive him as such, when canonically consecrated, and invested with the apostolic office and powers by the Right Reverend the Bishops hereafter named, and to render him all that canonical obedience and submission which, by the laws of Christ, and the constitution of our Church, is due to so important an office.

And we now address the Right Reverend the Bishops in the States of Connecticut, New York, and Pennsylvania, praying their united assistance in consecrating our said brother, and canonically investing him with the apostolic office and powers. This request we are induced to make, from a long acquaintance with him, and from a perfect knowledge of his being possessed of that love to God and benevolence to men, that piety, learning, and good morals, that prudence and discretion, requisite to so exalted a station, as well as that personal respect and attachment of the communion at large in these States, which will make him a valuable acquisition to the Order, and, we trust, a rich blessing to the Church.

Done at a meeting of the Presbyters whose names are underwritten, held at Salem, in the County of Essex, and Commonwealth of Massachusetts, the fourth day of June, Anno Salutis, 1789.

Samuel Parker, Rector of Trinity Church, Boston.
T. Fitch Oliver, Rector of St. Michael's Church, Marblehead.
John Cousens Ogden, Rector of Queen's Chapel, Portsmouth, N.H.
William Montague, Minister of Christ's Church, Boston.
Tillotson Brunson, Assistant Minister of Christ's Church, Boston.

A true copy. Attest: Samuel Parker.

At the meeting aforesaid,

Voted,—That the Rev. Samuel Parker be authorised and empowered to transmit copies of the foregoing Act, to be by him attested, to the Right Reverend the Bishops in Connecticut, New York, and Pennsylvania; and that he be appointed our agent, to appear at any Convocation to be holden at Pennsylvania or New York, and to treat upon any measures that may tend to promote an union of the Episcopal Church throughout the United States of America, or that may prove advantageous to the interests of said Church.

EDWARD BASS, Chairman.

A true copy. Attest: Samuel Parker.

A letter was also read from the Right Rev. Dr. Seabury, Bishop of the Church in Connecticut, to the Right Rev. Dr. White, and one from the same gentleman to the Rev. Dr. Smith.

Upon reading the said letters, it appearing that Bishop Seabury lay under some misapprehensions concerning an entry in the Minutes of a former Convention, as intending some doubt of the validity of his consecration,

Resolved unanimously,—That it is the opinion of this Convention, that the consecration of the Right Rev. Dr. Seabury to the Episcopal office is valid.

Mr. Burrows obtained leave of absence for Thursday.

Adjourned to 8 o'clock to-morrow morning.

Friday, July 31st, 1789.

The Convention met.

The Rev. Mr. Smith read prayers.

Dr. William Frisby produced his credentials as a Lay Deputy from the State of Maryland; which being approved, he took his seat.

The Rev. Dr. Ferguson, a Deputy from Maryland, and Mr. Philip Reading, a Deputy from Delaware, took their seats.

The Convention then went in procession to the German Reformed Church, in consequence of the invitation received from the Trustees of the University of Pennsylvania to attend the Commencement.

Friday, half-past 1, P.M.

The Convention having returned, they proceeded to business.

On motion, Resolved,—That a Committee, consisting of one Deputy from each State, be appointed to prepare a body of Canons for the government of this Church. And

The Rev. Dr. Beach, the Rev. Mr. Ogden, the Rev. Mr. Pilmore, the Rev. Mr. Couden, the Rev. Dr. Claggett, Mr. Andrews, and Mr. Brisbane, were appointed accordingly.

Resolved,—That on Monday next this Convention will resolve themselves into a Committee of the whole, for the purpose of taking into consideration the proposed Book of Common Prayer and Administration of the Sacraments.

Mr. Duff had leave of absence given him.

Resolved,—That the application of the Clergy of Massachusetts and New Hampshire to the Right Rev. Doctors Seabury, Provost, and White, be considered to-morrow in a Committee of the whole.

Mr. J. Cox and Mr. Ogden obtained leave of absence from Saturday evening till Monday.

Adjourned to 9 o'clock to-morrow.

SATURDAY, August 1st, 1786.

The Convention met.

The Rev. Mr. Ogden read prayers.

The Rev. Dr. Smith, from the Committee appointed to take into consideration the proposed Constitution of the Protestant Episcopal Church, and to recommend such alterations, additions, or amendments as they shall think necessary and proper, reported a Constitution for the same.

Ordered, that the said Constitution be read.

Ordered, that it be read a second time.

Samuel Powel, Esq., a Deputy from Pennsylvania, took his seat in the Convention.

The Constitution was then debated by paragraphs.

Resolved,—That the 1st, 2d, 4th, 5th, 6th, 7th, and 8th articles be adopted, and stand in this order—1, 2, 3, 4, 5, 6, 7; that they be a rule of conduct for this Convention; and that the remaining articles be postponed for the future consideration of this Convention.

The order for the day being called, the Convention resolved itself into a Committee of the whole, on the application of the Clergy of Massachusetts and New Hampshire to the Bishops in the States of Connecticut, New York, and Pennsylvania.

The Rev. Mr. Smith was called to the chair.

The Committee having made some progress in their business, rose, and reported progress, and obtained leave to sit again.

Adjourned to Monday morning, 9 o'clock.

MONDAY, August 3d, 1789.

The Convention met.

The Rev. Mr. Waddel read prayers.

The President having informed the Convention, by message, that the melancholy event of the death of the Rev. Dr. Griffith, which happened at his house this morning, necessarily detained him at home, the Rev. Dr. Smith was chosen President pro tempore.

Ordered, that the Rev. Dr. Moore, the Rev. Mr. Smith, Mr. Andrews, and Mr. Tench Coxe, be a Committee for settling the manner in which the Convention shall attend the funeral of the Rev. Dr. Griffith.

The Committee, after an adjournment of a few minutes, made the following Report:

Resolved,—That the senior Clergyman of the deputation of each State, except Virginia, attend the funeral of the Rev. Dr. Griffith as pall-bearer, and that the other members of this Convention attend as mourners, and that a Sermon be preached on the occasion.

Resolved,—That the Clergy of all denominations within this city be invited to attend his funeral.

This Report was agreed to, and the Rev. Dr. Smith was appointed to preach the funeral Sermon.

Resolved,—That the Rev. Dr. White, and Mr. Andrews, Lay Deputy from Virginia, be requested to walk as chief mourners, and direct all other matters relative to this melancholy event.

Adjourned to Tuesday, 9 o'clock A.M.

TUESDAY, August 4th, 1789.

The Convention met, and adjourned to the house of their President, to attend the funeral of the Rev. Dr. Griffith.

After the funeral, the Convention assembled, and adjourned to 4 o'clock, P.M.

TUESDAY, August 4th, P. M.

The Convention met.

On motion, resolved unanimously,—That the thanks of this Convention be given to the Rev. Dr. Smith, for his Sermon preached at the funeral of the Rev. Dr. Griffith, and that he be requested to furnish the Convention with a copy for publication.

The Convention resolved itself into a Committee of the whole, on the application of the Clergy of Massachusetts and New Hampshire.

The Committee having spent some time on the business, rose, and reported progress, and asked leave to sit again.

Dr. Claggett having been necessarily obliged to leave the Convention, the Rev. Mr. Bisset was appointed, in his stead, a member of the Committee for preparing a set of Canons.

The order for Monday being called up, it was, on motion, made the order of the day for Wednesday.

Adjourned to 9 o'clock to-morrow morning

WEDNESDAY, August 5, 1789.

The Convention met.

The Rev. Mr. Spieren read prayers.

The order of the day being called up, it was postponed.

The Convention then resolved itself into a Committee of the whole, on the application from the Clergy of Massachusetts and New Hampshire.

The Rev. Dr. Smith, in order to bring the business before them to a conclusion, offered the following resolves, viz.:

"The Committee of the whole, having had under their deliberate consideration the application of the Clergy of Massachusetts and New Hampshire, for the consecration of the Rev. Edward Bass, as their Bishop, do offer to the Convention the following resolves:

1st. Resolved,—That a complete Order of Bishops, derived as well under the English as the Scots line of Episcopacy, doth now subsist within the United States of America, in the persons of the Right Rev. William White, D.D., Bishop of the Protestant Episcopal Church in the State of Pennsylvania; the Right Rev. Samuel Provost, D.D., Bishop of the said Church in the State of New York, and the Right

Rev. Samuel Seabury, D.D., Bishop of the said Church in the State of Connecticut.

2d. Resolved,—That the said three Bishops are fully competent to every proper act and duty of the Episcopal office and character in these United States, as well in respect to the consecration of other Bishops, and the ordering of Priests and Deacons, as for the government of the Church, according to such rules, Canons, and institutions as now are, or hereafter may be duly made and ordained by the Church in that case.

3d. Resolved,—That in Christian charity, as well as of duty, necessity, and expediency, the Churches represented in this Convention ought to contribute, in every manner in their power, towards supplying the wants, and granting every just and reasonable request of their sister Churches in these States; and, therefore,

4th, Resolved,—That the Right Rev. Dr. White and the Right Rev. Dr. Provost be, and they hereby are requested to join with the Right Rev. Dr. Seabury, in complying with the prayer of the Clergy of the States of Massachusetts and New Hampshire, for the consecration of the Rev. Edward Bass, Bishop elect of the Churches in the said States; but that,before the said Bishops comply with the request aforesaid, it be proposed to the Churches in the New England States to meet the Churches of these States, with the said three Bishops, in an adjourned Convention, to settle certain articles of union and discipline among all the churches, previous to such consecration.

5th. Resolved,—That if any difficulty or delicacy, in respect to the Archbishops and Bishops of England, shall remain with the Right Rev. Drs. White and Provost, or either of them, concerning their compliance with the above request, this Convention will address the Archbishops and Bishops, and hope thereby to remove the difficulty.

These resolves were unanimously agreed to as the Report of the Committee.

The Committee having finished the business committed to them, rose, and reported to the Convention the above resolves.

On motion of the Rev. Dr. Smith, seconded by Mr. Andrews, this Report was unanimously agreed to.

Ordered,—That the different Committees appointed by this Convention, which have not yet reported, be called upon to report.

The Committee for preparing an address to the Most Reverend the Archbishops of Canterbury and York, informed the Convention that they were not yet ready to make a final report.

The Committee for preparing an address to the President of the United States, reported that they had not yet finished the business committed to their care.

Ordered, that Mr. T. Coxe be added to the above Committee.

The Committee on the Canons reported certain Canons, which were ordered to be read.

On motion, the Convention resolved themselves into a Committee of the whole on the said Canons, the Rev. Mr. Smith in the chair.

The Committee having made some progress in the business committed to them, rose and reported, and asked leave to sit again to-morrow.

Adjourned to 9 o'clock to-morrow morning.

THURSDAY, August 6th, 1789.

The Convention met.

The Rev. Mr. Couden read prayers.

On motion, Resolved,—That the Rev. Dr. Magaw, Mr. Tench Coxe, and Mr. Jones, be a Committee to assist the Secretary in revising and publishing the Minutes of the Convention.

The Committee for preparing an address to the President of the United States presented a draught, which was then read, and ordered to lie on the table.

The Convention then resolved themselves into a Committee of the whole on the Canons.

The Committee having spent some time on the business, rose and reported.

On motion, Resolved,—That the Report of the Committee lie on the table.

The address to the President of the United States was then read a second time.

It was afterwards read by paragraphs, and ordered to be engrossed for signing.

Adjourned to 9 o'clock to-morrow morning.

FRIDAY, August 7th, 1789.

The Convention met.

The Rev. Mr. Frazer read prayers.

The Rev. Dr. Smith laid before the Convention, "Proposals for printing, by subscription, a body of Sermons upon the most important branches of practical Christianity, together with an address upon the same subject," which here follow.

PHILADELPHIA, August 5, 1789.

TO THE RIGHT REVEREND AND REVEREND THE CLERGY AND THE WORTHY AND HONOURABLE LAY MEMBERS OF THE PROTESTANT EPISCOPAL CHURCH, IN THE STATES OF NEW YORK, NEW JERSEY, PENNSYLVANIA, DELAWARE, MARYLAND, VIRGINIA, AND SOUTH CAROLINA, NOW ASSEMBLED IN GENERAL CONVENTION.

MY WORTHY FRIENDS AND BRETHREN:

The Sermons and Discourses whereof the texts and titles follow, are the result of the Author's labours as a preacher of the blessed Gospel for near forty years past. Sundry of them, which were composed and delivered on special public occasions, have been already printed, and have passed through several editions, in Europe as well as America; but the main body of them were composed and delivered in the character of a Parish Minister, viz., in the years 1764 and 1765, at Christ Church and St. Peter's, in the city of Philadelphia; from thence forward to the year 1780, in the churches of the Oxford Mission, in the county of Philadelphia; and from the latter part of the year 1780, to July 1st, 1789, in Chester parish, Kent County, Maryland.

During the foregoing long period of ministerial service, the author hath frequently been solicited to print, or to give manuscript copies of many of the Sermons; and hath, as his leisure would allow, so often indulged some of his too partial friends and hearers in the latter way, that copies of sundry Sermons have been multiplied in manuscript, and circulated in a condition not only very incorrect, but wholly without those last improvements and touches which the best of them stand much in need of, and which the author had always designed to bestow on some of them, and bequeath them as a legacy to his surviving friends and hearers, if health and opportunity should permit: and if that should not be the case, he had directed those few, together with the whole remainder in the following list, to be suppressed from public view as hasty and unfinished compositions.

But the late change in the author's situation, the resignation of his parochial as well as collegiate charge in the State of Maryland, and his return to his former station in the college of Philadelphia (added to the consideration of his advanced age), rendering it probable that he can never again engage in any stated parochial duty, the applications of some of his former friends and hearers have been renewed for the publication of sundry of those Sermons, which had long since been delivered before them, and of which some of them had been supplied with manuscript copies.

In some late conversations with judicious and worthy persons, both of the Clergy and Laity, respecting the present state of our churches and people in America, it hath been further suggested, that the cause of religion and truth might be much promoted by the publication of a sufficient number of sermons, or discourses, digested, as nearly as possible, into a system or body of divinity, comprehending the most useful and important articles of the Christian doctrine, treated of in a scriptural and evangelical way, in an easy, affectionate, and correct style, suited to the minds and apprehensions of the young and those of inferior capacity, as well as edifying to those of riper years and more improved understanding; not running out into learned niceties or debates, to disturb common readers or hearers, but avoiding all speculative and controversial subjects, or touching upon them only to improve them, as far as possible, towards the purposes of practical godliness and vital Christianity.

Although the author hath not the vanity to imagine that the following Sermons are wholly sufficient to this good design, yet they may lay the foundation of a more perfect work; and he finds, upon an arrangement of them under proper heads, that, in order to form a tolerably complete system, only a few sermons would be wanting, and those chiefly upon speculative and controversial points, as the author hath ever avoided in the pulpit, but which (if thought necessary in a work of this kind) might be selected from some of the ablest and most orthodox divines of our Church.

Indeed, it may be said that a complete body of sermons and divinity might be selected or compiled in this way; and attempts of that kind have been made with good effect. But as every age and country is best pleased with its own forms, compositions, and phrases of speech, the author flatters himself, that if it should please God to enable him to finish those sermons in the way he proposes, they will be at least acceptable to those who have desired the publication of any of them. He further trusts, that if his design should meet with that approbation and countenance which he affectionately solicits from the members of the Convention, they will be of use to all well-disposed Christians, and especially to those of the following descriptions, viz.:

1. To heads of families who may think it their duty to devote the evenings of the Lord's day to the instruction of their own households.

2. To pious and well-disposed persons (remote from places of public worship, or unprovided with ministers or pastors) who may wish to collect their neighbours and friends to spend some parts of a Sunday in public worship, and in reading sermons and books of devotion.

3. To young clergymen and preachers, who, being ill supplied with books or a variety of sermons on proper subjects, may be assisted in their earlier compositions by the present work, which it is proposed to comprise in about four octavo volumes, in the same sized paper and letter as this address: two volumes to be published yearly, at the rate of one dollar per volume on the delivery of the same to the subscribers.

WILLIAM SMITH.

On motion of Mr. J. Cox,

Resolved unanimously,—That the Members of this Convention being fully persuaded that the interests of religion and practical godliness may be greatly promoted by the publication of a body of Sermons, upon the plan proposed above; and being well satisfied of the author's soundness in the faith, and eminent abilities for such a work, do testify their approbation of the same, and their desire to encourage it, by annexing their names thereto as subscribers.

[Here the names are subscribed.]

The Convention then took up the Report of the Committee of the whole upon the Canons, which were read, and engrossed.

The said Canons were then adopted, and ordered to be signed by the President and Secretary. They are as follow.

Canons

FOR THE GOVERNMENT OF THE PROTESTANT EPISCOPAL CHURCH IN THE UNITED STATES OF AMERICA, AGREED ON AND RATIFIED IN THE GENERAL CONVENTION OF SAID CHURCH, HELD IN THE CITY OF PHILADELPHIA, FROM THE 28TH DAY OF JULY TO THE 8TH DAY OF AUGUST, 1789, INCLUSIVE.

CANON 1.

In this Church there shall always be three Orders in the Ministry, viz., Bishops, Priests, and Deacons.

CANON 2.

Every Bishop elect, before his consecration, shall produce to the Bishops, to whom he is presented for that holy office, from the Convention by whom he is elected a Bishop, and from the General Convention, or a Committee of that body appointed to act in their recess, certificates, respectively in the following words, viz.:

Testimony from the Members of the Convention in the State from whence the person is recommended for Consecration.

We, whose names are underwritten, fully sensible how important it is, that the sacred office of a Bishop should not be unworthily conferred, and firmly persuaded that is is our duty to bear testimony on this solemn occasion without partiality or affection, do, in the presence of Almighty God, testify, that A. B. is not, so far as we are informed, justly liable to evil report, either for error in religion or for viciousness of life; and that we do not know or believe there is any impediment or notable crime for which he ought not to be consecrated to that holy office. We do, moreover, jointly and severally declare that, having personally known him for three years last past, we do in our consciences believe him to be of such sufficiency in good learning, such soundness in the faith, and of such virtuous and pure manners and godly conversation, that he is apt and meet to exercise the Office of a Bishop, to the honour of God and the edifying of his Church, and to be an wholesome example to the flock of Christ.

Testimony from the General Convention.

We whose names are underwritten, fully sensible how important it is that the sacred office of a Bishop should not be unworthily conferred, and firmly persuaded that it is our duty to bear our testimony on this solemn occasion without partiality or affection, do, in the presence of Almighty God, testify that A. B. is not, so far as we are informed, justly liable to evil report either for error in religion or for viciousness of life; and that we do not know or believe there is any impediment or notable crime, on account of which he ought not to be consecrated to that holy office, but that he hath, as we believe, led his life, for three years last past, piously, soberly, and honestly.

CANON 3.

Every Bishop in this Church shall, as often as may be convenient, visit the churches within his Diocese or district, for the purposes of examining the state of his Church, inspecting the behaviour of the Clergy, and administering the apostolic rite of Confirmation.

CANON 4.

Deacon's Orders shall not be conferred on any person until he shall be twenty-one years old, nor Priest's Orders on any one until he shall be twenty-four years old; and, except on urgent occasion, unless he hath been a Deacon one year. No man shall be consecrated a Bishop of this Church until he shall be thirty years old.

CANON 5.

No person shall be ordained either Deacon or Priest, unless he shall produce a satisfactory certificate from some Church, parish, or congregation, that he is engaged with them, and that they will receive him as their minister, and allow him a reasonable support; or unless he be engaged as a professor, tutor, or instructor of youth, in some college, academy, or general seminary of learning, duly incorporated; or unless the Standing Committee of the Church in the State for which he is to be ordained, shall certify to the Bishop their full belief and expectation, that he will be received and settled as a pastor by some one of the vacant churches in that State.

CANON 6.

Every candidate for Holy Orders shall be recommended to the Bishop by a Standing Committee of the Convention of the State wherein he resides, which recommendation shall be signed by the names of a majority of the Committee, and shall be in the following words:

We, whose names are hereunder written, testify that A. B., for the space of three years last past, hath lived piously, soberly, and honestly: Nor hath he at any time, as far as we know or believe, written, taught, or held, any thing contrary to the doctrine or discipline of the Protestant Episcopal Church. And, moreover, we think him a person worthy to be admitted to the sacred order of priest. In witness whereof we have hereunto set our hands. Dated the . . . day of . . . in the year of our Lord . . .

But before a Standing Committee of any State shall proceed to recommend any candidate, as aforesaid, to the Bishop, such candidate shall produce testimonials of his good morals and orderly conduct for three years last past, from the Minister and Vestry of the parish where he has resided, or from the Vestry alone if the parish be vacant; a publication of his intention to apply for Holy Orders having been previously made by such Minister or Vestry.

Canon 7.

In every State in which there is no Standing Committee, such Committee shall be appointed at its next ensuing Convention; and in the mean time every candidate for Holy Orders shall be recommended according to the regulations or usage of the Church in each State, and the requisitions of the Bishop to whom he applies.

Canon 8.

No person shall be ordained in this Church until he shall have satisfied the Bishop and the two Presbyters, by whom he shall be examined, that he is sufficiently acquainted with the New Testament in the original Greek, and can give an account of his faith in the Latin tongue, either in writing or otherwise, as may be required.

Canon 9.

Agreeably to the practice of the primitive Church, the stated times of Ordination shall be on the Sundays following the Ember weeks: viz., the Second Sunday in Lent, the Feast of Trinity, and the Sundays after the Wednesdays following the fourteenth day of September and the thirteenth of December.

Canon 10.

No person, not a member of this Church, who shall profess to be episcopally ordained, shall be permitted to officiate therein, until he shall have exhibited to the Vestry of the Church in which he shall offer to officiate, a certificate signed by the Bishop of the Diocese or district, or, where there is no Bishop, by three Clergymen of the Standing Committee of the Convention of that State, that his Letters of Orders are authentic, and given by some Bishop whose authority is acknowledged by this Church, and also satisfactory evidence of his moral character.

Signed by order of the Convention,

WILLIAM WHITE,

Bishop of the Protestant Episcopal Church in the Commonwealth of Pennsylvania, and President of the Convention.

FRANCIS HOPKINSON, Secretary.

Mr. Andrews moved the following resolve:

Whereas it appears that sundry other Canons are necessary for the good government of the Church,

Resolved,—That the Right Rev. Dr. White, the Rev. Dr. Smith, Rev. Dr. Magaw, Rev. Mr. Smith, Mr. Hopkinson, Dr. Clarkson, and Mr. T. Coxe, be a Committee to prepare and report to the next meeting of this Convention, such additional Canons as to them shall seem necessary.

Which was agreed to.

The Convention took into consideration the two Articles of the Constitution which had been postponed, and which they amended and agreed to.

Ordered, that the Constitution be engrossed for signing

The engrossed address to the President of the United States was read and signed by the Convention.

Ordered, that the Right Reverend Dr. Provost, the Rev. Mr. Smith, Mr. Andrews, Mr. John Cox, Mr. Brisbane, the Rev. Dr. Beach, the Rev. Dr. Moore, Mr. Rogers, the Rev. Mr. Ogden, Rev. Mr. Spieren, the Rev. Mr. Waddel, and the Hon. Mr.Duane, with such other gentlemen as have been deputed to this Convention, who may be in New York, be requested to present the same to the President of the United States.

Resolved,—That the said address, with the answer that may be received thereto, be printed in the Journals of the adjourned meeting of this Convention.

Adjourned to 9 o'clock to-morrow morning.

SATURDAY, August 8th, 1789.

The Convention met.

The Rev. Mr. Bisset read prayers.

The engrossed Constitution of the Protestant Episcopal Church was then read, and signed by the Convention; and is as follows.

A General Constitution

OF THE PROTESTANT EPISCOPAL CHURCH IN THE UNITED STATES OF AMERICA.

ART. 1. There shall be a General Convention of the Protestant Episcopal Church in the United States of America on the first Tuesday of August, in the year of our Lord, 1792, and on the first Tuesday of August in every third year afterwards, in such place as shall be determined by the Convention; and special meetings may be called at other times, in the manner hereafter to be provided for; and this Church, in a majority of the States which shall have adopted this Constitution, shall be represented, before they shall proceed to business, except that the representation from two States shall be sufficient to adjourn; and in all business of the Convention freedom of debate shall be allowed.

ART. 2. The Church in each State shall be entitled to a representation of both the Clergy and the Laity, which representation shall consist of one or more Deputies, not exceeding four of each Order, chosen by the Convention of the State: and in all questions, when required by the Clerical or Lay representation from any State, each Order shall have one vote; and the majority of suffrages by States shall be conclusive in each Order, provided such majority comprehend a majority of the States represented in that Order. The concurrence of both Orders shall be necessary to constitute a vote of the Convention. If the Convention of any State should neglect or decline to appoint Clerical Deputies, or if they should neglect or decline to appoint Lay Deputies, or if any of those of either Order appointed should neglect to attend, or be prevented by sickness or any other accident, such State shall nevertheless be considered as duly represented by such Deputy or Deputies as may attend, whether lay or clerical. And if, through the neglect of the Convention of any of the Churches which shall have adopted, or may hereafter adopt this Constitution, no Deputies, either Lay or Clerical, should attend at any General Convention, the Church in such State shall nevertheless be bound by the acts of such Convention.

ART. 3. The Bishops of this Church, when there shall be three or more, shall, whenever General Conventions are held, form a House of revision; and when any proposed act shall have passed in the General Convention, the same shall be transmitted to the House of revision for their concurrence. And if the same shall be sent back to the Convention, with the negative or non-concurrence of the House of revision, it shall be again considered in the General Convention, and if the Convention shall adhere to the said act by a majority of three-fifths of their body, it shall become a law to all intents and purposes, notwithstanding the non-concurrence of the House of revision; and all acts of the Convention shall be authenticated by both Houses. And in all cases, the House of Bishops shall signify to the Convention their approbation or disapprobation, the latter with their reasons in writing, within two days after the proposed act shall have been reported to them for concurrence, and in failure thereof it shall have the operation of a law. But until there shall be three or more Bishops as aforesaid, any Bishop attending a General Convention shall be a member ex officio, and shall vote with the Clerical Deputies of the State to which he belongs. And a Bishop shall then preside.

ART. 4. The Bishop or Bishops in every State shall be chosen agreeably to such rules as shall be fixed by the Convention of that State. And every Bishop of this Church shall confine the exercise of his Episcopal office to his proper Diocese or District, unless requested to ordain or confirm, or perform any other act of the Episcopal office, by any Church destitute of a Bishop.

ART. 5. A Protestant Episcopal Church in any of the United States not now represented, may, at any time hereafter, be admitted, on acceding to this Constitution.

ART. 6. In every State, the mode of trying Clergymen shall be instituted by the Convention of the Church therein. At every trial of a Bishop there shall be one or more of the Episcopal Order present: and none but a Bishop shall pronounce sentence of deposition or degradation from the Ministry on any Clergyman, whether Bishop, or Presbyter, or Deacon.

ART. 7. No person shall be admitted to Holy Orders, until he shall have been examined by the Bishop and by two Presbyters, and shall have exhibited such testimonials and other requisites as the Canons in that case provided may direct. Nor shall any person be ordained until he shall have subscribed the following declaration: "I do believe the Holy Scriptures of the Old and New Testament to be the word of God, and to contain all things necessary to salvation: and I do solemnly engage to conform to the doctrines and worship of the Protestant Episcopal Church in these United States." No person ordained by a foreign Bishop shall be permitted to officiate as a Minister of this Church, until he shall have complied with the Canon or Canons in that case provided, and have also subscribed the aforesaid declaration.

ART. 8. A Book of Common Prayer, Administration of the Sacraments, and other Rites and Ceremonies of the Church, Articles of Religion, and a form and manner of making, ordaining, and consecrating Bishops, Priests, and Deacons, when established by this or a future General Convention, shall be used in the Protestant Episcopal Church in these States, which shall have adopted this Constitution.

ART. 9. This Constitution shall be unalterable, unless in General Convention by the Church in a majority of the States which may have adopted the same; and all alterations shall be first proposed in one General Convention, and made known to the several State Conventions, before they shall be finally agreed to, or ratified, in the ensuing General Convention.

In General Convention, in Christ Church, Philadelphia, August the 8th, One thousand seven hundred and eighty-nine.

WILLIAM WHITE, D.D., Bishop of the Protestant Episcopal Church in the Commonwealth of Pennsylvania, and President of the Convention.

NEW YORK . . . ABRAHAM BEACH, D.D., Assistant Minister of Trinity Church, in the City of New York.

BENJAMIN MOORE, D.D., Assistant Minister of Trinity Church, in the City of New York.

MOSES ROGERS.

NEW JERSEY. . . WILLIAM FRAZER, Rector of St. Michael's Church, in Trenton, and St. Andrew's Church, in Amwell.

	UZAL OGDEN, Rector of Trinity Church, Newark.
	HENRY WADDELL, Rector of Shrewsbury and Middletown, New Jersey.
	GEORGE H. SPIEREN, Rector of St. Peter's, Amboy.
	JOHN COX.
	SAMUEL OGDEN.
	R. STRETTELL JONES.
PENNSYLVANIA	SAMUEL MAGAW, D.D., Rector of St. Paul's, Philadelphia.
	ROBERT BLACKWELL, D.D., Senior Assistant Minister of Christ Church and St. Peter's, Philadelphia.
	JOSEPH PILMORE, Rector of the United Churches of Trinity, St. Thomas, and All Saints.
	JOSEPH G. J. BEND, Assistant Minister of Christ Church and St. Peter's, Philadelphia.
	FRANCIS HOPKINSON.
	GERARDUS CLARKSON.
	TENCH COXE.
	SAMUEL POWEL, Esq.
DELAWARE . . .	JOSEPH COUDEN, A.M., Rector of St. Anne's.
	STEPHEN SYKES, A.M., Rector of St. Peter's and St. Matthew's, in Sussex [County.
	JAMES SYKES.
MARYLAND . . .	WILLIAM SMITH, D.D., a Clerical Delegate for Maryland, appointed in a Convention as Rector of Chester Parish, Kent County.
	COLIN FERGUSON, D.D., Rector of St. Paul's, Kent County.
	JOHN BISSETT, A.M., Rector of Shrews bury Parish, Kent County.
	RICHARD B. CARMICHAEL.
	WILLIAM FRISBY.
VIRGINIA	ROBERT ANDREWS.
SOUTH CAROLINA	ROBERT SMITH, Rector of St. Philip's Church, Charleston, and Principal of Charleston College.
	WILLIAM BRISBANE.
	W. W. BURROWS.

Proposals for an edition of the Holy Bible, by Mr. Isaac Collins, of Trenton, were laid before this Convention, and satisfactory information was given them, as to the proposer's abilities for the execution of the work.

Whereupon Resolved, on motion of Mr. Jones,

That the members of this Convention will assist Mr. Collins in the procuring of subscriptions.

The Committee for preparing an address to the Most Rev. the Archbishops of Canterbury and York, reported an address, which was read and adopted.

Ordered, that it be engrossed for signing, and that it be signed by the members of the Convention, as their address, and by the President officially.

Ordered, that it be published in the Journal of the adjourned meeting of this Convention.

On motion, Resolved,—That the Right Rev. Dr. White, Rev. Dr. Smith, Rev. Dr. Magaw, Hon. Mr. Hopkinson, Mr. T. Coxe, and Mr. Burrows, be a Committee to forward the above-mentioned address; to prepare and forward the necessary answers to the Rev. Mr. Parker and the Clergy of Massachusetts and New Hampshire, respecting their application for the consecration of the Rev. Edward Bass, their Bishop elect; to answer, as far as may be necessary, the Right Rev. Dr. Seabury's letters; to forward the minutes and proceedings of this Convention to the English Archbishops and Bishops; and also to the Right. Rev. Dr. Seabury, and to the Eastern and other Churches not included in this union, to notify to them the time and place to which this Convention should adjourn, and request their attendance at the same, for the good purposes of union and general government; and to call such special meetings of the Convention as may be necessary.

Resolved,—That this Convention adjourn, to meet at Philadelphia, on Tuesday, the 29th of September next, and that the Right Rev. Dr. Provost be requested to open the Convention with a Sermon.

Signed by order of the Convention,

WILLIAM WHITE,

Bishop of the Protestant Episcopal Church in the Commonwealth of Pennsylvania, and President of the Convention.

FRANCIS HOPKINSON, Secretary.

APPENDIX.

To all Persons to whom these presents shall come, or whom the same shall or may in any wise or at any time concern, we, John, by Divine Providence, Lord Archbishop of Canterbury, Primate of all England, and Metropolitan, send greeting:

Whereas by an Act of Parliament passed at Westminster, in the twenty-sixth year of the reign of our sovereign lord George the Third, King of Great Britain, France, and Ireland, entituled, "An Act to empower the Archbishop of Canterbury, or the Archbishop of York, for the time being, to consecrate to the Office of a Bishop, Persons, being Subjects or Citizens of Countries out of His Majesty's dominions,"—

It is enacted,—that it shall and may be lawful to and for the Archbishop of Canterbury, or the Archbishop of York for the time being, together with such other Bishops as they shall call to their assistance, to consecrate persons being subjects or citizens of countries out of his Majesty's dominions, Bishops for the purposes aforesaid, without the King's licence for their election, or the Royal mandate under the Great Seal for their confirmation and consecration, and without requiring them to take the oaths of allegiance and supremacy, and the oath of due obedience to the Archbishop for the time being. Provided always, that no persons shall be consecrated Bishops in the manner herein provided, until the Archbishop of Canterbury or the Archbishop of York, for the time being, shall have first applied for and obtained his Majesty's licence, by warrant under his Royal signet and sign manual, authorizing and impowering him to perform such consecration, and expressing the name or names of the persons so to be consecrated; nor until the said Archbishop has been fully ascertained of their sufficiency in good learning, of the soundness of their faith, and of the purity of their manners. Provided also, and be it hereby declared, that no person or persons consecrated to the office of a Bishop in the manner aforesaid, nor any person or persons deriving their consecration from or under any Bishop so consecrated, nor any person or persons admitted to the Order of Deacon or Priest by any Bishop or Bishops so consecrated, or by the successor or successors of any Bishop or Bishops so consecrated, shall be thereby enabled to exer cise his or their respective office or offices within his Majesty's dominions. Provided always, and be it farther enacted, that a certificate of such consecration shall be given under the hand and seal of the Archbishop who consecrates, containing the name of the person so consecrated, with the addition as well of the country whereof he is a subject or citizen, as of the Church in which he is appointed Bishop, and the farther description of his not having taken the said oaths, being exempted from the obligation of so doing by virtue of this Act.

Now know all men by these presents, that we the said John Lord Archbishop of Canterbury, having obtained his Majesty's licence, by warrant under his royal signet and sign manual, did, in pursuance of the said Act of Parliament, on Sunday, the fourth day of February, in the year of our Lord One thousand seven hundred and eighty-seven, in the Chapel of our Palace at Lambeth, in the county of Surry, admit our beloved in Christ, William White, Clerk, D.D., a subject or citizen of the State of Pennsylvania, in North America, and Rector of Christ Church and St. Peter's, in the city of Philadelphia, in the said State, of whose sufficiency in good learning, soundness in the faith, and purity of manners, we were fully ascertained, into the office of a Bishop of the Protestant Episcopal Church, in the State of Pennsylvania aforesaid, to which the said William White hath been elected by the Convention for the said State, as appears unto us by due testimony thereof by him produced, and him the said William White did then and there rightly and canonically consecrate a Bishop, according to the manner and form prescribed and used by the Church of England, his taking the oaths of allegiance, supremacy, and canonical obedience only excepted, he being exempted from the obligation of taking the said oaths by virtue of the above recited act. Provided, that neither he the said Bishop, nor any person or persons deriving their consecration from or under him, nor any person or persons admitted to the Order of Deacon or Priest by him, or his successor or successors, shall be enabled to exercise his or their respective office or offices within his Majesty's dominions. In testimony whereof we have caused our Archi-Episcopal seal to be affixed to these presents.—Given at Lambeth House the day and year above written, and in the fourth year of our translation.

J. [L. S.] CANTUAR.

We, William Lord Archbishop of York, Charles Lord

Bishop of Bath and Wells, and John Lord Bishop of Peterborough, were present, and assisting at the consecration within mentioned.

W. EBOR.
C. BATH AND WELLS.
J. PETERBOROUGH.

The signatures of the Archbishops of Canterbury and York, and of the Bishops of Bath and Wells, and Peterborough, were made in my presence, February 4th, 1787.

WM. DICKES,
(COPY.) SECRETARY TO THE ARCHBISHOP OF CANTERBURY.

On Sunday, the fourth day of February, in the year of our Lord One thousand seven hundred and eighty-seven, and in the fourth year of the translation of the Most Reverend Father in God, John, by Divine Providence Lord Archbishop of Canterbury, Primate of all England, and Metropolitan, in the chapel at the Palace at Lambeth, in the county of Surry, the said Most Reverend Father in God, by virtue and authority of a certain licence or warrant from his most gracious Majesty, and our sovereign Lord George the Third, by the grace of God of Great Britain, France, and Ireland, King, Defender of the Faith, and so forth, to him in this behalf directed, the Most Reverend Father in God, William, by the same Providence Lord Archbishop of York, Primate of England and Metropolitan, and the Right Reverend Fathers in God, Charles, by divine permission Lord Bishop of Bath and Wells, and John, by divine permission Lord Bishop of Peterborough, assisting him, consecrated the Rev. William White, Doctor in Divinity, Rector of Christ Church and St. Peter's, in the city of Philadelphia, a subject or citizen of the United States of North America, and the Reverend Samuel Provost, Doctor in Divinity, Rector of Trinity Church in the city of New York, a subject or citizen also of the United States of North America, to the Office of a Bishop respectively, the rites, circumstances, and ceremonies anciently used in the Church of England being observed and applied, according to the tenor of an Act passed in the twenty-sixth year of the reign of his said Majesty, entituled, "An Act to empower the Archbishop of Canterbury, or the Archbishop of York, for the time being, to consecrate to the Office of a Bishop, persons being subjects or citizens of countries out of his Majesty's dominions," in the presence of me, Robert Jenner, Notary Public, one of the Deputy Registers of the Province of Canterbury, being then and there present the Reverend and Worshipful William Backhouse, Doctor in Divinity, Archdeacon of Canterbury, the Rev. —— Lort, Doctor in Divinity, the Rev. —— Drake, Doctor in Divinity, William Dickes, Esquire, Notary Public, Secretary to his grace the said Lord Archbishop of Canterbury, with many others in great numbers then and there assem bled. Which I attest.

RT. JENNER,

(Copy.) Notary Public—Actuary assumed.

And we, the underwritten Notaries Public, by royal authority duly admitted and sworn, residing in Doctor's Commons, London, do hereby certify and attest, to all whom it may concern, that Robert Jenner, whose name is subscribed to the aforegoing act, was and is a Notary Public, and one of the Deputy Registers of the Province of Canterbury, and that the letters, name, and words, "Rt. Jenner, Notary Public," thereto subscribed, were and are of the proper handwriting and subscription of the said Robert Jenner; and that we saw him sign the same; and that full faith and entire credit is and ought to be given to all the acts, subscriptions, and attestations, of the said Robert Jenner, as well in judgment as out. In testimony whereof we have hereunto subscribed our names, to serve and avail as occasion may require, at Doctor's Commons, London, this fifth day of February, in the year of our Lord One thousand seven hundred and eighty-seven. Which we attest.

EDWARD COOPER, Notary Public.

(Copy.) WILLIAM ABBOT, Notary Public.

Note.—The Letter of Consecration of the Right Rev. Dr. Provost, will be annexed to the next Journal of the General Convention.

JOURNAL OF THE PROCEEDINGS

OF THE

BISHOPS, CLERGY AND LAITY,

OF THE

Protestant Episcopal Church

IN

THE UNITED STATES OF AMERICA,

IN

A CONVENTION

HELD IN

THE CITY OF PHILADELPHIA, FROM TUESDAY, SEPTEMBER 29TH, TO FRIDAY, OCTOBER 16TH, 1789.

PREFACE.

At a Convention of the Protestant Episcopal Church in the States of New York, New Jersey, Pennsylvania, Delaware, Maryland, Virginia, and South Carolina, held in Christ Church, in the city of Philadelphia, from July 28th to August 8th, 1789, upon the consideration of certain communications from the Bishop and Clergy of the Church in Connecticut, and from the Clergy in the Churches of Massachusetts and New Hampshire, it was resolved to adjourn to the 29th day of September following, in order to meet the said Churches, for the purpose of settling articles of union, discipline, uniformity of worship, and general government among all the Churches in the United States.

The following is a Journal of the proceedings of both Houses, (viz., of Bishops, and of Clerical and Lay Deputies) in the said adjourned Convention.

JOURNAL.

CHRIST CHURCH,
TUESDAY, September 29th, 1789.

The Right Rev. Dr. White, the Rev. Dr. William Smith, the Rev. Dr. Robert Smith, the Rev. Mr. Bend, Robert Andrews, Esq., and Dr. Gerardus Clarkson, met at Christ Church, but not being a sufficient number to proceed to business,

Adjourned until 10 o'clock to-morrow morning.

CHRIST CHURCH, WEDNESDAY, September 30th, 1789.

The Convention met.

The Right Rev. Dr. White presided, ex officio.

The Rev. Mr. Bracken read prayers.

The Rev. Mr. Bracken, Clerical Deputy from the Church in Virginia,* produced testimonials of his appointment, which being read and approved, he took his seat.

The Right Rev. Dr. Samuel Seabury, Bishop of the Protestant Episcopal Church in Connecticut, attended, to confer with the Convention, agreeable to the invitation given him, in consequence of a resolve passed at their late session; and the Rev. Dr. Samuel Parker, Deputy from the Churches in Massachusetts and New Hampshire, and the Rev. Mr. Bela Hubbard and the Rev. Mr. Abraham Jarvis, Deputies from the Church in Connecticut, produced testimonials of their appointment to confer with the Convention, in consequence of a similar invitation.

These testimonials were read, and deemed satisfactory.

The Right Rev. Dr. Seabury produced his Letters of Consecration to the holy office of a Bishop in this Church,

* This being an adjourned Convention, testimonials were only required from new members.

which were read, and ordered to be recorded. (See the Appendix.)

On motion, Resolved,—That the Secretary, the Hon. Francis Hopkinson, be permitted and requested to appoint an assistant Secretary, who is not a member of this Convention.

Resolved,—That this Convention will, to-morrow, go into a Committee of the whole, on the subject of the proposed union with the Churches in the States of New Hampshire, Massachusetts, and Connecticut, as now represented in Convention.

Resolved further,—That the hours of business in Convention, shall be from 9 o'clock in the morning until 3 in the afternoon.—Adjourned.

CHRIST CHURCH, THURSDAY, October 1st, 1789.

The Convention met.

The Rev. Mr. Rowe read prayers.

The Rev. Dr. Beach, from New York, the Rev. Mr. Frazer, and James Parker, Esq., from New Jersey, and James Sykes, Esq., from Delaware, took their seats in Convention.

Mr. Joseph Borden Hopkinson, was admitted as assistant Secretary.

Mr. John Rumsey produced credentials as a Lay Deputy from the State of Maryland, and was admitted to his seat.

The meeting in Christ Church being found inconvenient to the members in several respects,

On motion, Resolved,—That the Rev. Dr. William Smith and the Hon. Mr. Secretary Hopkinson, be appointed to wait upon his Excellency, Thomas Mifflin, Esq., the President of the State, and to request leave for the Convention to hold their meeting in some convenient apartment in the State House.

The Convention then resolved itself into a Committee of the whole, agreeably to the order of the day.

The Rev. Dr. Robert Smith in the chair.

And after some time rose and reported the following resolve, viz.:

Resolved,—That for the better promotion of an union of this Church with the eastern Churches, the General Constitution established at the last session of this Convention is yet open to amendment and alterations, by virtue of the powers delegated to this Convention.

The question being put on this Report, and a division called for, it was determined in the affirmative.

On motion, Resolved,—That a Committee be appointed to confer with the Deputies from the eastern Churches, on the subject of the proposed union with those Churches. Whereupon,

The Rev. Dr. William Smith, the Rev. Dr. Robert Smith, Rev. Dr. Benjamin Moore, Richard Harrison, and Tench Coxe, Esqrs., were chosen for this purpose.

The Rev. Dr. William Smith and Hon. Mr. Hopkinson reported, that the President of the State had very politely given permission to the Convention to hold their meetings at the State House, in the apartments of the General Assembly, until they shall be wanted for the public service.

Adjourned, to meet at the State House to-morrow morning.

STATE HOUSE, IN THE CITY OF PHILADELPHIA,
FRIDAY, October 2d, 1789.

The Convention met.

The Rev. Dr. Robert Smith read prayers.

The Rev. Dr. William Smith, from the Committee appointed to confer with the Deputies, from the Churches of New Hampshire, Massachusetts, and Connecticut, concerning a plan of union among all the Protestant Episcopal Churches in the United States of America, reported as follows, viz.

That they have had a full, free, and friendly conference with the Deputies of the said Churches, who, on behalf of the Church in their several States, and by virtue of sufficient authority from them, have signified that they do not object to the Constitution which was approved at the former session of this Convention, if the third article of that Constitution may be so modified as to declare explicitly the right of the Bishops, when sitting in a separate House, to originate and propose acts for the concurrence of the other House of Convention, and to negative such acts proposed by the other House as they may disapprove.

Your Committee conceiving this alteration to be desirable in itself, as having a tendency to give greater stability to the Constitution, without diminishing any security that is now possessed by the Clergy or Laity; and being sincerely impressed with the importance of an union to the future prosperity of the Church, do therefore recommend to the Convention a compliance with the wishes of their brethren, and that the third article of the Constitution may be altered accordingly. Upon such alteration being made, it is declared by the Deputies from the Churches in the eastern States, that they will subscribe the Constitution, and become members of this General Convention.

Upon special motion, the above Report was read a second time; whereupon the following resolution was proposed, viz.:

Resolved,—That the Convention do adopt that part of the Report of the Committee, which proposes to modify the Third Article of the Constitution, so as to declare explicitly "the right of the Bishops, when sitting in a separate House, to originate and propose acts for the concurrence of the other House of Convention, and to negative such acts proposed by the other House as they may disapprove, provided they are not adhered to by four-fifths of the other House."

After some debate, the resolution, with the proviso annexed, was agreed upon, and the Third Article was accordingly modified in the manner following, viz.:

ART. 3. The Bishops of this Church, when there shall be three or more, shall, whenever General Conventions are held, form a separate House, with a right to originate and propose acts for the concurrence of the House of Deputies, composed of Clergy and Laity; and when any proposed act shall have passed the House of Deputies, the same shall be transmitted to the House of Bishops, who shall have a negative thereupon, unless adhered to by four-fifths of the other House: and all acts of the Convention shall be authenticated by both Houses. And, in all cases, the House of Bishops shall signify to the Convention their approbation or disapprobation, the latter, with their reasons in writing, within three days after the proposed act shall have been reported to them for concurrence; and in failure thereof, it shall have the operation of a law. But until there shall be three or more Bishops as aforesaid, any Bishop attending a General Convention, shall be a member ex officio, and shall vote with the Clerical Deputies of the State to which he belongs: and a Bishop shall then preside.

On motion, Resolved,—That it be made known to the several State Conventions, that it is proposed to consider and determine, in the next General Convention, on the propriety of investing the House of Bishops with a full negative upon the proceedings of the other House.

Ordered, that the General Constitution of this Church, as now altered and amended, be laid before the Right Rev. Dr. Seabury, and the Deputies from the Churches in the eastern States, for their approbation and assent.

After a short time, they delivered the following testimony of their assent to the same viz.:

OCTOBER 2, 1789.

We do hereby agree to the Constitution of the Church, as modified this day in Convention.

SAMUEL SEABURY, D.D., Bishop of the Episcopal Church in Connecticut.
ABRAHAM JARVIS, A.M., Rector of Christ Church, Middletown:
BELA HUBBARD, A.M., Rector of Trinity Church, New Haven:
STATE OF CONNECTICUT.
SAMUEL PARKER, D.D., Rector of Trinity Church, Boston, and Clerical Deputy for Massachusetts and New Hampshire.

After subscribing as above, the Right Rev. Bishop Seabury, and the Clerical Deputies aforesaid, took their seats as members of the Convention.

On motion, the Rev. Dr. Parker and Rev. Mr. Jarvis, were added to the Committee for revising the Canons.

Adjourned.

STATE HOUSE, SATURDAY, October 3d, 1789.

The Convention met.

The Rev. Mr. Ogden read prayers.

Mr. Charles Goldsborough produced the credentials of his appointment as a Lay Deputy from the Church in Maryland, and took his seat accordingly.

The Right Rev. Bishop White informed the Convention that he had received certain letters from the Right Rev. Bishop Provost, with a request that they may be communicated to the Convention; which were read accordingly.

On motion, Resolved,—That, agreeably to the Constitution of the Church, as altered and confirmed, there is now in this Convention a separate House of Bishops.

The Bishops now withdrawing, the President's chair was declared vacant; whereupon the House of Clerical and Lay Deputies proceeded to the election of a President by ballot, and the Rev. William Smith, D.D., Clerical Deputy from Maryland (Provost of the College of Philadelphia) was duly chosen, and took the chair accordingly.

Resolved,—That seats be provided on the right hand of the chair, for the accommodation of the Bishops, when they shall choose to be present at the proceedings and debates of this House.

Here ends the Journal of the proceedings of the Convention, as consisting of a single House. The Journals of the two Houses will now follow, separately; to which will be prefixed the General Ecclesiastical Constitution, as subscribed and entered on the Book of Records, which will answer the intention, as well of exhibiting a List of the Members of both Houses in Convention, as of defining their separate rights and powers.

The Constitution

Of the Protestant Episcopal Church in the United States of America.

Art. 1. There shall be a General Convention of the Protestant Episcopal Church in the United States of America on the second Tuesday of September, in the year of our Lord 1792, and on the second Tuesday of September in every third year afterwards, in such place as shall be determined by the Convention; and special meetings may be called at other times, in the manner hereafter to be provided for; and this Church, in a majority of the States which shall have adopted this Constitution, shall be represented, before they shall proceed to business, except that the representation from two States shall be sufficient to adjourn; and in all business of the Convention, freedom of debate shall be allowed.

Art. 2. The Church in each State shall be entitled to a representation of both the Clergy and the Laity, which representation shall consist of one or more Deputies, not exceeding four of each Order, chosen by the Convention of the State: and in all questions, when required by the Clerical or Lay representation from any State, each Order shall have one vote; and the majority of suffrages by States shall be conclusive in each Order, provided such majority comprehend a majority of the States represented in that Order. The concurrence of both Orders shall be necessary to constitute a vote of the Convention. If the Convention of any State should neglect or decline to appoint Clerical Deputies, or if they should neglect or decline to appoint Lay Deputies, or if any of those of either Order appointed should neglect to attend, or be prevented by sickness or any other accident, such State shall nevertheless be considered as duly represented by such Deputy or Deputies as may attend, whether lay or clerical. And if, through the neglect of the Convention of any of the Churches which shall have adopted, or may hereafter adopt this Constitution, no Deputies, either Lay or Clerical, should attend at any General Convention, the Church in such State shall nevertheless be bound by the acts of such Convention.

Art. 3. The Bishops of this Church, when there shall be three or more, shall, whenever General Conventions are held, form a separate House, with a right to originate and propose acts for the concurrence of the House of Deputies, composed of Clergy and Laity; and when any proposed act shall have passed the House of Deputies, the same shall be transmitted to the House of Bishops, who shall have a negative thereupon unless adhered to by four-fifths of the other House. And all acts of the Convention shall be authenticated by both Houses. And in all cases, the House of Bishops shall signify to the Convention their approbation or disapprobation, the latter with their reasons in writing, within three days after the proposed act shall have been reported to them for concurrence, and in failure thereof it shall have the operation of a law.

But until there shall be three or more Bishops as aforesaid, any Bishop attending a General Convention shall be a member ex officio, and shall vote with the Clerical Deputies of the State to which he belongs; and a Bishop shall then preside.

ART. 4. The Bishop or Bishops in every State shall be chosen agreeably to such rules as shall be fixed by the Convention of that State. And every Bishop of this Church shall confine the exercise of his Episcopal office to his proper Diocese or District, unless requested to ordain or confirm, or perform any other act of the Episcopal office, by any Church destitute of a Bishop.

ART. 5. A Protestant Episcopal Church in any of the United States not now represented, may, at any time hereafter, be admitted, on acceding to this Constitution.

ART. 6. In every State, the mode of trying Clergymen shall be instituted by the Convention of the Church therein. At every trial of a Bishop there shall be one or more of the Episcopal Order present: and none but a Bishop shall pronounce sentence of deposition or degradation from the Ministry on any Clergyman, whether Bishop, or Presbyter, or Deacon.

ART. 7. No person shall be admitted to Holy Orders, until he shall have been examined by the Bishop and by two Presbyters, and shall have exhibited such testimonials and other requisites as the Canons in that case provided may direct. Nor shall any person be ordained until he shall have subscribed the following declaration: "I do believe the Holy Scriptures of the Old and New Testament to be the word of God, and to contain all things necessary to salvation: and I do solemnly engage to conform to the doctrines and worship of the Protestant Episcopal Church in these United States." No person ordained by a foreign Bishop shall be permitted to officiate as a Minister of this Church, until he shall have complied with the Canon or Canons in that case provided, and have also subscribed the aforesaid declaration.

ART. 8. A Book of Common Prayer, Administration of the Sacraments, and other Rites and Ceremonies of the Church, Articles of Religion, and a form and manner of making, ordaining, and consecrating Bishops, Priests, and Deacons, when established by this or a future General Convention, shall be used in the Protestant Episcopal Church in those States, which shall have adopted this Constitution.

ART. 9. This Constitution shall be unalterable, unless in General Convention by the Church in a majority of the States which may have adopted the same; and all alterations shall be first proposed in one General Convention, and made known to the several State Conventions, before they shall be finally agreed to, or ratified, in the ensuing General Convention.

Done in General Convention of the Bishops, Clergy, and Laity of the Church, the second day of October, 1789, and ordered to be transcribed into the Book of Records, and subscribed, which was done as follows, viz.:—

IN THE HOUSE OF BISHOPS.

SAMUEL SEABURY, D.D., Bishop of Connecticut.

WILLIAM WHITE, D.D., Bishop of the Protestant Episcopal Church, Pennsylvania.

IN THE HOUSE OF CLERICAL AND LAY DEPUTIES.

	WILLIAM SMITH, D.D., President of the House of Clerical and Lay Deputies, and Clerical Deputy from Maryland.
NEW HAMPSHIRE & MASSACHUSETTS	SAMUEL PARKER, D.D., Rector of Trinity Church, Boston.
CONNECTICUT . .	BELA HUBBARD, A.M., Rector of Trinity Church, New Haven.
	ABRAHAM JARVIS, A.M., Rector of Christ Church, Middletown.
NEW YORK . . .	BENJAMIN MOORE, D.D., ABRAHAM BEACH, D.D., } Assistant Ministers of Trinity Church, in the City of New York.
	RICHARD HARRISON, Lay Deputy from the State of New York.
NEW JERSEY. . .	UZAL OGDEN, Rector of Trinity Church, Newark.
	WILLIAM FRAZER, A.M., Rector of St. Michael's Church, Trenton, and St. Andrew's Church, Amwell.
	SAMUEL OGDEN, R. STRETTELL JONES, } Lay Deputies.
PENNSYLVANIA .	SAMUEL MAGAW, D.D., Rector of St. Paul's, Philadelphia.
	ROBERT BLACKWELL, D.D., Senior Assistant Minister of Christ Church and St. Peter's, Philadelphia.
	JOSEPH G. J. BEND, Assistant Minister of Christ Church and St. Peter's, Philadelphia.
	JOSEPH PILMORE, Rector of the United Churches of Trinity, St. Thomas, and All Saints.
	GERARDUS CLARKSON, TENCH COXE, FRANCIS HOPKINSON, SAMUEL POWEL, } Lay Deputies from the State of Pennsylvania.
DELAWARE . . .	JOSEPH COWDEN, A.M., Rector of St. Anne's.
	ROBERT CLAY, Rector of Emanuel and St. James's Churches.
MARYLAND . . .	JOHN BISSETT, A.M., Rector of Shrewsbury Parish, Kent County.
	JOHN RUMSEY, CHARLES GOLDSBOROUGH, } Lay Deputies.
VIRGINIA	JOHN BRACKEN, Rector of Bruton Parish, Williamsburg.
	ROBERT ANDREWS, Lay Deputy.
SOUTH CAROLINA	ROBERT SMITH, D.D., Rector of St. Philip's Church, Charleston.

WILLIAM SMITH, } Lay Deputies from
WILLIAM BRISBANE, } the State of South
Carolina.

Sundry other members attended this Convention at different times of sitting, but were absent on the day of signing the Constitution. See the names occasionally entered on the Journal.

JOURNAL

OF THE

House of Clerical and Lay Deputies.

STATE HOUSE, SATURDAY, October 3d, 1789.

The Bishops having withdrawn, and a President being chosen as aforesaid, the House of Clerical and Lay Deputies proceeded to business, as follows, viz.

The Committee on the Canons being called upon, reported progress, and had leave to sit again.

Resolved,—That a Committee be appointed to prepare a Calendar and tables of Lessons for Morning and Evening Prayer throughout the year; also Collects, Epistles, and Gospels;—and Rev. Dr. Parker, Rev. Dr. Moore, Rev. Mr. Bend, Dr. Clarkson, and Rev. Mr. Jarvis were chosen for this purpose.

Resolved,—That a Committee be appointed to prepare a Morning and Evening Service for the use of the Church. The Rev. Mr. Hubbard, Rev. Dr. Robert Smith, Rev. Dr. Blackwell, Mr. Rumsey, and Mr. Andrews, were chosen.

Resolved,—That a Committee be appointed to prepare a Litany, with occasional prayers and thanksgivings; and Rev. Dr. Beach, Rev. Mr. Bracken, Rev. Mr. Bisset, Mr. Hopkinson, and Mr. Goldsborough were chosen.

Resolved,—That a Committee be appointed to prepare an order for the administration of the Holy Communion; and Rev. Mr. Pilmore, Rev. Mr. Ogden, Col. Ogden, Rev. Mr. Frazer, and Mr. Sykes were appointed.

Adjourned to Monday morning.

MONDAY, October 5th, 1789.

The House met.

The Rev. Mr. Bisset read prayers.

William Smith, Esq., from South Carolina, took his seat in the House.

The Standing Committee appointed at the former session of this Convention, made report as follows:

That they had forwarded the address to the Most Reverend the Archbishops of Canterbury and York; and that they prepared and forwarded answers to the Rev. Dr. Parker and the Clergy of Massachusetts and New Hampshire; that they answered, as far as was necessary, the letters of the Right Reverend Bishop Seabury; that they notified the Church in the several States not included in this union, the time and place to which the Convention had adjourned, and requested their sending Deputies to the same, for the good purposes of union and general government; and that they inclosed, in each of the communications mentioned in this Report, a copy of the minutes and proceedings of this Convention at their last session.

The Rev. Mr. Bisset and the Rev. Mr. Bend were appointed to assist the Secretary in preparing the minutes for the press.

The Committee on the morning and evening service reported a morning service, which was read, and afterwards considered by paragraphs.

Adjourned.

TUESDAY, October 6th, 1789.

The House met.

The Rev. Mr. Bend read prayers.

The Committee on the Litany, etc., reported a Litany, which was read, and ordered to lie on the table.

Resolved,—That a Committee be appointed to report in what manner the Psalms should be used, whereupon the following members were elected by ballot for that service: Mr. Andrews, Mr. Hopkinson, Rev. Dr. Moore, Rev. Dr. Parker, and Rev. Dr. Robert Smith.

The Convention then resumed the consideration of the report on the morning service, and having made farther progress therein,

Adjourned to Thursday morning.

THURSDAY, October 8th, 1789.

The House met.

The Rev. Dr. Parker read prayers.

The Rev. Mr. Bloomer, from New York, Mr. Brisbane, from South Carolina, and the Rev. Dr. Magaw, from Pennsylvania, took their seats in the House.

The Rev. Mr. Hubbard was chosen Vice-President of this House.

The Convention resumed the consideration of the report on the morning service, and completed the same.

Ordered, that it be transcribed, and authenticated by the President and Secretary, and that the Rev. Dr. R. Smith and Mr. Andrews carry it to the House of Bishops for their concurrence.

Ordered, that the Rev. Dr. Parker and Rev. Mr. Bend, of the Committee on the Lessons, Calendar, etc., carry their report, as far as they have prepared it, to the House of Bishops for their consideration.

Mr. Harrison and Mr. Rumsey obtained leave of absence.

Adjourned.

FRIDAY, October 9th, 1789.

The House met.

The Rev. Dr. Magaw read prayers.

The Committee on the morning and evening service reported an evening service, which was read, and ordered to lie on the table.

The Committee on the Communion Service made a report, which was read, and ordered to lie on the table.

The report on the Litany was then taken up, and some progress made in the consideration thereof.

Adjourned.

SATURDAY, October 10th, 1789.

The House met.

The Rev. Mr. Frazer read prayers.

The Committee on the Calendar, etc., brought in the remainder of their report, which was ordered to be laid before the House of Bishops.

The House then resumed the consideration of the report on the Litany, and completed the same.

Ordered, that the Litany be transcribed, and authenticated by the President and Secretary.

The proposed tables of Lessons for Sundays and other Holy Days were returned by the House of Bishops, with some amendments.

On motion, the tables of Lessons for Sundays and other Holy Days, as amended by the House of Bishops, were recommitted to the Committee appointed to prepare them.

The Committee appointed to report in what manner the Psalms shall be used, made a report, which was read, agreed to, and directed to be transmitted to the House of Bishops.

The evening service was then considered, amended, and ordered to be transcribed and authenticated; and the Rev. Dr. Beach and Rev. Mr. Bisset were appointed to carry it to the House of Bishops for their concurrence.

The report on the Communion Service was taken up, and some progress made in the consideration thereof.

A message was received from the House of Bishops, with their assent to the Calendar, the Epistles and Gospels, and proposing certain amendments to the Collects laid before them; which amendments were agreed to.

Mr. Ogden had leave of absence.

It having been notified that the public service of the State of Pennsylvania would require the use of the State House during the present week,

Adjourned to meet at Christ Church on Monday morning next.

CHRIST CHURCH, MONDAY, October 12th, 1789.

The Convention met, and it being represented that convenient apartments might be had in the College of Philadelphia for the meeting of both Houses of Convention, during the remainder of the present session,

Adjourned to meet at the College immediately.

COLLEGE OF PHILADELPHIA.

The House met.

The Rev. Mr. Frazer read prayers.

A message was received from the House of Bishops, returning the proposed Litany and form of Morning Prayer, with amendments, and proposing a form of public baptism of infants.

The Committee appointed to consider the amendments of the House of Bishops to the tables of Lessons for Sundays, etc., advised a concurrence of this house in the said amendments.

Resolved,—That this report be agreed to, and that the said tables of Lessons be authenticated.

The house then took up the amendments proposed by the House of Bishops to the form of Morning Prayer and the Litany, some of which were adopted, and others non-concurred.

Ordered, that they be transmitted to the House of Bishops with the determination of this house.

A message was received from the House of Bishops, proposing a form for the solemnization of matrimony; also amendments to the report concerning the Psalms. These amendments were considered, some agreed to, and others non-concurred.

Ordered, that the House of Bishops be informed of the said determination.

A message was received from the House of Bishops, proposing an order for the visitation of the sick.

Resolved,—That, in future, this house will meet at 9 o'clock in the morning, and adjourn at 2 in the afternoon, to meet again at 4.

Adjourned till to-morrow morning.

TUESDAY, October 13th, 1789.

The House met.

The Rev. Dr. Beach read prayers.

The report on the Communion Service was resumed, considered by paragraphs, and agreed to.

A message was received from the House of Bishops, proposing a form of Burial Service, and the order in which the Psalter shall be used; and also requesting a conference with this house on the proposed amendments of the Morning Prayer and Litany.

It was agreed that this request should be complied with,

at 5 o'clock this afternoon. The Secretary was ordered to inform the House of Bishops of this, and he returned with their concurrence. Adjourned.

Four o'Clock, P.M.

The House met.

Resolved,—That the intended conference with the House of Bishops be deferred to a future time.

The Rev. Dr. Parker and Rev. Dr. Moore were desired to inform the House of Bishops of this resolution, and returned with the concurrence of that house.

Six additional Collects, reported by the Committee on the Communion Service, were considered and agreed to, and, with the Communion Service, ordered to be transcribed and transmitted to the House of Bishops.

A message was received from the House of Bishops, proposing the manner and form of setting forth the Book of Psalms in metre.

The Committee on the Litany, etc., reported certain occasional prayers and thanksgivings, which, with some few amendments, were adopted, and ordered to be transmitted to the House of Bishops.

The Convention then took up the form of Public Baptism of Infants, which they amended, and returned to the House of Bishops.

On motion, Resolved,—That the following clause be added to the Seventh Canon of this Church.

Unless it shall be recommended to the Bishop by two-thirds of the State Convention to which he belongs, to dispense with the aforesaid requisition in whole or in part: which recommendation shall only be for good causes moving thereunto, and shall be in the following words, with the signature of the names of the majority of such Convention: "We whose names are underwritten, are of opinion, that the dispensing with the knowledge of the Latin and Greek languages (or either of them, as the case may be) in the examination of A. B. for Holy Orders, will be of use to the Church of which we are the Convention, in consideration of other qualifications of the said A. B. for the Gospel ministry.

The above clause being sent to the House of Bishops, received their concurrence.

Adjourned.

WEDNESDAY, October 14th, 1789.

The House met.

The Rev. Dr. Parker read prayers.

The form for the Solemnization of Matrimony was considered and amended, and transmitted to the House of Bishops.

A message was received from the House of Bishops, informing that they had passed the form of Public Baptism of Infants, with the amendments of this house, and proposing a form for the private baptism of infants, and a form of baptism of those of riper years.—Adjourned.

Four o'clock, P.M.

The House met.

The Burial Service was considered, amended, and transmitted to the House of Bishops.

A message was received from the House of Bishops, with amendments to the Communion Service, and with the form for the Solemnization of Matrimony, which they had passed as amended by this house.

The amendments to the Communion Service were considered, amended, and transmitted to the House of Bishops; and the Service, thus amended, was, with the six additional Collects, assented to and returned by the said House.

Adjourned.

THURSDAY, October 15th, 1789.

The House met.

The Rev. Mr. Pilmore read prayers.

The order in which the Psalter shall be read, was considered and agreed to.

The house then went into a conference with the House of Bishops, which continued till 2 o'clock.—Adjourned.

Four o'clock, P.M.

The House met.

The Constitution, as copied in the Book of Records, was read and compared, and, having received an alteration as to the time of the future meetings of the Convention, was signed by both Houses of Convention.

The Committee on the Canons reported certain Canons,

which, being considered and amended, were ratified, and transmitted to the House of Bishops.

The house again went into a conference with the House of Bishops, in the course of which it was agreed, that the Book of Common Prayer, to be set forth by this Convention, shall be in use from the 1st day of October, 1790.

A message was received from the House of Bishops, pro posing a Catechism, Confirmation, and forms of prayer for families, and containing their assent to the Burial Service, except the first rubric; in their amendment to which this house concurred.

Dr. Parker obtained leave of absence after to-morrow noon.

On motion, the Rev. Dr. Blackwell, the Rev. Mr. Ogden, and Rev. Mr. Bisset, were appointed a Committee to report what further measures are necessary to perpetuate the succession of Bishops in America.—Adjourned.

FRIDAY, October 16th, 1789.

The Convention met.

The Rev. Dr. Beach read prayers.

The House of Bishops returned the Canons, with an amendment, in which this house concurred; and they also proposed a title-page to the Book of Common Prayer, which was read and passed.

The Canons now passed, together with those passed at the last session, being collected into one body, and ratified by both houses, were directed to be entered in the Book of Records, and printed with the Journal of this Convention. (See Appendix.)

The Rev. Mr. Bend proposed a table of proper Psalms for certain days, which was passed, and sent to the House of Bishops.

A preface and table of contents were sent to this house by the House of Bishops, which, with their concurrence, were referred to the Committee to be appointed to superintend the publication of the Book about to be issued by the Convention.

Tables for finding the Holy Days, and tables of the Moveable and Immoveable Feasts, which had been proposed by the House of Bishops, were passed.

The House of Bishops returned the order of Evening Prayer, with an amendment, to which this house agreed.

They also transmitted to this house amendments to the occasional prayers and thanksgivings, and a form for the churching of women, a form of thanksgiving for the fruits of the earth, additional prayers for the visitation of the sick, and a form of ratification of the Prayer Book.

The amendments of the House of Bishops to the occasional prayers and thanksgivings were considered and assented to.

A message was received from the House of Bishops, with their assent to the table of proper Psalms; and proposing a form of prayer to be used at sea, and a form of prayer for the visitation of prisoners, also an order for the communion of the sick.

The manner and form of setting forth the Book of Psalms in metre was considered, amended, and returned to the House of Bishops.

The additional prayers for the visitation of the sick were considered, and passed with an amendment, to which the House of Bishops agreed.

The order for the visitation, and the order for the communion of the sick, were agreed to.

The form of the ratification of the Book of Common Prayer was agreed to.

The House of Bishops proposed, for the adoption of this house, Articles of Religion, which, with the concurrence of the House of Bishops, were referred to a future Convention.

The form of the visitation of prisoners was then passed.

The form of thanksgiving for the fruits of the earth was assented to; also the form of prayer to be used at sea.

A message was received from the House of Bishops, with their assent to the amendments proposed to the manner and form of setting forth the Book of Psalms in metre.

The order for the administration of the baptism of those of riper years was considered and passed; also the form of private baptism of infants.

A message was sent to the House of Bishops, proposing that the Ash Wednesday Service, as set forth in the proposed book, should be adopted, instead of the commination formerly used; to which the House of Bishops assented.

The Confirmation, and the forms of family morning and evening prayer, were considered and adopted.

A message was received from the House of Bishops, proposing an alteration in the Litany, which was sent back with an amendment, in which the House of Bishops concurred.

A message was received from the House of Bishops, with their assent to the Morning Prayer, and the report on the Psalms.

Adjourned.

Four o'clock, P.M.

The House met.

The Catechism was considered, amended, and transmitted to the House of Bishops.

The form for the churching of women was agreed to; and it was resolved, with the concurrence of the House of Bishops, that the thanksgiving in the said form should be inserted among the occasional thanksgivings, and used, at the discretion of the Minister, instead of the whole Office.

Resolved,—That the Rev. Dr. William Smith, Rev. Dr. Magaw, Rev. Dr. Blackwell, Mr. Hopkinson, and Mr. Coxe, be a Committee to superintend the printing of the Book of Common Prayer, as set forth by this Convention, and that they advise with any person or persons who shall be appointed by the House of Bishops for the same purpose.

Resolved,—That the Committee appointed to superintend the printing of the Book of Common Prayer, etc., be instructed to have the selections of Psalms, set forth by this Church, printed immediately before the Psalter; and, besides a full and complete edition of the said book, printed in folio or octavo, or in both, to have an edition published, to contain only the parts in general use and the Collects of the day, with references to the Epistles and Gospels.

A message was received from the House of Bishops, with their assent to the Catechism, as amended; and with information that the Right Reverend Bishop White consents to advise with the Committee appointed by this house to superintend the printing of the Book of Common Prayer, etc.

Mr. Tench Coxe was elected Treasurer of the Convention.

The following gentlemen were appointed a Standing Committee, to act during the recess of the Convention:—The Reverend Dr. William Smith, ex officio, Reverend Dr. Parker, Reverend Mr. Hubbard, Reverend Dr. Beach, Mr. Harrison, Reverend Mr. Ogden, Mr. Jones, Reverend Dr. Blackwell, Mr. Hopkinson, Reverend Mr. Clay, Mr. Sykes, Reverend Mr. Bisset, Mr. Carmichael, Reverend Mr. Bracken, Mr. Andrews, Reverend Dr. Robert Smith, and Mr. Brisbane.

Resolved,—That this Committee, or a majority of them, have power to recommend to the Bishops the calling of special meetings of the Convention, when they think it necessary.

Resolved,—That it is the opinion of this house, that the Bishops have a right, when they think it necessary, to call special Conventions.

The Committee on the means of perpetuating the Episcopal succession in the United States of America, made the following report, which was read and adopted, viz.:

The Committee on the means of perpetuating the Episcopal succession in these United States, are of opinion,—

That the Standing Committee, which, agreeably to the Constitution, is chosen, as above, to act during the recess of the General Convention, ought, in the name of the Convention, to recommend for consecration any person who shall appear to them to be duly elected and qualified for the Episcopal office. That should any person, elected and qualified as above, be proposed, and should the answer from the English Archbishops be favourable to the intended plan of consecrating by the Right Rev. the Bishops Seabury, White, and Provoost, the Committee shall write to the said three Bishops, intimating that it is the will and desire of the General Convention, that such consecration should, as soon as convenient, take place. That, should the answer from England be unfavourable, or any obstacle occur, by the death of either of the three Bishops, or otherwise, the said Committee shall recommend any Bishop elect to England, for consecration.

Resolved,—That, with the concurrence of the House of Bishops, the next meeting of the Convention be in the city of New York.

Resolved,—That the Right Rev. Bishop Seabury be requested to preach a Sermon at the opening of the next Convention.

Signed by order of the House of Clerical and Lay Deputies.

WILLIAM SMITH, PRESIDENT.

FRANCIS HOPKINSON, Secretary.

JOURNAL

OF THE

House of Bishops.

IN CONVENTION OF THE PROTESTANT EPISCOPAL CHURCH IN THE UNITED STATES OF AMERICA, HELD AT THE STATE HOUSE, IN THE CITY OF PHILADELPHIA, ON MONDAY, THE 5TH DAY OF OCTOBER, IN THE YEAR OF OUR LORD, 1789.

After divine service in the House of Clerical and Lay Deputies, the House of Bishops met in the Committee Room of the Honorable House of Assembly. Present:

The Right Rev. Samuel Seabury, D.D., and
The Right Rev. William White, D.D.

The following rules are agreed on, and established, for the government of this house, viz.:

1st. The senior Bishop present shall be the President; seniority to be reckoned from the dates of the Letters of Consecration.

2d. This house will authenticate its acts by the signing of the names of, at least, the majority of its members.

3d. There shall be a Secretary to this house.

In addition to the above, it is now established as a temporary rule, that this house will attend divine service, during the Session, in the House of Clerical and Lay Deputies.

The Rev. Joseph Clarkson, A.M., is appointed the Secretary of this house.

This house went into a review of the Morning and Evening Prayer, and prepared some proposals on that subject.

Adjourned till 10 o'clock to-morrow morning.

STATE HOUSE, TUESDAY, October 6th, 1789.

After divine service,

Adjourned till 9 o'clock on Thursday morning.

THURSDAY, October 8th, 1789.

Divine service being over,

This house went into the consideration of the Litany, and of the other parts of the service connected with the Morning and Evening Prayer, and completed their proposals on that subject, excepting a few particulars, which they have noted as queries for their further consideration.

The house then proceeded to the consideration of the Collects, Epistles, and Gospels, and from them to the order for the administration of the Holy Communion; and having prepared their proposals on these parts of the service,

Adjourned till 9 o'clock to-morrow morning.

FRIDAY, October 9th, 1789.

Divine service being over,

The house went into a review of the service for the public baptism of infants, and prepared proposals on that subject.

The house then received a message from the House of Clerical and Lay Deputies, by the Rev. Dr. Parker and the Rev. Mr. Bend, informing that they had prepared tables of lessons for Sundays and other holy days, to be laid before this house, which were accordingly presented.

The house went immediately into the consideration of the above, during which there was received a message from the House of Clerical and Lay Deputies, by the Rev. Dr. Robert Smith and Robert Andrews, Esq., with information that they had prepared a form of Morning Prayer, to be laid before this house; which was accordingly presented.

The house then proceeded in their examination of the tables of lessons, and having prepared some amendments of the same,

Adjourned till 9 o'clock to-morrow morning.

SATURDAY, October 10th, 1789.

After divine service,

The house completed the instrument of amendments of the tables of lessons, and sent the same by their Secretary to the House of Clerical and Lay Deputies.

This house received a message from the House of Clerical and Lay Deputies, by the Rev. Dr. Parker and the Rev. Mr. Bend, with information that they had prepared proposals in regard to the Calendar, and in regard to the Collects, Epistles, and Gospels; which were accordingly presented.

The house then went into the consideration of the proposed form of Morning Prayer, during which they received a message from the House of Clerical and Lay Deputies, by the Rev. Dr. Beach and the Rev. Mr. Bisset, with information that they had prepared the Litany to be laid before this house; which was accordingly presented.

The house then went on with the consideration of the Morning Prayer, when they received another message from the House of Clerical and Lay Deputies, by the Rev. Dr. Robert Smith, and the Rev. Dr. Moore, with information that they had prepared a selection of Psalms; which was laid before the house.

The house, after preparing their amendments of the Morning Prayer for engrossing, proceeded to the consideration of the proposed Litany, and prepared their amendments of that service also for engrossing.

They then proceeded to the consideration of the proposed Calendar, and having assented to the same, returned it by their Secretary.

The house then proceeded to consider the proposals respecting the Collects, Epistles, and Gospels, and having prepared their amendments, sent them by their Secretary to the House of Clerical and Lay Deputies.

A message was received by the Rev. Dr. Parker, from the House of Clerical and Lay Deputies, representing that if this house were prepared to originate any parts of the service, it would be agreeable to the House of Clerical and Lay Deputies to receive them on Monday morning.

Accordingly the Secretary is desired to prepare a copy of the proposed form of public baptism of infants.

The public service requiring the use of the room where this house sit,

Adjourned to the Apparatus Room of the College, there to meet on Monday morning, at 9 o'clock.

College of Philadelphia,
Monday, October 12th, 1789.

Divine service being over,

The House of Bishops sent, by their Secretary, to the House of Clerical and Lay Deputies, their amendments of the Morning Prayer and of the Litany, together with the alterations, originated in this house, of the ministration of the public baptism of infants.

This house received a message from the House of Clerical and Lay Deputies, by the Rev. Dr. Parker, informing that they agree to the amendments proposed in regard to the tables of Lessons for Sundays, and other holy days, excepting the fourth amendment, on which they desire a conference.

This house withdrew the said fourth amendment, and desired Dr. Parker to report the same to the House of Clerical and Lay Deputies.

This house then prepared alterations of the form of solemnization of matrimony, which were accordingly reported by their Secretary to the House of Clerical and Lay Deputies.

The House of Clerical and Lay Deputies returned to this house, by the Hon. Mr. Hopkinson, their amendments of the Morning Prayer and Litany, with their concurrence in some articles and non-concurrence in others.

The house prepared alterations of the order for the visitation of the sick, which were accordingly reported to the House of Clerical and Lay Deputies.

The House of Clerical and Lay Deputies returned to this house the proposed amendments of the selection of Psalms, with their concurrence of some articles, and non-concurrence of others.

Adjourned till to-morrow at 9 o'clock.

TUESDAY, October 13th, 1789.

Divine service being over,

The House of Bishops proceeded to prepare,—the order how the Psalter is appointed to be read; the order how the rest of the Holy Scriptures is appointed to be read; and the order for the burial of the dead,—which being prepared, were sent by the Secretary to the House of Clerical and Lay Deputies, together with a message, requesting a conference with that house on the amendments of the proposed Morning Prayer and Litany, at such time and in such manner as they shall agree upon.

The house then proceeded to prepare a commination service, etc., when they received a message from the House of Clerical and Lay Deputies, by their Secretary, informing that, agreeably to the request of this house, they had appointed 5 o'clock this afternoon for a conference on the proposed Morning Prayer and Litany.

The room in which the House of Clerical and Lay Deputies meet was mutually agreed on, as most convenient for the business.

Adjourned till 4 o'clock this afternoon.

Four o'clock, P.M.

The House of Bishops received a message from the House of Clerical and Lay Deputies, by the Rev. Dr. Parker and the Rev. Dr. Moore, with information that, if agreeable to this house, the House of Clerical and Lay Deputies would postpone the conference agreed to be held this afternoon, until further communication; with which this house concurred.

This house then prepared the form and manner of setting forth the Psalms in metre, and sent the same, by their Secretary, to the House of Clerical and Lay Deputies; together with the form of Commination, etc., and tables of Moveable and Immoveable Feasts, with tables for finding the holy days.

The house then received a message from the House of Clerical and Lay Deputies, by the Rev. Dr. Beach, with information, that they had to propose prayers and thanksgivings for several occasions; which were accordingly presented.

Adjourned till 9 o'clock to-morrow morning.

WEDNESDAY, October 14th, 1789.

Divine service being over,

This house received a message from the House of Clerical and Lay Deputies, by the Rev. Dr. Parker, with amendments of the alterations of the Burial Service, originated in this house.

The amendments being concurred in, the alterations were passed, and returned.

This house then originated alterations of the services for private baptism, and for the baptism of adults, and sent the same, by their Secretary, to the House of Clerical and Lay Deputies.

A message from the House of Clerical and Lay Deputies, by the Hon. Mr. Hopkinson, was received by this house, which accompanied amendments of the alteration of the marriage service, originated in this house; which amendments being concurred in, the alterations were passed and returned.

This house received from the House of Clerical and Lay Deputies a proposed Communion Service, and made amendments.

Adjourned till 4 o'clock in the afternoon.

Four o'clock, P.M.

The house originated alterations of the Catechism—of the order of Confirmation—and a form of family prayer—and sent them to the House of Clerical and Lay Deputies, with the amendments of the Communion Service; which last were concurred in, except one, which being withdrawn by this house, the service was passed, and returned.

Adjourned till to-morrow morning, 9 o'clock.

THURSDAY, October 15th, 1789.

Divine service being over,

This house had returned to them, from the House of Clerical and Lay Deputies, by the Rev. Dr. Parker, the order how the Psalter is appointed to be read, and the order how the rest of the Holy Scripture is appointed to be read, with amendments; all of which were concurred in, except one, which was left for the conference, into which the house now went, agreeably to a former appointment, and in which they were employed during the morning of this day.

Adjourned till 4 o'clock this afternoon.

Four o'clock, P.M.

This house originated, and proposed to the House of Clerical and Lay Deputies, alterations of the title-page, a form of ratification of the Book of Common Prayer, a table of contents, a form or manner of printing the former preface, and those called "Of the Service of the Church," and "Of Ceremonies:" these, with the form of thanksgiving of women after child-birth, before prepared, and the amendments of the occasional prayers, were sent, by the Secretary, to the House of Clerical and Lay Deputies; after which the two houses proceeded in their conference.

Adjourned till to-morrow morning, 9 o'clock.

FRIDAY, October 16th, 1789.

Divine service being over,

This house received from the House of Clerical and Lay Deputies, by Dr. Blackwell, Canons, as reported by a Committee appointed at the former session.

This house acceded to the Canons proposed, except the amendment of one, in consequence of which it was proposed to withdraw the Canon, which being acceded to, this house passed the Canons.

This house received by Robert Andrews, Esq., the proposed order for Evening Prayer, of which they made an amendment, by proposing the insertion of two hymns, as alternatives to the Psalms already in the Service; which being agreed to, the order for Evening Prayer was passed.

The house received, by the Rev. Mr. Bend, a table of proper Psalms, which was passed.

The house received, by the Rev. Dr. Beach and Robert Andrews, Esq., the table of contents, and the other initial parts of the Book of Common Prayer, with a proposal that they should be referred to a Committee, to sit in the recess of this Convention; which was agreed to.

The house received by Rev. Mr. Ogden and Rev. Mr. Bend, amendments of the form of ratification of the Book of Common Prayer, and also the form of churching of women, which are to lay over for consideration.

This house originated and sent to the house of Clerical and Lay Deputies as follow: A proposed ratification of the Thirty-nine Articles, with an exception in regard to the thirty-sixth and thirty-seventh articles; a form for the Communion of the sick; a form for the visitation of prisoners; a form for thanksgivings for the fruits of the earth; and pray ers to be inserted in the visitation of the sick.

The House of Clerical and Lay Deputies returned, by the Rev. Mr. Bend, the proposed form of printing the Psalms in metre, with hymns, and proposed amendments of the same; which were agreed to, and the whole passed.

This house received, by the Rev. Mr. Bend, the visitation office and additional prayers, which being concurred in, the whole were passed; as was also the form of the ratification of the Book of Common Prayer.

This house received by Robert Andrews, Esq., the ratification of the articles, with a proposal for postponement, which was agreed to, the proposal for the Communion of the sick being first presented and passed.

This house received, by the Rev. Mr. Bisset, a proposal for retaining the service for Ash-Wednesday, as in the proposed book, with one alteration, which was agreed to.

This house returned the occasional prayers, passed.

The house then passed the Morning and Evening Prayer, the Litany, the selection of the Psalms, and the orders how the Psalter and the rest of the Holy Scripture is appointed to be read.

Four o'clock, P.M.

The house received from the House of Clerical and Lay Deputies, amendments of the Catechism; which being agreed to, the Service was passed.

This house returned to the House of Clerical and Lay Deputies, the office for the churching of women, and the occasional prayers, the amendments mutually proposed having been agreed to.

It is understood that the Services originated in this house, and not returned with amendments, have been agreed to.

This house received from the House of Clerical and Lay Deputies, a message, informing that they had appointed a Committee, to join with any person to be appointed by this house, in setting forth the Book of Common Prayer. In consequence of which the Right Rev. Bishop White agrees to assist the Committee in preparing tho book for publication.

The House of Clerical and Lay Deputies signified to this house that they were about to adjourn, to meet, the next stated time, in the city of New York, having previously appointed a Committee to act, if necessary, in their recess. On which, this house adjourned to the same time and place.

Signed as the Journal of the Convention, the sixteenth day of October, One thousand seven hundred and eighty-nine.

SAMUEL SEABURY, D.D.,
BISHOP OF CONNECTICUT, PRESIDENT.
WILLIAM WHITE, D.D., PENNSYLVANIA.

Attested: JOSEPH CLARKSON, Secretary.

APPENDIX.

Canons

FOR THE GOVERNMENT OF THE PROTESTANT EPISCOPAL CHURCH IN THE UNITED STATES OF AMERICA, AGREED ON AND RATIFIED IN THE GENERAL CONVENTION OF SAID CHURCH, HELD IN THE CITY OF PHILADELPHIA, FROM THE 29TH DAY OF SEPTEMBER TO THE 16TH DAY OF OCTOBER, 1789, INCLUSIVE.

CANON I.—Of the Orders of the Ministers in this Church.

In this Church there shall always be three Orders in the Ministry, viz: Bishops, Priests, and Deacons.

CANON II.—Certificates to be produced on the part of Bishops elect.

Every Bishop elect, before his consecration, shall produce to the Bishops, to whom he is presented for that holy office, from the Convention by whom he is elected a Bishop, and from the General Convention, or a Committee of that body to be appointed to act in their recess, certificates, respectively in the following words, viz.:

TESTIMONY FROM THE MEMBERS OF THE CONVENTION IN THE STATE FROM WHENCE THE PERSON IS RECOMMENDED FOR CONSECRATION.

We, whose names are underwritten, fully sensible how important it is, that the sacred office of a Bishop should not be unworthily conferred, and firmly persuaded that it is our duty to bear testimony on this solemn occasion without partiality or affection, do, in the presence of Almighty God, testify, that A. B. is not, so far as we are informed, justly liable to evil report, either for error in religion or for viciousness of life; and that we do not know or believe there is any impediment or notable crime for which he ought not to be consecrated to that holy office. We do, moreover, jointly and severally declare that, having personally known him for three years last past, we do in our consciences believe him to be of such sufficiency in good learning, such soundness in the faith, and of such virtuous and pure manners and godly conversation, that he is apt and meet to exercise the Office of a Bishop, to the honour of God and the edifying of his Church, and to be an wholesome example to the flock of Christ.

TESTIMONY FROM THE GENERAL CONVENTION.

We, whose names are underwritten, fully sensible how important it is that the sacred office of a Bishop should not be unworthily conferred, and firmly persuaded that it is our duty to bear our testimony on this solemn occasion without partiality or affection, do, in the presence of Almighty God, testify that A. B. is not, so far as we are informed, justly liable to evil report either for error in religion or for viciousness of life; and that we do not know or believe there is any impediment or notable crime, on account of which he ought not to be consecrated to that holy office, but that he hath, as we believe, led his life, for the three years last past, piously, soberly, and honestly.

Canon III.—Of Episcopal Visitation.

Every Bishop in this Church shall, as often as may be convenient, visit the churches within his Diocese or district, for the purposes of examining the state of his Church, inspecting the behaviour of the Clergy, and administering the apostolic rite of Confirmation.

Canon IV.—Of the Age of those who are to be Ordained or Consecrated.

Deacon's Orders shall not be conferred on any person until he shall be twenty-one years old, nor Priest's Orders on any one until he shall be twenty-four years old; and, except on urgent occasion, unless he hath been a Deacon one year. No man shall be consecrated a Bishop of this Church until he shall be thirty years old.

Canon V.—Of the Titles of those who are to be Ordained.

No person shall be ordained either Deacon or Priest, unless he shall produce a satisfactory certificate from some Church, parish, or congregation, that he is engaged with them, and that they will receive him as their minister, and allow him a reasonable support; or unless he be engaged as a professor, tutor, or instructor of youth, in some college, academy, or general seminary of learning, duly incorporated; or unless the Standing Committee of the Church in the State for which he is to be ordained, shall certify to the Bishop their full belief and expectation, that he will be received and settled as a pastor by some one of the vacant churches in that State.

Canon VI.—The Testimonials to be produced on the part of those who are to be Ordained.

Every candidate for Holy Orders shall be recommended to the Bishop by a Standing Committee of the Convention of the State wherein he resides, which recommendation shall be signed by the names of a majority of the Committee, and shall be in the following words:

We, whose names are hereunder written, testify that A. B., for the space of three years last past, hath lived piously, soberly, and honestly: Nor hath he at any time, as far as we know or believe, written, taught, or held, any thing contrary to the doctrine or discipline of the Protestant Episcopal Church. And, moreover, we think him a person worthy to be admitted to the sacred order of . . . In witness whereof we have hereunto set our hands. Dated the . . . day of . . . in the year of our Lord . . .

But before a Standing Committee of any State shall proceed to recommend any candidate, as aforesaid, to the Bishop, such candidate shall produce testimonials of his good morals and orderly conduct for three years last past, from the Minister and Vestry of the parish where he has resided, or from the Vestry alone if the parish be vacant—a publication of his intention to apply for Holy Orders having been previously made by such Minister or Vestry. In every State in which there is no Standing Committee, such Committee shall be appointed at its next ensuing Convention; and in the mean time, every candidate for Holy Orders shall be recommended according to the regulations or usage of the Church in each State, and the requisitions of the Bishop to whom he applies.

Canon VII.—Of the Learning of those who are to be Ordained.

No person shall be ordained in this Church until he shall have satisfied the Bishop and the two Presbyters, by whom he shall be examined, that he is sufficiently acquainted with the New Testament in the original Greek, and can give an account of his faith in the Latin tongue, either in writing or otherwise, as may be required. Unless it shall be recommended to the Bishop by two-thirds of the State Convention to which he belongs, to dispense with the aforesaid requisition in whole or in part: which recommendation shall only be for good causes moving thereunto, and shall be in the following words, with the signature of the names of the majority of such Convention: "We whose names are underwritten, are of opinion, that the dispensing with the knowledge of the Latin and Greek languages (or either of them, as the case may be) in the examination of A. B. for Holy Orders, will be of use to the Church of which we are the Convention, in consideration of other qualifications of the said A. B. for the Gospel ministry.

Canon VIII.—Of the Stated Times of Ordination.

Agreeably to the practice of the primitive Church, the stated times of Ordination shall be on the Sundays following the Ember weeks: viz., the Second Sunday in Lent, the Feast of Trinity, and the Sundays after the Wednesdays following the fourteenth day of September and the thirteenth of December.

Canon IX.—Of those who, having been ordained by foreign Bishops, settle in this Church.

No person, not a member of this Church, who shall profess to be episcopally ordained, shall be permitted to officiate therein, until he shall have exhibited to the Vestry of the Church in which he shall offer to officiate, a certificate signed by the Bishop of the Diocese or district, or, where there is no Bishop, by three Clergymen of the Standing Committee of the Convention of that State, that his Letters of Orders are authentic, and given by some Bishop whose authority is acknowledged by this Church, and also satisfactory evidence of his moral character.

CANON X.—Of the Use of the Book of Common Prayer.

Every minister shall, before all sermons and lectures, use the Book of Common Prayer, as the same shall be set forth and established by the authority of this or some future General Convention; and until such establishment of an uniform Book of Common Prayer in this Church, every minister shall read the Book of Common Prayer directed to be used by the Convention of the Church in the State in which he resides; and no other prayer shall be used besides those contained in the said book.

CANON XI.—Of the duty of Ministers in regard to Episcopal Visitation.

It shall be the duty of ministers to prepare children and others for the the holy ordinance of Confirmation. And on notice being received from the Bishop of his intention to visit any Church, which notice shall be at least one month before the intended visitation, the minister shall be ready to present for Confirmation those who shall have been previously instructed for the same, and shall deliver to the Bishop a list of the names of those presented.

And at every visitation it shall be the duty of the minister and of the church wardens, to give information to the Bishop of the state of the congregation, under such heads as shall have been committed to them in the notice given as aforesaid.

And further, the ministers and church wardens of such congregations as cannot be conveniently visited in any year, shall bring or send to the Bishop, at the stated meeting of the Convention of the diocese or district, information of the state of the congregation, under such heads as shall have been committed to them at least one month before the meeting of the Convention.

CANON XII.—Notorious Crimes and Scandals to be censured.

If any persons within this church offend their brethren by any wickedness of life, such persons shall be repelled from the Holy Communion, agreeably to the rubric, and may be further proceeded against, to the depriving of them of all privileges of church membership, according to such rules or process as may be provided, either by the General Convention or by the Conventions in the different States.

CANON XIII.—Sober conversation required in Ministers.

No ecclesiastical persons shall, other than for their honest necessities, resort to taverns or other places most liable to be abused to licentiousness. Further, they shall not give themselves to any base or servile labour, or to drinking or riot, or to the spending of their time idly. And if any offend in the above, they shall be liable to the ecclesiastical censure of admonition, or suspension, or degradation, as the nature of the case may require, and according to such rules or process as may be provided, either by the General Convention or by the Conventions in the different States.

Canon XIV.—Of the due celebration of Sundays.

All manner of persons within this Church shall celebrate and keep the Lord's day, commonly called Sunday, in hearing the word of God read and taught, in private and public prayer, in other exercises of devotion, and in acts of charity, using all godly and sober conversation.

Canon XV.—Ministers to keep a Register.

Every minister of this Church shall keep a register of baptisms, marriages, and funerals within his cure, agreeably to such rules as may be provided by the ecclesiastical authority where his cure lies; and if none such be provided, then in such a manner as in his discretion he shall think best suited to the uses of such a register.

And the intention of the register of baptisms is hereby declared to be, as for other good uses, so especially for the proving of the right of church membership of those who may have been admitted into this Church by the holy ordinance of baptism.

And further, every minister of this Church shall, within a reasonable time after the publication of this Canon, make out and continue a list of all adult persons within his cure, to remain for the use of his successor, to be continued by him and by every future minister in the same parish.

And no minister shall place on the said list the names of any persons except of those who, on due enquiry, he shall find to have been baptised in this Church; or who, having been otherwise baptised, shall have been received into this Church either by the holy rite of Confirmation, or by receiving the Holy Communion, or by some other joint act of the parties and of a minister of this Church, whereby such persons shall have attached themselves to the same.

Canon XVI.—A List to be made and published of the Ministers of this Church.

The secretary of the General Convention shall keep a register of all the Clergy of this Church, whose names shall be delivered to him, in the following manner: that is to say, every Bishop of this Church,—or, where there is no Bishop, the Standing Committee of that diocese or district,—shall, at the time of every General Convention, deliver, or cause to be delivered to the secretary, a list of the names of all the ministers of this Church in their proper diocese or district, annexing the names of their respective cures, or of their stations in any colleges or other incorporated seminaries of learning, or, in regard to those who have not any cures or such stations, their places of residence only. And the said list shall, from time to time, be published in the Journals of the General Convention,

And further, it is recommended to the several Bishops of this Church, and to the several Standing Committees, that, during the intervals between the meetings of the General Convention, they take such means of notifying the admission of ministers among them, as, in their discretion respectively, they shall think effectual to the purpose of preventing ignorant and unwary people from being imposed on, by persons pretending to be authorised ministers of this Church.

CANON XVII.—Notice to be given of the Induction and Dismission of Ministers.

It is hereby required, that on the induction of a minister into any Church or parish, the parties shall deliver, or cause to be delivered to the Bishop, or to the Standing Committee of the Diocese or district, notice of the same in the following form, or to this effect:

We, the church wardens (or, in case of an Assistant Minister, We, the rector and church wardens) do certify to the Right Rev. (naming the Bishop) that (naming the person) has been duly chosen Rector (or Assistant Minister as the case may be) of (naming the church or churches).

Which certificate shall be signed with the names of those who certify.

And if the Bishop, or the Standing Committee, be satisfied that the person so chosen is a qualified minister of this Church, he shall transmit the said certificate to the Secretary of the Convention, who shall record it in a book to be kept by him for that purpose.

But if the Bishop, or the Standing Committee, be not satisfied as above, he or they shall, at the instance of the parties, proceed to enquire into the sufficiency of the person so chosen, according to such rules as may be made in the States respectively, and shall confirm or reject the appointment, as the issue of that enquiry may be.

Passed, October 16th, 1789.

HOUSE OF BISHOPS:
SAMUEL SEABURY, Bishop of Connecticut,
PRESIDENT.
WILLIAM WHITE, Pennsylvania.

ATTESTED: JOSEPH CLARKSON, Secretary.

HOUSE OF CLERICAL AND LAY DEPUTIES:
WILLIAM SMITH, PRESIDENT.

ATTESTED: FRANCIS HOPKINSON, Secretary.

APPENDIX No. I.

An Address to the President of the United States, published agreeably to the following order, viz.:

IN CONVENTION, August 7th, 1789.

The Address to the President of the United States being read, and signed in Convention—

Resolved,—That the said Address, with the answer that may be received thereto, be printed in the Journals of the adjourned meeting of this Convention.

TO THE PRESIDENT OF THE UNITED STATES.

SIR:—We, the Bishops, Clergy, and Laity of the Protestant Episcopal Church in the States of New York, New Jersey, Pennsylvania, Delaware, Maryland, Virginia, and South Carolina, in General Convention assembled, beg leave, with the highest veneration, and the most animating national considerations, at the earliest moment in our power, to express our cordial joy on your election to the chief magistracy of the United States.

When we contemplate the short but eventful history of our nation; when we recollect the series of essential services performed by you in the course of the Revolution; the temperate yet efficient exertion of the mighty powers with which the nature of the contest made it necessary to invest you; and especially when we remember the voluntary and magnanimous relinquishment of those high authorities at the moment of peace; we anticipate the happiness of our country under your future administration.

But it was not alone from a successful and virtuous use of those extraordinary powers, that you were called from your honorable retirement to the first dignities of our government. An affectionate admiration of your private character, the impartiality, the persevering fortitude, and the energy with which your public duties have been invariably performed, and the paternal solicitude for the happiness of the American people, together with the wisdom and consummate knowledge of our affairs, manifested in your last military communication, have directed to your name *the universal wish*, and have produced, for the first time in the history of mankind, *an example of unanimous consent* in the appointment of the governor of a free and enlightened nation.

To these considerations, inspiring us with the most pleasing expectations as private citizens, permit us to add, that, as the representatives of a numerous and extended Church, we most thankfully rejoice in the election of a civil ruler, deservedly beloved, and eminently distinguished among the friends of genuine religion—who has happily united a tender regard for other churches with an inviolable attachment to his own.

With unfeigned satisfaction we congratulate you on the establishment of the new Constitution of government of the United States, the mild yet efficient operations of which, we confidently trust, will remove every remaining apprehension of those with whose opinions it may not entirely coincide, and will confirm the hopes of its numerous friends. Nor do these expectations appear too sanguine, when the moderation, patriotism and wisdom of the honorable members of the Federal legislature are duly considered. From a body thus eminently qualified, harmoniously co-operating with the Executive authority in constitutional concert, we confidently hope for the restoration of order and of our ancient virtues,—the extension of genuine religion,—and the consequent advancement of our respectability abroad, and of our substantial happiness at home.

We devoutly implore the Supreme Ruler of the Universe to preserve you long in health and prosperity,—an animating example of all public and private virtues,—the friend and guardian of a free, enlightened, and grateful people,—and that you may finally receive the reward which will be given to those whose lives have been spent in promoting the happiness of mankind.

WILLIAM WHITE, D.D., Bishop of the Protestant Episcopal Church, in the Commonwealth of Pennsylvania, and President of the Convention.

SAMUEL PROVOOST, D.D., Bishop of the Protestant Episcopal Church in the State of New York.

NEW YORK . . . BENJAMIN MOORE, D.D., Assistant Minister of Trinity Church, in the City of New York.

ABRAHAM BEACH, D.D., Assistant Minister of Trinity Church, in the City of New York.

NEW JERSEY. . . WILLIAM FRAZER, A.M., Rector of St. Michael's Church, Trenton, and St. Andrew's Church, Amwell.

UZAL OGDEN, Rector of Trinity Church, in Newark.

HENRY WADDEL, Rector of the churches of Shrewsbury and Middletown, New Jersey.

GEORGE H. SPIEREN, Rector of St. Peter's Church, Perth Amboy, New Jersey.

JOHN COX.

SAMUEL OGDEN.

ROBERT STRETTELL JONES.

PENNSYLVANIA . SAMUEL MAGAW, D.D., Rector of St. Paul's, and Vice-Provost of the University of Pennsylvania.

ROBERT BLACKWELL, D.D., Senior Assistant Minister of Christ Church and St. Peter's, Philadelphia.

JOSEPH PILMORE, Rector of the United Churches of Trinity, St. Thomas, and All Saints.

JOSEPH G. J. BEND, Assistant Minister of Christ Church and St. Peter's, Philadelphia.

FRANCIS HOPKINSON.

GERARDUS CLARKSON.

	TENCH COXE.
	SAMUEL POWEL.
DELAWARE . . .	JOSEPH COUDEN, A.M., Rector of St. Anne's.
	STEPHEN SYKES, A.M., Rector of the united Churches of St. Peter's and St. Matthew in Sussex Co.
	JAMES SYKES.
MARYLAND . . .	WILLIAM SMITH, D.D., Provost of the College and Academy of Philadelphia, and Clerical Deputy for Maryland, as late Rector of Chester Parish, in Kent County.
	THOMAS JOHN CLAGGET, Rector of St. Paul's, Prince George County.
	COLIN FERGUSON, D.D., Rector of St. Paul's, Kent County.
	JOHN BISSETT, A.M., Rector of Shrewsbury Parish, Kent County.
	WILLIAM FRISBY.
	RICHARD B. CARMICHAEL.
VIRGINIA	ROBERT ANDREWS.
SOUTH CAROLINA	ROBERT SMITH, D.D., Rector of St. Philip's Church, Charleston.
	W. W. BURROWS.
	WILLIAM BRISBANE.

THE PRESIDENT'S ANSWER.

TO THE BISHOPS, CLERGY, AND LAITY OF THE PROTESTANT EPISCOPAL CHURCH, IN THE STATES OF NEW YORK, NEW JERSEY, PENNSYLVANIA, DELAWARE, MARYLAND, VIRGINIA, AND SOUTH CAROLINA, IN GENERAL CONVENTION ASSEMBLED.

GENTLEMEN:

I sincerely thank you for your affectionate congratulation on my election to the chief magistracy of the United States.

After having received from my fellow-citizens in general the most liberal treatment—after having found them disposed to contemplate, in the most flattering point of view, the performance of my military services, and the manner of my retirement at the close of the war—I feel that I have a right to console myself, in my present arduous undertaking, with a hope that they will still be inclined to put the most favourable construction on the motives which may influence me in my future public transactions.

The satisfaction arising from the indulgent opinion entertained by the American people, of my conduct, will, I trust, be some security for preventing me from doing any thing, which might justly incur the forfeiture of that opinion. And the consideration that human happiness and moral duty are inseparably connected, will always continue to prompt me to to promote the progress of the former, by inculcating the practice of the latter.

On this occasion it would ill become me to conceal the joy I have felt in perceiving the fraternal affection which appears to encrease every day among the friends of genuine religion. It affords edifying prospects indeed, to see Christians of different denominations dwell together in more charity, and conduct themselves, in respect to each other, with a more Christian-like spirit than ever they have done in any former age, or in any other nation.

I receive, with the greatest satisfaction, your congratulations on the establishment of the New Constitution of Government; because I believe its mild, yet efficient, operations will tend to remove every remaining apprehension of those, with whose opinions it may not entirely coincide, as well as to confirm the hopes of its numerous friends; and because the moderation, patriotism, and wisdom of the present Federal Legislature seem to promise the restoration of order and our ancient virtues—the extension of genuine religion—and the consequent advancement of our respectability abroad, and of our substantial happiness at home.

I request, Most Reverend and respectable Gentlemen, that you will accept my cordial thanks for your devout supplications to the Supreme Ruler of the Universe in behalf of me. May you, and the people whom you represent, be the happy subjects of Divine Benediction both here and hereafter!

GEORGE WASHINGTON.

August 19, 1789.

APPENDIX.—No. II.

AN ADDRESS TO THE MOST REVEREND THE ARCHBISHOPS OF CANTERBURY AND YORK.

Most Venerable and Illustrious Fathers and Prelates:

We, the Bishops, Clergy, and Laity of the Protestant Episcopal Church in the States of New York, New Jersey, Pennsylvania, Delaware, Maryland, Virginia, and South Carolina, impressed with every sentiment of love and veneration, beg leave to embrace this earliest occasion, in General Convention, to offer our warmest, most sincere, and grateful acknowledgments to you, and (by your means), to all the venerable Bishops of the Church over which you preside, for the manifold instances of your former condescension to us, and solicitude for our spiritual welfare. But we are more especially called to express our thankfulness for that particular act of your fatherly goodness, whereby we derive, under you, a pure Episcopacy and succession of the ancient Order of Bishops, and are now assembled, through the blessing of God, as a Church duly constituted and organized, with the happy prospect before us of a future full and undisturbed exercise of our holy religion, and its extension to the utmost bounds of this continent, under an ecclesiastical constitution, and a form of worship, which we believe to be truly apostolical.

The growing prospect of this happy diffusion of Christianity, and the assurance we can give you, that our churches are spreading and flourishing throughout these United States, we know, will yield you more solid joy, and be considered as a more ample reward of your goodness to us, than all the praises and expressions of gratitude which the tongues of men can bestow.

It gives us pleasure to assure you, that, during the present sitting of our Convention, the utmost harmony has prevailed through all our deliberations; that we continue, as heretofore, most sincerely attached to the faith and doctrine of the Church of England, and that not a wish appears to prevail, either among our Clergy or Laity, of ever departing from that Church in any essential article.

The business of most material consequence which hath come before us, at our present meeting, hath been, an application from our sister churches in the Eastern States, expressing their earnest desire of a general union of the whole Episcopal Church in the United States, both in doctrine and discipline; and, as a primary means of such union, praying the assistance of our Bishops in the consecration of a Bishop elect for the States of Massachusetts and New Hampshire. We therefore judge it necessary to accompany this address with the papers which have come before us on that very interesting subject, and of the proceedings we have had thereupon, by which you will be enabled to judge concerning the particular delicacy of our situation, and, probably, to relieve us from any difficulties which may be found therein.

The application from the Church in the States of Massachusetts and New Hampshire is in the following words, viz.:

The good providence of Almighty God, the fountain of all goodness, having lately blessed the Protestant Episcopal Church in the United States of America, by supplying it with a complete and entire Ministry, and affording to many of her communion the benefit of the labours, advice, and government of the successors of the Apostles:

We, Presbyters of said Church in the States of Massachusetts and New Hampshire, deeply impressed with the most lively gratitude to the Supreme Governor of the universe, for his goodness in this respect, and with the most ardent love to his Church, and concern for the interest of her sons, that they may enjoy all the means that Christ, the great Shepherd and Bishop of souls, has instituted for leading his followers into the ways of truth and holiness, and preserving his Church in the unity of the spirit and the bond of peace, to the end that the people committed to our respective charges may enjoy the benefit and advantage of those offices, the administration of which belongs to the highest Order of the Ministry, and to encourage and promote, as far as in us lies, a union of the whole Episcopal Church in these States, and to perfect and compact this mystical body of Christ, do hereby nominate, elect and appoint, the Rev. Edward Bass, a Presbyter of said Church, and Rector of St. Paul's, in Newburyport, to be our Bishop; and we do promise and engage to receive him as such, when canonically consecrated, and invested with the apostolic office and powers by the Right Reverend the Bishops hereafter named, and to render him all that canonical obedience and submission which, by the laws of Christ, and the constitution of our Church, is due to so important an office.

And we now address the Right Reverend the Bishops in the States of Connecticut, New York, and Pennsylvania, praying their united assistance in consecrating our said brother, and canonically investing him with the apostolic office and powers. This request we are induced to make, from a long acquaintance with him, and from a perfect knowledge of his being possessed of that love to God and benevolence to men, that piety, learning, and good morals, that prudence and discretion, requisite to so exalted a station, as well as that personal respect and attachment to the communion at large in these States, which will make him a valuable acquisition to the Order, and, we trust, a rich blessing to the Church.

Done at a meeting of the Presbyters whose names are underwritten, held at Salem, in the County of Essex, and Commonwealth of Massachusetts, the fourth day of June, Anno Salutis, 1789.

SAMUEL PARKER, Rector of Trinity Church, Boston.
T. FITCH OLIVER, Rector of St. Michael's Church, Marblehead.
JOHN COUSENS OGDEN, Rector of Queen's Chapel, Portsmouth, New Hampshire.
WILLIAM MONTAGUE, Minister of Christ's Church, Boston.
TILLOTSON BRUNSON, Assistant Minister of Christ's Church, Boston.
A true copy.
Attest: SAMUEL. PARKER.

At the meeting aforesaid,

Voted,—That the Rev. Samuel Parker be authorised and empowered to transmit copies of the foregoing Act, to be by him attested, to the Right Reverend the Bishops in Connecticut, New York, and Pennsylvania; and that he be appointed our agent, to appear at any Convocation to be holden at Pennsylvania or New York, and to treat upon any measures that may tend to promote an union of the Episcopal Church throughout the United States of America, or that may prove advantageous to the interest of the said Church.

EDWARD BASS, CHAIRMAN.

A true copy.
Attest: SAMUEL PARKER.

This was accompanied with a letter from the Rev. Samuel Parker, the worthy Rector of Trinity Church, Boston, to the Right. Rev. Bishop White, dated June. 21st, 1789, of which the following is an extract:

"The Clergy here have appointed me their agent, to appear at any Convocation to be held at New York or Pennsylvania; but I fear the situation of my family and parish will not admit of my being absent so long as a journey to Philadelphia would take. When I gave you encouragement that I should attend, I was in expectation of having my parish supplied by some gentlemen from Nova Scotia, but I am now informed they will not be here till some time in August. Having, therefore, no prospect of attending in person at your General Convention next month, I am requested to transmit you an attested copy of an act of the Clergy of this and the State of New Hampshire, electing the Rev. Edward Bass our Bishop, and requesting the united assistance of the Right Reverend Bishops of Pennsylvania, New York, and Connecticut, to invest him with apostolic powers. This act I have now the honour of enclosing, and hope it will reach you before the meeting of your General Convention in July.

"The clergy of this State are very desirous of seeing an union of the whole Episcopal Church in the United States take place; and it will remain with our brethren at the southward to say, whether this shall be the case or not—whether we shall be an united or divided church. Some little difference in government may exist in different States, without affecting the essential points of union and communion."

In like spirit, the Right Rev. Dr. Seabury, Bishop of the Church in Connecticut, in his letter to the Rev. Dr. Smith, dated July 23d, writes on the subject of union, etc., as followeth:

"The wish of my heart, and the wish of the Clergy and of the Church people of this State, would certainly have carried me and some of the Clergy to your General Convention, had we conceived we could have attended with propriety. The necessity of an union of all the Churches, and the disadvantages of our present dis-union, we feel and lament equally with you; and I agree with you, that there may be a strong and efficacious union between churches, where the usages are different. I see not why it may not be so in the present case, as soon as you have removed those obstructions which, while they remain, must prevent all possibility of uniting. The Church of Connecticut consists, at present, of nineteen clergymen in full orders, and more than twenty thousand people they suppose, as respectable as the Church in any State in the union."

After the most serious deliberation upon this important business, and cordially joining with our brethren of the eastern or New England Churches in the desire of union, the following resolves were unanimously adopted in Convention, viz.:

Resolved,—1st, That a complete Order of Bishops, derived as well under the English as the Scots line of succession, doth now subsist within the United States of America, in the persons of the Right Rev. William White, D.D., Bishop of the Protestant Episcopal Church in the State of Pennsylvania; the Right Rev. Samuel Provoost, D.D., Bishop of the said Church in the State of New York; and the Right Rev. Samuel Seabury, D.D., Bishop of the said Church in the State of Connecticut.

2d. That the said three Bishops are fully competent to every proper act and duty of the Episcopal office and character in these United States; as well in respect to the consecration of other bishops, and the ordering of Priests and Deacons, as for the government of the Church, according to such Canons, Rules, and institutions as now are, or hereafter may be, duly made and ordained by the Church in that case.

3d. That in Christian charity, as well as of duty, necessity, and expediency, the Churches represented in this Convention onght to contribute, in every manner in their power, towards supplying the wants, and granting every just and reasonable request of their sister churches in these States; and therefore resolved,—

4th. That the Right Rev. Dr. White and the Right Rev. Dr. Provoost be, and they hereby are, requested to join with the Right Rev. Dr. Seabury, in complying with the prayer of the Clergy of the States of Massachusetts and New Hampshire, for the consecration of the Rev. Edward Bass, Bishop elect of the churches in the said States; but that, before the said Bishops comply with the request aforesaid, it be proposed to the churches in the New England States to meet the Churches of these States, with the said three Bishops, in an adjourned Convention, to settle certain articles of union and discipline among all the churches, previous to such consecration.

5th. That if any difficulty or delicacy, in respect to the Archbishops and Bishops of England, shall remain with the Right Rev. Drs. White and Provoost, or either of them, concerning their compliance with the above request, this Convention will address the Archbishops and Bishops, and hope thereby to remove the difficulty.

We have now, most venerable Fathers, submitted to your consideration whatever relates to this important business of union among all our churches in these United States. It was our original and sincere intention to have obtained three bishops, at least, immediately consecrated by the Bishops of England, for the seven States comprehended within our present union. But that intention being frustrated through unforeseen circumstances, we could not wish to deny any present assistance, which may be found in our power to give to any of our sister churches, in that way which may be most acceptable to them, and in itself legal and expedient.

We ardently pray for the continuance of your favour and blessing, and that, as soon as the urgency of other weighty concerns of the Church will allow, we may be favoured with that fatherly advice and direction, which to you may appear most for the glory of God and the prosperity of our Churches, upon the consideration of the foregoing documents and papers.

Done in Convention this eighth day of August, 1789, and directed to be signed by all the members as the act of their body, and by the President officially.

WILLIAM WHITE, D.D., Bishop of the Protestant Episcopal Church, in the Commonwealth of Pennsylvania, and President of the Convention.

NEW YORK . . . ABRAHAM BEACH, D.D., Assistant Minister of Trinity Church, in the City of New York.

BENJAMIN MOORE, D.D., Assistant Minister of Trinity Church, in the City of New York.

MOSES ROGERS, Lay Deputy from New York.

NEW JERSEY . . WILLIAM FRAZER, A.M., Rector of St. Michael's Church, in Trenton, and St. Andrew's Church, in Amwell.

UZAL OGDEN, Rector of Trinity Church, Newark.

HENRY WADDELL, Rector of the Churches of Shrewsbury and Middleton.

GEORGE H. SPIEREN, Rector of St. Peter's Church, Perth Amboy.

JOHN COX,
SAMUEL OGDEN,
ROBERT S. JONES, } Lay Deputies.

PENNSYLVANIA . SAMUEL MAGAW, D.D., Rector of St. Paul's, Philadelphia, and Vice-Provost of the University.

ROBERT BLACKWELL, D.D., Senior Assistant Minister of Christ Church and St. Peter's, Philadelphia.

JOSEPH PILMORE, Rector of the United Churches of Trinity, St. Thomas' and All Saints.

	JOSEPH G. J. BEND, Assistant Minister of Christ Church and St. Peter's, in Philadelphia.
	GERARDUS CLARKSON, TENCH COXE, FRANCIS HOPKINSON, } Lay Deputies.
DELAWARE . . .	JOSEPH COWDEN, ClericalDeputy.
	STEPHEN SYKES, Clerical Deputy.
	JAMES SYKES, Lay Deputy.
MARYLAND . . .	WILLIAM SMITH, D.D., Provost of the College and Academy of Philadelphia, and Clerical Deputy as late Rector of Chester Parish, Kent County, Maryland. And for
	THOMAS JOHN CLAGGETT, D. D., Rector of St. Paul's, Prince George's County.
	COLIN FERGUSON, D.D., Rector of St. Paul's, Kent County.
	JOHN BISSETT, A.M., Rector of Shrewsbury Parish.
	RICHARD B. CARMICHAEL, WILLIAM FRISBY, } Lay Deputies.
VIRGINIA	ROBERT ANDREWS, Professor of Mathematics in the College of William and Mary.
SOUTH CAROLINA	ROBERT SMITH, D.D., Rector of St. Philip's Church, and Principal of Charleston College.
	WILLIAM BRISBANE, WILLIAM BURROWS, } Lay Deputies.

APPENDIX.—No. III.

PAPERS RELATING TO THE SCOTS EPISCOPACY, AS CONNECTED WITH THE ENGLISH, AND THE CONSECRATION OF BISHOP SEABURY.

Extract from the Register of Archbishop Juxon, in the Library of his Grace the Archbishop of Canterbury, at Lambeth Palace.—FOL. 237.

"It appears that James Sharp was consecrated Archbishop of St. Andrew's—Andrew Fairfoull, Archbishop of Glasgow—Robert Leighton, Bishop of Doublenen (Dunblane)—and James Hamilton, Bishop of Galloway—on the 15th day of December, 1661, in St. Peter's Church, Westminister, by Gilbert, Bishop of London, Commissary to the Archbishop of Canterbury; and that the Right Rev. George, Bishop of Worcester, John, Bishop of Carlisle, and Hugh, Bishop of Landaff, were present and assisting."

Extracted this 3d day of June, 1789, by me,

WILLIAM DICKES, SECRETARY.

LONDON, JUNE 3d, 1789.

That the above is a true copy of an extract procured by order of Archbishop Moore, to be sent to Bishop Seabury, in Connecticut, is attested by us, Bishops of the Scottish Church, now in this place on business of importance to the said Church.

JOHN SKINNER, BISHOP.

WILLIAM ABERNETHY DRUMMOND, BISHOP.

JOHN STRÆCHAN, BISHOP.

A List of the Consecration and Succession of Scots Bishops since the Revolution, 1688, under William the Third as far as the Consecration of Bishop Seabury is concerned.

1693. FEB. 23. Dr. George Hicks, was consecrated Suffragan of Thetford, in the Bishop of Peterborough's chapel, in the parish of Enfield, by Dr. William Lloyd, Bishop of Norwich, Dr. Francis Turner, Bishop of Ely, and Dr. Thomas White, Bishop of Peterborough.

N. B Dr. Lloyd, Dr. Turner, and Dr. White, were three of the English Bishops who were deprived at the revolution, by the civil Power, for not swearing allegiance to William the Third. They were also three of the Seven Bishops who had been sent to the Tower by James the Second, for refusing to order an illegal proclamation to be read in their dioceses.

1705. JAN. 25. Mr. John Sage, formerly one of the Ministers of Glasgow, and Mr. John Fullarton, formerly Minister of Paisley, were consecrated at Edinburgh, by John Paterson, Archbishop of Glasgow, Alexander Rose, Bishop of Edinburgh, and Robert Douglas, Bishop of Dunblane.

N. B. Archbishop Paterson, Bishop Rose, and Bishop Douglas, were deprived at the revolution, by the civil power, because they refused to swear allegiance to William the Third.

1709. APRIL 28. Mr. John Falconar, Minister at Cairnbee, and Mr. Henry Chrystie, Minister at Kinross, were consecrated at Dundee, by Bishop Rose of Edinburgh, Bishop Douglas of Dunblane, and Bishop Sage.

1711. AUG. 25. The Honourable Archibald Campbell was consecrated at Dundee, by Bishop Rose of Edinbnrgh, Bishop Douglas of Dunblane, and Bishop Falconar.

1712. FEB. 24. Mr. James Gadderar, formerly Minister at Kilmaurs, was consecrated at London, by Bishop Hickes, Bishop Falconar, and Bishop Campbell.

1712. OCT. 22. Mr. Arthur Millar, formerly Minister at Inveresk, and Mr. William Irvine, formerly Minister at Kirkmichael, in Carrict, were consecrated at Edinburgh, by Bishop Rose of Edinburgh, Bishop Fullarton, and Bishop Falconar.

After the Bishop of Edinburgh's death.

1722. Oct. 7. Mr. Andrew Cant, formerly one of the Ministers of Edinburgh, and Mr. David Freebairn, formerly Minister of Dunning, were consecrated at Edinburgh, by Bishop Fullarton, Bishop Millar, and Bishop Irvine.

1727. June 4. Dr. Thomas Rattray, of Craighall, was consecrated at Edinburgh, by Bishop Gadderar, Bishop Millar, and Bishop Cant.

1727. June 18. Mr. William Dunbar, Minister at Cruden, and Mr. Robert Keith, Presbyter in Edinburgh, were consecrated at Edinburgh, by Bishop Gadderar, Bishop Millar, and Bishop Rattray.

N. B. They who were deprived of their Parishes at the revolution are, in this list called Ministers; but they who have not been parish Ministers under the civil establishment, are called Presbyters.

1736. June 24. Mr. Robert White, Presbyter at Cupar, was consecrated at Carsebank, near Forfar, by Bishop Rattray, Bishop Dunbar, and Bishop Keith.

1741. Sept. 10. Mr. William Falconar, Presbyter at Forres, was consecrated at Alloa, in Clacmannanshire, by Bishop Rattray, Bishop Keith, and Bishop White.

1742. Oct. 4. Mr. James Rait, Presbyter at Dundee, was consecrated at Edinburgh by Bishop Rattray, Bishop Keith, and Bishop White.

1743. Aug. 19. Mr. John Alexander, Presbyter at Alloa, in Clacmannanshire, was consecrated at Edinburgh, by Bishop Keith, Bishop White, Bishop Falconar, and Bishop Rait.

1747. July 17. Mr. Andrew Gerard, Presbyter in Aberdeen, was consecrated at Cupar, in Fife, by Bishop White, Bishop Falconar, Bishop Rait, and Bishop Alexander.

1759. Nov. 1. Mr. Henry Edgar was consecrated at Cupar, in Fife, by Bishop White, Bishop Falconar, Bishop Rait and Bishop Alexander, as co-adjutor to Bishop White, then Primus.

N. B. Anciently, no Bishop in Scotland had the stile of Archbishop, but one of them had a precedency, under the title of *Primus Scotiæ Episcopus.* And after the revolution they returned to their old stile, which they still retain, one of them being entitled Primus, to whom precedency is allowed, and deference paid in the Synod of Bishops.

1762. June 24. Mr. Robert Forbes was consecrated at Forfar, by Bishop Falconar, *Primus*, Bishop Alexander, and Bishop Gerard.

1768. Sept. 21. Mr. Robert Kilgour, Presbyter at Peterhead, was consecrated Bishop of Aberdeen, at Cupar, in Fife, by Bishop Falconar, Primus, Bishop Rait, and Bishop Alexander.

1777. Aug. 24. Mr. Charles Rose, Presbyter at Down, was consecrated Bishop of Dunblane, at Forfar, by Bishop Falconar, *Primus*, Bishop Rait, and Bishop Forbes.

1776. June 27. Mr. Arthur Petrie, Presbyter at Meikelfolla, was consecrated Bishop Co-adjutor at Dundee, by Bishop Falconar, *Primus*, Bishop Rait, Bishop Kilgour, and Bishop Rose, and appointed Bishop of Ross and Caithness, July 8th, 1777.

N. B. After the revolution, the Bishops in Scotland had no particular diocess, but managed their ecclesiastical affairs in one body as a College; but finding inconveniences in the mode, they took particular dioceses, which, though not exactly according to the limits of the dioceses under the former legal establishment, still retain their old names.

1778. Aug. 13. Mr. George Inness, Presbyter in Aberdeen, was consecrated Bishop of Brechen, at Alloa, by Bishop Falconar, *Primus*, Bishop Rose, and Bishop Petrie.

1782. Sept. 25. Mr. John Skinner, Presbyter in Aberdeen, was consecrated Bishop Co-adjutor, at Luthermuir, in the diocess of Brechen, by Bishop Kilgour, *Primus*, Bishop Rose, and Petrie.

☞ The foregoing list is taken from an attested copy, in the possession of Bishop Seabury.

1784. Nov. 14. Dr. Samuel Seabury, Presbyter, from the State of Connecticut, in America, was consecrated Bishop at Aberdeen, by Bishop Kilgour, *Primus*, Bishop Petrie, and Bishop Skinner,—as, by the deed of consecration, as follows, viz.:

IN DEI NOMINE.—Amen.

Omnibus ubique Catholicis per Presentes pateat,

Nos, Robertum Kilgour, miseratione divina, Episcopum Aberdonien—Arthurum Petrie, Episcopum Rossen et Moravien—et Joannem Skinner, Episcopum Coadjutorem; Mysteria Sacra Domini nostri Jesu Christi in Oratorio supradicti Joannis Skinner apud Aberdoniam celebrantes, Divini Numinis Præsidio fretos (presentibus tam e Clero, quam e Populo testibus idoneis) Samuelem Seabury, Doctorem Divinitatis, sacra Presbyteratus ordine jam decoratum, ac nobis præ Vitæ integritate, Morum probitate et Orthodoxia, commendatum, et ad docendum et regendum aptum et idoneum, ad sacrum et sublimem Episcopatus Ordinem promovisse, et rite ac canonice, secundum Morem et Ritus Ecclesiæ Scoticanæ, consecrasse, Die Novembris decimo quarto, Anno Æræ Christianæ Millesimo Septingentesimo Octagesimo Quarto.

In cujus Rei Testimonium, Instrumento huic (chirographis nostris prius munito) Sigilla nostra apponi mandavimus.

ROBERTUS KILGOUR, Episcopus, et Primus. [L. S.]

ARTHURUS PETRIE, Episcopus. [L. S.]

JOANNES SKINNER, Episcopus. [L. S.]

JOURNAL OF THE PROCEEDINGS

OF THE

BISHOPS, CLERGY, AND LAITY

OF THE

Protestant Episcopal Church

IN

THE UNITED STATES OF AMERICA,

IN

A CONVENTION

HELD IN

THE CITY OF NEW YORK, FROM TUESDAY, SEPTEMBER 11TH, TO WEDNESDAY, SEPTEMBER 19TH, 1792.

LIST OF THE MEMBERS OF THE HOUSE OF CLERICAL AND LAY DEPUTIES.

FROM THE STATE OF RHODE ISLAND.

Rev. John Bowden.
Samuel Marsh, Esq.

FROM THE STATE OF CONNECTICUT.

Rev. Abraham Jarvis, D.D.
Philip Nichols, Esq.
Thomas Belden, Esq.

FROM THE STATE OF NEW YORK.

Rev. Benjamin Moore, D.D.
Rev. Abraham Beach, D.D.
Rev. Thomas L. Moore.
Rev. Richard C. Moore.
Aquila Giles, Esq.
Dr. Samuel Martin.

FROM THE STATE OF NEW JERSEY.

Rev. Uzal Ogden.
Rev. William Frazer.
Rev. Henry Waddell.
Hon. Robert Morris.
Colonel Samuel Ogden.
John De Hart, Esq.

FROM THE STATE OF PENNSYLVANIA.

Rev. William Smith, D.D.
Rev. Samuel Magaw, D.D.
Rev. Joseph Pilmore.
Rev. Elisha Rigg.
John Campbell, Esq.

FROM THE STATE OF DELAWARE.

Rev. John Bisset.

FROM THE STATE OF MARYLAND.

Rev. John Bowie, D.D.
Rev. Joseph G. J. Bend.
Rev. John Coleman.
Colonel John Weems.
Major James Lloyd.
Dr. John Hindman.
Mr. James Howard.

FROM THE STATE OF VIRGINIA.

Rev. Samuel S. M'Croskey.
Robert Andrews, Esq.

FROM THE STATE OF SOUTH CAROLINA.

Rev. Thomas Frost.

JOURNAL

OF THE

House of Clerical and Lay Deputies.

NEW YORK,
TUESDAY, September 11th, 1792.

Clerical and Lay Deputies from the Churches in several of the States assembled in Trinity Church, at 10 o'clock A.M.; and after prayers by the Rev. Thomas L. Moore, judging it proper to wait for the arrival of the Deputies from other Churches,

Adjourned to 10 o'clock to-morrow morning.

WEDNESDAY, 10 o'clock, A.M.

The members met, and attended divine service performed by the Right Rev. Dr. Madison and Rev. Dr. Magaw, and a Sermon preached by the Right Rev. Dr. Seabury.

After the congregation was dismissed, the members assembled, the Rev. Dr. Smith, the President of the last Convention, in the Chair.

The Rev. John Bisset was appointed Secretary pro tempore.

The members proceeded to choose by ballot a President of the House; and the Rev. Dr. William Smith was elected.

They then proceeded to choose a Secretary by ballot; and the Rev. John Bisset was elected.

Resolved —That the Rev. Dr. Beach, Rev. Mr. Ogden,

and Major Lloyd be a Committee to examine the credentials of the members, and report thereon.

Resolved,—That the Rev. Dr. Moore, Mr. Andrews, Rev. Mr. Frazer, Mr. Campbell, and Mr. Marsh, be a Committee to report rules of order.

Resolved unanimously,—That the thanks of this house be given to the Right Rev. Dr. Seabury, for his Sermon delivered this day in Trinity Church; and that the Rev. Dr. Beach and Robert Andrews, Esq., be appointed to present the thanks of this house, and to request a copy of the Sermon for publication.

Ordered, that the Rev. Dr. Beach inform the House of Bishops, that this house is now organized, and ready to proceed to business, and to receive any communications from them, and to propose 10 o'clock A.M., as the stated hour of meeting.

The Bishops informed the House, by their Secretary, that they agree to the hour of 10 as the time of meeting.

Adjourned to 10 o'clock to-morrow morning.

THURSDAY, 10 o'clock, A.M.

The Rev. John Bisset read prayers.

Ordered, that the Rev. Mr. Ogden inform the Bishops, that seats are prepared for their accommodation on the right hand of the chair, whenever they may choose to be present at the debates of the house.

The Rev. Dr. Beach, from the Committee on the credentials of the members, brought in a report, which was read and concurred with.

Resolved,—That no person shall be capable of acting as a member of the House of Deputies, under the deputation of more than one Convention.

In consequence of this resolve, the Rev. John Bisset, who had been reported as elected by the Churches in Maryland and Delaware, took his seat as representative of the Church of Delaware.

The Rev. John Bowden and Samuel Marsh, Esq., two of the deputies from the Church in Connecticut, having produced a testimonial of their appointment by the Church in Rhode Island, took their seats as representatives of that Church.

The Rev. Dr. Moore, from the Committee for framing rules of order, brought in a report.

Ordered, that it be read.

Ordered, that it be read a second time, and considered by paragraphs.

Accordingly it was read and considered, and the following rules were adopted and ratified.

I. The business of every day shall be introduced by prayers.

II. When the President takes the chair, no member shall continue standing, or shall afterwards stand up, unless to address the Chair.

III. No member shall absent himself from the service of the Convention, unless he have leave, or be unable to attend.

IV. When any member is about to speak in debate, or deliver any matter to the Convention, he shall rise from his seat, and, without advancing, shall with due respect address himself to the President, confining himself strictly to the point in debate.

V. No member shall speak more than twice in the same debate without leave of the house.

VI. A question being once determined, shall stand as the judgment of the Convention, and shall not be again drawn into debate during the same session.

VII. While the President is putting any question, no one shall hold private discourse, stand up, walk into, out of, or across the house, or read any book.

VIII. Every member who shall be in the Convention when any question is put, shall, on a division, be counted, unless he be particularly interested in the decision.

IX. No motion shall be considered as before the house unless it be seconded, and reduced to writing when required.

X. When any question is before the Convention, it shall be determined on before any thing new is introduced, except the question for adjournment.

XI. The question on a motion for adjournment shall be taken before any other, and without debate.

XII. When the Convention is to rise, every member shall keep his seat until the President leave the chair.

The Rev. Dr. Magaw obtained leave of absence till Saturday morning.

Resolved,—That the house now go into a Committee of the whole on the State of the Church: Rev. Dr. Moore in the chair.

The Committee rose and reported progress, and asked leave to sit again.

Adjourned to 10 o'clock to-morrow morning.

FRIDAY, 10 o'clock A.M.

The Rev. Uzal Ogden read prayers.

It appearing to the Convention, that the Church in the State of Rhode Island had not acceded to the Constitution, but that the deputies from the Church in Connecticut were vested by the said Church in Rhode Island with full powers to act in all things on their behalf;

Resolved,—That the deputies from the Church in Connecticut are authorized to accede to the Constitution of the Protestant Episcopal Church in the United States of America, in the name and behalf of the Church in the State of Rhode Island.

Accordingly, the Clerical and Lay Deputies from the Church in Connecticut, subscribed the Constitution in the name of the Church in Rhode Island.

Satisfactory documents having been laid before the Convention of the appointment of the Rev. Thomas J. Claggett, D.D., to the Office of Bishop of the Protestant Episcopal Church in the State of Maryland, and also a testimony of the Convention of the Church in that State, in the form prescribed by the Canon;

Resolved,—That this house do now proceed to sign the testimony in such cases required from the General Convention.

Accordingly, the said testimony was signed by all the members, and delivered to the deputies from the Church in Maryland, to be presented to the Rev. Dr. Claggett.

Resolved,—That the Rev. Dr. Moore and Colonel Giles be a Committee to request of the Mayor and Aldermen of New York, the use of two apartments in the City Hall, for the accommodation of the Convention.

The house again resolved itself into a Committee of the whole, on the State of the Church.

The Rev. Dr. Moore, from the Committee of the whole,

reported, that a motion for ratifying the proposed amendment of the Constitution, by which the House of Bishops would be invested with a negative upon the proceedings of the other house, was negatived.

The Rev. Mr. Waddell obtained leave of absence for to-morrow.

Adjourned to 10 o'clock to-morrow morning.

SATURDAY, 10 o'clock, A.M.

The Rev. Joseph Pilmore read prayers.

The Rev. Dr. Moore reported, that the Mayor and Aldermen had granted the use of two apartments in the City Hall for the accommodation of the two Houses of Convention.

The house adjourned to the City Hall.

Ordered,—That Major Lloyd inform the House of Bishops, that this house request a conference with them on the general state of the Church, and propose that the Bishops appoint the time and place for holding such conference.

The Rev. Richard C. Moore obtained leave of absence till Monday morning.

It was moved to concur with the resolve of the Committee of the whole, on the question respecting the Bishops' negative.

The previous question was then moved—Shall the motion for concurrence be now put? and determined in the negative.

On motion, Resolved,—That it be made known to the several State Conventions, that it is proposed to consider and determine, in the next General Convention, on the propriety of investing the House of Bishops with a full negative upon the proceedings of the other house.

The house received from the House of Bishops, alterations of the Office of consecrating Bishops, and information that they agreed to enter immediately into conference with the Clerical and Lay Deputies in their house.

The house went into conference with the House of Bishops.

After the conference, in which the expediency of considering the articles of religion at this time was discussed,

Resolved,—That, as the Churches in some of the States are not represented in this Convention, and others only partially, the consideration of the Articles of Religion be postponed until the next General Convention.

The Office of Consecration, as altered by the House of Bishops, was taken up and read.

It was read a second time, and considered by paragraphs.

Resolved,—That it be agreed to and passed.

The house received information from the House of Bishops, that they had examined and approved the testimonials of the Rev. Dr. Claggett, Bishop elect of the Church in Maryland; and that they had appointed half after 10 o'clock on Monday morning as the time for his consecration.

Adjourned to 9 o'clock on Monday morning.

MONDAY, 9 o'clock A.M.

The Rev. Dr. Smith read prayers.

The house adjourned to attend divine service in Trinity Church, on occasion of the consecration of the Rev. Dr. Claggett, Bishop elect of the Church in Maryland.

After divine service the house met.

Resolved unanimously,—That the thanks of this house be given to the Rev. Dr. Smith, for his Sermon delivered this day in Trinity Church, and that he be requested to furnish a copy of the same for publication.

Resolved,—That a message be sent to the House of Bishops, requesting a conference with them at half after 9 o'clock to-morrow.

This message was carried by Major Lloyd, who returned and informed the house, that the Bishops agree to meet the house at the hour proposed.

A letter and copy of proceedings of the Clergy and Laity of the Church in North Carolina were laid before the house, expressing their approbation of the proceedings of the last General Convention held in Philadelphia, and their willingness to accede to the Constitution of the Protestant Episcopal Church in the United States of America.

Ordered,—That they be preserved by the Secretary among the records of the house.

A letter was received from Mr. Parry Hall, printer, in Philadelphia, which was read and ordered to lie on the table.

The Rev. Mr. Rigg and Rev. Mr. Bend obtained leave of absence for the remaining part of the session.

The house received from the House of Bishops, alterations

of the form and manner of ordering Priests; which were read.

Adjourned to 9 o'clock to-morrow morning.

TUESDAY, 9 o'clock, A.M.

The Rev. Dr. Smith read prayers.

The form of ordering Priests was again read, and considered by paragraphs, and with two amendments was passed.

Ordered,—That the House of Bishops be informed thereof by Mr. Bisset; who returned and reported that they concurred with the amendments proposed by this house.

The house went into conference with the House of Bishops on the State of the Church.

When the Bishops withdrew, the President reported, that the two houses had agreed to appoint a joint Committee to compare the printed edition of the Book of Common Prayer with the original acts of the last General Convention, where they may judge it necessary, and to prepare a mode of authenticating the book by some certain standard, and of publishing future editions of the same in the Churches in the different States.

Resolved,—That the Rev. Dr. Magaw, Rev. Dr. Moore, Rev. Mr. Jarvis, Col. Ogden, John De Hart, Esquire, and Dr. Hindman, be a Committee on the part of this House for the above purpose.

The President also reported, that the two houses had agreed to appoint a joint committee for preparing a plan of supporting missionaries to preach the gospel on the frontiers of the United States.

Resolved,—That the Rev. Dr. Beach, Rev. Mr. Bowden, Rev. Mr. M'Croskey, Rev. Mr. Frost, Samuel Marsh, Esq., Dr. Martin, Major Lloyd, and Mr. Campbell, be a Committee on the part of this house for the above purpose.

The Rev. Mr. Frazer, Rev. Mr. Coleman, Mr. Andrews, and Mr. Marsh, had leave of absence after to-morrow morning.

Resolved,—That the next meeting of the General Convention be held in the city of Philadelphia; and that the House of Bishops be requested to appoint one of their body to open the Convention with a Sermon.

Ordered, that the Rev. Mr. Frost communicate to the

House of Bishops the above resolve, and appointment of committees.

The House of Bishops informed the house that they had appointed Bishops Seabury and White a Committee to act in conjunction with a Committee appointed by this house, to compare the Book of Common Prayer with the original acts, etc.; and Bishops Madison and Claggett a Committee to act with the Committee appointed for preparing a plan of supporting missionaries, etc.

The house received from the House of Bishops alterations of the form and manner of making Deacons.

Ordered that they be read.

A message was received from the House of Bishops, informing this house that they agreed to the resolve of holding the next meeting of the General Convention in Philadelphia, and that they had appointed the Right Rev. Dr. Provoost to open the Convention with a Sermon.

The form of making Deacons was again taken up and considered by paragraphs, and, with some amendments, was agreed to.

Ordered, that Mr. Bisset carry it to the House of Bishops and request their concurrence with the amendments proposed.

The House of Bishops informed the house, that they concurred with the amendments proposed to the form of making Deacons.

The house received from the House of Bishops additional Canons, and a resolve for printing in one book the form of ordaining Deacons, Priests, and Bishops.

Ordered that the Canons be read.

Adjourned to 9 o'clock to-morrow morning.

WEDNESDAY, 9 o'clock, A.M.

The Rev. Dr. Magaw read prayers.

The Rev. Dr. Magaw, from the Committee appointed for comparing the printed edition of the Book of Common Prayer with the original acts, etc., brought in a report, which was read, and ordered to lie on the table.

The Rev. Dr. Beach, from the Committee appointed for preparing a plan for supporting missionaries, etc., brought in a report, which was read, and ordered to lie on the table.

The additional Canons were again taken up, and considered by paragraphs.

Six additional Canons were, with amendments, agreed to and enacted; and, with an amendment of the 7th Canon, ordered to be sent by Mr. Bisset to the House of Bishops, for their concurrence in the amendments of this house.

The House of Bishops informed the house, that they concurred with the amendments proposed by this house to the Canons, except to the amendment to the 4th.

Resolved,—That the house concur with the resolve of the House of Bishops, for printing in one book the form of ordaining Deacons, Priests, and Bishops, and that the Rev. Dr. Moore be appointed, on the part of this house, for that purpose.

Resolved,—That the house adhere to their amendment of the 4th Canon; and that Colonel Ogden inform the House of Bishops thereof.

The report of the Committee on the Book of Common Prayer was again taken up, and considered by paragraphs; and, with amendments, sent by the Secretary to the House of Bishops for their concurrence.

The House of Bishops informed the House, that they recede from their disagreement to the amendment of the 4th Canon, and agree to the resolve respecting the negative of the House of Bishops.

The report of the Committee on the plan for supporting missionaries, etc., was again taken up and considered by paragraphs, and some amendments were proposed and agreed to.

A message was received from the House of Bishops, proposing that a joint Committee be appointed for publishing Journals of the two houses, and that the Lists of Clergy be printed in an Appendix.

The Rev. Dr. Bowie and Dr. Hindman obtained leave of absence.

Adjourned to 5 o'clock P.M.

Five o'clock, P.M.

The house met, and proceeded in the consideration of the report on the plan for supporting missionaries, etc., which was agreed to with amendments; and the Secretary was desired to carry it to the House of Bishops for their concurrence.

Ordered, that the Presiding bishop be requested to forward to his Grace the Archbishop of Canterbury, thirty copies of the Journal for his use, and for the use of the Right Rev. the Bishops of England.

The house proceeded to appoint a Standing Committee, and the following gentlemen were chosen:

For New Hampshire, the Hon. Mr. Livermore.

For Massachusetts, the Rev. Dr. Parker.

For Rhode Island, the Rev. William Smith.

For Connecticut, the Rev. Abraham Jarvis.

For New York, the Rev. Dr. Moore, Rev. Dr. Beach, Richard Harrison, Esq.

For New Jersey, the Rev. Uzal Ogden, Mr. J. M. Wallace, Colonel Ogden.

For Pennsylvania, the Rev. Dr. Magaw, Rev. Dr. Blackwell, Rev. Mr. Pilmore, Hon. Mr. Powell, Dr. Rush, Mr. John Wilcocks.

For Delaware, the Rev. Mr. Thorne, Nicholas Ridgely, Esq.

For Maryland, the Rev. John Bisset, Major Lloyd.

For Virginia, Rev. Mr. M'Croskey, Robert Andrews, Esq.

For South Carolina, the Rev. Dr. Smith, Hon. Mr. Izard.

Ordered, that the President of this house is chairman of the above Committee, and is empowered to call together the members.

The House of Bishops proposed an amendment to the report respecting missionaries, which was agreed to.

The house proceeded to appoint a Committee for carrying into effect the act respecting missionaries; and the Rev. Dr. Smith, Rev. Dr. Magaw, Rev. Dr. Blackwell, Rev. Dr. Andrews, Hon. Mr. Powell, Mr. John Wood, and Dr. Rush, were chosen:

Ordered, that the Secretary inform the House of Bishops thereof.

The House of Bishops informed the house that they agree to the amendment of the 7th Canon of the last Convention, and propose that the annexed certificate be altered, to correspond with it; and that the Canon so altered, be published as a Canon of this Convention.

Resolved,—That the above proposal be agreed to.

The house proceeded to appoint a Committee on the part of this house, for publishing and authenticating the Book of Common Prayer, agreeably to an act of Convention passed for that purpose; and the Rev. Dr. Moore, Rev. Dr. Beach, and Dr. Johnson were chosen.

Ordered, that the House of Bishops be informed thereof by the Secretary, who reported that they had appointed the Right Rev. Dr. Provoost.

Resolved unanimously,—That the thanks of this house be given to the Mayor and Aldermen of New York for the use of the City Hall; and that the Rev. Dr. Moore and Colonel Giles communicate the same.

Resolved,—That the Rev. Dr. Moore, Rev. Dr. Beach, and the Secretary, be a Committee on the part of this house, for revising, correcting and publishing the Journals.

Ordered, that one thousand copies of the Journals be printed.

Resolved,—That the thanks of the house be given to the President and Secretary for their attention and services.

The house rose.

Signed by order of the House of Clerical and Lay Deputies.

WILLIAM SMITH, President.

Attest: J. Bisset, Secretary.

JOURNAL

OF THE

House of Bishops.

NEW YORK,
SEPTEMBER 11th, 1792.

The Right Rev. Dr. Seabury, Bishop of the Protestant Episcopal Church in the States of Connecticut and Rhode Island, attended in Trinity Church at 10 o'clock, A.M., and, after prayers,

Adjourned till 10 o'clock to-morrow morning.

WEDNESDAY, 10 o'clock, A.M.

The members met. Present: the Right Rev. Dr. Seabury, Right Rev. Dr. Provoost, Bishop of the Protestant Episcopal Church in New York; Right Rev. Dr. White, Bishop of the Protestant Episcopal Church in Pennsylvania; and the Right Rev. Dr. Madison, Bishop of the Protestant Episcopal Church in Virginia.

They then attended divine service. The Right Rev. Dr. Madison read prayers, and the Right Rev. Dr. Seabury preached, agreeably to the appointment of the last General Convention.

After divine service, they proceeded to the choice of a Secretary, and the Rev. Samuel Keene was appointed pro tem.

The House of Clerical and Lay Deputies informed the Bishops that they were organized, and ready to proceed to business, and that they propose 10 o'clock A.M., as the stated hour of meeting.

The Bishops agreed to meet at the same hour, and desired their Secretary to notify the same to the House of Clerical and Lay Deputies.

The Bishops took into consideration the form and manner of making, ordaining, and consecrating Bishops, Priests, and Deacons; and, after some deliberation, agreed to postpone the farther consideration thereof till Friday next.

Adjourned.

THURSDAY, 10 o'clock, A.M.

The Bishops met, and attended prayers in the House of Clerical and Lay Deputies.

The first rule for the government of the House of Bishops, as agreed on at the last Convention, was re-considered.

Resolved,—That the said rule be rescinded—that the following be adopted instead thereof, viz.: The office of President of this house shall be held in rotation, beginning from the North; reference being had to the Presidency of this house in the last Convention.

In consequence of the above rule, the Right Rev. Dr. Provoost took the chair. Adjourned.

FRIDAY, 10 o'clock, A.M.

The house met. Present: the Right Rev. Dr. Provoost, Right Rev. Dr. Seabury, Right Rev. Dr. White, and Right Rev. Dr. Madison; and attended prayers in the House of Clerical and Lay Deputies.

The house went into the consideration of the form and manner of making, ordaining, and consecrating Bishops, Priests, and Deacons, agreeably to the postponement of Wednesday last.

A message being received from the House of Clerical and Lay Deputies, by the Rev. Dr. Moore, informing this house that they had appointed a Committee to apply for the use of an apartment in the City Hall; and that, if it meet with the concurrence of this house, application will also be made for another apartment to accommodate the Bishops.

Resolved,—That the Rev. Dr. Moore be requested to inform the House of Clerical and Lay Deputies, that this house do concur in their proposition.

The house proceeded in the consideration of the form of ordaining or consecrating a Bishop; and having agreed on sundry alterations of the same, appointed Bishops White and Madison a Committee to prepare a draft of the said alterations, to be laid before the House of Clerical and Lay Deputies to-morrow morning.

Adjourned.

SATURDAY MORNING.

The house met—present as yesterday.

The Rev. Mr. Keene being obliged to resign the office of Secretary, the Rev. L. Cutting was chosen in his stead.

The house received a message by the Rev. Dr. Moore, that rooms were prepared in the City Hall for the reception of the two Houses of Convention.

The house received a message by the Rev. Dr. Beach, asking this house to concur with them in thanking the Right Rev. Bishop Seabury for his Sermon delivered at the opening of the Convention, and in requesting a copy of the same, to be printed.

Resolved,—That this house concurs with the House of Clerical and Lay Deputies, in thanking the Right Rev. Bishop Seabury for his Sermon, delivered at the opening of the Convention, and in requesting a copy of the same, to be printed.

The Clerical and Lay deputies from the State of Maryland, presented to this house the Rev. Thomas John Claggett, D.D., as Bishop elect of the Church in the said State, requesting that his consecration might be expedited. The said deputies laid before the house the proceedings of the Convention held in Annapolis, in May, 1792, respecting the election of the Rev. Dr. Claggett, together with the certificates required by the 2d Canon.

Adjourned to the Senate Chamber in the City Hall, agreeably to the determination of yesterday.

SENATE CHAMBER, CITY HALL.

The Committee reported a draft of the alterations in the Consecration Service.

The house received a message from the Clerical and Lay

deputies by Hon. Mr. Lloyd, requesting a conference with them on the general state of the Church.

Resolved,—That the alterations in the Consecration Service be sent to the House of Clerical and Lay Deputies for their concurrence; and that they be informed this house is now ready to meet them in their room on the proposed conference.

The house went into a conference with the House of Clerical and Lay Deputies, in which the President of this house was requested to take the chair, when the following motion was made.

Agreed, that as the churches in some of the States are not represented in this Convention, and others only partially, the consideration of the Articles of Religion be postponed until the next General Convention—which passed in the negative in the House of Bishops, and in the affirmative in the House of Clerical and Lay Deputies.

The house having considered the testimonials respecting the election of the Rev. Dr. Claggett, and found them satisfactory,

Resolved,—That the consecration of the Rev. Dr. Thomas John Claggett take place on Monday morning at half-past 10.

Adjourned.

MONDAY MORNING, 9 o'clock.

House met. Present as on Saturday.

The house took under consideration the offices for ordaining Priests and Deacons, and having made some advance therein, proceeded to Trinity Church, to the consecration of the Rev. Thomas John Claggett, D.D.; and after divine service returned to their house, when the Right Rev. Bishop Claggett took his seat.

A message from the House of Clerical and Lay Deputies, reporting that they concurred with the House of Bishops in their alterations in the form of consecrating Bishops.

A message from the House of Clerical and Lay Deputies, requesting a conference between the two houses to-morrow morning, at half-past 9 o'clock.

In consideration of the resolve of the House of Clerical and Lay Deputies, respecting the articles, this house agree to postpone the same.

Resolved,—That a record of the certificate of the consecration of the Right Rev. Bishop Claggett be entered on the Journals of this house; and that the Rector, Church Wardens, and Vestry of Trinity Church, be requested to enter it on their church book.

Resolved,—That it be proposed to the House of Clerical and Lay Deputies to publish, in one book, the form and manner of making, ordaining, and consecrating Bishops, Priests, and Deacons, conformably to the alterations agreed on between the two houses.

Adjourned till half-past 9 o'clock to-morrow morning.

TUESDAY MORNING, half-past 9.

House met. Present, the Right Rev. Bishops Provoost, Seabury, White, Madison, and Claggett.

The house originated certain Canons, and sent them to the House of Clerical and Lay Depnties for their concurrence.

The house received a message by the Rev. Mr. Bisset, from the House of Clerical and Lay Deputies, proposing two amendments in the Office for ordaining Priests; to both which the house agreed.

The house went into a conference with the House of Clerical and Lay Deputies. The President of this house was requested to take the chair—in which conference the following propositions were agreed to.

Resolved,—That a joint Committee be appointed to compare the printed edition of the Common Prayer Book with the original acts of the last General Convention, where they may judge it necessary, and to adopt a mode of authenticating the book by some certain standard, and for publishing future editions of the same in the churches of the different States.

Resolved,—That a joint Committee of both houses be appointed to report a plan for supporting missionaries to preach the Gospel on the frontiers of the United States.

Resolved,—That the Right Rev. Bishops Seabury and White be a Committee from this house on the first proposition; and the Right Rev. Bishops Madison and Claggett be a Committee on the last.

The house received a message from the House of Clerical and Lay Deputies, proposing that the next General Convention be held in the city of Philadelphia, and that this house would appoint one of their body to open the Convention with a Sermon.

Resolved,—That this house agree to the above, and request the Right Rev. Bishop Provoost to preach the Sermon.

The house originated alterations in the Office for ordaining Deacons; and alterations of the Preface, and of the Title of the book of ordination and consecration, and sent them to the House of Clerical and Lay Deputies, requesting their concurrence.

The house received from the House of Clerical and Lay Deputies, amendments to the additions in the Office for ordaining Deacons, and in the Preface; in which the house concurred.

Adjourned.

WEDNESDAY, September 19.

The house met. Present as yesterday, except Bishop Claggett.

The house received a message from the House of Clerical and Lay Deputies, asking the concurrence of the house in a resolve of thanks to the Rev. Dr. Smith, for his Sermon delivered before them on the occasion of the consecration of Bishop Claggett, and that he be requested to furnish a copy of the same for publication.

Resolved,—That this house concur in the same.

The Committee appointed yesterday to compare the printed edition, etc., also the Committee appointed to prepare a plan for supporting missionaries to preach the Gospel on the frontiers of the United States, made report.

Resolved,—That the several members of this house deliver to the Secretary the Lists of the Clergy of their respective dioceses, and that the House of Clerical and Lay Deputies be requested to send to this house the lists from the several States in which there are no Bishops, agreeably to the 16th Canon, and that the said Lists be printed as an Appendix to the Journal.

This house received a message from the House of Clerical and Lay Deputies, proposing as follows:

That it be made known to the several State Conventions, that it is proposed to consider and determine, in the next

General Convention, on the propriety of investing the House of Bishops with a full negative on the proceedings of the other house.

This house concurs in the above, and agrees to the amendment of the 4th Canon.

The house received from the House of Clerical and Lay Deputies their concurrence with the proposal concerning the publication of the ordination and consecration services. In that proposal, the President of this house was named on the joint Committee by this house, and the Rev. Dr. Moore is appointed on the part of the Clerical and Lay Deputies.

The house received from the House of Clerical and Lay Deputies, amendments of the report of the joint Committee to compare the printed edition of the Prayer Book, etc.; to which this house agreed, and passed the report.

The house sent information to the House of Clerical and Lay Deputies, that they propose to adjourn to 6 o'clock this evening.

The house received from the House of Clerical and Lay Deputies, amendments of the report of the joint Committee on the plan for supporting missionaries to preach the Gospel on the frontiers of the United States, to which this house proposed an addition.

The house also received from the House of Clerical and Lay Deputies, a proposal of sending Journals of this Convention to the Archbishop of Canterbury, for the purpose of informing his Grace, and the other Prelates of England, of the state and proceedings of this Church.

Resolved,—That the house concur therein.

The House of Clerical and Lay Deputies concurred in the report of the plan for the support of missionaries, etc., and named the requisite Committee; with which this house agreed.

The house received a proposal from the House of Clerical and Lay Deputies, for printing one thousand copies of the Journal; also a message as to the mode of authenticating the acts of the Convention.

This house agreed to the former, and proposed the acts to be authenticated by the signatures of the Presidents of the respective houses.

The house received a message from the House of Clerical and Lay Deputies, with information that they had appointed a Committee to superintend the printing a correct edition of the Common Prayer Book, requesting that a Committee be appointed from this house for the same purpose; when Bishop Provoost was accordingly appointed.

A message, reporting that the House of Clerical and Lay Deputies concur with the proposal respecting the 7th Canon.

The house received from the House of Clerical and Lay Deputies, their concurrence to the proposal of printing a List of the Clergy, in an Appendix to the Journal.

A message was received, desiring the concurrence of this house to the appointing a Committee for printing their Journal; when Bishop Provoost was appointed.

On motion, Resolved,—That the thanks of this house be given to the Rev. L. Cutting, for his services as Secretary.

The house rose.

Signed by order of the House of Bishops.

SAMUEL PROVOOST,

PRESIDENT.

Attest: L. CUTTING, Secretary.

THE CERTIFICATE OF THE CONSECRATION OF THE RIGHT REV. BISHOP CLAGGETT.

Know all men by these presents, that we, Samuel Provoost, D.D., Bishop of the Protestant Episcopal Church in the State of New York, Presiding Bishop; Samuel Seabury, D.D., Bishop of Connecticut and Rhode Island; William White, D.D., Bishop of the Protestant Episcopal Church in the Commonwealth of Pennsylvania; James Madison, D.D., Bishop of the Protestant Episcopal Church in the State of Virginia; under the protection of Almighty God, in Trinity Church, in the city of New York, on Monday, the seventeenth of September, in the year of our Lord One thousand seven hundred and ninety-two, did then and there rightly and canonically consecrate our beloved in Christ, Thomas John Claggett, D.D., late Rector of St. James's parish in the State of Maryland, of whose sufficiency in good learning, ssundness in the faith, and purity of manners, we were fully ascertained, into the office of Bishop of the Protestant Episcopal Church in the said State, to which the said Thomas John Claggett hath been elected by the Convention of the said State. In testimony whereof we have signed our names and caused our seals to be affixed.

Given in the city of New York this nineteenth day of September, in the year of our Lord One thousand seven hundred and ninety-two.

SAMUEL PROVOOST. [L. S.]
S. SEABURY. [L. S.]
WM. WHITE. [L. S.]
J. MADISON. [L. S.]

A true copy of the Certificate of the Consecration of the Right Rev. Dr. Thomas John Claggett, as compared with the original, by

LEOC. CUTTING,
SECRETARY OF THE HOUSE OF BISHOPS.
J. BISSET,
SECRETARY OF THE HOUSE OF CLERICAL AND LAY DEPUTIES.

Additional Canons.

I.

For a more full accomplishment of the good purposes to be answered by the 16th Canon, enacted by the last General Convention, it is hereby required, that every Clergyman claiming to be a Minister of this Church, shall deliver in his name to the Bishop, or if there be no Bishop, to the chairman or some member of the Standing Committee of the Church in the State in which he resides, on or before Easter Monday, 1793; or, if he be not within any of the States which have acceded to the Constitution of this Church, then within three months after he shall come to reside in any of the said States. And every Clergyman, during his neglect of conformity to this Canon, shall not be known as a Clergyman of this Church, or be admitted to minister in any offices of the same.

II.

If a Clergyman of the Church in any diocese or district within this union shall, in any other diocese or district, conduct himself in such a way as is contrary to the rules of this Church, and disgraceful to his office, the bishop, or, if there be no bishop, the Standing Committee, shall give notice thereof to the ecclesiastical authority of the diocese or district to which such offender belongs, exhibiting, with the information given, the proofs of the charges made against him.

III.

Whenever a Clergyman shall be degraded, agreeably to the Canons of any particular Church in the union, the Bishop who pronounces sentence, shall, without delay, cause the sentence of degradation to be published from every pulpit where there may be an officiating minister, throughout the diocese or district in which the degraded minister resided; and also shall give information of the sentence to all the Bishops of this Church, and, where there is no Bishop, to the Standing Committee.

IV.

In regard to the first certificate required in favour of a Bishop elect, by the 2d Canon of the last General Convention, and the certificate required in favour of a candidate for Priest's or Deacon's Orders by the 6th Canon, if there be any members of the bodies respectively concerned who have not the requisite personal knowledge of the parties, such persons may prefix the following declaration to their signatures:

"We believe the testimony contained in the above Certificate, and we join in the recommendation of A. B. to the office of . . . on sufficient evidence offered to us of the facts set forth."

Provided, that in the case of a Priest or Deacon, two at least of the Standing Committee sign the same, as being personally acquainted with the candidate.

V.

No stranger shall be permitted to officiate in any congregation of this Church, without first producing the evidences of his being a minister thereof to the minister, or, in case of vacancy or absence, to the church wardens, vestrymen, or trustees of the congregation. And in case any person not regularly ordained shall assume the ministerial office, and perform any of the duties thereof in this Church, the minister, or, in case of vacancy or absence, the church wardens, vestrymen, or trustees of the congregation where such offence may be committed, shall cause the name of such person, together with the offence, to be published in as many of the public papers as may be convenient.

VI.

No clergyman belonging to this church shall officiate, either by preaching or reading prayers, in the parish, or within the parochial cure of another clergyman, unless he have received express permission for that purpose from the minister of the parish or cure, or, in his absence, from the church wardens, vestrymen, or trustees of the congregation.

The Seventh Canon of the last General Convention, as altered and amended by this Convention.

Of the Learning of those who are to be Ordained.

No person shall be ordained in this Church until he shall have satisfied the Bishop and the two Presbyters, by whom he shall be examined, that he is sufficiently acquainted with the New Testament in the original Greek, and can give an account of his faith in the Latin tongue, either in writing or otherwise, as may be required; and that he hath a competent knowledge of moral philosophy, church history, and the belles lettres, and hath paid attention to rhetoric and pulpit eloquence, as the means of giving additional efficacy to his labours. Unless it shall be recommended to the Bishop by two-thirds of the State Convention to which he belongs, to dispense with the aforesaid requisition in whole or in part: which recommendation shall only be for good causes moving thereunto, and shall be in the following words, with the signatures of the names of the majority of such Convention:

"We whose names are underwritten, are of opinion, that the dispensing with the knowledge of the Latin and Greek languages [or either of the other requisites specified in the Seventh Canon, as the case may be] in the examination of A. B. for Holy Orders, will be of use to the Church of which we are the Convention, in consideration of other qualifications of the said A. B. for the Gospel ministry."

Enacted, September 19th, 1792.

House of Bishops:
SAMUEL PROVOOST, President.
Attest: L. Cutting, Secretary.

House of Clerical and Lay Deputies:
WILLIAM SMITH, President.
Attest: J. Bisset, Secretary.

An Act of the General Convention, for supporting Missionaries to preach the Gospel on the frontiers of the United States.

1. Resolved,—That it be recommended to the ministers of this Church to preach a sermon in each of the churches under their care, on the first Sunday of September in every year; and, if that day should not be adapted to the purpose, then on such other Sunday as the minister and vestry or trustees of the congregation shall appoint, for the purpose of collecting money in order to carry into effect this charitable design.

2. That the money so collected be entered in a record to be kept by the vestries or trustees of each congregation; and by the minister and church wardens or trustees be delivered to a treasurer appointed by each State Convention, and by him transmitted to a treasurer who shall be appointed as herein after directed.

3. That such missionaries as may be employed by this Church, be authorized to make collections of money from such congregations on the frontiers as may contribute, and render an accurate account to the bishop of this Church in the State of Pennsylvania, and the Standing Committee to be appointed by this Convention, of the sums thus collected.

4. That the bishop of this Church in Pennsylvania, and the said Standing Committee, frame an address to the members of this Church, recommending this charitable design to their particular attention, which address shall be read by every minister on the day appointed for the collection.

5. That the bishop of this Church in Pennsylvania, and the said Standing Committee, have authority to appoint a secretary and a treasurer, the first to carry on the correspondence, and the other to keep the accounts and the moneys of the institution.

6. That when it shall appear to the bishop of this Church in Pennsylvania, and the Standing Committee to be appointed as aforesaid, that sufficient funds have been provided for the above purpose, they shall then employ such missionaries, allow such salaries, and make such arrangements, as to them shall seem best, reporting regularly their proceedings to each General Convention.

An Act of the General Convention for publishing future Editions of the Book of Common Prayer, in the Churches in the different States.

Resolved,—That a committee be appointed by the General Convention for the purpose of publishing the Book of Common Prayer, and securing the copy right to them and their assigns, in trust for the Convention; and that this committee be empowered and directed to convey a right to print the book to any printer or printers in any of the States, who may be recommended for that purpose by the State Convention, or their

Standing Committee, free from any premium for copy right; such State Convention or Standing Committee to superintend, and correct the press according to the standard book.

The Rev. J. L. Wilson, Clerical Deputy from the State of North Carolina, having been detained by contrary winds, did not arrive in the city of New York till the 28th instant, the Convention having risen a few days before.

J. BISSET, Secretary.

APPENDIX.

List of the Clergy

OF THE

PROTESTANT EPISCOPAL CHURCH.

DELIVERED IN AND PUBLISHED AGREEABLY TO THE 16TH CANON OF THE LAST GENERAL CONVENTION.

From NEW HAMPSHIRE and MASSACHUSETTS no list was delivered in.

RHODE ISLAND.

The Rev. Moses Badger, Rector of King's church, Providence.
The Rev. William Smith, Rector of Trinity church, Newport.

CONNECTICUT.

The Rev. Ebenezer Dibble, Rector of St. John's church Stamford.
Rev. George Ogilvie, St. Paul's church, Norwalk.
Rev. Philo Shelton, Stratfield.
Rev. Dr. Bela Hubbard, Trinity church, New Haven.
Rev. Philo Perry, Christ church, Newtown.
Rev. David Perry, Reading, etc.
Rev. Truman Marsh, New Milford.
Rev. Ashbel Baldwin, Litchfield.
Rev. Ambrose Todd, Symsbury.
Rev. Abraham Lynsen Clarke, Huntington.
Rev. Dr. Richard Mansfield, Derby.
Rev. Reuben Ives, Cheshire.
Rev. Dr. Abraham Jarvis, Christ Church, Middleton.
Rev. Daniel Fogg, Brooklyn.
Rev. John Tyler, Christ church, Norwich.
Rev. Chauncey Prindle, Westbury.
Rev. John Bowden, residing at Stratford.
Rev. Edward Blakslee, Deacon, Woodbridge.
Rev. Solomon Blakslee, Deacon, East Haddam.
Rev. David Belden, Deacon, ——.
Rev. Seth Hart, Deacon, Waterbury.
Rev. David Butler, Deacon, North Guilford.

NEW YORK.

Rev. Jeremiah Leaming, D.D., residing in New York.
Rev. Abraham Beach, D.D., Assistant Minister of Trinity church, New York.
Rev. Benjamin Moore, D.D., Assistant Minister of Trinity church, New York.
Rev. Thomas L. Moore, Rector of St. George's church, South Hempstead.
Rev. Thomas Ellison, Rector of St. Peter's church, Albany.
Rev. Richard C. Moore, Rector of St. Andrew's church, Staten Island.
Rev. Daniel Foote, Rector of the United churches at Rye and White Plains.
Rev. George H. Spierin, Rector of the United churches at Newburgh and Wallkill.
Rev. Elias Cooper, Rector of St. John's church, Philipsburgh.
Rev. Andrew Fowler, Rector of the United churches at Peek's Kill and Highlands.
Rev. Theodosius Bartow, Rector of the church at New Rochelle.
Rev. William Hammel, Rector of the United churches at Jamaica, New-town, and Flushing.
Rev. Ambrose Hull, Rector of the church at Brooklyn.
Rev. Ammi Rogers, Rector of the United churches at Schenectady and Ballstown.
Rev. Gideon Bostwick officiates every third Sunday at Hudson.
Rev. James Nicholls officiates every third Sunday at Camden.
Rev. Daniel Barber, officiates every third Sunday at Kingsbury.
Rev. Elisha D. Rattoone, Professor of the Greek and Latin languages in Columbia College.
Rev. Samuel Nesbit, residing in New York.

NEW JERSEY.

Rev. Uzal Ogden, Rector of Trinity church, Newark.
Rev. Samuel Spraggs, Rector of St. John's church, Elizabethtown.
Rev. Henry Vandyke, Rector of St. Peter's church, Amboy, and Christ church, New Brunswick.
Rev. Henry Waddell, Rector of Christ church, Shrewsbury, and Christ church, Middletown.
Rev. Levi Heath, Rector of St. Mary's church, Burlington.
Rev. William Frazer, Rector of St. Michael's church, Trenton, and St. Andrew's church, Amwell.
Rev. John Croes, Rector of —— church, Swedesburgh.
Rev. Samuel Gray, Rector of —— church, Salem.
Rev. William Ayres, Rector of St. Peter's church, Spotswood.

PENNSYLVANIA.

Rev. William Smith, D.D.
Rev. Samuel Magaw, D.D., Rector of St. Paul's church, Philadelphia.
Rev. John Andrews, D.D., Vice-Provost of the University of Pennsylvania.
Rev. Robert Blackwell, D.D., Assistant Minister of Christ Church and St. Peter's, in the city of Philadelphia.
Rev. Joseph Hutchins, D.D.
Rev. John Campbell, Rector of the churches in York and Huntington.
Rev. Joseph Pilmore, Assistant Minister of St. Paul's church, Philadelphia.

Rev. Slator Clay, Rector of St. David's, Radnor, St. Peter's in the Valley, and St. James's, Perkiomen.
Rev. Elisha Rigg, Rector of St. James's, Lancaster.
Rev. Joseph Clarkson.
Rev. Robert Ayres, Rector of the Episcopal churches in Redstone, and the parts adjacent.
Rev. Francis Reno, Deacon in Westmoreland county.
Rev. Joseph H. Turner, Deacon in the churches of Chester, Marcus Hook, and Concord.
Rev. Joseph Doddridge, Deacon in Washington county.

DELAWARE.

Rev. Robert Clay, Emanuel church, New Castle county.
Rev. Sydenham Thorne, Christ church, Kent county.
Rev. William Skelly, Christ church, Sussex county.

MARYLAND.

Rev. Clement Brooke, St. Mary's county.
Rev. John W. Compton, William and Mary parish.
Rev. John Weems, Port Tobacco parish.
Rev. Hatch Dent, Trinity parish, Charles county.
Rev. Joseph Messenger, St. John's parish.
Henry Moscrop, St. Anne's parish, Prince George's county.
Rev. Edward Gault, Christ church parish.
Rev. Thomas J. Chew, All Saints' parish, Calvert county.
Rev. Thomas J. Claggett, D.D., St. James's parish.
Rev. Walter M'Pherson, All Hallows parish.
Rev. Ralph Higinbotham, St. Anne's parish.
Rev. Mason L. Weems, St. Margaret's, Westmoreland parish, Anne Arundel county.
Rev. Thomas Read, Prince George's parish, Montgomery county.
Rer. George Bower, All Saints parish.
Rev. Townshend Dade, Frederick county.
Rev. Joseph G. J. Bend, St. Paul's parish.
Rev. William Duke, Baltimore county.
Rev. John Coleman, St. John's parish.
Rev. John Ireland, Harford county.
Rev. John Bisset, St. Stephen's parish, Cecil county.
Rev. Archibald Walker, Chester parish.
Rev. Colin Ferguson, St. Paul's parish, Kent county.
Rev. Samuel Keene, D.D., St. Luke's parish.
Rev. Samuel Keene, Jun., St. Paul's parish.
Rev. Owen F. Magrath, Christ Church parish, Queen Anne's county.
Rev. John Bowie, D.D., St. Michael's parish.
Rev. James Conner, St. Peter's parish, Talbot county.
Rev. Thomas Gordon, St. Mary's, White Chapel parish, Carolina county.
Rev. James Kemp, Great Choptank parish, Dorchester county.
Rev. George Dasheill, Stepney parish.
Rev. Hamilton Bell, Somerset parish.
Rev. Samuel Tingley, Coventry parish, Somerset county.
Rev. John White, All Hallows parish, Worcester county.
Rev. Thomas Scott, one of the Tutors of St. John's College.

VIRGINIA.

Rev. Isaac Darneille, rector of Amherst parish.
Rev. Alexander Hay, rector of Antrim parish.
Rev. Devereux Jarratt, rector of Bath parish.
Rev. Hugh Corrans Boggs, rector of Berkeley parish.
Rev. Price Davies, rector of Brisland parish.
Rev. John Cameron, rector of Bristol parish.
Rev. John Iredall, rector of Broomfield parish.
Rev. Alexander M'Farland, rector of Brunswick parish.
Rev. John Bracken, rector of Bruton parish.
Rev. Samuel Shield, rector of Charles parish.
Rev. Samuel Klug, Christ church parish.
Rev. David Ball, Christ church parish.
Rev. James Elliott, rector of Cople parish.
Rev. James Craig, rector of Cumberland parish.
Rev. Needler Robinson, rector of Dale parish.
Rev. Spence Grayson, rector of Dettingen parish.
Rev. Jesse Carter, rector of Drysdale parish.
Rev. Henry Skyrin, rector of Elizabeth city parish.
Rev. James Whitehead, rector of Elizabeth river parish.
Rev. Brian Fairfax, rector of Fairfax parish.
Rev. Alexander Balmain, rector of Frederick's parish.
Rev. Matthew Maury, rector of Fredericksville parish.
Rev. James Craig, rector of Hamilton's parish.
Rev. John Buchanan, rector of Henrico parish.
Rev. Samuel S. M'Croskey, rector of Hungars parish.
Rev. James Thompson, rector of Leeds parish.
Rev. Charles Crawford, rector of Lexington parish.
Rev. Elkanah Talley, rector of Littleton parish.
Rev. Isaac Wm. Gibern, rector of Lunenburg parish.
Rev. Anthony Walke, rector of Lynhaven parish.
Rev. Wm. Cameron, rector of Manchester parish.
Rev. John J. Spooner, rector of Martins Brandon parish.
Rev. William Hubard, rector of Newport parish.
Rev. Henry J. Burgess, Nottoway parish.
Rev. Robert Buchan, rector of Overwharton parish.
Rev. Arthur Emerson, rector of Portsmouth parish.
Rev. John Brunskill, rector of Raleigh parish.
Rev. Alexander Lundie, rector of St. Andrew's parish.
Rev. John Matthews, St. Anne's parish.
Rev. James Morris, rector of St. Bride's parish.
Rev. Reuben Clopton, rector of St. David's parish.
Rev. William Vere.
Rev. John Woodville, rector of St. George's parish.
Rev. Charles Hopkins, rector of St. James, Northam parish.
Rev. James Price, rector of St. John's parish.
Rev. Joseph Gurley, rector of St. Luke's parish.
Rev. Archibald Dick, Rector of St. Margaret's parish.
Rev. James Stevenson, rector of St. Mark's parish.
Rev. Peter Nelson, St. Martin's parish.
Rev. Abner Waugh, rector of St. Mary's parish.
Rev. William Stewart, rector of St. Paul's parish.
Rev. Benjamin Blagrove, rector of St. Peter's parish.

Rev. Thomas Davis, rector of St. Stephen's parish.
Rev. John Hyde Saunders, rector of Southam parish.
Rev. Andrew Sim, rector of South Farnham parish.
Rev. Samuel Butler, rector of Southwark parish.
Rev. James Taylor, rector of Suffolk parish.
Rev. Lee Massey, rector of Truro parish.
Rev. James Henderson, rector of Westover parish.
Rev. James Maury Fontaine, rector of Ware parish.
Rev. John Bryan, rector of Wicomico parish.

SOUTH CAROLINA.

Rev. Dr. Smith.
Rev. Mr. Frost.
Rev. Dr. Purcell.
Rev. Dr. Gates.
Rev. Mr. Jenkins.
Rev. Mr. Nixon, Master of an Academy.
Rev. Mr. White, Charleston.
Rev. Mr. Mills, St. Andrews.
Rev. Mr. Ellington, St. James's, Goose Creek.
Rev. Mr. M'Culley, St. Luke's.
Rev. Mr. Tate, St. Helen's.
Rev. Mr. Sykes, Prince George's.
Rev. Mr. Blackwall.
Rev. Mr. Ireland, St. Bartholomew's.
Rev. Mr. Graham, Edisto.

JOURNAL OF THE PROCEEDINGS

OF THE

BISHOPS CLERGY, AND LAITY

OF THE

Protestant Episcopal Church

IN

THE UNITED STATES OF AMERICA,

IN

A CONVENTION

HELD IN

THE CITY OF PHILADELPHIA, FROM TUESDAY, SEPTEMBER 8TH, TO FRIDAY, SEPTEMBER 18TH, 1795.

LIST OF THE MEMBERS OF THE HOUSE OF CLERICAL AND LAY DEPUTIES.

FROM THE STATE OF NEW YORK.

Rev. John Bisset.
Rev. George H. Spierin.

FROM THE STATE OF NEW JERSEY.

Rev. Henry Waddell.
Rev. John Croes.
Joshua M. Wallace, Esq.

FROM THE STATE OF PENNSYLVANIA.

Rev. William Smith, D.D.
Rev. John Andrews, D.D.
Rev. Samuel Magaw, D.D.
Rev. Robert Blackwell, D.D.
Joseph Swift, Esq.
Francis Gurney, Esq.
Mr. J. B. Gilpin.
Mr. William Stevenson.

FROM THE STATE OF DELAWARE.

Rev. Joseph Clarkson.
Rev. George Dashiell.

FROM THE STATE OF MARYLAND.

Rev. Joseph G. J. Bend.
Rev. John Coleman.
Rev. James Kemp.
Rev. Samuel Keene.
Samuel Johnson, Esq.
David Kerr, Esq.

FROM THE STATE OF VIRGINIA.

Rev. Samuel S. M'Croskey, D.D.
Robert Andrews, Esq.

FROM THE STATE OF SOUTH CAROLINA.

Rev. Henry Purcell, D.D.

JOURNAL

OF THE

House of Clerical and Lay Deputies.

PHILADELPHIA,
TUESDAY, September 8th, 1795.

Clerical and Lay Deputies from the Churches in several of the States assembled in Christ Church, at 10 o'clock A.M.; and not being a sufficient number to enter upon business,

Adjourned to 10 o'clock to-morrow morning.

WEDNESDAY, 10 o'clock, A.M.

The members met, and a quorum being formed,

The Rev. Mr. Bisset read prayers.

Resolved,—That this house appoint a Secretary, who is not a member. Whereupon,

The Rev. James Abercrombie, second assistant minister of Christ Church and St. Peter's, was unanimously chosen.

The deputies then proceeded to the election of a President, when the Rev. Dr. William Smith was unanimously chosen.

Ordered, that Mr. Andrews inform the House of Bishops that this house is now formed, and ready to proceed to business.

Resolved,—That the Rules of Order, adopted by the House of Clerical and Lay Deputies of the last General Convention, be the rules for the government of this house.

Resolved, with the concurrence of the House of Bishops, that Mr. Swift be appointed to request of the Mayor the use of two apartments in the City Hall, for the accommodation of the Convention during their present session.

The House of Bishops having transmitted to this house a message, informing that Bishop Provost is ready to preach before the Convention, agreeably to the appointment of the last General Convention, and proposing that the delivery of the Sermon be postponed to Friday next, in order that sufficient notice may be given.

Resolved,—That this house agree to the said proposal, and that the Rev. Mr. Bisset inform the House of Bishops thereof.

Resolved,—That Mr. Wallace, the Rev. Mr. Bisset, the Rev. Mr. Clarkson, Mr. Andrews, and the Rev. Dr. Purcell, be a Committee to examine the credentials of the members.

Mr. Swift informed the house, that the use of two apartments in the City Hall was granted, agreeably to application.

Resolved, with the concurrenee of the House of Bishops, that the hours of sitting be from 10 to 3 o'clock.

Adjourned, to meet in the City Hall to-morow, at 10 o'clock, A.M.

CITY HALL, THURSDAY, 10 o'clock, A.M.

The house met, and the Rev. Mr. Bend read prayers.

The Committee appointed to examine the credentials of the members, reported, that the Deputies from the States of New York, New Jersey, Pennsylvania, Delaware, Maryland, Virginia and South Carolina, had produced satisfactory testimonials of their appointment.

Resolved,—That this house will to-morrow go into a Committee of the whole on the State of the Church.

Mr. Andrews presented a proposed Canon, to alter Canon 6 of the year 1789, and Canon 4 of the year 1792, respecting the testimonials necessary to be produced by candidates for Holy Orders.

Resolved,—That the same be referred to the Committee of the whole on the State of the Church.

A letter was received from the Right Rev. Dr. White, of the House of Bishops, enclosing sundry testimonials, respecting the Rev. Dr. Samuel Peters, as Bishop elect of the Church in the State of Vermont, which were read, and ordered to lie on the table.

Mr. Andrews presented a proposed Canon to alter Canon 6 of the year 1792, respecting the officiating of ministers in the parish, or within the parochial cure of another clergyman, which was read and referred to the Committee of the whole on the State of the Church.

The House of Bishops transmitted to this house, by their Secretary, a letter addressed "to the Bishops, Clergy, and Laity of the Protestant Episcopal Church of the United States of America, in Convention, Philadelphia," accompanied with the following message:

"The House of Bishops have read the letter from Person Parish, in North Carolina, directed to the General Convention, but not finding it of such a nature as they can act upon it, they propose to the House of Clerical and Lay Deputies, that such answer be returned, signed by the Presidents of both houses, as to the Presidents may appear most proper."

The letter was read, and it was

Resolved,—That this house agree to the proposal contained in the above message.

Adjourned to 10 o'clock to-morrow morning.

FRIDAY, 10 o'clock, A.M.

The house met, and adjourned to attend divine service in Christ Church, which was performed by the Rev. Mr. Waddell, who read prayers, and the Right Rev. Dr. Provoost, who preached the occasional Sermon. Immediately after which the House returned to the City Hall.

A proposed Canon to prevent a congregation in any diocese or State, from uniting with a Church in any other diocese or State, was received from the House of Bishops, and after being read, was referred to the Committee of the whole on the State of the Church.

Dr. Andrews presented a proposed Canon to alter the 7th Canon of the year 1789, and the 7th Canon of the year 1792, concerning the learning of those who are to be ordained, which was referred to the same Committee.

Resolved unanimously,—That the thanks of this house be given to the Right Rev. Dr. Provoost, for his Sermon, delivered before the Convention this morning in Christ Church, and that the Rev. Dr. Blackwell and Joshua M. Wallace, Esq., be appointed to present the thanks of this house, and to request a copy of the Sermon for publication.

The Rev. Dr. Purcell presented testimonials from the Convention of the State of South Carolina, relative to the election of the Rev. Robert Smith, D.D., to the office of Bishop of the Protestant Episcopal Church in that State; which were read, and ordered to lie upon the table.

Resolved,—That the order of the day be postponed till to-morrow.

The attention of the house was called by the Rev. Dr. Andrews to the consideration of a pamphlet lately published, entitled, "Strictures on the Love of Power in the Prelacy, by a Member of the Protestant Episcopal Association in the State of South Carolina," which he declared to be a virulent attack upon the doctrines and discipline of our Church, and a libel against the House of Bishops, and which was alleged to be written by a member of this house.

Resolved,—That it be the order of the day for Monday next, that the house, in Committee of the whole, enter upon the investigation of this charge.

Adjourned to 10 o'clock to-morrow morning.

SATURDAY, 10 o'clock, A.M.

The house met, and the Rev. Mr. Abercrombie read prayers.

The members present signed the testimonial, in such cases prescribed by the Canon, in favour of the Rev. Robert Smith, D.D., who had been elected to the office of Bishop of the Protestant Episcopal Church in the State of South Carolina, and transmitted it by the Rev. Dr. Purcell to the House of Bishops.

The house resolved itself into a Committee of the whole, to take into consideration the general state of the Church; and the Rev. Dr. Blackwell was appointed chairman.

After some time the Committee rose, and the chairman reported that they had, according to order, taken under consideration the proposed Canon to them referred, entitled a Canon concerning the testimonials of those who are to be ordained, to which they have made several amendments; also a Canon, to regulate the officiating of ministers in the parishes or parochial cures of other clergymen, to which an amendment had been made.

Resolved,—That the report be taken up on Monday next.

The chairman further reported, that the Committee not having had time to go through the whole business referred to them, had directed him to ask for leave to sit again; which was granted.

The House of Bishops presented, by their Secretary, the two following messages, which were read, and ordered to lie on the table.

"Whereas the present Convention, from particular unavoidable circumstances,(1) is deprived of many of its members who were anxious to be present,

"Resolved,—That this house propose to the House of Clerical and Lay Deputies to defer the discussion of Articles until the meeting of the next General Convention, when a more full representation of this Church may be expected.

"The House of Bishops took into consideration a resolution of the House of Clerical and Lay Deputies, as in preceding Convention, which resolution was in these words: 'Resolved, that it be made known to the several State Conventions that it is proposed to consider and determine, in the next General Convention, on the propriety of investing the House of Bishops, with a full negative upon the proceedings of the other house;'

"Whereupon, resolved, that the following message be sent to the House of Clerical and Lay Deputies, viz.,

"The House of Bishops have not, in any former Convention, expressed their sense upon the aforesaid subject; but they now propose to the House of Clerical and Lay Deputies, that the legislative power of the House of Bishops shall remain as fixed by the third article of the Constitution of this Church."

The House of Bishops also informed this house, that they had examined and approved the testimonials in favour of the Rev. Dr. Robert Smith, Bishop elect of the Church in South Carolina, and that they had appointed to-morrow morning as the time for his consecration at Christ Church.

Adjourned to 10 o'clock on Monday morning.

(1) The intercourse between New York and Philadelphia had been suspended by public authority some time before the meeting of the Convention.

MONDAY, 10 o'clock, A.M.

The house met, and the Rev. Mr. Clarkson read prayers.

Dr. Andrews presented a proposed Canon to alter Canon 3d of the year 1789, respecting Episcopal visitation, which was read, and ordered to be referred to the Committee of the whole on the State of the Church.

Mr. Bisset presented a proposed Canon to alter the 4th Canon of the year 1789; which was read, and ordered to be referred to the same Committee.

The house took up the proposed Canon concerning the testimonials of those who are to be ordained; which was read and passed.

The proposed Canon, to regulate the officiating of ministers in the parish or parochial cure of another clergyman, was taken up, and the question on the proposed amendment was taken by States, and lost; whereupon an addition to the Canon was moved by Mr. Bisset, read, and ordered to be postponed.

A proposed Canon, for the better accomplishing of the objects of the 6th Canon of the year 1792, respecting the preaching of Clergymen in different parishes, was received from the House of Bishops, read, and ordered to lie on the table.

The house then resolved itself into a Committee of the whole, on the order of the day, the Rev. Dr. Blackwell in the chair; and after some time the Committee rose, and the chairman reported the following resolution.

Resolved,—That the pamphlet entitled "Strictures on the Love of Power in the Prelacy, by a Member of the Protestant Episcopal Association in the State of South Carolina," contains very offensive and censurable matter.

This resolution was adopted by the house.

The Committee then asked leave to sit again, which was granted.

The Rev. Mr. Spierin obtained leave of absence.

Adjourned to 10 o'clock to-morrow morning.

TUESDAY, 10 o'clock A.M.

The house met, and the Right Rev. Dr. Madison read prayers.

The proposed Canon respecting the testimonials to be

produced on the part of those who are to be ordained, was sent to the House of Bishops by the Rev. Mr. Bisset.

Dr. Magaw presented a proposed Canon on the preparatory exercises of a candidate for the ministry; which was read, amended, and sent to the House of Bishops.

The House of Bishops returned the Canons on the testimonials to be produced on the part of those who are to be ordained, with an amendment; which was agreed to, and returned by Mr. Wallace, with an additional amendment, which was concurred in by the House of Bishops.

The proposed Canon respecting the officiating of Clergymen within the parish or parochial cure of another Clergyman, was passed, and transmitted by the Rev. Mr. Bisset to the House of Bishops.

The Rev. Mr. Croes presented a proposed Canon, empowering the Bishop in each diocese, to compose a form of prayer or thanksgiving for extraordinary occasions, which was read, and ordered to lie on the table.

The Canon, proposed by the House of Bishops, for the better accomplishing of the objects of the 6th Canon of the year 1792, was returned to the House of Bishops, with an amendment, which was agreed to.

The proposed Canon respecting the preparatory exercises of candidates for Holy Orders, was agreed to, and sent to the House of Bishops by the Rev. Mr. Bisset.

The house resolved itself into a Committee of the whole, on the State of the Church, the Rev. Dr. Blackwell in the chair.

The Committee rose, and the chairman reported

A Canon of Episcopal visitation, a Canon of the learning of candidates for Holy Orders, and a Canon of the age of those who are to be ordained or consecrated.

The Rev. Mr. Keene, the Rev. Mr. Kemp, and Mr. Kerr, obtained leave of absence.

Adjourned till 9 o'clock to-morrow morning.

WEDNESDAY, 9 o'clock, A.M.

The house met, and the Rev. Mr. Waddell read prayers.

The proposed Canon respecting Episcopal visitation was read, passed, and sent by the Rev. Mr. Clarkson to the House of Bishops.

The proposed Canon, respecting the learning of candidates for Holy Orders, was read, passed, and sent by the Rev. Mr. Bisset to the House of Bishops; also the proposed Canon respecting the age of those who are to be ordained.

The Rev. Mr. Bisset presented additional documents respecting the formation of a congregation in Person parish, in the State of North Carolina; which, after being read, were referred to the Presidents of both houses.

The house then resolved itself into a Committee of the whole, with a view to determine who was the author of the pamphlet entitled "Strictures on the Love of Power in the Prelacy, by a member of the Protestant Episcopal Association in the State of South Carolina."

While they were engaged in this business, a message came from the House of Bishops, which the Committee rose to receive, and which is in the following words:

"The House of Bishops propose a conference with the House of Clerical and Lay Deputies, upon a matter which they are anxious to lay before the house."

The house agreed to the conference, which was immediately gone into, the President of the House of Bishops in the chair.

After some time the conference ended, and the President took the chair.

A paper was laid before the house, concerning the pamphlet entitled "Strictures on the Love of Power in the Prelacy," which it was resolved should be referred to a Committee of the whole to-morrow.

The House of Bishops returned the Canon respecting the learning of those who are to be ordained, with an amendment, which being read, was negatived.

An amendment was also proposed by the House of Bishops to the Canon respecting Episcopal visitation, which was read and concurred in.

The Bishops returned the Canon respecting the age of those who are to be ordained or consecrated, with their concurrence.

The House of Bishops requested a conference on the Canon, Of the learning of those who are to be ordained.

Ordered, that the Rev. Mr. Bend inform the House of Bishops, that this house agrees to the conference on the proposed Canon respecting the learning of those who are to be ordained.

The conference accordingly took place.

The proposed Canon, respecting the empowering of the Bishop of each State, to compose a form of prayer or thanksgiving for extraordinary occasions, was read, agreed to, and sent to the House of Bishops by the Secretary.

The House of Bishops returned the said Canon, with their concurrence.

Resolved unanimously,—That the thanks of this House be presented to the Rev. Dr. Smith, for his Sermon delivered at the consecration of the Right Reverend Dr. Robert Smith, and that he be desired to furnish a copy of the same to be printed.

The Canon respecting the preparatory exercises of a candidate for the ministry, was returned by the House of Bishops, with amendments, which were adopted.

Adjourned to 9 o'clock to-morrow morning.

THURSDAY, 9 o'clock, A.M.

The house met, and the Rev. Mr. Croes read prayers.

Dr. Andrews proposed an amendment of an amendment proposed by the House of Bishops, on the proposed Canon respecting the learning of those who are to be ordained; and the question being taken by States, was agreed to, and sent to the House of Bishops.

The House of Bishops returned the said Canon with their concurrence.

On motion of the Rev. Dr. Magaw,

Resolved,—That a Committee be appointed, consisting of four members, who (in concurrence with a Committee of the House of Bishops, if they shall appoint such Committee, and independently of what relates to the printing of the Minutes) shall arrange the Canons and principal papers belonging to the Convention, causing them to be fairly transcribed in a proper bound book, in order that they may be faithfully preserved for the perpetual use of the Houses of the General Convention of this Church, to recur to, as occasion may require; and the said Committee may, if they think proper, employ a clerk, or transcriber, to be paid out of such monies as may be provided for defraying the necessary incidental expenses of Convention. Whereupon,

Resolved,—That the President of this house, the Rev. Dr.

Andrews, the Rev. Dr. Magaw, and the Rev. Dr. Blackwell, be the members of the above Committee, and that the Rev. Mr. Bisset, the Secretary of the House of Clerical and Lay Deputies in the last General Convention, be requested to collect and deliver to the said Committee, all the documents belonging to the Convention which may be in his hands, and to assist the Committee in the execution of their duties as far as may be in his power.

A message was received from the House of Bishops, informing this house that they had concurred in the above resolve, and appointed Bishop White on their part.

The house resolved itself into a Committee of the whole, on the paper referred to them yesterday, and on other business referred to them.

The Committee rose, and their chairman reported that they had considered the paper referred to them yesterday, which was from the author of the pamphlet entitled "Strictures on the Love of Power in the Prelacy," in which he professes his sorrow for the publication, and that they were of opinion the house should accept it as a satisfactory concession.

Resolved,—That the house adopt the above report.

The Committee also reported certain Canons and resolutions, without amendment.

Ordered, that the paper referred to in this report be carried by the Rev. Mr. Bisset to the House of Bishops.

The following message was received from the House of Bishops:

"The Bishops request the House of Clerical and Lay Deputies to appoint a Committee, to confer with a Committee of their house on a subject which has been already before them."

A Committee of five was accordingly appointed, viz., the Rev. Dr. Andrews, the Rev. Mr. Bend, the Rev. Mr. Waddell, Colonel Gurney, and Mr. Johnson; who, at the request of the House of Bishops, repaired to their chamber, and on their return made a report, referring to some alterations which may be proper in the Minutes, in consequence of the concession made by the author of the pamphlet entitled "Strictures on the Love of Power in the Prelacy," which was agreed to.

Adjourned till 9 o'clock to-morrow morning.

FRIDAY, 9 o'clock, A.M.

The house met, and the Rev. Dr. Purcell read prayers.

The Canon, entitled "a Canon to prevent a congregation in any diocese or State to unite with the Church in any other diocese or State," which was proposed by the House of Bishops, was read, amended, and being sent to the House of Bishops, was returned with their concurrence.

Resolved,—That the testimonials from the State of Vermont, respecting the consecration of the Rev. Dr. Samuel Peters, sent by the House of Bishops, be returned to them, with a request, that they will answer it in whatever manner they shall think best.

The message from the House of Bishops, respecting the Articles of Religion, was read and concurred in.

The following resolve was sent by the Rev. Dr. Andrews to the House of Bishops, and returned with their concurrence:

Resolved,—That it be earnestly recommended to the Churches in the several States, not to fail to send deputies to the next General Convention, as it appears inexpedient that the consideration of the Articles of Religion should be postponed beyond the period of that meeting.

The Secretary of the Committee for carrying into effect the act for supporting Missionaries to preach the Gospel on the frontiers of the United States, reported to this house the progress made by said Committee in the execution of the business entrusted to them. Whereupon,

Resolved,—That it be recommended to the different State Conventions, to continue, either by an annual Sermon, or by soliciting private contributions, to provide for the establishment of Missionaries to preach the Gospel on the frontiers of the United States; and that, instead of committing the general management of the fund, as by the act of the last General Convention, to a Standing Committee of any State, the Convention of each State shall appoint such Committee to have the management of the money contributed in that State, and the application of the same to the support of a Missionary or Missionaries in such part of the United States as they may think proper; and the money heretofore collected in any State, and remitted to the treasurer of the former Standing Committee, shall be returned to such State Committees when they are appointed, and shall call for the same.

The act passed on this subject in the year 1792 is hereby rescinded.

Resolved,—That a Committee of both houses be appointed to digest and report to the next General Convention a Course of Study for Candidates for Holy Orders, and that the following gentlemen be appointed by this house: the Rev. Dr. Moore, the Rev. Dr. Andrews, the Rev. Dr. Magaw, the Rev. Dr. Smith, and the Rev. Mr. Bend.

Resolved, with the concurrence of the House of Bishops, that it be made known to the several State Conventions, that it is proposed to consider and determine in the next General Convention, on the following addition to the second article of the Constitution, in the 9th line, after the word "Convention," viz.:

"But if the Church shall not be represented in both Orders in a majority of the States, then the vote shall be given by States without regard to Orders."

Resolved unanimously, with the concurrence of the House of Bishops, that the thanks of this Convention be given to Matthew Clarkson, Esq., Mayor of the city, for the use of the City Hall, and that Colonel Gurney and Joseph Swift, Esq., be a Committee to communicate the same.

Resolved, with the concurrence of the House of Bishops, that eight hundred copies of the Journals be printed.

The house proceeded to appoint a Standing Committee,(1) and the following gentlemen were chosen:

For New Hampshire, the Hon. Mr. Livermore.

For Massachusetts, the Rev. Dr. Parker.

For Rhode Island, the Rev. William Smith.

For Connecticut, the Rev. Mr. Baldwin.

For New York, the Rev. Dr. Moore, the Rev. Dr. Beach, Robert Watts, Esq.

For New Jersey, the Rev. Mr. Waddell, the Rev. Mr. Croes, Joshua M. Wallace, Esq.

For Pennsylvania, the Rev. Dr. Magaw, the Rev. Dr. Blackwell, the Rev. Dr. Andrews, Colonel Gurney, Joseph Swift, Esq., Mr. J. B. Gilpin.

For Delaware, the Rev. Mr. Clarkson, the Rev. Mr. Clay, Nicholas Ridgley, Esq.

(1) For the powers and duties of the Standing Committee, see page 19 of the Journal of the House of Clerical and Lay Deputies, in Convention, Sept. 1789. [*Vide* P. 113 of this Reprint.]

For Maryland, the Rev. Mr. Bend, Samuel Johnson, Esq., General Lloyd.

For Virginia, the Rev. Dr. M'Croskey, Robert Andrews, Esq.

For South Carolina, the Rev. Mr. Frost, Rev. Dr. Purcell, the Hon. William Smith.

Ordered, that the President of this house is chairman of the above Committee, and is empowered to call together the members.

Resolved,—That the thanks of this house be given to the President for his able and impartial management in his place, and to the Secretary for his correct attention and services.

Resolved,—That the next meeting of the General Convention be held in the city of Philadelphia.

The house rose.

WILLIAM SMITH, President.

James Abercrombie, Secretary.

JOURNAL

OF THE

House of Bishops.

PHILADELPHIA,
SEPTEMBER 8th, 1795.

This being the day of the meeting of the General Convention of the Protestant Episcopal Church, the Right Rev. Bishop White attended in Christ Church.

IN THE VESTRY ROOM OF CHRIST CHURCH,
WEDNESDAY, September 9.

The house met. Present:

The Right Rev. Bishop White of the State of Pennsylvania, who, by the rules of the house made at the last meeting, presided; the Right Rev. Bishop Provoost, of the State of New York; the Right Rev. Bishop Madison, of the State of Virginia.

The Rev. Joseph Turner was chosen Secretary.

The house received a message from the House of Clerical and Lay Deputies, informing them that their house was formed and ready to proceed to business.

The house received another message, informing them that the House of Clerical and Lay Deputies propose to this house the adjourning to the City Hall.

The proposal for removing is agreed to.

This house sent a message to the House of Clerical and Lay Deputies, informing them that Bishop Provoost is ready to preach before the Convention, agreeably to the appointment of the last Convention, and proposing Friday next as the time for the delivery of the Sermon.

Information was received that the House of Clerical and Lay Deputies concurred.

A message was received from the House of Clerical and Lay Deputies, proposing that the hours of sitting of the Convention, shall be from 10 in the morning to 3 in the afternoon, with which this house concurred.

Resolved,—That during the session of the Convention, the house will attend divine service in the House of Clerical and Lay Deputies.

Adjourned to meet to-morrow morning in the City Hall.

CITY HALL, THURSDAY, SEPTEMBER 10.

The house met. Present:

The Right Rev. Bishop White, President; Right Rev. Bishop Provoost; Right Rev. Bishop Madison; Right Rev. Bishop Claggett.

The Rev. Mr. Bisset presented to this house, from the House of Clerical and Lay Deputies, an application from the Vestry of the Protestant Episcopal Church in Person county, North Carolina.

This house resolved, that it be proposed to the House of Clerical and Lay Deputies, that as the said letter cannot be acted on by the Convention, the Presidents of the two houses be desired to send such an answer to the same, as in their judgments shall be proper.

Adjourned to 10 o'clock to-morrow morning.

FRIDAY MORNING, 10 o'clock.

The house met. Present as yesterday.

This house proceeded with the House of Clerical and Lay Deputies to Christ Church, where the Rev. Mr. Waddell read prayers; after which the Right Rev. Bishop Provoost delivered a Sermon, suited to the occasion of the present meeting, as appointed at the last Convention.

After divine service, this house returned to the City Hall, and entered upon business.

Resolved,—That the thanks of this house be given to the Right Rev. Bishop Provoost for his Sermon delivered this morning, and that he be desired to furnish a copy of it for the press.

This house originated a Canon, and sent it to the house of Clerical and Lay Deputies, restricting any individual congregation from associating with the Church of any other diocese or State, than that in which they are situated.

The house then adjourned.

SATURDAY MORNING, 10 o'clock.

The house met. Present as yesterday.

This house received from the House of Clerical and Lay Deputies, the testimonials of the Rev. Robert Smith, D.D., Bishop elect of this Church in the State of South Carolina.

A message was sent from this house to the House of Clerical and Lay Deputies, informing them that they had examined and approved the testimonials of the Rev. Dr. Smith, of South Carolina, and that the consecration will take place to-morrow morning, in Christ Church.

The following message was sent from this house to the House of Clerical and Lay Deputies:

Whereas the present Convention, from particular unavoidable circumstances is deprived of many of its members,

Resolved,—That this house propose to the House of Clerical and Lay Deputies, to defer the discussion of the Articles until the meeting of the next General Convention, when a more full representation of this Church may be expected.

The following message was also sent to the House of Clerical and Lay Deputies, viz.:

This house took into consideration a resolution of the House of Clerical and Lay Deputies, in a preceding Convention, which resolution is in these words—

"Resolved,—That it be made known to the several State Conventions, that it is proposed to consider and determine, in the next General Convention, on the propriety of investing the House of Bishops with a full negative upon the proceedings of the other house."

Thereupon resolved,—That the following message be sent to the House of Clerical and Lay Deputies, viz., The House of Bishops have not expressed their sense in any former Convention upon the subject aforesaid; but they now propose to the House of Clerical and Lay Deputies, that the legislative power of the House of Bishops shall remain as fixed by the third article of the Constitution of this Church.

The house then adiourned to Monday, 10 o'clock.

MONDAY MORNING, Sept. 14.

The house met. Present as on Saturday.

The Right Rev. Dr. Smith, who had been yesterday consecrated Bishop of this Church in South Carolina, took his seat in this house.

A proposed Canon was sent to the House of Clerical and Lay Deputies, intended to accomplish more fully the object of the Sixth Canon, passed in Convention in 1792.

The Right Rev. Bishop Claggett obtained leave of absence.

The house then adjourned.

TUESDAY MORNING.

The house met. Present as yesterday, except Bishop Claggett.

This house received from the House of Clerical and Lay Deputies, a proposed Canon respecting the testimonials of those who are to be ordained.

This house returned the above proposed Canon to the House of Clerical and Lay Deputies, with an amendment.

The same Canon was again presented to this house with an amendment from the House of Clerical and Lay Deputies, with which this house concurred.

This house received a proposed Canon from the House of Clerical and Lay Deputies, on the preparatory exercises of the candidates for the ministry.

This house returned the same with amendments.

The proposed Canon, that originated in this house, for the more full accomplishing of the object of the sixth Canon of 1792, which had been sent to the House of Clerical and Lay Deputies was returned to this house with an amendment.

The proposed Canon respecting preparatory exercises of

candidates for the ministry, was returned to the House of Clerical and Lay Deputies with an amendment.

The house then adjourned to 9 o'clock to-morrow morning.

WEDNESDAY MORNING, 9 o'clock.

The house met. Present as yesterday.

A message was sent from this house to the House of Clerical and Lay Deputies, desiring a conference with their house upon a matter which they are desirous to lay before them.

The conference was agreed to, and the House of Bishops met the House of Clerical and Lay Deputies in the chamber of the latter; when the President, by desire, took the chair.

The conference being ended, this house returned to their chamber.

This house received from the House of Clerical and Lay Deputies their concurrence with the amendment to the proposed Canon, respecting exercises to be required of persons who are to be ordained.

Resolved,—That the said Canon now pass, and be returned to the House of Clerical and Lay Deputies.

This house received from the House of Clerical and Lay Deputies, a proposed Canon concerning the learning of those who are to be ordained.

This house received from the House of Clerical and Lay Deputies, a proposed Canon to alter the third Canon of 1789, on Episcopal visitation.

This house received from the House of Clerical and Lay Deputies, a proposed Canon to alter the Canon concerning the age of persons to be ordained.

This house returned to the House of Clerical and Lay Deputies their proposed Canon concerning the learning of persons to be ordained, with an amendment, and also the proposed Canon to alter the third Canon of 1789, with an amendment.

This house passed the proposed Canon to alter the Canon respecting the age of persons to be ordained.

The house passed the Canon to alter the 6th Canon of 1792, Of officiating in the parishes or parochial cures of other ministers.

The House of Clerical and Lay Deputies signified their non-concurrence with the amendment of the proposed Canon concerning the learning of persons to be ordained.

Resolved,—That a conference be requested on the said proposed Canon, at such hour as the House of Clerical and Lay Deputies may appoint.

This house received a message from the House of Clerical and Lay Deputies, informing that they agreed to the conference.

The two houses then went into conference, and after some time spent therein, this house returned to their chamber.

This house received from the House of Clerical and Lay Deputies a proposed Canon, authorising the Bishop of any diocese to appoint forms of prayer or thanksgiving for extraordinary occasions; which was passed and returned.

Resolved unanimously,—That the thanks of this house be presented to the Rev. Dr. William Smith, for his Sermon, delivered in Christ Church at the consecration of the Right Rev. Dr. Robert Smith, and that he be requested to furnish a copy of the same, to be printed.

The Right Rev. Bishop Madison obtained leave of absence.

The house then adjourned to 9 o'clock to-morrow morning.

THURSDAY MORNING, 9 o'clock.

This house met. Present as yesterday, except the Right Rev. Bishop Madison.

This house returned to the House of Clerical and Lay Deputies, the proposed Canon of the learning of persons to be ordained, with an amendment.

The above proposed Canon was returned to the house with an amendment, with which this house concurred.

This house received a resolution from the House of Clerical and Lay Deputies, for the appointment of a Committee for the arrangement of the Canons and other papers belonging to this Convention, desiring the concurrence of this house.

This house concurred in the same.

This house requested the House of Clerical and Lay Deputies to appoint a Committee of their house to meet a Committee of the House of Bishops.

The Committee of this house is Bishop White and Bishop Provoost.

The House of Clerical and Lay Deputies agreed to the request of this house, and the joint Committee met in the Bishops' chamber.

This being done, this house returned to their chamber.

A message came to this house from the House of Clerical and Lay Deputies, that they had agreed to the report of the joint Committee with a small amendment, which was agreed to.

Bishop Provoost obtained leave of absence.

The house then adjourned to 9 o'clock to-morrow morning.

FRIDAY MORNING, 9 o'clock.

The house met. Present, the Right Rev. Bishop White and the Right Rev. Bishop Smith.

There was returned to this house the proposed Canon from the House of Clerical and Lay Deputies, to prevent any Church from uniting themselves to any other diocese than to that in the State in which they belong, with an amendment to the said Canon; which amendment was agreed to, and the Canon passed.

The house received from the House of Clerical and Lay Deputies, papers respecting the election of Dr. Peters to be Bishop in the State of Vermont.

The President of this house is desired to give such an answer as the nature of the case requires, and particularly to mention, in the said answer, that the Bishops cannot with propriety consecrate a Bishop for the Church in any State, until such Church shall have acceded to the general Ecclesiastical Constitution of the Church in the United States.

This house received a resolution from the House of Clerical and Lay Deputies, proposing that the monies collected for the purpose of sending Missionaries to the frontiers, be returned to the churches in the States in which they were respectively collected; and proposing that the object of the institution be pursued by the churches in the individual States; with which this house agreed.

This house received a proposed constitutional alteration of the manner of voting in the House of Clerical and Lay Deputies; in which this house concurred.

This house received a resolution from the House of Clerical and Lay Deputies, to appoint a Committee that may digest and report to the next Convention, a course of studies for candidates for Holy Orders, in which this house concurred, and the Right Rev. Bishop White, Bishop Provoost and

Bishop Madison are the Committee from this house for the above purpose.

The House of Bishops concurred with the House of Clerical and Lay Deputies in thanks to the Mayor of the city for the use of the Hall.

The house of Clerical and Lay Deputies inform this house, that 800 copies of the Journals of this Convention are proposed to be printed; which was agreed to.

The House of Clerical and Lay Deputies sent a message to this house, expressing their intention of rising; and that they had appointed Philadelphia for the place of meeting of the next General Convention.

The thanks of the House of Bishops were given to the Rev. Joseph Turner, for his services as Secretary.

Signed by order of the house,

WILLIAM WHITE, PRESIDING BISHOP.

ATTEST: JOSEPH TURNER, Secretary.

THE CERTIFICATE OF THE CONSECRATION OF THE RIGHT REV. BISHOP SMITH IS AS FOLLOWS.

Know all men by these presents, that we, William White, D.D., Bishop of the Protestant Episcopal Church in the State of Pennsylvania, Presiding Bishop; Samuel Provoost, D.D., Bishop of the Protestant Episcopal Church in the State of New York; James Madison, D.D., Bishop of the Protestant Episcopal Church in the State of Virginia; and Thomas John Claggett, D.D., Bishop of the Protestant Episcopal Church in the State of Maryland, under the protection of Almighty God, in Christ Church, in the city of Philadelphia, on Sunday, the thirteenth day of September, in the year of our Lord One thousand seven hundred and ninety-five, did then and there rightly and canonically consecrate our beloved in Christ, Robert Smith, D.D., Provost of Charleston College, and Rector of St. Philip's Church, Charleston, in the State of South Carolina, of whose sufficiency in good learning, soundness in the faith, and purity of manners, we were fully ascertained, into the office of Bishop of the Protestant Episcopal Church in the said State, to which the said Robert Smith hath been elected by the Convention of the said State.

In testimony whereof we have signed our names and caused our seals to be affixed.

Given in the city of Philadelphia this fourteenth day of September, in the year of our Lord One thousand seven hundred and ninety-five.

WILLIAM WHITE. [L. S.]
SAMUEL PROVOOST. [L. S.]
JAMES MADISON. [L. S.]
THOMAS JOHN CLAGGETT. [L. S.]

APPENDIX.

Canons.

Canon I.—Of Episcopal Visitation.

Every bishop in this Church shall visit the churches within his diocese or district, for the purposes of examining the state of his Church, inspecting the behaviour of the Clergy, and administering the apostolic rite of Confirmation. And it is deemed proper that such visitations be made once in three years at least, by every bishop to every church within his diocese or district, which shall make provision for defraying the necessary expenses of the bishop at such visitation. And it is hereby declared to be the duty of the minister and vestry of every church or congregation, to make such provision accordingly.

The bishop of any diocese or State district may, on the invitation of the Convention or Standing Committee of the church in any State where there is not a bishop, visit and perform the episcopal offices in that State, or part of the State, as the case may be, provision being made for defraying his expenses as aforesaid: and such State, or part of a State, shall be considered as annexed to the district or diocese of such bishop, until a bishop is duly elected and consecrated for such State, or until the invitation given by the Convention or Standing Committee be revoked. But it is to be understood, that to enable the Bishop to make the aforesaid visitations, it shall be the duty of the clergy, in such reasonable rotation as may be devised, to officiate for him in any parochial duties which belong to him. And no State shall proceed to the election or appointment of a bishop, unless there be at least six presbyters residing and officiating therein, a majority of whom, at least, shall concur in such election. But the Conventions of two or more States, having together nine or more settled and officiating presbyters, may associate, and join in the election of a bishop.

The Third Canon of the year 1789 is hereby rescinded.

Canon II.—Of the Testimonials to be produced on the part of those who are to be Ordained.

Every candidate for Holy Orders shall be recommended to the Bishop by a Standing Committee appointed by the Convention of the church in that State wherein he resides, which recommendation shall be signed by the names of a majority of the Committee, and shall be in the following words:

We, whose names are hereunder written, testify that A. B. hath laid before us satisfactory testimonials, that for the space of three years last past, he hath lived piously, soberly, and honestly: and hath not written, taught, or held, any thing contrary to the doctrine or discipline of the Protestant Episcopal Church. And, moreover, we think him a person worthy to be admitted to the sacred order of . . . In witness whereof we have hereunto set our hands, this . . . day of . . . in the year of our Lord . . . . .

But before a Standing Committee in any State shall proceed to recommend any candidate, as aforesaid, to the Bishop, such candidate shall produce from the minister and vestry of the parish where he resides, or from the vestry alone if the parish be vacant, or if there be no vestry, from at least twelve respectable persons of the Protestant Episcopal Church in the neighbourhood in which he resides, testimonials of his good morals and orderly conduct for three years last past, and that he has not, so far as they know and believe, written, taught, or held any thing contrary to the doctrine or discipline of the Protestant Episcopal Church; a publication of his intention to apply for Holy Orders having been previously made by such minister or vestry. He shall also lay before the Standing Committee, testimonials to the same effect, signed by at least one respectable clergyman of the Protestant Episcopal Church in the United States, from his personal knowledge of the candidate for at least one year.

In every State in which there is no Standing Committee, such Committee shall be appointed at its next ensuing Convention; and in the mean time, every candidate for Holy Orders shall be recommended according to the regulations or usage of the Church in each State, and the requisitions of the bishop to whom he applies.

The 6th Canon, passed in October, 1789, concerning the testimonials to be produced on the part of those who are to be ordained, and so much of the 4th Canon passed in 1792, as relates to the subject of this Canon, are hereby rescinded

Canon III.—Of the Age of those who are to be Ordained or Consecrated.

Deacon's Orders shall not be conferred on any person until he shall be twenty-one years old, nor Priest's Orders on any one until he shall be twenty-four years old; and unless he shall have been a Deacon one year. No man shall be consecrated a bishop of this Church until he shall be thirty years old.

The 4th Canon of the year 1789 is hereby rescinded.

Canon IV.—Of the Learning of those who are to be Ordained.

No person shall be ordained in this Church until he shall have satisfied the Bishop and the two Presbyters by whom he shall be examined, that he is well acquainted with the Holy Scriptures, can read the New Testament in the original Greek, and give an account of his faith in the Latin tongue; and that he hath a competent knowledge of natural and moral philosophy and church history, and hath paid attention to composition and pulpit eloquence as means of giving additional efficacy to his labours; unless the bishop shall judge it proper to dispense with the above requisites in part, in consideration of certain other qualifications in the candidate, peculiarly fitting him for the Gospel ministry.

The 7th Canon of the year 1789 is hereby rescinded.

Canon V.—Of the Officiating of Ministers of this Church in the Churches or within the Parochial Cures of other Clergymen.

No clergyman belonging to this Church shall officiate, either by preaching or reading prayers, in the parish, or within the parochial cure of another clergyman, unless he have received express permission for that purpose, from the minister of the parish or cure, or in his absence, from the church wardens and vestrymen, or trustees of the congregation. But if any minister of a church shall, from inability or any other cause, neglect to perform the regular services to his congregation, and shall refuse his consent to any other minister of this Church to officiate within his cure, the church wardens, vestrymen, or trustees of such congregation shall, on proof of such neglect and refusal before the bishop of the diocese, or, if there be no bishop, before the Standing Committee, or before such persons as may be deputed by him or them, or before such persons as may be, by the regulations of this Church in any State, vested with the power of hearing and deciding on complaints against clergymen, have power to open the doors of their churches to any regular minister of the Protestant Episcopal Church.

The 6th Canon of 1792 is hereby rescinded.

Canon VI.—Of the Preparatory Exercises of a Candidate for the Ministry.

Every candidate for the ministry shall give notice of his intention to the bishop, or to such body as the Church in the State in which the candidate resides, may have appointed to superintend the instruction of candidates for Holy Orders, at least one year before his ordination. And if there be a bishop within the State or district where the candidate resides, he shall apply to no other bishop for ordination, without the permission of the former. And the said candidate shall pass through the preparatory exercises which the bishop, or such body aforesaid, may appoint: such as composing of theses, homilies or sermons, one or more, to be delivered either publicly or privately, in his or their presence, at such time or times as may be appointed by the authority aforesaid.—And this Canon shall be in force from and after the first day of January next.

Canon VII.—For the better accomplishing of the Objects of the Sixth Canon of 1792.

Whereas there is no provision made in the 6th Canon of 1792, for the case of such a vicinity of two or more churches, as that there can be no local boundaries drawn between their respective cures, it is hereby ordained that, in every such case, no minister of this Church, other than the parochial clergy of the said cures, shall preach within the common limits of the same, in any other place than in one of the churches thereof, without the consent of the major number of the parochial clergy of the said churches.

CANON VIII.—To prevent a Congregation in any Diocese or State to unite with a Church in any other Diocese or State.

Whereas a question may arise, whether a congregation within the diocese of any bishop, or within any State in which there is not yet any bishop settled, may unite themselves with the Church in any other diocese or State, it is hereby determined and declared, that all such unions shall be considered as irregular and void; and that every congregation of this Church shall be considered as belonging to the body of the Church of the diocese, or of the State, within the limits of which they dwell or within which there is seated a Church to which they belong. And no clergyman having a parish or cure in more than one State, shall have a seat in the Convention of any State, other than that in which he resides.

CANON IX.—To empower the Bishop in each Diocese or District to compose Forms of Prayer or Thanksgiving for extraordinary occasions.

The bishop of each diocese or district may compose forms of prayer or thanksgiving, as the case may require, for extraordinary occasions, and transmit them to each clergyman within his diocese or district, whose duty it shall be to use such forms in his church on such occasions. And the Clergy in those States in which there is no Bishop, may use the forms of prayer or thanksgiving composed by the Bishop of any other State.

Done in Convention, and signed by order of the House of Bishops.

WILLIAM WHITE, D.D., PRESIDING BISHOP.
WILLIAM SMITH, D.D.,
PRESIDENT OF THE HOUSE OF CLERICAL AND LAY DEPUTIES.

List of the Clergy

OF THE

PROTESTANT EPISCOPAL CHURCH,

DELIVERED IN AND PUBLISHED AGREEABLY TO THE 16TH CANON OF THE GENERAL CONVENTION OF 1789.

From NEW HAMPSHIRE and MASSACHUSETTS no lists were delivered in.

The Lists from RHODE ISLAND and CONNECTICUT are the same as those in the last Journal, no new Lists having been delivered in.

RHODE ISLAND.

The Rev. Moses Badger, Rector of King's church, Providence.
The Rev. William Smith, Rector of Trinity church, Newport.

CONNECTICUT.

Right Rev. Samuel Seabury, D.D., Bishop.
The Rev. Ebenezer Dibble, Rector of St. John's church Stamford.
Rev. George Ogilvie, St. Paul's church, Norwalk.
Rev. Philo Shelton, Stratfield.
Rev. Dr. Bela Hubbard, Trinity church, New Haven.
Rev. Philo Perry, Christ church, Newtown.
Rev. David Perry, Reading, etc.
Rev. Truman Marsh, New Milford.
Rev. Ashbel Baldwin, Litchfield.
Rev. Ambrose Todd, Symsbury.
Rev. Abraham Lynsen Clarke, Huntington.
Rev. Dr. Richard Mansfield, Derby.
Rev. Reuben Ives, Cheshire.
Rev. Dr. Abraham Jarvis, Christ Church, Middleton.
Rev. Daniel Fogg, Brooklyn.
Rev. John Tyler, Christ church, Norwich.
Rev. Chauncey Prindle, Westbury.
Rev. John Bowden, residing at Stratford.
Rev. Edward Blakslee, Deacon, Woodbridge
Rev. Solomon Blakslee, Deacon, East Haddam.

Rev. David Belden, Deacon, ——.
Rev. Seth Hart, Deacon, Waterbury.
Rev. David Butler, Deacon, North Guilford.

NEW YORK.

Right Rev. Samuel Provoost, D.D., Bishop.
Rev. Jeremiah Leaming, D.D., residing in New York.
Rev. Abraham Beach, D.D., Assistant Minister of Trinity church, New York.
Rev. Benjamin Moore, D.D., Assistant Minister of Trinity church, New York.
Rev. Thomas L. Moore, Rector of St. George's church, South Hempstead.
Rev. Thomas Ellison, Rector of St. Peter's church, Albany.
Rev. John Bisset, Assistant Minister of Trinity Church, New York.
Rev. Richard C. Moore, Rector of St. Andrew's church, Staten Island.
Rev. George H. Spieren, Rector of Christ church, Poughkeepsie.
Rev. Samuel Nesbit, Rector of St. Anne's church, Brooklyn.
Rev. Elias Cooper, Rector of St. John's church, Philipsburgh.
Rev. Andrew Fowler, Rector of —— church, Bedford.
Rev. Theodosius Bartow, Rector of Trinity church at New Rochelle.
Rev. William Hammel, Rector of the churches at Jamaica, Newtown, and Flushing.
Rev. John J. Sands, Minister of Christ church, Rye.
Rev. Elijah D. Rattoone, Professor of the Greek and Latin Languages in Columbia College.
Rev. Ammi Rogers, Rector of the churches at Schenectady and Ballston.
Rev. John Ireland, Rector of St. Peter's church, West Chester.
Rev. David Belden, Rector of Christ church, Duanesburgh.
Rev. Frederick Van Horne, Minister of St. Andrew's church, Ulster county.
Rev. Walter C. Gardiner, Minister of Christ church, Hudson.
Rev. Samuel Haskell, Minister of —— church, Peekskill.
Rev. James Nicholls officiates every third Sunday at Camden.
Rev. Daniel Barber, officiates every third Sunday at Kingsbury.

NEW JERSEY.

Rev. Uzal Ogden, Rector of Trinity church, Newark.
Rev. Henry Waddell, Rector of Christ church, Shrewsbury, and Christ church, Middletown.
Rev. Henry Vandyke, Rector of St. Mary's church, Burlington.
Rev. William Ayres, Rector of St. Peter's church, Spotswood.
Rev. John Croes, Rector of Trinity church, Swedesborough.
Rev. Richard C. Moore, Rector of St. Peter's church, Amboy, but residing in the State of New York.
Rev. Elisha D. Rattoone, Assistant Minister of Trinity church, Newark, but residing in New York.
Rev. John Wade, residing at present at Colestown.

PENNSYLVANIA.

The Right Rev. William White, D.D., Bishop.
Rev. William Smith, D.D.
Rev. Samuel Magaw, D.D., Rector of St. Paul's church, Philadelphia.

Rev. John Andrews, D.D., Vice-Provost of the University of Pennsylvania.
Rev. Robert Blackwell, D.D., Assistant Minister of Christ Church and St. Peter's, in the city of Philadelphia.
Rev. Joseph Hutchins, D.D.
Rev. John Campbell, Rector of the Episcopal churches in York and Huntingdon.
Rev. Slator Clay, Rector of St. David's, Radnor, St. Peter's in the Valley, and St. James's, Perkiomen.
Rev. Elisha Rigg, Rector of St. James's, Lancaster.
Rev. Levi Heath, Rector of Pequea and Bangor churches, Lancaster county.
Rev. Robert Ayres, Rector of Emanuel church and St. Peter's church in Washington and Fayette counties.
Rev. Francis Reno, Westmoreland county.
Rev. Joseph H. Turner, Rector of St. Paul's church, Chester, and St. Martin's church, Marcus Hook.
Rev. Caleb Hopkins, Rector of Christ church, Derry township, and Christ church, Turbut township, Northumberland county.
Rev. Thomas Davis, Washington connty.
Rev. James Abercrombie, Assistant Minister of Christ church and St. Peter's, in the city of Philadelphia.
Rev. Joseph Doddridge, Deacon in Washington county.
Rev. John Taylor, Deacon in Northumberland county.
Rev. Absalom Jones, (a black man), Deacon in the African church of St. Thomas, Philadelphia.

DELAWARE.

Rev. Joseph Clarkson, Rector of Trinity church, Wilmington.
Rev. Robert Clay, Emanuel church, New Castle.
Rev. George Dasheille, St. Anne's church, Middletown, Newcastle county.
Rev. William Pryce, Christ church, Kent county.
Rev. William Skelly, Christ church, Sussex county.
Rev. James Wiltbank, St. Peter's church, Sussex county.

MARYLAND.

The Right Rev. Thomas J. Claggett, D.D., Bishop.
Rev. Andrew Elliott, Rector of King and Queen.
Rev. Francis Walker, St. Andrew's.
Rev. Charles Smoot, William and Mary, St. Mary's county.
Rev. John W. Compton, William and Mary.
Rev. John Weems, Port Tobacco parish.
Walter Harrison, Durham, Charles county.
Rev. Edward Gantt, Jun., All Saints, Calvert.(1)
Rev. Joseph Messenger, St. John's parish.(1)
Rev. Joseph Jackson, Queen Anne's, Prince George.
Rev. Clement Brook.
Rev. Walter Addison.
Rev. Andrew T. Macormick, residing in Prince George.
Rev. Thomas Scott, St. James's.(1)
Rev. Henry Moscrop, All Hallows.
Rev. Ralph Higinbottom, St. Anne's.

Rev. Stephen Sykes, Anne Arundel.
Rev. Thomas Read, Prince George's parish.(1)
Rev. George Ralph, Washington.
Rev. Edward Gantt, M.D.
Rev. Nicholas W. Lane, St. Peter's, Montgomery.
Rev. George Bower, Rector of All Saints, Frederick.
Rev. Joseph G. J. Bend, St. Paul's parish.(1)
Rev. T. Fitch Oliver, St. Thomas's, Baltimore.
Rev. John Coleman, St. John's parish.(1)
Rev. John Allen, St. George's.
Rev. John Ireland, Harford county.
Rev. William Duke, St. Mary Anne's.(1)
Rev. Jeremiah Cosden, St. Stephen's, Cecil.
Rev. Colin Ferguson, D.D., St. Paul's parish, Kent county.(1)
Rev. Archibald Walker, Kent.
Rev. Samuel Keene, D.D., St. Luke's parish.
Rev. Samuel Keene, Jun., Queen Anne's.(1)
Rev. Owen F. Magrath, St. Peter's.
Rev. John Bowie, D.D., St. Michael's, Talbot.
Rev. James Kemp, Great Choptank parish, Dorchester county.(1)
Rev. Samuel Tingeley.
Rev. Samuel Sloan, Somerset.
Rev. David Ball, Rector of All Hallows parish, Worcester.

VIRGINIA.

The Right Rev. James Madison, D.D., Bishop.
Rev. Charles O'Neill, rector of Amherst parish.
Rev. Alexander Hay, rector of Antrim parish.
Rev. Devereux Jarratt, rector of Bath parish.
Rev. Samuel Gray, Botetourt parish.
Rev. Hugh Corrans Boggs, rector of Berkeley parish.
Rev. Benjamin Brown, rector of Brisland parish.
Rev. John Syme, rector of Bristol parish.
Rev. John Cameron, D.D., rector of ——
Rev. Alexander M'Farland, rector of Brunswick parish
Rev. John Bracken, D.D., rector of Bruton parish.
Rev. John Camm, rector of Charles parish.
Rev. Henry Heffernam.
Rev. David Ball, Christ church parish.
Rev. James Elliott, rector of Cople parish.
Rev. Needler Robinson, rector of Dale parish.
Rev. Spence Grayson, rector of Dettingen parish.
Rev. Jesse Carter, rector of Drysdale parish.
Rev. John J. Spooner, Elizabeth city parish.
Rev. James Whitehead, rector of Elizabeth river parish.
Rev. Thomas Davis, Fairfax parish.
Rev. Alexander Balmain, rector of Frederick parish.
Rev. Matthew Maury, rector of Fredericksville parish.
Rev. James Craig, rector of Hamilton parish.
Rev. John Buchanan, D.D., rector of Henrico parish.
Rev. Samuel S. M'Croskey, rector of Hungars parish.
Rev. James Thompson, rector of Leeds parish.
Rev. Charles Crawford, rector of Lexington parish.

Rev. William Crawford, Lexington parish.
Rev. Elkanah Talley, rector of Littleton parish.
Rev. Isaac Wm. Gibbern, rector of Lunenburg parish.
Rev. Anthony Walke, rector of Lynhaven parish.
Rev. Wm. Cameron, rector of Manchester parish.
Rev. William Hubard, rector of Newport parish.
Rev. Henry J. Burgess, Nottoway parish.
Rev. Robert Buchan, rector of Overwharton parish.
Rev. Arthur Emerson, rector of Portsmouth parish.
Rev. John Brunskill, rector of Raleigh parish.
Rev. Alexander Lundie, rector of St. Andrew's parish.
Rev. John Matthews, St. Bride's parish.
Rev. Reuben Clopton, ——
Rev. Cave Jones, St. George's parish.
Rev. Isaac Foster, ——.
Rev. James Stenvenson, rector of St. George's parish.
Rev. Charles Hopkins, rector of St. James, Northam parish.
Rev. James Price, rector of St. John's parish.
Rev. Archibald Dick, rector of St. Margaret's parish.
Rev. John Woodville, St. Mark's parish.
Rev. Peter Nelson, St. Martin's parish.
Rev. Abner Waugh, rector of St. Mary's parish.
Rev. William Stewart, rector of St. Paul's parish.
Rev. John Parsons, ——.
Rev. John Seward, St. Stephen's parish.
Rev. John Hyde Saunders, rector of Southam parish.
Rev. Samuel Butler, rector of Southwark parish.
Rev. Lee Massey, rector of Truro parish.
Rev. Sewal Chapin, rector of Westover parish.
Rev. James Henderson, rector of York parish.
Rev. John Bryan, rector of Wicomico parish.
Rev. John O'Donnel, rector of Hampshire parish.
Rev. Thomas Hughes, rector of Petsworth parish.
Rev. Joseph Wilson.
Rev. Stephen Johnson.
Rev. John Wade.
Rev. Armistead Smith, rector of Matthews parish.

SOUTH CAROLINA.

The Right Rev. Robert Smith, D.D., Bishop.
Rev. Mr. Frost.
Rev. Dr. Purcell, St. Michael's.
Rev. Dr. Gates.
Rev. Mr. Jenkins.
Rev. Mr. Nixon, Master of an Academy.
Rev. Mr. White, Charleston.
Rev. Mr. Mills, St. Andrew's.
Rev. Mr. M'Culley, St. Luke's.
Rev. Mr. Tate, St. Helen's.
Rev. Mr. Blackwall, St. Bartholomew's.
Rev. Mr. Connor, Edisto.

Those gentlemen whose names are marked (1) were elected members of the Standing Committee in the State Convention of 1795.

JOURNAL OF THE PROCEEDINGS

OF THE

BISHOPS, CLERGY, AND LAITY

OF THE

Protestant Episcopal Church

IN

THE UNITED STATES OF AMERICA,

IN

A CONVENTION

HELD IN

THE CITY OF PHILADELPHIA, FROM TUESDAY, JUNE 11TH, TO WEDNESDAY, JUNE 19TH, 1799.

LIST OF THE MEMBERS OF THE HOUSE OF CLERICAL AND LAY DEPUTIES.

FROM THE STATE OF MASSACHUSETTS.

Rev. William Walter, D.D.

FROM THE STATE OF RHODE ISLAND.

Rev. Abraham Lynsen Clarke.

FROM THE STATE OF CONNECTICUT.

Rev. William Smith, D.D.
Rev. Ashbel Baldwin.
Benjamin Hall, Esq.

FROM THE STATE OF NEW YORK.

Rev. John Bisset.
Rev. Ammi Rogers.

FROM THE STATE OF NEW JERSEY.

Rev. Uzal Ogden, D.D.
Rev. Henry Waddell.
Rev. John Croes.
Rev. Menzies Rayner.
John Rutherford, Esq.
Mr. Jeffery Clarke.
Mr. John Dennis.

FROM THE STATE OF PENNSYLVANIA.

Rev. William Smith, D.D.
Rev. John Andrews, D.D.
Rev. Samuel Magaw, D.D.
Rev. Robert Blackwell, D.D.
General Francis Gurney.
John C. Stocker, Esq.
Mr. Joseph Sims.
Mr. J. B. Gilpin.

FROM THE STATE OF DELAWARE.

Rev. Robert Clay.
Rev. Joseph Carkson.
Rev. William Pryce.
Rev. Walter C. Gardiner.
Joseph Burn, Esq.

FROM THE STATE OF VIRGINIA.

Rev. John Bracken, D.D.
Robert Andrews, Esq.

JOURNAL

OF THE

House of Clerical and Lay Deputies.

PHILADELPHIA, CHRIST CHURCH,
TUESDAY, JUNE 11, 1799.

A SUFFICIENT number of Clerical and Lay Deputies to form a Convention not appearing, the members present adjourned to meet at the State House to-morrow morning at 10 o'clock.

STATE HOUSE, WEDNESDAY, June 12.

The members met agreeably to adjournment, and a quorum being formed,

The Right Rev. Dr. White read prayers.

Deputies from seven States appearing, the house proceeded to the appointment, by ballot, of a President; and a majority of the votes were found for the Rev. William Smith, D.D.

The Rev. James Abercrombie, one of the Assistant-Ministers of Christ Church and St. Peter's, was appointed Secretary to the Convention.

Resolved,—That the Rev. Dr. Andrews inform the House of Bishops, that the House of Clerical and Lay Deputies is formed, and ready to proceed to business.

Resolved,—That the rules of order established by the

House of Clerical and Lay Deputies, of the two preceding General Conventions, be adopted.

The Rev. William Walter, D.D., Clerical deputy from the State of Massachusetts; the Rev. Abraham Lynsen Clark, Clerical deputy from the State of Rhode Island; the Rev. John Bisset and the Rev. Ammi Rogers, Clerical deputies from the State of New York; the Rev. Uzal Ogden, D.D., the Rev. Henry Waddell, and the Rev. John Croes, Clerical deputies, and Mr. Jeffery Clarke, Lay deputy from the State of New Jersey; Rev. William Smith, D.D., the Rev. John Andrews, D.D., the Rev. Samuel Magaw, D.D., and the Rev. Robert Blackwell, D.D., Clerical deputies, General Francis Gurney, and Mr. Joseph Sims, Lay deputies from the State of Pennsylvania; the Rev. Joseph Clarkson, the Rev. William Price, and the Rev. Walter C. Gardiner, Clerical deputies, and Joseph Burn, Esq., Lay deputy from the State of Delaware; and the Rev. John Bracken, D.D., Clerical Deputy, and Robert Andrews, Esq., Lay deputy from the State of Virginia, delivered in, at the Secretary's table, certificates of their appointment, which were read, and determined to be satisfactory.

Mr. Bisset proposed the following resolution, viz.: That a Committee, consisting of —— members, be appointed to revise the Canons, to propose amendments, and to report the whole in one regular series. This resolution was read, and ordered to lie on the table.

Adjourned to 10 o'clock to-morrow morning.

THURSDAY, June 13.

Prayers being read by the Secretary, the house proceeded to business.

The Rev. William Smith, D.D., and the Rev. Ashbel Baldwin, Clerical deputies, and Benjamin Hall, Esq., Lay deputy from the State of Connecticut, presented their testimonials, which were approved, and they took their seats accordingly. Mr. John Dennis, a Lay deputy from the State of New Jersey, and John C. Stocker, Esq., a Lay deputy from the State of Pennsylvania, took their seats.

Mr. Bisset's proposed resolution of yesterday, was taken up and carried, and the blank ordered to be filled up with the word "five.

The members appointed were, Rev. Dr. Smith of Connecticut, Rev. Mr. Bisset of New York, Rev. Mr. Waddell of New Jersey, Gen. Gurney of Pennsylvania, and Mr. Hall of Connecticut.

The house resolved itself into a Committee of the whole on the State of the Church.

The Rev. Dr. Walter in the chair.

After some time the Committee rose, and the Chairman reported the following resolution, viz.

Resolved,—That the consideration of the resolution, for an alteration in the Constitution of this Church, proposed in the last General Convention, in these words: "But if the Church shall not be represented in both Orders, by a majority of the States, then the votes shall be given by States without regard to Orders," be postponed to the next General Convention.

This resolution was disagreed to by the house.

Resolved,—That this house will now go into a Committee of the whole, to take into consideration the second resolution of the General Convention of Friday, Sept. 18, 1795, and to report thereon.

The house resolved itself accordingly, Dr. Walter in the chair.

The Chairman of the Committee of the whole reported, that the Committee had risen and requested leave to sit again.

Resolved,—That in the places of Dr. Moore and Mr. Bend, who are absent, Dr. Smith of Connecticut, and Mr. Bisset, be added to the other three members, viz., Dr. Smith of Pennsylvania, Dr. Andrews, and Dr. Magaw, the Committee appointed by the last General Convention to digest and report a course of study for candidates for Holy Orders, and that they be requested to report the same during the present session.

Resolved,—That Dr. Andrews and Mr. Andrews be a Committee to bring in a Canon prescribing the mode of calling special meetings of the General Convention.

Resolved,—That the Secretary be requested to officiate as Chaplain to the Convention during the present session.

Adjourned to 10 o'clock to-morrow morning.

FRIDAY, June 14.

The house met, and the Chaplain read prayers.

The Rev. Menzies Rayner, a Clerical deputy from the State of New Jersey, and the Rev. Robert Clay, a Clerical deputy from the State of Delaware, took their seats.

Mr. Andrews, from the Committee appointed to report a Canon for calling special Conventions, reported a Canon, prescribing the mode of calling special Conventions; which was read the first time, and ordered for a second reading.

On motion, the Canon prescribing the mode of calling special Conventions was read a second time, amended, and ordered to be fairly transcribed for a third reading. It was then passed, and sent for concurrence, by the Secretary, to the House of Bishops.

Mr. Croes presented testimonials from the State Convention of New Jersey, recommending the Rev. Uzal Ogden, D.D., as Bishop of that State.

Ordered to lie on the table.

On motion of Mr. Baldwin, the house resolved itself into a Committee of the whole, to take into consideration the propriety of framing Articles of religion. Dr. Walter in the chair.

The Chairman of the Committee reported the following resolution, viz.

Resolved,—That the articles of our faith and religion, as founded on the Holy Scriptures of the Old and New Testaments, are sufficiently declared in our Creeds and Liturgy, as set forth in the Book of Common Prayer established for the use of this Church, and that further articles do not appear necessary.

This resolution was disagreed to by the house.

The House of Bishops sent for concurrence a form of consecration of a church or chapel; which was ordered to lie on the table.

The Rev. Mr. Clarkson asked leave of absence till Tuesday, which was not granted.

Adjourned to 6 o'clock this evening.

FRIDAY EVENING, 6 o'clock.

The house met.

The Canon, prescribing the mode of calling special Conventions, was returned with amendments from the House of Bishops, which were agreed to.

The form of consecration of a church or chapel, sent to this house by the Bishops, was read, and referred to a Committee of the whole house to-morrow morning.

On motion, resolved, that the testimonials respecting the Bishop elect of New Jersey be read, which was done.

Resolved,—That the consideration of this subject be postponed till to-morrow.

Adjourned to 9 o'clock to-morrow morning.

SATURDAY, June 15.

The house met, and the Chaplain read prayers.

The house proceeded to the consideration of the testimonials in favour of the Bishop elect of New Jersey; and, after discussion, the subject was postponed.

A resolution was proposed by Mr. Bisset, that the Convention now proceed to the framing of Articles of religion for this Church.

The question was taken by Yeas and Nays as follows.

CLERGY—Massachusetts, No; Connecticut, Yea; Rhode Island, Yea; New York, Yea; New Jersey, Yea; Pennsylvania, No; Delaware, Yea; Virginia, No.

LAITY—Connecticut, Yea; New Jersey, Yea; Pennsylvania, Yea; Virginia, No.

So it was carried in the affirmative.

Resolved,—That the Committee shall consist of a member from each State now represented, who were chosen, and were as follows.

Massachusetts, Dr. Walter; Connecticut, Dr. Smith; New York, Mr. Bisset; New Jersey, Mr. Waddell; Pennsylvania, Dr. Andrews; Delaware, Mr. Clay; Virginia, Dr. Bracken.

Resolved,—That leave be given to Mr. Baldwin to bring in a Canon to regulate the qualifications of Ministers to vote in State and General Conventions.

A message was received from the House of Bishops, communicating "a resolution for altering the 1st Article of the Constitution," and "a proposal of a Prayer, to be used at the meetings of Conventions."

The house resolved itself into a Committee of the whole, to take into consideration the communications from the House of Bishops. Dr. Walter in the chair.

The Committee rose, and reported certain amendments in

the "form of consecration of a church or chapel;" also, amendments to the resolution for the time of meeting of future General Conventions, together with an amendment to the "Prayer to be used during the sitting of Convention;" all of which were concurred in by the house.

Resolved,—That leave be given to Mr. Andrews to bring in a Canon respecting the consecration of Bishops in the recess of the General Convention; which was presented, read, and ordered to lie on the table.

Adjourned to 9 o'clock on Monday morning.

MONDAY MORNING, June 17.

The house met, and the Chaplain read prayers.

Mr. Baldwin presented "A Canon to regulate the qualifications of Ministers to vote in State and General Conventions; which was read, and ordered to lie on the table.

The proposed Canon respecting the consecration of Bishops in the recess of the Convention, was read a second time, amended, and ordered to be sent to the House of Bishops.

The communications from the House of Bishops, with the amendments proposed by the House of Clerical and Lay Deputies, were returned by the House of Bishops, with their concurrence.

The Chairman of the Committee for revising and amending the Canons, made a report, which was read, and ordered to be recommitted.

At 11 o clock the house adjourned for two hours, in order that the several Committees might finish their reports.

MONDAY, 1 o'clock, P.M.

The house met.

Mr. Andrews solicited leave to bring in a Canon, repealing in part the Canon of 1795, "Concerning the learning of those who are to be ordained," which was granted; and the Canon was read, approved, and sent for concurrence to the House of Bishops.

On motion of Mr. Bisset, Resolved,—That the Committee appointed to review and arrange the Canons be discharged, and that all the Canons which have been passed in preceding General Conventions, together with those which may be passed during the present session, shall be arranged under the respective years in which they were enacted, and printed at the end of the Journal of this Convention. Provided, nevertheless, that if any Canon of the preceding Conventions has been repealed, it shall be mentioned by its number and title only, followed by a notification of its having been repealed.

A motion was made by Mr. Bisset, that it be made known to the several State Conventions, that it is proposed to consider and determine in the next General Convention, on the following addition to the second article of the Constitution. to be introduced in the 9th line, after the word "Convention," viz.

"But if the Church shall not be represented in both Orders in a majority of the States, then the votes shall be by States, without regard to Orders."

The previous question, "Shall the main question be put?" was taken, and determined in the negative.

John Rutherford, Esq., Lay deputy from the State of New Jersey, took his seat.

On motion of Mr. Croes, the recommendation of the Church in New Jersey, in favour of their Bishop elect, was taken up; and after some discussion, it was resolved that the consideration of the same be postponed till to-morrow.

The House of Bishops returned the Canon repealing in part the Canon of 1795, "Concerning the learning of those who are to be ordained," with their approbation; and a substitute for the Canon respecting the consecration of Bishops during the recess of the General Convention, which was adopted.

Adjourned to 10 o'clock to-morrow morning.

TUESDAY MORNING, June 18.

The House met, and the Chaplain read prayers.

The proposed Canon, respecting the qualification of Ministers to vote in State and General Conventions, was read, amended, and ordered to be sent for concurrence to the House of Bishops; which was done.

Mr. J. B. Gilpin, a Lay deputy from the State of Pennsylvania, took his seat.

The chairman of the Committee on the Articles reported seventeen Articles of religion, which were read. Whereupon, on motion of Mr. Bisset,

Resolved unanimously,—That on account of the advanced period of the present session, and the thinness of the Convention, the consideration of the Articles now reported and read be postponed, and that the Secretary transcribe the Articles into the Journal of this Convention, to lie over for the consideration of the next General Convention.

Dr. Bracken asked leave to bring in a Canon, supplementary to the 2d Canon of 1795, "Concerning the testimonials to be produced on the part of those who are to be ordained," which was read twice, and, upon the question for the third reading, was negatived.

The testimonials of the Bishop elect of New Jersey being called up, the following resolution passed:

Whereas doubts have arisen in the minds of some members of the Convention, whether all the Priests who voted in the election of the Rev. Uzal Ogden, D.D., to the office of a Bishop in the State of New Jersey, were so qualified as to constitute them a majority of the resident and officiating priests in the said State, according to the meaning of the Canon in this case made and provided. And whereas, in a matter of so great importance to the interest of religion and the honour of our Church, it is not only necessary that they who concur in recommending to an office so very sacred, should have a full conviction of the fitness of the person they recommend, but that they should also be perfectly satisfied with respect to the regularity of every step which had been taken in the business,—

Resolved, therefore, that in the opinion of the House of Deputies, all proceedings respecting the consecration of the Rev. Uzal Ogden, D.D., ought to be suspended, until a future Convention of the State of New Jersey shall declare their sense of the subject.

The House of Bishops returned the Canon, "to regulate the qualifications of Ministers, etc.," with amendments. The amended title was adopted; the other proposed amendment was rejected.

The House of Bishops receded from their amendment of the Canon, explanatory of the 1st Canon of 1795.

Resolved,—That the next General Convention, to be held agreeably to the Constitution on the second Tuesday of September, 1801, shall meet in the city of Trenton.

Resolved,—That the Right Rev. Dr. White be requested to preach at the opening of the next General Convention.

Resolved,—That the House of Bishops be informed that this house is ready to adjourn.

Mr. Bisset was requested to communicate the two preceding resolves to the House of Bishops.

Resolved,—That the thanks of this house be given to their President, the Rev. Dr. Smith, and to their Secretary and Chaplain, the Rev. Mr. Abercrombie, for their attention and services.

Mr. Bisset reported, "That the Right Rev. Dr. White would comply with the request of this house; and that the House of Bishops, having no further communications to make, concurred in the resolution of adjournment.

Ordered, that 570 copies of the Journal be printed.

The house adjourned, sine die.

Signed by order of the House of Clerical and Lay Deputies.

WILLIAM SMITH, President.

James Abercrombie, Secretary.

APPENDIX.

ARTICLES OF RELIGION.

Extract from the Journal of the House of Clerical and Lay Deputies, in Convention met, 1799.

Resolved unanimously,—That on account of the advanced period of the present Session, and the thinness of the Convention, the consideration of the Articles, now reported and read, be postponed; and that the Secretary transcribe the Articles into the Journal of this Convention, to lie over for the consideration of the next General Convention.

The Articles referred to are as follow.

I. Of faith in the Holy Trinity.

There is but one living and true God, everlasting; of infinite power, wisdom, and goodness; the maker and preserver of all things, visible and invisible. And in the unity of this Godhead there are three persons —the Father, the Son, and the Holy Ghost; our Creator, Redeemer, and Sanctifier.

II. Of the Holy Scripture.

Holy Scripture containeth all things necessary to salvation; so that whatsoever is not read therein, and cannot be proved thereby, is not to be received as an article of faith, nor deemed necessary to salvation.

By Holy Scripture, we understand the canonical books of the Old and New Testament.

THE NAMES AND NUMBER OF THE CANONICAL BOOKS IN THE OLD TESTAMENT.

		CHAPS.			CHAPS.
1.	Genesis	having 50	21.	Ecclesiastes	having 12
2.	Exodus	" 40	22.	The Song of Solomon	" 8
3.	Leviticus	" 27	23.	Isaiah	" 66
4.	Numbers	" 36	24.	Jeremiah	" 52
5.	Deuteronomy	" 34	25.	Lamentations	" 5
6.	Joshua	" 24	26.	Ezekiel	" 48
7.	Judges	" 21	27.	Daniel	" 12

		CHAPS.
8.	Ruth	having 4
9.	The 1st Book of Samuel	31
10.	The 2d Book of Samuel	24
11.	The 1st Book of Kings	22
12.	The 2d Book of Kings	25
13.	The 1st Book of Chronicles	29
14.	The 2d Book of Chronicles	36
15.	Ezra.	" 10
16.	Nehemiah	" 13
17.	The Book of Esther	" 10
18.	The Book of Job	" 42
19.	The Psalms	" 150
20.	The Proverbs	" 31

		CHAPS.
28.	Hosea	having 14
29.	Joel	" 3
30.	Amos	" 9
31.	Obadiah	" 1
32.	Jonah	" 4
33.	Micah	" 7
34.	Nahum	" 3
35.	Habakuk	" 3
36.	Zephaniah	" 3
37.	Haggai	" 2
38.	Zechariah	" 14
39.	Malachi	" 4

CANONICAL BOOKS OF THE NEW TESTAMENT.

1.	St. Matthew	having 28
2.	St. Mark	" 16
3.	St. Luke	" 24
4.	St. John	" 21
5.	The Acts of the Apostles	28
6.	Epistle to the Romans	" 16
7.	1st Epistle to the Corinthians	16
8.	2d Epistle to the Corinthians	13
9.	Epistle to the Galatians.	5
10.	Epistle to the Ephesians	6
11.	Epistle to the Philipians	4
12.	Epistle to the Colossians	4
13.	1st Epistle to the Thessalonians	5
14.	2d Epistle to the Thessalonians	3

15.	1st Epistle to Timothy	having 6
16.	2d Epistle to Timothy	" 4
17.	Epistle to Titus	" 3
18.	Epistle to Philemon	" 1
19.	Epistle to the Hebrews	" 13
20.	Epistle of St. James	" 5
21.	1st Epistle of St. Peter	" 5
22.	2d Epistle of St. Peter	" 3
23.	1st Epistle of St. John	" 5
24.	2d Epistle of St. John	" 1
25.	3d Epistle of St. John	" 1
26.	Epistle of St. Jude	" 1
27.	Revelation of St. John, the Divine	" 22

The Apocryphal books are read by the Church, for example of life and instruction of manners, not for the establishment of discipline or doctrine.

III. Of the Old and New Testament

There is a perfect harmony and accordance between the Old and New Testament; for in both, "Pardon of sin and everlasting life are offered to mankind through Christ, who is the only mediator between God and man;" and although Christians are not bound to obey the civil and ceremonial precepts, yet are they obliged to observe all the moral commandments of the Mosaic dispensation.

IV. Of the Creeds.

The Nicene Creed and the Apostles' Creed ought to be retained and believed, because every Article contained in them may be proved by Holy Scripture.

V. Of the Transgression of our first Parents.

By the transgression of our first parents they lost that primitive innocence and perfect holiness in which God had created them; and thus the nature of man became corrupted, and prone to evil, so that there is no man living who sinneth not.

VI. Of Justification.

We are justified, or pardoned by God, not on account of our own good works, but only through the merits and mediation of our blessed Redeemer and Advocate, Jesus Christ. But although good works cannot put away our sins, nor appear perfect before God, yet are they pleasing and acceptable to God in Christ, and essentially necessary to salvation—for Scripture assures us, that "faith without works is dead," and that without holiness no man shall see the Lord.

VII. Of Predestination and Election.

Being well assured, from Holy Scripture, of the eternal purpose or promise of redemption, according to which God sent his Son to be the propitiation for the sins of the whole world, and Christ Jesus gave himself a ransom for all; we receive the doctrine of predestination as consistent with, and agreeable to, this most gracious and general scheme of salvation, which we believe to be universal in the intention, however partial the wickedness of mankind may render it in the application. Under the impression of this belief, it is the duty of Christians to be satisfied with and attend to the promises of God, as they are generally set forth to us in Holy Scripture, without seeking to be "wise above what is written," or plunging into the unrevealed secrets of either past or future eternity, but always remembering the distinction which in such cases Moses lays down —"Secret things belong unto the Lord our God, but the things which are revealed belong unto us and to our children for ever, that we may do all the words of this law."

VIII. Of Salvation by Christ alone.

Holy Scripture declares, that "there is none other name under heaven given among men whereby we must be saved, but only the name of our Lord Jesus Christ." But we are not authorised to assert, that men shall not be saved by the name of Jesus Christ, to whom his Gospel has not been promulgated. We leave them to the uncovenanted mercies of God.

IX. Of the Church.

The visible Church of Christ is the whole multitude of believers, of whatsoever nation or language, dwelling on the face of the earth, among whom the pure word of God is preached, the Sacraments duly administered, and the order of the priesthood observed, according to Christ's ordinance and appointment.

X. Of the authority of the Church.

The Church hath power to ordain, change, and abolish rites and ceremonies, and to determine controversies of faith; but it is not lawful for the Church to ordain or command any thing to be received or believed which is contrary to the Canon of Scripture, or to expound one part of the same so as to be repugnant to another. The Church, also, is the witness or keeper of Holy Writ, and must neither adulterate, nor add to, nor take from the same.

XI. Of ministering in the Church.

It is not lawful for any man to take upon him the office of public preaching, or administering the Holy Sacraments, until he be regularly ordained, and sent to execute the same. And those we judge lawfully sent, who are ordained by the Bishops of the Church.

XII. Of the Sacraments.

Sacraments were ordained by Christ, not only to be badges or tokens of Christian profession, but to be outward and visible signs of inward and spiritual grace, by which He doth work invisibly in us, and doth not only quicken, but doth also strengthen and confirm our faith in Him.

XIII. Of Baptism.

Baptism is an ordinance by which we are regenerated and born again of water and the Holy Ghost, received into Christ's Church, and made living members of the same.

XIV. Of the Lord's Supper.

The Supper of the Lord is not only a token of the love that Christians ought to have towards one another, but rather a pledge of our redemption by Christ's death. To such as worthily receive the same, the bread which is broken is a partaking of the body of Christ, and the cup of blessing is a partaking of the blood of Christ; both which are spiritually received, for the preservation of our souls and bodies unto everlating life.

XV. Of the Oblation of Christ.

The oblation of the body of Christ, once made, is that perfect sacrifice, propitiation, and satisfaction, which was offered for the sins of the whole world. And there is no other sacrifice, satisfaction, or atonement for sin, but that only.

XVI. Of excommunicated Persons.

Whosoever is publicly excommunicated by the governors of the Church, and cut off from the unity of the same, is to be considered as an alien from the promises of the Gospel, until he be openly reconciled, and received again into communion.

XVII. Of the power of the Civil Magistrate.

The power of the civil magistrate extendeth to all men, as well Clergy as Laity, in all things temporal—but hath no authority in things purely spiritual. And we hold it to be the duty of all men who are professors of the gospel, to pay a respectful obedience to the civil authority, regularly and legitimately constituted.

JOURNAL

OF THE

House of Bishops.

PHILADELPHIA, CHRIST CHURCH,
TUESDAY, June 11th, 1799.

This being the day of a Special Meeting of the General Convention of the Protestant Episcopal Church, duly summoned, the Right Rev. Bishop White of the House of Bishops, attended, and appointed to meet the next day at 10 o'clock, in the Committee Room of the House of Assembly; leave having been given to meet there by his Excellency the Governor.

WEDNESDAY, June 12, 1799.

In the Committee Room of the House of Assembly.

Present as before, together with the Right Rev. Bishop Provoost, of the State of New York, and the Right Rev. Bishop Bass of the State of Massachusetts.

This being a special meeting, and the Bishop whose turn it would have been to preside, agreeably to the rules of this house, not attending, Bishop White, the President of the last Convention, was requested to preside.

Resolved,—That during the session of the Convention, the house will attend divine service in the House of Clerical and Lay Deputies.

The house received a message by the Rev. Dr. Andrews, from the House of Clerical and Lay Deputies, informing that they are organized and ready to proceed to business. This house declared, that they also are ready to proceed.

After some time, the house adjourned until to-morrow morning at ten o'clock.

THURSDAY, June 13.

The house met. Present as yesterday.

The Rev. John Henry Hobart was appointed Secretary.

The Right Rev. Bishop Provoost proposed to the consideration of this house, a form of consecration of a church or chapel, which was read, and made the order of the day for to-morrow.

The house adjourned till 10 o'clock to-morrow morning.

FRIDAY, June 14.

The house met. Present as yesterday.

The House of Clerical and Lay Deputies presented, by their Secretary, a proposed Canon, prescribing the mode of calling special meetings of the General Convention.

The house then went into the consideration of the form of consecration of a church or chapel; which, after amendment, they adopted, and sent to the House of Clerical and Lay Deputies for their concurrence.

The house returned to the House of Clerical and Lay Deputies the proposed Canon, prescribing the mode of calling special meetings of the General Convention, with amendments.

The house then adjourned to 9 o'clock to-morrow morning.

SATURDAY, June 15.

The house met. Present as yesterday.

The house agreed to a resolve, respecting an alteration in the first article of the General Constitution, and sent it to the House of Clerical and Lay Deputies for their concurrence.

The house proposed to the House of Clerical and Lay Deputies a prayer to be used at the meeting of the Convention, and to be printed with the Journal of the present Convention.

The house adjourned to Monday morning, 9 o'clock.

MONDAY, June 17, 1799.

The house met. Present as on Saturday.

The House of Clerical and Lay Deputies returned to this house, by their Secretary, the resolution for altering the first article of the General Constitution, with an amendment. Also, the Prayer to be used at meetings of the Convention, with an amendment. Also, the form of consecration of a church or chapel, with sundry amendments.

The house passed the resolution respecting the alteration of the first article of the General Constitution, with the proposed amendment; which resolution is as follows, viz.

Resolved,—That it be made known to the several State Conventions, that it is proposed to consider and determine in the next General Convention, on the following alteration of the first Article of the Constitution:

"Article I. There shall be a General Convention of the Protestant Episcopal Church in the United States of America, on the third Tuesday in May, in the year of our Lord 1805, and on the third Tuesday in May every fifth year afterwards, in such place," etc., as before.

The house passed the Prayer to be used at meetings of the Convention, with the proposed amendment.

The house approved of the amendments to the form of consecration of a church or chapel, with an exception to one, which they ordered to be returned to the House of Clerical and Lay Deputies.

A message was received from the House of Clerical and Lay Deputies, that they had receded from their amendment to the form of consecration of a church or chapel, which amendment had been disagreed to by this house.

The form of consecration was then passed as amended.

A proposed Canon was received from the House of Clerical and Lay Deputies, respecting the consecration of Bishops in the recess of the General Convention.

The above Canon was returned to the House of Clerical and Lay Deputies, with a proposed substitute.

The house received from the House of Clerical and Lay Deputies a proposed Canon, repealing in part the Fourth Canon of 1795, concerning the learning of those who are to be ordained.

The house passed the above Canon.

The Right. Rev. Bishop Provoost obtained leave of absence.

The house adjourned to 10 o'clock to-morrow morning.

TUESDAY, June 18, 1799.

The house met. Present as yesterday, except the Right Rev. Bishop Provoost.

The House of Clerical and Lay Deputies informed the house, that they had agreed to the proposed substitute to the Canon respecting the consecration of Bishops in the recess of the General Convention.

The House of Clerical and Lay Deputies presented to this house a proposed Canon, to regulate the qualification of Ministers to vote in the State and General Conventions.

The aforesaid Canon was returned to the House of Clerical and Lay Deputies, with a substitute for the title, and another proposed amendment.

The house concurred in the following resolution, which they received from the House of Clerical and Lay Deputies.

Resolved,—That Trenton, in New Jersey, be the place of meeting of the next General Convention.

The House of Clerical and Lay Deputies informed this house that they had concurred in the amendments to the proposed Canon, prescribing the mode of calling special meetings of the General Convention.

The house then passed the above Canon.

The House of Clerical and Lay Deputies informed this house, that they had concurred in the proposed substitute to the title of a Canon which originated in their house, and that they had disagreed to the proposed amendment.

The house receded from the amendment, and passed the Canon, in title as follows:

"A Canon explanatory of part of the 1st Canon of 1795."

The House of Clerical and Lay Deputies informed this house that they had finished the business before them, and were ready to rise.

The house declared that they also are ready to rise.

The house rose.

Signed by order of the House of Bishops.

WILLIAM WHITE,
PRESIDING BISHOP.

Attest: JOHN HENRY HOBART, Secretary.

APPENDIX.

Canons

For the Government of the Protestant Episcopal Church in the United States of America.

The following Canons were agreed on, and ratified in the General Convention of said Church, held in the City of Philadelphia, from the 29th day of September to the 16th day of October, 1789, inclusive.

Canon I.—Of the Orders of the Ministers in this Church.

In this Church there shall always be three Orders in the Ministry, viz., Bishops, Priests, and Deacons.

Canon II.—Certificates to be produced on the part of Bishops elect.

Every bishop elect, before his consecration, shall produce to the Bishops, to whom he is presented for that holy office, from the Convention by whom he is elected a Bishop, and from the General Convention, or a Committee of that body to be appointed to act in their recess, certificates, respectively in the following words, viz.:

TESTIMONY FROM THE MEMBERS OF THE CONVENTION IN THE STATE FROM WHENCE THE PERSON IS RECOMMENDED FOR CONSECRATION.

We, whose names are underwritten, fully sensible how important it is, that the sacred office of a bishop should not be unworthily conferred, and firmly persuaded that it is our duty to bear testimony on this solemn occasion without partiality or affection, do, in the presence of Almighty God, testify, that A. B. is not, so far as we are informed, justly liable to evil report, either for error in religion or for viciousness of life; and that we do not know or believe there is any impediment or notable crime for which he ought not to be consecrated to that holy office. We do, moreover, jointly and severally declare that, having personally known him for three years last past, we do in our consciences believe him to be of such sufficiency in good learning, such soundness in the faith, and of such virtuous and pure manners and godly conversation, that he is apt and meet to exercise the Office of a Bishop, to the honour of God and the edifying of his Church, and to be an wholesome example to the flock of Christ.

TESTIMONY FROM THE GENERAL CONVENTION.

We whose names are underwritten, fully sensible how important it is that the sacred office of a Bishop should not be unworthily conferred, and firmly persuaded that it is our duty to bear our testimony on this solemn occasion without partiality or affection, do, in the presence of Almighty God, testify that A. B. is not, so far as we are informed, justly liable to evil report either for error in religion or for viciousness of life; and that we do not know or believe there is any impediment or notable crime, on account of which he ought not to be consecrated to that holy office, but that he hath, as we believe, led his life, for the three years last past, piously, soberly, and honestly.

Canon III.—Of Episcopal Visitation.

Repealed by Canon I. of 1795.

Canon IV.—Of the Age of those who are to be Ordained or Consecrated.

Repealed by Canon III. of 1795.

Canon V.—Of the Titles of those who are to be Ordained.

No person shall be ordained either Deacon or Priest, unless he shall produce a satisfactory certificate from some church, parish, or congregation, that he is engaged with them, and that they will receive him as their minister, and allow him a reasonable support; or unless he be engaged as a professor, tutor, or instructor of youth, in some college, academy, or general seminary of learning, duly incorporated; or unless the Standing Committee of the Church in the State for which he is to be ordained, shall certify to the Bishop their full belief and expectation, that he will be received and settled as a pastor by some one of the vacant churches in that State.

Canon VI.—The Testimonials to be produced on the part of those who are to be Ordained.

Repealed by Canon II. of 1795.

Canon VII.—Of the Learning of those who are to be Ordained.

Repealed by Canon IV. of 1795.

Canon VIII.—Of the Stated Times of Ordination.

Agreeably to the practice of the primitive Church, the stated times of

Ordination shall be on the Sundays following the Ember weeks: viz., the Second Sunday in Lent, the Feast of Trinity, and the Sundays after the Wednesdays following the fourteenth day of September and the thirteenth of December.

Canon IX.—Of those who, having been ordained by foreign Bishops, settle in this Church.

No person, not a member of this Church, who shall profess to be episcopally ordained, shall be permitted to officiate therein, until he shall have exhibited to the Vestry of the Church in which he shall offer to officiate, a certificate signed by the Bishop of the Diocese or district, or, where there is no Bishop, by three Clergymen of the Standing Committee of the Convention of that State, that his Letters of Orders are authentic, and given by some Bishop whose authority is acknowledged by this Church, and also satisfactory evidence of his moral character.

Canon X.—Of the Use of the Book of Common Prayer.

Every minister shall, before all sermons and lectures, use the Book of Common Prayer, as the same shall be set forth and established by the authority of this or some future General Convention; and until such establishment of an uniform Book of Common Prayer in this Church, every minister shall read the Book of Common Prayer directed to be used by the Convention of the Church in the State in which he resides; and no other prayer shall be used besides those contained in the said book.

Canon XI.—Of the duty of Ministers in regard to Episcopal Visitation.

It shall be the duty of ministers to prepare children and others for the the holy ordinance of Confirmation. And on notice being received from the Bishop of his intention to visit any Church, which notice shall be at least one month before the intended visitation, the minister shall be ready to present for Confirmation those who shall have been previously instructed for the same, and shall deliver to the Bishop a list of the names of those presented.

And at every visitation it shall be the duty of the minister and of the church wardens, to give information to the bishop of the state of the congregation, under such heads as shall have been committed to them in the notice given as aforesaid.

And further, the ministers and church wardens of such congregations as cannot be conveniently visited in any year, shall bring or send to the Bishop, at the stated meeting of the Convention of the diocese or district, information of the state of the congregation, under such heads as shall have been committed to them at least one month before the meeting of the Convention.

Canon XII.—Notorious Crimes and Scandals to be censured.

If any persons within this church offend their brethren by any wickedness of life, such persons shall be repelled from the Holy Communion, agreeably to the rubric, and may be further proceeded against, to the depriving of them of all privileges of church membership, according to such rules or process as may be provided, either by General Convention or by the Conventions in the different States.

Canon XIII.—Sober conversation required in Ministers.

No ecclesiastical persons shall, other than for their honest necessities, resort to taverns or other places most liable to be abused to licentiousness. Further, they shall not give themselves to any base or servile labour, or to drinking or riot, or to the spending of their time idly. And if any offend in the above, they shall be liable to the ecclesiastical censure of admonition, or suspension, or degradation, as the nature of the case may require, and according to such rules or process as may be provided, either by the General Convention or by the Conventions in the different States.

Canon XIV.—Of the due celebration of Sundays.

All manner of persons within this Church shall celebrate and keep the Lord's day, commonly called Sunday, in hearing the word of God read and taught, in private and public prayer, in other exercises of devotion, and in acts of charity, using all godly conversation.

Canon XV.—Ministers to keep a Register.

Every minister of this Church shall keep a register of baptisms, marriages, and funerals within his cure, agreeably to such rules as may be provided by the ecclesiastical authority where his cure lies; and if none such be provided, then in such a manner as in his discretion he shall think best suited to the uses of such a register.

And the intention of the register of baptisms is hereby declared to be, as for other good uses, so especially for the proving of the right of church membership of those who may have been admitted into this Church by the holy ordinance of baptism.

And further, every minister of this Church shall, within a reasonable time after the publication of this Canon, make out and continue a list of all adult persons within his cure, to remain for the use of his successor, to be continued by him and by every future minister in the same parish.

And no minister shall place on the said list the names of any persons except of those who, on due enquiry, he shall find to have been baptised in this Church; or who, having been otherwise baptised, shall have been received into this Church either by the holy rite of Confirmation, or by receiving the Holy Communion, or by some other joint act of the parties and of a minister of this Church, whereby such persons shall have attached themselves to the same.

Canon XVI.—A List to be made and published of the Ministers of this Church.

The secretary of the General Convention shall keep a register of all the Clergy of this Church, whose names shall be delivered to him, in the following manner: that is to say, every Bishop of this Church,—or, where there is no Bishop, the Standing Committee of that diocese or district,—shall, at the time of every General Convention, deliver, or cause to be delivered to the secretary, a list of the names of all the ministers of this Church in their proper diocese or district, annexing the names ot their respective cures, or of their stations in any colleges or other incorporated seminaries of learning, or, in regard to those who have not any cures or such stations, their places of residence only. And the said list shall, from time to time, be published in the Journals of the General Convention.

And further, it is recommended to the several Bishops of this Church, and to the several Standing Committees, that, during the intervals between the meetings of the General Convention, they take such means of notifying the admission of ministers among them, as, in their discretion respectively, they shall think effectual to the purpose of preventing ignorant and unwary people from being imposed on, by persons pretending to be authorised ministers of this Church.

Canon XVII.—Notice to be given of the Induction and Dismission of Ministers.

It is hereby required, that on the induction of a minister into any Church or parish, the parties shall deliver, or cause to be delivered to the Bishop, or to the Standing Committee of the Diocese or district, notice of the same in the following form, or to this effect:

We, the church wardens [or, in case of an Assistant Minister, We, the rector and church wardens] do certify to the Right Rev. [naming the Bishop] that [naming the person) has been duly chosen Rector [or Assistant Minister as the case may be] of [naming the church or churches].

Which certificate shall be signed with the names of those who certify.

And if the Bishop, or the Standing Committee, be satisfied that the person so chosen is a qualified minister of this Church, he shall transmit the said certificate to the Secretary of the Convention, who shall record it in a book to be kept by him for that purpose.

But if the Bishop, or the Standing Committee, be not satisfied as above, he or they shall, at the instance of the parties, proceed to enquire into the sufficiency of the person so chosen, according to such rules as may be made in the States respectively, and shall confirm or reject the appointment, as the issue of that enquiry may be.

Passed Oct. 16th, 1789.

House of Bishops.

SAMUEL SEABURY, Bp. Connect., Pres.

WILLIAM WHITE, Pennsylvania.

Attested: Joseph Clarkson, Secretary.

House of Clerical and Lay Deputies.

WILLIAM SMITH, President.

Attested: Francis Hopkinson, Secretary.

ADDITIONAL CANONS.

Passed 1792.

I. Of Clergymen claiming to be Ministers of this Church.

For a more full accomplishment of the good purposes to be answered by the 16th Canon, enacted by the last General Convention, it is hereby required, that every Clergyman claiming to be a Minister of this Church, shall deliver in his name to the Bishop, or if there be no Bishop, to the chairman or some member of the Standing Committee of the Church in the State in which he resides, on or before Easter Monday, 1793; or, if he be not within any of the States which have acceded to the Constitution of this Church, then within three months after he shall come to reside in any of the said States. And every Clergyman, during his neglect of conformity to this Canon, shall not be known as a Clergyman of this Church, or be admitted to minister in any offices of the same.

II. Of a Clergyman in any Diocese chargeable with Misdemeanor in any other.

If a Clergyman of the Church in any diocese or district within this union shall, in any other diocese or district, conduct himself in such a way as is contrary to the rules of this Church, and disgraceful to his office, the bishop, or, if there be no bishop, the Standing Committee, shall give notice thereof to the ecclesiastical authority of the diocese or district to which such offender belongs, exhibiting, with the information given, the proofs of the charges made against him.

III. Of publishing the sentence of degradation against a Clergyman.

Whenever a Clergyman shall be degraded, agreeably to the Canons of any particular Church in the union, the Bishop who pronounces sentence, shall, without delay, cause the sentence of degradation to be published from every pulpit where there may be an officiating minister, throughout the diocese or district in which the degraded minister resided; and also shall give information of the sentence to all the Bishops of this Church, and, where there is no Bishop, to the Standing Committee.

IV. Of the Declaration which may be prefixed to certain Signatures.

In regard to the first certificate required in favour of a Bishop elect, by the 2d Canon of the last General Convention, and the certificate required in favour of a candidate for Priest's or Deacon's Orders by the 6th Canon, if there be any members of the bodies respectively concerned who have not the requisite personal knowledge of the parties, such persons may prefix the following declaration to their signatures:

"We believe the testimony contained in the above Certificate, and we join in the recommendation of A. B. to the office of . . . on sufficient evidence offered to us of the facts set forth."

Provided, that in the case of a Priest or Deacon, two at least of the Standing Committee sign the same, as being personally acquainted with the candidate.

V. Of the officiating of Strangers.

No stranger shall be permitted to officiate in any congregation of this Church, without first producing the evidences of his being a minister thereof to the minister, or, in case of vacancy or absence, to the church wardens, vestrymen, or trustees of the congregation. And in case any person not regularly ordained shall assume the ministerial office, and perform any of the duties thereof in this Church, the minister, or, in case of vacancy or absence, the church wardens, vestrymen, or trustees of the congregation where such offence may be committed, shall cause the name of such person, together with the offence, to be published in as many of the public papers as may be convenient.

VI. Of one Clergyman officiating within the Parochial Cure of another Clergyman.

Repealed by Canon V. of 1795.

HOUSE OF BISHOPS:

SAMUEL PROVOOST, PRESIDENT.

ATTEST: L. CUTTING, Secretary.

HOUSE OF CLERICAL AND LAY DEPUTIES:

WILLIAM SMITH, PRESIDENT.

ATTEST: J. BISSET, Secretary.

CANONS.---Passed 1795.

CANON I.—Of Episcopal Visitation.

Every bishop in this Church shall visit the churches within his diocese or district, for the purposes of examining the state of his Church, inspecting the behaviour of the Clergy, and administering the apostolic rite of Confirmation. And it is deemed proper that such visitations be made once in three years at least, by every bishop to every church within his diocese or district, which shall make provision for defraying the necessary expenses of the bishop at such visitation. And it is hereby declared to be the duty of the minister and vestry of every church or congregation, to make such provision accordingly.

The bishop of any diocese or State district may, on the invitation of the Convention or Standing Committee of the church in any State where there is not a bishop, visit and perform the episcopal offices in that State, or part of the State, as the case may be, provision being made for defraying his expenses as aforesaid: and such State, or part of a State, shall be considered as annexed to the district or diocese of such bishop, until a bishop is duly elected and consecrated for such State, or until the invitation given by the Convention or Standing Committee be revoked. But it is to be understood, that to enable the Bishop to make the aforesaid visitations, it shall be the duty of the clergy, in such reasonable rotation as may be devised, to officiate for him in any parochial duties which belong to him. And no State shall proceed to the election or appointment of a bishop, unless there be at least six presbyters residing and officiating therein, a majority of whom, at least, shall concur in such election. But the Conventions of two or more States, having together nine or more settled and officiating presbyters, may associate, and join in the election of a bishop.

The Third Canon of the year 1789 is hereby rescinded.

Canon II.—Of the Testimonials to be produced on the part of those who are to be Ordained.

Every candidate for Holy Orders shall be recommended to the Bishop by a Standing Committee appointed by the Convention of the church in that State wherein he resides, which recommendation shall be signed by the names of a majority of the Committee, and shall be in the following words:

We, whose names are hereunder written, testify that A. B. hath laid before us satisfactory testimonials, that for the space of three years last past, he hath lived piously, soberly, and honestly: and hath not written, taught, or held, any thing contrary to the doctrine or discipline of the Protestant Episcopal Church. And, moreover, we think him a person worthy to be admitted to the sacred order of . . . In witness whereof we have hereunto set our hands, this . . . day of . . . in the year of our Lord . . . . .

But before a Standing Committee in any State shall proceed to recommend any candidate, as aforesaid, to the Bishop, such candidate shall produce from the minister and vestry of the parish where he resides, or from the vestry alone if the parish be vacant, or if there be no vestry, from at least twelve respectable persons of the Protestant Episcopal Church in the neighbourhood in which he resides, testimonials of his good morals and orderly conduct for three years last past, and that he has not, so far as they know and believe, written, taught, or held any thing contrary to the doctrine or discipline of the Protestant Episcopal Church; a publication of his intention to apply for Holy Orders having been previously made by such minister or vestry. He shall also lay before the Standing Committee, testimonials to the same effect, signed by at least one respectable clergyman of the Protestant Episcopal Church in the United States, from his personal knowledge of the candidate for at least one year.

In every State in which there is no Standing Committee, such Committee shall be appointed at its next ensuing Convention; and in the mean time, every candidate for Holy Orders shall be recommended according to the regulations or usage of the Church in each State, and the requisitions of the bishop to whom he applies.

The 6th Canon, passed in October, 1789, concerning the testimonials to be produced on the part of those who are to be ordained, and so much of the 4th Canon passed in 1792, as relates to the subject of this Canon, are hereby rescinded.

CANON III.—Of the Age of those who are to be Ordained or Consecrated.

Deacon's Orders shall not be conferred on any person until he shall be twenty-one years old, nor Priest's Orders on any one until he shall be twenty-four years old; and unless he shall have been a Deacon one year. No man shall be consecrated a bishop of this Church until he shall be thirty years old.

The 4th Canon of the year 1789 is hereby rescinded.

CANON IV.—Of the Learning of those who are to be Ordained.

No person shall be ordained in this Church until he shall have satisfied the Bishop and the two Presbyters by whom he shall be examined, that he is well acquainted with the Holy Scriptures, can read the New Testament in the original Greek, and give an account of his faith in the Latin tongue; and that he hath a competent knowledge of natural and moral philosophy and church history, and hath paid attention to composition and pulpit eloquence as means of giving additional efficacy to his labours; [unless the bishop shall judge it proper to dispense with the above requisites in part, in consideration of certain other qualifications in the candidate, peculiarly fitting him for the Gospel ministry.]

The 7th Canon of the year 1789 is hereby rescinded.

N.B. The last clause of this Canon, marked thus [ ], was repealed by the 4th Canon of 1799.

CANON V.—Of the Officiating of Ministers of this Church in the Churches or within the Parochial Cures of other Clergymen.

No clergyman belonging to this Church shall officiate, either by preaching or reading prayers, in the parish, or within the parochial cure of another clergyman, unless he have received express permission for that purpose, from the minister of the parish or cure, or in his absence, from the church wardens and vestrymen, or trustees of the congregation. But if any minister of a church shall, from inability or any other cause, neglect to perform the regular services to his congregation, and shall refuse his consent to any other minister of this Church to officiate within his cure, the church wardens, vestrymen, or trustees of such congregation shall, on proof of such neglect and refusal before the bishop of the diocese, or, if there be no bishop, before the Standing Committee, or before such persons as may be deputed by him or them, or before such persons as may be, by the regulations of this Church in any State, vested with the power of hearing and deciding on complaints against clergymen, have power to open the doors of their churches to any regular minister of the Protestant Episcopal Church.

The 6th Canon of 1792 is hereby rescinded.

CANON VI.—Of the Preparatory Exercises of a Candidate for the Ministry.

Every candidate for the ministry shall give notice of his intention to the bishop, or to such body as the Church in the State in which the candidate resides, may have appointed to superintend the instruction of candidates for Holy Orders, at least one year before his ordination. And if there be a bishop within the State or district where the candidate resides, he shall apply to no other bishop for ordination, without the permission of the former. And the said candidate shall pass through the preparatory exercises which the bishop, or such body aforesaid, may appoint: such as composing of theses, homilies or sermons, one or more, to be delivered either publicly or privately, in his or their presence, at such time or times as may be appointed by the authority aforesaid.—And this Canon shall be in force from and after the first day of January next.

CANON VII.—For the better accomplishing of the Objects of the Sixth Canon of 1792.

Whereas there is no provision made in the 6th Canon of 1792, for the case of such a vicinity of two or more churches, as that there can be no local boundaries drawn between their respective cures, it is hereby ordained that, in every such case, no minister of this Church, other than the parochial clergy of the said cures, shall preach within the common limits of the same, in any other place than in one of the churches thereof, without the consent of the major number of the parochial clergy of the said churches.

CANON VIII.—To prevent a Congregation in any Diocese or State to unite with a Church in any other Diocese or State.

Whereas a question may arise, whether a congregation within the diocese of any bishop, or within any State in which there is not yet any bishop settled, may unite themselves with the Church in any other diocese or State, it is hereby determined and declared, that all such unions shall be considered as irregular and void; and that every congregation of this Church shall be considered as belonging to the body of the Church of the diocese, or of the State, within the limits of which they dwell or with in which there is seated a Church to which they belong. And no clergy man having a parish or cure in more than one State, shall have a seat in the Convention of any State, other than that in which he resides.

CANON IX.—To empower the Bishop in each Diocese or District to compose Forms of Prayer or Thanksgiving for extraordinary occasions.

The bishop of each diocese or district may compose forms of prayer or thanksgiving, as the case may require, for extraordinary occasions, and transmit them to each clergyman within his diocese or district, whose duty it shall be to use such forms in his church on such occasions. And the Clergy in those States in which there is no Bishop, may use the forms of prayer or thanksgiving composed by the Bishop of any other State.

Done in Convention, and signed by order of the House of Bishops.

WILLIAM WHITE, D.D., PRESIDING BISHOP.
WILLIAM SMITH, D.D.,
PRESIDENT OF THE HOUSE OF CLERICAL AND LAY DEPUTIES.

CANONS.---Passed 1799.

CANON I.—Of the mode of calling Special Meetings of the General Convention.

The right of calling special meetings of the General Convention shall be in the Bishops. This right shall be exercised by the presiding bishop, or, in the case of his death, by the Bishop who, according to the rules of the House of Bishops, is to preside at the next General Convention; provided that the summons shall be with the consent, or on the requisition of a majority of the Bishops expressed to him in writing.

The place of holding any special Convention shall be that fixed on by the preceding General Convention, for the meeting of the next General Convention, unless circumstances, to be judged of by the Bishops, shall render a meeting at such place unsafe; in which case, the Bishops shall appoint some other place.

CANON II.—Of the Consecration of Bishops in the recess of the General Convention.

If, during the recess of the General Convention, the Church in any State should be desirous of the consecration of a Bishop, the Standing Committee of the Church in such State may, by their president, or by some other person or persons specially appointed, communicate the desire to the Standing Committees of the churches in the different States, together with copies of the necessary testimonials; and if the major number of the Standing Committees shall consent to the proposed consecration, the Standing Committee of the State concerned may communicate the evidences of such consent, together with the other testimonials, to any three Bishops of this Church, who may thereon proceed to the consecration. The evidences of the consent of the different Standing Committees shall be in the form prescribed for the General Convention in the 2d Canon of 1789. And without the aforesaid requisites, no consecration shall take place during the recess of the General Convention.

CANON III.—Explanatory of part of the 1st Canon of 1795.

No clergyman employed by the year, or for any limited time, shall be considered as a regularly officiating and resident Minister of the Church in any State, for the purpose expressed in the two concluding sentences of the 1st Canon of 1795, entitled, "A Canon concerning Episcopal Visitation."

CANON IV.—Repealing in part the 4th Canon of 1795, concerning the "Learning of those who are to be ordained."

Whereas, by the Canon of 1795, entitled "Of the learning of those who are to be ordained," a power is vested in the Bishops of dispensing with certain enumerated requisites in part, which power is not only too indefinitely expressed, but may be abused; so much therefore of the said Canon as authorises Bishops to dispense with any of the qualifications required in candidates for Holy Orders, is hereby repealed.

BY ORDER OF THE HOUSE OF BISHOPS:
WILLIAM WHITE, D.D., PRESIDING BISHOP.

BY ORDER OF THE HOUSE OF CLERICAL AND LAY DEPUTIES:
WILLIAM SMITH, PRESIDENT.

A Prayer,

To be used at the Meetings of the Convention.

Almighty and everlasting God, who, by thy Holy Spirit, didst preside in the Council of the blessed Apostles, and hast promised, through thy Son Jesus Christ, to be with thy Church to the end of the world: We beseech thee to be present with the Council of thy Church here assembled in thy name and presence. Save them from all error, ignorance, pride, and prejudice; and of thy great mercy vouchsafe, we beseech thee, so to direct, sanctify, and govern us in our present work, by the mighty power of the Holy Ghost, that the comfortable Gospel of Christ may be truly preached, truly received, and truly followed, in all places, to the breaking down the kingdom of sin, satan, and death; till at length the whole of thy dispersed sheep, being gathered into one fold, shall become partakers of everlasting life, through the merits and death of Jesus Christ our Saviour. Amen.

List of the Clergy

OF THE

PROTESTANT EPISCOPAL CHURCH,

In the different States, 1799.

NEW HAMPSHIRE.

Rev. Joseph Willard, rector of St. John's church, Portsmouth.
Rev. Robert H. Fowle, rector of —— church, Haldernesse.
Rev. Daniel Barber, Rector of —— church, Clairmont.

MASSACHUSETTS.

The Right Rev. Edward Bass, D.D., Bishop.
Rev. W. W. Wheeler, rector of —— church, Scituate.
Rev. William Walter, D.D., rector of Christ Church, Boston.
Rev. Samuel Parker, D.D., Rector of Trinity church, Boston.
Rev. John Sylvester J. Gardner, Assistant Minister of Trinity church, Boston.
Rev. Nathaniel Fisher, rector of —— church, Salem.
Rev. William Harris, rector of St. Michael's church, Marblehead.
Rev. Wm. Montague, rector of —— church, Deedham.
Rev. Daniel Burhams, rector of —— church, Lanesborough.
Rev. Ezra Bradlee, rector of —— church, Barrington.
Rev. James Bowers, deacon, Pittston.

RHODE ISLAND.

Rev. Abraham Lynsen Clarke, rector of St. John's church, Providence.
Rev. John Usher, rector of St. Michael's church, Bristol.
Rev. Joseph Warren, rector of St. Paul's church, North Kingstown.
Rev. Theodore Dehon, deacon, rector of Trinity church, Newport.

CONNECTICUT.

The Right Rev. Abraham Jarvis, D.D., Bishop.
Rev. Jeremiah Leaming, residing at New Haven.

CONNECTICUT.

The Right Rev. Abraham Jarvis, D.D., Bishop.
Rev. Jeremiah Leaming, residing at New Haven.
Rev. John Bowden, D.D., Principal of the Episcopal Academy at Cheshire.
Rev. Richard Mansfield, D.D., Rector of Christ Church at Derby, and of the Churches of Oxford and Great Hill.
Rev. Bela Hubbard, Trinity church, New Haven, and Christ church, West Haven.
Rev. John Tyler, Christ church, Norwich.
Rev. Daniel Fogg, rector of —— church, Pomphret
Rev. William Smith, D.D., rector of St. Paul's church, Norwalk.
Rev. Philo Shelton, rector of Trinity church, Stratfield, St. John's, Fairfield, and a church in Weston.
Rev. Ashbel Baldwin, rector of Christ church, Stratford, and Trinity church, Trumbul.
Rev. Chauncey Prindle, rector of Christ church, Watertown, and St. Peter's, Plymouth.
Rev. Reuben Ives, rector of St. Peter's church, Cheshire, and the churches at Hamden and Southington.
Rev. Tillotson Brownson, rector of St. Peter's church at Waterbury, and of the churches at Salem.
Rev. Truman Marsh, rector of St. John's church, New Milford, and the churches of Roxbury and New Preston.
Rev. Ambrose Todd, rector of St. Andrew's church, Symsbury, and St. Peter's church, Granby.
Rev. Solomon Blakesley, rector of St. Stephen's church in East Haddam.
Rev. Seth Hart, rector of St. Paul's church, Wallingsford, and a church in Berlin.
Rev. Charles Seabury, rector of St. James's church, New London.
Rev. Smith Miles, rector of the churches at Chatham & Middle Haddam.
Rev. David Butler, rector of Christ church, Reading, and the church at Ridgefield.
Rev. Alexander V. Griswold, rector of St. Matthew's church, Bristol, St. Mark's, Harwington, and a church in Northfield.
Rev. William Green, rector of St. John's, Seabrook.
Rev. Calvin White, Deacon, St. John's church, Stamford, and a church at Horseneck.
Rev. Evan Rogers, Deacon, the churches of Hebron and Pomphret.
Rev. Bethel Judd, Deacon.

NEW YORK.

The Right Rev. Samuel Provoost, D.D., Bishop.
Rev. Benjamin Moore, D.D., Assistant Minister of Trinity church, New York.
Rev. Abraham Beach, D.D., Assistant Minister of Trinity church, New York.
Rev. John Bisset, Assistant Minister of Trinity church, New York.
Rev. Thomas Ellison, rector of St. Peter's church, Albany.
Rev. Ammi Rogers, rector of Christ church, Battstown, St. James's, Milton, St. John's, Stillwater, and Trinity church, Waterford.
Rev. Robert. G. Wetmore, rector of St. George's church, Schenectady, and Christ church, Duanesborough.

Rev. John Urquhart, rector of St. John's church, Johnstown, and —— church, Fort Hunter.
Rev. Richard C. Moore, rector of St. Andrew's church, Staten Island.
Rev. Elias Cooper, rector of St. John's church, Philipsburgh.
Rev. Theodosius Bartow, rector of Trinity church, New Rochelle.
Rev. Elijah D. Rattoone, rector of Grace church, Jamaica, and St. George's, Flushing.
Rev. John Ireland, rector of St. Anne's church, Brooklyn.
Rev. Frederick Van Horne, rector of St. Andrew's church, in Ulster county.
Rev. Amos Pardee, rector of —— church, Hampton.
Rev. Philander Chase, Missionary of the Protestant Episcopal church in the State of New York.
Rev. Samuel Nesbit, resident minister in New York.
Rev. John J. Sands, Minister of the churches in Islop and Brookhaven.
Rev. Samuel Haskill, rector of Christ church in Rye.
Rev. Henry Van Dyke, rector of St. James's church, Newtown.
Rev. Daniel Nash, Minister of the churches in Otsego.

NEW JERSEY.

Rev. Charles H. Wharton, D.D., rector of St. Mary's church, in Burlington.
Rev. Uzal Ogden, D.D., rector of Trinity church, Newark.
Rev. Henry Waddell, rector of St. Michael's church, Trenton.
Rev. John Croes, rector of Trinity church, Swedesborough.
Rev. Menzies Rayner, rector of St. John's church, Elizabethtown.
Rev. Andrew Fowler, rector of St. Peter's church, Spotswood.
Rev. John Henry Hobart, Deacon of Christ church, New Brunswick.

PENNSYLVANIA.

The Right Rev. William White, D.D., Bishop.
Rev. William Smith, D.D.
Rev. Samuel Magaw, D.D., rector of St. Paul's church, in the city of Philadelphia.
Rev. John Andrews, D.D., Vice-Provost of the University of Pennsylvania.
Rev. Robert Blackwell, D.D., Assistant Minister of Christ Church and St. Peter's, in the city of Philadelphia.
Rev. Joseph Hutchins, D.D.
Rev. John Campbell, rector of the Episcopal churches of York and Huntingdon.
Rev. Slator Clay, rector of St. David's, Radnor; St. Peter's in the Valley, and St. James's, Perkiomen.
Rev. Joseph Clarkson, rector of St. James's, Lancaster, and of Pequea and Carnarvon, Lancaster connty.
Rev. Robert Ayres, rector of Emanuel church and St. Peter's church, in Washington and Fayette counties.
Rev. Francis Reno, Westmoreland county.
Rev. Joseph Turner, rector of St. Paul's church, Chester, and St. Martin's, Marcus Hook.

Rev. Caleb Hopkins, rector of Christ church, Derry Township, and Christ church, Turbut township, Northumberland county.
Rev. Thomas Davis, Washington county.
Rev. James Abercrombie, Assistant Minister of Christ church and St. Peter's, in the city of Philadelphia.
Rev. Absalom Jones (a black man), Deacon in the African church of St. Thomas's, Philadelphia.

DELAWARE.

The Rev. Robert Clay, Emanuel church, New Castle.
Rev. Walter C. Gardiner, Christ church, Dover.
Rev. William Pryce, Christ church, Kent county.
Rev. James Wiltbank, St. Peter's church, Sussex.

MARYLAND.

The Right Rev. Thomas J. Claggett, D.D., Bishop.
Rev. Charles Smoot, rector of William and Mary parish, St. Mary's.
Rev. Henry Lyon Davis, St. Mary's.
Rev. John Weems, Port Tobacco, Charles.
Rev. Mr. ——, William and Mary, Charles.
Rev. Hatch Dent, Trinity, Charles.
Rev. Edward Gant, Jun., Christ church, Calvert.
Rev. Nicholas W. Lane, All Saints, Calvert.
Rev. Francis Walker, residing in Calvert.
Rev. George Ralph, rector of Queen Ann's parish, St. George's county.(1)
Rev. John Mesinger, St. John's, Prince George's county.
Rev. Andrew M'Cormick, Washington, Prince George's county.
Rev. Clement Brook, residing in Prince George's county.
Rev. Walter D. Addison, residing in Prince George's county.
Rev. John W. Compton, St. James', Anne Arundel.
Rev. Ralph Higinbothom, St. Anne's, Anne Arundel.
Rev Owen F. Magrath, residing in Anne Arundel.
Rev. Henry Moscrop, residing in Anne Arundel.
Rev. Thomas Read, Prince George's, Montgomery.(1)
Rev. William Swan, St. Peter's, Montgomery.
Rev. Edward Gantt, residing in Montgomery.
Rev. George Bower, rector of All Saints, Frederick.
Rev. Joseph G. J. Bend, and Rev. John Ireland, associate rectors of St. Paul's, Baltimore.
Rev. John Coleman, St. Thomas's, Baltimore.
Rev. John Allen, St. George's, Harford.
Rev. Jeremiah Cosden, St. Stephen's, Cecil.
Rev. George Dashiell, Shrewsbury.
Rev Archibald Walker, D.D., Chester, Kent.
Rev. Colin Ferguson, D.D., residing in Kent county.
Rev. William Duke, residing in Kent.
Rev. Samuel Keene, D.D., St. Luke's, Queen Anne's.
Rev. Elisha Rigg, St. Paul's, Queen Anne's.(1)
Rev. Joseph Jackson, St. Peter's, Talbot.

Rev. John Bowie, D.D., St. Michael's, Talbot.
Rev. James Kemp, Great Choptank parish, Dorchester county.(1)
Rev. Joshua Reece, Stepney, Somerset.
Rev. Thomas Scott, Somerset, Somerset.
Rev. Isaac Foster, Coventry, Somerset.(1)
Rev. Samuel Sloan, residing in Somerset.
Rev. David Ball, Rector of All Hallows parish, Worcester.(1)
Rev. Samuel Tingeley, Worcester, Worcester.

(1) Members of the Standing Committee this year.

VIRGINIA.

The Right Rev. James Madison, D.D., Bishop.
Rev. Charles O'Neill, rector of Amherst parish.
Rev. Alexander Hay, rector of Antrim parish.
Rev. Devereux Jarratt, rector of Bath parish.
Rev. Samuel Gray, Botetourt parish.
Rev. Hugh Corrán Boggs, rector of Berkeley parish.
Rev. Benjamin Brown, rector of Brisland parish.
Rev. Andrew Syme, rector of Bristol parish.
Rev. John Cameron, D.D., rector of ——
Rev. Alexander M'Farland, rector of Brunswick parish.
Rev. Henry Spiering.
Rev. John Bracken, D.D., rector of Bruton parish.
Rev. John Camm, rector of Charles parish.
Rev. Henry Heffernen, Christ church.
Rev. James Elliott, rector of Cople parish.
Rev. Needler Robinson, rector of Dale parish.
Rev. Spence Grayson, rector of Dettingen parish.
Rev. Jesse Carter, rector of Drysdale parish.
Rev. Daniel M'Naughton, Christ church.
Rev. John J. Spooner, Elizabeth city parish.
Rev. James Whitehead, rector of Elizabeth river parish.
Rev. Thomas Davis, Fairfax parish.
Rev. Alexander Balmain, rector of Frederick parish.
Rev. John V. Weylie, Lecturer, Frederick.
Rev. Matthew Maury, rector of Fredericksville parish.
Rev. James Craig, rector of Hamilton parish.
Rev. John Buchanan, D.D., rector of Henrico parish.
Rev. Samuel S. M'Croskey, D.D., rector of Hungars parish.
Rev. James Thompson, rector of Leeds parish.
Rev. Charles Crawford, rector of Lexington parish.
Rev. William Crawford, Lexington parish.
Rev. James Dickinson, Littleton.
Rev. George Young, Lunenburg.
Rev. Anthony Walke, rector of Lynhaven parish.
Rev. John Dunn, Manchester.
Rev. William Hubard, rector of Newport parish.
Rev. Jacob Keeling, Nansemond.
Rev. Robert Buchan, rector of Overwharton parish.
Rev. Arthur Emerson, rector of Portsmouth parish.
Rev. John Brunskill, rector of Raleigh parish.
Rev. Alexander Lundie, rector of St. Andrew's parish.
Rev. John Matthews, St. Bride's parish.

Rev. Reuben Clopton, ——
Rev. Cave Jones, St. George's parish.
Rev. James Stevenson, rector of St. George's parish.
Rev. Charles Hopkins, rector of St. James, Northam parish.
Rev. James Price, rector of St. John's parish.
Rev. Thomas Hughes, rector of St. David's.
Rev. Archibald Dick, rector of St. Margaret's parish.
Rev. John Woodville, St. Mark's parish.
Rev. Abner Waugh, rector of St. Mary's parish.
Rev. William Stewart, rector of St. Paul's parish.
Rev. John Parsons, ——.
Rev. John Seward, St. Stephen's parish.
Rev. John Hyde Saunders, rector of Southam parish.
Rev. Samuel Butler, rector of Southwark parish.
Rev. Samuel Chapin, rector of Westover parish.
Rev. James Evans, Yorkhampton.
Rev. John O'Donnel, rector of Hampshire parish.
Rev. Lee Massey, rector of Truro parish.
Rev. Armistead Smith, Matthews.
Rev. John C. Brockenboroug, Washington.
Rev. Duncan M'Naughton, Wicomico.
Rev. Joseph Wilson:
Rev. Stephen Johnson:
Rev. John Wade:
Rev. Cornelius Carvert—Cures not known.

SOUTH CAROLINA.

The Right Rev. Robert Smith, D.D., Bishop.
Rev. Thomas Frost, St. Philip's.
Rev. Hev. Henry Purcell, D.D., St. Michael's, Charleston.
Rev. Edward Jenkins, St. Michael's, Charleston.
Rev. Milwood Pogson, St. James's, Goose Creek, St. George's, Dorchester
Rev. Peter M. Parker, St. John's, Berkley.
Rev. John Thompson, St. Thomas's.
Rev. Thomas Mills, St. Andrew's, James' Island, St. Andrew's, Main.
Rev. Edmund Matthews, St. John's, Edisto.
Rev. Mr. Nixon, St. Bartholomew's.
Rev. Thomas D. Bladen, St. James', Santee.
Rev. James Connor, St. Stephen's.
Rev. George H. Spierin, Prince George's.
Rev. John O'Donnel, All Saints.
Rev. Hugh Frazier, Prince Frederick's.
Residents in the State without cures:
Rev. Dr. Gates.
Rev. Mr. Cotton, Teacher in Charleston College.
Rev. Mr. M'Culley, Master of an Academy, Beaufort.
Rev. Mr. Blackwall.
Rev. Mr. Best, Master of an Academy, Charleston.

JOURNAL OF THE PROCEEDINGS

OF THE

BISHOPS, CLERGY, AND LAITY

OF THE

Protestant Episcopal Church

IN

THE UNITED STATES OF AMERICA,

IN

A CONVENTION

HELD IN

THE CITY OF TRENTON, IN NEW JERSEY, FROM TUESDAY, SEPTEMBER 8, TO SATURDAY, SEPTEMBER 12, 1801.

LIST OF THE MEMBERS OF THE HOUSE OF CLERICAL AND LAY DEPUTIES.

FROM THE STATE OF MASSACHUSETTS.

Rev. Samuel Parker, D.D.
Rev. William Harris.

FROM THE STATE OF CONNECTICUT.

Rev. Ashbel Baldwin.
Rev. Philo Shelton.
Rev. Evan Rogers.
James Clark, Esq.

FROM THE STATE OF NEW YORK.

Rev Abraham Beach, D.D.
Rev. Isaac Wilkins.
Rev. John Ireland.
Rev. John Henry Hobart.
John Read, Esq.
William Ogden, Esq.

FROM THE STATE OF NEW JERSEY.

Rev. Uzal Ogden, D.D.
Rev. Charles H. Wharton, D.D.
Colonel Samuel Ogden.
Matthias Williamson, Jun., Esq.
John Dennis, Esq.

FROM THE STATE OF PENNSYLVANIA.

Rev. William Smith, D.D.
Rev. Robert Blackwell, D.D.

FROM THE STATE OF DELAWARE.

Rev. Robert Clay.
Rev. William Pryce.
Joseph Burn, Esq.

FROM THE STATE OF MARYLAND.

Rev. James Kemp.
Rev. Joseph G. J. Bend.
Rev. John Coleman.
Rev. George Dashiell.
David Kerr, Esq.
William Helmsley, Esq.

JOURNAL

OF THE

House of Clerical and Lay Deputies.

TRENTON, STATE OF NEW JERSEY,
ST. MICHAEL'S CHURCH, Sept. 8, 1801.

A SUFFICIENT number of Clerical and Lay Deputies to form a quorum not appearing, the members present adjourned to meet at the Church to-morrow morning at 9 o'clock.

WEDNESDAY, Sept. 9, 1801.

The house met, and the Rev. Mr. Ireland read prayers.

The members then adjourned to the State House, when a sufficient number of Clerical and Lay Deputies to form a house appearing, and a quorum being formed, the house proceeded to the appointment, by ballot, of a President, and a majority of votes was found for the Rev. Abraham Beach, D.D. The Rev. Ashbel Baldwin was appointed Secretary and Chaplain to the Convention.

Resolved,—That the Rev. Dr. Parker and William Ogden, Esq., inform the House of Bishops, that the House of Clerical and Lay Deputies is formed and ready to proceed to business.

Resolved,—That the rules of order established by the House of Clerical and Lay Deputies of the three preceding Conventions, be adopted by this house.

The Rev. Samuel Parker, D.D., and the Rev. William Harris, Clerical deputies from Massachusetts; the Rev. Ashbel Baldwin, Rev. Philo Shelton, and Rev. Evan Rogers, Clerical deputies, and James Clarke, Esq., Lay deputy from Connecticut; the Rev. Abraham Beach, D.D., Rev. Isaac Wilkins, Rev. John Ireland, and Rev. John Henry Hobart, Clerical deputies, and John Read and William Ogden, Esqs., Lay deputies from New York; the Rev. Uzal Ogden, D.D., Clerical deputy, and Col. Samuel Ogden and John Dennis, Esq., Lay deputies from New Jersey; the Rev. William Smith, D.D., and Rev. Robert Blackwell, D.D., Clerical deputies from Pennsylvania; the Rev. James Kemp, Clerical deputy, and David Kerr, Esq., Lay deputy from Maryland, delivered in, at the Secretary's table, certificates of their appointment, which were read, and determined to be satisfactory.

Dr. Parker proposed the following resolution, which was adopted, viz., That during the Session of the present Convention, they shall meet each day at 9 o'clock, A.M., and adjourn at 1 o'clock P.M., and meet again at 4 o'clock, P.M.

Dr. Parker was requested by this house to give information to the House of Bishops of the foregoing resolution, who reported that they acceded to the same.

The Rev. Dr. Beach presented the testimonial required by the Canons, from the State Convention of New York, in favour of the Rev. Benjamin Moore, D.D., the Bishop elect of that State.

On motion, the following message was sent by the Rev. Mr. Hobart to the House of Bishops: "The House of Clerical and Lay Deputies wish to know from the House of Bishops, whether they have received any communication from Bishop Provoost, on the subject of his resignation of his Episcopal jurisdiction in the State of New York."

A communication was received from the House of Bishops, on the subject of the foregoing message from this house.

The house then proceeded to sign the testimonial required by the Canons in favour of the Rev. Benjamin Moore, D.D., Bishop elect of the State of New York; which, together with the testimonial from the State Convention of New York, was ordered to be presented to the House of Bishops.

The house then adjourned until 4 o'clock.

WEDNESDAY, 4 o'clock, P.M.

The house met.

The Rev. Charles H. Wharton, D.D., Clerical deputy from the State of New Jersey, and the Rev. Joseph G. J. Bend, a Clerical deputy from the State of Maryland, presented their testimonials, which were approved, and they took their seats accordingly.

Resolved,—That the proceedings of this house shall be read at the opening of the house every morning.

The question being called for upon the alteration of the first Article of the Constitution, as proposed by the last General Convention; and the votes being taken by States, it was negatived.

The house then adjourned until 9 o'clock to-morrow morning.

THURSDAY MORNING, Sept. 10.

The house met according to adjournment, and the Chaplain read prayers.

Matthias Williamson, Jun., Esq., Lay deputy from the State of New Jersey; the Rev. Robert Clay and the Rev. William Price, Clerical deputies, and Joseph Burn, Esq., Lay deputy from the State of Delaware; the Rev. John Coleman and Rev. George Dashiell, Clerical Deputies, and William Helmsley, Esq., a Lay deputy from the State of Maryland, presented their testimonials, which were read and approved, and they took their seats accordingly.

A message was received from the House of Bishops, informing this house that they had read and approved the testimonials in favour of the Rev. Dr. Benjamin Moore, Bishop elect of the State of New York, and had appointed to-morrow morning, 10 o'clock, for his consecration.

On motion, Resolved,—That the Rev. Mr. Bend inform the House of Bishops, that this house will attend the consecration of the Rev. Dr. Moore at the appointed time.

On motion of the Rev. Dr. Wharton, Resolved,—That the following addition be made to the 4th Canon of 1799, viz., "Unless when such candidate come recommended by the General Convention."

The Rev. Dr. Wharton was requested to carry the foregoing resolution to the House of Bishops for their concurrence.

The following resolution was moved by Mr. Kerr.

Whereas the House of Clerical and Lay Deputies of the General Convention of the Protestant Episcopal Church, held at Philadelphia in June, 1799, resolved that all proceedings respecting the consecration of the Rev. Uzal Ogden, D.D., ought to be suspended until a future Convention of the State of New Jersey shall declare their sense of the subject;

Resolved,—That the proceedings and declaration of the State Convention of the Protestant Episcopal Church in New Jersey, on the subject to them referred, be read, and that the testimonials of this house, requisite on such occasions, be given by this house.

The proceedings of the State Convention of the Protestant Episcopal Church in New Jersey, respecting the election of Dr. Ogden as Bishop for that State, were accordingly read and fully considered; and the question upon signing the requisite testimonial being taken by States, it was negatived.

Adjourned to 4 o'clock this evening.

THURSDAY, 4 o'clock, P.M.

The house met.

A communication from the House of Bishops, respecting the Articles of religion, was read;

And, on motion, a Committee, consisting of a Clerical member from each State, viz., Dr. Parker, Mr. Baldwin, Mr. Wilkins, Dr. Ogden, Dr. Smith, Mr. Clay, and Mr. Kemp, were appointed to take into consideration the foregoing communication from the House of Bishops, and were ordered to report to this house to-morrow.

A message was received from the House of Bishops, disagreeing to the resolution of this house, making an addition to the fourth Canon of 1799, and proposing instead thereof, that the fourth Canon of 1795 be revived, with the following addition, viz., "In which case the Bishop shall record the reasons of the aforesaid dispensation; and the reasons so recorded shall be liable to be called for at any meeting of the State Convention, and if said Convention think proper, shall be entered on their Journals"—the fourth Canon of 1799 to be repealed.

This house disagreed to the proposed substitute from the House of Bishops to their resolution, and requested a conference. Dr. Parker, Rev. Mr. Wilkins, and Rev. Mr. Kemp, were appointed a Committee on the part of this house; and the Rev. Mr. Hobart was requested to inform the House of Bishops thereof.

The following resolution was received from the House of Bishops, and agreed to by this house, viz.

Resolved,—That it be made known to the State Conventions, that it is proposed to consider and determine, in the next General Convention, on the following alteration of the first Article of the Constitution, viz.

"Article I. There shall be a General Convention of the Protestant Episcopal Church in the United States of America, on the third Tuesday of May, 1808, and on the third Tuesday of May every third year afterwards," etc. as before.

A proposed Canon was received from the House of Bishops, respecting those persons who shall discontinue, without lawful cause, all exercise of the ministerial office; which was considered by this house, and agreed to.

On motion, Resolved,—That the following clause be added to the sixth rule of order—"without the consent of two-thirds of the house."

On motion of Mr. Kerr, Resolved,—That the Presiding Bishop in the House of Bishops be requested to appoint a clergyman of this house to perform divine service, and preach a sermon every evening during the present Session.

On motion of the Rev. Mr. Bend, Resolved,—That it be recommended to the several State Conventions of this Church to cause as great a number as possible of the Constitution and Canons of the Protestant Episcopal Church in the United States, and of the Constitutions and Canons of their respective churches, to be printed and distributed among their respective congregations.

The foregoing resolution was transmitted to the House of Bishops, and a message was received from them, informing this house that they had concurred in the same.

The Rev. Mr. Rogers, from Connecticut, asked leave of absence during the remainder of the Session, which was granted.

The Rev. Mr. Ireland, from the State of New York, asked leave of absence during the remainder of the session; granted.

Adjourned to 9 o'clock to-morrow morning.

FRIDAY, Sept. 11.

The House met, and the Chaplain read prayers.

The Rev. Mr. Harris, from Massachusetts, asked leave of absence during the remainder of the Session, which was granted.

The house then adjourned to attend divine service at St. Michael's Church, Trenton, on occasion of the consecration of the Rev. Dr. Moore, Bishop elect of the church in New York.

After divine service, the house met at 4 o'clock, P.M.

On motion, Resolved,—That the thanks of this house be presented to the Right Rev. Bishop White, for his Sermon delivered this day, at the consecration of the Rev. Dr. Moore, and that he be requested to furnish a copy of the same for publication.

A proposed Canon was received from the House of Bishops, limiting the operation of the 4th Canon of 1795.

The foregoing Canon was adopted with an amendment.

The Rev. Dr. Parker, Rev. Mr. Shelton, and James Clark, Esq., were appointed a Committee to consider certain memorials presented to this house from Churches in New Hampshire and Vermont, and to report thereon.

The Committee appointed to consider the communication from the House of Bishops, respecting the Articles of religion, made a report, which was unanimously adopted, and sent to the House of Bishops for their concurrence.

The Rev. Mr. Wilkins presented the following proposed Canon.

"No Lay deputy shall be admitted as a member of this house, who shall not have been a communicant of the Protestant Episcopal Church for at least one year previous to his appointment."

The question was taken by States on the foregoing Canon, and the Yeas and Nays were as follows:

CLERGY—Massachusetts, No; Connecticut, Yea; New York, Yea; New Jersey, No; Pennsylvania, No; Delaware, No; Maryland, No.

LAITY—Connecticut, No; New York, Yea; Delaware, No; Maryland, No.

So it was determined in the negative.

Resolved,—That the Secretaries of the former Conventions and the Secretaries of the present Convention, be requested to transmit all the papers to the Committee who were appointed for the purpose of arranging and recording the Journals of the General Convention; and when these papers are recorded, they shall be deposited with the Bishop of this Church in Pennsylvania, to be transmitted to the next General Convention.

The House of Bishops informed this house, that they had concurred in the amendment proposed by this house, to the proposed Canon limiting the operation of the 4th Canon of 1795.

Adjourned to 8 o'clock to-morrow morning.

SATURDAY, 8 o'clock, A.M.

The house met, and the Chaplain read prayers.

The Committee appointed to consider the memorials from certain churches in New Hampshire and Vermont, made the following report, which was read, and unanimously adopted, viz.:

REPORT OF THE COMMITTEE.

It appears from the memorials of certain churches in the western part of the state of New Hampshire, and the eastern part of the state of Vermont, that, having agreed to and adopted the General Constitution of the Protestant Episcopal Church in the United States, they are desirous of forming a junction, and uniting themselves, for the purpose of holding Conventions, and effecting a due organization of their churches; and, on account of the impracticability of joining with the other churches in said respective states, they are desirous of being considered as a separate district. Your Committee are of opinion, that the 8th Canon of 1795 militates against the wishes of said memorialists, but that their local situation requires a dispensation from the operation of said Canon, more especially as many valuable tracts of land have been granted to the Episcopal Church in those towns, and others in the vicinity, which land requires the attention of a duly organized Church for its preservation and improvement. Your Committee are therefore of opinion, that, from their peculiar circumstances, they ought to be allowed to put themselves under the jurisdiction of a Bishop of one of the neighbouring states, until a Bishop shall be duly consecrated and settled in said states, as the only measure that can relieve them under their peculiar situation and circumstances. Signed by order,

S. PARKER.

The above report was sent to the House of Bishops, and returned with their concurrence.

The Rev. Mr. Hobart proposed a Canon, prescribing the mode of publishing authorized editions of the Common Prayer Book, etc., which was read and adopted, and sent to the House of Bishops.

The House of Bishops returned the foregoing Canon, with an amendment, in which this house concurred.

The House of Bishops also returned to this house the resolution respecting the Articles of religion, with amendments, which were read and adopted.

[For this resolution respecting Articles of religion, as agreed to by the House of Bishops and the House of Clerical and Lay Deputies, see Appendix.]

This house adopted, and sent to the House of Bishops, a resolution respecting certain spurious editions of the Book of Common Prayer.

The House of Bishops informed this house, that they disagreed to the above named resolution, and proposed another as a substitute, which was adopted by this house.

The Rev. Dr. Smith proposed a Canon, making an addition to the 1st Canon of 1795, of Episcopal visitation; which was read and adopted, and sent to the House of Bishops.

The House of Bishops informed this house, that they concurred in the foregoing Canon.

On motion of the Rev. Mr. Bend, Resolved,—That the House of Bishops be requested to consider of and establish a course of theological studies, proper for Candidates for Holy Orders, and to report the same to the next General Convention.

The House of Bishops concurred in the foregoing resolution.

On motion, Resolved,—That the Rev. Mr. Bend, Rev. Mr. Ireland (of Baltimore), Rev. Mr. Kemp, Rev. Mr. Coleman, and Rev. Mr. Dashiell, be appointed a Committee to report to this House, at the next General Convention, such additional hymns as they shall think are adapted to Christian worship.

On motion, Resolved,—That the Rev. Dr. Beach, Rev. Mr. Hobart, with the Secretary of this house, be a Committee on the part of this house, to revise and publish the Journals, etc., of this Convention, and also to superintend the printing of Bishop White's Sermon, delivered before this Convention.

Ordered, that 500 copies of the Journals, and the same number of the Sermon, be printed.

On motion, Resolved,—That the next meeting of the General Convention be held in the city of New York.

The House of Bishops concurred in the foregoing resolution.

On motion, Resolved,—That the Right Rev. Bishop Moore be requested to preach a Sermon at the opening of the next General Convention; and that the Rev. Mr. Hobart inform the House of Bishops of the foregoing resolution, and that this house is ready to adjourn.

On motion, Resolved,—That the Rev. Mr. Waddell, Secretary of the House of Bishops, be requested to return the thanks of this Convention to the Governor, for the use of the rooms in the State House.

Resolved,—That the thanks of this house be given to their President, the Rev. Dr. Beach, and to their Secretary and Chaplain, the Rev. Mr. Baldwin, for their attention and services.

The Rev. Mr. Hobart reported, that the Right Rev. Bishop Moore would comply with the request of this house, to preach a Sermon at the opening of the next General Convention; and that the House of Bishops, having no further communications to make, concurred in the resolution of adjournment.

The house adjourned sine die.

Signed by order of the House of Clerical and Lay Deputies.

ABRAHAM BEACH, President.

Ashbel Baldwin, Secretary.

JOURNAL

OF THE

House of Bishops.

TRENTON, STATE OF NEW JERSEY,
ST. MICHAEL'S CHURCH, Sept. 8, 1801.

This being the day of the Meeting of the General Convention of the Protestant Episcopal Church, the Right Rev. Bishop White, of Pennsylvania, appeared, and appointed to meet to-morrow, at 9 o'clock.

WEDNESDAY, Sept. 9, 1801.

Present as before, together with the Right Rev. Bishop Claggett, of Maryland, and the Right Rev. Bishop Jarvis, of Connecticut.

The house attended divine service with the House of Clerical and Lay Deputies.

His Excellency the Governor having granted permission to the Convention to meet in the State House,

Resolved,—That this house do adjourn to meet immediately in the Council Chamber of the same.

The house met at the State House.

Some doubt arising in regard to the meaning of the rule of this house, in the year 1792 substituted in the place of the 1st rule of this house in 1789, Resolved,—That until the same shall be considered and explained by this house, the Right. Rev. Bishop White be requested to preside at the present Session.

The Rev. Henry Waddell was appointed Secretary of this house.

A message was received from the House of Clerical and Lay Deputies, by the Rev. Mr. Kemp, informing this house that they were organized, and ready to proceed to business. This house informed them that they were ready for the same.

A letter was laid before this house from the Right Rev. Bishop Provoost, addressed to Bishop White, as follows:

NEW YORK, SEPT. 7, 1801.

Right rev. and dear sir:

I think it my duty to request that, as President of the House of Bishops, you will inform that venerable body, that, induced by ill health, and some melancholy occurrences in my family, and an ardent wish to retire from all public employment, I resigned, at the last meeting of our Church Convention, my jurisdiction as Bishop of the Protestant Episcopal Church in the state of New York.

I am, with great regard, dear and right rev. sir,

Your affectionate brother,

SAMUEL PROVOOST.

Right Rev. Bishop White.

A message from the House of Clerical and Lay Deputies was read, as follows: — "The House of Clerical and Lay Deputies wish to know from the House of Bishops, whether they have received any communication from Bishop Provoost, on the subject of the resignation of his Episcopal jurisdiction in the State of New York."

The House of Bishops having considered the subject brought before them by the letter of Bishop Provoost, and by the message from the House of Clerical and Lay Deputies, touching the same, can see no grounds on which to believe, that the contemplated resignation is consistent with ecclesiastical order, or with the practice of Episcopal churches in any ages, or with the tenor of the Office of Consecration. Accordingly, while they sympathize most tenderly with their brother Bishop Provoost, on account of that ill health, and those melancholy occurrences which have led to the design in question, they judge it to be inconsistent with the sacred trust committed to them, to recognize the Bishop's act as an effectual resignation of his Episcopal jurisdiction. Nevertheless, being sensible of the present exigencies of the church of New York, and approving of their making provision for the actual discharge of the duties of the Episcopacy, the

Bishops of this house are ready to consecrate to the Office of a Bishop, any person who may be presented to them with the requisite testimonials from the General and State Conventions, and of whose religious, moral, and literary character, due satisfaction may be given. But this house must be understood to be explicit in their declaration, that they shall consider such a person as assistant or co-adjutor Bishop during Bishop Provoost's life, although competent, in point of character, to all the Episcopal duties; the extent in which the same shall be discharged by him, to be dependent on such regulations as expediency may dictate to the Church in New York, grounded on the indisposition of Bishop Provoost, and with his concurrence.

The Secretary not being present, Bishop Jarvis is requested to deliver the above as a message to the House of Clerical and Lay Deputies, and to furnish that house with a copy of Bishop Provoost's letter.

A message was received from the House of Clerical and Lay Deputies, by the Rev. Dr. Parker, informing that the meetings of that house, during the session, are appointed to be at 9 o'clock in the forenoon, and at 4 in the afternoon.

This house agreed on the same hours, and informed the House of Clerical and Lay Deputies thereof, by the Rev. Dr. Parker.

Adjourned to 4 o'clock, P.M.

WEDNESDAY, 4 o'clock, P.M.

The house met. Present as yesterday.

The Rev. Henry Waddell took his place as Secretary to this house.

The house agreed on a form and manner of setting forth the Articles of religion, and agreed that the same be sent to the House of Clerical and Lay Deputies for their concurrence; which was done accordingly.

The house then adjourned to 9 o'clock to-morrow morning.

THURSDAY, Sept. 10, 9 o'clock, A.M.

The house met. Present as yesterday.

The testimonial from the Convention of the Church in the State of New York, in favour of the Rev. Dr. Benj. Moore, as Bishop elect of the Church in that State; and also the testimonial from the House of Clerical and Lay Deputies, now sitting, in favour of the said Dr. Moore; being received and read, and found agreeable to the prescribed forms;

Resolved,—That the House of Clerical and Lay Deputies be informed that the Bishops now present are ready to proceed to the consecration of the Rev. Dr. Moore, to-morrow morning at 10 o'clock.

The House of Clerical and Lay Deputies informed this house by the Rev. Mr. Bend, that they will attend the consecration of the Rev. Dr. Moore at the time appointed.

This house received, by the Rev. Mr. Bend, a message, as follows.

"The question being taken in the House of Clerical and Lay Deputies, upon the following alteration in the 1st Article of the Constitution, viz., 'ART. I. There shall be a General Convention of the Protestant Episcopal Church in the United States of America on the third Tuesday of May, in the year of our Lord 1805, and on the third Tuesday of May in every fifth year afterwards,' etc. And the votes being taken, it was determined in the negative."

This house Resolved,—That it be proposed to the House of Clerical and Lay Deputies to propose to the next General Convention, that the first Article of the Constitution shall be as follows, viz., "ART. I. There shall be a General Convention of the Protestant Episcopal Church in the United States of America, on the third Tuesday in May, 1808, and in every third year," etc., as before.

A message was received from the House of Clerical and LayDeputies, by the Rev. Dr. Wharton, proposing an addition to the 4th Canon of 1799. This house disagreed to the said proposal, and instead thereof proposed to the House of Clerical and Lay Deputies the revival of, and an addition to, that part of the 4th Canon of 1795, which had been repealed, together with the repeal of the 4th Canon of 1799.

The house then adjourned to the afternoon.

THURSDAY, 4 o'clock, P.M.

The house met. Present as before.

A message was received from the House of Clerical and Lay Deputies, by the Rev. Mr. Hobart, informing this house that they disagree to the proposal made to them by this house for the revival of, and an addition to, that part of the 4th Canon of 1795 which had been repealed, together with the repeal of the 4th Canon of 1799, and requesting a conference on the subject with this house; whereupon the Right Rev. Bishop Claggett was appointed a Committee on the part of this house, to meet and confer with a Committee of the House of Clerical and Lay Deputies on the subject aforesaid.

The house adjourned till 9 o'clock to-morrow morning.

FRIDAY, Sept. 11, 9 o'clock.

The house met. Present as yesterday.

The house adjourned, in order to attend the consecration of the Bishop elect of the Church in the State of New York.

FRIDAY, 4 o'clock, P.M.

The house met. Present as before.

A message was received from the House of Clerical and Lay Deputies, by the Rev. Mr. Baldwin, with the following resolution:

"Resolved,—That it be recommended to the several State Conventions of this Church, to cause as great a number as possible of the Constitution and Canons of the Protestant Episcopal Church in the United States, and of the Constitutions and Canons of their respective churches, to be printed and distributed among their respective congregations."

Whereupon, it was Resolved,—That this house do concur in the aforesaid resolution.

The Right Rev. Bishop Moore, who was consecrated this morning, appeared in the house and took his seat.

A proposed Canon, limiting the operation of the 4th Canon of 1795, was adopted, and sent to the House of Clerical and Lay Deputies for their concurrence.

The House of Clerical and Lay Deputies returned the above Canon as adopted by them, with an amendment, which was agreed to by this house.

The Right Rev. Bishop Claggett asked and obtained leave of absence.

The house adjourned to 8 o'clock to-morrow morning.

SATURDAY, September 12, 8 o'clock, A.M.

The house met. Present, the Right Rev. Bishop White, the Right Rev. Bishop Jarvis, and the Right Rev. Bishop Moore.

A message was received from the House of Clerical and Lay Deputies, by the Rev. Dr. Smith, with a proposed Canon, making an addition to the 1st Canon of 1795. The proposed Canon was agreed to by this house.

This house agreed to a resolution received from the House of Clerical and Lay Deputies, respecting Articles of religion.

This house received from the House of Clerical and Lay Deputies applications from certain churches of New Hampshire and Vermont, respecting certain arrangements on account of their local circumstances, which papers were accompanied with a resolution of the House of Clerical and Lay Deputies concerning the same. This house concurred in the resolution.

This house received from the House of Clerical and Lay Deputies, by the Rev. Mr. Hobart, a proposed Canon, prescribing the mode of publishing authorised editions of the Common Prayer Book, etc.; which Canon this house agreed to, with an amendment.

This house received from the House of Clerical and Lay Deputies a proposal, that the next meeting of the Convention should be in the city of New York; in which this house concurred.

The House of Clerical and Lay Deputies returned the amendment of this house to the proposed Canon prescribing the mode of publishing authorised editions of the Common Prayer Book, etc., with their concurrence.

The House of Clerical and Lay Deputies sent to this house a proposed resolution, requesting this House to consider of and establish a course of ecclesiastical studies, proper for Candidates for Holy Orders, and to report the same to the next General Convention.

This house concurred in the foregoing resolution.

This house received from the House of Clerical and Lay Deputies a proposed resolution concerning certain spurious editions of the Common Prayer, which this house disagreed to, and proposed the following as a substitute, viz.

"Whereas this Convention has received information, that

certain unauthorised books of Common Prayer have been published, in which some parts of the authorised book are omitted, and other matters added;

Resolved,—That it shall be the duty of every Bishop to make inquiry into, and report at every meeting of the Convention, such cases of this sort as may have come within his knowledge.

This house received from the House of Clerical and Lay Deputies, their concurrence in the foregoing resolution.

This house received from the House of Clerical and Lay Deputies a proposed resolve, that the Right Rev. Bishop Moore be requested to preach a Sermon at the next General Convention; which resolve was adopted by this house.

This house received a message from the House of Clerical and Lay Deputies, naming a Committee on their part for revising and publishing the Journals; and the Right Rev. Bishop Moore was appointed a Committee on the part of this house.

A resolution was received from the House of Clerical and Lay Deputies, requesting the Rev. Mr. Waddell, to return the thanks of this Convention to the Governor, for the use of the rooms in the State House.

This house concurred in the foregoing resolution.

A message was received from the House of Clerical and Lay Deputies, informing this house that they are ready to adjourn.

Resolved,—That this house are also ready to adjourn.

Resolved,—That the thanks of this house be returned to the Rev. Mr. Waddell, their Secretary, for his attention and services.

The house rose.

Signed by order of the House of Bishops.

WILLIAM WHITE,
PRESIDING BISHOP.

Attest: HENRY WADDELL, Secretary.

THE CERTIFICATE OF THE CONSECRATION OF THE RIGHT REV. BISHOP MOORE IS AS FOLLOWS.

Know all men by these presents, that we, William White, D.D., Bishop of the Protestant Episcopal Church in the State of Pennsylvania, Presiding Bishop; Thomas John Claggett, D.D., Bishop of the Protestant Episcopal Church in the State of Maryland, and Abraham Jarvis, D.D., Bishop of the Protestant Episcopal Church in the State of Connecticut, under the protection of Almighty God, in St. Michael's Church, in the city of Trenton, on Friday, the eleventh day of September, in the year of our Lord One thousand eight hundred and one, did then and there rightly and canonically consecrate our beloved in Christ, Benjamin Moore, D.D., Rector of Trinity Church, in the city of New York, of whose sufficiency in good learning, soundness in the faith, and purity of manners, we were fully ascertained, into the office of Bishop of the Protestant Episcopal Church in the State of New York, to which the said Benjamin Moore, D.D., hath been elected by the Convention of the said State, in consequence of the inability of the Right Rev. Bishop Provoost, and of his declining all Episcopal jurisdiction within the said State.

In testimony whereof we have signed our names and caused our seals to be affixed.

Given in the city of Trenton, this eleventh day of September, in the year of our Lord One thousand eight hundred and one.

WILLIAM WHITE. [L. S.]
THOMAS JOHN CLAGGETT. [L. S.]
ABRAHAM JARVIS. [L. S.]

APPENDIX.

Resolution of the Bishops, the Clergy, and Laity of the Protestant Episcopal Church in the United States of America, in Convention, in the city of Trenton, the 12th day of September, in the year of our Lord 1801, respecting Articles of Religion.

The Articles of Religion are hereby ordered to be set forth with the following directions, to be observed in all future editions of the same; that is to say—

The following to be the title, viz.:

"Articles of Religion, as established by the Bishops, the Clergy, and the Laity of the Protestant Episcopal Church in the United States of America, in Convention, on the 12th day of September, in the year of our Lord 1801."

The Articles to stand as in the Book of Common Prayer of the Church of England, with the following alterations and omissions, viz.:

In the 8th Article, the word "three" in the title, and the words "three —Athanasius's creed" in the Article, to be omitted, and the Article to read thus:

"ART. VIII. OF THE CREEDS.

"The Nicene Creed, and that which is commonly called the Apostles' Creed, ought thoroughly to be received and believed, for they may be proved by most certain warrants of Holy Scripture."

Under the title "Article 21," the following Note to be inserted, viz.:

"The 21st of the former Articles is omitted, because it is partly of a local and civil nature, and is provided for, as to the remaining parts of it, in other Articles."

The 35th Article to be inserted with the following note, viz.

"This Article is received in this Church, so far as it declares the Books of Homilies to be an explication of Christian doctrine, and instructive in piety and morals. But all references to the constitution and laws of England are considered as inapplicable to the circumstances of this Church; which also suspends the order for the reading of said homilies in churches until a revision of them may conveniently be made, for the clearing of them, as well from obsolete words and phrases, as from the local references."

The 36th Article, entitled "Of Consecration of Bishops and Ministers," to read thus:

"The Book of Consecration of Bishops, and ordering of Priests and Deacons, as set forth by the General Convention of this Church in 1792, doth contain all things necessary to such consecration and ordering: neither hath it any thing, that, of itself, is superstitious and ungodly: and, therefore whosoever are consecrated or ordered according to said form, we decree all such to be rightly, orderly, and lawfully consecrated and ordered."

The 37th Article to be omitted, and the following substituted in its place:

"OF THE POWER OF THE CIVIL MAGISTRATE.

"The power of the civil magistrate extendeth to all men, as well Clergy as Laity, in all things temporal—but hath no authority in things purely spiritual. And we hold it to be the duty of all men who are professors of the gospel, to pay respectful obedience to the civil authority, regularly and legitimately constituted."

ADOPTED BY THE HOUSE OF BISHOPS.
WILLIAM WHITE, D.D., PRESIDING BISHOP.

ADOPTED BY THE HOUSE OF CLERICAL AND LAY DEPUTIES.
ABRAHAM BEACH, D.D., PRESIDENT.

Canons.

PASSED 1801.

CANON I.—Respecting tnose who discontinue all exercise of the Ministerial Office without lawful cause, etc.

If any person, having been ordained in this Church, or having been otherwise regularly ordained and admitted a minister in this church, shall discontinue all exercise of the ministerial office without lawful cause, or shall avow that he is no longer a minister of this Church, or shall live in the habitual disuse of the public worship, or of the Holy Eucharist, according to the offices of this Church—such person, on due proof of the same, or on his own confession, shall be liable to be degraded from the Ministry.

CANON II.—Limiting the operation of the 4th Canon of 1795.

The Bishop of this Church, in any State, with the advice and consent of all the Clerical members of the Standing Committee of his diocese, may dispense with the knowledge of the Latin and Greek languages, and other branches of learning not strictly ecclesiastical, which are required by the 4th Canon of 1795.

Canon III.—Prescribing the mode of publishing authorised editions of the Common Prayer Book, etc.

The Bishop of this Church, in any state, or where there is no Bishop, the standing committee are authorised to appoint, from time to time, some suitable person or persons to compare and correct all new editions of the Common Prayer Book, Book of Offices, etc., by some standard book, and a certificate of their having been so compared and corrected shall be published with said books. And in case any edition shall be published without such correction, it shall be the duty of the Bishop, or where there is no Bishop, of the standing committee, to give public notice that such edition is not authorised by the Church. The Bishop of this Church in Pennsylvania is hereby authorised to set forth an edition of the Articles of religion, which, when published, shall be the standard copy. The octavo edition of the Common Prayer Book, published in New York in 1793, by Hugh Gaine, and the quarto edition of the Book of Offices, etc., of the same year, published in the same place, are hereby established as standard books, with the exception of errors evidently typographical—the correction of which errors is confided to such person or persons as the Bishop or standing committee may appoint for superintending any publication.

Canon IV.—Making an addition to the 1st Canon of 1795, concerning Episcopal Visitation.

It shall be the duty of every Bishop of this Church to keep a register of his proceedings at every visitation of his diocese, and particularly of the names and age of the persons confirmed, and to report a copy of such register to the House of Bishops, at every triennial meeting of the General Convention of this Church, in order that the same may be communicated to the House of Clerical and Lay Deputies, to be preserved among the general records of the Church.

The above Canons passed in Convention, September, 1801.

By Order of the House of Bishops:
WILLIAM WHITE, D.D., Presiding Bishop.

By Order of the House of Clerical and Lay Deputies:
ABRAHAM BEACH, D.D., President.

List of the Clergy

OF THE

PROTESTANT EPISCOPAL CHURCH,

In the different States, 1801.

Delivered in and published agreeably to the 16th Canon of 1789.

NEW HAMPSHIRE.

Rev. Joseph Willard, rector of St. John's church, Portsmouth.
Rev. Robert H. Fowle, rector of —— church, Holdernesse.
Rev. Daniel Barber, Rector of —— church, Clermont.

The list from this State is the same as in the Journal of the last Convention, no new list having been delivered in.

MASSACHUSETTS.

The Right Rev. Edward Bass, D.D., Bishop.
Rev. William Willard Wheeler, rector of St. Michael's church, Scituate, and St. Peter's, Marshfield.
Rev. Nathaniel Fisher, rector of St Peter's church, Salem.
Rev. Samuel Parker, D.D., Rector of Trinity church, Boston.
Rev. John Sylvester J. Gardner, Assistant Minister of Trinity church, Boston.
Rev. Samuel Haskill, rector of Christ church, Boston.
Rev. Wm. Montague, rector of St. Paul's church, Deedham, and —— Quincy.
Rev. William Harris, rector of St. Michael's church, Marblehead.
Rev. James Bowers, deacon, Pittston.

RHODE ISLAND.

Rev. John Usher, rector of St. Michael's church, Bristol.
Rev. Abraham Lynsen Clarke, Assistant Minister of St. Michael's church, Bristol.
Rev. Theodore Dehon, rector of Trinity church, Newport.

Rev. Abraham Brunson, Deacon, Assistant Minister of Trinity church, Newport.
Rev. Nathaniel Bowen, Deacon, Providence.

CONNECTICUT.

The Right Rev. Abraham Jarvis, D.D., Bishop.
Rev. Jeremiah Leaming, residing at New Haven.
Rev. John Bowden, D.D., Principal of the Episcopal Academy, Cheshire.
Rev. Richard Mansfield, D.D., Rector of Christ Church at Derby, and of the Churches of Oxford and Great Hill.
Rev. Bela Hubbard, D.D., Trinity church, New Haven, and Christ church. West Haven.
Rev. John Tyler, rector of Christ church, Norwich.
Rev. Daniel Fogg, rector of —— church, Pomfret.
Rev. Philo Shelton, rector of Trinity church, Fairfield, St. John's, Stratfield, and —— church in Weston.
Rev. Ashbel Baldwin, rector of Christ church, Stratford, and Trinity church, Trumbul.
Rev. Chauncey Prindle, rector of Christ church, Watertown, and St. Peter's, Plymouth.
Rev. Reuben Ives, rector of St. Peter's church, Cheshire, and the churches of Hamden and Southington.
Rev. Tillotson Bronson, rector of St. John's church, Waterbury, and —— church, Salem.
Rev. Truman Marsh, rector of —— church, Litchfield.
Rev. Ambrose Todd, rector of St. Panl's church, Huntingdon.
Rev. Daniel Burhans, rector of Trinity church, Newtown, and —— church, Brookfield.
Rev. David Butler, rector of Christ church, Reading, and the churches of Danbury and Ridgefield.
Rev. Alexander V. Griswold, rector of St. Matthew's church, Bristol, St. Mark's, Harwinston, and —— church, Norfield.
Rev. Solomon Blakslee, rector of St. Stephen's church, East Haddam.
Rev. Charles Seabury, rector of St. James's church, New London.
Rev. Smith Miles, rector of the churches at Chatham & Middle Haddam.
Rev. Evan Rogers, rector of St. Peter's, Hebron, and —— church, Marlborough.
Rev. Joseph Warren, rector of Christ church, Middletown.
Rev. William Green, residing in New London.
Rev. Calvin White, Rector of St. John's, Stamford, and —— church, Horseneck.
Rev. Menzies Rayner, rector of —— church, Hartford.
Rev. Jasper D. Jones, Deacon.
Rev. Nathan B. Burges, Deacon, officiating at Guilford and North Bristol.
Rev. Henry Whitlock, Deacon, officiating at Norwalk and Dilton.
Rev. Bethuel Judd, Deacon, officiating at Woodbury and Roxbury.

NEW YORK.

The Right Rev. Benjamin Moore, D.D., Bishop.
Rev. Abraham Beach, D.D., Rev. John Henry Hobart, Rev. Cave Jones; Assistant Ministers of Trinity church, New York.
Rev. Thomas Ellison, rector of St. Peter's church, Albany.
Rev. Richard C. Moore, rector of St. Andrew's church, Staten Island.
Rev. Henry Van Dyke, rector of St. James's church, Newtown.
Rev. Seth Hart, rector of St. George's church, Hempstead.

Rev. Elijah D. Rattoone, rector of Grace church, Jamaica, and St. George's, Flushing.
Rev. Isaac Wilkins, rector of St. Peter's church, West Chester, and St. Paul's church, East Chester.
Rev. Theodosius Bartow, rector of Trinity church, New Rochelle.
Rev. John Ireland, rector of St. Anne's church, Brooklyn.
Rev. Elias Cooper, rector of St. John's church, Yonkers.
Rev. Frederick Van Horne, rector of St. Andrew's church, Orange co.
Rev. Robert G. Wetmore, rector of St. George's church, Schenectady, and Christ church, Duanesborough.
Rev. John Urquhart, rector of St. John's church, Johnstown, and —— church, Fort Hunter.
Rev. Philander Chase, rector of Christ church, Poughkeepsie, and Trinity church, Fishkill.
Rev. Gamaliel Thatcher, rector of Christ church, Balstown, and other churches.
Rev. Daniel Nash, Rector of the churches in Otsego.
Rev. Amos Pardee, rector of —— church, Hampton.
The Right Rev. Bishop Provoost, Rev. William Smith, D.D., Rev. Samuel Nesbitt, residing in New York.

NEW JERSEY.

Rev. Uzal Ogden, D.D., rector of Trinity church, Newark.
Rev. Charles H. Wharton, D.D., rector of St. Mary's church, Burlington.
Rev. Henry Waddell, rector of St. Michael's church, Trenton.
Rev. John Croes, rector of Christ church, New Brunswick.
Rev. Andrew Fowler, rector of —— church, Middletown.
Rev. Frederick Beasley, Deacon, St. John's church, Elizabethtown.
Rev. — Cotten, residing at present in New Brunswick.

PENNSYLVANIA.

The Right Rev. William White, D.D., Bishop.
Rev. William Smith, D.D.
Rev. Samuel Magaw, D.D., rector of St. Paul's church, in the city of Philadelphia.
Rev. John Andrews, D.D., Vice-Provost of the University of Pennsylvania.
Rev. Robert Blackwell, D.D., Assistant Minister of Christ Church and St. Peter's, in the city of Philadelphia.
Rev. Joseph Hutchins, D.D.
Rev. John Campbell, rector of the Episcopal churches of York and Huntingdon.
Rev. Slator Clay, rector of St. David's, Radnor; St. Peter's in the Valley, and St. James's, Perkiomen.
Rev. Joseph Clarkson, rector of St. James's, Lancaster, —— church, Pequea, and —— church, Carnarvon.
Rev. Robert Ayres, rector of Emanuel church, Washington county, and St. Peter's church, Fayette county.
Rev. Francis Reno, Westmoreland county.
Rev. Joseph Turner, rector of St. Paul's church, Chester, and St. Martin's, Marcus Hook.
Rev. Caleb Hopkins, rector of Christ church, Derry Township, and Christ church, Turbut township, Northumberland county.
Rev. Thomas Davis, Washington county.

Rev. James Abercrombie, Assistant Minister of Christ church and St. Peter's, in the city of Philadelphia.

Rev. Absalom Jones (a black man), Deacon in the African church of St. Thomas's, Philadelphia.

DELAWARE.

The Rev. Robert Clay, Emanuel church, New Castle.
Rev. William Pryce, Trinity church, Wilmington.
Rev. Joshua Reese, St. Anne's church, Middletown.
Rev. James Wiltbank, St. George's church, Sussex county.

MARYLAND.

The Right Rev. Thomas J. Claggett, D.D., Bishop.
Rev. Charles Smoot, rector of William and Mary parish, St. Mary's.
Rev. Henry Lyon Davis, King and Queen parish, St. Mary's county.
Rev. — Brockenbury, Deacon, William and Mary parish, Charles county.
Rev. John I. Sayrs, Durham parish, Charles county.
Rev. George Ralph, Trinity parish, Charles county.
Rev. Edward Gant, Jun., Christ church, Calvert.
Rev. Joseph Messenger, St. John's, Prince George's county.
Rev. Walter D. Addison, residing in Prince George's.
Rev. Andrew M'Cormick, Washington, Prince George's county.
Rev. John W. Compton, St. James', Anne Arundel.
Rev. Ralph Higinbothom, St. Anne's, Anne Arundel.
Rev. Nicholas W. Lane, All Hallows, Anne Arundel.
Rev Owen F. Magrath, residing in Annapolis, Anne Arundel.
Rev. Henry Moscrop, Westminster, Anne Arundel.
Rev. William Swan, St. Margaret's, Anne Arundel.
Rev. Thomas Read, Prince George's, Montgomery.(1)
Rev. Edward Gantt, sen., residing at Georgetown, Montgomery.
Rev. Thomas Scott, St. Peter's, Montgomery.
Rev. George Bower, rector of All Saints, Frederick.
Rev. Joseph G. J. Bend, associate rector of St. Paul's, Baltimore.(1)
Rev. John Ireland, associate rector of St. Paul's, Baltimore.
Rev. John Coleman, St. Thomas's, Baltimore.(1)
Rev. Francis Barclay, residing in Baltimore.
Rev. John Allen, St. George's, Harford.
Rev. James Jones Wilmer, St. John's, Harford.
Rev. William Duke, residing in Cecil county.
Rev. Colin Ferguson, D.D., residing in Kent county.
Rev Archibald Walker, D.D., residing in Kent county.
Rev. George Dashiell, Chester and St. Paul's, Kent county.
Rev. Samuel Keene, D.D., St. Luke's, Queen Anne's.
Rev. Samuel Keene, Jun., residing in St. Luke's, Queen Anne's.
Rev. Elisha Rigg, St. Paul's, Queen Anne's.(1)
Rev. Joseph Jackson, St. Peter's, Talbot.
Rev. James Kemp, Great Choptank, Dorchester.
Rev. William Price, Somerset, Somerset.
Rev. Samuel Sloan, residing in Somerset.
Rev. David Ball, All Hallows, Worcester.

(1) Members of the Standing Committee this year.

VIBGINIA.

The Right Rev. James Madison, D.D., Bishop.
Rev. Charles O'Neill, rector of ——, Amherst.

Rev. Alexander Hay, rector of Antrim parish.
Rev. Samuel Gray, Botetourt parish.
Rev. Hugh Corrans Boggs, rector of Berkley parish.
Rev. Levi Heath, Berkley.
Rev. Benjamin Brown, rector of Brisland parish.
Rev. Andrew Syme, rector of Bristol parish.
Rev. John Cameron, D.D., rector of ——
Rev. Alexander M'Farland, rector of Brunswick parish.
Rev. John Bracken, D.D., rector of Bruton parish.
Rev. John Camm, rector of Charles parish.
Rev. Henry Heffernam, Christ church.
Rev. James Elliott, rector of Cople parish.
Rev. Needler Robinson, rector of Dale parish.
Rev. Spence Grayson, rector of Dettingen parish.
Rev. Jesse Carter, rector of Drysdale parish.
Rev. Daniel M'Naughton, Christ church.
Rev. James Whitehead, rector of Elizabeth river parish.
Rev. Thomas Davis, Fairfax parish.
Rev. Alexander Balmain, rector of Frederick parish.
Rev. John O'Weylie, Lecturer, Frederick.
Rev. Matthew Maury, rector of Fredericksville parish.
Rev. John Hooker Reynolds, Hardy.
Rev. John Buchanan, D.D., rector of Henrico parish.
Rev. Samuel S. M'Croskey, D.D., rector of Hungars parish.
Rev. John Thompson, rector of Leeds parish.
Rev. Charles Crawford, rector of Lexington parish.
Rev. William Crawford, Lexington parish.
Rev. James Dickinson, Littleton.
Rev. George Young, Lunenburg.
Rev. Anthony Walke, rector of Lynhaven parish.
Rev. Armistead Smith, Matthews.
Rev. John Dunn, Manchester.
Rev. James Leach, Mecklenberg.
Rev. William Hubard, rector of Newport parish.
Rev. Jacob Keeling, Nansemond.
Rev. Robert Buchan, rector of Overwharton parish.
Rev. Arthur Emerson, rector of Portsmouth parish.
Rev. John Brunskill, rector of Raleigh parish.
Rev. Alexander Lundie, rector of St. Andrew's parish.
Rev. James Stevenson, rector of St. George's parish.
Rev. Charles Hopkins, rector of St. James, Northam parish.
Rev. James Price, rector of St. John's parish.
Rev. Thomas Hughes, rector of St. David's.
Rev. Archibald Dick, rector of St. Margaret's parish.
Rev. John Woodville, St. Mark's parish.
Rev. Abner Waugh, rector of St. Mary's parish.
Rev. John Parsons, ——.
Rev. John Seward, St. Stephen's parish.
Rev. John Hyde Saunders, rector of Southam parish.
Rev. Samuel Butler, rector of Southwark parish.
Rev. Lee Massey, rector of Truro parish.
Rev. Samuel Chapin, rector of Westover parish.
Rev. James Evans, Yorkhampton.
Rev. John C. Brockenboroug, Washington.

Rev. Duncan M'Naughton, Wicomico.
Rev. Joseph Wilson:
Rev. Stephen Thomson:
Rev. Cornelius Carvert—Cures not known.

SOUTH CAROLINA.

The Right Rev. Robert Smith, D.D., Bishop.
Rev. Thomas Frost, St. Philip's, Charleston.
Rev. Henry Purcell, D.D., St. Michael's, Charleston.
Rev. Edward Jenkins, St. Michael's, Charleston.
Rev. Milwood Pogson, St. James's, Goose Creek, St. George's, Dorchester.
Rev. Peter M. Parker, St. John's, Berkley.
Rev. John Thompson, St. Thomas's.
Rev. Thomas Mills, St. Andrew's, James' Island, St. Andrew's, Main.
Rev. Edmund Matthews, St. John's, Edisto.
Rev. William Nixon, St. Bartholomew's.
Rev. Thomas D. Bladen, St. James', Santee
Rev. George H. Spierin, Prince George's.
Rev. James Connor, St. Stephen's.
Rev. John O'Donnel, All Saints.
Rev. Hugh Frazier, Prince Frederick's.
Residents in the State without cures:
Rev. Thomas Gates, D.D.
Rev. Mr. M'Culley, Master of an Academy, Beaufort.
Rev. Mr. Blackwall.
Rev. Mr. Best, Master of an Academy, Charleston.

The list from this State is the same as in the Journal of the last Convention, no new list having been delivered in.

JOURNAL OF THE PROCEEDINGS

OF THE

BISHOPS, CLERGY, AND LAITY

OF THE

Protestant Episcopal Church

IN

THE UNITED STATES OF AMERICA,

IN

A CONVENTION

HELD IN

THE CITY OF NEW YORK, FROM TUESDAY, SEPTEMBER 11TH, TO TUESDAY, SEPTEMBER 18TH, 1804.

LIST OF THE MEMBERS OF THE HOUSE OF CLERICAL AND LAY DEPUTIES.

FROM THE STATE OF MASSACHUSETTS

Rev. Samuel Parker, D.D.
Rev. Samuel Haskell.

FROM THE STATE OF CONNECTICUT.

Rev. Ashbel Baldwin.
Rev. Philo Shelton.
Rev. Tillotson Bronson.
Rev. Daniel Burhans.
Nathan Smith, Esq.
Andrew Hilliar, Esq.

FROM THE STATE OF NEW YORK.

Rev. Abraham Beach, D.D.
Rev. Isaac Wilkins.
Rev. William Harris.
Rev. John Henry Hobart.
William Ogden, Esq.

FROM THE STATE OF NEW JERSEY.

Rev. Uzal Ogden, D.D.
Rev. John Croes.
Rev. Samuel Lilly.
Colonel Samuel Ogden.

FROM THE STATE OF PENNSYLVANIA.

Rev. Robert Blackwell, D.D.
Rev. Joseph Clarkson.
Thomas Cumpston, Esq.
Gen. Francis Gurney.
Mr. Levi Bull.

FROM THE STATE OF DELAWARE.

Rev. William Pryce.

FROM THE STATE OF MARYLAND.

Rev. Joseph G. J. Bend, D.D.
Rev. James Kemp, D.D.
Rev. John Coleman.
Rev. Joseph Jackson.
William Helmsley, Jun., Esq.
Richard Key Heath, Esq.

JOURNAL

OF THE

House of Clerical and Lay Deputies.

NEW YORK, September 11, 1804.

This being the day appointed for the meeting of the General Convention of the Protestant Episcopal Church in the United States of America, several Clerical and Lay Deputies attended at 10 o'clock, A.M., in Trinity Church, but not being a quorum, adjourned to meet at 5 o'clock, P.M., in a room of the building belonging to the Episcopal Charity School.

Five o'clock, P.M.

A quorum of the house appearing, they proceeded to the election, by ballot, of a President and Secretary, when the Rev. Dr. Abraham Beach was duly chosen President, and the Rev. John H. Hobart, Secretary.

The testimonials of the Clerical and Lay Delegates were then read and approved of, and the following gentlemen took their seats in the house.

From Massachusetts, the Rev. Dr. Samuel Parker, Rev. Samuel Haskell. From Connecticut, the Rev. Ashbel Baldwin, Rev. Philo Shelton, Rev. Tillotson Bronson, Rev. Daniel Burhans. From New York, Rev. Dr. Abraham Beach, Rev. Isaac Wilkins, Rev. William Harris, Rev. John H. Hobart. From New Jersey, Rev. Dr. Uzal Ogden, Rev. Samuel Lilly, Colonel Samuel Ogden. From Delaware, Rev.

William Pryce. From Maryland, Rev. Dr. James Kemp, Rev. Joseph Jackson, Richard Key Heath, Esq.

The house not judging it expedient to do business the first day of the Session, adjourned to meet to-morrow morning at 9 o'clock.

WEDNESDAY, September 12, 1804, 9 o'clock, A.M.

The house met.

The testimonials of the Clerical and Lay Deputies from the State of Pennsylvania were read and approved of. And General Francis Gurney, Thomas Cumpston, Esq., and Mr. Levi Bull, Lay deputies from the State of Pennsylvania; the Rev. John Croes, Clerical deputy from New Jersey; the Rev. Joseph G. J. Bend, D.D., Clerical deputy, and William Helmsley, Jun., Esq., Lay deputy from the State of Maryland; and Nathan Smith, Esq., Lay deputy from the State of Connecticut, appeared and took their seats in the house.

A message was sent to the House of Bishops, informing them that this house was organized, and ready to proceed to business.

The House of Bishops returned for answer, that they also were organized, and ready to proceed to business.

The rules of order established by the House of Clerical and Lay Deputies of the Convention of 1792 and the following Conventions, were adopted as the rules of order of this house, with the following addition to the 6th rule—" unless with the consent of two-thirds of the house."

The record of the appointment of the Rev. Samuel Parker to the office of Bishop of the Protestant Episcopal Church in the State of Massachusetts, and also the requisite testimony from the Convention of the Church in that State, were presented and read.

Whereupon it was unanimously Resolved,—That the house do sign, in favour of the Rev. Dr. Parker, the testimony required by the Canons in the election of a Bishop. The testimony was accordingly signed, and, together with the testimony from the Convention of the Church in Massachusetts, was laid before the House of Bishops.

On motion, Resolved,—That the hours of meeting each day shall be from 9 o'clock, A.M., to three o'clock P.M., and notice of this resolution was transmitted to the House of Bishops.

A message was received from the House of Bishops, informing this house that they had approved the testimonies in favour of the Rev. Dr. Parker, Bishop elect of this Church in the State of Massachusetts, and that they had appointed Friday morning for his consecration. They also informed this house, than they concurred in the resolution as to the hours of meeting.

The house then attended divine service in Trinity Church, where prayers were read by the Right Rev. Bishop Claggett, and a Sermon on the occasion of the meeting of the Convention delivered by the Right Rev. Bishop Moore.

The house having returned after divine service to their place of sitting,

On motion, it was unanimously Resolved,—That the thanks of the Convention be returned to the Right Rev. Bishop Moore, for his Sermon preached before the Convention this day, and that he be requested to furnish a copy for publication. The House of Bishops concurred in the above resolution, and informed this house that the Right Rev. Bishop Moore had consented to furnish a copy of his Sermon for the purpose aforesaid.

The house then took up and agreed to the alteration proposed at the last General Convention, in the 1st article of the General Constitution, in the words following, viz.

"ART. I. There shall be a General Convention of the Protestant Episcopal Church in the United States of America, on the third Tuesday in May, 1808, and in every third year," etc., as before.

Information of the above ratification of the proposed alteration in the Constitution was sent to the House of Bishops, who returned for answer that they concurred in the same.

The following resolution was moved and seconded, viz.

Resolved,—That a Committee be appointed to enquire, whether any and what alterations of, or additions to, the Canons of the Church are necessary, and to report.

The question being taken on the above resolution, it was determined in the negative.

The house adjourned.

THURSDAY, Sept. 13, 1804, 9 o'clock, A.M.

The house met, and prayers were read by the Secretary as Chaplain to the house.

The Rev. Dr. Robert Blackwell and Rev. Joseph Clarkson, Clerical deputies from the State of Pennsylvania; Andrew Hillier, Esq., a Lay deputy from the State of Connecticut; and William Ogden, Esq., a Lay deputy from the State of New York, appeared and took their seats in the house.

On motion, Resolved,—That a Committee be appointed to prepare an Office of induction into the rectorship of parishes. The following members were appointed a Committee: Rev. Dr. Parker, Rev. Mr. Baldwin, Rev. Mr. Harris, Rev. Dr. Ogden, Rev. Dr. Blackwell, Rev. Mr. Price, Rev. Dr. Bend.

A proposed Canon concerning dioceses was taken up and considered, and the question being taken thereon, it was determined in the negative.

The following proposed Canons, viz., "A Canon concerning Ministers moving from one diocese or State to another;" a Canon making an addition to the 17th Canon of 1789, entitled, "Notice to be given of the induction and dismission of Ministers;" a Canon altering the 7th Canon of 1795; and a Canon repealing the 2d Canon of 1801, which limits the operation of the 4th Canon of 1795; were passed, and sent to the House of Bishops for their concurrence.

The house adjourned.

FRIDAY, Sept. 14, 1804, 9 o'clock, A.M.

The house met, and prayers were read by the Secretary, as Chaplain to the house.

The Committee appointed to prepare an Office of induction reported an Office; and the house, after having entered on the consideration of the same, proceeded to attend divine service in Trinity Church, on the occasion of the consecration of the Rev. Dr. Parker, Bishop elect of the Protestant Episcopal Church in the State of Massachusetts.

Prayers were read by the Rev. Dr. Bend, and a Sermon delivered by the Right Rev. Bishop White; who, assisted by the Right Rev. Bishop Claggett, of Maryland, the Right Rev. Bishop Jarvis, of Connecticut, and the Right Rev.

Bishop Moore, of New York, performed the Office of consecration.

After divine service, the house returned to their place of sitting.

On motion, it was unanimously Resolved,—That the thanks of this house be returned to the Right Rev. Bishop White, for the Sermon delivered at the consecration of the Rev. Dr. Parker, and that he be requested to furnish a copy for publication.

The above resolution was sent to the House of Bishops, who returned it with their concurrence; and informed the house, that the Right Rev. Bishop White had consented to furnish a copy of his Sermon for publication.

The house resumed the consideration of the Office of induction, and having made progress in the same, adjourned.

SATURDAY, Sept. 15, 1804, 9 o'clock, A.M.

The House met, and prayers were read by the Secretary, as Chaplain to the house.

The house finished the consideration of the Office of induction; and having agreed to the same, sent it to the House of Bishops for their concurrence.

A message was received from the House of Bishops, informing this house that they proposed a substitute to the Canon concerning Ministers moving from one diocese or State to another; that they did not concur in the Canon altering the 7th Canon of 1795; and that they proposed a substitute to the Canon repealing the 2d Canon of 1801, which limits the operation of the 4th Canon of 1795.

The house agreed to the substitute proposed by the House of Bishops, to the Canon concerning Ministers moving from one diocese to another, with an amendment, which was sent to the House of Bishops, and adopted by them.

The house took up the consideration of the substitute proposed by the House of Bishops to the Canon repealing the 2d Canon of 1801, which limits the operation of the 4th Canon of 1795; and the question being taken on agreeing to the same, it was determined in the negative.

A memorial was presented from the Vestry of Trinity Church, Newark, New Jersey, stating that a very unhappy difference, which appears to threaten the very existence of their Church, subsists between the Rector and the congregation of said Church, and praying the Convention to devise some means for their relief.

The above memorial was referred to the following Committee, to report thereon. The Rev. Dr. Blackwell, Rev. Mr. Haskell, Rev. Mr. Brunson, Rev. Mr. Hobart, Rev. Mr. Price, Rev. Dr. Kemp, William Ogden, Thomas Cumpston and Richard K. Heath, Esqrs.

The following Canons, viz., a Canon additional to the 6th Canon of 1795, and a Canon limiting the operation of the 6th Canon of 1795, were sent from the House of Bishops. The first Canon was read and concurred in by this house.

The office of induction was received from the House of Bishops with amendments, which were adopted by this house.

Leave of absence was granted to the Rev. Mr. Lilly and Andrew Hilliar and Nathan Smith, Esqrs., during the remainder of the Session.

A proposed Canon concerning Lay Readers was adopted, and sent to the House of Bishops, who returned it with their concurrence.

A proposed Canon was adopted, entitled "A Canon providing for an accurate view of the state of the Church from time to time," and sent to the House of Bishops for their concurrence.

The house adjourned.

MONDAY, Sept. 17, 1804, 9 o'clock, A.M.

The house met.

Prayers were read by the Secretary, as Chaplain to the house.

The Committee appointed on the memorial from Trinity Church, Newark, New Jersey, made report.

On motion, the report was recommitted to the same Committee.

The house adopted a proposed substitute to the Canon sent from the House of Bishops, limiting the operation of the 6th Canon of 1795, and sent it to the House of Bishops for their concurrence.

Leave of absence for the remainder of the Session was granted to Richard K. Heath, Esq.

A proposed Canon was adopted concerning candidates coming from places within the United States, in which the Constitution of the Church has not been acceded to. A proposed Canon was also adopted, respecting the dissolution of all pastoral connection between Ministers and their congregations.

The above Canons were sent to the House of Bishops.

The following message was received from the House of Bishops:

"The House of Bishops communicate to the House of Clerical and Lay Deputies, the following extract from their Journal.

'The papers presented to this house by the President, from the Rev. Ammi Rogers, of Connecticut, requesting their attention to sundry matters affecting his standing in the Church and his private character, were taken into consideration. Whereupon,

'Resolved,—That there be declared to the House of Clerical and Lay Deputies, the desire of the House of Bishops, that if any members of that house possess information respecting the conduct of said Ammi Rogers, in the matters brought before the House of Bishops, which matters will be communicated by the Bishops to any members of the house aforesaid who may desire it, such members will lay before the House of Bishops the information possessed by them at 12 o'clock.'"

Whereupon the house Resolved,—That any members who may have any thing to communicaté to the House of Bishops, on the subject of the above message, have leave to withdraw at the hour mentioned.

The House of Bishops also informed this house that they had concurred in the following Canons, viz.: A Canon providing for an accurate view of the state of the Church from time to time; and the proposed substitute to the Canon limiting the operation of the 6th Canon of 1795; and the Canon concerning candidates coming from places within the United States which have not acceded to the Constitution of the Church; and that they proposed to connect the Canon respecting the dissolution of all pastoral connection between Ministers and their congregations, with the Canon making an addition to the 17th Canon of 1789; in which proposition the house concurred.

A proposed Canon respecting differences between Ministers and their congregations was adopted, and sent to the House of Bishops for their concurrence.

A Canon was received from the House of Bishops, entitled,

"Notice to be given of the election of Ministers," which was agreed to, with amendments, and the change of the title to "Canon concerning the election and induction of Ministers into parishes or churches."

A proposed Canon concerning Clergymen ordained by foreign Bishops, and desirous of settling in this Church, was adopted, and sent to the House of Bishops for their concurrence. On motion, the Committee appointed at the last Convention to report such additional hymns as they may think are adapted to Christian worship, was discharged.

The house adjourned.

TUESDAY, September 18, 1804, 9 o'clock, A.M.

The house met, and prayers were read by the Secretary, as Chaplain to the house.

A message was received from the House of Bishops, stating that they disagreed to the amendments to the Canon concerning the election and induction of Ministers into parishes or churches, and request a conference on the subject; that they had negatived the Canon concerning Clergymen ordained by foreign Bishops, and that they had passed the Canon respecting differences between Ministers and their congregations, with amendments.

The house agreed to the amendments of the House of Bishops to the last-mentioned Canon, and to the conference requested.

Resolved,—That the Rev. Dr. Blackwell, Rev. Dr. Kemp, and Rev. Mr. Hobart, be a Committee to manage the conference on the part of this house; and that, with the concurrence of the House of Bishops, they make the proposed Canon concerning foreign clergymen a subject of the conference.

The Committee withdrew, and the Rev. Dr. Bend was requested to officiate in the Secretary's stead, during his absence.

The Committee on the Memorial of Trinity Church, Newark, made the following report:

"The Committee on the Memorial of the Vestry of Trinity Church, Newark, whose report was yesterday recommitted to them, made report, that as this Convention have passed a Canon providing for such cases as that of the Vestry of said Church, the Committee think it unnecessary that this house should go into an investigation of the affair."

This report was agreed to by the house.

Resolved,—That 1000 copies of the Journals, 1000 copies of the Office of induction, and 1000 copies of each of the Sermons preached before the Convention, be published.

The President, Secretary, and the Rev. Mr. Harris were appointed a Committee, in conjunction with the Right Rev. Bishop Moore, to publish the Journals. The House of Bishops concurred in the appointment of this Committee.

The house took into consideration the place at which the next meeting of the General Convention should be held, and unanimously determined that the meeting should be at Baltimore.

It was moved and seconded, that those parts of the Minutes which respect the petition from Trinity Church, Newark, be expunged.

Resolved unanimously,—That they be not expunged.

Resolved,—That the Right Rev. Bishop Parker be requested to preach a Sermon at the opening of the next General Convention.

The Committee of Conference returned, and reported that the House of Bishops had receded from their negative to the amendment proposed by this house to the Canon concerning the election and induction of Ministers into parishes or churches, and proposed another amendment, which amendment was agreed to by this house; and also that they receded from their negative to the Canon concerning Clergymen ordained by foreign Bishops, and proposed a substitute, which was agreed to by this house.

A message was received from the House of Bishops, informing that they had established a course of study for candidates for Orders, which will be published with their Journal.

A proposed Canon, concerning the studies of candidates for Orders, was adopted, and sent to the House of Bishops for their concurrence.

A proposed Canon, concerning subscription to the Articles of the Church, was negatived, under the impression that a sufficient subscription to the Articles is already required by the 7th Article of the Constitution.

A proposed Canon, concerning candidates who may be refused orders, was adopted, and sent to the House of Bishops for their concurrence.

On motion, Resolved,—That it be made known to the different State Conventions, that it is proposed in the next General Convention to consider and determine on the following proposed alteration to the General Constitution of the Church, viz., that in Art. III., the words "unless adhered to by four-fifths of the other house," be struck out.

The above resolution was sent to the House of Bishops.

A resolution was adopted concerning the arrangement and publication of the Constitution and all the Canons of the Church, and sent to the House of Bishops for their concurrence.

A message was received from the House of Bishops, that they had agreed to the resolution respecting a proposed alteration in the Constitution; to the Canon concerning candidates who may be refused Orders; to the resolutions concerning printing the Journals, Office of induction, and Sermons; and that they proposed an amendment to the resolution concerning the arrangement and publication of the Constitution and all the Canons of the Church—which amendment was agreed to, and the resolution passed as follows, viz.

Resolved,—That the Committee appointed to publish the Journals be authorised to publish the Constitution and all the Canons of the Church in the order of their enaction, making a reference by asterisk, at the end of every Canon, to a note pointing out the various other Canons which refer to the subject of that particular Canon.

The Constitution and Canons published by the above Committee, and the Office of induction, are to be considered as authorised and standard copies.

The House of Bishops also informed this house that they had negatived the Canon concerning the studies of candidates for Orders.

The following message was also received from the House of Bishops, viz.

"The House of Bishops propose to the House of Clerical and Lay Deputies, that the adjournment of the Convention be accompanied by prayer, in the presence of the two houses —the presiding Bishop to officiate."

The house unanimously concurred in the above resolution.

On motion, Resolved,—That the thanks of this house be returned to the President and Secretary for their services.

The House of Bishops then attended in the chamber of the House of Clerical and Lay Deputies, when prayers were read by the Right Rev. Bishop White, as presiding Bishop.

The house rose.

Signed by order of the House of Clerical and Lay Deputies,

ABRAHAM BEACH, President.

John Henry Hobart, Secretary.

JOURNAL

OF THE

House of Bishops.

NEW YORK, Sept. 11, 1804.

This being the day appointed for the Meeting of the General Convention of the Protestant Episcopal Church in the United States of America, the Right Rev. Bishop Moore attended in Trinity Church; no other member of this house appearing, adjourned till to-morrow, at 9 o'clock A.M., to meet in the house of the Episcopal Charity School.

WEDNESDAY, Sept. 12, 1804, 9 o'clock, A.M.

The house met. Present, the Right Rev. Bishop White, of Pennsylvania; the Right Rev. Bishop Claggett, of Maryland; and the Right Rev. Bishop Moore, of New York.

Resolved,—That it be a standing rule of this house, that the senior Bishop present at the opening of any Convention, shall preside.

The Right Rev. Bishop White, in consequence, took his seat as presiding Bishop.

The Rev. Cave Jones was appointed Secretary to this house.

The Right Rev. Bishop Jarvis, of Connecticut, appeared and took his seat.

This house received a message from the House of Clerical

and Lay Deputies, informing them that they were organized, and ready to proceed to business.

This house returned information that they were also ready for the same.

A resolution, communicated from the House of Clerical and Lay Deputies, was agreed to by this house, "That the hours of meeting, during the Session, shall be from 9 o'clock A.M., to 3 o'clock P.M."

This house received from the House of Clerical and Lay Deputies, the requisite testimonials of the Rev. Dr. Parker, Bishop elect of the State of Massachusetts.

A message was transmitted to the said house, informing that the House of Bishops approve of the said testimonials, and will proceed to the consecration of Dr. Parker on Friday next.

Adjourned, to attend divine service at Trinity Church.

The Right Rev. Bishop Claggett performed service, and the Right Rev. Bishop Moore preached a Sermon adapted to the occasion of the meeting of this Convention.

After which the house again met.

A message was received from the House of Clerical and Lay Deputies, informing that a resolution had passed that house, "That the thanks of the Convention be presented to the Right Rev. Bishop Moore for his Sermon preached before them this morning, and that he be requested to furnish a copy for publication."

This house concurred in the said resolution, and the Right Rev. Bishop Moore consented to comply with their request.

This house concurred in a resolution received from the House of Clerical and Lay Deputies, ratifying the alteration of the first Article of the Constitution, as proposed at the last General Convention.

The house then adjourned.

THURSDAY, Sept. 13, 1804, 9 o'clock, A.M.

Present as yesterday

This house came to a resolution to attend prayers, during the Session, in the chamber of the House of Clerical and Lay Deputies. The house attended accordingly.

The following proposed Canons were presented from the House of Clerical and Lay Deputies, viz., a Canon concerning ministers removing from one diocese or State to another; a Canon making an addition to the 17th Canon of 1789; a Canon repealing the 2d Canon of 1801, which limits the operation of the 4th Canon of 1795; a Canon altering the 7th Canon of 1795.

The proposed Canon, entitled "A Canon concerning Ministers removing from one diocese or State to another," was taken into consideration, and a substitute was agreed to, and sent to the House of Clerical and Lay Deputies.

The house then adjourned.

FRIDAY, Sept. 4, 1804, 9 o'clock, A.M.

Present as yesterday.

A message was received from the House of Clerical and Lay Deputies, informing that the said house was ready to attend the consecration of the Rev. Dr. Parker, when this house shall see proper.

This house informed the House of Clerical and Lay Deputies, that they were ready to proceed immediately to the consecration.

The house then adjourned for the above purpose.

The Rev. Dr. Bend read prayers, and the Right Rev. Bishop White delivered a Sermon, and, as presiding Bishop, performed the Consecration service, assisted by the other Bishops present.

The house again met.

A message was received from the House of Clerical and Lay Deputies, informing that the said house had come to a resolution, "That the thanks of the Convention be presented to the Right Rev. Bishop White for his Sermon preached before them this day, at the consecration of the Rev. Dr. Parker, and that he be requested to furnish a copy for publication."

This house concurred in the above resolution; and Bishop White acceded to the request.

The proposed Canon, entitled "A Canon repealing the 2d Canon of 1801, which limits the operation of the 4th Canon of 1795," was returned to the House of Clerical and Lay Deputies, with a substitute.

A memorial was laid on the table by the President, from the Rev. Ammi Rogers, accompanied with sundry documents and a letter, requesting that a day may be appointed for the consideration of the points therein stated.

Monday next was assigned for the above purpose, and notice thereof was given to Mr. Rogers.

The house adjourned.

SATURDAY, Sept. 15, 1804, 9 o'clock, A.M.

The house met. Present as yesterday.

The Right Rev. Dr. Parker, who was yesterday consecrated, in Trinity Church, Bishop of this Church in the State of Massachusetts, took his seat in this house.

A Canon was passed, entitled, "A Canon limiting the operation of the 6th Canon of 1795," and was sent to the House of Clerical and Lay Deputies.

A proposed Office was presented from the House of Clerical and Lay Deputies, entitled "An Office of induction."

A proposed Canon was adopted by this house, and sent to the House of Clerical and Lay Deputies, entitled, "A Canon additional to the 6th Canon of 1795."

The substitute to the Canon, entitled "Concerning Ministers moving from one diocese or State to another," which was sent from this house to the House of Clerical and Lay Deputies, was returned from said house, with an amendment, which was adopted by this house.

The proposed office, entitled "An Office of induction," etc., was returned to the House of Clerical and Lay Deputies, with amendments.

The Canon which originated in this house, entitled "A Canon additional to the 6th Canon of 1795," was returned from the House of Clerical and Lay Deputies, with a message that it had passed that house.

The proposed substitute, which was sent by this house to the House of Clerical and Lay Deputies, for the proposed Canon, entitled "A Canon repealing the 2d Canon of 1801, which limits the operation of the 4th Canon of 1795," was returned from that house, with a message that they did not concur in the same.

A message was received from the House of Clerical and Lay Deputies, informing that the amendments proposed by this house to the "Office of induction," etc., had been adopted by that house.

A proposed Canon, entitled "Canon respecting Lay Readers," was presented from the House of Clerical and Lay Deputies, and was immediately taken up and passed by this house.

The house then adjourned till Monday morning.

MONDAY, Sept. 17, 1804, 9 o'clock, A.M.

The house met. Present as on Saturday.

A proposed Canon was presented from the House of Clerical and Lay Deputies, entitled "Canon providing for an accurate view of the state of the Church from time to time," which was immediately taken up and passed.

A proposed substitute was presented from the House of Clerical and Lay Deputies, to the Canon entitled "Canon limiting the operation of the 6th Canon of 1795," which passed this house.

The papers presented to this house by the President, from the Rev. Ammi Rogers, of Connecticut, requesting their attention to sundry matters affecting his standing in the Church and his private character, were then taken into consideration.

Whereupon Resolved,—That there be declared to the House of Clerical and Lay Deputies the desire of the House of Bishops, that if any members of that house possess information respecting the conduct of the said Ammi Rogers, in the matters brought before the House of Bishops, which matters will be communicated by the House of Bishops to any members of the house aforesaid who may desire it, such members will lay before the House of Bishops the information possessed by them at 12 o'clock.

Resolved,—That information of the above message be communicated to the Rev. Ammi Rogers, in order that, if he have any further matters to lay before the House of Bishops, the same may be done at the said hour.

The information required in the above resolution was accordingly communicated.

A proposed Canon was presented from the House of Clerical and Lay Deputies, entitled "Canon of Candidates coming from places within the United States, in which the Constitution of this Church has not been acceded to;" which Canon passed this house.

This house received from the House of Clerical and Lay Deputies a proposed Canon, entitled, "Canon respecting the dissolution of all pastoral connection between Ministers and congregations;" which was taken into consideration. Also the proposed Canon presented on Thursday last, entitled "Canon making addition to the 17th Canon of 1789," was taken up.

These two Canons passed this house with amendments, and an incorporation of both into one Canon.

A proposed Canon, entitled, "Notice to be given of the election of Ministers," passed this house.

Agreeably to the resolution of the last General Convention, this house considered and established a Course of Ecclesiastical Studies for candidates for Holy Orders.

Twelve o'clock.

The Clerical Members from the State of Connecticut were admitted to a hearing on the subject of the Rev. Ammi Rogers; when Mr. Rogers was also called in.

The Rev. Mr. Baldwin asked for leave to make a statement of the case, which was granted.

Documents on both sides were then read, and a hearing was given to the parties concerned.

While the subject of Mr. Rogers was under consideration, several Canons were presented from the House of Clerical and Lay Deputies, as follow.

A Canon respecting differences between Ministers and their congregations; proposed.

Canon respecting the dissolution of all pastoral connection between ministers and congregations, and a Canon making addition to the 17th Canon of 1789;" passed the House of Clerical and Lay Deputies with amendments, and an incorporation into one Canon, as proposed by this house.

"Notice to be given of the election of Ministers," returned with amendments, and an alteration of the title.

"Of Clergymen ordained by foreign Bishops, and desirous of settling in this Church;" proposed.

The house then adjourned till 7 o'clock, P.M.

Seven o'clock, P.M.

The amendments to the Canon entitled "Notice to be given of the election of Ministers," were considered, and not agreed to; and a conference thereupon was requested.

The Canon respecting differences between Ministers and their congregations, was passed with an amendment.

The Canon, "Of Clergymen ordained by foreign Bishops, and desirous of settling in this Church," was negatived.

The Rev. Ammi Rogers appeared, and asked permission to see one of the papers presented to this house by the Clerical Deputies from Connecticut. Whereupon it was

Resolved,—That nothing shall be done in the business except in the presence of both parties.

Bishop Claggett obtained leave of absence.

The house then adjourned till to-morrow, 8 o'clock A.M.

TUESDAY, Sept. 18, 1804, 8 o'clock, A.M.

The house met. Present as yesterday, except Bishop Claggett.

A message was delivered from the House of Clerical and Lay Deputies, informing that the said house had agreed to the conference requested on the amendments to the Canon, entitled "Notice to be given of the election of Ministers." This house agreed to enter immediately on the business.

The Rev. Dr. Blackwell, Rev. Dr. Kemp, and Rev. Mr. Hobart, appeared as a Committee from the House of Clerical and Lay Deputies, to enter upon the conference proposed. After which conference, this house receded from their non-concurrence, on condition of a small additional amendment.

A conference was then proposed by the House of Clerical and Lay Deputies on the Canon, entitled "Of Clergymen ordained by foreign Bishops," etc., which Canon was negatived by this house. The conference was assented to, and the aforementioned gentlemen appeared as a Committee from the house on the subject. Whereupon a substitute was proposed by this house, and sent by the above Committee.

A message was sent to the House of Clerical and Lay Deputies informing that, agreeably to a requisition of the last General Convention, this house have prepared a Course of Ecclesiastical Studies, which they intend to publish with their Journals.

The Rev. Mr. Shelton appeared, and asked permission to lay further testimony before the house in the case of Mr. Ammi Rogers.

Leave was given, on condition that Mr. Rogers be also informed.

Both parties were then introduced, and further hearing was given them.

A proposed Canon was received from the House of Clerical and Lay Deputies, entitled, "Of candidates who may be refused Orders," which was passed.

Also a proposed Canon, entitled, "Concerning the studies of candidates for Orders;" which was negatived.

A message was received from the House of Clerical and Lay Deputies in the following words:—"The House of Clerical and Lay Deputies have acceded to the amendment proposed by the House of Bishops to the Canon respecting differences between Ministers and their congregations; and have agreed to the substitute for the Canon concerning Clergymen ordained by foreign Bishops; and to the amendment to the Canon entitled 'Canon concerning the election and induction of Ministers into parishes or churches.'"

Also a message was received, informing that the House of Clerical and Lay Deputies have agreed to the following resolution:

Resolved,—That it be made known to the different State Conventions, that it is proposed in the next General Convention to consider and determine on the following proposed alteration to the General Constitution of the Church, viz., that in Art. III., the following words be stricken out, "unless adhered to by four-fifths of the other house."

The above resolution was concurred in by this house.

Another resolution was received from the House of Clerical and Lay Deputies, in the following words:

Resolved,—That the Committee appointed to publish the Journals be authorised to publish the Constitution and all the Canons of the Church in the order of their enaction, noting at the end of each Canon the various other Canons which refer to the subject of that particular Canon."

An amendment was proposed and carried in this house, to strike out from the word "noting," and insert the following words: "making a reference by asterisk, at the end of every Canon, to a note pointing out the various other Canons which refer to the subject of that particular Canon."

This amendment was concurred in by the House of Clerical and Lay Deputies.

A message was received in the following words:

"The House of Clerical and Lay Deputies request the concurrence of the House of Bishops to a resolution for printing 1000 copies of the Journals, 1000 copies of the Office of induction, and 1000 copies of each of the Sermons preached before the Convention; a resolution appointing the Rev. Dr. Beach, the Rev. Mr. Harris, and the Rev. Mr. Hobart, in conjunction with Bishop Moore, to arrange the Canons of this Church; a resolution unanimously passed by the house, that the General Convention meet next at Baltimore; and a resolution that Bishop Parker be requested to preach at the opening of the next General Convention.

"The house also inform the House of Bishops, that it is their wish, if possible, that an adjournment of the Convention should take place this morning."

This house concurred in these several resolutions.

On motion of the Right Rev. Bishop Jarvis, Resolved,—That it be proposed to the House of Clerical and Lay Deputies, that the adjournment of the Convention be accompanied by prayer, in the presence of the two houses—the presiding Bishop to officiate."

The House of Clerical and Lay Deputies sent their concurrence.

A message was received from the House of Clerical and Lay Deputies, informing that said house are ready to adjourn.

The house then attended prayers in the chamber of the House of Clerical and Lay Deputies.

This house adjourned to meet at Bishop Moore's at 7 o'clock, P.M.

Seven o'clock, P.M.

The House of Bishops met at Bishop Moore's dwelling.

Present: Right Rev. Bishop White, Right Rev. Bishop Moore, Right Rev. Bishop Parker.

The house resumed the consideration of the matters brought before them by the Rev. Ammi Rogers, and came to the following determination concerning the same.

After full inquiry, and fair examination of all the evidence that could be procured, it appears to this house, that the said Ammi Rogers had produced to the Standing Committee of New York (upon the strength of which he obtained Holy Orders) a certificate, signed with the name of the Rev. Philo Perry, which certificate was not written nor signed by him.

That the conduct of the said Ammi Rogers, in the State of Connecticut, during his residence in that State, since he left New York, has been insulting, refractory, and schismatical in the highest degree; and were it tolerated, would prove subversive of all order and discipline in the Church; and that the statement which he made in justification of his conduct, was a mere tissue of equivocation and evasion, and of course served rather to defeat than to establish his purpose.

Therefore this house do approve of the proceedings of the Church in Connecticut, in reproving the said Ammi Rogers, and prohibiting him from the performance of any ministerial duties within that diocese; and, moreover, are of opinion, that he deserves a severe ecclesiastical censure, that of degradation from the ministry.

In regard to the question, To what authority is Mr. Rogers amenable? this house are sensible, that there not having been, previously to the present Convention, any sufficient provision for a case of a Clergyman removing from one diocese to another, it might easily happen that different sentiments would arise as to this point. We are of opinion, that Mr. Rogers' residence being in Connecticut, it is to the authority of that diocese he is exclusively amenable. But as the imposition practiced with a view to the Ministry was in New York, we recommend to the Bishop and Standing Committee of that State, to send to the Bishop in Connecticut such documents, duly attested, of the measure referred to, as will be a ground of proceedure in that particular.

We further direct the Secretary to deliver a copy of the above to the Clerical Deputies from Connecticut, and another copy to the Rev. Ammi Rogers. And we further direct, that either of the aforesaid parties be permitted to have any documents respectively delivered in by them, a copy of it being first taken; except the petition and affidavit of the Rev. Ammi Rogers, of which he may have a copy if desired—as may either of the parties have of any document delivered by the other party.

Resolved,—That the thanks of this house be given to the Rev. Mr. Jones for his services as Secretary.

The house rose.

Signed by order of the House of Bishops.

WILLIAM WHITE,
PRESIDING BISHOP.

Attest: CAVE JONES, Secretary H. B.

APPENDIX.

Course of Ecclesiastical Studies,

ESTABLISHED BY THE HOUSE OF BISHOPS IN THE CONVENTION OF 1804, IN PURSUANCE OF A RESOLUTION OF THE PRECEDING GENERAL CONVENTION.

In attending to this subject, a considerable difficulty occurs, arising out of the difference of the circumstances of students, in regard not only to intellectual endowments and preparatory knowledge of languages and science, but to access to authors, and time to be devoted to a preparation for the ministry. For in accommodating to those whose means are slender, we are in danger of derogating from the importance of religious knowledge; while, on the other hand, although we should demand all that is desirable, we shall be obliged to content ourselves, in some cases, with what is barely necessary.

In consideration of the above, it will be expedient to set down such a course of study, as is accommodated to a moderate portion of time and means; and afterwards to suggest provision, as well for a more limited as for a more enlarged share of both.

Let the student be required to begin with some books in proof of the divine authority of Christianity, such as Grotius on the Truth of the Christian Religion, Jenkins on the Reasonableness of Christianity, Paley's Evidences, Lesly's Methods with the Jews and Deists; Stillingfleet's Origines Sacra, and Butler's Analogy. To the above should be added some books which give a knowledge of the objections made by Deists. For this Leland's view may be sufficient, except that it should be followed by answers to deistical writers since Leland, whose works and the answers to them may be supposed known to the student. It would be best, if circumstances permit, that he should read what the Deists themselves have written.

After the books in proof of Revelation, let the student, previously to the reading of any system of divinity, study the Scriptures with the help of some approved commentators,—such as Patrick and Lowth on the Old Testament, and Hammond, or Whitby, or Doddridge on the New: being aware, in regard to the last-mentioned author, of the points on which he differs from our Church, although it be with moderation and candour. During such his study of the Scriptures, let him read some work or works which give an account of the design of the different books, and the grounds on which their respective authority is asserted; for instance, Father Simon's Canon of Scripture, Collier's Sacred Interpreter, Gray's Key to the Old Testament, and Percy's Key to the New. Let the student read the Scriptures over and over, referring to his commentators as need may require, until he can give an account of the design and character of each book, and explain the more difficult passages of it. He is supposed to know enough of profane history to give an account of that also, whenever it mixes with the sacred. There are certain important subjects which may be profitably attended to, as matters of distinct study, during the course of the general study of Scripture. For instance: the student having proceeded as far as the Deluge, may read some author who gives a larger account than the commentators of the particulars attached to that crisis, and also the principles on which are founded the different systems of chronology: all of which will be found clearly done in the Universal History. In reading the book of Leviticus, it will be useful to attend to some connected scheme of the sacrifices, such as is exhibited by Bishop Kidder in his Introduction to the Pentateuch, and by Mr. Joseph Mede in some of his discourses. A more full and interesting interpretation of the Prophecies than can be expected from the commentators, will be desirable; and for this purpose, let Bishop Newton's work be taken. Between the study of the Old Testament and that of the New, should be read Prideaux and Shuckford's Connections. With the New Testament should be taken some book relating to the Harmony of the Gospels, as M'Knight's or Bishop Newcome's. Let the student, before entering on the Gospels, read Dr. Campbell's Introductory Dissertations. Towards the close of the Gospels, the subject of the Resurrection should be particularly attended to; for which purpose let there be taken either Mr. West on the subject, or Bishop Sherlock's Trial of the Witnesses.

After the study of the Scriptures, let attention be given to ecclesiastical history, so far as the Council of Nice. This period is distinctly taken from a desire that the portion of history preceding it, as well as the opinions then entertained, may be learned from original writers; which may be considered as one of the best expedients for the guarding of the student against many errors of modern times. The writers of that interval are not numerous or bulky. Eusebius is soon read through, and so are the Apostolic Fathers. Even the other writers are not voluminous, except Origen, the greater part of whose works may be passed over. The Apostolic Fathers may be best read in Cotelerius's edition; but there are translations of most of them by Archbishop Wake and the Rev. William Reeves. Cave's Lives of the Apostles and Fathers may be profitably read at this period.

This stage of the student's progress seems the most proper for the study of the two questions, of our Lord's divinity and of Episcopacy. The aspect of early works on these subjects, best enables us to ascertain in what shape they appeared to the respective writers. And it is difficult to suppose, on the ground of what we know of human nature, that during the first three centuries, either the character of Christ should have been conceived of as materially different from what had been the representation of it by the first teachers of our religion; or, that there should have been a material change of Church government, without opposition to the innovation. For the former question, let the works of Bishop Bull and the Rev. Charles Lesly be taken; to which may well be added the late controversy between Bishop Horsley and Dr. Priestley; and for the latter, Mr. Hooker's Ecclesiastical Polity, Archbishop Potter on Church Government, and Daubeny's Guide to the Church. As the Lord Chancellor King published a book on the Discipline of the Primitive Church, in which he has rested Episcopacy on insufficient grounds, unwarily admitted by many on his authority, let the student read his book, and the refutation of it in Mr. Slater's Original Draft of the Primitive Church.

After this, let the student go on with the history of the fourth century, from Mosheim. But it will be of advantage to him to turn to Fleury's history for the epitomies there given of the writings of the eminent men who abounded in that century and part of the next. Let him then return to Mosheim, and go on with that writer to the Reformation. Here let him pause and study, as the main hinges of Popery, its pretences to supremacy and infallibility; on which there will be found satisfactory matter in Mr. Chillingworth's Religion of Protestants a Safe Way to Salvation, and Dr. Barrow's treatise Of the Pope's Supremacy. Here also let there be read Father Paul's History of the Council of Trent. Then let the student resume Mosheim. But it will be best if, for a more minute knowledge of the History of the Church of England since the Reformation, he take along with him Collier's History—a very able work, but in the reading of which some allowance must be made for peculiar prejudices. On coming, in the reign of Elizabeth, to the questions which arose between the Divines of the Established Church and the Presbyterians, then known by the name of Puritans, let recourse be had again to Mr. Hooker's work and to the London Cases. Then let Mosheim be proceeded with to the end.

After these studies, and not before, let Divinity be read in a systematic method. Bishop Pearson's Exposition of the Creed may be considered as a small system, and on account of the excellence of the work is recommended; as also Bishop Burnet's Exposition of the Thirty-nine Articles. Then let a larger system be taken; suppose Stackhouse's Body of Divinity, with the addition of the following modern works:—Elements of Christian Theology, by the present Bishop of Lincoln, and the Scholar Armed. That many works of this sort are not mentioned, is because we think their utility is principally confined to arrangement, and suppose that the knowledge they convey is to be obtained from the Scriptures and judicious commentators.

It seems necessary to this course of study, to recommend the Sermons of some of the most distinguished preachers; who have so abounded in the Church of England for some ages past, that the only matter will be, from among many of great name, to select a convenient number. And for this purpose we refer to the list at the end.

It seems not unnecessary to require attention to the History of the Common Prayer, the grounds on which the different Services are constructed, and the meaning of the Rubrics. Perhaps a careful study of Dr. Wheatley on the Common Prayer, and of the late work of Mr. Reeves, will be sufficient.

Some books should be read on the duties of the Pastoral office; such as St. Chrysostom on the Priesthood, Bishop Burnet on the Pastoral Care, and Bishop Wilson's Parochialia. It is, however, to be remembered, that one reason of studying carefully the Book of Common Prayer and its Rubrics, is that, by the help of these, in connection with what belongs in Scripture to the ministerial character, sufficient information of its duties may be had.

A knowledge of the Constitution and the Canons should be held absolutely necessary. And it is to be hoped that they will, on this account, be soon published, detached from the Journals.

To set down what books shall be essential, no student to be ordained without being fully prepared to answer on them, is more difficult. The lowest requisition is as follows:—Paley's Evidences; Mosheim, with a reference to Mr. Hooker for the Episcopacy; Stackhouse's Body of Divinity, and Mr. Reeves on the Common Prayer; the Constitution and Canons of the Church; allowing in the study of the Scriptures a latitude of choice among the approved commentators; it being understood, that if the student cannot, on the grounds contained in some good Commentary, give an account of the different books, and explain such passages as may be proposed to him, this is of itself a disqualification.

In the beginning it was intimated, that the course to be recommended would be disproportioned to the means of some, and fall short of what would be within the compass of others. For the benefit of the latter, we publish the following list of books on the different branches of ecclesiastical knowledge.

During the whole course of study, the student will endeavour, by the grace of God, to cultivate his heart by attention to devotional and practical treatises, several of which will be mentioned in the general list that follows.

LIBRARY OF A PARISH MINISTER,

Prefixed to "Elements of Christian Theology," published by the Right Rev. the present Bishop of Lincoln.

The books mentioned are divided into four classes.

The first containing such as relate to the exposition of the Old and New Testaments; the second, such as serve to establish the divine authority of the Scriptures; the third, such as explain the doctrines and discipline of the Church and the duties of its Ministers; and the fourth, miscellaneous, including Sermons and Ecclesiastical History.

CLASS THE FIRST.

Bible, with marginal references, 8vo.
Crutwell's Concordance of Parallels, 4to.
Butterworth's Concordance, 8vo.
Patrick, Lowth, and Whitby, on the Old and New Testament, 6 vols. fol.
Doddridge's Family Expositor, 6 vols. 8vo.
Pool's Synopsis, 5 vols. folio.
Collier's Sacred Interpreter, 2 vols. 8vo.
Jenning's Jewish Antiquities, 2 vols. 8vo.
Lowman's Rationale of the Hebrew Ritual, 8vo.
Gray's Key to the Old Testament, 8vo.
Home's Scripture History of the Jews, 2 vols. 8vo.
Parkhurst's Greek Lexicon, 4to.
Campbell's Translation of the Gospels, 2 vols. 4to.
Marsh's Michaelis, 3 vols. 8vo.

Bowyer's Conjectures on the New Testament, 4to.
Macknight's Harmony, 4to.
Macknight on the Epistles, 3 vols. 4to.
Lowman on the Revelation, 8vo.
Oliver's Scripture Lexicon, 8vo.
Macbean's Dictionary of the Bible, 8vo.

CLASS THE SECOND.

Stillingfleet's Origines Sacræ, 2 vols. 8vo.
Clarke's Grotius, 8vo.
Clarke's Evidences of Natural and Revealed Religion, 8vo.
Lardner's Works, 11 vols. 8vo.
Paley's Evidences, 2 vols. 8vo.
Paley's Horæ Paulinæ, 8vo.
Jenkins on the Certainty and Reasonableness of Christianity, 2 vols. 8vo.
Leland on the Advantage and Necessity of Revelation, 2 vols. 8vo.
Leland's View of Deistical Writers, 2 vols. 8vo.
Butler's Analogy, 8vo.
Campbell on Miracles, 2 vols. 8vo.
Newton on the Prophecies, 2 vols. 8vo.
Kett's History the Interpreter of Prophecy, 3 vols. 12mo.
Leland on the Divine Authority of the Old and New Testament, 2 vols.

CLASS THE THIRD.

Burnet's History of the Reformation, 3 vols. folio.
Burnet's Exposition of the Thirty-nine Articles, 8vo.
Burnet's Pastoral Care, 8vo.
Pearson on the Creed, 2 vols. 8vo.
Nicholls on the Common Prayer, 8vo.
Wheatley on the Common Prayer, 8vo.
Shepherd on the Common Prayer, 8vo.
Wilson's Parochialia, 12mo.
Wall on Infant Baptism, 2 vols. 8vo.
Secker on the Catechism, 12mo.
Secker's Charges, 8vo.
The Homilies, by Sir Adam Gordon, 8vo.
Daubeny's Guide to the Church.
Daubeny's Appendix to the same, 2 vols.

CLASS THE FOURTH.

Cudworth's Intellectual System, 2 vols. 4to.
Hooker's Ecclesiastical Polity, 3 vols. 8vo.
Bingham's Antiquities, 2 vols. folio.
Broughton's Dictionary of all Religions, 2 vols. folio.
Shuckford's Connection, 4 vols. 8vo.
Prideaux's Connection, 4 vols. 8vo.
Echard's Ecclesiastical History, 2 vols. 8vo.
Mosheim's Ecclesiastical History, 6 vols. 8vo.
Burns' Ecclesiastical Law, 4 vols. 8vo.
Common Place Book to the Holy Bible, 4to.
Barrow's Works, 3 vols: folio.
Tillotson's Works, 3 vols. folio.
Clarke's Sermons, 8 vols. 8vo.

Sherlock's Sermons, 5 vols. 8vo.
Secker's Sermons, 9 vols. 8vo.
Scott's Christian Life, 5 vols. 8vo.
Whole Duty of Man, 12mo.
Scholar Armed, 2 vols. 8vo.
Tracts by Society for Christian Knowledge, 12 vols. 12mo.

In addition to the preceding, may be recommended the following list of Sermons and devotional and practical books.

Sermons by Bishop Pearce, Bishop Wilson, Bishop Horne, Bishop Porteus, Dr. Jortin, Dr. Brady; by the late Right Rev. Bishop Seabury of this Church; by the late Rev. Dr. Smith, of the same; Bishop Gibson's Tracts; Bishop Horne's Commentary on the Psalms; Rev. Wm. Jones's (of Nayland) Works; Nelson's Festivals and Fasts of the Church, Nelson's Practice of True Devotion; Nelson's Christian Sacrifice; Bishop Taylor's Rule of Holy Living and Dying; Scougall's Life of God in the Soul of Man; Dr. Sherlock on Death,—on Judgment,—on a Future State,—on Providence.

By Order of the House of Bishops:
WILLIAM WHITE, D.D., Presiding Bishop.

Canons.

Passed in 1804.

Canon I.—Concerning the Election and Induction of Ministers into Parishes or Churches.

It is hereby required, that on the election of a Minister into any church or parish, the Vestry shall deliver, or cause to be delivered to the bishop, or, where there is no bishop, to the standing committee of the diocese, notice of the same, in the following form, or to this effect.

"We the church wardens [or in case of an associated rector or assistant minister, We, the rector and church wardens] do certify to the Right Rev. [naming the bishop], or to the rev. [naming the President of the standing committee] that [naming the person] has been duly chosen rector [or associated rector, or assistant minister, as the case may be] of [naming the parish, or church, or churches]."

Which certificate shall be signed with the names of those who certify.

And if the bishop or the standing committee be satisfied that the person so chosen is a qualified minister of this church, the bishop, or the president of the standing committee, shall transmit the said certificate to the secretary of the Convention, who shall record it in a book to be kept by him for that purpose. And if the minister elect be a presbyter, the bishop, or the president of the standing committee, shall proceed to have him inducted according to the Office established by this Church. But if he be a Deacon, the act of induction shall not take place till after he shall have received priest's orders, when it shall be the duty of the bishop or president to have it performed.

But if the bishop or the standing committee be not satisfied as above, he or they shall, at the instance of the parties, proceed to inquire into the sufficiency of the person so chosen, according to such rules as may be made in the respective dioceses, and shall confirm or reject the appointment, as the issue of that enquiry may be.

No minister, who may be hereafter elected into any parish or church, shall be considered as a regularly admitted and settled parochial minister in any diocese or state, or shall, as such, have any vote in the choice of a bishop, until he shall have been inducted according to the Office prescribed by this Church.

The 17th Canon of 1789, and the third Canon of 1799, are hereby repealed.

Canon II. Respecting the dissolution of all pastoral connection between Ministers and their Congregations.

When any minister has been regularly inducted or settled in a parish or church, he shall not be dismissed without the concurrence of the ecclesiastical authority of the diocese or state; and in case of his dismission without such concurrence, the Vestry or congregation of such parish or Church shall have no right to a representation in the Convention of the state, until they have made such satisfaction as the Convention may require. Nor shall any minister leave his congregation against their will, without the concurrence of the ecclesiastical authority aforesaid; and if he shall leave them without such concurrence, he shall not be allowed to take a seat in any Convention of this Church, or be eligible into any Church or parish within the states which have acceded to the Constitution of this Church, until he shall have made such satisfaction as the ecclesiastical authority of the diocese or state may require.

In the case of the regular and canonical dissolution of the connection between a minister and his congregation, the bishop, or if there be no bishop, the standing committee shall direct the secretary of the Convention to record the same. But if the dissolution of the connection between any minister and his congregation be not regular or canonical, the bishop or standing committee shall lay the same before the Convention of the diocese or state, in order that the above-mentioned penalties may take effect.

Canon III.—Concerning Ministers removing from one Diocese or State to another.

No minister, removing from one diocese to another, or coming from any state which may not have acceded to the Constitution of this church, shall be received as a minister by any congregation of this Church, until he shall have presented to the Vestry thereof a certificate from the ecclesiastical authority of the diocese or state to which he is about to remove, that he has produced to them satisfactory testimonials that he has not been justly liable to evil report, for error in religion or viciousness of life, during the three years last past; which testimonials shall be signed by the bishop or bishops, or, where there is no bishop, by the majority of the clerical members of the standing committee or committees of the diocese or dioceses wherein he has resided; which committee or committees shall, in all cases, be duly convened: or, in case he comes from a state not in connection with this Church, and having no Convention, by three clergymen of this Church. Nor shall any minister, so removing, be received by any Vestry, or acknowledged by any bishop or Convention, as a minister of the Church to which he removes, until he shall have produced the aforesaid testimonials.

Every minister shall be amenable for any offences committed by him, in any diocese, to the ecclesiastical authority of the diocese in which he resides.

Canon IV.—Respecting differences between Ministers and their Congregations.

In cases of controversy between ministers who now, or may hereafter hold the rectorship of churches or parishes, and the vestry or congregation of such churches or parishes, which controversies are of such a nature as cannot be settled by themselves, the parties, or either of them, shall make application to the bishop of the diocese, or, in case there be no bishop, to the Convention of the state. And if it appear to the bishop and his presbyters, or, if there be no bishop, to the Convention, or the standing committee of the diocese or state, if the authority should be committed to them by the Convention, that the controversy has proceeded to such lengths, as to preclude all hope of its favourable termination, and that a dissolution of the connection which exists between them is indispensably necessary to restore the peace and promote the prosperity of the Church: the Bishop and his presbyters, or, if there be no bishop, the Convention, or the standing committee of the diocese or state, if the authority should be committed to them by the Convention, shall recommend to such ministers to relinquish their titles to their rectorships, on such conditions as may appear reasonable and proper to the bishop and his presbyters, or, if there be no bishop, to the Convention, or the standing committee of the diocese or state, if the authority should be committed to them by the Convention. And if such rectors or congregations refuse to comply with such recommendations, the Bishop and his presbyters, or, if there be no bishop, the Convention or the standing committee of the diocese or state, if the authority should be committed to them by the Convention, with the aid and consent of a bishop, may, at their discretion, proceed according to the Canons of the Church, to suspend the former from the exercise of any ministerial duties within the diocese or state, and prohibit the latter from a seat in the Convention, until they retract such refusal, and submit to the terms of the recommendation; and any minister so suspended shall not be permitted, during his suspension, to exercise any ministerial duties in any other diocese or state. This Canon shall apply also to the cases of associated rectors and assistant ministers and their congregations.

Canon V.—Of Clergymen ordained by foreign Bishops, and desirous of settling in this Church.

A clergyman coming from a foreign country, and professing to be regularly ordained, shall, before he be permitted to officiate in any parish or church, exhibit to the Vestry thereof satisfactory evidence of his moral character, and a certificate signed by the bishop of the diocese, or, where there is no bishop, by three clerical members of the standing committee, that his letters of Orders are authentic, and given by some bishop whose authority is acknowledged by this Church. And should any such clergyman desire to settle in any diocese, he shall first obtain the license of the bishop, or, where there is no bishop, the permission of three clerical members of the standing committee, to officiate within the diocese or state. And if, within one year, he shall be guilty of any unworthy conduct, the bishop, or, where there is no bishop, three clerical members of the standing committee, shall withdraw this license or permission; nor shall he be allowed to discharge the clerical functions, till he shall have produced to the bishop such testimonials as are prescribed in the 2d Canon of 1795, or to the clerical members of the standing committee, such credentials as would induce them to give said testimonials.

And in any case, before he shall be entitled to be inducted into a parish or church, he shall have resided one year in the United States.

And if any such foreign clergyman shall remove from one diocese to another, before one year have expired, he shall not be allowed by the ecclesiastical authority of the diocese to which he goes, to officiate in said diocese, till he shall have complied with the requisitions of the Canon concerning ministers removing from one diocese or state to another.

The 9th Canon of the Convention of 1789 is hereby repealed.

CANON VI.—Limiting the operation of Canon 6, of 1795.

When a minister of any other denomination of Christians shall apply for Orders in this Church, the Bishop to whom application is made, being satisfied that he is a man of piety and unexceptionable character, that he holds the doctrines of the Church, and that he possesses all the literary and other qualifications required, and being furnished with testimonials from the standing committee duly convened, may ordain him as soon as is convenient. In all such cases the standing committee may insert in their testimonials the words, "We believe him to be sincerely attached to the doctrines and discipline of the Protestant Episcopal Church," instead of the words, "and hath not written, taught, or held any thing contrary to the doctrine or discipline of the Protestant Episcopal Church."

CANON VII.—Additional to Canon 6, of 1795.

Every candidate for Holy Orders, who may be recommended by a standing committee of any Church destitute of a bishop, if he have resided for the greater part of the three years last past within the diocese of any bishop, shall apply to such bishop for ordination. And such candidate shall produce the usual testimonials, as well from the committee of the diocese in which he has resided, as from the committee of the Church in the state for which he is to be ordained.

CANON VIII.—Of Candidates coming from places within the United States, in which the Constitution of this Church has not been acceded to.

It is hereby declared, that the Canons of this Church, which respect candidates for Holy Orders, shall affect as well those coming from places in the United States in which the Constitution of this Church has not been acceded to, as those residing in States in which it has been adopted; and in such cases, every candidate shall produce to the bishop, to whom he may apply for Holy Orders, the requisite testimonials, subscribed by the standing committee of the diocese.

CANON IX.—Of Candidates who may be refused Orders.

No bishop shall ordain any candidate until he has required of him, whether he has ever, directly or indirectly, applied for Orders in any other diocese or state; and if the bishop has reason to believe that the candidate has been refused Orders in any other diocese or state, he shall write to the bishop of the diocese, or, if there be no bishop, to the standing committee, to know whether any just cause exists why the candidate should not be ordained. When any bishop rejects the application of any candidate for Orders, he shall immediately give notice to the bishop of every state or diocese, or, where there is no bishop, to the standing committee.

CANON X.—Respecting Lay Readers.

No candidate for Holy Orders shall take upon him to perform devotional service in any Church, but by the permission of the bishop or ecclesiastical authority of the state in which said candidate may wish to perform such service. And it shall be the duty of the bishop or ecclesiastical authority to limit and confine every such candidate to such part o parts of the Common Prayer Book, to such dress, and to such stations in the Church, as are appropriate only to lay readers: and also to point out what sermons or homilies he shall or may read to his congregation. And a non-conformity on the part of the candidate to such restrictions, shall be deemed in all cases a disqualification for Holy Orders.

CANON XI.—Providing for an accurate view of the State of the Church from time to time.

As a full and accurate view of the State of the Church, from time to time, is highly useful and necessary, it is hereby ordered, that every minister of this Church shall present or forward, at every annual Convention, to the bishop of the diocese, or, where there is no bishop, to the president of the Convention, a particular account of the state of his parish or Church; and these parochial reports shail be read, and entered on the Journals of the Convention. At every General Convention, the Journals of the different State Conventions since the last General Convention, together with such other papers, viz., Episcopal charges, addresses, and pastoral letters, as may tend to throw light on the state of the Church in each diocese, shall be presented to the House of Clerical and Lay Deputies. And the parochial reports inserted on those journals, together with the Episcopal addresses and the Episcopal registers, specified in the 2d Canon of 1801, shall be read in the said house. These journals and documents shall then be sent by the House of Clerical and Lay Deputies to the House of Bishops, who shall be requested to draw up a view of the state of the Church, adding such remarks or counsel as they may think proper: the whole in the form of a Pastoral Letter from the House of Bishops, which shall be read in the House of Clerical and Lay Deputies, and printed with the Journals of the Convention, for the general information of the Church.

It shall be the duty of the Secretary of the Convention of every diocese or state, or of the person or persons with whom the journals, or other Ecclesiastical papers are lodged, to forward to the House of Clerical and Lay Deputies, at every General Convention, the documents and papers specified in this Canon. At the first General Convention held after the passing of this Canon, the Journals of the state Conventions, since the organization of those Conventions, with the Constitutions and Canons of the Church in each state respectively, with all other useful Ecclesiastical documents, shall be presented to the House of Clerical and Lay Deputies, and sent, as before directed, to the House of Bishops.

BY ORDER OF THE HOUSE OF BISHOPS:
WILLIAM WHITE, D.D.,
PRESIDING BISHOP.

Attest: CAVE JONES, Secretary.

BY ORDER OF THE HOUSE OF CLERICAL AND LAY DEPUTIES:
ABRAHAM BEACH, D.D., PRESIDENT.

Attest: J. H. HOBART, Secretary.

The next General Convention will be held in the city of Baltimore, on the third Tuesday in May, 1808.

List of the Clergy

OF THE

PROTESTANT EPISCOPAL CHURCH,

In the United States of America, 1804.

Delivered in and published agreeably to the 16th Canon of 1789.

NEW HAMPSHIRE.

Rev. Joseph Willard, rector of St. John's church, Portsmouth.
Rev. Robert H. Fowle, rector of —— church, Holdernesse.
Rev. Daniel Barber, rector of —— church, Clairmont.

MASSACHUSETTS.

The Right Rev. Samuel Parker, D.D., Bishop, and rector of Trinity church, Boston.
Rev. William Willard Wheeler, rector of St. Michael's church, Scituate, and St. Peter's, Marshfield.
Rev. Nathaniel Fisher, rector of St. Peter's church, Salem.
Rev. John Sylvester I. Gardner, Assistant Minister of Trinity church, Boston.
Rev. Samuel Haskill, rector of St. Ann's church, Gardiner.
Rev. William M. Montague, rector of St. Paul's church, Dedham.
Rev. James Bowers, rector of St. Michael's church, Marblehead.
Rev. Timothy Hilliard, Minister of the church at Portland.
Rev. James Morss, Minister of St. Paul's, Newburyport.
Rev. Amos Pardy, rector of St. Luke's church, Lanesborough.
Rev. Samuel Griswold, rector of St. James's church, Great Barrington, and the church at Lenox.

RHODE ISLAND.

Rev. Theodore Dehon, rector of Trinity church, Newport.
Rev. Alexander V. Griswold, rector of St. Michael's church, Bristol.
Rev. Joseph Warren, rector of St. Paul's church, Narraganset.

CONNECTICUT.

The Right Rev. Abraham Jarvis D.D., Bishop.

Rev. Jeremiah Leaming, residing at New Haven.

Rev. William Smith, D.D., Principal of the Episcopal Academy, Cheshire.

Rev. Richard Mansfield, D.D., Rector of Christ Church at Derby, and of the Churches of Oxford and Great Hill.

Rev. Bela Hubbard, D.D., rector of Trinity church, New Haven and Christ church, West Haven.

Rev. John Tyler, rector of Christ church, Norwich.

Rev. Daniel Fogg, rector of —— church, Pomfret.

Rev. Philo Shelton, rector of Trinity church, Fairfield, St. John's, Stratfield, and —— church in Weston.

Rev. Ashbel Baldwin, rector of Christ church, Stratford, and Trinity church, Trumbull.

Rev. Chauncey Prindle, rector of Christ church, Watertown, and St. Peter's, Plymouth.

Rev. Reuben Ives, rector of St. Peter's church, Cheshire, and the churches of Hamden and Southington.

Rev. Tillotson Bronson, rector of St. John's church, Waterbury, and —— church, Salem.

Rev. Truman Marsh, rector of —— church, Litchfield.

Rev. Ambrose Todd, rector of St. Paul's church, Huntingdon.

Rev. Daniel Burhans, rector of Trinity church, Newtown, and —— church, Brookfield.

Rev. Solomon Blakesley, rector of St. Stephen's church, East Haddam.

Rev. Charles Seabury, rector of St. James's church, New London.

Rev. Smith Miles, rector of the churches at Chatham and Middle Haddam.

Rev. Menzies Rayner, rector of —— church, Hartford.

Rev. Nathan B. Burges, rector of the churches at Guilford and North Bristol.

Rev. Henry Whitlock, rector of the churches at Norwalk and Wilton.

Rev. Clement Merriam, rector of Christ church, Middletown.

NEW YORK.

The Right Rev. Benjamin Moore, D.D., Bishop, and rector of Trinity church, New York.

Rev. Peter Anthony Albert, rector of the French church De le St.-Esprit, New York.

Rev. Theodosius Bartow, rector of Trinity church, New Rochelle.

Rev. Edmund D. Barry, Assistant Minister of the church De le St.-Esprit, New York.

Rev. Abraham Beach, D.D., Assistant Ministers of Trinity church, New York.

Rev. Frederick Beasley, rector of St. Peter's church, Albany.

Rev. John Bowden, D.D., Professor of Moral Philosophy, Logic, and Rhetoric in Columbia College, New York.

Rev. Richard Bradford, rector of St. Luke's church, Catskill.

Rev. David Butler, officiating at Troy and Lansinburgh.

Rev. Philander Chase, rector of Christ church, Poughkeepsie, and Trinity church, Fishkill.

Rev. Abraham L. Clarke, rector of St. James's church, Newtown, and St. George's, Flushing.

Rev. Elias Cooper, Rector of St. John's church, Yonkers.

Rev. William Harris, rector of St. Mark's church, Bowery, New York.
Rev. Seth Hart, rector of St. George's church, Hempstead, with which is connected Christ Church, North Hempstead.
Rev. John Henry Hobart, an Assistant Minister of Trinity church, New York.
Rev. John Ireland, rector of St. Anne's church, Brooklyn.
Rev. Cave Jones, an Assistant Minister, Trinity church, New York.
Rev. Bethel Judd, rector of Christ church, Hudson.
Rev. Jonathan Judd, Deacon, Missionary in the western part of the State.
Rev. Richard C. Moore, rector of St. Andrew's church, Staten Island.
Rev. Daniel Nash, rector of St. John's church, Otsego, St. Luke's, Richfield, and Harmony church, Butternuts.
Rev. Samuel Nesbitt, residing in New York.
Rev. Philo Perry, officiating in the Church, New Stamford.
Rev. Davenport Phelps, Missionary in the western part of the State.
Rev. Joseph Pilmore, rector of Christ church, New York.
The Right Rev. Bishop Provoost, New York.
Rev. Evan Rogers, rector of Christ church, Rye.
Rev. George Strebeck, Deacon, officiating in the congregations at Bedford and its vicinity.
Rev. Gamaliel Thatcher, Missionary in the western part of the State.
Rev. John Urquhart, Principal of the Academy at Johnstown.
Rev. Frederick Van Horne, rector of St. Andrew's church, Orange co.
Rev. Isaac Wilkins, rector of St. Peter's church, West Chester, and St. Paul's church, East Chester.

NEW JERSEY.

Rev. Uzal Ogden, D.D., rector of Trinity church, Newark.
Rev. Charles H. Wharton, D.D., rector of St. Mary's church, Burlington.
Rev. Henry Waddell, rector of St. Michael's church, Trenton.
Rev. John Croes, rector of Christ church, New Brunswick, and St. Peter's church, Spotswood.
Rev. Andrew Fowler, rector of Christ church, Shrewsbury, and Christ church, Middletown.
Rev. Jasper D. Jones, Rector of St. Peter's church, Perth Amboy.
Rev. Henry I. Feltus, Minister at Trinity church, Swedesborough.
Rev. Samuel Lilly, rector of St. John's church, Elizabethtown.

PENNSYLVANIA.

The Right Rev. William White, D.D., Bishop.
Rev. Samuel Magaw, D.D.
Rev. John Andrews, D.D., Vice-Provost of the University of Pennsylvania.
Rev. Robert Blackwell, D.D., Assistant Minister of Christ Church and St. Peter's, in the city of Philadelphia.
Rev. Joseph Hutchins, D.D.
Rev. John Campbell, rector of the Episcopal churches of York and Huntingdon.
Rev. Slator Clay, rector of St. David's, Radnor; St. Peter's in the Valley, and St. James's, Perkiomen.
Rev. Joseph Clarkson, rector of St. James's, Lancaster, —— church, Pequea, and —— church, Carnarvon.
Rev. Robert Ayres, rector of Emanuel church, Washington county, and St. Peter's church, Fayette county.

Rev. Francis Reno, Westmoreland county.
Rev. Joseph Turner, rector of St. Paul's church, Chester, and St. Martin's, Marcus Hook.
Rev. Caleb Hopkins, rector of Christ church, Derry Township, and Christ church, Turbut township, Northumberland county.
Rev. Thomas Davis, Washington county.
Rev. James Abercrombie, Assistant Minister of Christ church and St. Peter's, Philadelphia.
Rev. Absalom Jones (a black man), rector of the African church of St. Thomas's, Philadelphia.
Rev. John Taylor, Pittsburgh.

DELAWARE.

The Rev. Robert Clay, Emanuel church, New Castle.
Rev. William Pryce, Trinity church, Wilmington.
Rev. James Wiltbank, St. Peter's church, Lewes.
Rev. William L. Gibson, St. Paul's church, Georgetown.

MARYLAND.

The Right Rev. Thomas J. Claggett, D.D., Bishop, and rector of St. Paul's parish, Prince George's county.
Rev. Charles Smoot, rector of William and Mary parish, St. Mary's.
Rev. George Ralph, All Faith, St. Mary's.
Rev. Francis Walker, St. Andrew's, St. Mary's.
Rev. Benjamin Contee, William and Mary, Charles.
Rev. Owen F. Magrath, King and Queen, Charles.
Rev. Edward Gant, Jun., Christ church, Calvert.
Rev. Joseph Messinger, St. John's, Prince George's county.
Rev. Thomas Scott, Queen Anne's, Prince George's.
Rev. Walter D. Addison, residing in Prince George's.
Rev. John W. Compton, St. James', Anne Arundel.
Rev. William Duke, St. Anne's, Anne Arundel.
Rev. Nicholas W. Lane, All Hallows, Anne Arundel.
Rev. Ralph Higinbothom, residing in Annapolis, Anne Arundel.
Rev. Thomas Read, Prince George's, Montgomery.
Rev. — Reynolds, St. Peter's, Montgomery.
Rev. George Bower, rector of All Saints, Frederick.
Rev. John Kewley, Emanuel, Albany.
Rev. Joseph G. J. Bend, D.D., St. Paul's parish, Baltimore county.
Rev. Elijah D. Rattoone, D.D., St. Paul's parish, Baltimore county.
Rev. John Coleman, St. James's and St. Thomas's, Baltimore county.
Rev. William Swan, residing in Baltimore county.
Rev. George Dashiell, St. Peter's, Baltimore.
Rev. John Allen, rector of St. George's, Harford.
Rev. Henry Lyon Davis, St. Stephen's, Cecil.
Rev. Simon Wilmer, Shrewsbury, Kent.
Rev. John Armstrong, St. Paul's, Kent.
Rev. Colin Ferguson, D.D., residing in Chestertown, Kent county.
Rev Archibald Walker, near Chestertown, Kent county.
Rev. Samuel Keene, D.D., residing in Queen Anne's.
Rev. Samuel Keene, Jun., residing in Queen Anne's.
Rev. Joseph Jackson, St. Peter's, Talbot.
John Price, St. Michael's, Talbot.
Rev. Francis Barclay, residing in Easton, Talbot.

Rev. James Kemp, Great Choptank, Dorchester.
Rev. William M. Stone, Stepney, Somerset.
Rev. Samuel Sloan, residing in Somerset.
Rev. David Ball, All Hallows, Worcester.
Rev. James Jones Wilmer, place of residence not known.

Resident in that part of the District of Columbia, formerly part of Maryland:

Rev. John I. Sayrs.
Rev. Andrew M'Cormick.
Rev. Edward Gantt.

VIRGINIA.

The Right Rev. James Madison, D.D., Bishop.
Rev. Charles O'Neill, rector of ——, Amherst.
Rev. Alexander Hay, Antrim.
Rev. — Gray Bottetourt.
Rev. Hugh Corran Boggs, Berkeley.
Rev. — Heath, Berkley.
Rev. Benjamin Brown, Blisland.
Rev. Andrew Syme, Bristol.
Rev. John Cameron, D.D., rector of ——
Rev. Alexander M'Farland, Brunswick.
Rev. John Bracken, D.D., Bruton.
Rev. John Camm, Charles.
Rev. — Heffernen, Christ Church.
Rev. James Elliot, Cople.
Rev. Needler Robinson, Dale.
Rev. Spence Grayson, Dettingen.
Rev. Daniel M'Naughton, Christ Church.
Rev. James Whitehead, Elizabeth River.
Rev. Thomas Davis Fairfax.
Rev. Alexander Balmain, Frederick.
Rev. John O'Weylie, Lecturer, Frederick.
Rev. Matthew Maury, Fredericksville.
Rev. John Hooker Reynolds, Hardy.
Rev. John Buchanan, D.D., Henrico.
Rev. John Thompson, Leeds.
Rev. Charles Crawford, Lexington.
Rev. William Crawford, ——
Rev. James Dickinson, Littleton.
Rev. — Young, Lunenburg.
Rev. Anthony Walke, Lynhaven.
Rev. Armistead Smith, Matthews.
Rev. John Dunn, Manchester.
Rev. James Leach, Mecklenburg.
Rev. William Hubard, Newport.
Rev. Jacob Keeling, Nansemond.
Rev. Robert Buchan, Overwharton.
Rev. Arthur Emerson, Portsmouth.
Rev. John Brunskill, Raleigh.
Rev. — Stevenson, St. George's.
Rev. Charles Hopkins, St. James's, Northam.
Rev. James Price, St. John's.

Rev. Thomas Hughes, St. David.
Rev. Archibald Dick, St. Margaret's.
Rev. John Woodville, St. Mark's.
Rev. Abner Waugh, St. Mary's.
Rev. John Parsons, ——
Rev. John Seward, St. Stephen's.
Rev. John Hyde, Saunders, Southam.
Rev. Samuel Butler, Southwark.
Rev. Lee Massey, Truro.
Rev. Samuel Chapin, Westover.
Rev. James Evans, Yorkhampton.
Rev. John C. Brockenboroug, Washington.
Rev. Duncan M'Naughton, Wicomico.
Rev. Joseph Wilson, Rev. Stephen Thomson, Rev. Cornelius Carvert, cures not known.

The list from this State is the same as in the Journal of the last General Convention, no new list having been delivered in.

SOUTH CAROLINA.

Rev. Edward Jenkins, D.D., St. Michael's, Charleston.
Rev. Nathanael Bowen, St. Michael's, Charleston.
Rev. Milwood Pogson, St. James's, Goose Creek, St. George's, Dorchester.
Rev. John Thompson, St. Thomas's.
Rev. Thomas Mills, St. Andrew's, James' Island, St. Andrew's, Main.
Rev. Edmund Matthews, St. John's, Edisto.
Rev. — Nixon, St. Bartholomew's.
Rev. Thomas D. Bladen, St. James', Santee.
Rev. James Connor, St. Stephen's.
Rev. George H. Spierin, Prince George's.
Rev. John O'Donnel, All Saints.
Rev. — Frazier, Prince Frederick's.
Rev. — Gates, D.D.
Rev. — Hicks, Minister of the church at Beaufort.

Residents in the State without cures:

Rev. — M'Culley, Master of an Academy, Beaufort.
Rev. — Blackwall.
Rev. — Best, Master of an Academy, Charleston.

No new list from this State has been delivered in. The list published is probably inaccurate, as it was drawn up from imperfect information.

JOURNAL OF THE PROCEEDINGS

OF THE

BISHOPS, CLERGY, AND LAITY

OF THE

Protestant Episcopal Church

IN

THE UNITED STATES OF AMERICA,

IN

A CONVENTION

HELD IN

THE CITY OF BALTIMORE, FROM TUESDAY, MAY 17, TO THURSDAY, MAY 26, 1808.

LIST OF THE MEMBERS OF THE HOUSE OF CLERICAL AND LAY DEPUTIES.

FROM THE STATE OF RHODE ISLAND.

Rev. Theodore Dehon.

FROM THE STATE OF CONNECTICUT.

Rev. Ashbel Baldwin.
Rev. Daniel Burhans.
Burrage Beach, Esq.
Mr. Joseph Nicoll.

FROM THE STATE OF NEW YORK.

Rev. Abraham Beach, D.D.
Rev. Richard C. Moore, D.D.
Rev. John Henry Hobart, D.D.
Dr. John Onderdonk.
John Moore, Esq.

FROM THE STATE OF NEW JERSEY.

Joshua M. Wallace, Esq.

FROM THE STATE OF PENNSYLVANIA.

Rev. Robert Blackwell, D.D.
Rev. Joseph Clarkson.
Rev. Levi Bull.
John Lardner, Esq.
Dr. P. F. Glentworth.
Joseph Sims, Esq.

FROM THE STATE OF DELAWARE.

Rev. William Pryce.
Mr. Joseph Burn.

FROM THE STATE OF MARYLAND.

Rev. Joseph G. J. Bend, D.D.
Rev. James Kemp, D.D.
Rev. George Dashiell.
Rev. Simon Wilmer.
William H. Dorsey, Esq.
James Ringgold, Esq.
John C. Weems, Esq.
George Robertson, Esq.

JOURNAL

OF THE

House of Clerical and Lay Deputies.

BALTIMORE, May 17, 1808.

This being the day appointed for the meeting of the General Convention of the Protestant Episcopal Church in the United States of America, several Clerical and Lay Deputies attended at 12 o'clock, A.M., in St. Paul's Church, but not being a quorum, adjourned to meet at 5 o'clock, P.M.

Five o'clock, P.M.

A quorum of the house appearing, the President of the house in the last Convention took the chair, and the Secretary of the house in the last Convention acted as Secretary pro tempore.

The house then proceeded to read the testimonials of the Clerical and Lay Delegates, which were severally approved, and the following gentlemen took their seats in the house.

From Rhode Island—The Rev. Theodore Dehon.

From Connecticut—The Rev. Ashbel Baldwin, Rev. Daniel Burhans, Burrage Beach, Esq., and Mr. Joseph Nicoll.

From New York, the Rev. Abraham Beach, D.D., Rev. Richard C. Moore, D.D., the Rev. John H. Hobart, D.D., Dr. John Onderdonk, and John Moore, Esq.

From Pennsylvania—The Rev. Joseph Clarkson, John Lardner, Esq., and Dr. P. F. Glentworth.

From Delaware—Rev. William Pryce and Mr. Jos. Burns.

From Maryland—The Rev. Joseph G. J. Bend, D.D., the Rev. James Kemp, D.D., the Rev. George Dashiell, the Rev. Simon Wilmer, James Ringgold, Esq., and William H. Dorsey, Esq.

The house proceeded to the election of a President and Secretary, when it appeared that the Rev. Abraham Beach was unanimously chosen President, and the Rev. J. H. Hobart, Secretary.

A message was sent to the House of Bishops, informing them that this house was organized, and ready to proceed to business.

The House of Bishops returned for answer that they also were organized, and ready to proceed to business.

The house took into consideration the rules of order of preceding Houses of Clerical and Lay Deputies, and adopted the same, as follows, with some small alterations.

I. The business of every day shall be introduced with the Morning Service of the Church.

II. When the President takes the chair, no member shall continue standing, or shall afterwards stand up, unless to address the chair.

III. No member shall absent himself from the service of the house, unless he have leave, or be unable to attend.

IV. When any member is about to speak in debate, or deliver any matter to the house, he shall rise from his seat, and, without advancing, shall, with due respect, address himself to the President, confining himself strictly to the point in debate.

V. No member shall speak more than twice in the same debate, without leave of the house.

VI. A question being once determined, shall stand as the judgment of the house, and shall not be again drawn into debate during the same session, unless with the consent of two-thirds of the house.

VII. While the President is putting any question, no one shall hold private discourse, stand up, walk into, out of, or across the house, or read any book.

VIII. Every member who shall be in the house when any question is put, shall, on a division, be counted, unless he be particularly interested in the decision.

IX. No motion shall be considered as before the house, unless it be seconded, and reduced to writing when required.

X. When any question is before the house, it shall be determined on before any thing new is introduced, except the question for adjournment.

XI. The question on a motion for adjournment shall be taken before any other, and without debate.

XII. When the house is to rise, every member shall keep his seat until the President leaves the chair.

On motion Resolved,—That the Clergy of the Protestant Episcopal Church, who may be in the city of Baltimore, and who are not members of this house, shall be admitted to the sittings of the same.

This house Resolved,—That in consequence of the decease of the Right Rev. Bishop Parker, who had been appointed to open the meeting of this Convention with a Sermon, the House of Bishops be requested to appoint one of their number to perform that duty; and the Rev. Dr. Bend was appointed to communicate this request to the House of Bishops.

The Rev. Dr. Bend returned with a message from the House of Bishops, that the Right Rev. Bishop White intends to open the Convention with a discourse to-morrow, at the hour which has been publicly notified for divine service.

On motion Resolved,—That the hour of meeting each day shall be at 9 o'clock, A.M.

The Rev. Mr. Dashiell, the rector of St. Peter's, gave notice that there would be divine service and sermon in that church every evening during the Session.

The Rev. Dr. Bend informed the house, that the Church of St. Paul's and Christ Church were not fitted for service by candle-light.

WEDNESDAY, May 18, 1808, A.M.

The house attended divine service in St. Paul's church.

The Rev. Dr. Beach performed the service, and the Right Rev. Bishop White preached a Sermon adapted to the occasion of the meeting of the Convention.

After divine service the house met.

The Rev. Levi Bull, a Clerical deputy from Pennsylvania, and George Robertson, Esq., a Lay deputy from Maryland, appeared and took their seats.

The testimonial of the appointment of deputies from New Jersey was read and approved of, and Joshua M. Wallace,

Esq., a Lay deputy from New Jersey, appeared and took his seat.

On motion, Resolved unanimously,—That the thanks of the Convention be returned to the Right Rev. Bishop White for his Sermon preached before the Convention this morning, and that he be requested to furnish a copy for publication.

The House of Bishops concurred in this resolution, and informed this house that the Right Rev. Bishop White would furnish a copy of his Sermon for the purpose aforesaid.

On motion Resolved,—That a Committee be appointed to revise the Canons, and to report the same for the consideration of this house.

The following gentlemen were appointed the Committee. The Rev. Dr. Kemp, Rev. Mr. Baldwin, Rev. Dr. Hobart, Dr. John Onderdonk, and Joshua M. Wallace, Esq.

The house took up the alteration proposed by the last General Convention, in the Constitution of the Church, viz., that in Article III. the words, "unless adhered to by four-fifths of the other house," be struck out; and the further consideration thereof postponed until to-morrow.

A memorial to the General Convention was presented and read from the Convention of the Clergy and the Lay Delegates of the Protestant Episcopal Church in New Hampshire, praying the Convention to rescind a resolution of the General Convention of 1801, relative to the permission of an union between certain churches in New Hampshire and the church in Vermont. The memorial was referred to the Rev. Mr. Baldwin, Rev. Mr. Burhans, and Burrage Beach, Esq., to report thereon.

The house adjourned.

THURSDAY, May 19, 1808.

The house met, and Morning Service was performed by the Secretary, as Chaplain to the house.

The Rev. Robert Blackwell, D.D., a Clerical deputy from Pennsylvania; Joseph Sims, Esq., a Lay deputy from Pennsylvania; and John C. Weems, Esq., a Lay deputy from Maryland, appeared and took their seats.

The house resumed the consideration of the resolution proposed by the last General Convention, viz.

Resolved,—That in Article III. of the Constitution of the

Protestant Episcopal Church in the United States of America, the words, "unless adhered to by four-fifths of the other house," be struck out.

The question being taken by States on the above resolution, it was agreed to as follows:

Rhode Island—Clergy, Aye.	Aye.
Connecticut—Clergy, Aye; Laity, Aye.	Aye.
New York—Clergy, Aye; Laity, Aye.	Aye.
New Jersey—Laity, Aye.	Aye.
Pennsylvania—Clergy, Aye; Laity, No.(1)	Divided.
Delaware—Clergy, Aye; Laity, Aye.	Aye.
Maryland—Clergy, Aye; Laity, Aye.	Aye.

The Rev. Dr. Bend and the Rev. Dr. Moore were requested to carry the above resolution to the House of Bishops, who returned it with their concurrence.

Agreeably to the 11th Canon of 1804, the Journals of the State Conventions and other ecclesiastical documents were presented; and after the parochial reports and episcopal addresses contained on those Journals were read, the Journals and documents were transmitted to the House of Bishops, with a request that they would draw up a view of the state of the Church, adding such remarks or counsel as they might think proper, in the form of a Pastoral Letter from the House of Bishops, agreeably to the 11th Canon of 1804.

The Deputies from the Church in Maryland informed the house, that they were instructed by the Convention of said Church, to call the attention of the General Convention to the expediency of adopting the English Canon concerning marriages, and inserting the same in future editions of the Book of Common Prayer; and to the expediency of setting forth a Companion for the Altar; and they stated that they were also instructed to enforce the necessity of adopting an additional number of hymns.

In consequence of the above communication, the house adopted the following resolutions:

Resolved,—That the communication from the Convention of the Church in Maryland, on the subject of the English

(1) Joseph Sims, Esq., and Dr. P. F. Glentworth, Lay deputies from this State, were in favour of the resolution, but voted in the negative, because they supposed it necessary that they should have received instructions on the subject from the Convention of the State, which instructions they had not received.

Canon concerning marriages, be referred to the House of Bishops, with a request that they will consider the same, if they deem it expedient, during the present or at some future Convention, and will make any communication to this house which they may deem proper.

Resolved,—That it is not expedient to take any order on the subject of setting forth a Companion for the Altar. The above resolutions were sent to the House of Bishops for their concurrence.

Resolved,—That it is expedient to add thirty hymns to the present number contained in the Prayer Book, provided that a Rubric be annexed thereto, directing that a certain portion, or portions, of the Psalms of David, in metre, be sung at every celebration of divine service.

The following gentlemen were appointed a Committee to prepare and report hymns for the consideration of this house. The Rev. Dr. Moore, Rev. Dr. Kemp, Rev. Mr. Dashiell, Rev. Mr. Burhans, and Joshua M. Wallace, Esq.

The Deputies from the Church in Maryland also informed the Convention, that they were instructed to use their endeavours to have the 1st and 2d Canons of the General Convention of 1804 reconsidered, so far as they relate to the induction of Ministers into churches or parishes.

On motion, Resolved,—That the subject of induction be referred to the Committee on the Canons.

The house adjourned.

FRIDAY, May 20, 1808, 9 o'clock, A.M.

The house met, and Morning Prayer was performed by the Secretary as Chaplain to the house.

Leave of absence was granted to Mr. Burns, the Lay deputy from the State of Delaware.

The Committee on the Canons made a report in part, which was read.

A message was received from the House of Bishops, with an extract from their Minutes, and a letter from William H. Winder, Esq., enclosing a petition from Ammi Rogers. The Clerical and Lay Deputies from the State of Connecticut, at their own request, were permitted to withdraw.

Whereupon, Resolved unanimously,—That it is the opinion of this house, that agreeably to the 6th Article of the Constitution, the General Convention have no cognizance of the case of Ammi Rogers, and that he therefore have leave to withdraw his petition.

Ordered, that the Secretary carry a copy of the above resolution to the House of Bishops, and furnish a copy of the same to William H. Winder, Esq., who transmitted the petition of Ammi Rogers to the House of Bishops.

The house adjourned.

SATURDAY, May 21, 1808, 9 o'clock, A.M.

The house met, and Morning Service was performed by the Secretary, as Chaplain to the house.

The Committee on the Canons made a further report, which was read.

On motion, Resolved,—That the Prayer to be used at the meetings of Convention, adopted in General Convention, 1799, be inserted in all future editions of the Book of Common Prayer, among the Occasional Prayers.

The above resolution was sent to the House of Bishops for their concurrence.

The Committee on the memorial from the Convention of the Protestant Episcopal Church in the State of New Hampshire, made a report. Whereupon,

Resolved,—That a Committee of two or more persons from the State of Connecticut, Rhode Island, or Massachusetts, be appointed, whose duty it shall be to give notice to the parties interested, to give them a hearing if requested, and to make a report to any two of the Bishops of this Church, whose decision shall be final till the meeting of the next General Convention.

Resolved,—That the Rev. Ashbel Baldwin, the Rev. Philo Shelton, the Rev. Daniel Burhans, Burrage Beach, Esq., and Mr. Joseph Nicolls, be the Committee.

Resolutions, proposing the appointment of a Committee to address the Church in certain dioceses, were read, and ordered to lie on the table.

A message from the House of Bishops, on the subject of the English canon concerning marriages, was received and read.

The house then adjourned.

MONDAY, May 23, 1808, 9 o'clock, A.M.

The house met, and prayers were read by the Secretary as Chaplain to the house.

The resolutions proposed and laid on the table on Saturday, proposing the appointment of a Committee to address the Church in certain districts, and for other purposes, were read and adopted, and sent to the House of Bishops for their concurrence.

The Committee appointed to prepare an additional number of hymns made report.

The house took up the consideration of the Canons, as reported by the Committee appointed to digest and revise the same, and made some progress therein.

A message was received from the House of Bishops, with a "Pastoral address," prepared in pursuance of the 11th Canon of 1804, which was read in part.

The house then adjourned to meet at 5 o'clock, P.M.

MONDAY, 5 o'clock, P.M.

The house met, and resumed and finished the reading of the Pastoral Letter from the House of Bishops, transmitted to them by said house.

A message was received from the House of Bishops, with a substitute to the resolutions for the appointment of a Committee to address the Church in certain districts, and for other purposes.

The house then resumed the consideration of the Canons as reported by the Committee, and made further progress therein.

The Secretary was directed to communicate to the House of Bishops the revised Canons, as far as they have been agreed to by this house, with the necessary information relative to them.

The house adjourned.

TUESDAY, May 24, 1808, 9 o'clock A.M.

The house met, and Morning Service was performed by the Secretary as Chaplain to the house.

A memorial to this Convention, signed by the Rev. Nat. Bowen, Rev. Andrew Fowler, and Robert I. Turnbull, and

David Alexander, Clerical and Lay deputies from the Convention of the Protestant Episcopal Church in South Carolina, stating that they were unable to attend the meeting of the General Convention; and that it was the wish of the Church in South Carolina, that there should be a repeal or modification of certain Canons—was presented and read, and ordered to be sent to the House of Bishops.

The house resumed the consideration of the report of the Committee on the Canons, and made further progress therein.

The house adjourned until 5 o'clock.

TUESDAY, 5 o'clock P.M.

The house met, and finished the consideration of the report of the Committee on the Canons.

The Secretary was desired to communicate the remainder of the revised Canons to the House of Bishops, with the necessary information relative to them.

Leave of absence was granted to George Robertson, Esq., a Lay deputy from the State of Maryland.

The house adjourned.

WEDNESDAY, May 25, 1808, 9 o'clock A.M.

The house met, and prayers were read by the Secretary, as Chaplain to the house.

The house considered the substitute of the House of Bishops to the proposed resolutions of this house, for the appointment of a Committee to address the Church in certain districts, and for other purposes, and agreed to the same with amendments. These amendments were sent to the House of Bishops, and concurred in by them, and the resolutions finally adopted as follows.

1. Resolved,—That a Committee be appointed, consisting of three of the Bishops of this Church, and two of the Clergy, and two of the Lay members of the same, to make a solemn and affectionate address to the Churches represented in both Orders in this Convention, urging upon them the propriety, necessity, and duty of sending regularly a deputation to the General Convention; and that the said address contain a respectful appeal to every Bishop of this Church, on the subject of attendance on his part.

2. Resolved,—That the same Committee be authorised and

desired to address the Protestant Episcopal Church, in every State in which it is organized, but which has not acceded to the Constitution of this Church, inviting it to accede to the same.

3. Resolved,—That the same Committee address the Clergy of the several States or Territories of the United States, in which the Church hath not been organized; also, some of the most respectable lay members of the Church in such States or Territories, and invite them to organize themselves, and accede to the Constitution of the Protestant Episcopal Church in the United States of America.

4. Resolved,—That the same Committee be authorised and desired to consider of and determine on the proper mode of sending a Bishop into said States or Territories; and, in case of a reasonable prospect of accomplishing this object, to elect a person to such Episcopacy; and the certificate being given in the usual terms by the Standing Committees of this Church, as prescribed in the Canon for the consecration of Bishops in the recess of the General Convention, any three Bishops of the same be authorized to consecrate to the Episcopacy the person elected as above; provided that the jurisdiction assigned him shall not interfere with the rights of any State or diocese which shall hereafter adopt the Constitution of the Church in the United States.

5. Resolved,—That the Right Rev. Bishop White, Right Rev. Bishop Claggett, the Right Rev. Bishop Moore, the Rev. Dr. Beach, the Rev. Dr. Hobart, General Mathew Clarkson, and Dr. John Onderdonk, be the Committee for the purposes aforesaid, any four of whom shall be a quorum, provided it include one Bishop, one presbyter, and one layman.

6. Resolved,—That the said Committee render an account of their proceedings to the next General Convention.

On motion, Resolved,—That it be made known to the several State Conventions of this Church, that it is proposed to consider of, and determine on, at the next General Convention, the propriety of the following addition to the 8th article of the Constitution of the Church: "No alteration or addition shall be made in the Book of Common Prayer, or other offices of the Church, unless the same shall be proposed in one General Convention, and by a resolve thereof made known to the Convention of every diocese or State, and adopted at the subsequent General Convention."

This resolution was sent to the House of Bishops, and returned with their concurrence.

The report of the Committee appointed to prepare an additional number of hymns, was read and adopted.

This report, with the resolutions relative to an additional number of hymns, were sent by the Rev. Dr. Moore and the Rev. Mr. Dashiell, to the House of Bishops for their concurrence.

The Committee on the Canons, to whom was referred the office of induction, reported certain resolutions, which were adopted by this house, sent to the House of Bishops, and returned with their concurrence, as follows, viz.

1. Resolved,—That the title of the Office of induction be changed to "Office of institution," and that the corresponding alterations of expression be made in the Office itself.

2. Resolved,—That the following Rubric be prefixed to the Letter of institution in said Office.

"In any State or diocese, the concluding paragraph in the Letter of institution may be omitted, where it interferes with the usages, laws, or charters of the Church in the same."

3. Resolved,—That in the first Rubric, the words, "as prescribed by the 1st Canon of 1804," be changed, and the word "shall" be changed to "may."

Certain proposed resolutions on the subject of duels and divorces, were read and adopted, and sent to the House of Bishops for their concurrence.

A message was received from the House of Bishops with proposed amendments to the revised Canons, in which they requested the concurrence of this house.

The house then adjourned to 5 o'clock, P.M.

Five o'clock, P.M.

A further message from the House of Bishops, proposing amendments in the revised Canons, was received.

The house took up the consideration of the amendments proposed by the House of Bishops, to the revised Canons.

The House of Clerical and Lay Deputies concurred in these amendments, with the exception of one amendment; proposed further amendments; and ordered notice of the same to be sent by the Secretary to the House of Bishops.

The house adjourned until to-morrow, 8 o'clock.

THURSDAY, May 26, 1808, 8 o'clock A.M.

The house met.

A message was received from the House of Bishops, informing this house that they had receded from the amendment to one of the Canons, to which this house had non-concurred; had concurred in other amendments proposed by this house; had proposed a further amendment; and also that they had postponed the resolution concerning the insertion of the Prayer at the opening of the Convention among the Occasional Prayers in the Common Prayer Book.

They also returned the resolutions concerning duels and divorces, with a proposed amendment, which was concurred in by this house, and the resolutions passed, as follows:

1. Resolved,—That the Ministers of this Church ought not to perform the funeral service, in the case of any person who shall give or accept a challenge to a duel.

2. Resolved,—That it is the sense of this Church, that it is inconsistent with the law of God, and the Ministers of this Church, therefore, shall not unite in matrimony any person who is divorced, unless it be on account of the other party having been guilty of adultery.

This house also concurred in the further amendments of the House of Bishops, to one of the Canons.

A further message was received from the House of Bishops, with the proposed hymns, and the resolution relative to the same, which they had passed, with a substitute for one of the hymns.

In this proposed substitute the house concurred.

Certain petitions addressed to the General Convention, communicated by Ammi Rogers to the House of Bishops, which they had not opened, were sent by them to this house. Whereupon the delegates from the State of Connecticut were, at their request, permitted to withdraw; and on motion, it was

Resolved,—That as this house have already decided that they have no cognizance of the case of Ammi Rogers, he have leave to withdraw these petitions.

The following proposed resolution was passed unanimously:—

Whereas, associated Rectorships are inconsistent with the usages of the Protestant Episcopal Church, and in many respects inconvenient;

Resolved,—That it be recommended to the different State Conventions of this Church not to authorise, in future, associated Rectorships, and that when the existing associated Rectorships shall expire, not to renew the same.

The above resolution was sent to the House of Bishops, and returned with their concurrence.

The following resolutions were also passed by this house, sent by the Secretary of this house to the House of Bishops, and returned with an amendment, in which this house concurred.

Resolved,—That the Hymns set forth by this Convention, together with those now authorized, be printed in a small volume, under the direction of the Right Rev. Bishop Moore of New York, and the President and Secretary of the House of Clerical and Lay Deputies; that the said Committee be directed to annex tables to the Hymns and Psalms, suiting them to particular subjects and occasions; that these Hymns and tables be inserted in all future editions of the Book of Common Prayer, under the regulations of the Canon prescribing the mode of publishing authorised editions of the Book of Common Prayer; and that the edition of the Hymns, thus set forth by the authority of this Convention, be the standard copy.

Resolved,—That the Secretary of the House of Clerical and Lay Deputies prepare the Journals and other acts of this Convention for publication; and that the said Secretary, with the President of the house, and the Right Rev. Bishop Moore, be a Committee to publish the same, together with the Sermon preached at the opening of this Convention, and the Pastoral Letter of the House of Bishops; and that the Book of Canons and the Office of institution, published by said Committee, be authorised as standard copies.

Resolved,—That the city of New Haven, in the State of Connecticut, be the place for the meeting of the next General Convention, which will be held, agreeably to the Constitution, on the third Tuesday of May, A. D. 1811.

Resolved,—That the Right Rev. Bishop Claggett be requested to preach a Sermon at the opening of the next General Convention; and that, in case of his absence, the House of Bishops be requested to appoint one of their Order to preach a Sermon.

On motion, Resolved,—That the thanks of this house be returned to the President and Secretary.

This day being the Festival of the Ascension, the House of Bishops, and the House of Clerical and Lay Deputies, attended Divine service in St. Paul's Church.

Service was celebrated by the Right Reverend Bishop White.

ABRAHAM BEACH, PRESIDENT.

ATTESTED:
JOHN HENRY HOBART, Secretary.

JOURNAL

OF THE

House of Bishops.

City of Baltimore, Tuesday, May 17, 1808.

Nine o'clock, A.M.

Agreeably to a resolution of the last General Convention of the Protestant Episcopal Church, appointing this city as the place of the next meeting; and this being the day of their said meeting, fixed by the Constitution of the said Church, there met, in St. Paul's Church, of the House of Bishops, the Right Rev. Bishop White, of Pennsylvania, and the Right Rev. Bishop Claggett, of Maryland; who adjourned to five o'clock in the afternoon of the same day.

Tuesday Afternoon.

Present as in the forenoon.

The House of Bishops adjourned to the house of the Rev Dr. Bend, in the vicinity of St. Paul's Church.

Resolved,—That, agreeably to the offer of the Rev. Dr. Bend, his house be the place of meeting during the sitting of the Convention.

The Rev. Dr. James Whitehead, associate Rector of St. Paul's parish, in this city, was appointed Secretary of this house.

This house received by the Rev. Dr. Bend, a message from the House of Clerical and Lay Deputies, informing that they were organized, and ready to proceed to business.

Resolved,—That the Rev. Dr. Bend be desired to inform the House of Clerical and Lay Deputies that this house are also ready to proceed to business.

This house also received a message from the House of Clerical and Lay Deputies, stating, that the Right Rev. Bishop Parker, who had been appointed to open this Convention with a Sermon, having departed this life, it is the wish of the House of Clerical and Lay Deputies, that the said service may be performed by a member of this house.

Whereupon Resolved,—That the desire be complied with, and the Rev. Dr. Bend is authorised to inform the House of Clerical and Lay Deputies, that Bishop White intends to open the Convention with a discourse to-morrow, at the hour which has been publicly notified for divine service.

The house adjourned.

WEDNESDAY, May 18, 9 o'clock, A.M.

The house met, and adjourned to attend divine service in St. Paul's Church. The Rev. Dr. Beach performed service, and a Sermon, adapted to the occasion of the meeting of the Convention, was preached by the Right Rev. Bishop White. After service, the Bishops returned to their place of meeting. Present as yesterday.

Resolved,—That this house will attend divine service, during the Session, in the House of Clerical and Lay Deputies; and the hours of business appointed by said house be observed by this house.

A message was received from the House of Clerical and Lay Deputies, by the Rev. Dr. Hobart, with a communication of the thanks of the said house to the Right Rev. Bishop White, for his Sermon preached this morning, and with a request that he furnish a copy of the same for publication. With this request the Right Rev. Bishop White complied.

The house adjourned.

THURSDAY, May 19, 8 o'clock, A.M.

The house met. Present as yesterday.

A message was received by the Rev. Drs. Bend and Moore, with the following communication from the House of Clerical and Lay Deputies.

"Resolved,—That in Article the third of the Constitution, the words, 'unless adhered to by four-fifths of the other house,' be struck out;" to which resolution this house gave their concurrence.

A message was also received by the Rev. Mr. Bull, with the following communication from the House of Clerical and Lay Deputies, viz., "The house resolved that the Journals of the different State Conventions, Episcopal addresses, parochial reports, and other Ecclesiastical documents presented, and some of them read in this house, be forwarded to the House of Bishops, in order that they may draw up a Pastoral Letter from the House of Bishops, to be read in this house, and published agreeably to the eleventh Canon of 1804."

A message was received from the House of Clerical and Lay Deputies, by the Rev. Dr. Kemp, with a resolution against the expediency of setting forth a Companion for the Altar; in which resolution this house concurred.

This house also received the following resolution.

"Resolved,—That the communication of the Church in Maryland, requesting the attention of the General Convention to the English Canon respecting marriages, and the expediency or inexpediency of adopting the same, and ordering it to be inserted in the future editions of the Book of Common Prayer, be referred to the House of Bishops, to take up the subject if they deem it expedient, during the present or some future Convention, and to make any communication to this house which they may think proper."

The house adjourned.

FRIDAY, May 20, 9 o'clock, A.M.

The house met. Present as yesterday.

There was presented to this house a letter, signed "William H. Winder," enclosing two documents, signed "Ammi Rogers." Mr. Winder informs this house, that he is counsel for the said Ammi Rogers, who, in the documents referred to, appeals to the General Convention from a sentence of degradation said to have been passed on him, without trial or hearing, by the Right Rev. Bishop Jarvis, of Connecticut.

This house having considered the contents of the aforesaid papers, are of opinion that, agreeably to the Constitution of this Church, they have no authority to act on an appeal in regard to the matter stated; and there is no existing mode by which any Bishop or Bishops of this Church can take cognizance of the conduct of any other Bishop, unless at the desire of the Convention of the diocese to which such a Bishop should belong, and conformably to tha rules of process by them established.

And whereas this house acted on the concerns of the said Ammi Rogers, in the Session of 1804, as appears by the Minutes, they now wish it to be known that their proceedings at that time originated in his own petition, relative to the following points.

1st. Whether he belonged to the diocese of Connecticut, or to that of New York.

2dly. The recalling, which he proposed, of a circular letter written by Bishop Jarvis, forbidding the petitioner to perform divine service in the diocese, and the Clergy and Laity of the same to countenance him as a Minister.

3dly. A candid and impartial inquiry into his conduct and character.

On the first of the said points, the house then assembled, being assured that both the parties were disposed to submit to their determination, declared it to be, that Ammi Rogers, was a Clergyman not of New York, but of Connecticut.

The second point being a matter of internal concern of the Church in Connecticut, was not acted on judicially by this house; although, as their opinion was expected on both sides, they expressed it as it was, approbatory of the measure.

On the third point, they were of opinion that Ammi Rogers, far from having been treated with injustice, had not received a sentence sufficiently severe.

To the opinions thus given, no addition or alteration is intended by this house; and they finally dismiss the subject from their consideration.

This house, wishing the House of Clerical and Lay Deputies to be informed of their proceedings on the application now before them, direct that the Secretary deliver to them a copy of the minute now made, with the papers on which it is grounded. They also direct the Secretary to deliver a copy of the minute to William H. Winder, Esq., and for the further information of that gentleman, to deliver with it a copy of the Constitution of this Church.

The above was accordingly communicated to the House of Clerical and Lay Deputies, and a message was received from them, containing the following unanimous resolution.

That it is the opinion of this house, that agreeably to the 6th Article of the Constitution, the General Convention have no cognizance of the case of Ammi Rogers, and that he therefore have leave to withdraw his petition.

The house adjourned.

SATURDAY, May 21, 9 o'clock, A.M.

The house met. Present as yesterday.

In consequence of the message received by this house from the House of Clerical and Lay Deputies concerning the English Canon about marriages, the following message was sent.

The House of Bishops having taken into consideration the message sent to them by the House of Clerical and Lay Deputies, relative to the subject of marriage, as connected with the table of degrees, within which, according to the Canons of the Church of England, marriage cannot be celebrated, observe as follows:

Agreeably to the sentiment entertained by them, in relation to the whole Ecclesiastical system, they consider that table as now obligatory on this Church, and as what will remain so; unless there should hereafter appear cause to alter it, without departing from the Word of God, or endangering the peace and good order of this Church. They are, however, aware, that reasons exist for making an express determination as to the light in which this subject is to be considered. They conceive so highly of the importance of it, and it is connected with so many questions, both sacred and civil, that they doubt the propriety of entering on it, without maturer consideration than any expected length of the present Session will permit; and this opinion derives additional weight, both from there being but few of their house present, and from there being several of the churches not represented in this Convention.

Accordingly, they content themselves with recommending the subject to be considered and acted on at a future Convention.

This house received a message from the House of Clerical

and Lay Deputies, with certain resolutions, grounded on the memorial of the Convention of the Protestant Episcopal Church in the State of New Hampshire, in which resolutions this house concurred.

This house also received from the House of Clerical and Lay Deputies, a resolution relative to the "Prayer to be used at the meetings of the Convention."

The house adjourned.

MONDAY, May 23, 1808, 9 o'clock, A.M.

The house met. Present as on Saturday.

This house, in consequence of the communication from the House of Clerical and Lay Deputies of the Journals, parochial reports, and other Ecclesiastical documents, and agreeable to the 11th Canon of the General Convention of 1804, agreed on a "Pastoral Letter from the House of Bishops of the Protestant Episcopal Church to the members of the same," which was sent by the Secretary to the House of Clerical and Lay Deputies, in order to be read in said house.

A message was received from the House of Clerical and Lay Deputies, with certain resolutions on the subject of appointing a Committee to address the Church in certain districts, and for other purposes, which resolutions the house considered, and sent to the House of Clerical and Lay Deputies a substitute therefor.

Five o'clock, P.M.

The house received from the House of Clerical and Lay Deputies a draft of the Canons, as revised by said house; and the Rev. Dr. Hobart, who delivered this message, was permitted, agreeably to a request of the said house, to give the necessary information relative to said Canons.

The house entered on the consideration of them, and adjourned without finishing the same.

TUESDAY, May 24, 1808, 9 o'clock, A.M.

The house met. Present as yesterday.

The house proceeded in the consideration of the Canons, as revised and amended by the House of Clerical and Lay Deputies.

Five o'clock, P.M.

This house received from the House of Clerical and Lay Deputies the remainder of the Canons, revised and amended, with certain information relative to them, by the Secretary of said house.

WEDNESDAY, May 25, 1808, 9 o'clock, A.M.

The house met. Present as yesterday.

This house received from the House of Clerical and Lay Deputies, by the Rev. Mr. Clarkson, the proposed substitute from this house to the resolutions appointing a Committee to address the Church in certain districts, and for other purposes, with proposed amendments, in which this house concurred. And also a resolution to make known to the State Conventions, a proposed addition to the Constitution of the Church, in which this house concurred.

This house received from the House of Clerical and Lay Deputies, by the Rev. Dr. Moore and the Rev. Mr. Dashiell, a resolution relative to Hymns, with a proposed additional number of Hymns.

A further message was received from the House of Clerical and Lay Deputies, by the Rev. Dr. Hobart, with certain resolutions proposing alterations in the Office of induction, in which this house concurred; and this house also received certain resolutions on the subject of duels and divorces.

This house proceeded in the consideration of the revised Canons received from the House of Clerical and Lay Deputies, and having passed several of them, with amendments, sent them to the House of Clerical and Lay Deputies for their concurrence.

Five o'clock, P.M.

This house finished the consideration of the revised Canons, and returned them, with amendments, to the House of Clerical and Lay Deputies.

This house sent to the House of Clerical and Lay Deputies the following resolve, concerning persons who have already been received as candidates for Orders.

Resolved,—That the Canon regulating the preparatory exercises of candidates for Orders, shall not affect those persons who have already been received as candidates, but that their cases shall be governed by the Canons on said subject, which were in existence at the commencement of the present Convention.(1)

The house adjourned to 8 o'clock to-morrow morning.

THURSDAY, May 26, 1808, 8 o'clock, A.M.

The house met. Present as yesterday.

This house received from the House of Clerical and Lay Deputies, by the Rev. Dr. Hobart, a message, that the said house had non-concurred in one of the amendments proposed by this house, to one of the revised Canons, had concurred in the other amendments, and proposed further amendments. In these amendments this house concurred.

They also receded from their proposed amendment, returned by the House of Clerical and Lay Deputies, and proposed a further amendment, in which they were afterwards informed the House of Clerical and Lay Deputies concurred.

This house adopted the resolutions sent from the House of Clerical and Lay Deputies, relative to duels and divorces, with an amendment, in which the said house concurred.

This house returned to the House of Clerical and Lay Deputies, the resolution concerning the Prayer to be used at the opening of the Convention, wishing to delay the insertion of the same, among the Occasional Prayers in the Book of Common Prayer, until some future occasion.

This house took up the consideration of the resolution from the House of Clerical and Lay Deputies, relative to an additional number of Hymns, and adopted the same; they also adopted the proposed Hymns, with the exception of one Hymn, instead of which they proposed another.

This house also received a message, by the Rev. Dr. Hobart, from the House of Clerical and Lay Deputies, stating that the said house had agreed to the substitute to one of the Hymns; and requesting the concurrence of this house in a

(1) With the approbation of the Presiding Bishop, the Secretary of the House of Clerical and Lay Deputies states, that through inadvertence, this resolution was not transmitted to the House of Clerical and Lay Deputies, but that from the sentiments expressed in said house, during the consideration of the Canons, it appeared to be understood, that the Canon concerning the preparatory exercises was not designed to affect those persons who had already been received as candidates for Orders.

resolution disapproving of associated Rectorships, and to sundry resolutions relative to the setting forth of the Hymns, the publishing of the Journals, the place of meeting of the next General Convention and the preacher at the opening of the same. The house passed the aforesaid resolutions, with an amendment to the resolution concerning the setting forth of the Hymns, in which amendment the House of Clerical and Lay Deputies concurred.

Certain petitions were received from Ammi Rogers, which, as this house had resolved to dismiss the subject of his case finally from their consideration, they did not open, but ordered them to be sent to the House of Clerical and Lay Deputies, who informed this house that they had granted leave to the said Ammi Rogers to withdraw these petitions.

Resolved,—That the thanks of this house be given to the Rev. Dr. Bend, for the accommodations which they have received in the use of his parlour, and in other attentions, during the Session of the Convention.

The house rose, after attending, with the House of Clerical and Lay Deputies, divine service at St. Paul's Church—this day being the Festival of the Ascension.

Divine service was celebrated by the Right Rev. Bishop White.

Signed by order of the House of Bishops.

WILLIAM WHITE,
PRESIDING BISHOP.

Attested: JAMES WHITEHEAD, Secretary.

N.B. The Canons passed at this Convention are published with the Constitution of this Church, in a distinct pamphlet.—[NOTE TO ORIGINAL EDITION.]

List of the Clergy

OF THE

PROTESTANT EPISCOPAL CHURCH,

In the United States of America, 1808.

Delivered in and published agreeably to the 16th Canon of 1789.

NEW HAMPSHIRE.

St. John's church, Portsmouth, vacant.
Rev. Robert H. Fowle, rector of —— church, Holdernesse.
Rev. Daniel Barber, rector of —— church, Clermont.
Rev. Mr. Catlin officiates at Plainfield.
Rev. Samuel Mead.

MASSACHUSETTS.

Rev. William Willard Wheeler, rector of St. Michael's church, Scituate, and St. Peter's, Marshfield.
Rev. Nathaniel Fisher, rector of St. Peter's church, Salem.
Rev. John Sylvester I. Gardner, rector of Trinity church, Boston.
Rev. Mr. Eaton, rector of Christ church, Boston.
Rev. Samuel Haskill, rector of St. Ann's church, Gardiner.
Rev. William Montague, rector of St. Paul's church, Dedham.
Rev. James Bowers, rector of St. Michael's church, Marblehead.
Rev. Timothy Hilliard, Minister of the church at Portland.
Rev. James Morss, Minister of St. Paul's, Newburyport.
Rev. Amos Pardy, rector of St. Luke's church, Lanesborough.
Rev. Samuel Griswold, rector of St. James's church, Great Barrington, and the church at Lenox.

RHODE ISLAND.

Rev. Theodore Dehon, rector of Trinity church, Newport.
Rev. Alexander V. Griswold, rector of St. Michael's church, Bristol.
Rev. Mr. Ward, Assistant Minister of Trinity church, Newport.
Rev. Nathan B. Crocker, rector of —— church, Providence.

CONNECTICUT.

The Right Rev. Abraham Jarvis, D.D., Bishop.
Rev. Tillotson Bronson, Principal of the Episcopal Academy, Cheshire.
Rev. Richard Mansfield, D.D., Rector of Christ Church Derby, and of the Churches of Oxford and Great Hill.
Rev. Bela Hubbard, D.D., rector of Trinity church, New Haven, and Christ church, West Haven.
Rev. John Tyler, rector of Christ church, Norwich.
Rev. Daniel Fogg, rector of —— church, Pomfret.
Rev. Philo Shelton, rector of Trinity church, Fairfield, St. John s, Stratfield, and —— church, Weston.
Rev. Ashbel Baldwin, rector of Christ church, Stratford, and Trinity church, Trumbull.
Rev. Chauncey Prindle, rector of the churches of Oxford and Salem.
Rev. Reuben Ives, rector of St. Peter's church, Cheshire, and the churches of Hamden and Southington.
Rev. Truman Marsh, rector of the associated churches, Litchfield.
Rev. Ambrose Todd, rector of St. Paul's church, Huntingdon.
Rev. Daniel Burhans, rector of Trinity church, Newtown, and St. Luke's church, Brookfield.
Rev. Solomon Blakslee, rector of St. Stephen's church, East Haddam.
Rev. Charles Seabury, rector of St. James's church, New London.
Rev. Smith Miles, rector of the churches at Chatham and Middle Haddam.
Rev. Menzies Rayner, rector of the church, Hartford.
Rev. Henry Whitlock, rector of the churches at Norwalk and Wilton.
Rev. Calvin White, Assistant Minister of Christ church, Derby.
Rev. Nathan B. Burges, rector of the church, Hebron.
Rev. Roger Searl, rector of St. Mark's church, Harrington, and the church in Northfield.
Rev. Horace Virgil Barber, rector of St. John's church, Waterbury.
Rev. Russel Wheeler, rector of Christ church, Watertown, and the church in Bethlehem.
Rev. Asa Cornwall, rector of the churches in Simsbury and Granby.
Rev. Elijah G. Plumb, Deacon in the churches of Danbury, Reading, and Ridgefield.
Rev. Benjamin Benham, Deacon in St. Peter's church, New Milford, and the churches of Roxbury and New Preston.
Rev. David Baldwin, Deacon in the churches of Guilford and North Bristol.

NEW YORK.

The Right Rev. Benjamin Moore, D.D., Bishop, and rector of Trinity church, New York.
Rev. Amos G. Baldwin, rector of Trinity church, Utica.
Rev. Theodosius Bartow, rector of Trinity church, New Rochelle.
Rev. John F. Bartow, Deacon, St. Michael's church, Bloomingdale, New York.
Rev. Edmund D. Barry, Principal of the Episcopal Academy, New York, officiates at Christ church, Jamaica.
Rev. Abraham Beach, D.D., Assistant Minister of Trinity church, New York.
Rev. Frederick Beasley, rector of St. Peter's church, Albany.

Rev. John Bowden, D.D., Professor of Moral Philosophy, Logic, and Rhetoric in Columbia College, New York.
Rev. David Butler, officiating at Troy and Lansinburgh.
Rev. Barzillai Buckley, rector of Christ church, Poughkeepsie, and Trinity church, Fishkill.
Rev. James Chapman, Deacon, Trinity church, New York.
Rev. Abraham L. Clarke, rector of St. James's church, Newtown, and St. George's, Flushing.
Rev. Elias Cooper, Rector of St. John's church, Yonkers.
Rev. Joab G. Cooper, Deacon, Christ church, Hudson.
Rev. Henry I. Feltus, St. Anne's church, Brooklyn.
Rev. William Harris, rector of St. Mark's church, Bowery, New York.
Rev. Seth Hart, rector of St. George's church, Hempstead, with which is connected Christ Church, North Hempstead.
Rev. John Henry Hobart, D.D., an Assistant Minister of Trinity church, New York.
Rev. Thomas Y. How, Deacon, Trinity church, New York.
Rev. Cave Jones, an Assistant Minister, Trinity church, New York.
Rev. Jonathan Judd, Rector of St. John's church, Johnstown, and —— church, Fort Hunter.
Rev. Thomas Lyell, rector of Christ church, New York.
Rev. Richard C. Moore, D.D., rector of St. Andrew's, Staten Island.
Rev. David Moore, Deacon, Staten Island.
Rev. Daniel Nash, rector of St. John's church, Otsego, St. Luke's, Richfield, and Harmony church, Butternuts.
Rev. Samuel Nesbitt, residing in New York.
The Right Rev. Bishop Provoost, New York.
Rev. Davenport Phelps, Missionary in the western part of the State.
Rev. Philo Perry, rector of Christ church, Ballstown.
Rev. Joseph Prentiss, Deacon, Athens and Cocksackie.
Rev. Joseph Reed, St. Luke's church, Catskill.
Rev. Evan Rogers, rector of Christ church, Rye.
Rev. Cyrus Stebbins, rector of St. George's church, Schenectady.
Rev. George Strebeck, rector of St. Stephen's church, New York.
Rev. John Urquhart.
Rev. Frederick Van Horne.
Rev. Joseph Warren, St. Peter's church, Peekskill, and St. Philip's church, Philipstown.
Rev. Isaac Wilkins, rector of St. Peter's church, West Chester, and St. Paul's church, East Chester.

NEW JERSEY.

Rev. Charles H. Wharton, D.D., rector of St. Mary's church, Burlington.
Rev. Henry Waddell, rector of St. Michael's church, Trenton.
Rev. John Croes, rector of Christ church, New Brunswick, and St. Peter's church, Spotswood.
Rev. Jasper D. Jones, Rector of St. Peter's church, Perth Amboy.
Rev. Joseph Willard, D.D., rector of Trinity church, Newark.
Rev. John C. Rudd, rector of St. John's church, Elizabethtown.
Rev. Simon Wilmer, Trinity church, Swedesborough.

PENNSYLVANIA.

The Right Rev. William White, D.D., Bishop.
Rev. Samuel Magaw, D.D.

Rev. John Andrews, D.D., Vice-Provost of the University of Pennsylvania.
Rev. Robert Blackwell, D.D., Assistant Minister of Christ Church and St. Peter's, in the city of Philadelphia.
Rev. Joseph Hutchins, D.D.
Rev. John Campbell, rector of the churches of York and Huntingdon.
Rev. Joseph Pilmore, D.D., rector of St. Paul's church, Philadelphia.
Rev. Slator Clay, rector of St. David's, Radnor; St. Peter's in the Valley, and St. James's, Perkiomen.
Rev. Joseph Clarkson, rector of St. James's, Lancaster, St. John's church, Pequea, and Bangor church, Carnarvon.
Rev. Robert Ayres, rector of Emanuel church, Washington county, and St. Peter's church, Fayette county.
Rev. Francis Reno, Westmoreland county.
Rev. Joseph Turner, rector of St. Paul's church, Chester, and St. Martin's, Marcus Hook.
Rev. Caleb Hopkins, rector of Christ church, Derry Township, and Christ church, Turbut township, Northumberland county.
Rev. Thomas Davis, Washington county.
Rev. James Abercrombie, D.D., Assistant Minister of Christ church and St. Peter's, Philadelphia.
Rev. Absalom Jones (a black man), rector of the African church of St. Thomas's, Philadelphia.
Rev. John Taylor, Pittsburgh.
Rev. Levi Bull, rector of St. Gabriel's church, Berks county, and St. Mary's church, Chester county.
Rev. Robert Ayres.

DELAWARE.

The Rev. Robert Clay, Emanuel church, New Castle.
Rev. William Pryce, Trinity church, Wilmington.
Rev. James Wiltbank, St. Peter's church, Lewes.
Rev. Hamilton Bell, St. Paul's church, Georgetown.

MARYLAND.

The Right Rev. Thomas J. Claggett, D.D., Bishop.
Rev. Francis Barclay, A.M., rector of William and Mary parish, St. Mary's.
Rev. George Ralph, Rector of All Faith parish, St. Mary's county.
Rev. Benjamin Contee, William and Mary, Charles.(1)
Rev. John Weems, rector of Port Tobacco parish, Charles county.
Rev. Nicholas W. Lane, residing in Calvert county.
Rev. Edward Gant, Jun., residing in Calvert co.
Rev. Thomas Scott, rector of Queen Anne's, Prince George's.(1)
Rev. Walter D. Addison, rector of St. John's parish, Prince George's.
Rev. Joseph Messinger, residing in St. John's, Prince George's county.
Rev. William Swan, residing iu St. Paul's parish, Prince George's county.
Rev. Bethel Judd, A.M., Principal of St. John's College, and Rector of St. Anne's, Anne Arundel.
Rev. John W. Compton, St. James', Anne Arundel.
Rev. Ralph Higinbothom, residing in Annapolis, Anne Arundel.
Rev. Joseph G. J. Bend, D.D., associate rector of St. Paul's parish, Baltimore county.(1)
Rev. James Whitehead, D.D., associate rector of St. Paul's parish, Baltimore.(1)

Rev. George Dashiell, A.M., St. Peter's, Baltimore.
Rev. John Armstrong, rector of St. Thomas's, Baltimore county.
Rev. John Coleman, St. James's parish, Baltimore.
Rev. Elijah D. Rattoone, D.D., residing in Baltimore.
Rev. John Allen, A.M., rector of St. George's, Harford county.
Rev. George D. Handy, rector of St. John's parish, Harford county.
Rev. Thomas Read, Prince George's, Montgomery.
Rev. George Bower, A.M., rector of All Saints, Washington county.
Rev. Andrew T. M'Cormick, rector of Washington parish, Columbia.
Rev. John I. Sayres, A.M., Minister of St. John's church, Washington parish, Columbia.
Rev. John Kewley, M.D., rector of Chester parish, Kent county.(1)
Rev. Archibald Walker, D.D., Kent county.
Rev. William Briscoe, Deacon, Kent county.
Rev. William Duke, A.M., St. Mary Anne's parish, Cecil county.
Rev. Henry Lyon Davis, A.M., rector of St. Stephen's, Cecil county.(1)
Rev. John H. Reynolds, rector of St. Paul's, Queen Anne's county.
Rev. Joseph Jackson, St. Peter's, Talbot.
Rev. Samuel Keene, D.D., Talbot county.
Rev. John Price, Talbot county.
Rev. James Kemp, D.D., rector of Great Choptank parish, Dorchester county.(1)
Rev. William M. Stone, rector of Stepney parish, Somerset county.
Rev. James Laird, A.M., rector of Somerset parish, Somerset county.
Rev. David Ball, rector of All Hallows parish, Worcester county.

Those Clergymen marked thus (1), were elected members of the Standing Committee at the last Convention in this diocese.

VIRGINIA.

The Right Rev. James Madison, D.D., Bishop.

No list of the Clergy was received from this State.

SOUTH CAROLINA.

Rev. Edward Jenkins, D.D., St. Philip's, Charleston.
Rev. Nathanael Bowen, St. Michael's, Charleston.
Rev. William Percy, D.D., officiating at St. Philip's and St. Michael's, Charleston.
Rev. J. D. Simons, Deacon, Charleston.
Rev. Thomas Mills, rector of St. Andrew's parish.
Rev. Andrew Fowler, rector of St. Bartholomew's.
Rev. Galen Hicks, rector of St. Helena's church in Beaufort.
Rev. John T. Nankivel, rector of St Thomas and St. Dennis.
Rev. Hugh Frazier, rector of Prince Frederick's.
Rev. Christopher E. Gadsden, Deacon, St. John's, Berkley.
Rev. J. T. Tsheudy, Deacon, Clermont.
Rev. Thomas Gates, D.D., residing in St. George's parish, Dorchester.
Rev. Milward Pogson, residing in Charleston.
Rev. Paul Trapier Gervais, Deacon, Charleston.

Vacant parishes in this State are, Prince George Winyah, Georgetown; St. Stephen's, Santee; St. James's, Goose Creek; St. George's, Dorchester; St: John's, Colleton; St. Helena, on the Island of St. Helena; St. Luke's, St. Peter's, All Saints, St. Matthews, Christ Church—most of them able and willing to support Ministers.

JOURNAL OF THE PROCEEDINGS

OF THE

BISHOPS, CLERGY, AND LAITY

OF THE

Protestant Episcopal Church,

IN

THE UNITED STATES OF AMERICA,

IN

A GENERAL CONVENTION,

HELD IN

THE CITY OF NEW HAVEN FROM MAY 21 TO MAY 24, A. D. 1811

LIST OF THE MEMBERS OF THE HOUSE OF CLERICAL AND LAY DEPUTIES.

NEW HAMPSHIRE.

The Hon. James Sheafe.

MASSACHUSETTS.

Rev. James Bowers,
Rev. William Montague,
Shubael Bell.
Rev. John S. J. Gardiner,
Rev. James Morss,

RHODE ISLAND.

Rev. Alexander Viets Griswold,
Rev. Nathan B. Crocker,
John Russel.
Rev. Salmon Wheaton,
Benjamin Gardiner,

VERMONT.

Rev. Abraham Brownson,
Anson J. Sperry.
Rev. Parker Adams,

CONNECTICUT.

Rev. Bela Hubbard, D. D.,
Rev. John Kewly, M. D.,
Rev. Ashbel Baldwin,
Col. William Moseley.
Rev. Henry Whitlock,
Burrage Beach,
Gen. Matthias Nicoll,

NEW YORK.

Rev. John H. Hobart, D. D.,
Rev. Isaac Wilkins,
Rev. Elias Cooper,
Hon. Rufus King,
Hon. Philip S. Van Rensselaer,
Dr. John Onderdonk.

NEW JERSEY.

Rev. Charles H. Wharton, D. D.,
Rev. John Croes,
Rev. John C. Rudd,
John Dennis.
Joshua M. Wallace,
Peter Kean,
Edward Carpenter,

PENNSYLVANIA.

Rev. Joseph Pilmore, D. D.,
Rev. Levi Bull,
Hon. James Milnor,
P. F. Glentworth, M. D.,
Thomas M'Euen,
Ephraim Clark.

MARYLAND.

Rev. Joseph G. I. Bend, D. D.,
Rev. George Dashiel,
Rev. James Kemp, D. D.,
Joseph Cotman.
Rev. Henry Lyon Davis,
George Robertson,
Edward De Courcy,

JOURNAL

OF THE

House of Clerical and Lay Deputies.

NEW HAVEN, May 21, 1811.

This being the day appointed for the meeting of the General Convention of the Protestant Episcopal Church in the United States of America, several Clerical and Lay Deputies attended at 10 o'clock A. M. in the Trinity Church; and a quorum of the House being present, the Rev. Dr. Wharton was requested to take the chair, and the Rev. Dr. Hobart to act as Secretary *pro tempore.*

The House then proceeded to read the testimonials of the Clerical and Lay Deputies; which were severally approved, and the following gentlemen took their seats in the House.

From New Hampshire, the Hon. James Sheafe. From Massachusetts, the Rev. James Bowers, and the Rev. William Montague. From Rhode Island, the Rev. Alexander Viets Griswold, the Rev. Nathan B. Crocker, Benjamin Gardiner, and John Russel. from Vermont, the Rev. Abraham Brownson—he having previously presented a certificate that the State of Vermont had acceded to the Constitution of this Church. From Connecticut, the Rev. Bela Hubbard, D. D., the Rev. John

Kewly, M. D., Rev. Ashbel Baldwin, Burrage Beach, Gen. Matthias Nicoll, and Col. William Moseley. From New York, the Rev. John H. Hobart, D. D., Hon. Rufus King, and the Hon. Philip S. Van. Rensselaer. From New Jersey, the Rev. Charles H. Wharton, D. D., the Rev. John Croes, the Rev. John C. Rudd, Joshua M. Wallace, and Peter Kean. From Pennsylvania, the Rev. Joseph Pilmore, D. D., the Rev. Levi Bull, the Hon. James Milnor, P. F. Glentworth, M. D., Thomas M'Euen, and Ephraim Clark. From Maryland, the Rev. Joseph G. I. Bend, D. D., the Rev. George Dashiel, the Rev. James Kemp, D. D., the Rev. Henry Lyon Davis, George Robertson, Edward De Courcy, and Joseph Cotman.

The House proceeded to the election of a President and Secretary, when it appeared that the Rev. Isaac Wilkins was chosen President, and the Rev. Ashbel Baldwin, Secretary.

A message was sent to the House of Bishops, informing them that this house was organized and ready to proceed to business.

The House of Bishops returned for answer, that they also were organized, and ready to proceed to business.

The House took into consideration the rules of order, and adopted the following.

1. The business of every day shall be introduced with the Morning Service of the Church.

2. When the President takes the chair, no member shall continue standing, or shall afterwards stand up, unless to address the chair.

3. No member shall absent himself from the service of the House, unless he have leave, or be unable to attend.

4. When any member is about to speak in debate, or deliver any matter to the House, he shall, with due respect, address himself to the President, confining himself strictly to the point in debate.

5. No member shall speak more than twice in the same debate, without leave of the House.

6. A question being once determined, shall stand as the judgment of the House, and shall not be again drawn into debate during the same session, unless with the consent of two-thirds of the House.

7. While the President is putting any question, the members shall continue in their seats, and shall not hold any private discourse.

8. Every member who shall be in the House when any question is put, shall, on a division, be counted, unless he be personally interested in the decision.

9. No motion shall be considered as before the House, unless it be seconded, and, when required, reduced to writing.

10. When any question is before the House, it shall be determined on before any thing new is introduced, except the question of adjournment.

11. The question on the motion for adjournment shall be taken before any other, and without debate.

12. When the House is about to rise, every member shall keep his seat until the President shall leave his chair.

On motion, Resolved, That the Clergy of the Protestant Episcopal Church, who may be in the city of New Haven, and who are not members of this House, shall be admitted to the sittings of the same.

This House resolved, that in consequence of the absence of the Right Rev. Bishop Clagget, who had been appointed to open this Convention with a sermon, the House of Bishops be requested to appoint one of their number to perform that duty; and the Rev. Dr. Kemp was appointed to communicate this request to the House of Bishops.

The Rev. Dr. Kemp returned with a message from the House of Bishops, that the Right Rev. Bishop White intends to open the Convention, with a discourse, to-morrow, at the hour which has been appointed for divine service.

On motion, Resolved, that the hour of meeting each day shall be at nine o'clock, A. M.

This House adjourned to meet at the court-house to-morrow.

WEDNESDAY, May 22, 1811.

The House met.

The Rev. Parker Adams, a Clerical Deputy, and Anson J. Sperry, a Lay Deputy from the State of Vermont; the

Rev. John S. J. Gardiner, and the Rev. James Morss, Clerical Deputies, and Shubael Bell, a Lay Deputy, from Massachusetts; the Rev. Isaac Wilkins and the Rev. Elias Cooper, Clerical Deputies, and Dr. John Onderdonk, a Lay Deputy, from New York; the Rev. Salmon Wheaton, a Clerical Deputy from Rhode Island; and the Rev. Henry Whitlock, a Clerical Deputy from Connecticut, appeared and took their seats.

The House attended divine service in Trinity Church.

The Rev. Isaac Wilkins performed divine service, and the Right Rev. Bishop White preached a sermon adapted to the occasion of the meeting of the Convention.

After divine service the house met.

On motion, Resolved unanimously, That the thanks of the Convention be returned to the Right Rev. Bishop White, for his sermon preached before the Convention this morning, and that he be requested to furnish a copy for publication.

The House of Bishops concurred in this resolution, and informed this House that the Right Rev. Bishop White would furnish a copy of his sermon for the purpose aforesaid.

On motion, by the Hon. Rufus King, Resolved, That the following extract from the Journals of a Special Convention, held in Trinity Church, New York, May 15, A. D. 1811, be entered on the Journals of this House:—"Resolved, that the Convention will now proceed to the choice of a Bishop; to assist Bishop Moore in the duties of his Episcopal office, and to succeed him in case of survivorship. The Convention then proceeded to the election; and on counting the ballots, it appeared that the Rev. John H. Hobart, D. D., was elected by a majority of both orders."

On motion, Resolved, That this House will now proceed to sign the testimonials in favour of the Rev. John H. Hobart, D. D., Bishop elect for the State of New-York; which testimonials were unanimously signed by the House, agreeably to the third Canon of this Church.

The Rev. Mr. Gardiner made a communication to this House, that the Rev. Alexander Viets Griswold had been canonically elected Bishop of the diocese, composed of the States of New Hampshire, Massachusetts, Rhode Island, and Vermont.

On motion, Resolved, That this House will now proceed to sign the testimonials in favour of the Rev. Alexander V. Griswold, Bishop elect of the Eastern Diocese; which testimonials were unanimously signed by the House, agreeably to the third Canon of this Church.

The House adjourned.

THURSDAY, May 23, 1811.

The House met.

John Dennis and Edward Carpenter, Lay Delegates from the State of New Jersey, appeared and took their seats.

On motion, Resolved, That the delegation from the State of New York be requested to present the testimonials signed by this House in favour of the Rev. John H. Hobart, D. D., Bishop elect, to the House of Bishops.

On motion, Resolved, That the delegation from the States of New Hampshire, Massachusetts, Rhode-Island, and Vermont, be requested to present to the House of Bishops the testimonials signed by this House, in favour of the Rev. Alexander V. Griswold, Bishop elect.

The Rev. Mr. Bartow presented a certificate of his appointment to attend the Convention, signed by the wardens and vestry of the Episcopal Church in the city of Savannah, State of Georgia, which was read. Whereupon, Resolved, That the Protestant Episcopal Church in the State of Georgia, not being organized, and not having, in Convention, acceded to the Constitution of the Protestant Episcopal Church in the United States of America, the Rev. Mr. Bartow cannot be admitted a member of this House, but that he be allowed the privilege of an honorary seat.

This day being the Festival of the Ascension, the House attended divine service in Trinity Church,

The Rev. Dr. Pilmore performed service, and the Rev. Dr. Wharton delivered a sermon.

After divine service the House met.

The House of Bishops informed this House, that they desired an interview with the Deputies of the Churches in those States in which the Rev. Mr. Griswold has been elected to the Episcopal chair.

On motion, Resolved, that the Deputies from New Hampshire, Massachusetts, Rhode Island, and Vermont, be requested to wait on the House of Bishops.

Agreeably to the 45th Canon of the Church, the journals of several State Conventions were handed into the House—the parochial reports, and Episcopal addresses inserted in those journals were read by the Secretary, and a particular inquiry was made into the State of the Church in each diocese. The Rev. Dr. Kemp, Rev. Dr. Hobart, Rev. Mr. Montague, Dr. Glentworth, and Burrage Beach, Esq., were appointed a committee to lay before this house a view of the state of the Church, agreeably to the 45th Canon.

The House of Bishops informed this House, that having received from them the testimonials of two Reverend Gentlemen elected to the Episcopacy, they lament that they cannot proceed to the consecration of those two Reverend Gentlemen during the session of this Convention, there being only two Bishops present; but they propose (God willing) to carry this design into effect in the City of New-York, as soon as possible after the rising of this Convention.

A petition was presented to this House, signed by Benajah Hawley, which was read and ordered to lie on the table.

The House of Bishops informed this House, that in reference to the object of the appointment of a committee at the last Convention to act in the recess, for the devising measures for sending a Bishop into the Western States, that whenever the said business shall be taken up by this Convention, the House of Bishops are in possession of some communications which they think worthy of consideration.

The house adjourned.

FRIDAY, May 26, 1811.

The House met, and morning service was performed by the Secretary, in Trinity Church.

The Committee appointed at the last General Convention on the memorial from the Convention of the Protestant Episcopal Church in the State of New Hampshire, reported, That they had made no progress on the subject of their appointment. Whereupon resolved, That inasmuch as this House has received information, that the object of said Committee has been happily accomplished, said Committee is consequently discharged from any further attention to this business.

The Committee appointed at the last General Convention to address the Church in certain districts, and for other purposes, made the following report, which was read, and sent to the House of Bishops.

"The Committee appointed at the last General Convention to address the Church in certain districts, and for other purposes, Report, That a quorum of the said Committee resident in the city of New York, met and appointed the Right Rev. Bishop Moore to draft and to transmit the several addresses specified in the first three resolutions. This duty was discharged by him accordingly. The Committee not having any reasonable prospect of accomplishing the object contemplated in the 4th resolution, of sending a Bishop into those States or territories which have not acceded to the Constitution of the Protestant Episcopal Church in the United States of America, did not proceed to elect a person to said office, or to take any measures in that business.

JOHN H. HOBART,
Secretary of the Committee.

A message was received from the House of Bishops, with certain documents on the subject of a western Episcopacy, which were read.

On motion, Resolved, That the documents from the House of Bishops, relative to the western Episcopacy, be returned to them, with a request from this House, that they will take what order on the subject they may deem advisable.

There was laid before this House, by the House of Bishops, a petition, addressed to this Convention by the Rev. William Smith, D. D. of Norwalk, in the State of Connecticut, relative to a book of music composed by him, entitled, "The Churchman's Choral Companion to his Prayer Book." Whereupon, Resolved, That it is inexpedient to take any order on that subject; which resolve was sent to the House of Bishops.

The House of Bishops proposed to the House of Clerical and Lay Deputies the appointment of a Committee for further attention to the object of the 4th resolution (recorded page 14 in the journal of the last Convention), and that the Bishops in Pennsylvania and Virginia be requested to correspond with each other, for the devising means whereby the congregations west of the Allegany mountains may be benefitted by any measures to be adopted by the Committee, the appointment of which is hereby recommended.

The foregoing communication was considered by this House; whereupon, Resolved, That the Bishops in Pennsylvania and Virginia be requested to devise means for supplying the Congregations of this Church, west of the Allegany mountains, with the ministrations and worship of the same, and for the organizing the Church in the western States,—any thing in the 37th Canon to the contrary notwithstanding. The foregoing resolves were ordered to be sent to the House of Bishops.

The petition, signed by Benajah Hawley, which was yesterday read before the House, was again considered. On motion, Resolved, That it is the sense of this House, that the prayer of the petitioner cannot be granted, and that he have leave to withdraw his petition.

A memorial signed by the Rev. Benjamin Benham and the Rev. Virgil H. Barber, was presented to this House, and read by the Secretary.

On motion, Resolved, That it is inexpedient to take any order on the aforesaid memorial.

On motion, Resolved, That the presiding Bishop of the House of Bishops be respectfully requested to address a letter, in behalf of this Convention, to the venerable Society in England for propagating the Gospel in Foreign Parts, informing them that the Church in the State of Vermont is duly organized, and in union with the Protestant Episcopal Church of the United States, being placed under the jurisdiction of the Bishop of New-Hampshire, Massachusetts, Rhode-Island, and Vermont. That a Board of Trustees of Donations to the Church has been incorporated in the State of Massachusetts; and that, in the opinion of this Convention, the Society may safely confide the care of their lands in Vermont to such attorney or attornies as may be recommended by the said Board of Trustees, and approved by the Ecclesiastical Convention of Vermont.

The foregoing resolution was ordered to be sent to the House of Bishops.

A Canon repealing the 46th Canon, for making known the Constitution and Canons of this Church, was proposed and adopted.

The Rev. Dr. Bend was requested to carry the above Canon to the House of Bishops, who returned it with their concurrence.

On motion, Resolved, that the following addition to the 8th article of the Constitution, proposed at the last General Convention be agreed to.

"No alteration or addition shall be made in the Book of Common Prayer, or other offices of the Church, unless the same shall be proposed in one General Convention, and by a resolve thereof made known to the Convention of every Diocese or State, and adopted at the subsequent General Convention;" which resolution was directed to be sent to the House of Bishops.

The House of Bishops informed this House, that they concur with them in the proposed addition to the 8th article of the constitution.

The House of Bishops inform the House of Clerical and Lay deputies, that the presiding Bishop undertakes, (God willing) to perform the service requested of him, in relation to certain lands in Vermont belonging to the venerable Society in England, for the propagation of the Gospel.

On motion, Resolved, that the resolution passed by the last Convention, on the subject of duelling, be considered as not precluding any Minister from performing the burial service, when the person giving or receiving a challenge has afterwards exhibited evidences of sincere repentance.

The foregoing resolve was sent to the House of Bishops, and returned with their concurrence.

Resolved, That when this House shall adjourn, they will adjourn to meet at 7 o'clock this evening.

Leave of absence was granted to the Rev. Mr. Croes, and Anson J. Sperry, Esq. during the remainder of the session.

The House adjourned.

FRIDAY, 7 o'clock P. M.

The House met.

On motion, Resolved, That the city of Philadelphia be the place for the meeting of the next General Convention, which will be held on the third Tuesday in May, 1814; which resolve was ordered to be sent to the House of Bishops.

The Committee appointed to draft a report of the state of the Church to be laid before the House of Bishops, made the following report, which was read and accepted, and directed to be sent to that House.

"The House of Clerical and Lay Deputies, in compliance with the requisitions of the 45th Canon, have taken a general view of the state of the Church, and respectfully offer to the House of Bishops the result of their inquiries. Time would not admit them to enter into a minute detail of every particular; but from the few observations they have made, and the documents that will accompany them, they hope the House of Bishops will be able to comply with the requisition of the above mentioned Canon, in regard to a pastoral letter.

NEW-HAMPSHIRE.

"The number of Churches in this State has not increased, but respect for, and attachment to the Church seem to be growing in several places; and were there more Ministers there is reason to hope that it would soon be in a state of prosperity.

MASSACHUSETTS.

"In some parts of this commonwealth, it is greatly to be lamented that the Churches are in a state of derangement and decay; while in other places the congregations have increased.

RHODE-ISLAND.

"The congregations in this State, though few, are large, and, with the exception of the Church in Narraganset, there appears to be a degree of zeal and regularity that promises the happiest effect.

VERMONT.

"We are highly gratified to find that the Church in this State is now organized, and that zealous exertions are making to promote its interest and advancement.

EASTERN DIOCESE IN GENERAL.

"Although in these States, now formed into a diocese, some irregularities have taken place, and there has been a want of attention to the Canons and Rules of the Church, particularly to the Canon which requires parochial reports to be made, yet the arrangements lately formed, and the exertions made to organize the Church, and to obtain for it an Episcopal head, yield a ground of hope that this branch of the Church of Christ will not only preserve, but even extend more and more the light of the blessed Gospel.

CONNECTICUT.

"In Connecticut we have reason to believe that the Canons and Rules of the Church are duly observed. Since the last General Convention between four and five hundred families have been added to the Church; the congregations are in a flourishing condition; a number of new Churches have been built, and, with the zeal and exertions of the Clergy, we may cherish the expectation, that the power as well as the form of godliness will greatly advance.

NEW YORK.

"Here it is believed that the Church is orderly and regular. Congregations are every year forming, and the old ones seem to maintain their usual ground. In the city of New York, in particular, several new Churches have been built, and in the Diocese in general prosperity seems to attend the Church.

NEW JERSEY.

"In this State the Church appears to conduct her affairs with regularity and attention. The congregations are not numerous, but they are generally orderly and attentive.

PENNSYLVANIA.

"From the documents laid before us, it appears that although the Bishop has called the attention of the Clergy to the requisition of the 45th Canon, still they have not presented their parochial reports, and the Convention is very partially attended. Many, however, of the Clergy and Laity are zealous and attentive. In the city of Philadelphia, and in some of the neighbouring counties new congregations have been formed, and churches built, and the affairs of the Church are managed with attention and regularity.

MARYLAND

"The Church in Maryland is still in a deplorable condition; the zeal, however, manifested in some parts of the State, yield a hope, that she will again rise, and become a distinguished part of the Church in the United States.

"There being no representation from the States of Delaware, Virginia, and South Carolina, and no copies of the journals of the Conventions of those States, this House are unable to speak with certainty as to the situation of the Churches in those districts. They fear, indeed, that the Church in Virginia is, from various causes, so depressed, that there is danger of her total ruin, unless great exertions, favoured by the blessing of Providence, are employed to raise her. In South Carolina, there is reason to believe, that a lively zeal for the interests of the Church prevails, which, guided by sound principles, has already suggested various measures, which promise great and lasting benefit. The House of Clerical and Lay Deputies beg leave to observe to the House of Bishops, that while the review, in which they have been engaged, of the state of the Church, affords too much cause for deploring her declension in some places where she once flourished, her prosperity in other parts, and her general situation justify the most sanguine hopes of her friends. With an increasing attachment to her Apostolic ministry, and her primitive forms, they trust there is a corresponding increase of that power of godliness, which the outward order of the Church is designed to excite and nourish.

"They pray, for the Church and for themselves, your counsel, and the blessing of Almighty God.

"Signed by order of the House of Clerical and Lay Deputies.

ISAAC WILKINS, President."

On motion, Resolved, That this Convention have understood, with satisfaction, that the Convention of the Church in Connecticut are engaged in obtaining for the Episcopal Academy in that State a charter empowering the trustees to grant degrees, and this Convention do express their earnest wish for the success of this measure. This resolution was sent to the House of Bishops, and returned with their concurrence.

A message was received from the House of Bishops, informing this House, that they concur with them in appointing the city of Philadelphia for the meeting of the next General Convention.

A "Pastoral Address," prepared in pursuance of the 45th Canon, was received from the House of Bishops.

On motion, Resolved, That the House of Bishops be

requested to appoint one of their own order to preach a sermon at the opening of the next General Convention; which was sent to the House of Bishops, and returned with the following message: "The House of Bishops state to the House of Clerical and Lay Deputies, that they hope, under the blessing of God, for the attendance of their brother, the Right Rev. Bishop Clagget, at the next General Convention, and for his performance of the duty looked for from him, had his health permitted, at the opening of the present. But should there be a disappointment in this respect, the two Bishops now present (God willing) intend to provide by correspondence between themselves, or with some one of their Right Reverend Brethren, for the performance of this duty."

On motion, Resolved, That the Secretary of the House of Clerical and Lay Deputies prepare the journals of this Convention for publication; and that the said Secretary, with the Rev. Dr. Hobart, the Hon. Rufus King, and Dr. John Onderdonk, be a Committee to publish the same, together with the sermon preached at the opening of the Convention, and the Pastoral Address of the House of Bishops.

On motion, Resolved, That the thanks of this House be presented to the President and Secretary.

ISAAC WILKINS, President.

Attested, Ashbel Baldwin, Secretary.

JOURNAL

OF THE

House of Bishops.

CITY OF NEW HAVEN, Tuesday, May 21, 1811.

This being the day appointed by the Constitution of the Protestant Episcopal Church in the United States of America, for the meeting of the General Convention of said Church; and agreeably to a resolve of the last General Convention of the Church, in the city of Baltimore, the city of New Haven being appointed the place of meeting, the Right Rev. Bishop White, of Pennsylvania, and the Right Rev. Bishop Jarvis, of Connecticut, met in Trinity Church, in the aforesaid city. It appeared that Bishop Clagget, who engaged to open the Convention with a sermon, had left his place of residence, on his way to this city, but was obliged, by indisposition, to return

The Right Rev. Bishop Provost,, and the Right Rev. Bishop Moore were prevented from attending by bodily disability, and the Right Rev. Bishop Madison by engagements, which, in his estimation, did not admit of being dispensed with at this time.

The House of Bishops received a communication from the House of Clerical and Lay Deputies, by the Rev. Dr. Bend, informing them that they were organized, and ready to proceed to business. Dr. Bend was desired to inform the House of Clerical and Lay Deputies, that the House of Bishops was also ready.

This House was informed by the Rev. Dr. Kemp, that it was the desire of the House of Clerical and Lay Deputies, that the House of Bishops would provide one of their own order to deliver a sermon to-morrow morning at 10 o'clock. They returned for answer, that the Right Rev. Bishop White would deliver a discourse at the afore-mentioned time.

Resolved, That this House attend divine service with the House of Clerical and Lay Deputies during the session.

Resolved, That this House adjourn to 9 o'clock to-morrow morning, to meet in the State-House.

WEDNESDAY, 9 o'clock, A.M.

Met according to adjournment. Present as yesterday.

This House was informed, by the Rev. Dr. Hubbard, that the House of Clerical and Lay Deputies were ready to proceed to Church for divine service. This House joined the procession, and went to Trinity Church. The Rev. Mr. Wilkins read prayers, and the Right Rev. Bishop White delivered a sermon. After divine service they returned to the State-House.

Resolved, That the Rev. Philo Shelton act as Secretary to this House.

A message was received, by the Rev. Dr. Bend, from the House of Clerical and Lay Deputies, that they returned the thanks of that House to the Right Rev. Bishop White, for his sermon delivered this day before the Convention, and that he be requested to furnish a copy for publication.

Their request was complied with.

This House adjourned to 9 o'clock to-morrow morning.

THURSDAY, 9 o'clock, A.M.

Met according to adjournment. Present as yesterday.

At 10 o'clock this House joined the procession of Clerical and Lay Deputies, and went to Trinity Church, where divine service was read by the Rev. Dr. Pilmore, and a sermon delivered by the Rev. Dr. Wharton; they then returned to the State-House, and resumed their business.

This House received from the House of Clerical and Lay Deputies, the testimonials in favour of the Rev. John H. Hobart, D. D., as Bishop elect for the diocese of New York; also testimonials in favour of the Rev. Alexander Viets Griswold, for the Churches of Rhode Island, Massachusetts, New Hampshire and Vermont.

In reference to the election of the Rev. John H. Hobart, D. D., there was laid before this House the following letter from the Right Rev. Bishop Moore.

New York, May 18, 1811.

"Brethren:—You will perceive by the proceedings of the Convention lately held in this State, that the Rev. Dr. John Henry Hobart has been elected Assistant Bishop in this Diocese. My design in addressing these few lines to you, is to express my heartfelt approbation of the above measure.

Your affectionate brother,

BENJAMIN MOORE.

By his son Clement C. Moore.

To the Right Rev., the Bishops of the Protestant Episcopal Church in the United States of America, assmbled in General Convention, at New Haven, in Connecticut."

It not appearing on the face of the testimonials of the Rev. Alexander V. Griswold, how far the Convention of the Churches for which he was elected had given their respective sanctions to his election, this House sent the following message to the House of Clerical and Lay Deputies.

"The House of Clerical and Lay Deputies are informed by the House of Bishops, that they desire an interview with the Deputies of the Churches in those States in which the Rev. Alexander V. Griswold has been elected to the Episcopal chair."

In consequence of the above message, there appeared

from the House of Clerical and Lay Deputies, a delegation from Massachusetts, New Hampshire, and Vermont, which gave this House satisfaction, that the Rev. Alexander V. Griswold was unanimously elected by the Convention of the Church in Massachusetts, and so far as the election affected the Church in the other States, it was concurred in by their respective Conventions, and reported to their several constituents, and approved of by them. With this evidence the House was satisfied.

On the subject of the consecration of the Bishops elect, the House sent the following message to the House of Clerical and Lay Deputies.

"The House of Bishops inform the House of Clerical and Lay Deputies, that having received from them the testimonials of two Reverend Gentlemen elected to the Episcopacy, they lament that they cannot proceed to the consecration of those two Reverend Gentlemen during the session of this Convention, there being only two Bishops present; but they propose (God willing) to carry this design into effect in the city of New York, as soon as possible after the rising of this Convention."

The House of Bishops inform the House of Clerical and Lay Deputies, in reference to the object of the appointment of a committee to act in the recess, for the devising of measures for the sending of a Bishop into the Western States, that whenever the said business shall be taken up by this Convention, the House of Bishops are in possession of some communications which they think worthy of consideration.

This House adjourned to 9 o'clock to-morrow A. M.

FRIDAY, 10 o'clock, A.M.

The House, after attending divine service in Trinity Church, met in the State-House. Present as the day before.

This House received, by the Rev. Dr. Bend, a message from the House of Clerical and Lay Deputies the following resolution.

"Resolved, That the documents from the House of

Bishops relative to the Western Episcopacy be returned to them, with the request of this House, that they will take what order upon this subject they may deem advisable."

There was laid before this House and read, a letter addressed to both Houses, by the Rev. Dr. Smith, residing in Norwalk, in this State, relative to a book of music composed by him, called, "The Churchman's Choral Companion to his Prayer Book."

Resolved, That the said letter be communicated to the House of Clerical and Lay Deputies; which was accordingly done by their Secretary.

The following message was received, by the Rev. Mr. Davis, from the House of Clerical and Lay Deputies.

"There was laid before this House, by the House of Bishops, a petition addressed to this Convention by the Rev. William Smith, D. D., residing in Norwalk, in the State of Connecticut, relative to a book of music composed by him, entitled, 'The Churchman's Choral Companion to his Prayer Book.'"

Resolved, That it is inexpedient for the Convention to take any order on the subject."

Resolved, That in the above resolution this House concur.

This House received from the House of Clerical and Lay Deputies a report from the Committee appointed at the last General Convention to address the Church in the western districts, and for other purposes.

The following message was sent to the House of Clerical Deputies:

"The House of Bishops propose to the House of Clerical and Lay Deputies the appointment of a Committee for further attention to the object of the 4th resolution (recorded page 14 in the journal of the last Convention), and that the Bishops in Pennsylvania and in Virginia be requested to correspond with each other, for the devising means whereby the congregations in those States westward of the Allegany mountains may be benefited by any measures to be adopted by the Committee, the appointing of which is hereby recommended."

This House received, by Dr. Kemp, from the House of Clerical and Lay Deputies, the following resolution:

"Resolved, That the Bishops in Pennsylvania and Virginia be requested to devise means for supplying the congregations of this Church west of the Allegany mountains with the ministrations and worship of the same, and for organizing the Church in the Western States, anything in the 37th Canon to the contrary notwithstanding."

The above resolution was concurred in by this House.

This House received by the Rev. Dr. Hubbard, from the House of Clerical and Lay Deputies, the following resolve:

"Resolved, That the presiding Bishop of the House of Bishops be respectfully requested to address a letter, in behalf of this Convention, to the venerable Society in England for propagating the Gospel in Foreign Parts, informing them that the Church in the State of Vermont is duly organized, and in union with the Protestant Episcopal Church of the United States of America, being placed under the jurisdiction of the Bishop of the Diocese of New Hampshire, Massachusetts, Rhode Island, and Vermont. That a Board of Trustees of Donations to the Church has been incorporated in the State of Massachusetts; and that, in the opinion of this Convention, the Society may safely confide the care of their lands in Vermont to such attorney or attornies as may be recommended by the said Board of Trustees, and approved by the Ecclesiastical Convention of Vermont."

The House of Bishops informed the House of Clerical and Lay Deputies that the presiding Bishop will, by the providence of Almighty God, perform the services requested of him, in relation to certain lands in Vermont, belonging to the venerable Society of England for propagating the Gospel.

This House received from the House of Clerical and Lay Deputies, a proposed Canon, repealing the 46th Canon for making known the Constitution and Canons of the Church.

The House of Bishops concur with the House of Clerical and Lay Deputies in the repealing the aforesaid Canon.

The House of Bishops concur with the House of Clerical and Lay Deputies in the proposed addition to the 8th article of the Constitution by them resolved, viz.

"Resolved, That the following addition to the 8th article of the Constitution, proposed at the last General Convention be agreed to.

"No alteration or addition shall be made in the Book of Common Prayer, or other offices of the Church, unless the same shall be proposed in one General Convention, and by a resolve thereof made known to the Convention of every Diocese or State, and adopted at the subsequent General Convention."

This House received from the House of Clerical and Lay Deputies a resolution on the subject of duelling, in which resolution this House concurred.

This House adjourned to meet at 7 o'clock, P. M.

FRIDAY, 7 o'clock, P. M.

The House met according to adjournment.

This House received from the House of Clerical and Lay Deputies, by the hand of the Rev. Dr. Bend, the following resolution:

"On motion, Resolved, That the next meeting of the General Convention be in the city of Philadelphia."

In the above resolution this House concur.

This House received from the House of Clerical and Lay Deputies, the following resolve:

"Resolved, That this Convention have understood, with satisfaction, that the Convention of the Church in Connecticut are engaged in obtaining for the Episcopal academy in Cheshire, a charter, empowering the trustees to grant degrees; and this Convention do express their earnest wish for the success of this measure."

In the above resolve this House concur.

The House of Bishops, agreeably to the 45th Canon, providing for a review of the state of the Church adopted a Pastoral Address; which was sent to the House of Clerical and Lay Deputies.

This House received, by the hands of the Rev. Dr. Hubbard, from the House of Clerical and Lay Deputies, a resolve in the following words:

"Resolved, That the House of Bishops be requested to appoint one of their own order to preach a sermon at the opening of the next General Convention."

This House state to the House of Clerical and Lay Deputies, that they hope, under the blessing of God, for the attendance of their brother, the Right Rev. Bishop Clagget, at the next General Convention, and for his performance of the duty looked for from him, had his health permitted, at the opening of the present. But should there be a disappointment in this respect, the two Bishops now present (God willing) intend to provide, by correspondence between themselves, or with some one of their Right Reverend Brethren, for the performance of that duty.

The House adjourned.

Signed by order of the House of Bishops:

WILLIAM WHITE,
PRESIDING BISHOP.

Attested, PHILO SHELTON, Secretary.

CANON—Repealing the 46th Canon.

The 46th Canon, providing for making known the Constitution and Canons of the Church, is hereby repealed.

Addition to the 8th Article of the Constitution.

No alteration or addition shall be made in the Book of Common Prayer, or other Offices of the Church, unless the same shall be proposed in one General Convention, and by a resolve thereof made known to the Convention of every Diocese or State, and adopted at the subsequent General Convention.

HOUSE OF CLERICAL AND LAY DUPUTIES.
ISAAC WILKINS, PRESIDENT.

ASHBEL BALDWIN, Secretary.

HOUSE OF BISHOPS.
WILLIAM WHITE, PRESIDING BISHOP.

PHILO SHELTON, Secretary.

The following Clergy attended the General Convention, and were admitted to the sittings of the House of Clerical and Lay Deputies.

The Rev. John V. Bartow, Georgia.
William Gibson, Virginia.
Oliver Norris, Maryland.
Elijah G. Plumb, Conn.
Benjamin Benham, "
Daniel Burhans, "
Richard Mansfield, D.D. "
Calvin White, "
Russel Wheeler, "
Virgil H. Barber, "
Truman Marsh, "
Chauncy Prindle, "
Tillotson Brunson, "
Asa Eaton, Massachusetts.

The Rev. Simon Wilmer, New Jersey.
Thomas Lyell, New York.
Samuel F. Jarvis, "
Joseph D. Welton, Conn.
Roger Searle, "
Menzies Rayner, "
Smith Miles, "
John Tyler, "
Charles Seabury, "
Solomon Blakely, "
David Baldwin, "
Daniel M'Donald, "
Isaac Jones, "

List of the Clergy

OF THE

PROTESTANT EPISCOPAL CHURCH

In the United States of America,

Delivered in and published agreeably to the Canons, 1808.

EASTERN DIOCESE.

Composed of the States of Massachusetts, Rhode Island, New Hampshire, and Vermont.

The Right Rev. Alexander Viets Griswold, Bishop.

NEW HAMPSHIRE.

The Rev. Charles Burroughs, Deacon, St. John's Church, Portsmouth.
The Rev. John H. Fowle, Rector of —— Church, Holderness.
The Rev. Daniel Barber, Rector of —— Church, Claremont.
The Rev. Mr. Catlin, officiates at Plainfield.
The Rev. Samuel Mead.

MASSACHUSETTS.

The Rev. John Sylvester J. Gardiner, Rector of Trinity Church, Boston
The Rev. Asa Eaton, Rector of Christ Church, Boston.
The Rev. Nathaniel Fisher, Rector of St. Peter's Church, Salem.
The Rev. James Bowers, Rector of St. Michael's Church. Marblehead.
The Rev. William Montague, Rector of St. Paul's Church, Dedham.
The Rev. James Morse, Rector of St. Paul's Church, Newburyport.
The Rev. Amos Purdy, Rector of St. Luke's Church, Lanesborough.
The Rev. Samuel Griswold, Rector of St. James's Church, Great Barrington, and the Church at Lenox.
St. Michael's Church, Scituate, and St. Peter's, Mansfield, vacant
St. Ann's Church, Gardiner, vacant.
The Church at Portland vacant.
The Church at Hanover, vacant.

RHODE-ISLAND.

The Right Rev. Alexander V. Griswold, Rector of St. Michael's Church, Bristol.
The Rev. Nathan B. Crocker, Rector of St. John's Church, Providence.
The Rev. Salmon Wheaton, Rector of Trinity Church, Newport.

VERMONT.

The Rev. Abraham Bronson, Manchester and Arlington.
The Rev. Parker Adams, Deacon, Vergennes, Middlebury and Charlotte.

CONNECTICUT.

The Right Rev. Abraham Jarvis, D.D., Bishop.
The Rev. Tillotson Brunson, Principal of the Episcopal Academy, Cheshire.
The Rev. Richard Mansfield, D.D., Rector of Christ Church, Derby, and the Churches of Oxford and Great Hill.
The Rev. Bela Hubbard, D.D., Rector of Trinity Church, New-Haven, and Christ Church, West-Haven.
The Rev. John Tyler, Rector of Christ Church, Norwich.
The Rev. Daniel Fogg, Rector of ——— Church, Pomfret.
The Rev. Philo Shelton, Rector of Trinity Church, Fairfield, St. John's, Stratfield, and the Church at Weston.
The Rev. Ashbel Baldwin, Rector of Christ Church, Stratford, and Trinity Church, Trumbull.
The Rev. Chauncy Prindle. Rector of the Churches of Oxford and Salem.
The Rev. Reuben Ives, Rector of St. Peter's Church, Cheshire, and officiating in the Churches at Hambden and Wallingford.
The Rev. Truman Marsh, Rector of the Associated Churches in Litchfield.
The Rev. Daniel Burhans, Rector of Trinity Church, Newtown, and St. Luke's, Brookfield.
The Rev. Solomon Blakesly, Rector of St. Stephen's Church, East Haddam.
The Rev. Charles Seabury, Rector of St. James's Church, New London.
The Rev. Smith Miles, Rector of the Churches of Chatham and Middle Haddam.
The Rev. Menzies Rayner, Rector of the Church, Hartford.
The Rev. Calvin White, Assistant Minister of the Church in Derby.
The Rev. John Kewley, M. D., Rector of Christ Church, Middletown.
The Rev. Henry Whitlock, Rector of St. Paul's Church, Norwalk, and the Church at Wilton.
The Rev. Roger Searle, Rector of St. Peter's Church, Plymouth, and St. Matthew's, Bristol.
The Rev. Virgil H. Barber, Rector of St. John's Church, Waterbury.
The Rev. Russell Wheeler, Rector of Christ Church, Watertown.
The Rev. Asa Cornwall, Rector of the Churches in Simsbury and Granby.
The Rev. Elijah G. Plumb, Minister of the Churches in Reading, Danbury, and Ridgefield.
The Rev. Benjamin Benham, Rector of St. John's Church, New Milford, and the Churches of New Preston and Bridgewater.
The Rev. David Baldwin, Rector of the Churches of Guilford and North Bristol.
The Rev. Joseph D. Welton, officiating in the Churches of Woodbury, Roxbury and Bethlehem.

The Rev. Sturgis Gilbert, officiating in the Churches of Kent and Sharon.
The Rev. Daniel M'Donald, Deacon, and assistant instructor in the Episcopal Academy, Cheshire.
The Rev. Nathaniel Huse, Deacon, officiating at Warehouse Point.
The Rev. William Smith, D. D., resident at Norwalk.

NEW YORK.

The Right Rev. Samuel Provoost, D. D.,
The Right Rev. Benjamin Moore, D. D., } Bishops.
The Right Rev. John Henry Hobart, D. D.,
The Rev. Amos G. Baldwin, Rector of Trinity Church, Utica.
The Rev. Theodosius Bartow, Rector of Trinity Church, New Rochelle.
The Rev. Edmund D. Barry, Principal of the Protestant Episcopal Academy, New York; officiating at St. Matthew's Church, Jersey City.
The Rev. Abraham Beach, D. D., Assistant Rector of Trinity Church, New York.
The Rev. William Berrian, Deacon, residing in New York; officiating at Belville, New Jersey.
The Rev. John Bowden, D. D., Professor of Rhetoric and Moral Philosophy in Columbia College.
The Rev. Nathaniel Bowen, Rector of Grace Church, New York.
The Rev. David Butler, Rector of St. Paul's Church, Troy, and Trinity Church, Lansingburgh.
The Rev. Barzillai Bulkley, Rector of St. George's Church, Flushing, Long Island.
The Rev. Nathan B. Burgess, Caroline Church, Brookhaven, Long Island.
The Rev. William Clark, Deacon, Missionary.
The Rev. Timothy Clowes, Deacon, St. Peter's Church, Albany.
The Rev. Elias Cooper, Rector of St. John's Church, Yonkers.
The Rev. Joab G. Cooper, Christ Church, Hudson, Columbia County.
The Rev. Adam Empie, Deacon, Hempstead, Long Island.
The Rev. Henry J. Feltus, Rector of St. Ann's Church, Brooklyn, Long Island.
The Rev. Samuel Fuller, Deacon, Missionary.
The Rev. Nathan Felch, Churches at Bedford and North Castle, West Chester County.
The Rev. William Harris, Rector of St. Mark's Church, New York.
The Rev. Seth Hart, Rector of St. George's Church, Hempstead, and Christ Church, North Hempstead, Long Island.
The Rev. Samuel Haskill, Rector of Christ Church, Rye, West Chester County.
The Rev. Thomas Y. How, an Assistant Minister of Trinity Church, New York.
The Rev. Reuben Hubbard, Duanesborough.
The Rev. Sam'l F. Jarvis, St. Michael's Church, Bloomingdale, New York.
The Rev. Cave Jones, an Assistant Minister of Trinity Church, N. York.
The Rev. Jonathan Judd, Rector of St. John's Church, Johnstown, and St. Ann's Church, Fort Hunter, Montgomery County.
The Rev. Thomas Lyell, Rector of Christ Church, New York
The Rev. Richard C. Moore, D. D., Rector of St. Stephen's Church, N. Y.
The Rev. David Moore, Deacon, St. Andrew's Church, Staten Island.

The Rev Daniel Nash, Rector of St. John's Church, Otsego, St. Luke's Church, Richfield, Harmony Church, Butternutts, and other Churches in Otsego County.
The Rev. Samuel Nesbit, residing in New York.
The Rev. Joseph Perry, Christ Church, Balltown.
The Rev. Davenport Phelps, Missionary in the Western Part of the State.
The Rev. Joseph Prentice, Rector of Trinity Church, Athens, Greene Co.
The Rev. Wm. Powell, Dea., St. Andrew's Church, Coldenham, Orange Co.
The Rev. John Reed, Rector of Christ Church, Poughkeepsie, Duchess Co.
The Rev. Gilbert H. Sayres, Deacon, Grace Church, Jamaica, Long Island.
The Rev. Cyrus Stebbins, Rector of St. George's Church, Schenectady.
The Rev. George Strebeck, residing in New York.
The Rev. John Urquhart, Peekskill and Phillip's Town, Duchess County.
The Rev. Frederick Van Horne, residing at Coldenham.
The Rev. Isaac Wilkins, Rector of St. Peter's Church, West Chester, and St. Paul's Church, East Chester.
The Rev. Seth Williston, Deacon, Zion Church, New York.
The Rev. William E. Wyatt, Deacon, St. James's Church, Newtown, Long Island.

NEW JERSEY.

The Rev. Chas. H. Wharton, D. D., Rector, St Mary's Church, Burlington.
The Rev. John Croes, Rector of Christ Church, New Brunswick, and St. Peter's Church, Spotswood.
The Rev. Joseph Willard, Rector of Trinity Church, Newark.
The Rev. John C. Rudd, Rector of St. John's Church, Elizabeth Town.
The Rev. Simon Wilmer, Rector of Trinity Church, Swedesborough.
The Rev. James Chapman, St. Peter's Church, Perth Amboy.
The Rev. Daniel Higbee, St. Andrew's Church, Mount Holly, and St. Mary's Church, Colestown.
The Rev. John Croes, jr. Deacon; officiating in St. Peter's Church, Freehold, Christ Church, Shrewsbury, and Christ Church, Middletown.

PENNSYLVANIA.

The Right Rev. William White, D. D., Bishop.
The Rev. Samuel Magaw, D. D.
The Rev. John Andrews, D. D., Provost of the University of Pennsylvania.
The Rev. Robert Blackwell, D. D.
The Rev. Joseph Hutchins, D. D.
The Rev James Abercrombie, D. D., Assistant Minister of Christ Church, St. Peter's and St. James's, Philadelphia.
The Rev. Jos. Pilmore, D. D., Rector of St. Paul's Church, Philadelphia.
The Rev. William Ayres.
The Rev. Slater Clay, Rector of St. James's Perkiomen, and St. Peter's in the Valley.
The Rev. Joseph Clarkson, Rector of St. James's, Lancaster, St. John's Church, Pequea, and Bangor Church, Carnarvon.
The Rev Robert Ayres.
The Rev. Francis Reno, Westmoreland County.
The Rev. Joseph Turner, Rector of St. Martin's Church, Marcus Hook.
The Rev. Caleb Hopkins, Rector of Christ Church, Derry Township, and Christ Church, Turbutt Township, Northumberland County.

The Rev. Thomas Davis, Somerset County.
The Rev. James Wiltbank, Rector of Trinity Church, Oxford, and All Sain s, Pequeston.
The Rev. Absalom Jones (a black man), Rector of the African Church of St. Thomas, Philadelphia.
The Rev. John Taylor, Rector of the Episcopal Church in Pittsburgh.
The Rev. Levi Bull, Rector of St. Gabriel's Church, Berk's County, and St. Mary's, Chester County.
The Rev. Joseph Hulbert Turner, A. M., Deacon.
The Rev. Jackson Kemper, A. M., Deacon, Assistant Minister of Christ Church, St. Peter's and St. James's, Philadelphia.

DELAWARE.

No list of the Clergy was received from this State.

MARYLAND.

The Right Rev. Thomas John Claggett, D. D., Bishop.
*The Rev. Benj Contee, Rector of William and Mary, Charles County.
The Rev. John Weems, Rector of Port Tobacco Parish, Charles County.
The Rev. William Swann, residing in Port Tobacco, Charles County.
The Rev. William Duncan, Rector of Durham, Charles County.
The Rev. Nicholas W. Lane, residing in Calvert County.
The Rev. Thomas Scott, Rector of Queen Anne's, Prince George's County.
*The Rev. Bethel Judd, A. M., Principal of St. John's College, and Rector of St. Anne's Parish.
The Rev. Ralph Higinbothom, Vice-Principal, residing in Annapolis, Anne Arundel County.
The Rev. John W. Compton, Rector of St. James's Parish, Anne Arundel.
The Rev. William Hind, Rector of Margaret, Westmoreland, "
The Rev. Oliver Norris, Rector of Queen Caroline, Anne Arundel.
The Rev. Walter D. Addison, Rector of John's, Territory of Columbia.
The Rev. Andrew T. M'Cormick, Rector of Washington, Territory of Columbia.
The Rev. Thomas Read, Rector of Prince George's, Montgomery County.
The Rev. John Chandler, Rector of St. Peter's, Montgomery County.
The Rev. George Bower, Rector of St. John's, Montgomery County.
The Rev. George Bower, Rector of St. John's, Washington County.
*The Rev. Joseph G. I. Bend, D. D., Associate Rector of St. Paul's Parish, Baltimore County.
The Rev. Frederic Beasley, D. D., Associate Rector of St. Paul's Parish, Baltimore County.
The Rev. George Ralph, A. M., residing in St. Paul's Parish, Baltimore County.
The Rev. Henry Moscrop, residing in St. Paul's Parish, Baltimore County.
*The Rev. George Dashiel, Rector of St. Peter's, Baltimore County.
The Rev. John Coleman, Rector of St. James's, Baltimore County.
The Rev. George D. Handy, Rector of St. John's, Harford County.
The Rev. John Allen, Rector of St. George's, Harford County.
*The Rev. Henry L. Davis, Rector of St. Stephen's, Cecil County.
The Rev. William Duke, residing in Elkton, Cecil County.

This mark * denotes members of the Standing Committee.

The Rev. William H. Wilmer, Rector of Charlestown, Kent County.
The Rev. Daniel Stephens, Rector of St. Luke's, Queen Anne's County.
*The Rev. Joseph Jackson, St. Peter's, Talbot County.
The Rev. James Kemp, D. D., Rector of Great Choptank, Dorchester Co.
The Rev. William M. Stone, Rector of Stepney, Somerset County.
The Rev. James Laird, Rector of Somerset, Somerset County.
The Rev. David Ball, Rector of All-Hallow's, Worcester County.

VIRGINIA.

The Right Rev. James Madison, D D., Bishop.
No list of the Clergy was received from this State.

SOUTH CAROLINA.

The Rev. Theodore Dehon, D. D., Rector of St. Michael's Church, Charleston.
The Rev. James D. Simons, Rector of St. Philips.
The Rev Christopher Edward Gadsden, Assistant Minister of St. Philip's Church, Charleston
The Rev. William Percy, Rector of the third Episcopal Church, Charleston.
The Rev. Thomas Mills, D. D., Rector of St. Andrews Parish.
The Rev. Andrew Fowler.
The Rev Charles Blair Snowden, Rector of St. Stephen's Parish.
The Rev. John T. Tschudy, Rector of Claremont Parish.
The Rev. Solomon Halling, Rector of Prince George, Winyah, Georgetown.
The Rev. John Barnwell Campbell, Rector of St. Helena's Church, Beaufort.
The Rev. Hugh Fraser, Rector of Prince Frederick's Parish.
The Rev. Jos. Warren, Rector of the Episcopal Church on Edisto Island.

CLERGYMEN IN THE STATE NOT HAVING CURES.

The Rev. Thomas Gates, D. D.
The Rev. Milward Pogson.
The Rev. Paul T. Gervais.
The Rev. Galen Hicks.

GEORGIA.

The Rev. John V. Bartow, Rector of Christ Church, Savannah.

On Wednesday, the 29th day of May, in Trinity Church, in the city of New York, the Right Rev. Bishop White, of Pennsylvania, being presiding Bishop, the Right Rev. Bishop Provoost, of New York, and the Right Rev. Bishop Jarvis, of Connecticut, being present, and assisting, the Rev. John Henry Hobart, D. D., of New York, and the Rev. Alexander V. Griswold, of Bristol, Rhode Island, were consecrated Bishops: the former for the Diocese of New York, and the latter for the Eastern Diocese, composed of the States of Massachusetts, Rhode Island, New Hampshire and Vermont.

The following are the certificates of consecration:

Know all men by these presents, that we, William White, D. D., Bishop of the Protestant Episcopal Church in the State of Pennsylvania, presiding Bishop, Samuel Provoost, D. D., Bishop of the Protestant Episcopal Church in the State of New York, and Abraham Jarvis, D. D., Bishop of the Protestant Episcopal Church in the State of Connecticut, under the protection of Almighty God, in Trinity Church, in the City of New York, on Wednesday, the twenty-ninth day of May, in the year of our Lord one thousand eight hundred and eleven, did then and there rightly and canonically consecrate our beloved in Christ, John Henry Hobart, D. D, an Assistant Minister of Trinity Church, in the city of New York, of whose sufficiency in good learning, soundness in the faith, and purity of manners we were fully ascertained, into the office of Bishop of the Protestant Episcopal Church in the State of New York, to which he hath been elected by the Convention of said State; to assist the Bishops of the Church in said State in the duties of the Episcopal office, and to succeed in case of survivorship.

Given in the city of New York, this twenty-ninth day of May, in the year of our Lord one thousand eight hundred and eleven.

WILLIAM WHITE.
SAMUEL PROVOOST.
ABRAHAM JARVIS.

Know all mon by these presents, that we, William White, D. D., Bishop of the Protestant Episcopal Church in the State of Pennsylvania, presiding Bishop, Samuel Provoost, D. D., Bishop of the Protestant Episcopal Church in the State of New York, and Abraham Jarvis, D. D., Bishop of the Protestant Episcopal Church, in the State of Connecticut, under the protection of Almighty God, in Trinity Church, in the city of New York, on Wednesday, the twenty-ninth day of May, in the year of our Lord one thousand eight hundred and eleven, did then and there rightly and canonically consecrate our beloved in Christ, Alexander Viets Griswold, Rector of St. Michael's Church, Rhode Island, of whose sufficiency in good learning, soundness in the faith, and purity of manners we were fully ascertained, into the office of Bishop of the Protestant Episcopal Church in the Eastern Diocese, composed of the States of Massachusetts, Rhode Island, New Hampshire, and Vermont, to which he hath been elected by the Convention of said States.

Given in the city of New York, this twenty-ninth day of May, in the year of our Lord one thousand eight hundred and eleven.

WILLIAM WHITE.
SAMUEL PROVOOST.
ABRAHAM JARVIS.

JOURNAL OF THE PROCEEDINGS

OF THE

BISHOPS, CLERGY, AND LAITY

OF THE

Protestant Episcopal Church,

IN

THE UNITED STATES OF AMERICA,

HELD IN

THE CITY OF PHILADELPHIA, FROM MAY 17TH, TO MAY 24TH, 1814, INCLUSIVE.

JOURNAL.

LIST OF THE MEMBERS OF THE HOUSE OF CLERICAL AND LAY DEPUTIES

who attended the Convention of the Protestant Episcopal Church, in the United States, held in Philadelphia, in May, 1814.

CLERICAL DEPUTIES.

VERMONT.

John P. K. Henshaw.

MASSACHUSETTS.

John Sylvester,
John Gardiner, D. D.,
Asa Eaton,
James Morss.

CONNECTICUT.

Ashbel Baldwin,
Philo Shelton.

RHODE ISLAND.

Salmon Wheaton,
Nathan B. Crocker.

NEW YORK.

John Kewley, M. D.,
Thomas Y. How, D D.

NEW JERSEY.

Charles Henry Wharton, D. D.,
John Croes, D. D.,
John C. Rudd.

PENNSYLVANIA.

Joseph Pilmore, D. D.,
James Abercrombie, D. D.,
James Wiltbank,
Levi Bull.

DELAWARE.

William Pryce, Robert Clay.

MARYLAND.

James Kemp, D. D., George Dashiel, William M. Stone, Daniel Stephens.

VIRGINIA.

William A. Wilmer, Oliver Norris, Hugh C. Boggs.

SOUTH CAROLINA.

John S. Tschudy, Christopher E. Gadsden.

LAY DEPUTIES.

MASSACHUSETTS.

John Deane, Esq.

RHODE ISLAND.

Benjamin Gardner, Esq., Abel Jones, Esq.

CONNECTICUT.

Charles Sigourney, Esq.

NEW YORK.

Hon. Philip S. Van Rensselaer, Doctor John Onderdonk.

NEW JERSEY.

Joshua M. Wallace, Esq., Hon. William Coxe, Joseph Higby, Esq., Josiah Harrison, Esq.

PENNSYLVANIA.

General Francis Gurney, Thomas M'Euen, Esq., John M'Elroy, Esq., Jacob Warren, Esq.

DELAWARE.

Joseph Burn, Esq., Joseph Reynolds, Esq.

MARYLAND.

Robert Dunn, Esq., John C. Herbert, Esq.

VIRGINIA.

George Deneale, Esq., Edward M'Guire, Col. Hugh Mercer.

LIST OF THE CLERGY

who were admitted to attend the sittings of the Convention of 1814, not being members of the same.

NEW YORK.

Timothy Clowes,
John Brady,
David Moore.

NEW JERSEY.

Simon Wilmer.

PENNSYLVANIA.

Joseph Hutchins, D. D.,
Joseph Turner,
Frederick Beaseley, D. D.,
Jehu C. Clay.

MARYLAND.

Henry Lyon Davis,
Purnell F. Smith,
Samuel F. Turner.

JOURNAL

OF THE

House of Clerical and Lay Deputies.

PHILADELPHIA, Tuesday, May 17, 1814.

This being the day appointed for the meeting of the General Convention of the Protestant Episcopal Church in the United States of America, several Clerical and Lay Deputies attended at 12 o'clock, A. M., in St. James' Church, and adjourned to meet at 5 o'clock, P. M.

Same day, 5 o'clock, P. M.

A quorum of the House appearing, the Secretary of the House in the last Convention acted as Secretary *pro tempore.*

The House then proceeded to read the Testimonials of the Clerical and Lay Deputies, which were severally approved, and the following gentlemen took their seats in the House.

From Massachusetts, Rev. John S. J. Gardiner, D. D., Rev. James Morss, and John Deane, Esq. From Rhode Island, Rev. Salmon Wheaton, Rev. Nathan B. Crocker, Benjamin Gardner, and Abel Jones, Esq. From Connecticut, Rev. Ashbel Baldwin, Rev. Philo Shelton, and Charles Sigourney, Esq. From New York, Rev. John Kewley, M. D., Rev. Thomas Y. How, D. D., and Hon. Philip S. Van Rensselaer. From New Jersey, Rev. Charles H. Wharton, D. D., Rev. John Croes, D. D., Rev. John C.

Rudd, Joshua M. Wallace, Esq., Hon. William Coxe, and Joseph Higby, Esq. From Pennsylvania, Rev. James Wiltbank, Rev. Levi Bull, Rev. James Abercrombie, D. D., Rev Joseph Pilmore, D. D., General Francis Gurney, Thomas M'Euen, and John M'Elroy, Esqrs. From Delaware, Rev. William Pryce. From Virginia, Rev. Hugh C. Boggs. From Maryland, Rev. Daniel Stephens, Rev. James Kemp, D. D., Rev. William M. Stone, and Robert Dunn, Esq. From South Carolina, Rev. John J. Tschudy, and Rev. Christopher E. Gadsden.

The House proceeded to the election of a President and Secretary, when it appeared that the Rev. John Croes, D. D. was chosen President, and the Rev. Ashbel Baldwin, Secretary.

On motion, resolved unanimously, That James Milnor, Esq., be invited to assist the Secretary in the duties of his office.

The following rules of order were then read and adopted:

1. The business of every day shall be introduced with the morning service of the Church.

2. When the President takes the chair, no member shall continue standing, or shall afterwards stand up, unless to address the chair.

3. No member shall absent himself from the service of the House, unless he have leave, or be unable to attend.

4. When any member is about to speak in debate, or deliver any matter to the House, he shall, with due respect, address himself to the President, confining himself strictly to the point in debate.

5. No member shall speak more than twice in the same debate without leave of the House.

6. A question being once determined, shall stand as the judgment of the House, and shall not be again drawn into debate during the same session, unless with the consent of two-thirds of the House.

7. While the President is putting any question, the members shall continue in their seats, and shall not hold any private discourse.

8. Every member, who shall be in the House when any question is put, shall, on a division, be counted, unless he be personally interested in the decision.

9. No motion shall be considered as before the House, unless it be seconded, and, when required, reduced to writing.

10. When any question is before the House, it shall be determined on before any thing new is introduced, except the question of adjournment.

11. The question on a motion for adjournment shall be taken before any other, and without debate.

12. When the House is about to rise, every member shall keep his seat until the President shall leave his chair.

Doctor How presented a certificate, signed by the Clerk of the Vestry, of the Protestant Episcopal Church at Lexington, in the State of Kentucky, of the appointment of Mr. John D. Clifford, to represent the Church of that State in this Convention, which was read.

Whereupon, Resolved, that the Protestant Episcopal Church in the State of Kentucky not being organized, and not having in convention, acceded to the Constitution of the Protestant Episcopal Church in the United States of America, Mr. Clifford cannot be admitted a member of this House, but that he be allowed the privilege of an honorary seat.

Dr. Kemp was appointed to inform the House of Bishops, that this House was organized and ready to proceed to business.

Dr. Kemp reported that he had performed that service, and that he was requested by the House of Bishops, to inform this House, that they also were prepared to proceed to business.

It having been stated that the Rev. Mr. Henshaw, although a resident in Vermont, at the time of his election as a Clerical Delegate from that State, had since removed, and was a resident in another State, it was on motion Resolved, that Mr. Henshaw be admitted to a seat as a member of this Convention:

And Mr. Henshaw took his seat accordingly.

On motion, Resolved, that the Clergy of the Protestant Episcopal Church, who may be in this City during the sitting of this Convention, and who are not members, be admitted to attend the same, as visitors.

On motion, ordered, that unless otherwise directed, the hour of meeting, be in future at 9 o'clock, A. M.

Adjourned.

Wednesday, May 18, 1814, St. James' Church.

House met.

The following gentlemen appeared and took their seats in this House.

From Virginia, Rev. William H. Wilmer, Rev. Oliver Norris, George Deneale, Esq., Edward C. M'Guire, and Col. Hugh Mercer. From Maryland, Rev. George Dashiel, John C. Herbert, Esq. From Delaware, Joseph Burn, and Alexander Reynolds, Esq. From Massachusetts, Rev. Asa Eaton. From Pennsylvania, Jacob Warren, Esq. From New York, Dr. John Onderdonk.

A certified extract from the minutes of the Convention of the Protestant Episcopal Church of the State of Virginia, stating the election by that body of the Rev. Richard Channing Moore, as bishop of that diocese, was presented and read. Whereupon,

Resolved,—That the members of this house, do now proceed to sign the testimonials required by the Canons in favour of Dr. Richard Channing Moore, in order to his consecration as Bishop of the diocese of Virginia; which was accordingly done, and the certificate in proper form transmitted to the house of bishops.

The house then rose for the purpose of attending Divine Service, and Sermon by the Right Rev. Bishop Hobart, on occasion of the meeting of this Convention and the Consecration of Dr Moore. After which the house resumed their session; and it was on motion,

Resolved unanimously,—That the thanks of this Convention be communicated to Bishop Hobart, for his appropriate and excellent Sermon, and that he be requested to furnish a copy of the same, for publication.

The Rev. Dr. Wharton was appointed to communicate the foregoing resolution to the house of Bishops for their concurrence, and if concurred in by them, to wait upon the Right Rev. Bishop Hobart with the same.

Dr. Wharton reported that he had performed the services assigned him; that the resolution had been concurred in by the house of Bishops, and communicated to Bishop Hobart; who promised to comply with the request of the Convention.

On motion, Resolved,—That a Committee, consisting of one member from each State represented in this house, be appointed to examine the Journals of the different State Conventions, Episcopal charges, addresses, and pastoral letters, which have been or may be, laid before this house during the present session, to make inquiry into the state of the Church in each diocese, and into the attention paid to the Canons and Rules of the Church; to draw up a view of the state of the Church, and report the same to the house, agreeably to the 45th Canon.

The following gentlemen were appointed to compose said Committee:—

From Vermont, Rev. Mr. Henshaw. From Massachusetts, Rev. Dr. Gardiner. From Rhode Island, Rev. Mr. Wheaton. From Connecticut, Rev. Mr. Shelton. From New York, Rev. Dr. How. From New Jersey, Rev. Mr. Rudd. From Pennyslvania, Rev. Dr. Abercrombie. From Delaware, Rev. Mr. Pryce. Virginia, Rev. Mr. Wilmer. South Carolina, Mr. Tschudy.

Divine Service and Sermon having been announced as intended to take place in this church to-morrow morning, at 10 o'clock, the house agreed to meet at that time for the purpose of attending the same, and immediately afterwards to proceed to the transaction of business.

Adjourned.

Thursday, May 19th, 1814.

House attended Divine Service in St. James' Church. Divine Service was performed by the Reverend Simon Wilmer, and a Sermon preached by the Reverend Doctor How.

After Divine Service House met.

Josiah Harrison, Esq., a lay delegate from New Jersey, appeared and took his seat.

On motion, Resolved unanimously,—That at the next General Convention, and at all future conventions, the session shall be opened, in addition to the prayers and Sermon, usual on such occasions, with the celebration of the Lord's Supper; in which resolution the house of Bishops concurred.

The following resolution was submitted for consideration by Mr. Herbert, and ordered to lie on the table.

Resolved,—That the following clause be added as an amendment to the 9th Canon:

"Provided always, that the Bishop, with the advice and consent of two-thirds of the Standing Committee, may dispense with the knowledge of the Latin and Greek Languages in candidates for Deacon's orders."

The following documents were laid before the House, in compliance with the 45th Canon:

From Massachusetts, a certified copy from the records of the Church of that State, up to the year 1813, inclusive.

From Rhode Island, a certified abstract of the returns made to the convention of the Church in that State.

From Connecticut, a printed journal of the proceedings of the convention of that diocese, for the years 1811, 1812, and 1813.

From New York, printed journals from the year 1785 to the year 1813, inclusive.

From New Jersey, printed journals for the years 1811, 1812, and 1813, and a report containing the substance of the three journals.

From Pennsylvania, printed journals for the years 1811, 1812, and 1813.

From Maryland, printed journals for the years 1811, 1812, and 1813.

From Virginia, journals up to the year 1813, inclusive.

From South Carolina, journals up to the year 1813, inclusive.

The following resolution was communicated by the House of Bishops, as adopted by them, in which they requested the concurrence of this House:

Resolved,—That the journals of the General Convention of the Protestant Episcopal Church in the United States of America, from the commencement of the said conventions; together with an appendix, containing the Constitution and Canons of the Church, be published under the superintendence of the Bishop of this Church in Pennsylvania; provided a number be engaged for, sufficient for the encouragement of a bookseller: which resolution was read and concurred in by this House.

Mr. Higby asked for, and obtained, leave of absence during the remainder of the session.

Adjourned until to-morrow morning at 10 o'clock.

FRIDAY, May 20, 1814.

The House attended Divine Service in St. James' Church. The President performed Divine Service, and the Right Reverend Bishop Griswold preached a sermon.

After Divine service the House met.

The Rev. Robert Clay, a Clerical Delegate, from the State of Delaware, appeared and took his seat.

Mr. Wallace asked and obtained leave of absence for Mr. Coxe, during the remainder of the session.

The following resolution was offered by the Rev. Mr. Gadsden, and ordered to lie on the table until to-morrow.

Resolved,—That with the consent of the House of Bishops, a joint committee of both houses, be appointed to take into consideration, the institution of a Theological Seminary, and if they should deem the same expedient, to report a plan for the raising of funds, and generally for the accomplishment of the object.

A message was received from the House of Bishops, communicating a declaration of that House, explanatory of the 19th Canon, so far as concerns the place of officiating and the dress of Lay Readers which was read and returned to said House.

A message was received from the House of Bishops, communicating a declaration, proposed to be made by this Convention, of the identity of the Protestant Episcopal Church, in the United States of America, with the body heretofore known by the name of the Church of England, and of the present entire independence of the former of the Civil and Ecclesiastical authority of any foreign country, which declaration was concurred in, and returned to the House of Bishops.

A message was received from the House of Bishops, communicating a Canon, which had been adopted by that House, entitled "a Canon altering and explaining the 29th Canon, concerning the election and institution of Ministers," in which they requested the concurrence of this House; on motion it was ordered to lie on the table.

Mr. Burns asked for, and obtained leave of absence, during the remainder of the session.

A message was received from the House of Bishops, transmitting a proposition for directing the Bishop, or other

Ecclesiastical authority in each State or Diocese, to furnish themselves with a copy or copies of the Book of Homilies, and requiring the same to be studied by candidates, for the ministry; which on motion was ordered to lie on the table.

Adjourned, until 10 o'clock, to-morrow morning.

SATURDAY, May 21, 1814.

The House attended Divine Service in St. James's Church. The Rev. Mr. Wheaton performed Divine Service, and the Right Rev. Bishop Dehon preached a sermon.

After Divine Service, House met.

The Rev. Mr. Henshaw asked for, and obtained leave of absence, until Tuesday next.

The Rev. Mr. Wilmer proposed the following resolution:

Resolved,—That the next Session of the General Convention be holden at

On motion, the said resolution was laid on the table.

The Committee appointed to examine the Journals of the different State Conventions, Episcopal charges, addresses and pastoral letters, and to draw up a view of the state of the Church, made report as follows:

The House of Clerical and Lay Deputies, in compliance with the requisitions of the 45th Canon, have taken a general view of the state of the Church, and respectfully offer to the House of Bishops, the result of their inquiries. From these observations, and the accompanying documents, it is hoped, that the House of Bishops will be able to comply with the requisition of the above mentioned Canon, in regard to a Pastoral Letter.

EASTERN DIOCESE.

NEW HAMPSHIRE.

The Church in this State appears to be stationary; no material alteration having taken place for several years past. The Congregations, though not numerous, are attached to the worship of the Church, and perform their devotional exercises with order and regularity.

MASSACHUSETTS.

In this State, the general appearance of the Church is highly flattering. Two new church edifices have been erected; new congregations have been formed; and some of the former ones considerably enlarged. A growing zeal for the cause of religion, and an attachment to the interests of the Church are visible in many parts of the State, and promise increasing prosperity. Though some instances have occurred, in which the Rubrics and Canons have not been regarded, it is believed that such instances are less frequent than on former occasions, and that an attachment to the prescribed order and worship of the Church, is daily increasing.

RHODE ISLAND.

The state of the Church in this part of the Eastern Diocese, is also flourishing. The congregations are all, except one, large and prosperous. Some have much increased, both in the number of families and the number of communicants; order and regularity generally prevail, and every deviation from the established regulations of the Church, meets with decided disapprobation.

VERMONT.

The great question, in regard to the Church lands in this State, yet remains undecided. Consequently, the difficulty of providing support, for a sufficient number of pious and active Clergymen, presents an insuperable obstacle, to the growth of the Church here. The labours, however, of those two or three Clergymen, who have officiated here, have in general, been crowned with success, and several congregations formed, which are zealous and flourishing.

EASTERN DIOCESE, GENERALLY.

From the returns made by the Bishop of the Eastern Diocese, composed of the above mentioned States, it appears that there have been since the last General Convention, the following ordinations, viz.: the Rev. Parker Adams, Rev. Charles Burroughs, Rev. Nathaniel Huse, (for Connecticut.)—Priests. Aaron Humphrey, John Prentice Kewley Henshaw, Evan Malbone Johnson, (for Connecticut,) and Titus Strong, Deacons.

The number of confirmations, in three years have been 1504.—The Rev. Joab G. Cooper, has been instituted Rector of the Church in Hanover, and the Rev. Charles Burroughs, Rector of the Church in Portsmouth, (N. H)—Six persons have been admitted as candidates for holy orders.

CONNECTICUT.

The Church in this State appears to be increasing in numbers, and in vital religion. Though frowned upon, in the removal of her venerable Bishop, by death, yet the Diocese continues regular in holding Conventions, and in a due attention to the Canons of the Church. The Clergy are zealous in the discharge of their duties. The vacancy of the episcopate it is believed will be filled, as soon as provision is made for its support. This desirable object is in a train favourable to its accomplishment, in the establishment of a permanent fund. Several new church edifices have been erected, since the last General Convention; there is also, an increased solicitude, on the part of the Laity, to provide means for the support of the Clergy, and to have the places for public worship kept in decent repair.

The number of confirmations in the last two years of the Bishop's life was 464.

During the year 1811, (since which there appear no returns of ordination,) the Rev. Samuel F. Jarvis was ordained Priest, and Frederick Holcombe, Stephen Jewett, and Orin Clark, Deacons.

NEW YORK.

The congregations in this Diocese, are very numerous and respectable, and supplied with the constant, or occasional services of stated Clergymen, or Missionaries.

The Parochial Reports are regularly exhibited. In 1812, the Right Rev. Bishop Hobart visited thirty-seven Congregations, in various parts of the State, and administered the rite of confirmation in twenty-one congregations to 500 persons.

In the year 1813, thirty-two congregations were visited, and the rite of confirmation administered in sixteen congregations to 1100.

Since the last General Convention, in May, 1811, and

until the State convention in October, 1813, six persons,—John Brady, John M'Vickar, David Huntington, Benjamin T. Onderdonk, Lewis P. Bayard, (of New Jersey,) and James Thompson, have been admitted to the holy order of Deacons;--and thirteen Deacons, David Moore, Adam Empie, Ralph Williston, Wm. Berrian, Gilbert H. Sayres, Wm. A. Clark, John M'Vickar, Orin Clark, John Brady, Timothy Clowes, John Croes, (of N. J.) Wm. Powell, Isaac Jones, (of Connecticut,) Wm. E. Wyatt, and Stephen Jewett have been admitted to the holy order of Priests—Several persons have been admitted as candidates, for Deacon's orders.

During the period above mentioned, the following institutions have taken place: The Rev. Wm. Berrian, an assistant minister of Trinity Church, of New York, the Rev. Joseph Perry, Rector of St. Paul's Church, Ballston Spa., and St. James' Church, Newton; the Rev. John Kewley, Rector of St. George's Church, New York; the Rev. John Brady, assistant minister of the same; the Rev. Ralph Williston, Rector of Zion Church, New York, and Timothy Clowes, Rector of St. Peter's Church, Albany.—During the same period, the Rev. Jonathan Judd, and the Rev. Reuben Hubbard, removed to the Diocese of Connecticut; the Rev. Adam Empie, to North Carolina, and the Rev. Dr. Abraham Beach, to New Jersey.

The following Churches have been consecrated: St. James' Church, Hyde Park, Dutchess County; St. James' Church, Milton, Saratoga County; St. Peter's Church, Auburn, Cayuga County; St. Luke's Church, Richfield, Otsego County; St. James' Church, Goshen; Grace Church, Waterford; and Christ Church, Hampton.

The following missionaries have also been employed in the part of the State, west of Albany, viz., the Rev. Samuel Fuller, the Rev. Wm. A. Clark, the Rev. Orin Clark, and the Rev. Davenport Phelps, lately deceased, who is justly regarded as the founder of the congregations, in the most western counties of the State, whom he attached, not merely to his personal ministrations, but to the doctrines, the order, and the liturgy of our Church.

On the whole, there is every reason to believe, that in this Diocese, the Canons of the Church are faithfully observed, and the clergy regular and zealous in their ministrations. And in consequence, under the Divine blessing, the congregations increase, not only in numbers, but in attachment to the principles of the Church, and in the spirit of Evangelical piety, as exhibited in her Articles and Liturgy.

NEW JERSEY.

From the journals and reports of the Convention in this State, it appears that the number of congregations, duly organized, is twenty-seven. Of this number, only seven enjoy the constant services of the ministry; four or five others have their churches regularly, though but a part of the time, opened on Sundays, by Clergymen. To provide the remaining congregations, which are unable to maintain Clergymen for themselves, with the administration of the word and ordinances, a fund has been raised by the Convention, which is always in a state of gradual augmentation. There are in the Diocese six instituted Rectors; the whole number of officiating ministers, is nine.

An Episcopal Society has been recently established in the Diocese, principally in the northern part, for the purpose of gratuitously distributing Bibles, Prayer books, and religious Tracts, and if the funds admit of it, giving aid to young men designed for the ministry.

The congregations, belonging to this Convention, appear to be, in general, strongly attached to the services and usages of the Church, and in the management of their affairs, to be actuated by a strict and sincere regard to the Rubrics and Canons. Since the last General Convention, there has been an increased attention to the concerns of religion, and the Church, which has manifested itself, particularly in repairing and improving the places of public worship; and it is believed, that the number of pious churchmen has been considerably enlarged.

PENNSYLVANIA.

There is every reason to believe that there is an increased attention to the concerns of the Church in this State. The conventions have of late been well attended, and the Clergy have in a great measure been punctual in presenting their parochial reports; from these reports it appears that the number of communicants, in the several congregations throughout the State, has been considerably augmented, particularly in those in the city of Philadelphia. It is highly gratifying to find, that since the last General Convention, exertions have been made for the establishment of an Episcopal Fund. A society has been formed for the advancement of Christianity, which at present promises extensive usefulness to the Church in this State. "Most of the vacant Churches," says the Bishop, in one of his addresses, "have been visited under the directions of this Society, and from the satisfaction given, we may hope that, under the Divine blessing, there will be an increasing usefulness of the institution." The venerable head of this Diocese, has been enabled to visit, during the two last years, some of the country congregations; the happy effects of these visits, are forcibly illustrated by the fact, that in 1811, he reported to the Convention that, during the past year, 61 persons had been confirmed; in 1812, he reported that 306 had received this holy rite; in 1813, he announced that, during the last year, the number amounted to 581. These circumstances are auspicious; it is hoped they will be followed by a rapid increase of vital Godliness, among all the members of our Apostolic Church, in this quarter,—and in general the Rubrics are duly observed. Since the last General Convention, until the present time, five persons, Samuel Halbert Turner, Jackson Kemper, Charles Blair Snowden, (of South Carolina,) Richard D. Hall, and Jehu Curtis Clay, have been admitted to the holy order of Deacons; and seven Deacons, Daniel Higbee, (of New Jersey,) John Barnwell Campbell, (of South Carolina,) Charles Blair Snowden, (of South Carolina,) William King, (of Virginia,) Samuel Halbert Turner, (of Maryland,) Jackson Kemper, and Richard D. Hall, have been admitted to the holy order of Priests.

DELAWARE.

The condition of the Church in this State, is truly distressing, and the prospect gloomy. Of the eleven congregations in Delaware, two are supplied by the Rev. Mr. Clay, and one by the Rev. Mr. Davis, from Maryland; it is, however, gratifying to learn, that there is an increasing anxiety manifested for obtaining Clergymen. Some of the vacant congregations have the service performed on Sundays, by Laymen. Where the Sacrament of the Lord's Supper has been administered, by visiting Clergymen, the communicants have been numerous. Could the Church in this State be supplied with zealous and pious ministers, there is every reason to believe that their labours would be crowned with success, in advancing the interests of the Church, and vital godliness.

MARYLAND.

The Church in Maryland, still continues in a state of depression; many parishes are without ministers, and a considerable number of the churches are in a decayed condition; the Clergy are so ill provided for, that, except in Baltimore and Georgetown, their livings are quite insufficient for the support of their families, and of course they are obliged to resort to some other means. In these cities the Clergy are well supported, and the churches kept in good repair, and there appear to be evident symptoms of the increase of piety; in some parts of the State, by the exertions of pious and zealous ministers, there seems to be a revival of religion, —churches have been repaired, and some built; the prevailing vices have been checked, and greater attention to Divine worship has appeared; besides there is an increasing disposition to relish the fine service of our Church, and to comply with her ordinances, so that if it should please God to raise up pious, enlightened, and zealous ministers, who would continue to labour in this part of our Divine Master's vineyard, the Church in Maryland might still be raised, and prove a nursery for good principles, enlightened devotion, and pure piety. As the charges and returns of the Bishop are but partially inserted on the journals of the Convention, and as no account of his proceedings during the last year has been received, it is impossible to state the number of churches consecrated, or Clergymen ordained, since the last General Convention.

VIRGINIA.

From a variety of causes, not necessary, and perhaps not proper to detail here, the Church in this State has fallen into a deplorable condition; in many places her ministers have thrown off their sacred profession; her Liturgy is either contemned or unknown, and her sanctuaries are desolate. It would rend any feeling heart, to see spacious temples, venerable even in their dilapidation and ruins, now the habitations of the wild beasts of the forest.

But amidst this gloomy scene, a ray of light breaks in upon the prospect, cheering the hearts of the friends of the Church. Her members in Virginia have been taught, by a dreadful experience, the value of their peculiar institutions. They look back with regret, and sigh when they talk of former days, when they were wont to go with joy into the courts of Zion; they are ready and desirous to return to that fold, from which they have wandered so long, as sheep having no shepherd; they anxiously seek the restoration of their primitive and apostolical form of worship, and sound doctrine, and pray that ministers of zeal and piety may come and help them. Perhaps no place in the United States presents a more extensive field for the faithful labourer.—Here are the best of materials, and here are the noblest inducements of duty, of honour, and reward.

The dispositions of the people, and especially of some eminent Laymen, who have come forward with interest and zeal, afford pleasing pledges of those good fruits which their active exertions will not fail to produce. A magnificent Church has sprung up in Richmond, from the ashes of the theatre; it has the patronage and support of men of the greatest talents, and highest rank in Virginia. They have chosen, as their pastor, the Rev R. C. Moore, D. D., who is now the Bishop of the Diocese, and under whose auspices there is reason to hope for the most favourable results.

The corner stone of a large and respectable church has been laid in Fredericksburg, on the site of the old building, which has gone to decay. For Leesburgh also, they have obtained a subscription, adequate to the expense of erecting a respectable church; and in the counties of Frederick and Spottsylvania, and perhaps in other places, from which reports have not been received, the state of the Church is improving. In Alexandria, there are two large and respectable congregations. From the present excitement, which is manifest throughout the State, nothing more seems wanting, under the blessing of God, than faithful ministers, to realize the hopes which are entertained of the future prosperity of this important part of our Zion. Let all who wish her well, pray the Lord of the harvest, to send forth labourers into His harvest.

SOUTH CAROLINA.

There is cause of rejoicing to the friends of the Church in this Diocese. There is an evident revival of religion, and a visible growth in piety. From various causes, not necessary, and perhaps not expedient to state, the Church in this State had sunk very low; but, through the blessing of the Almighty on the zealous exertions of the visible head of it, much has been done for its good, and more is to be confidently expected.

The various parishes are making exertions to provide for their ministers, and to re-establish Divine Service in the vacant churches. A resolution has also been entered into by the Clergy to supply the services and ordinances of the Church, as often as possible, to the vacant parishes. It appears from the Bishop's address, in 1812, that two new Episcopal congregations were collected and organized; one at Columbia, the seat of government, and one at Camden; and that, for the former, a Lay reader was provided by the Protestant Episcopal Society for the advancement of Christianity in South Carolina. It appears also, from the same address, that Dr. Frederick Dalcho, of Charleston, had been received as a candidate for holy orders, and the Rev. Christian Hankle, formerly of Burlington, New Jersey, had been admitted to the order of Deacon.

In the year 1813—14 Episcopal visitations were made, and 516 persons confirmed. Two candidates for holy orders, viz. Maurice Harvey Lance and Albert Muller, were received, and Dr. Frederick Dalcho was admitted to the order of Deacons. The Parish of St. George Winyaw was deprived by death of its Rector, the Rev. Dr. Halling.

The state of the Church, in this Diocese, will appear from the following extract from the last address of the Bishop. "In the view," says he, "which I am required, by a useful Canon of the Church, to give you of the affairs of the Diocese, since the last meeting of the Convention, it will fall within the scope of the regulation, to congratulate you on the degree of concord and Christian fellowship with which our Churches are blessed. It is hardly possible, that in any society, composed of many parts, and all the parts of frail and fallible beings, there should exist such an entire unity of opinion and community of feelings, as to produce always a perfectly harmonious co-operation towards an accomplishment of the same ends; as near an approach to this happy state, as is compatible with the condition and infirmities of man, is, through the good blessing of God, at present enjoyed by us, in this Diocese. In a degree, which is gratifying to me to remark, as it has doubtless been pleasing to you to notice, the Clergy of the Diocese are kindly affectioned, one to another, with brotherly love; and their respective parishes being knit together, and compacted by that which every joint supplieth, are, it is humbly hoped, making some increase of the body, to the edifying of itself in love. Thus far there is unity, and all will ever be concerned for the interests and feelings of all, if we be actuated by the genuine spirit of the religion of Jesus Christ."

It ought to be mentioned, that in South Carolina a Society has been instituted for the advancement of Christianity, which has met with great success, and been instrumental in establishing two Churches in a section of the country where our worship was never before held. This Society, by distributing books, illustrative of the distinctive principles of our Church, and by assisting a young man of genius and piety, a candidate for the ministry, has done much to advance the interests of our religion, and of our excellent Church.

It is also to be stated, that the Rubrics and Canons are here conscientiously and strictly observed.

The House of Clerical and Lay Deputies, in laying the preceding statement before the venerable House of Bishops, pray for themselves and the Church, their counsel, and the blessing of Almighty God.

Signed, by order of the House of Clerical and Lay Deputies,

JOHN CROES, PRESIDENT.

May 21, 1814.

The said report having been read and considered, was adopted, directed to be signed by the President, and sent to the House of Bishops, which things were accordingly done.

A Message was received from the House of Bishops, communicating a Canon adopted by them, entitled "A Canon concerning the alms and contributions, at the Holy Communion," in which they requested the concurrence of this house. The said Canon was considered, concurred in by the house, and returned to the House of Bishops.

A communication was received from the House of Bishops, on the subject of devising means, for supplying the congregations of this Church, west of the Alleghany mountains; and respecting a correspondence with the venerable Society in England, for propagating the gospel in foreign parts, on the subject of certain lands, to which the Church has a claim, in the State of Vermont; which commuication was read, and returned to the House of Bishops, agreeably to their request, to be entered upon their journals.

The Canon sent yesterday from the House of Bishops, altering and explaining the 29th Canon, concerning the election, and institution of ministers, was taken up for consideration, concurred in, and sent back to that house.

The proposition sent yesterday, from the House of Bishops, respecting the Book of Homilies, was taken up for consideration. concurred in, and returned to that house.

A resolution was adopted, and sent to the House of Bishops, for their concurrence, respecting the preparation, and transmission of reports from the State Conventions to the General Convention.

A Message was received from the House of Bishops, communicating a proposition, submitted to them, for the publication of certain Anthems, with their determination thereon; and also a general resolution adopted by them, with respect to the recommendation of proposed publications, which, after being read, were returned to the House of Bishops, with the respectful thanks of this house, for the judicious course adopted by them, in reference to these subjects.

A resolution, respecting the posture of minister and people, during the singing of the metre psalms and hymns, was received from the House of Bishops; which after having been read was postponed until Monday next.

The Rev. Messrs. Stone, Eaton, and Morss, Mr. Harrison, and Dr. Onderdonk, asked and obtained leave of absence, during the remainder of the session.

Adjourned.

MONDAY, May 23, 1814.

House attended Divine Service in St. James's Church. Divine Service was performed by the Rev. A. Baldwin, Secretary of this house, and a sermon preached by the Rev. Dr. Croes, President of the same.

After Divine Service, house met.

The recommendation of the House of Bishops, relative to the posture of ministers and people, during the singing of the metre, psalms and hymns, was taken up for consideration, approved of, and agreeably to request, returned to that house, to be entered on their journal.

Mr. Gadsden's resolution, respecting a Theological Seminary, was taken up for consideration, and after some debate, it was moved and seconded, to postpone the further consideration of the same. The votes being required, to be taken by States, the ayes and noes on the question of postponement, were as follows:

Massachusetts—Clergy, No; Laity, ——.
Connecticut—Clergy, Aye; Laity, No.
Rhode Island—Clergy, No; Laity, No.
New York—Clergy, No; Laity, No.
New Jersey—Clergy, No; Laity, No.
Pennsylvania—Clergy, Aye; Laity, Aye.
Delaware—Clergy, No; Laity, ——.
Maryland—Clergy, Aye; Laity, divided.
Virginia—Clergy, No; Laity, No.
South Carolina—Clergy, No; Laity, ——.

And so the motion for postponement was negatived.

The question on the resolution recurring, the vote thereon was required to be taken by States, and the ayes and the noes were as follow:

Massachusetts—Clergy, Aye; Laity, ——.

Connecticut—Clergy, No; Laity, No.
Rhode Island—Clergy, Aye; Laity, Aye.
New York—Clergy, No; Laity, No.
New Jersey—Clergy, No; Laity, Aye.
Pennsylvania—Clergy, No; Laity, No.
Delaware—Clergy, No; Laity, ——.
Maryland—Clergy, No; Laity, divided.
Virginia—Clergy, Aye; Laity, Aye.
South Carolina—Clergy, Aye; Laity, ——.

And so the resolution was negatived.

The House of Bishops communicated a written opinion, explanatory of the 9th and 40th Canons, which was considered, approved of, and returned to that house.

The following resolution was proposed and adopted.

Resolved,—That a committee of two persons be appointed to confer with the House of Bishops, on the expediency of securing to the General Convention, the right of the Book of Common Prayer, and to report to the house.

The Rev. Mr. Wilmer, and the Rev. Doctor How, were appointed a committee, on the part of this house, for the purpose expressed in the foregoing resolution.

Mr. Warren asked, and obtained leave of absence.

The following resolution was proposed and adopted.

Whereas, the mode heretofore adopted, for making known the Constitution and Canons of the Church, has fallen short of that desirable end, and in order that the interest of the Church may be advanced by a more general knowledge of the said Constitution and Canons, and also that the proceedings of the General Convention may be promulgated, to the members of the Church at large; Resolved that it be recommended to the ecclesiastical authorities in the several Dioceses, to cause the same to be made known in the congregations respectively within their bounds, by such measures as may be deemed expedient, and accommodated to local circumstances.

The said resolution was sent to the House of Bishops, for their concurrence, and was concurred in by them.

On motion, Resolved, that the thanks of this Convention be presented to the Bishops, who have preached before the Convention, during the present Session, and that they be requested to furnish copies of their sermons, for publication.

The said resolution was sent to the House of Bishops, for their concurrence, and the said House concurred in the same, with an amendment, inserting the words "and the President of the House of Clerical and Lay Deputies," which amendment was agreed to by this house. Dr. Kemp and Mr. Herbert were appointed on the part of this house, to carry the same into effect.

The committee appointed to confer with the House of Bishops, upon the expediency of securing to the General Convention, a copy right of the Book of Common Prayer, reported that they had performed that duty; that the House of Bishops return for answer, that they will appoint a committee to confer with the committee of this house, and report at a convenient season.

Mr. Wilmer's resolution, as to the place of meeting of the next General Convention was taken up, and the blank left therein filled with the word "New York."

The vote having been required to be taken by States, the ayes and noes thereon, were as follow:

Vermont—Clergy, No; Laity, ——.
Massachusetts—Clergy, Aye; Laity, ——.
Connecticut—Clergy, Aye; Laity, Aye.
Rhode Island—Clergy, Aye; Laity, Aye.
New York—Clergy, Aye; Laity, Aye.
Pennsylvania—Clergy, Aye; Laity, No.
Delaware—Clergy, No; Laity, ——.
Maryland—Clergy, No; Laity, No.
Virginia—Clergy, No; Laity, ——.
South Carolina—Clergy, No; Laity, ——.

The House of Bishops informed this house, that they had appointed the Right Rev. Bishops White and Hobart, a committee on their part, on the subject of a copy right, for the book of Common Prayer.

The following Message was received from the House of Bishops, together with a pastoral letter, prepared by said house.

The House of Bishops, having examined and considered the report of the House of Clerical and Lay Deputies, presented agreeably to the provisions of the 45th Canon, transmit to them agreeably to the same Canon, a pastoral letter, founded on the report. The House of Bishops, reciprocating the affectionate sentiments of the House of Clerical and Lay Deputies, accompanying their report, request their aid in all proper measures of the Episcopacy, for the extending of the influence of religion, and the increase of the Church; imploring the Divine blessing on them individually, and on the Churches which they respectively represent.

The resolution sent to the House of Bishops, on the subject of the preparation, and transmission of reports, from each State Convention, on the state of the Church, was returned with an amendment, in which this house concurred. The resolution, as amended and finally agreed to, is as follows:

Resolved,—That it be recommended, that the ecclesiastical authority of the Church in every State or diocese, prepare a report on the state of the Church, in their State or diocese, previously to the meeting of every General Convention, for the purpose of aiding the Committee on the State of the Church, appointed by the House of Clerical and Lay Deputies, in drafting their report.

The committee appointed on the part of this house, to return the thanks of the convention to the Bishops, and the President of this house, for the sermons preached by them respectively, and to request copies for publication, reported, that they had performed that service, and that the Reverend gentlemen would comply with the request of the convention.

Adjourned.

TUESDAY, May 24, 1814.

The house attended Divine Service in St. James's Church, which was performed by the Rev. W. A. Wilmer.

After Divine Service, house met.

The pastoral letter of the House of Bishops, transmitted to this house yesterday, was read, and then returned to the House of Bishops.

The joint committee of the two houses, on the question of a copy right for the book of Common Prayer, report as follows. That they are informed on credible authority, that the same object was contemplated in the year 1789, on the editing of the book, as it is now established by the authority of this Church, but was relinquished, in consequence of perceiving that complaints were likely to arise from the apprehension that the price would be thereby enhanced. The objection was, that an appropriation of the proceeds, to a purpose both religious and charitable, would not reconcile the members of this Church to a tax, which, it was alledged was thus imposed; the book being of a character which it was a duty to possess. Whether the objection may not be guarded against by a contract, in which the prices of books should be fixed agreeably to their different sizes; and whether in this case, there ought to be regarded the complaints, which would still be made of an alledged unreasonableness of price, the committee submit to the consideration of the Convention. The committee are not sufficiently informed of the operation of law, on the present subject, so as to judge of the practicability of the measure proposed; nor have they had either time, or the authority of the convention, to take advice thereon,—but, they propose that law advice should be taken, before further progress. Further, it has not occurred to the committee, how the copy right may be so contrived, as to be made consistent with the 8th article of the Ecclesiastical Constitution. That some alteration must be made in the present book, to bring it under the exclusive claim of a copy right, is evident. If the alteration should affect the book, as described by its known name, the difficulty here noticed must present itself. But if the alteration should be made in any of the instruments of this Church, which are usually bound up with the Book of Common Prayer, it would seem that the latter might be still published, without legal interference. On the ground of the premises, the joint committee propose to the two houses as follows:

Resolved,—That it be referred to the Bishops to consider of the propriety of granting a copy-right in the Book of Common Prayér; to inquire in their respective dioceses, and elsewhere, as circumstances may permit, whether the said measure can be adopted, consistently with law, and the approbation of the Conventions in the different dioceses, and to report to the next General Convention.

The foregoing report having been adopted in the House

of Bishops, on motion, this house concurred in the adoption of the same.

The following resolution was proposed and adopted.

Resolved,—That this Convention contemplate with much pleasure the rise and progress of institutions for the advancement of Christianity, in several of the dioceses in the United States, and that they recommend such institutions to the patronage of all the friends of our Church.

A message was received from the House of Bishops communicating a resolution which originated in, and had been adopted by that house, on the subject of a Theological Seminary; in which this house concurred.

The Rev. Mr. Wilmer, and Mr. Maguire asked for and obtained leave of absence.

A message was received from the House of Bishops communicating a Canon which had passsd that house, entitled "A Canon repealing a part of the 45th Canon of 1808," which was concurred in by this house.

A resolution was received from the House of Bishops for the addition of a second appendix to the volume of Journals proposed to be reprinted; said seeond appendix, to contain the pastoral letters of the House of Bishops for the two last and the present Conventions, which resolution was concurred in by this house.

On motion, Resolved,—That the thanks of this house be presented to the President, Secretary and assistant Secretary, for the services rendered by them respectively during the present session.

On motion, Resolved,—That the House of Bishops be requested to appoint one of their own order to preach a sermon at the opening of the next General Convention.

The foregoing resolution having been communicated to the House of Bishops, a message was returned from that house, informing of their concurrence in the same, and stating their hope, that it may be consistent with the state of health of their brother the Right Reverend Bishop Clagget to be present and to preach; and in case of his absence their resolution that the next Bishop in seniority, who may not already have preached at the opening of a convention, be requested to perform the duty.

The Rev. Doctor Abercrombie, Mr. M'Euen, and Mr.

Milnor the assistant Secretary, were appointed a committee to superintend the publication of the Journal of the proceedings of this house at the present Convention.

In pursuance of a request from this house, the Right Reverend members of the House of Bishops attended in the same, for the purpose of closing the Session of the Convention by solemn prayer, which was performed by the Right Reverend Doctor White, presiding Bishop: after which

Adjourned *sine die.*

JOURNAL

OF THE

House of Bishops.

CITY OF PHILADELPHIA, Tuesday, May 17th, 1814.

This being the day appointed by the Constitution of the Protestant Episcopal Church in the United States of America, for the meeting of the General Convention of said Church; and agreeably to a resolve of the last General Convention of the Church in the city of New Haven, the city of Philadelphia being appointed the place of meeting, the Right Rev. Bishop White, of Pennsylvania, the Right Rev. Bishop Hobart of New York, the Right Rev. Bishop Griswold, of the Eastern Diocese, and the Right Rev. Bishop Dehon, of South Carolina, met in the vestry-room of St. James's Church at 12 o'clock in the aforesaid city. It appeared that Bishop Clagget, who was to have opened the Convention with a sermon, was prevented from attending by indisposition.

The House, having chosen the Rev. Jackson Kemper to act as Secretary, adjourned to meet at 5 o'clock, P. M.

5 o'clock, P. M.

Met according to adjournment.

The House received a communication from the House of Clerical and Lay Deputies, by the Rev. Mr. Kemp, informing them that they were organized, and ready to proceed to business. Dr. Kemp was desired to inform the House of Clerical and Lay Deputies, that the House of Bishops was also ready.

The House adjourned to 9 o'clock to-morrow morning.

WEDNESDAY, 9 o'clock, A. M.

Met according to adjournment. Present as yesterday.

This House received from the House of Clerical and Lay Deputies the testimonials required by the Canons, from the Convention of the Church in Virginia, and from the said House, in favour of the Rev. Richard Channing Moore, D. D., as Bishop elect for the diocese of Virginia; whereupon this House approved the said testimonials and resolved to proceed to the consecration.

At 10 o'clock the House attended Divine Service. Morning prayers were read by the Rev. Dr. How, and a sermon, on the occasion of the opening of the Convention, was preached by Bishop Hobart; after which, the Rev. Dr. Moore was consecrated Bishop; the Right Rev. Bishop White, as presiding Bishop, performing the office of consecration, assisted by the Bishops present.

Divine Service being ended, the House returned to the vestry-room, when the Right Rev. Bishop Moore took his seat in the House.

A message was received, by the Rev. Dr. Wharton, from the House of Clerical and Lay Deputies, informing, that a resolution had passed that House, "that the thanks of the Convention be presented to the Right Rev. Bishop Hobart, for his sermon preached before them this morning, and that he be requested to furnish a copy for publication."

This House concurred in the said resolution, and the Right Rev. Bishop Hobart consented to comply with their request.

The following resolution was proposed: That the Journals of the General Convention of the Protestant Episcopal Church in the United States of America, from the commencement of the said Conventions, together with an appendix, containing the Constitution and the Canons of the Church, be published under the superintendence of the Bishop of this Church in Pennsylvania; provided a number be engaged for, sufficient for the encouragement of a bookseller. If the House of Clerical and Lay Deputies should concur in this resolve, the design will be forwarded by a knowledge of the number of copies which could be engaged for in the respective States.

The above resolution was adopted, and ordered to be sent

to the House of Clerical and Lay Deputies for their concurrence.

On motion, The House agreed to attend Divine Service every morning in the House of Clerical and Lay Deputies.

The House adjourned to meet at 10 o'clock to-morrow morning.

THURSDAY MORNING, May 19th, 1814.

The House met after having attended Divine Service, in the House of Clerical and Lay Deputies. Present, Bishop White, Bishop Hobart, Bishop Griswold, Bishop Dehon, Bishop Moore.

The House received from the House of Clerical and Lay Deputies, by Joshua Wallace, Esq., a resolution relative to the administering of the Lord's Supper at the opening of the General Convention; in which resolution, the House of Bishops concurred.

A message was received from the House of Clerical and Lay Deputies by their Secretary, the Rev. Mr. Baldwin, informing this House that they agreed with them in the resolution concerning the publishing of the Journals of the General Conventions.

Adjourned to meet to-morrow at 10, A. M.

FRIDAY MORNING, May 20th, 1814.

The following declaration was proposed and agreed to.

It having come to the knowledge of this House, that some doubts have arisen in certain districts, in reference to the sense of some of the provisions of the 19th Canon; they hold it expedient to make the following declaration, to record it on their minutes, and to communicate it to the House of Clerical and Lay Deputies.

So far as concerns regulations, in reference to the place of officiating, and to ministerial dress, the Bishops suppose that the prohibitions of the Canon, were grounded merely on the propriety of guarding against popular mistakes;

which, might otherwise, rank among the number of the clergy a person not ordained. Accordingly they conceive, that the design of the Canon reaches every circumstance of position and of dress, which the custom of the Church and the habits of social life may render liable to misconception in the premises. On this ground, the House of Bishops consider it as contrary to the design of the Canon for candidates to read sermons from the places usually considered as appropriated to ordained ministers, or to appear in bands, or gowns, or surplices.

The Secretary communicated the above declaration to the House of Clerical and Lay Deputies.

The following declaration was proposed and agreed to:

It having been credibly stated to the House of Bishops, that on questions, in reference to property devised before the revolution to congregations belonging to "the Church of England," and to uses connected with that name, some doubts have been entertained in regard to the indentity of the body to which the two names have been applied, the House think it expedient to make the declaration, and to request the concurrence of the House of Clerical and Lay Deputies therein—that "The Protestant Episcopal Church in the United States of America" is the same body heretofore known in these States, by the name of "The Church of England;" the change of name, although not of religious principle in doctrine, or in worship, or in discipline, being induced by a characteristic of the Church of England, supposing the independence of the Christian Churches, under the different sovereignties, to which, respectively, their allegiance in civil concerns belongs. But that when the severance alluded to took place, and ever since, this Church conceives of herself, as professing and acting on the principles of the Church of England, is evident from the organization of our Conventions, and from their subsequent proceedings, as recorded on the Journals; to which, accordingly, this Convention refer for satisfaction in the premises. But it would be contrary to fact, were any one to infer, that the discipline exercised in this Church, or that any proceedings therein, are at all dependent on the will of the civil or of the ecclesiastical authority of any foreign country.

The above declaration having been communicated to the

House of Clerical and Lay Deputies, they returned for answer that they concurred therein.

A Canon, altering and explaining the 29th Canon, concerning the election and institution of ministers, was proposed and agreed to, and sent to the other House for their concurrence.

The following Resolution, concerning the Book of Homilies, was proposed and adopted, and sent to the House of Clerical and Lay Deputies for their concurrence.

The House of Bishops, taking into consideration, that the two Books of Homilies are referred to in the 35th Article of this Church, as containing a body of sound Christian doctrine; and knowing, by their respective experience, the scarcity of the volume, rendering it difficult for some candidates in the ministry to possess opportunities of studying its contents, propose to the House of Clerical and Lay Deputies, to make it a standing instruction to every Bishop, and to the Ecclesiastical authority in every State destitute of a Bishop, to be furnished (as soon as may be) with a copy or copies of said work, and to require it to be studied by all candidates for the ministry within their respective bounds: under the expectation, that when offering for ordination, the knowledge of its contents will be indispensably required.

A Canon, concerning the alms and contributions at the Holy Communion, was proposed and adopted.

Adjourned to meet to-morrow morning at 10 o'clock.

SATURDAY MORNING, May 21st, 1814.

The Canon, concerning the alms and contributions at the Holy Communion, was taken to the House of Clerical and Lay Deputies, by the Secretary, for their concurrence.

A communication was made to this House by the President, respecting two matters committed to him by the last triennial Convention.

Whereupon, Resolved, That information of the same be transmitted to the House of Clerical and Lay Deputies; to be returned to this House and entered on their Journal. The communication is as follows:

The President requests the attention of the House, to

those passages in the Journal of 1811, where it appears, that there were laid on him two acts of duty, which consequent circumstances have prevented from being carried into effect.

The President, and the Bishop of this Church in Virginia, were requested "to devise means for supplying the congregations of this Church, west of the Alleghany mountains, with the ministration and worship of the same, and for organizing the Church in the Western States." In consequence of this request, the President had begun a correspondence with Bishop Madison; but all further progress was arrested by the decease of the said Right Rev. Brother. This did not hinder the President from submitting to the Convention of this Church, in Pennsylvania, a proposal which was complied with, designed so far to meet the desires of some members of this Church, in the Western Country, as that in the event of the settlement of a Bishop therein, the congregations in the Western counties of the State might be under his superintendence; on such a plan as would not affect the integrity of the Church, in the State of Pennsylvania, as a component member of the body of this Church throughout our union, in contrariety to the constitution.

The President was further requested to address a letter in behalf of the Convention to the venerable Society in England for propagating the Gospel in foreign parts, in reference to certain lands held by them in the State of Vermont, and intended in the original grant for the benefit of the Episcopal Church therein. It was necessary to the execution of this commission, that the President should have been furnished with certain documents. These were delayed by some circumstances not under his control, until the occurrence of the present war; which rendered a correspondence in the premises improper.

The above information was carried to the House of Clerical and Lay Deputies, by the Secretary.

The following recommendation was proposed and adopted.

The House of Bishops propose to the House of Clerical and Lay Deputies the following recommendation, to be considered of by the House, and if agreeable, to be returned to this House and entered on their Journal.

Whereas, a diversity of custom has of late years prevailed in the posture of ministers and of the people, during the act of singing the psalms and the hymns in metre; the former practice of sitting during this part of the service gradually giving way to the more comely posture of standing; it is hereby recommended by this Convention, that it be considered as the duty of the ministers of this Church, to encourage the use of the latter posture, and to induce the members of their congregations, as circumstances may permit, to do the same; allowance to be made for cases in which it may be considered inconvenient by age, or by infirmity. Practice under this recommendation is to begin from the time when suitable information shall have been given by the Clergy to their respective flocks. And it shall be the duty of every minister to give notice of this recommendation to his congregation at such time as in his discretion may be the most proper.

The carrying into effect of the contemplated change, may be delayed by the Bishop of any Diocese, or, where there is no Bishop, by the Ecclesiastical Authority therein, until there shall have been time and opportunity of explaining satisfactorily the grounds of the measure.

This recommendation was taken by the Secretary to the House of Clerical and Lay Deputies.

The following proposition was submitted and agreed to, and communicated to the House of Clerical and Lay Deputies.

The House of Bishops communicate to the House of Clerical and Lay Deputies, the following resolve, and the following rule of the House of Bishops, to be entered on their Journal after being returned by the House of Clerical and Lay Deputies.

There was laid before the House an address from the Rev. Dr. Wm. Smith, of Connecticut, together with sundry anthems selected from Holy Scripture, and adapted to certain Fasts and Feasts of the Church. The object of the address is to induce the establishment of the said anthems, as parts of the Liturgy.

Whereupon, Resolved, That it is not expedient, during this Convention, to go into a review, either in whole or in part, of the Book of Common Prayer. It could not, however, but give satisfaction to the Bishops to recollect, that anthems taken from Scripture, and judiciously arranged, may, according to the known allowance of this Church, be sung in congregations at the discretion of their respective ministers. On this occasion, a question arose, how far it may be proper at any meeting of the Convention, to give their sanction, or that of this House in particular, to any work, however tending to religious instruction, or to the excitement of pious affections. In reference to this subject, it is the unanimous opinion of the Bishops present, that no such sanction should be given. And it is hereby made a rule of the House, that if any application should be made, tending to such effect, it shall not be considered as regularly brought before them.

A message was received from the House of Clerical and Lay Deputies, communicating their concurrence in the Canon concerning the alms and contributions at the Holy Communion.

A message was received from the House of Clerical and Lay Deputies, informing, that they agreed to the Canon concerning the election and institution of ministers, and to the resolution concerning the Book of Homilies.

The House of Clerical and Lay Deputies returned to the House of Bishops their communication concerning anthems, with the thanks of said House for the course adopted by the House of Bishops. They likewise returned the communication respecting a Bishop for the Western Country, and the correspondence which the President of this House was requested to hold with the venerable Society in England for propagating the Gospel in foreign parts, relative to lands in Vermont.

A resolve was received from the House of Clerical and Lay Deputies, concerning the appointment of a committee in each Diocese, to prepare a report on the state of the Church in that State or Diocese, previous to the meetings of the General Convention.

The above resolution was ordered to lie on the table.

A report on the state of the Church, signed by the President of the House of Clerical and Lay Deputies, agreeably to the 45th Canon, was received from said house.

Adjourned to meet at 9 o'clock Monday morning.

MONDAY MORNING, May 23d, 1814.

Present as usual.

The Resolution of the House of Clerical and Lay Deputies concerning the preparation of a report on the state of the Church, was agreed to with an amendment, which was sent to said house for their concurrence.

The House of Clerical and Lay Deputies returned the recommendation concerning posture during the singing of the metre psalms, with their concurrence.

The following message was sent to the House of Clerical and Lay Deputies.

The House of Bishops transmit to the House of Clerical and Lay Deputies the following opinions, the result of attention to an application of the Clerical deputies from Connecticut. If approved of, it will be entered on the Journal of the former House.

The Clerical Deputies from the diocese of Connecticut, by direction of the Convention of the same, requested the opinions of the Bishops present, on the meaning of two passages of the Canons: 1st, Of this phrase in the 9th Canon—"In consideration of certain other qualifications of the candidates;" and 2ndly, Of this phrase in the 40th Canon—"or by some other joint act of the parties, and of a minister of this Church."

In explanation of the former phrase, the Bishops are of opinion, that if a candidate should possess extraordinary strength of natural understanding, a considerable extent of theological erudition, although not derived through the medium of the original languages of Scripture, a peculiar aptitude to preach, and a large share of prudence; those qualifications may be a ground of the dispensation here referred to.

In reference to the phrase in the 40th Canon, it would perhaps be difficult to define the various ways in which the consent spoken of may be satisfactorily evidenced. But the Bishops are of opinion, that any person duly baptized in any religious society extraneous to this communion, joining himself to any congregation of this communion, and possessing an interest in its concerns, in consequence of express or implied permission, may be properly entered by the minister, on the list of the names of persons under his parochial care. But the Bishops do not consider themselves as now called on to consider, whether it may not be expedient to make provision for a more definite mode, for the receiving into this Church of persons not baptized within its pale, but joining it on conviction and with fair characters.

A message was received from the House of Clerical and Lay Deputies, by their Secretary, signifying the concurrence of that House with the proposed amendment to the resolution concerning the preparation of a report on the state of the Church; and their approbation of the opinions with respect to the 9th and 40th Canons.

A message was received from the Honse of Clerical and Lay Deputies, requesting the concurrence of this House in a resolution respecting the securing of a copyright of the Book of Common Prayer.

This House appointed Bishops White and Hobart a committee to consult with the Rev. Dr. How, and the Rev. Mr. Wm. Wilmer, a committee of the House of Clerical and Lay Deputies, upon the above-mentioned subject.

The report on the state of the Church transmitted to this House by the House of Clerical and Lay Deputies, was read by the Secretary.

A pastoral letter was proposed and adopted, and sent to the House of Clerical and Lay Deputies.

A message was received from the House of Clerical and Lay Deputies, requesting the concurrence of this House in a resolution concerning the making better known the Constitution, Canons, &c. of the Church.

Dr. Kemp and Mr. Herbert were the bearers of a resolve from the House of Clerical and Lay Deputies, concerning the publication of the sermons delivered by the Bishops before the Convention, which resolve, after being so amended by the House of Bishops as to include the sermon preached by the President of the House of Clerical and Lay Deputies, was agreed to by this house.

The House of Clerical and Lay Deputies concurred in the amendment.

Adjourned to meet to-morrow morning at 9 o'clock.

TUESDAY MORNING, May 24th, 1814.

This house attended Divine Service as usual in the House of Clerical and Lay Deputies.

The joint committee of the two houses on securing the copyright of the Book of Common Prayer, reported; which report was adopted by both houses.

Resolved,—That to the volume of Journals already directed to be reprinted, there be added a second appendix containing the two pastoral letters read in the last two preceding Conventions, and the pastoral letters read in this Convention.

This resolution was taken to the House of Clerical and Lay Deputies, and returned with their concurrence.

Resolved,—That it be referred to the Bishops; and, in those Dioceses in which there are no Bishops, to the Standing Committees therein, to inquire in the respective Dioceses or States, and to consider for themselves, concerning the expediency of establishing a Theological Seminary, to be conducted under the general authority of this Church; and to report to the next General Convention.

The House of Clerical and Lay Deputies concurred in the above resolution.

The resolution concerning the making known the Constitution, Canons, &c. was considered, agreed to, and sent back to the House of Clerical and Lay Deputies.

The house received from the House of Clerical and Lay Deputies, a resolution respecting institutions for the advancement of Christianity, in which they concurred.

This house agreed with the House of Clerical and Lay Deputies, in appointing the next General Convention to be held at New York.

Information having been received from the House of Clerical and Lay Deputies, that they had appointed a committee of their house to superintend the publication of the Journal, &c. Bishop White was requested to act as a committee on the part of this house.

This house received from the House of Clerical and Lay Deputies a resolve, requesting the House of Bishops to appoint one of their own order to preach a sermon at the opening of the next General Convention.

A Canon, repealing part of the 45th Canon of 1808, was

adopted and sent to the House of Clerical and Lay Deputies, in which they concurred.

This House returned for answer to the resolve of the House of Clerical and Lay Deputies, requesting the House of Bishops to appoint one of their own order to preach a sermon at the opening of the next General Convention.

"The Bishops concur in the above resolve; hoping that it may be consistent with the state of health of their brother the Right Rev. Bishop Clagget to be present, and to preach; and in the case of his absence, resolving, that the next Bishop in seniority, who may not already have preached at the opening of a Convention, be requested to perform the duty."

The House of Bishops being ready to adjourn, and having received information from the House of Clerical and Lay Deputies that they were also ready, the business of the Convention was concluded with solemn prayer by the presiding Bishop.

Signed, by order of the House of Bishops,

WILLIAM WHITE,

PRESIDING BISHOP.

Attested: JACKSON KEMPER, Secretary.

Canons.

CANON—Concerning the alms and contributions at the Holy Communion.

Whereas, it appears, that no direction has been made, as to the mode in which the alms and contributions at the administration of the Holy Communion are to be applied, it is hereby declared, that they shall be deposited with the minister of the parish, or with such Church officer as shall be appointed by him, to be applied by the minister or under his superintendence, to such pious and charitable uses as shall be thought fit.

HOUSE OF BISHOPS ADOPTED May 20th, 1814.

JACKSON KEMPER, SECRETARY.

ADOPTED IN HOUSE OF CLERICAL AND LAY DEPUTIES, May 21st, 1814.

ASHBEL BALDWIN, SECRETARY.

CANON—Altering and explaining the 29th Canon, concerning the election and institution of ministers.

So much of the 29th Canon of 1808, as requires the institution of an assistant minister in order to his being considered as a regularly admitted and settled parochial minister in any Diocese or State, and his having a voice in the choice of a Bishop, in consequence of his not having been instituted, and as excludes a Deacon from a seat and vote in any Convention where he is not excluded by the constitution and Canons of the Church in any Diocese, is hereby repealed. It is also declared, in explanation of the said Canon, that the provision concerning the use of the office of institution, is not to be considered as applying to any congregation destitute of a house of worship.

HOUSE OF BISHOPS, ADOPTED May 20th 1814.

JACKSON KEMPER, SECRETARY.

ADOPTED IN HOUSE OF CLERICAL AND LAY DEPUTIES, May 21st, 1814.

ASHBEL BALDWIN, SECRETARY.

CANON—Repealing part of the 45th Canon of 1808.

That part of the 45th Canon of 1808 which requires that the parochial reports inserted on the Journals of each State or Diocesan Convention, shall be read in the House of Clerical and Lay Deputies in General Convention, is hereby repealed.

HOUSE OF BISHOPS, ADOPTED May 24th, 1814.

JACKSON KEMPER, SECRETARY.

ADOPTED IN HOUSE OF CLERICAL AND LAY DEPUTIES, May 24th, 1814.

ASHBEL BALDWIN, SECRETARY.

List of the Clergy

OF THE

PROTESTANT EPISCOPAL CHURCH

In the United States.

EASTERN DIOCESE.

Composed of the States of Massachusetts, Rhode Island, New Hampshire, and Vermont.

The Right Rev. Alexander Viets Griswold, Bishop.

NEW HAMPSHIRE.

The Rev. Charles Burroughs, Rector of St. John's Church, Portsmouth.
The Rev. John H. Fowle, Rector of —— Church, Holderness.
The Rev. Daniel Barber, Rector of Union Church, Claremont.
The Rev. Mr. Catlin, officiates at Plainfield.
The Rev. Samuel Mead.

MASSACHUSETTS.

The Rev. John Sylvester J. Gardiner, Rector of Trinity Church, Boston.
The Rev. Asa Eaton, Rector of Christ Church, Boston, of St. Mary's, Newton, and of Christ Church, Cambridge.
The Rev. John P. K. Henshaw, Deacon, officiates at Marblehead.
The Rev. William Montague, Rector of St. Paul's Church, Dedham.
The Rev. James Morss, Rector of St. Paul's Church, Newburyport.
The Rev. Amos Purdy, Rector of St. Luke's Church, Lanesborough.
The Rev. Samuel Griswold, Rector of St. James's Church, Great Barrington, and the Church at Lenox.
The Rev. Joel G. Cooper, Rector of St. Andrew's Church, Hanover, and officiates also at Marshfield, and Quincy.
The Rev. Aaron Humphrey, Deacon, officiates in St. Ann's Church, Gardiner.
The Rev. Titus Strong, Deacon, officiates at Greenfield.

RHODE-ISLAND.

The Right Rev. Alexander V. Griswold, D.D., Rector of St. Michael's Church, Bristol.
The Rev. Nathan B. Crocker, Rector of St. John's Church, Providence.
The Rev. Salmon Wheaton, Rector of Trinity Church, Newport.
The Rev. James Bowers, officiates in Narragansett.

VERMONT.

The Rev. Abraham Bronson, Manchester and Arlington.

CONNECTICUT.

The Rev. Richard Mansfield, D.D., Rector of Christ Church, Derby, and the Church in Great Hill.
The Rev. John Tyler, Rector of Christ Church, Norwich.
The Rev. Daniel Fogg, Rector of the Church, Pomfret.
The Rev. Philo Shelton, Rector of Trinity Church, Fairfield, St. John's, Stratfield, and the Church in Weston.
The Rev. Ashbel Baldwin, Rector of Christ Church, Stratford, and Trinity Church, Trumbull.
The Rev. Tillotson Brownson, D.D., Principal of the Episcopal Academy, Cheshire.
The Rev. William Smith, D.D., residing at Norwalk.
The Rev. Chauncy Prindle, Rector of the Churches of Oxford and Salem.
The Rev. Reuben Ives, Rector of St. Peter's Church, Cheshire, and officiating in the Churches in Hamden, Wallingsford, Southington and Meriden.
The Rev. Truman Marsh, Rector of the Associated Churches in Litchfield.
The Rev. Daniel Burhans, Rector of Trinity Church, Newtown.
The Rev. Solomon Blakesly, Rector of St. Stephen's Church, East Haddam.
The Rev. Charles Seabury, Rector of St. James's Church, New London.
The Rev. Smith Miles, Rector of the Churches of Chatham and Glastenbury.
The Rev. Philander Chase, Rector of Trinity Church, Hartford.
The Rev. Menzies Rayner, Rector of the Churches in Huntington.
The Rev. Calvin White, Assistant Minister of the Church in Derby.
The Rev. Bethel Judd, Rector of St. Paul's Church, Norwalk, and the Church at Wilton.
The Rev. Henry Whitlock, Rector of Trinity Church, New Haven, and St. Matthew's, Bristol.
The Rev. Roger Searle, Rector of St. Peter's Church, Plymouth.
The Rev. Virgil H. Barber, Rector of St. John's Church, Waterbury.
The Rev. Asa Cornwall Assistant in the Episcopal Academy, Cheshire.
The Rev. Jonathan Judd, minister of the Churches in Stamford and Horsneck.
The Rev. Elijah G. Plumb Minister of the Churches in Branford, East Haven, North Branford and Northford.
The Rev. Benjamin Benham, Rector of St. John's Church, New Milford, and the Churches of Bridgewater and Brookfield.
The Rev. David Baldwin, Rector of the Churches of Guilford, North Guilford and North Bristol.
The Rev. Joseph D. Wilton, Minister of the Churches in Woodbury, Roxbury and Kent.

The Rev. Isaac Jones, Assistant Minister in the Churches, Litchfield.
The Rev. Sturges Gilbert, Minister in the Churches of Kent and Sharon.
The Rev. Nathaniel Huss, Minister of the Church at East Windsor.
The Rev. Frederick Holcomb, Minister of the Churches in Harwington and Northfield.
The Rev. Birdsley G. Nobles, Deacon, officiating at Christ Church, Middletown.
The Rev. Nathan B. Burgis, residing at Milford.
The Rev. Jasper D. Jones, residing at Simsbury.

NEW YORK.

The Right Rev. Samuel Provoost, D. D.
The Right Rev. Benjamin Moore, D. D., Bishop and Rector of Trinity Church, New York.
The Right Rev. John Henry Hobart, D.D., Assistant Bishop, and assistant Rector of Trinity Church, New York.
The Rev. Parker Adams, Trinity Church, Lansingburgh, Rensselaer County, and Grace Church, Waterford, Saratoga County.
The Rev. Amos G. Baldwin, Rector of Trinity Church, Utica, Oneida County.
The Rev. Virgil H. Barber, principal of the academy, and minister of Trinity Church, Fairfield, Herkimer County.
The Rev. Theodosius Barlow, Rector of Trinity Church, New Rochelle, Westchester County.
The Rev. Edmund D. Barry, Principal of the Protestant Episcopal Academy, New York; and officiating at St. Matthew's Church, City of Jersey.
The Rev. William Berrian, an Assistant Minister of Trinity Church, New York.
The Rev. John Bowden, D.D., Professor of Rhetoric and moral Philosophy, in Columbia College, New York.
The Rev. Nathaniel Bowen, D.D., Rector of Grace Church, New York.
The Rev. John Brady, Assistant Minister of St. George's Church, New York.
The Rev. David Butler, Rector of St. Paul's Church, Troy, Rensselaer County.
The Rev. Barzillai Bulkley, Rector of St. George's Church, Flushing, Long Island.
The Rev. William A. Clark, Missionary, Onondaga County, and parts adjacent.
The Rev. Orin Clark, Trinity Church, Geneva, Ontario County.
The Rev. Timothy Clowes, Rector of St. Peter's Church, Albany.
The Rev. Elias Cooper, Rector of St. John's Church, Yonkers, Westchester County.
The Rev. Harry Croswell, Deacon, Christ Church, Columbia County.
The Rev. Adam Empie, West Point.
The Rev. Henry J. Feitus, Rector of St. Ann's Church, Brooklyn, Long Island.
The Rev. Samuel Fuller, Missionary, Albany and Green Counties.
The Rev. N. Feltch, residing in West Chester County.
The Rev. William Hammel, residing in New York.
The Rev. William Harris, D.D., Rector of St. Mark's Church, New York, and President of Columbia College, New York.

The Rev. William Hart, Rector of St. George's Church, Hempstead, and Christ Church, North Hempstead, Long Island.
The Rev. Samuel Haskill, Rector of Christ Church, Rye, Westchester County.
The Rev. Thomas Y. How, D.D., an Assistant Minister of Trinity Church, New York.
The Rev. David Huntington, Deacon, St. Paul's Church, Charlton, Saratoga County.
The Rev. Samuel F. Jarvis, St Michael's Church, Bloomingdale, and St. James', Hamilton Square, New York.
The Rev. Stephen Jewett, Christ Church, Hampton, Washington County.
The Rev. Cave Jones, residing in the City of New York.
The Rev. Evan Malbone Johnson, Deacon, Grace Church, New York.
The Rev. John Kewley, Rector of St. George's Church, New York.
The Rev. William B. Lacey, Deacon, St. Paul's Church, Paris, Oneida County.
The Rev. Thomas Lyell, Rector of Christ Church, New York.
The Rev. Daniel M'Donald, St. Peter's Church, Auburn, Cayuga County.
The Rev. John M'Vickar, St. James' Church, Hyde Park, Dutchess County.
The Rev. David Moore, St. Andrew's Church, Staten Island.
The Rev. Henry Moscrop, residing in New York.
The Rev. Daniel Nash, Rector of the Churches in Otsego County.
The Rev. Benjamin T. Onderdonk, Deacon, an Assistant Minister of Trinity Church, New York.
The Rev. Joseph Perry, Rector of St. James' Church, Milton, and Christ Church, Ballston, Saratoga County.
The Rev. Joseph Prentice, Rector of Trinity Church, Athens, Green County.
The Rev. William Powel, St. Andrew's Church, Coldenham, and St. James' Church, Goshen, Orange County.
The Rev. John Reed, Rector of Christ Church. Poughkeepsie, Dutchess County.
The Rev. Gilbert H. Sayres, Grace Church, Jamaica, Long Island.
The Rev. Cyrus Stebbins, Rector of St. George's Church, Schenectady.
The Rev. James Thompson, Deacon, Missionary, Greene and Delaware Counties.
The Rev. Frederick Vanhorne, residing in Coldenham.
The Rev. Alanson W. Welton, Deacon, Missionary, Ontario and adjacent Counties.
The Rev. Russel Wheeler, Missionary, Harmony Church, Butternuts, St. Matthew's Church, Unadilla, Otsego County, and parts adjacent.
The Rev. Eli Wheeler, Deacon, Hempstead.
The Rev. Isaac Wilkins, D.D., Rector of St. Peter's Church, West Chester, and St. Paul's Church, East Chester.
The Rev. Joseph Willard, residing in New York.
The Rev. Ralph Williston, Rector of Zion Church, New York.

NEW JERSEY.

The Rev. Abraham Beach, D.D., residing near New Brunswick.
The Rev. Charles H. Wharton, D.D., Rector of St. Mary's Church, Burlington.
The Rev. John Croes, D.D., Rector of Christ Church, New Brunswick.
The Rev. John C. Rudd Rector of St. John's Church, Elizabeth Town.

The Rev. Simon Wilmer, Rector of Trinity Church, Swedesborough.
The Rev. James Chapman, Rector of St. Peter's Church, Perth Amboy.
The Rev. John Croes, jun., Rector of Christ Church, Shrewsbury.
The Rev. Daniel Higbee, St. Andrew's Church, Mount Holly.
The Rev. Lewis P. Bayard, Deacon, Trinity Church, Newark.

PENNSYLVANIA.

The Right Rev. William White, D. D., Bishop, and Rector of Christ Church, St. Peter's Church, and St. James' Church, Philadelphia.
The Rev. Robert Blackwell, D. D., residing in Philadelphia.
The Rev. Joseph Hutchins, D. D., residing in Philadelphia.
The Rev. James Abercrombie, D. D., senior Assistant Minister of Christ Church, St. Peter's, and St. John's, Philadelphia.
The Rev. Joseph Pilmore, D. D., Rector of St. Paul's Church, Philadelphia.
The Rev. Frederick Beasley, D. D., Provost of the University of Pennsylvania.
The Rev. William Ayres, residing in Philadelphia.
The Rev. John Campbell, Rector of Carlisle.
The Rev. Joseph Turner, Rector of St. Martin's, Marcus Hook.
The Rev. Slator Clay, Rector of St. James', Perkiomen, St. Peter's, Great Valley, and St. Thomas', Whitemarsh.
The Rev Joseph Clarkson, Rector of St. James', Lancaster, St. John's, Pequea, and Bangor Church, Carnarvon.
The Rev. James Wiltbank, Rector of Trinity Church, Oxford, and All Saints, Lower Dublin.
The Rev. Robert Ayres, residing in Brownsville.
The Rev. Francis Reno, officiating in the Counties of Beaver and Allegany.
The Rev. Caleb Hopkins, Rector of Christ Church, Derry township; St. Paul's, Bloom township; and Christ Church, Turbit Township, Northumberland County.
The Rev. Absalom Jones (a colored man), Rector of the African Church of St. Thomas, Philadelphia.
The Rev. John Taylor, Rector of Trinity Church, Pittsburgh.
The Rev. Levi Bull, Rector of St. Gabriel's, Berk's County, and St. Mary's, Chester County.
The Rev. John Armstrong, Rector of St. John's, Yorktown.
The Rev. Jackson Kemper, Assistant Minister of Christ Church, St. Peter's and St. James's, Philadelphia.
The Rev. Richard D. Hall, Rector of St. James the Greatest, Bristol.
The Rev. Jehu Curtis Clay, Deacon, officiating at St. David's, Radnor.

DELAWARE.

The Rev. Robert Clay, Rector of Emanuel's Church, New Castle.
The Rev. William Pryce, Rector of St. James', Newport.

MARYLAND.

The Right Rev. Thomas John Claggett, D. D., Bishop.
The Rev. Dr. James Kemp, first Rector, St. Paul's, Baltimore.
The Rev. William C. Wyatt, second Rector, St. Paul's, Baltimore.
The Rev. Galen Hicks, Rector of Trinity, Baltimore.
The Rev. George Dashiell, Rector of St. Peter's, Baltimore.
The Rev. Dr. Benj. Contee, Rector of William and Mary Charles County.

The Rev. John Weems, Rector of Port Tobacco Parish, Charles County.
The Rev. Noble Young, Rector of Durham.
The Rev. William Gibson, Rector of Queen Ann's, Prince George's County.
The Rev. William Ninde, Rector of St. Ann's Parish, Annapolis.
The Rev. Purnell F. Smith, Rector of St. James' Parish, Prince George Co.
The Rev. George Lemmon, Rector of Queen Caroline, Prince George Co.
The Rev. Walter D. Addison, Rector of St. John's, Territory of Columbia.
The Rev. Andrew M'Cormick, Rector of Washington, Territory of Columbia.
The Rev. Thomas Read, Rector of Prince George's, Montgomery County.
The Rev. John Chandler, Rector of St. Mark's, Montgomery County.
The Rev. Thomas P. Irving, Rector of St John's, Montgomery County.
The Rev. John Allen, Rector of St. George's, Harford County.
The Rev. Henry L. Davis, Rector of St. Stephen's, Cecil County.
The Rev. William Duke, residing in Elkton.
The Rev. Samuel H. Turner, Rector of Chester Parish, Kent County.
The Rev. Daniel Stephens, Rector of St. Paul's, Queen Anne's County.
The Rev. Thomas Bayne, Rector of St. Peter's, Talbot County.
The Rev. William Stone, Rector of Stepney Parish, Somerset County.
The Rev. James Laird, Rector of Somerset Parish, Somerset County.

VIRGINIA.

No list of the Clergy in this State was furnished to the Convention.

SOUTH CAROLINA.

The Right Rev. Theodore Dehon, D. D., Bishop.
The Rev. John Barnwell Campbell, Rector of St. Helena's Church, Beaufort.
The Rev. Frederick Dalcho, Deacon, officiating in St. Paul's, Stono.
The Rev. Andrew Fowler, Rector of the Church on Edisto Island.
The Rev. Hugh Fraser, Rector of All Saints.
The Rev. Christopher Edward Gadsden, Assistant Minister of St. Philip's Church, Charleston.
The Rev. Christian Hankel, Deacon, officiating in St. Luke's Parish.
The Rev. Philip Matthews, Rector of the Church, on St. Helena's Island.
The Rev. Thomas Mills, D. D., Rector of St. Andrews Parish.
The Rev. William Percy, D. D., Rector of the third Episcopal Church, Charleston.
The Rev. James Dewar Simons, Rector of St. Philip's Church, Charleston.
The Rev Charles Blair Snowden, Rector of St. Stephen's.
The Rev. John Jacob Tschudy, Rector of St. John's Parish, Berkeley.
The Rev. Joseph Weaver, Rector of St. Thomas and St. Dennis.

CLERGYMEN NOT HAVING CURES.

The Rev. Thomas Gates, D. D.
The Rev. Milward Pogson.
The Rev. Paul Feropier Gervais.
The Rev. James O'Farrell.

CERTIFICATE OF BISHOP MOORE'S CONSECRATION.

Know all men by these presents, that we, William White, D. D., Bishop of the Protestant Episcopal Church in the State of Pennsylvania, presiding Bishop, John Henry Hobart, D. D., Assistant Bishop of the Protestant Episcopal Church in the State of New York, Alexander Viets Griswold, D. D., Bishop of the Protestant Episcopal Church in the Eastern Diocese, and Theodore Dehon, D. D., Bishop of the Protestant Episcopal Church in the State of South Carolina, under the protection of Almighty God, in St. James' Church, in the city of Philadelphia, on Wednesday, the eighteenth day of May, in the year of our Lord one thousand eight hundred and fourteen, did then and there rightly and canonically consecrate our beloved in Christ, Richard Channing Moore, D. D., Rector of St. Stephen's Church in the city of New York, of whose sufficiency in good learning, soundness in the faith, and purity of manners we were fully ascertained, into the office of Bishop of the Protestant Episcopal Church in the State of Virginia, to which he hath been elected by the Convention of said State.

Given in the city of Philadelphia, this eighteenth day of May, in the year of our Lord one thousand eight hundred and fourteen.

WILLIAM WHITE, (L. S.)
JOHN HENRY HOBART, (L. S.)
ALEXANDER V. GRISWOLD, (L. S.)
THEODORE DEHON, (L. S.)

JOURNAL OF THE PROCEEDINGS

OF THE

BISHOPS, CLERGY, AND LAITY

OF THE

Protestant Episcopal Church,

IN

THE UNITED STATES OF AMERICA,

IN

A GENERAL CONVENTION.

HELD IN

TRINITY CHURCH, IN THE CITY OF NEW YORK, FROM THE 20TH TO THE 27TH DAY OF MAY INCLUSIVE, A. D. 1817.

LIST OF THE ATTENDING MEMBERS.

HOUSE OF BISHOPS.

The Right Rev. William White, D. D., of Pennsylvania, presiding Bishop.

The Right Rev. John Henry Hobart, D. D., of New York.

The Right Rev. Alexander Viets Griswold, D. D., of the Eastern Diocese, composed of the States of New Hampshire, Massachusetts, Vermont and Rhode Island.

The Right Rev. Theodore Dehon, D. D., of South Carolina.

The Right Rev. Richard Channing Moore, D. D., of Virginia.

The Right Rev. James Kemp, D. D., of Maryland.

The Right Rev. John Croes, D. D., of New Jersey.

HOUSE OF CLERICAL AND LAY DEPUTIES.

CLERICAL DEPUTIES.

NEW HAMPSHIRE.

The Rev. Charles Burroughs.

MASSACHUSETTS.

The Rev. Thomas Carlile, The Rev. Titus Strong.

VERMONT.

The Rev. Stephen Beach.

RHODE ISLAND.

The Rev. Salmon Wheaton, The Rev. Nathan B. Crocker.

CONNECTICUT.

The Rev. Ashbel Baldwin, The Rev. Harry Croswell.
The Rev. Roger Searle,

NEW YORK.

The Rev. Isaac Wilkins, D. D.,
The Rev. Thomas Y. How, D. D.,
The Rev. David Butler,
The Rev. William Harris, D. D.

NEW JERSEY.

The Rev. Charles H. Wharton, D. D.,
The Rev. John C. Rudd,
The Rev. Simon Wilmer,
The Rev. James Chapman.

PENNSYLVANIA.

The Rev. Frederic Beasley, D. D.,
The Rev. Levi Bull,
The Rev. Jackson Kemper,
The Rev. Joseph Clarkson,
The Rev. James Montgomery.*

DELAWARE.

The Rev. William Wickes.

MARYLAND.

The Rev. Henry L. Davis,
The Rev. Walter D. Addison,
The Rev. William E. Wyatt,
The Rev. Samuel H. Turner.

VIRGINIA.

The Rev. John Dunn,
The Rev. William H. Wilmer,
The Rev. Oliver Norris.

SOUTH CAROLINA.

The Rev. Andrew Fowler.

LAY DEPUTIES.

RHODE ISLAND.

Hon. Benjamin Gardiner,
Col. Thomas Lloyd Halsey
Alexander Jones, Esq.

VERMONT.

Mr. Orange Ferris,

CONNECTICUT.

Burrage Beach, Esq.,
Elijah Boardman, Esq.

NEW YORK.

Hon. Rufus King,
Hon. Philip S. Van Rensselaer,
Dr. John Onderdonk,
Mr. William Ogden.

NEW JERSEY.

Joshua M. Wallace, Esq.,
Joseph Higbie, Esq.,
Robert Boggs, Esq.

*The Rev. Dr. Beasley having resigned his seat in the House, in consequence of intelligence requiring his return to his family, the Rev. Mr. Montgomery, by a rule of the Convention of Pennsylvania, was appointed to fill his place.—*Committee of Publication.*

PENNSYLVANIA.

Thomas McEuen, Esq., Richard Dale, Esq.,
Plunket F. Glentworth, M. D., William Meredith, Esq.

MARYLAND.

Tench Tilghman, Esq., Francis S. Key, Esq.,
Alexander C. Magruder, Esq., Beddingfield Hands, Esq.

VIRGINIA.

Hon. Charles F. Mercer, Col. Hugh Mercer.

NORTH CAROLINA.

Mr. Moses Jarvis.

The following Clergy, not members of the Convention, were admitted to attend the sittings of the same.

MASSACHUSETTS.—The Rev. George T. Chapman.

CONNECTICUT.—The Rev. Daniel Burhans, The Rev. Joseph D. Welton, The Rev. Smith Miles, The Rev. Birdsey G. Noble, The Rev. David Baldwin, The Rev. Reuben Hubbard, The Rev. Reuben Sherwood, The Rev. Charles Smith.

NEW YORK.—The Rev. Gregory T. Bedell, The Rev. William Berrian, The Rev. Nathaniel Bowen, D. D., The Rev. John Brown, The Rev. Barzillai Bulkley, The Rev. Richard F. Cadle, The Rev. Orin Clark, The Rev. Timothy Clowes, The Rev. William Creighton, The Rev. Henry J. Feltus, The Rev. Seth Hart, The Rev. Samuel Haskill, The Rev. John P. K. Henshaw, The Rev. Samuel F. Jarvis, The Rev. Evan M. Johnson, The Rev. Ravaud Kearney, The Rev. Thomas Lyell, The Rev. James Milnor, The Rev. David Moore, The Rev. Benjamin T. Onderdonk, The Rev. Henri L. P. F. Peneveyre, The Rev. William Powell, The Bev. John Reed, The Rev. Gilbert H. Sayres, The Rev. Hugh Smith, The Rev. George Weller.

NEW JERSEY.—The Rev. Lewis P. Bayard, The Rev. John Croes, jr., The Rev. George Y. Morehouse.

PENNSYLVANIA.—The Rev. Joseph R. Walker.

JOURNAL

OF THE

House of Clerical and Lay Deputies.

NEW YORK, Tuesday, May 20, 1817.

This being the day appointed for the meeting of the General Convention of the Protestant Episcopal Church in the United States of America, several Clerical and Lay Deputies attended in Trinity Church, at half past six o'clock, P. M., and a quorum of the house being present, the Rev. Dr. Wharton was requested to take the chair, *pro tempore*, and the Secretary of the house in the last Convention acted as Secretary *pro tempore*.

The house then proceeded to read the testimonials of the Clerical and Lay Deputies, which were severally approved, and the following gentlemen took their seats in the house.

CLERICAL DEPUTIES.

From New Hampshire, Rev. Charles Burroughs. From Massachusetts, Rev. Titus Strong, Rev. Thomas Carlile. From Rhode Island, Rev. Salmon Wheaton, Rev. Nathan B. Crocker. From Vermont, Rev. Stephen Beach. From Connecticut, Rev. Ashbel Baldwin, Rev. Roger Searle. From New York, Rev. Thomas Y. How, D. D., Rev. Isaac Wilkins, D. D., Rev. David Butler. From New Jersey, Rev. Charles H. Wharton, D. D., Rev. John C. Rudd, Rev. Simon Wilmer, Rev. James Chapman. From Pennsylvania, Rev. Frederic Beasley, D. D., Rev. Joseph Clarkson, Rev. Levi Bull, Rev. Jackson Kemper. From Delaware, Rev.

William Wickes. From Maryland, Rev. Walter D. Addison, Rev. William E. Wyatt, Rev. Samuel H. Turner, Rev. Henry L. Davis. From Virginia, Rev. William H. Wilmer, Rev. Oliver Norris, Rev. John Dunn.

LAY DEPUTIES.

From Rhode Island, Hon. Benjamin Gardiner, Alexander Jones, Esq., Col. Thomas Lloyd Halsey. From Connecticut, Barrage Beach, Esq. From New York, Dr. John Onderdonk, Hon. Philip S. Van Rensselaer, Mr. William Ogden. From New Jersey, Joshua M. Wallace, Esq., Joseph Higbie, Esq., Robert Boggs, Esq. From Pennsylvania, Thomas McEuen, Esq., Plunket F. Glentworth, M. D., Richard Dale, Esq., William Meredith, Esq. From Maryland, Tench Tilghman, Esq., Alexander C. Magruder, Esq., Francis S. Key, Esq., Riddingfield Hands, Esq. From Virginia, Hon. Charles F. Mercer, Col. Hugh Mercer.

The house proceeded to the election of a President and Secretary, when it appeared that the Rev. Isaac Wilkins, D. D., was chosen President, and the Rev. Ashbel Baldwin, Secretary.

On motion, Resolved,—That the Rev. Mr. Rudd be requested to assist the Secretary in the duties of his office.

On motion, Resolved,—That Clergymen of the Protestant Episcopal Church, who may be in the city of New York during the session of this Convention, and not members thereof, be admitted to the sittings of the same.

The Rev. Dr. How and Rev. Mr. Butler were appointed to inform the House of Bishops, that this house was organized, and ready to proceed to business.

The House of Bishops returned for answer, that they also were organized, and ready to proceed to business.

The following message was received from the House of Bishops:

"The House of Bishops inform the House of Clerical and Lay Deputies, that as they deem it proper to have the business of the Convention opened by the celebration of Divine Service, they propose an adjournment until to-morrow morning, at the hour publicly notified for said service."

Whereupon, Resolved,—That this house adjourn until that time.

WEDNESDAY, May 21, 1817.

The house attended Divine Service in Trinity Church. Service was performed by the Rev. Isaac Wilkins, D. D., and a sermon preached by the Right Rev. Bishop Griswold.

After Divine Service the house met.

The Rev. Andrew Fowler, a clerical deputy from South Carolina, and Mr. Orange Ferris, a lay deputy from Vermont, appeared, produced the testimonials of their appointment, and took their seats.

The Rev. William Harris, D. D., a clerical deputy, and the Hon. Rufus King, a lay deputy from New York, appeared and took their seats.

The following rules of order were read and adopted:

1. The morning service of the Church shall be performed every day during the session of the Convention.

2. When the President takes the chair, no member shall continue standing, or shall afterwards stand up unless to address the chair.

3. No member shall absent himself from the service of the house, unless he have leave, or be unable to attend.

4. When any member is about to speak in debate, or deliver any matter to the house, he shall, with due respect, address himself to the President, confining himself strictly to the point in debate.

5. No member shall speak more than twice in the same debate, without leave of the house.

6. A question being once determined, shall stand as the judgment of the house, and shall not be again drawn into debate during the same session, unless with the consent of two thirds of the house.

7. While the President is putting any question, the members shall continue in their seats, and shall not hold any private discourse.

8. Every member, who shall be in the house when any question is put, shall, on a division, be counted, unless he be personally interested in the decision.

9. No motion shall be considered as before the house, unless it be seconded, and, when required, reduced to writing.

10. When any question is before the house, it shall be determined before any thing new is introduced, except the question of adjournment.

11. The question on a motion for adjournment shall be taken before any other, and without debate.

12. When the house is about to rise, every member shall keep his seat until the President shall leave his chair.

On motion, Resolved,—That the thanks of this Convention be presented to the Right Rev. Bishop Griswold, for his appropriate sermon delivered this morning, and that he be requested to furnish a copy for publication.

The Rev. Dr. Harris and the Rev. Dr. Beasley were appointed a committee to communicate the foregoing resolution to the House of Bishops.

A message was received from the House of Bishops, informing this house that they concurred in the vote of thanks to Bishop Griswold for his sermon, and in requesting a copy for publication, and that Bishop Griswold would comply with the request of the Convention.

On motion, Ordered,—That unless otherwise directed, the hour of meeting be in future at nine o'clock, A. M.

On motion, Resolved,—That a committee, consisting of one member from each State represented in this Convention, be appointed to examine the Journals of the different State Conventions, Episcopal Charges, Addresses, and Pastoral Letters, which have been, or may be laid before this house during the present session; to make inquiry into the state of the Church in each Diocese, and into the attention paid to the Canons and rules of the Church; to draw up a view of the state of the Church, and report the same to the house, agreeably to the 45th Canon.

The following gentlemen were appointed to compose said committee.

From New Hampshire, Rev. Mr. Burroughs. From Vermont, Rev. Mr. Beach. From Massachusetts, Rev. Mr. Carlile. From Rhode Island, Rev. Mr. Wheaton. From Connecticut, Rev. Mr. Searle. From New York, Rev. Dr. How. From New Jersey, Rev. Dr. Wharton. From Pennsylvania, Rev. Dr. Beasley. From Delaware, Rev. Mr. Wickes. From Maryland, Rev. Mr. Addison. From Virginia, Rev. Mr. Dunn. From South Carolina, Rev. Mr. Fowler.

The following documents, which have been laid before the house in conformity with the 45th Canon, were referred to the above committee.

From Vermont, a written Constitution and Journal of the Convention.

Eastern Diocese, Bishop Griswold's Pastoral Letter and Address, together with several papers and reports.

From Connecticut, printed Journals from 1813 to 1817.

From New York, printed Journals for the years 1814, 1815, and 1816, with one Charge, a Pastoral Letter, and several Addresses by the Bishop of that Diocese.

From New Jersey, printed Journals for 1815 and 1816, together with a written report on the state of the Church in that Diocese.

From Pennsylvania, printed Journals for 1814, 1815, 1816, and 1817.

From Delaware, printed Journals for 1810 and 1816.

From Maryland, printed Journals for 1814, 1815, 1816, and an Address to the members of the Church in that Diocese.

From Virginia, printed Journals for 1815 and 1816.

From South Carolina, printed Journals for 1815, 1816 and 1817.

A message was received from the House of Bishops, informing this house that they had received a communication from the Secretary of a Convention of the Protestant Episcopal Church in North Carolina, containing a copy of the Constitution of that Diocese, and a Journal of the first Convention of the same, together with a request to be received into union with the General Convention, (all which were sent with the message,) and that the House of Bishops recognized the Protestant Episcopal Church in North Carolina as a member of this union.

The documents accompanying the foregoing message were then read, and this house concurred with the House of Bishops in admitting the Church in North Carolina as a member of this Convention.

Mr. Moses Jarvis jr., a lay deputy from North Carolina, appeared, produced the testimonial of his appointment, and took his seat.

Mr. Jarvis was added to the committee on the state of the Church; and the Constitution and Journal contained in the communications from North Carolina were referred to the said committee.

Adjourned.

THURSDAY, May 22, nine o'clock, A. M.

The house met.

Elijah Boardman, Esq., a lay deputy from the Diocese of Connecticut, appeared and took his seat.

The President of this house stated, that from his difficulty of hearing, he found it inconvenient to himself to discharge the duties of his office, and therefore offered his resignation which was accepted.

The house then proceeded to the choice of a President when, upon counting the ballots, it was found that the Rev. William H. Wilmer was duly elected.

The Rev. Mr. Rudd asked, and obtained leave of absence for Robert Boggs, Esq., until Saturday next.

On motion of the Rev. Mr. Strong, Resolved,—That a committee be appointed to inquire into the expediency of an additional number of Hymns.

The following gentlemen were appointed the committee—Rev. Mr. Strong, Rev. Mr. Searle, Rev. Dr. How, Rev. Dr. Wharton, Rev. Mr. Bull, Rev. Mr. Wickes, Rev. Mr. Davis, Rev. Mr. Norris, and Rev. Mr. Fowler.

Francis S. Key, Esq., submitted the following resolution for consideration, which was ordered to lie on the table

"Resolved,—That the Clergy of this Church be, and they are hereby enjoined to recommend sobriety of life and conversation to the professing members of their respective congregations, and that they be authorized and required to state it, as the opinion of this Convention, that conforming to the vain amusements of the world, frequent horse races, theatres, and public balls, playing cards, or being engaged in any other kind of gaming, are inconsistent with Christian sobriety, dangerous to the morals of the members of the Church, and peculiarly unbecoming the character of communicants."

The house adjourned to attend Divine Service. Service was performed by the Rev. Dr. Beasley, and a sermon preached by the Right Rev. Bishop White.

After Divine Service, the house met.

The Rev. Dr. Wilkins was appointed a committee to unite with a committee on the part of the House of Bishops, to receive from the Right Rev. Bishop Griswold the copy of his sermon preached before the Convention yesterday morning.

The Episcopal Addresses inserted in the Journals of the several Diocesan Conventions were read, in conformity with the 45th Canon.

The Rev. Dr. Beasley stated, that he had just received information, that circumstances of a domestic nature required his immediate return to his family; he therefore resigned his seat in this house.

The Secretary presented a certificate signed by the Clerk of the Protestant Episcopal Church at Zanesville, in the State of Ohio, of the appointment of Dr. Horace Reed, to represent that Church in this Convention, which was read.

Whereupon, Resolved,—That the Protestant Episcopal Church in the State of Ohio not having in Convention acceded to the Constitution of the Protestant Episcopal Church in the United States of America, Dr. Reed cannot be admitted a member of this house, but that he be allowed the privilege of an honorary seat.

The Rev. James Montgomery, of Pennsylvania, by a rule of the Convention of that Diocese, having been appointed to fill the place vacated by the resignation of Dr. Beasley, appeared, and took his seat as a member of this house.

The following resolutions were offered by the Rev. Dr. Wharton for the consideration of the house, and ordered to lie on the table:

1. Resolved,—That it is expedient to provide for the better education of candidates for the ministry in the Church.

2. Resolved,—That a committee consisting of one Clergyman and one Layman from each State, be appointed to bring in a report on the best manner of carrying the above resolution into execution.

Adjourned.

FRIDAY, May 23, nine o'clock, A. M.

The house met.

The Rev. Harry Croswell, a clerical deputy from Connecticut, appeared and took his seat.

The committee appointed to inquire into the expediency of an additional number of Hymns, reported the following resolution:

Resolved,—That the House of Bishops be requested to make a selection of Hymns, leaving out such of the present Hymns in the Book of Common Prayer, and adding such others as they may think proper, and report to the next General Convention:—which resolution was indefinitely postponed.

On motion, Resolved,—That Mr. Key's resolution, laid on the table yesterday, be called up for the consideration of the house to-morrow morning.

The house adjourned to attend Divine Service. Service was performed by the Rev. William H. Wilmer, and a sermon preached by the Right Rev. Bishop Dehon.

After Divine Service the house met.

A message was received from the House of Bishops, communicating sundry papers and facts relative to the state of the Protestant Episcopal Church westward of the Alleghany mountains, together with certain resolutions of the House of Bishops relative to the Western States, and a Canon limiting the operation of the 2d and 37th Canons.

The documents accompanying this message were then read.

The resolutions of the House of Bishops, and the Canon sent from the same house, were then considered, concurred in by this house, and information of this concurrence conveyed to the House of Bishops.

On motion, Resolved,—That the list of organized parishes in the State of Ohio, which has just been read before this house, be entered on the Journal.

The following is the list:

St. Peter's Church, in Ashtabula, County of Ashtabula.
Trinity Church, in Cleveland, County of Cuyahoga.
St. Mark's Church, in Columbia, County of Cuyahoga.
St. John's Church, in Liverpool, County of Medina.
St. Paul's Church, in Medina, County of Medina.
St. Luke's Church, in Ravenna, County of Portage.
Grace Church, in Parkman, County of Portage.
St. Stephen's Church, in Middlebury, County of Portage.
St. James's Church, in Boardman, County of Trumbull.
Christ Church, in Windsor, County of Ashtabula.
Grace Church, in Berkshire, County of Delaware.
St. Michael's Church, in Norton, County of Delaware.
St. John's Church, in Worthington, County of Franklin.
St. Paul's Church, Chilicothe.
St. James's Church, in Zanesville, County of Muskingum.
——— Church, in Cambridge, County of Guernsey.
——— Church, in Morristown, County of Belmont.
——— Church, in St. Clairville, County of Belmont.
——— Church, in Steubenville, County of Jefferson.

The Rev. Mr. Chapman asked, and obtained leave of absence for the remainder of the session.

Adjourned.

SATURDAY, May 24, nine o'clock, A. M.

The house met.

The Rev. Mr. Rudd asked, and obtained leave of absence for Joseph Higbie, Esq., for the remainder of the session.

Mr. Key's resolution was called up for discussion.

The house adjourned to attend Divine Service. Service was performed by the Rev. Mr. Norris, and a sermon preached by the Right Rev. Bishop Moore.

After Divine Service the house met, and proceeded to the further consideration of Mr. Key's resolution.

The Rev. Dr. How moved the following resolution:

Resolved,—That inasmuch as ample provision is already made for the purposes of Christian discipline in the cases specified in the foregoing resolution, by the Constitution, Canons, Rubricks, Homilies, and Liturgy of the Church, it is unnecessary at this time to pass any resolution on the subject of the discipline of the Church.

On motion, Resolved,—That the consideration of this subject be postponed, in order to attend to a message from the House of Bishops.

A communication from the House of Bishops was then read on the subject of a Theological Seminary; whereupon, the resolutions offered on Thursday by the Rev. Dr. Wharton were taken up, and passed in the affirmative. A committee, consisting of the following gentlemen, was then appointed:

From New Hampshire, Rev. Mr. Burroughs.
Massachusetts, Rev. Mr. Carlile.
Rhode Island, Rev. Mr. Crocker, Col. Halsey.
Vermont, Rev. Mr. Beach, Mr. Ferris.
Connecticut, Rev. Harry Croswell, B. Beach, Esq.
New York, Rev. Dr. Harris, Hon. Mr. King.
New Jersey, Rev. Dr. Wharton, J. M. Wallace, Esq.
Pennsylvania, Rev. Mr. Clarkson, W. Meredith, Esq.
Delaware. Rev. Mr. Wickes.
Maryland, Rev. Mr. Davis, T. Tilghman, Esq.
Virginia Rev. Mr. Dunn, Hon. C. F. Mercer,
North Carolina, Mr. Moses Jarvis, jun.
South Carolina, Rev. Mr. Fowler.

On motion, Resolved,—That the papers sent to this house from the House of Bishops, on the subject of a Theological Seminary, be referred to said committee.

A communication was read from the House of Bishops, recommending the attention of the Clergy to the 22d Canon.

The Rev. Mr. Bull, Rev. Mr. Carlile, Rev. Mr. Strong, and Mr. Ferris, asked, and obtained leave of absence for the remainder of the session.

The house then proceeded to consider the Rev. Dr. How's resolution, when a motion was made for an adjournment, which motion prevailed, and the house adjourned.

MONDAY, May 26—nine o'clock A. M.

The house met, and proceeded to the further consideration of the resolution offered on Saturday by the Rev. Dr. How. This subject was postponed to receive the following report of the committee on the state of the Church, which was read, accepted, and sent to the House of Bishops.

REPORT.

The House of Clerical and Lay Deputies, in compliance with the 45th Canon, have taken a general view of the state of the Church, and offer to the House of Bishops the result of their inquiries, respectfully requesting that venerable body to draw up, and cause to be published, a Pastoral Letter to the members of the Church.

EASTERN DIOCESE.

NEW HAMPSHIRE.

Since the last General Convention the Church in this State has greatly increased. An Episcopal congregation has been formed in Concord, the seat of the State Legislature; and Episcopal service is regularly performed there on Sundays by a clergyman or a lay reader. We trust that they will soon be able to erect a building for public worship. A new Church has been established at Bradford, and another at Hopkinton. An Episcopal Church has also been incorporated at Drewsville, which is a part of Walpole, and they annually derive a hundred and thirty dollars from their Church lands. St. John's Church, at Portsmouth, contains more than seventy families, and has about seventy communicants. The Church at Cornish is without a clergyman, but Divine Service is generally performed on Sundays by a lay reader. Union Church at Claremont, and Trinity Church at Holderness, we trust, continue to improve under the labours of their respective ministers. The necessity of encouragement of Missionary Societies will appear, when it is suggested, that five of the few Churches in this State want either the ability or the opportunity to provide themselves with pastors. We feel much pleasure in stating, that the aid and visitations of the Right Rev. Bishop of the Eastern Diocese have been, through the great goodness of the Divine Head of the Church, an essential blessing to the Churches of this State.

MASSACHUSETTS.

In this State we are gratified to observe an increase of Churches, and a growing attention to our doctrine and discipline. With but few exceptions, the congregations are regularly supplied, and a zeal is manifested among those who are not favoured with stated ministrations, to contribute as much as is in their power to obtain this desirable object. From the formation of societies for the distribution of Prayer Books and Episcopal Tracts much good has resulted. And, it is presumed, at no former time have such efforts been made for the increasing prospects of the Church—nor any been crowned with greater success.

VERMONT.

The aspect of the Church in this State is much more pleasing than it was at the time of the sitting of the last General Convention. The question in regard to the Church lands remains yet undecided; but, it is thought, is in a way soon to be decided in favour of the Church. There are at present two clergymen only who officiate in this State. The Rev. Mr. Bronson officiates at Arlington and Manchester; his congregations are large and respectable. "Mr. Beach," says Bishop Griswold, "is now officiating at Fairfield, St. Albans, and Sheldon, in Vermont; and of his success we have the most pleasing intelligence. A very considerable number of communicants have already been added to these Churches. Large congregations attend his preaching. A spirit of religious inquiry and awakened concern for the one thing needful, extensively prevails in those parts of the State where he labours; and cheering are the prospects of still greater increase, both in members and piety. At Fairfield they are erecting a house for the worship of God, and already is this pious work in great forwardness. Indeed, the number of churches which are now building, or will probably soon be commenced, is one of the best proofs of the increasing zeal amongst our people, for the service of God, and the support of his holy worship." At Bellows' Falls, also at Windsor and Middlebury, are churches now erecting. All that is wanting for the rapid growth of the Church in Vermont, is a number of zealous clergymen. O that the Lord of all would send more labourers into His harvest!

RHODE ISLAND.

The Church in Rhode Island, through the Divine blessing, is in a flourishing condition. Since the last General Convention a new congregation has been formed in the village of Pawtucket, and a neat and spacious church edifice nearly completed. The other churches of this State are also prosperous. It has pleased the Lord to awaken many to righteousness; so that large additions have been made to our communion, and our congregations considerably increased. Much good is expected to result from societies which have been instituted for the distribution of the Book of Common Prayer and religious Tracts.

EASTERN DIOCESE—GENERALLY.

Since the last Convention, there have been admitted to the order of Deacons, Silas S. Safford, (since deceased), Walter Cranston, John L. Blake, Stephen Beach, Thomas Carlile, Chever Felche, George S. White, Joseph R. Andrus, George T. Chapman, Gideon W. Olney, Jonathan M. Wainwright, George Leonard, and Benjamin B. Smith; and Titus Strong, John L. Blake, Thomas Carlile, George S. White, and Joseph R. Andrus, Deacons, have been ordained Priests. The Rev. Titus Strong has been instituted Rector of St. James's Church, Greenfield; and the Rev. Thomas Carlile, Rector of St. Peter's Church, in Salem. Six hundred and seventy-five persons have been confirmed. There are fourteen candidates for Holy Orders.

In May, of 1815, Bishop Griswold, being invited according to the directions of the 20th Canon, visited some of the Churches in Connecticut, confirmed 131 persons, and admitted Ezekiel G. Gear and Reuben Sherwood to the order of Deacons; and the Rev. Birdsey G. Noble, Alpheus Gear, Harry Croswell, and Aaron Humphrey, Deacons, to that of Priests.

CONNECTICUT.

In the Diocese of Connecticut the prospects of the Church are in a high degree flattering. A rapid increase of numbers—a growing zeal—and a proportionate measure of industry and liberality, on the part of both the Clergy and Laity, are among the circumstances on which we calculate, through the blessing of God, for raising the Church from its late depressed state, and for ensuring its lasting prosperity. From the journals of the Diocesan Conventions, it appears that there has been a considerable accession of members to our communion since the last report: and as the balance of emigration is against the Diocese, it is evident that these additions have been principally drawn from other denominations: and that the liberality of our people has been proportionate to this increase, is manifest from the great number of edifices which have been erected for the celebration of the ordinances and worship of our Church—and from the munificence displayed in the construction of these edifices. Trinity Church, in New Haven, which was consecrated in February, 1816, is surpassed by very few, if any in the Union, for size, convenience, or simple elegance. The Church in this Diocese has laboured under very serious inconvenience since the death of its late lamented Diocesan, Bishop Jarvis, by being in a great measure deprived of the benefit of Episcopal visitations. This inconvenience, however, is now in a considerable degree remedied, by an arrangement with the Right Rev. Bishop Hobart, of New York, who has been regularly invited by the Convention of the State, under the 20th Canon of the General Convention, to take temporary charge of the Diocese ; and has accordingly done so.

Under this arrangement, Bishop Hobart has visited a part of the Diocese—consecrated several churches—and administered the right of confirmation to about 1600 persons. Still, however, the want of a resident Diocesan is much felt; and we confidently hope that the time is not far distant, when the fund for the support of a Bishop, amounting already to little less than 15,000 dollars, will be sufficient to supply this necessity, and to meet the wishes, and fulfil the most sanguine expectations of the friends of the Church throughout the Diocese.

NEW YORK.

We have reason to be thankful to the great Head of the Church for the degree of prosperity with which he has blessed that portion of it which forms the Diocese of New York. Fidelity in the Clergy, and an encouraging spirit of zeal and devotion in the Laity, very generally prevail. And this fidelity, zeal, and devotion, are marked with a scrupulous adherence to the Canons, Rubrics, and edifying usages of our excellent Church. The sufficiency of her provisions to secure the influence and happy consequences of evangelical piety, has been, in some instances, most eminently displayed. In illustration of this remark, we refer to the following extract from the address of the Bishop of this Diocese to the Convention of 1816.

"In St. Paul's Church, Troy, 78 received confirmation, principally young persons; many of whom at the first opportunity, came to the communion. I deem it of importance to state, that in this congregation, during a season of unusual religious excitement, its Rector did not find it necessary to deviate, in any degree from the forms of our Church; but by more frequency in the use of them, and by greater assiduity in his parochial duties and instructions, he was happily instrumental in increasing the piety of his flock."

Since the period embraced in the last report, twenty-nine persons have been admitted by the Right Rev. Bishop Hobart, to the holy order of Deacons, viz., William B. Lacey, Harry Croswell (since removed to Connecticut), John Brown, William Creighton, George Boyd (since removed to Pennsylvania), Alpheus Gear, of Connecticut, Eli Wheeler, of Connecticut (since settled in this Diocese), Alanson W. Welton, of Connecticut (since settled in this Diocese), George Y. Morehouse, of New Jersey, at Perth-Amboy, New Jersey, where, previously to the election of a Bishop in that Diocese, Bishop Hobart was invited to hold an ordination, by the Standing Committee of the same; Gregory T. Bedell, William Hawley (since removed to the city of Washington), William H. Hart (since removed to Virginia), Abiel Carter, (since removed to Pennsylvania), William J. Bulkley, of Connecticut, Charles W. Hamilton, Henri L. P. F. Peneveyre (from the Protestant Church of Luzerne, in Switzerland), Henry U. Onderdonk, Thomas C. Brownell, Professor in Union College, Schenectady, Ravaud Kearney, Petrus S. Ten Broeck, George Weller, James F. Hull, of New Orleans, Samuel Johnston, Joshua M. Rogers, Hugh Smith, Henry Anthon, Richard F. Cadle, Nathaniel Bruce, M. D. and Charles Smith, of Connecticut.

Twenty Deacons have been admitted to the holy order of Priests, viz. the Rev. James Thompson, the Rev. David Huntington, the Rev. Eli Wheeler, the Rev. Benjamin T. Onderdonk, the Rev. Lewis P. Bayard, of New Jersey, at Newark, (N. J.) where Bishop Hobart was invited prior to the election of a Bishop in that State, by the Standing Committee of the same, to hold an ordination; the Rev. Alanson W. Welton, the Rev. John Brown, the Rev. William B. Lacey, the Rev. Henri L. P. F. Peneveyre, the Rev. Henry U. Onderdonk, the Rev.

John P. K. Henshaw, (since removed to Maryland); the Rev. James F. Hull, of New Orleans; the Rev. Thomas C. Brownell; the Rev. Walter Cranston, of Georgia, at New Haven, in Connecticut, the Rev. Reuben Sherwood, of Connecticut, at Norwalk, in that Diocese in which Diocese Bishop Hobart had been invited by the Convention of the same, agreeably to the 20th Canon of the General Convention, to perform Episcopal offices; the Rev. Evan M. Johnson, the Rev. William Creighton, the Rev. Ravaud Kearney, the Rev. Petrus S. Ten Broeck, and the Rev. George Weller.

Since the last General Convention, the following Institutions have taken place in this Diocese: of the Rev. John M'Vickar to the Rectorship of St. James's Church, Hyde Park, Dutchess County; of the Rev. Henry J. Feltus, to that of St. Stephen's Church, New York; of the Rev. Samuel F. Jarvis, to that of St. James's Church, New York; of the Rev. Charles Seabury, to that of Caroline Church Brookhaven, Long Island; of the Rev. Eli Wheeler, to that of St. John's Church, Johnstown; of the Rev. John P. K. Henshaw, (since removed to Maryland), to that of St. Ann's Church, Brooklyn, Long Island; of the Rev. Parker Adams, to that of Trinity Church, Lansingburgh, Rensselaer County, and Grace Church, Waterford, Saratoga County; of the Rev. Joseph Prentice, to that of St. Luke's Church, Cattskill, Greene County; of the Rev. David Moore, to that of St. Andrew's Church, Staten Island; of the Rev. James Milnor, to that of St. George's Church, New York; of the Rev. William Creighton, to that of St. Mark's Church, New York; of the Rev. Henri L. P. F. Peneveyre, to that of the French Church Du St. Esprit, New York—where the services of our Church are celebrated in the French language.

The Right Rev. John Henry Hobart, D. D., has been appointed Rector; the Rev. Thomas Y. How, D. D., Assistant Rector; and the Rev. Benjamin T. Onderdonk, an Assistant Minister of Trinity Church, New York. The Rev. Evan M. Johnson has been settled as Minister of St. James's Church, Newtown, Long Island; the Rev. Gregory T. Bedell, Deacon of Christ Church, Hudson, Columbia County; the Rev. John Brown, of St. George's Church, Newburgh, Orange County; the Rev. William Powell, of St. John's Church, Yonkers, West Chester County; the Rev. Henry Anthon, Deacon of ——— Church, Redhook, Dutchess County; the Rev. Ravaud Kearney, of St. Paul's Church, East Chester, West Chester County; the Rev. Petrus S. Ten Broeck, of Trinity Church, Fishkill, and St. Phillip's Church, Phillipstown, Dutchess County, and

St. Peter's Church, Peekskill, Putnam County; and the Rev. Daniel Mc Donald, of Trinity Church, Fairfield, Herkimer County.

The following clergymen are at present employed as Missionaries in this State, by, and under the direction of, the ecclesiastical authority of the Diocese; the Rev. Daniel Nash, the Rev. Samuel Fuller, the Rev. William A. Clark, the Rev. James Thompson, the Rev. William B. Lacey, the Rev. Russel Wheeler, the Rev. Alanson W. Welton, the Rev. Ezekiel G. Gear, Deacon, the Rev. Orin Clark, the Rev. Stephen Jewett, the Rev. Professor Thomas C. Brownell (who performs missionary services on Sundays, in destitute congregations in the vicinity of Union College;) the Rev. Charles W. Hamilton, Deacon. the Rev. Henry U. Onderdonk, the Rev. George Weller, the Rev. Samuel Johnston, Deacon, the Rev. Joshua M. Rogers, Deacon, and the Rev. Charles Seabury. And here it is proper to mention that, from the Missionary Fund in this Diocese, a salary is also given to Mr. Eleazar Williams, a young man of Indian extraction, who resides with the Oneida tribe in this State, and performs the very useful offices of lay reader, catechist, and school-master among his Indian brethren. His religious exercises are the services of our Church, and approved sermons, both translated into the Mohawk language. His labours have been very faithful, and promise great success.

The Church in this Diocese has experienced incalculable advantage from the faithful labours of Missionaries. Some of the best established parishes, now affording competent support to their pastors, owe their existence, under God, to these labours. They have preserved the services of the sanctuary where, from a variety of opposing causes, there was danger of their loss. They have revived them in churches long vacated; and they are now carrying their consolations and their benefits to the remotest parts of the Diocese. As their happy consequence, sacred edifices, commodious, neat, not unfrequently elegant, are fast beautifying tracts of our State, which, but lately, were an entire wilderness.

Among the changes that have taken place in this Diocese since the last General Convention, we have to notice the decease of the Right Rev. Samuel Provoost, D. D., the Right Rev. Benjamin Moore, D. D., and the Rev. Elias Cooper, the late pious and useful Rector of St. John's Church, Yonkers, and the oldest Presbyter in the Diocese.

The Confirmations reported by the Bishop in 1814, were 800; in 1815—400; in 1816—1000. Total, 2200. For the administration of this ordinance, and for the discharge of other Episcopal dutiess the Bishop regularly and frequently visits every parish in this extensive Diocese.

Since the last report the following parishes have been duly organized in this Diocese, and received into union with the Convention; St. Paul's Church, Oxford, Chenango County; Trinity Church, Coventry, Chenango County; St. Paul's Church, Preble and Tully, Courtlandt County; Trinity Church, Granville, Washington County; St. Andrew's Church, Genoa, Cayuga County; Zion Church, Onondaga, Onondaga County; St. Stephen's Church, Smithfield, Madison County; and St. Paul's Church, Durham, Greene County.

The following churches have been consecrated by the Bishop: St. Matthew's Church, Unadilla, Otsego County; Trinity Church, Athens, Greene County; Christ Church, Manlius, Onondaga County; Trinity Church, Rensselaerville, Albany County; St. George's Church, New York, (re-built, after destruction by fire); St. James's Church, North Salem, West Chester County; Trinity Church, Granville, Washington County; St. John's Church, Canandaigua, Ontario County.

The whole number of organized congregations in the Diocese amounts to 115, and the number of clergy to 68.

A short time previous to the last General Convention, St. George's Church, in the city of New York, was destroyed by fire. Since that period, our brethren in that city have been again visited with the same calamity. Zion Church, belonging to a small but respectable congregation, who, a few years since, conformed to our communion, and have uniformly evinced their strong attachment to our doctrines and worship, has been burnt. This unhappy circumstance so deranged the affairs of the parish, as to render necessary the removal of the worthy Rector, the Rev. Ralph Williston, whose useful services are now transferred to another Diocese. The re-building of this church has progressed only in part.

It is matter of sincere felicitation to the members of our Church in this Diocese, that although peculiar circumstances have, in some measure, threatened her temporal prosperity, her members have not suffered it to decline, but have made efforts proportioned to the emergency. This has been particularly manifested in many country parishes, where unprecedented exertions have been made in building and repairing places of public worship, and meeting other parochial expenses.

Not least among the means that have been blessed to the good of the Church in this Diocese, are the voluntary associations formed by her members for the promotion of pious objects. The number of Bible and Common Prayer Book Societies has considerably increased. One, established in the city of New York, by young men of our Church, as auxiliary to that which was instituted in 1809, has set an unprecedented example of activity and zeal in the diffusion of religious truth. The young men of the same city have also lately distinguished themselves by forming another association, promising the most beneficial consequences. Its object is to raise funds for the support of Missionaries employed by the Bishop, and the Committee for propagating the Gospel, (appointed by the Convention), with whom is lodged the only authority to manage the missionary concerns of the Diocese.

To conclude: although it must be confessed that much still remains to be done in this Diocese, yet, thankful for the prosperity it has heretofore enjoyed, we cherish the humble hope, that the vigilant superintendence with which it is blessed, the fidelity of its pastors, and the zeal, devotion and liberality of its members, will be sanctified to its further increase and its instrumentality in promoting the glory of God, and the salvation of men.

NEW JERSEY.

The state of the Church, in this Diocese, through the goodness of God, continues, on the whole, to improve. Its progress is not rapid, but steady and substantial.

The Churches at Newark, Elizabeth Town, Perth-Amboy, New Brunswick, and Burlington, remain under the care of the Pastors who had the charge of them when the last report was made. They are flourishing, both in their temporal and spiritual concerns; and afford every reason for the conclusion that, with the Divine blessing, they will continue so. Within the last three years, the congregation at Perth-Amboy have erected a convenient and handsome house for the accommodation of their Rector. The same valuable object is in progress at Elizabeth Town.

Of the Churches at Shrewsbury, Middletown, and Freehold, united under the pastoral care of the clergyman formerly reported, the first named has considerably increased both in number of families and communicants. The congregation has also repaired and painted its handsome church. The other two congregations remain as before stated.

The congregation of St. Andrew's Church, Mount Holly, has also much increased. Formerly it enjoyed only part of the services of a clergyman; but, within the last two years, it has been able to give entire support to one. The Rev. George Y. Morehouse is now the Rector of that Church.

St. John's Church at Salem, vacant for more than forty years, with the exception of a few months in 1792 and 1793, has, within a short time, revived, and considerably improved. It now enjoys, in conjunction with St. George's, Penn's Neck, which had also, for a long time, been vacant, and St. Mary's, Colestown, lately much increased, the ministrations of the Pastor formerly of St. Andrew's, Mount Holly.

The respectable Church at Swedesborough, though still large, has, since the last report, from some cause not accurately known, experienced a considerable diminution in the number of its communicants. The Rector formerly named has still the charge of it.

The Churches at Jersey, Berkley, Mullica's Hill, Glassborough, Woodbridge, Trenton, Spotswood, Newton, Knowlton, Hardwick, Piscataway, Alexandria, Amwell, Allen-Town, and Chew's Landing, still remain vacant. The first five have the benefit of Divine Service, performed by licensed candidates and other laymen: and the whole occasionally enjoy the ministrations of the Bishop and the neighbouring Rectors. The difficulty, for some time past, of procuring a suitable clergyman to act as a Missionary, has occasiond the state of the vacant Churches generally. to be less favourable than it would otherwise have been. That difficulty will, no doubt, shortly be removed, as means are in progress for obtaining one.

There is a prospect, also, that a new Church will shortly be instituted at the manufacturing town of Paterson.

The Bishop of the Diocese, since his consecration in November, 1815, has visited the Churches at Newark, Elizabeth Town, Shrewsbury, Spotswood, Mount-Holly, Swedesborough, Salem, Berkeley, Mullica's Hill, and Glassborough, and administered the holy rite of Confirmation in those of them which follow, viz. at Swedesborough, Mount-Holly, Elizabeth Town, Shrewsbury, New-Brunswick, and Newark. The number confirmed in these Churches was 198.

He also admitted to the holy order of Priests, the Rev. George Y. Morehouse, who, shortly after, was instituted Rector of St. Andrew's Church, at Mount-Holly.

Samuel C. Stratton and Francis H. Cuming have been admitted candidates for holy orders since the last General Convention. Within the same time, the Rev. Lewis P. Bayard has been ordained Priest, and instituted Rector of Trinity Church Newark.

It is with pleasure likewise stated, that the Missionary Fund, which, on a former report, was $ 2,307.42, has, by a report made in August last to the State Convention, increased to $ 2,611.04.

The Fund for the support of the widows and children of clergymen has also considerably increased.

The Permanent Fund of the Episcopal Society has advanced from $ 156, the sum stated in the former report, to $ 475. The Society has also distributed a considerable number of Bibles, Prayer Books, and Tracts.

It is further stated, and with great satisfaction, that the females of the churches of Newark and Elizabeth-Town, have established Bible and Prayer-Book Societies, auxiliary to the Episcopal Society.

A Missionary Society has also been instituted in Trinity Church, Newark, in aid of the General Fund.

Sunday Schools have likewise been established in several congregations, principaly by ladies, which promise much good.

Since the last Convention, the number of officiating clergymen has increased from 8 to 9, and the instituted rectors from 6 to 8.

On an examination of the progress of the Church in this Diocese, since the termination of the Revolutionary war, in 1783, it is found that it has increased by the addition of Trinity Church, Swedesborough; St. George's Church, Penn's-Neck; St. John's Church, Chew's Landing; St. Thomas's Church, Glassborough; St. Matthew's Church, City of Jersey; and St. Stephen's Church, Mullica's Hill.

PENNSYLVANIA.

The Church in this Diocese has always been small, and principally limited to the City of Philadelphia and its immediate neighborhood. We have, however, satisfactory evidence, that it is increasing in numbers, strengh, and zeal, and, we trust, in piety.

Prayer Books, and many valuable tracts, have been distributed by the Society for the Advancement of Christianity in this State. This Society has likewise, by means of its Missionaries supplied several vacant congregations with occasional services, and formed new congregations in the north-western part of the Diocese.

Since the last General Convention, two churches have been consecrated to the worship of Almighty God. The communicants of some congregations have greatly increased, and a growing attention to the best interests of the soul is evidently perceptible.

During last year a new Society was formed in this Diocese, for the express purpose of sending Missionaries into the western States. Under its direction, a young clergyman has visited, with success, many parts of Ohio, Kentucky, and Tennessee.

The most gratifying intelligence from this Diocese is, that a very considerable number of young men have directed their attention to the Gospel ministry. There are, at present, twelve candidates for holy orders.

During the years 1814, 1815, and 1816, 487 persons have been confirmed.

Since the last General Convention, the following persons have received Deacon's orders: James Milnor, Samuel Phinney, George Sheets, Jacob Morgan Douglass, James Montgomery, Thomas P. May, Charles M. Dupuy, and Joseph R. Walker.

During the same period, the following have received Priest's orders: Rev. James Milnor, Rev. Jehu Curtis Clay, Rev. George Boyd, Rev. Abiel Carter, and Rev. Samuel Phinney.

The members of this Diocese have been zealous in distributing the Bible.

DELAWARE.

This Diocese was once an important portion of the Protestant Episcopal Church. In this small State there are the remains of eleven congregations, which, at no very distant period, were all supplied with the ministrations of the Divine Word by clergymen of our Church. Owing, however, to causes of which we can now have but a very indistinct view, and which probably cannot, by any, be correctly traced, this Diocese preesnts a most deplorable picture of departure from its first love. There are but two of the congregations in this Diocese that are regularly supplied by ministers of our Church. From the year 1810 till 1816 there was no regular Convention held. In the last mentioned year, a Convention was called, at which some regulations were entered into, which, should they be carried into effect, it is hoped, and with some confidence expected, that, through the Divine blessing, the situation of the Church in this State will be greatly meliorated. Distressing as is the condition of the Church in this Diocese, still there is every reason to believe that her prospects are brighter than they have been for many years. Among some things which induce this belief may be reckoned this pleasing circumstance, that, within the last eighteen months, there have been admitted, as candidates for holy orders, of this State, four young men of piety and talents, of whom the most encouraging hopes are entertained. Another circumstance in the present prospects of our Church here, and which seems to offer the most effectual means of her restoration, is the establishment of an Episcopal Missionary Society in Wilmington. If the zeal of our members can be excited so as to afford sufficient pecuniary aid to this institution, we expect, both from the benefits which have already resulted from missionary exertions in one Church, and from the peculiar state of feeling on this subject in this Diocese, that, through God's grace, the Church may be raised to a degree of strength and respectability exceeding the most sanguine expectations of past years. In Wilmington efforts have been making to raise a spacious building for the service of God; but there are so many difficulties in the way of their success, and so few to contend with them, that some fear is entertained as to the final accomplishment of the object.

MARYLAND.

The members of the Church in this Diocese appear to be increasing in piety and zeal. New churches have been erected, the number of communicants has increased, greater regard is had to the discipline and forms of worship of the Church, and more anxiety is discovered to keep in decent repair the houses of worship, and to provide for the comfortable support of the ministry; yet, in many parts of the Diocese, the Church is still in a low and depressed state, and its members are deprived of the ministrations of the sanctuary. If pious and zealous clergymen could be procured, there is every reason to believe that, in these parishes, the Church would flourish, and religion would prosper. Some societies have been formed for the distribution of religious tracts; and, at the last meeting of the Convention, steps were taken to raise a fund for the support of Missionaries, and the education of young men for the ministry.

In the Convention of 1814 a Suffragan Bishop was appointed in this Diocese, and its venerable Bishop (who has since, after a long life of piety and usefulness, been called away to receive the reward of his labours), commissioned him to perform all Episcopal duties on the Eastern Shore of this State. Part of the Diocese was shortly after visited by Bishop Kemp, and the rite of Confirmation administered by him to about 330 persons before the meeting of the last Convention. The ill health of Bishop Claggett, for some years before his death, prevented him from attending some of the Conventions, and communicating the Episcopal duties performed by him.

VIRGINIA.

The Church here has risen from that gloom and depression which caused her friends to mourn and weep. She now is in a prosperous state. A spirit of true religion is reviving in almost every part of the Diocese; and a sincere attachment to the pure doctrine and worship of our Church is increasing among her members. In Fredericksburgh a large church has been erected and consecrated. In Leesburgh a church has been built and consecrated. In several parishes, churches that were in a ruinous state have been repaired. In Warrenton a handsome church is building, and will be ready for consecration in a few weeks. In Charlestown a spacious church is building, and will be finished in the course of the present year. In Port Royal an adequate sum of money has been subscribed for building a church there. A sufficient sum of money has been subscribed for erecting a church in Lunenburgh.

In the city of Richmond there are two numerous and very respectable congregations. In Norfolk there is a large and respectable congregation. In Petersburgh the Church is more prosperous than formerly. In Alexandria there are two large and very respectable congregations. A Prayer-Book and Tract Society has been established here. By the blessing of Almighty God, our worthy and zealous Bishop has been instrumental in conducing much to the prosperity of our Zion, wherever he has visited in his Diocese.

NORTH CAROLINA.

There is a well-grounded hope, that the Church in this Diocese (now first received into union with the General Convention) will increase in strength (with Divine aid) so as, in a few years, to be able to dispense the Word of God to a large number of souls that are now scattered over a wide tract of country, a great part of whom are almost strangers to the sound of the Gospel.

There are at present but three Churches in the State that are blessed with settled pastors—those at Fayetteville, Wilmington, and Newbern.

At the first of these places the congregation has lately settled the Rev. Bethel Judd, from the Diocese of Connecticut.

At Wilmington there is a church of considerable size, and generally well attended. The congregation have evinced by their attention to the Church a strong and ardent wish for its prosperity. They have at present the Rev. Adam Empie, from the Diocese of New York, for their pastor, who is much beloved by the congregation.

At Newbern the church has lately undergone some alterations and repairs, and affords a very comfortable and decent house of worship. Since the first of April, the Rev. Jehu Curtis Clay, from the Diocese of Pennsylvania, has been the pastor of this congregation, and he has had the satisfaction of having the church numerously and respectably attended. The number of communicants on last Easter Day exceeded thirty, and there is but little doubt that this Church will increase, should the present minister continue his services amongst this people, who, for about twelve months before his arrival, were destitute of a pastor.

At Edenton there is a neat church, but, unfortunately for the congregation, they have no minister, nor have they had one since the Rev. Mr. Hatch left them, about two years since.

The town of Washington, and its vicinity, has lately met with a loss in the death of the Rev. Mr. Blunt, who, for many years before his decease, was in the habit of making appointments in different parts of the county in which he resided, where he would preach, baptize children, and, at stated times, administer the Sacrament of the Lord's Supper. These families, not a few in number, are now entirely deprived of hearing the Word of God preached, and of having the bread of life broken to them by an Episcopal minister.

SOUTH CAROLINA.

It is with peculiar satisfaction we report the increasing progress of the Church in this Diocese. It appears, that since the last meeting of the General Convention, some new congregations have been formed, and some new churches have been erected in this section of the Protestant Episcopal Communion; particularly a spacious and elegant church in the city of Charleston, a neat and handsome church on John's Island, a church in St. Mark's, and one in All-Saints' parish. In some other parts of this Diocese, funds have been raised, and exertions are making for rebuilding their places of public worship; and several have lately been fully completed, and the cemeteries enclosed.

It also appears that the Canons and Rules of the Church have here been observed; that the public offices of our holy religion have, with much uniformity, been performed according to the rubrics of the Book of Common Prayer; and that great harmony and love subsist between the Bishop and his Clergy, as well as among the Clergy themselves.

It furthermore appears that Mr. John Chandler, Mr. Henry

Gibbs, Mr. David J. Campbell, and Mr. —— Wilson, have been admitted by the Bishop as candidates for holy orders; that Mr. Morris H. Lance, Mr. Thomas Frost, and Mr. Albert Muller, natives of this Diocese, have been received into the holy order of Deacons; and that the Rev. Christian Hankel has been advanced to the holy order of Priests.

It appears, however, that there is yet cause to lament the ruinous state of many churches, and the want of clergymen in various parts of this Diocese. "The harvest is truly great, but the labourers are few." We have also to lament, that since the last meeting of this Convention, two clergymen, viz. the Rev. James Dewar Simons, and the Rev. Joseph Warren, have been removed by death.

The Society instituted for the *Advancement of Christianity* in this Diocese has been productive of much good, and its funds and influence are rapidly increasing. The baptisms and the communicants have greatly multiplied within the last year; and the public worship of Almighty God has not only been more generally and devoutly attended, but religious knowledge and practice seem to be progressive. The visitations of the Bishop have been frequent, and the sacred rite of Confirmation has been duly administered.

From the unremitted zeal and exertions of the Bishop and Clergy of this Diocese, there is reason to cherish the most flattering expectations, that the power as well as the form of religion, under the blessing of God, will continue to increase.

THE WESTERN STATES.

The most gratifying intelligence relative to our Church in this extensive part of the United States has been laid before this Convention. A respectable and flourishing congregation in the city of Lexington, State of Kentucky, has for several years been blessed with the regular ministrations of our Church, and the care of an active and zealous pastor. In the State of Ohio, nineteen congregations have been regularly organized; and steps taken for constituting a Diocese. The measures adopted by this Convention, added to the zeal and attachment to the Church manifested by the scattered members of our communion in these States, and the disinterested labours of a few clergymen who have been among them, will, it is hoped, through the blessing of God, tend to their speedy enjoyment of Episcopal superintendence.

In laying the preceding statement before the House of Bishops, the House of Clerical and Lay Deputies solicit their counsel, and their prayers for the blessing of Almighty God.

Signed, by order of the House of Clerical and Lay Deputies,

WILLIAM H. WILMER, PRESIDENT.

NEW YORK, May 26, 1817.

The house adjourned to attend Divine Service. Service was performed by the Rev. Mr. Wyatt, and a sermon preached by the Right Rev. Bishop Kemp.

After Divine Service, the house met, and resumed the consideration of the Rev. Dr. How's resolution, which was passed in the affirmative.

The Rev. Mr. S. Wilmer, offered the following resolution, which was laid upon the table:

Resolved,—That the next General Convention be holden at ———.

The Hon. Charles Fenton Mercer submitted the following resolution and proposed alterations of the Constitution of the Protestant Episcopal Church, which were read and laid upon the table:

Resolved,—That it be made known to the several State Conventions of this Church, that it is proposed to consider at the next General Convention, and, if deemed expedient, finally to ratify, the following alterations of the Constitution of the Church:—

1st. To strike out from the beginning of the second Article to the end of the first period, which terminates with the word "Convention," and to insert in lieu thereof, the following provisions:— Every State or Territory of the United States, may be made to constitute, of itself, or in union with the whole or certain portions of any other State or Territory, one Diocese, or be divided into two or more Dioceses by the General Convention, with the consent of the local Ecclesiastical authority or authorities affected thereby. Each Diocese shall be entitled to a representation of the clergy and laity, to consist of deputies chosen in such manner as the Convention of the Diocese may prescribe; the number of clerical deputies of each Diocese to be in the proportion of one deputy for every five ministers resident, and the number of lay deputies, of one for every ten congregations organized therein; provided, that every Diocese shall be entitled to at least two clerical and two lay deputies, and that no Diocese shall be entitled to more than twelve Clerical and eight Lay Deputies in the General Convention. In all questions submitted to the House of Clerical and Lay Deputies, the decision thereupon, if required by the representation of any Diocese, shall be by orders; each order having one vote expressed by a majority of the voices therein, and the concurrence of both orders shall be necessary in such case, to constitute a vote of the house.

2d. Wherever the word "State" or "States" occurs in the present Constitution or Canons of the Church, without being followed by the word "Diocese" or "Dioceses," such word shall be deemed to be supplied by the preceding amendment of the Constitution, if a just exposition of the sense of the Constitution or Canon require it.

The Rev. Dr. Wharton, from the committee on a Theological Seminary, made the following report, which was read, and ordered to lie on the table.

The committee appointed to consider the subject of establishing a Theological Seminary for the Protestant Episcopal Church, beg leave to report the following resolutions:

1. Resolved,—That a Seminary for the better education of candidates for the ministry be established, to be called "The Theological Seminary of the Protestant Episcopal Church in the United States of America.

2. Resolved,—That the government of said Seminary be vested in a Board of Trustees, to be appointed by the General Convention of the Church; said Board to consist of twenty-two members, of whom the senior Bishop and the Bishop of the Diocese where said Seminary shall be established, shall be two, with ten clergymen and ten laymen, and nine members shall constitute a quorum.

3. Resolved,—That the appointment of the professors and other officers in said Seminary be made by the Board of Trustees, who also shall make by-laws for their own government and that of the Seminary.

4. Resolved,—That once every year, or oftener, the said Board of Trustees meet in the said Seminary, to take cognizance of, and regulate all matters relating to the same.

5. Resolved,—That a committee be appointed to accelerate the establishment of this institution, and to enter upon

this important duty, as soon as in their judgment sufficient funds, or a reasonable prospect of them, will authorize the undertaking.

6. Resolved,—That the said Seminary be established at ———, in the Diocese of ———.

A message was received from the House of Bishops, communicating two Canons for the consideration of this house, which were laid on the table.

On motion, Resolved,—That when this house adjourn, it adjourn to meet this evening at six o'clock.

Adjourned.

MONDAY, six o'clock P. M.

The house met.

The report of the committee on the Theological Seminary, was taken up, read, and considered by sections.

A message was received from the House of Bishops, communicating four resolutions of that body, on the subject of a Theological Seminary, which was read.

A communication was received from the House of Bishops, on the subject of the French Prayer Book, which was laid upon the table.

The house adjourned to meet at eight o'clock to-morrow morning.

TUESDAY, May 27, eight o'clock A. M.

The house met,

The report of the committee on the subject of a Theological Seminary was called up and read.

On motion, Resolved,—That the further consideration of said report be postponed, for the purpose of taking up the resolutions of the House of Bishops on the same subject.

The house adjourned to attend Divine Service. Service was performed by the Rev. Dr. Wharton, and a sermon preached by the Right Rev. Bishop Croes.

After Divine Service, the house met, and proceeded to the consideration of the resolutions of the House of Bishops on a Theological Seminary, which, after discussion, were concurred in by this house. Whereupon,

Resolved,—That the resolutions offered by the committee of this house on the same subject, be indefinitely postponed.

A message was received from the House of Bishops, accompanying a Pastoral letter.

The house adjourned to meet at half past six o'clock this evening.

TUESDAY, half past six o'clock P. M.

The house met.

The resolutions of the House of Bishops on the subject of the French Prayer Book, were taken up, read, and concurred in by this house.

A communication from the House of Bishops on the subject of amusements, was read before this house.

Two Canons sent to this house yesterday by the House of Bishops, one "*to govern in the case of a minister declaring that he will no longer be a minister of this Church,*" and the other "*for carrying into effect the design of the second rubric before the communion service,*" were taken up, read, and concurred in by this house, and returned to the House of Bishops.

The Pastoral Letter received from the House of Bishops was then read and returned to that house.

This house received a report of the House of Bishops on the subject of a copy-right in the Book of Common Prayer, which was read and agreed to by this house.

The house proceeded to the choice of a committee pursuant to the 4th resolution on the subject of a Theological Seminary. Upon counting the ballots, the following gentlemen were declared duly elected.

Of the Clergy, The Rev. Dr. Wharton, The Rev. Dr. How, The Rev. Dr. Harris.

Of the Laity, Hon. Rufus King, William Meredith, Esq., Hon. Charles F. Mercer.

The Rev. Mr. Wilmer's resolution as to the place of meeting of the next General Convention, was taken and carried, and the blank left therein filled with the word "Philadelphia."

On motion, Resolved,—That the House of Bishops be requested to appoint one of their own order to preach a sermon at the opening of the next General Convention.

A message was received from the House of Bishops, communicating the concurrence of that house in the resolution that the next General Convention be holden at Philadelphia; and informing that, with the divine permission, the Right Rev. Bishop Dehon will preach at the opening of the same.

There was laid before this house a resolution of the House of Bishops, to have the blank in the 3d resolution on the subject of a Theological Seminary filled with the word *three*.

Resolved,—That this House concur therein, and that information of this concurrence be sent to the House of Bishops.

The House of Bishops communicated to this house two resolutions, proposing an alteration of the first article of the Constitution, so far as it regards the time of the meeting of this Convention, which were read, and concurred in by this House.

A request was received from the House of Bishops, that this House would appoint a committee of their own body, to unite with the Right Rev. Bishop Hobart, on the part of the House of Bishops, to superintend the printing of the Journals, Bishop Griswold's Sermon, and the Pastoral Letter.

Whereupon, the Rev. Dr. How, the Rev. Mr. Rudd, and Mr. William Ogden, were appointed the committee.

On motion, Resolved,--That the thanks of this house be presented to the Right Rev. the Bishops who have preached before this Convention during the present session, and that they be requested to furnish copies of their sermons for publication.

The Rev. Mr. Searle moved the following resolution, which was read and passed in the affirmative, and sent to the House of Bishops.

"Resolved,—That the Right Rev. the House of Bishops be respectfully requested to designate and establish some specific edition of the Old and New Testaments, without note or comment, to be considered as the authentic version or standard by which the genuineness of all copies of the Holy Scriptures used by the members of this Church, is to be ascertained; thereby, to secure them against perversions, and the people of our communion from error, either in discipline or doctrine."

The following communication was received from the House of Bishops:

"The House of Bishops, deeming the fulfilment of the request of the House of Clerical and Lay Deputies on the subject of an authentic version of the Holy Bible, a matter requiring very serious attention and deliberation, have resolved, that its members will give such attention and deliberation to the subject, previously to the next meeting of the General Convention, and report at the said meeting."

On motion, Resolved,—That the thanks of this house be presented to the President, Secretary, and Assistant Secretary, for the services rendered by them respectively during the present session.

In pursuance of a request from this house, the Right Rev. the members of the House of Bishops attended in the same, for the purpose of closing the session of the Convention by solemn prayer, which was performed by the Right Rev. Bishop White, presiding Bishop; after which the house adjourned *sine die.*

Signed, by order of the House of Clerical and Lay Deputies,

WILLIAM H. WILMER, PRESIDENT.

Attested, ASHBEL BALDWIN, Secretary.

JOURNAL

OF THE

House of Bishops.

NEW YORK, Tuesday, May 20, 1817.

This being the day prescribed by the Constitution of the Protestant Episcopal Church in the United States of America for the meeting of the General Convention of the same, and the city of New York having been appointed by the last Convention as the place of meeting at this time, the Right Rev. William White, D. D. of the Diocese ot Pennsylvania; the Right Rev. John Henry Hobart, D. D. of the Diocese of New York; the Right Rev. Alexander Viets Griswold, D. D. of the Eastern Diocese, (composed of the States of New Hampshire, Massachusetts, Rhode Island, and Vermont); the Right Rev. Theodore Dehon, D. D. of the Diocese of South Carolina; the Right Rev. Richard Channing Moore, D. D. of the Diocese of Virginia; the Right Rev. James Kemp, D. D. of the Diocese of Maryland; and the Right Rev. John Croes, D. D. of the Diocese of New Jersey; met in the Vestry-Room of Trinity Church at half past six o'clock P. M.

Agreeably to the established rules of order of the House of Bishops, the Right Rev. Bishop White, being senior Bishop, took the chair as presiding Bishop in the house.

The Rev. Benjamin T. Onderdonk was appointed Secretary to the house.

The Rev. Dr. How, and the Rev. Mr. Butler, as a committee from the House of Clerical and Lay Deputies, brought information that the said house was organized, and ready to proceed to business; and they were requested to state to the House of Clerical and Lay Deputies, that the House of Bishops was also ready to proceed to business.

Resolved,—That the following message be transmitted, by the Secretary of this house, to the House of Clerical and Lay Deputies.

The House of Bishops inform the House of Clerical and Lay Deputies, that as they deem it proper to have the business of the Convention opened by the celebration of divine service, they propose an adjournment until to-morrow morning, at the hour publicly notified for said service.

The House of Clerical and Lay Deputies agreeing to the above proposal, the House of Bishops accordingly adjourned until to-morrow morning at half past ten o'clock.

WEDNESDAY, May 21.

The Bishops attended Divine Service in Trinity Church with the House of Clerical and Lay Deputies, at half past ten o'clock A. M. Morning Prayer was celebrated by the Rev. Isaac Wilkins, D. D. of New York, President of the House of Clerical and Lay Deputies, and a sermon, adapted to the occasion of the meeting of the Convention, was delivered by the Right Rev. Alexander Viets Griswold, D. D. of the Eastern Diocese. The Holy Communion was then administered, agreeably to a resolution of the last Convention, by the Right Rev. the presiding Bishop, assisted by other Bishops present. After Divine Service the house assembled in the Vestry-Room. Present as yesterday.

The Rev. Dr. Harris, and the Rev. Dr. Beasley, informed this house, that the House of Clerical and Lay Deputies had passed a resolution to tender the thanks of this Convention to the Right Rev. Bishop Griswold, for the sermon preached by him this morning, and request a copy for publication.

Resolved,—That this house concur with the House of Clerical and Lay Deputies in the above resolution. The Secretary was ordered to communicate this concurrence to the House of Clerical and Lay Deputies.

A communication was received from the Secretary of a Convention of the Protestant Episcopal Church in the State of North Carolina, containing a copy of the Journal of said Convention; from which it appeared that they had acceded to the Constitution of the Protestant Episcopal Church in the United States of America, and desired to be received into union with the General Convention thereof.

Whereupon, Resolved,—That this Convention have received with great satisfaction the aforesaid communication, and recognize the Protestant Episcopal Church in the State of North Carolina as a member of this union.

Resolved,—That the foregoing resolution be sent to the House of Clerical and Lay Deputies for their concurrence; and that the documents from North Carolina be also sent to that house.

A message was received from the House of Clerical and Lay Deputies, by the Rev. Dr. Beasley, stating, that they were ready to adjourn until nine o'clock to-morrow morning.

On motion, Resolved,—That this house adjourn until the same time.

Adjourned accordingly.

THURSDAY, May 22.

The house met pursuant to adjournment. Present as yesterday. The minutes of the proceedings on Tuesday and Wednesday were read, and approved.

The following commnnication was received from the House of Clerical and Lay Deputies, by the Rev. Dr Wharton:

"The House of Clerical and Lay Deputies concur with the House of Bishops, in admitting the Convention of the Church in North Carolina as a member of this union."

Resolved,—That the House of Clerical and Lay Deputies be informed that this house is ready to adjourn for the attendance of the Bishops on public worship.

Adjourned accordingly.

Morning Prayer was celebrated by the Rev. Frederic Beasley, D. D, of Pennsylvania; and a sermon preached by the Right Rev. the presiding Bishop. After which the house again met. Present as before.

The following report, with documents accompanying, was made by the presiding Bishop, upon the subjects therein mentioned, which had been submitted to him by the Convention.

REPORT.

The subscriber, the presiding Bishop of this house, submits to his brethren a report, on two subjects committed to him by the General Convention of 1811, and recognized by that of 1814; and on another subject, which originated in the Convention the last referred to.

One of the subjects was an application from the Church in the State of Vermont, to the Soicety (in England) for Propagating the Gospel. It was committed to the subcriber, to certify to that venerable body, certain facts in favour of the application. At the time of the last General Convention, he had not been furnished with the necessary documents; there having been an intended delay of the design, owing to the circumstances of the public concerns. The desire of the Convention has been since complied with; and the necessary communications were sent by the Honorable and Rev. Mr. Stewart, lately of the Province of Quebec, on his return to England.

The next subject was the taking of preparatory measures for the organizing of the Church in the States, and parts of States, westward of the Alleghany mountains. The subscriber has had some correspondence on the subject; and has provided, so far as is in his power, for a comprehension of the counties of Pennsylvania westward of said mountains, under the projected organization; although on such terms as shall not destroy the unity of the Church in that State. Relatively to the contemplated measure, there have been sent to the subscriber sundry documents from the Western States, herewith delivered. It is understood, that there is now in this city, a lay gentleman, commissioned to confer with the Convention on their contents.

The last subject referred to, is the republication of the Journals, with the Constitution, the Canons, and the Pastoral Letters, under the superintendence of the subcriber. This has been accomplished in an octavo volume, by Mr. John Bioren, bookseller, of Philadelphia. A considerable number of the books is now for sale in this city, in the hands of Messrs. Swords, booksellers. It is to be hoped, that the members of this Convention either have taken, or will take such measures in the States to which they respectively belong, as may prevent Mr. Bioren from suffering loss, and even ensure to him a gain, from this his exertion to serve the Church.

WILLIAM WHITE.

Whereupon, Resolved—That the thanks of the Convention be presented to the presiding Bishop, for his attention to these subjects, and his communication now made concerning them.

Among the documents accompanying the above communications, were petitions from several congregations and Episcopalians inhabiting the western country, asking leave to form a Convention, to include, for the present, all the western country, to be placed, provisionally, under the care of the Bishop of Pennsylvania.

Whereupon, Resolved,—That the General Convention cherish a lively interest in the spiritual concerns of their brethren in the western country, and are exceedingly solicitous to extend among them the ministrations of our Church.

Resolved,—That it is expedient to enact the following Canon:

"A Canon limiting the operation of the 2d and 37th Canons." *

Resolved,—That it be recommended to the Episcopal congregations in the States referred to in the above communications, where Conventions are not already organized, to organize Conventions, which may be received into union with this Convention, and, when expedient, may unite, according to the Canons, in the choice of a Bishop, having jurisdiction over those States; and that this Convention have received with much satisfaction information of the measures which have been already adopted in the State of Ohio, for the organization of the Church in that State.

Resolved,—That though the measure of a Convention comprising sundry States in the western country, may be a measure of temporary expediency, it cannot be authorized by this Convention consistently with the general Constitution of the Church, which recognizes only a Convention of the Church in each State.

* The Canon is published, with the others passed at this session, at the end of the Journal.

Resolved,—That it be earnestly recommended to the authorities of this Church, in each State respectively, to adopt measures for sending Missionaries to our destitute brethren in the Western States. Such Missionaries to be subject to the direction of the ecclesiastical authority of the State or States in which they may officiate.

Resolved,—That the presiding Bishop be requested to transmit the foregoing resolutions to such person or persons as he may judge proper.

The following communication from the House of Clerical and Lay Deputies was handed to this House by the Rev. Dr. Wilkins:—

"The Rev. Dr. Wilkins was appointed a committee, to unite with a committee on the part of the House of Bishops, to receive from the Right Rev. Bishop Griswold the copy of his sermon preached before the Convention yesterday morning."

The Right Rev. Bishop Hobart was appointed the committee of this house for the above mentioned purpose.

The Rev. Mr. Rudd appeared from the House of Clerical and Lay Deputies, with information that that body were ready to adjourn until nine o'clock to-morrow morning.

Resolved,—That this house adjourn until the same time.

Adjourned accordingly.

FRIDAY, May 23.

The house met pursuant to adjournment. Present as yesterday.

The minutes of the proceedings yesterday were read and approved.

The report of the presiding Bishop, which was yesterday read, together with the documents accompanying, and the resolutions founded thereon, was transmitted to the House of Clerical and Lay Deputies.

Resolved,—That this house adjourn for the purpose of attending Divine Service; and that notice of this resolution be sent to the House of Clerical and Lay Deputies.

Notice was accordingly sent and the house adjourned.

Morning prayer was celebrated by the Rev. William H.

Wilmer, of Virginia, President of the House of Clerical and Lay Deputies, and a sermon preached by the Right Rev. Theodore Dehon, D. D., of South Carolina.

After which the house again met. Present as before.

The following communication was handed to the house by the Rev. Mr. Rudd :—

"The House of Clerical and Lay Deputies respectfully inform the House of Bishops, that they have concurred in the adoption of the 'Canon limiting the 2d and 37th Canons;' and that the House of Clerical and Lay Deputies concur in the resolutions accompanying said Canon."

A message was received from the House of Clerical and Lay Deputies, through the Rev. Mr. Baldwin, informing that that house was ready to adjourn until to-morrow morning at nine o'clock.

Resolved,—That this house adjourn until the same hour.

Adjourned accordingly.

SATURDAY, May 24.

The house met. Present as yesterday.

The minutes of the proceedings yesterday were read, and approved.

Agreeably to a resolution of the last General Convention, referring it to the Bishops, and, where there are no Bishops, to the Standing Committees, to inquire in the respective Dioceses or States, and to consider for themselves concerning the expediency of establishing a Theological Seminary, to be conducted under the authority of this Church, and to report to this Convention;—the Bishops composing this house, rendered their respective reports.

Resolved,—That this house adjourn for the purpose of attending Divine Service; and that information of this resolution be sent to the House of Clerical and Lay Deputies.

Adjourned accordingly.

Morning prayer was celebrated by the Rev. Oliver Norris, of Virginia, and a sermon preached by the Right Rev. Richard C. Moore, D. D., of the same Diocese.

The house then again assembled for business.

The reports of the Bishops on the subject of a Theological

Seminary were transmitted to the House of Clerical and Lay Deputies.

Resolved,—That a committee of this house be appointed to take into consideration the "table of kindred and affinity" on the subject of marriage, established by the civil and ecclesiastical laws of England, and to report to the next Convention.

Resolved,—That said committee consist of the presiding Bishop and two other members of this house.

The Right Rev. Bishop Kemp, and the Right Rev. Bishop Croes, were accordingly appointed.

Resolved,—That the following be entered on the Journal of this house, and be communicated to the House of Clerical and Lay Deputies.

The House of Bishops, impressed with the importance of informing the youth and others in the Doctrines, Constitution, and Liturgy of the Church, deem it their duty to call the attention of the Clergy to the 22d Canon, which enjoins on them diligence in catechetical instruction and lectures. The Bishops consider these as among the most important duties of clergymen, and among the most effectual means of promoting religious knowledge and practical piety.

Resolved,—That the house adjourn until Monday morning, nine o'clock; and that information of this resolution be sent to the House of Clerical and Lay Deputies.

Adjourned accordingly.

MONDAY, May 26.

The house met. Present as on Saturday.

The minutes of the proceedings on Saturday were read, and approved.

The presiding Bishop read a letter from Mr. A. Robertson, Secretary of the American Academy of the Fine Arts, directed to the Right Rev. Bishop Hobart, and enclosing tickets of admission to the exhibition of the gallery of said Academy, sent by order of the President and Board of Directors of the same, to the members of this house, with an invitation to them to visit the gallery as often as convenient during their stay in this city.

Whereupon, Resolved,—That the Right Rev. Bishop Hobart be requested to present, through Mr. Robertson, to the President and Directors of the Academy, the acknowledgements of the members of this house; and an assurance of the pleasure it will afford them, should the business of the Convention permit, to avail themselves of their polite invitation.

"A Canon to govern in the case of a minister declaring that he will no longer be a minister of this Church," was proposed and adopted.

Resolved,—That the house adjourn for the purpose of attending Divine Service; and that information of this step be sent to the House of Clerical and Lay Deputies.

Adjourned accordingly.

Morning prayer was celebrated by the Rev. William E. Wyatt, of Maryland, and a sermon preached by the Right Rev. James Kemp, D. D., of the same Diocese.

After which the house again met. Present as before.

"A Canon for carrying into effect the design of the second "Rubric before the Communion Service" was proposed and adopted.

This, together with the other Canon passed this morning, was sent to the House of Clerical and Lay Deputies for their concurrence.

The report of the House of Clerical and Lay Deputies on the state of the Church, sent to this house, agreeably to the requisitions of the 45th Canon, was read, and committed to the Right Rev. the presiding Bishop, with a request that he would draw up the Pastoral Letter of this house, contemplated by the said Canon, and requested by the House of Clerical and Lay Deputies.

After which, on information that the House of Clerical and Lay Deputies had adjourned until six o'clock this evening,

Resolved,—That this house adjourn until the same time.

Adjourned accordingly.

Six o'clock, P. M.

The house met pursuant to adjournment. Present as before.

The Right Rev. Bishop Hobart stated to the house, that

there is in the city of New York the Church du St. Esprit, which was erected in an early period of the province, by Protestant emigrants from the kingdom of France. It appears that the Church is now under the superintendence of Bishop Hobart—that there is still a portion of the congregation who worship in the French language—that he has lately ordained, and instituted as their Rector, the Rev. Mr. Peneveyre, a native of Switzerland, and that this clergyman officiates according to a French translation of the Liturgy of this Church.

Whereupon, Resolved,—That it be recommended to the Right Rev. Bishop Hobart to cause the said French Liturgy to be examined, in order to ascertain how far the translation is correct; and to confirm the use thereof, with such amendments and improvements as the case may call for; and to declare it to be the Liturgy which may be used by any minister of this Church who may officiate in a congregation to whom the French language is familiar.

Resolved,—That the above provision be extended to a translation in the French language of the Book of Psalms and Hymns in metre, and of any of the Offices comprehended in the worship of this Church.

The above resolutions were sent to the House of Clerical and Lay Deputies for their concurrence.

The following resolutions were then proposed and adopted:

Resolved,—That it is expedient to establish, for the better education of the candidates for holy orders in this Church, a general Theological Seminary, which may have the united support of the whole Church in these United States, and be under the superintendence and control of the General Convention.

Resolved,—That this seminary be located in the city of New York.

Resolved,—That —— persons be appointed by the House of Bishops to visit the several parts of the United States, and solicit contributions towards funds for founding and endowing such an institution.

Resolved,—That a Committee be appointed, to consist of the presiding Bishop, and the Bishops of this Church in New York and New Jersey, with three clergymen, and three laymen, to be appointed by the House of Clerical and Lay Deputies; which committee shall be empowered to receive and manage such funds as shall be collected—to devise a plan for establishing and carrying into operation such an institution; which plan shall be communicated to the several Bishops of this Church—and in the event of sufficient funds being obtained, if a majority of the Bishops shall have approved the plan, to carry it into immediate operation.

These resolutions were sent to the House of Clerical and Lay Deputies for their concurrence.

And this house adjourned until nine o'clock to-morrow morning.

TUESDAY, May 27.

The house met. Present as yesterday.

Resolved,—That the following be entered on the Journal of this house, and be sent to the House of Clerical and Lay Deputies, to be read therein:—

The House of Bishops, solicitous for the preservation of the purity of the Church, and the piety of its members, are induced to impress upon the clergy the important duty, with a discreet but earnest zeal, of warning the people of their respective cures, of the danger of an indulgence in those worldly pleasures which may tend to withdraw the affections from spiritual things. And especially on the subject of gaming, of amusements involving cruelty .to the brute creation, and of theatrical representations, to which some peculiar circumstances have called their attention,—they do not hesitate to express their unanimous opinion, that these amusements, as well from their licentious tendency, as from the strong temptations to vice which they afford, ought not to be frequented. And the Bishops cannot refrain from expressing their deep regret at the information that in some of our large cities, so little respect is paid to the feelings of the members of the Church, that theatrical representations are fixed for the evenings of her most solemn festivals.

A copy of the foregoing was accordingly sent to the House of Clerical and Lay Deputies.

Resolved,—That this house adjourn for the purpose of attending Divine Service; and that information of this step be sent to the House of Clerical and Lay Deputies.

Adjourned accordingly.

Morning Prayer was celebrated by the Rev. Charles H. Wharton, D. D., of New Jersey, and a sermon preached by the Right Rev. John Croes, D. D., of the same Diocese.

The house then again assembled. Present as before.

The Minutes of the proceedings yesterday were read and approved.

The presiding Bishop proposed a Pastoral Letter to the members of the Protestant Episcopal Church in the United States—which Letter was unanimously adopted by this house, to be published agreeably to the provisions of the 45th Canon; and was sent to the House of Clerical and Lay Deputies.

Agreeably to a reference made to the members of this house by the last General Convention, to consider the propriety of granting a copy-right in the Book of Common Prayer, the following report was adopted, and sent to the House of Clerical and Lay Deputies:—

The House of Bishops, on the subject referred to them by the last General Convention, relatively to the granting of a copy-right in the Book of Common Prayer, report as their opinion, and as the opinion prevalent in their respective Dioceses, so far as they are informed, that the said measure ought not to be adopted.

The two following resolutions were adopted and ordered to be sent to the House of Clerical and Lay Deputies:—

Resolved,—That it is expedient to alter the first article of the Constitution of this Church, so far as it fixes the time of the meeting of the General Convention thereof, by striking out the words—"third Tuesday in May, in the year of our Lord 1808, and on the third Tuesday in May;" and inserting instead thereof, the words—*first Tuesday in October, in the year of our Lord* 1823, *and on the first Tuesday in October*.

Resolved,—That in conformity with the 9th article of the Constitution, the Secretaries of this Convention, after the adjournment thereof, make known the proposed alteration to the several State Conventions.

It was then Resolved,—That this house adjourn until half past six o'clock this evening, and that information thereof be sent to the House of Clerical and Lay Deputies.

Half past six o'clock, P. M.

The house met. Present as before.

A message was received from the House of Clerical and Lay Deputies, communicating the concurrence of that house in the resolution of the House of Bishops, on the subject of a Theological Seminary—in the report of the House of Bishops on the subject of a copy-right in the Book of Common Prayer—and in the resolutions of the House of Bishops on the subject of the Book of Common Prayer in the French language.

A Canon "to govern in the case of a minister declaring that he will no longer be a minister of this Church;" and a Canon "for carrying into effect the design of the second Rubric before the Communion Service;" which were adopted yesterday in this house, and sent to the House of Clerical and Lay Deputies, were received from that house with the concurrence of the same.

Resolved,—That the blank in the third resolution on the subject of a Theological Seminary, be filled with the word *three.*

This resolution was sent to the House of Clerical and Lay Deputies, and returned with their concurrence.

Whereupon, Resolved,—That this house proceed now to the appointments contemplated by the third resolution on the subject of a Theological Seminary.

Resolved,—That the Rev. Daniel Burhans, of Newtown, in Connecticut, be appointed to visit the States of New Hampshire, Massachusetts, Vermont, Rhode Island, and Connecticut; that the Rev. Nathaniel Bowen, D. D., of the city of New York, be appointed to visit the States of New York, New Jersey, Pennsylvania, Delaware and Maryland;—and that the Rev. William H. Wilmer, of Alexandria, in the District of Columbia, be appointed to visit the States of Virginia, North Corolina, South Carolina, and Georgia; to solicit contributions for the founding and endowing of the Theological Seminary of the Protestant Episcopal Church in the United States of America.

Resolved,—That the above gentlemen be furnished by the presiding Bishop each with a certificate of his appointment, and a copy of the resolutions of the Convention on this subject; and further, that they be authorized to defray their expenses from the monies which they may obtain for the promotion of the business committed to them, and that they render a detailed account of their receipts and expenditures to the committee who have care of this business.

Resolved,—That in the event of either of the above gentlemen declining his appointment, or being removed from opportunity to discharge its duties, by death, his place may be filled by the above mentioned committee.

Resolved,—That the gentlemen hereby appointed, or substitutes which may be chosen agreeably to the last resolution, shall be subject to any instruction or advice which the committee above mentioned may deem it expedient to give.

On motion, Resolved,—That the House of Clerical and Lay Deputies be requested to appoint a committee on the part of that house, to unite with the Right Rev. Bishop Hobart, on the part of this house, to superintend the printing of the Journal of this Convention, the Pastoral Letter of the House of Bishops, and the Sermon of the Right Rev. Bishop Griswold.

This resolution was sent to the House of Clerical and Lay Deputies, who returned for answer, that they had appointed the Rev. Dr. How, the Rev. Mr. Rudd, and Mr. William Ogden, for the purpose specified.

The following extract from the Journal of the House of Clerical and Lay Deputies was received from that house, and read :—

"On motion, Resolved,—That the thanks of this house be presented to the Right Rev. the Bishops who have preached before this Convention during the present session, and that they be requested to furnish copies of their sermons for publication."

A message was received from the House of Clerical and Lay Deputies, communicating two resolutions—the first, that the House of Bishops be requested to appoint one of their own order to preach at the opening of the next General Convention;—and the second, that the next session of the General Convention be holden in the city of Philadelphia.

The Secretary of this house was directed to inform the House of Clerical and Lay Deputies, that with the Divine permission, the Right Rev. Bishop Dehon will preach at the opening of the next General Convention; and that this house concur in the resolution to hold the meeting of said Convention in the city of Philadelphia.

The House of Clerical and Lay Deputies informed this house, that the Rev. Dr. Wharton, the Rev. Dr. How, the Rev. Dr. Harris, the Hon. Rufus King, William Meredith, Esq., and the Hon. Charles F. Mercer, had been appointed, agreeably to the provisions of the fourth resolution, on the subject of a Theological Seminary.

A message was received from the House of Clerical and Lay Deputies, with information that that house concurred in the proposed alteration to the first article of the Constitution.

The following extract from the Journal of the House of Clerical and Lay Deputies was received by this house and read:—

"Resolved,—That the Right Rev. the House of Bishops be respectfully requested to designate and establish some specific edition of the Old and New Testaments, without note or comment, to be considered as the authentic version or standard by which the genuineness of all copies of the Holy Scriptures used by the members of this Church, is to be ascertained; thereby, to secure them against perversions, and the people of our communion from error, either in discipline or doctrine."

Whereupon, the following resolution was adopted, and ordered to be sent to the House of Clerical and Lay Deputies.

The House of Bishops, deeming the fulfilment of the request of the House of Clerical and Lay Deputies, on the subject of an authentic version of the Holy Bible, a matter requiring very serious attention and deliberation, resolve, that its members will give such attention and deliberation to the subject, previously to the next meeting of the General Convention, and report at the said meeting.

A message was received from the House of Clerical and Lay Deputies, with information that that house was ready to rise, and requested the House of Bishops to unite with them in closing the session of the Convention with solemn Prayer.

Resolved,—That this house will attend in the House of Clerical and Lay Deputies, for the purpose specified in the above message.

The presiding Bishop officiated, by the use of several appropriate Prayers and Collects of the Liturgy; and dismissed the members of the Convention with the Blessing.

After which the house adjourned *sine die.*

Signed by order of the House of Bishops.

WILLIAM WHITE, D. D.,
PRESIDING BISHOP.

Attested: BENJAMIN T. ONDERDONK, Secretary.

Canons

PASSED IN GENERAL CONVENTION, 1817.

CANON I.—Limiting the Operation of the second and the thirty-seventh Canons.

In the event of their being a Bishop consecrated for any State or States westward of the Alleghany Mountains, it shall be lawful for the Episcopal congregations in Pennsylvania and Virginia, westward of the said mountains, or for those of either of the said States, to place themselves, with the consent of the Bishops of these States respectively, under the provisionary superintendence of the Bishop the first referred to; the thirty-seventh Canon to the contrary notwithstanding. Further; it shall be lawful for such congregations in Pennsylvania, and for those in Virginia, the majority in each case concurring, to unite in Convention with the Church in any western State or States. These provisions are to cease whenever the consent for the continuance of them on the part of the Bishop of the Church in Pennsylvania or in Virginia, as the case may be, with the approbation of the General Convention, shall be withdrawn. In the case above referred to, the number of Clergymen specified in the second Canon shall not be requisite.

CANON II.—To govern in the Case of a Minister declaring that he will no longer be a Minister of this Church.

If any minister of this Church shall declare to the Bishop of the Diocese to which he belongs, or to any Ecclesiastical authority for the trial of clergymen, or, where there is no Bishop, to the Standing Committee, his renunciation of the ministry, and his design not to officiate in future in any of the offices thereof; it shall be the duty of the Bishop, or, where there is no Bishop, of the Standing Committee, to record the declaration so made. And it shall be the duty of the Bishop to admonish or to suspend him, and to pronounce and record, in the presence of two or three clergymen, that the person so declaring has been admonished, or suspended, or displaced from his grade of the ministry in this Church. In any Diocese in which there is no Bishop, the same sentence may be pronounced by the Bishop of any other Diocese, invited by the Standing Committee to attend for that purpose. In the case of displacing from the ministry as above provided for, it shall be the duty of the Bishop to give notice thereof to every Bishop of this Church, and to the Standing Committee in every Diocese wherein there is no Bishop.

CANON III.—For carrying into Effect the design of the second Rubric before the Communion Service.

There being the provision in the second Rubric before the Communion Service, requiring that every minister repelling from the Communion, shall give an account of the same to the ordinary; it is hereby provided, that on the information to the effect stated being laid before the ordinary, that is the Bishop, it shall not be his duty to institute an inquiry, unless there be complaint made to him in writing by the expelled party. But on receiving complaint, it shall be the duty of the Bishop to institute an inquiry, as may be directed by the Canons of the Diocese in which the event has taken place. And the notice given as above by the minister shall be a sufficient presentation of the party expelled, for the purpose of trial.

Done in General Convention, at New York, in the month of May, in the year of our Lord 1817.

BY ORDER OF THE HOUSE OF BISHOPS:

WILLIAM WHITE, D.D.,

PRESIDING BISHOP.

Attested: BENJAMIN T. ONDERDONK, Secretary.

BY ORDER OF THE HOUSE OF CLERICAL AND LAY DEPUTIES.

WILLIAM H. WILMER, PRESIDENT.

Attested: ASHBEL BALDWIN, Secretary.

List of the Clergy

OF THE

PROTESTANT EPISCOPAL CHURCH

In the United States of America.

Delivered in, and published agreeably to the 41st Canon.

EASTERN DIOCESE.

Composed of the States of New Hampshire, Massachusetts, Vermont, and Rhode Island.

The Right Rev. Alexander Viets Griswold, D. D., Bishop.

NEW HAMPSHIRE.

The Rev. Charles Burroughs, Rector of St. John's Church, Portsmouth.
The Rev. John H. Fowle, Rector of —— Church, Holderness.
The Rev. Daniel Barber, Rector of Union Church, Claremont.
The Rev. Joseph R. Andrus, Missionary in Concord, Hopkinton, and Bradford.

MASSACHUSETTS.

The Rev. John S. J. Gardiner, D. D., Rector of Trinity Church, Boston.
The Rev. Asa Eaton, Rector of Christ Church, Boston, St. Mary's, Newton, and Christ Church, Cambridge.
The Rev. James Morss, Rector of St. Paul's Church, Newburyport.
The Rev. Amos Pardee, Rector of St. Luke's Church, Lanesborough.
The Rev. Samuel Griswold, Rector of St. James's Church, Great Barrington, and —— Church, Lenox.
The Rev. Titus Strong, Rector of St. James's Church, Greenfield.
The Rev. Thomas Carlile, Rector of St. Peter's Church, Salem.
The Rev. George S. White, Missionary in Bridgewater, and other places.
The Rev. Chever Felch, Deacon, Chaplain in the Navy, residing at Boston, and occasionally officiating in vacant churches.
The Rev. Gideon W. Olney, Deacon, Minister of St. Ann's Church, Gardiner.
The Rev. Benjamin B. Smith, Deacon, Minister of St. Andrew's Church, Hanover.
The Rev. William Montague, residing at Dedham.
The Rev. James Bowers.

VERMONT.

The Rev. Abraham Bronson, Manchester and Arlington.
The Rev. Stephen Beach, Deacon, Fairfield, Sheldon, and St. Albans.
The Rev. George T. Chapman, Deacon, Minister of Trinity Church, Rutland, and Immanuel Church, Bellows' Falls.
The Rev. George Leonard, Deacon, officiating in the eastern parts of the State.

RHODE-ISLAND.

The Right Rev. Alexander V. Griswold, D.D., Rector of St. Michael's Church, Bristol.
The Rev. Nathan B. Crocker, Rector of St. John's Church, Providence.
The Rev. Salmon Wheaton, Rector of Trinity Church, Newport.
The Rev. John L. Blake, Rector of St. Paul's Church, North Providence.

CONNECTICUT.

The Right Rev. John Henry Hobart, D. D., of New York, performing Episcopal offices under the 20th Canon of the General Convention, by invitation of the Convention of the Diocese.
The Rev. Richard Mansfield, D. D., Rector of Christ Church, Derby, and —— Church, Great Hill.
The Rev. John Tyler, Rector of Christ Church, Norwich.
The Rev. William Smith, D. D., residing at Milford.
The Rev. Philo Shelton, Rector of St. John's Church, Stratfield, and Trinity Church, Fairfield.
The Rev. Ashbel Baldwin, Rector of Christ Church, Stratford.
The Rev. Tillotson Brownson, D.D., Principal of the Episcopal Academy, Cheshire.
The Rev. Chauncy Prindle, residing at Oxford.
The Rev. Reuben Ives, Rector of St. Peter's Church, Cheshire and officiating in the Churches in Hamden, Wallingford, Southington and Meriden.
The Rev. Truman Marsh, Rector of the Associated Churches in Litchfield.
The Rev. Daniel Burhans, Rector of Trinity Church, Newtown.
The Rev. Solomon Blakesly, Rector of St. James's Church, New London.
The Rev. Smith Miles, Rector of the Churches at Chatham and Glastenbury.
The Rev. Menzies Rayner, Rector of the Churches in Huntington.
The Rev. Calvin White, Assistant Minister of —— Church, Derby.
The Rev. Roger Searle, Rector of St. Peter's Church, Plymouth.
The Rev. Asa Cornwal, Assistant in the Episcopal Academy, Cheshire.
The Rev. Jonathan Judd, Rector of the Churches in Stamford and Horseneck.
The Rev. Elijah G. Plumb, Minister of the Churches in Branford, East Haven, North Branford and Northford.
The Rev. Benjamin Benham, Rector of St. John's Church, New Milford, and the Churches of Bridgewater and Brookfield.
The Rev. David Baldwin, Rector of the Churches of Guilford, North Guilford and North Bristol.
The Rev. Joseph D. Wilton, Minister of Trinity Church, Trumbull.
The Rev. Isaac Jones, Assistant Minister of the Churches in Litchfield.
The Rev. Sturges Gilbert, Minister of —— Church, Woodbury.
The Rev. Nathaniel Huse, Minister of the Churches in Simsbury and Granby.

The Rev. Frederick Holcomb, Minister of the Churches in Watertown and Northfield.
The Rev. Birdsey G. Nobles, Rector of Christ Church, Middletown.
The Rev. Jasper D. Jones, residing at Simsbury.
The Rev. Harry Croswell, Rector of Trinity Church, New Haven.
The Rev. Reuben Hubbard, Rector of the Churches in Danbury, Reading, and Ridgefield.
The Rev. Reuben Sherwood, Rector of St. Paul's Church, Norwalk.
The Rev. Aaron Humphrey, Rector of the Churches in Oxford.
The Rev. Nathan B. Burges, residing at Litchfield.
The Rev. Alpheus Gear, Rector of St. John's Church, Waterbury.
The Rev. Jonathan M. Wainwright, Deacon, Minister of Trinity Church, Hartford.
The Rev. Charles Smith, Deacon, Minister of —— Church, Wilton.

NEW YORK.

The Right Rev. John Henry Hobart, D.D., Bishop, and Rector of Trinity Church, including St. Pauls and St. John's Chapels, New York.
The Rev. Parker Adams, Rector of Trinity Church, Lansingburgh, Rensselaer County, and Grace Church, Waterford, Saratoga County.
The Rev. Henry Anthon, Deacon, Minister of —— Church, Redhook, Dutchess County.
The Rev. Amos G. Baldwin, Rector of Trinity Church, Utica, Oneida County.
The Rev. Theodosius Bartow, Rector of Trinity Church, New Rochelle, Westchester County.
The Rev. Gregory T. Bedell, Deacon, Minister of Christ Church, Hudson.
The Rev. William Berrian, an Assistant Minister of Trinity Church, New York.
The Rev. John Bowden, D.D., Professor of Rhetoric and Moral Philosophy, in Columbia College, New York.
The Rev. Nathaniel Bowen, D. D., Rector of Grace Church, New York.
The Rev. John Brown, Minister of St. George's Church, Newburgh Orange County.
The Rev. Thomas C. Brownell, Professor of Rhetoric and Belles-Letters, Union College, Schenectady.
The Rev. Nathaniel F. Bruce, M. D., Deacon, Minister of Christ Church, Duanesburgh, Schenectady County.
The Rev. Barzillai Bulkley, Rector of St. George's Church, Flushing, Long Island.
The Rev. David Butler, Rector of St. Paul's Church, Troy, Rensselaer County.
The Rev. Richard F. Cadle, Deacon, Minister of St. Luke's Church, Goshen, Orange County.
The Rev. Orin Clark, Rector of Trinity Church, Geneva, Ontario County.
The Rev. William A. Clark, Missionary, Manlius, Onondaga County, and the counties adjacent.
The Rev. Timothy Clowes, Rector of St. Peter's Church, Albany.
The Rev. William Creighton, Rector of St. Mark's Church, New York.
The Rev. Asahel Davis, Deacon.
The Rev. N. Felch, residing in Putnam County.
The Rev. Henry J. Feltus, Rector of St. Stephen's Church, New York.
The Rev. Samuel Fuller, Missionary, Albany and Green Counties.

The Rev. Ezekiel G. Gear, Deacon, Missionary, Onondaga County, and Counties adjacent.
The Rev. Charles W. Hamilton, Deacon, Missionary, Washington County, and parts adjacent.
The Rev. William Hammel, residing in New York.
The Rev. William Harris, D.D., President of Columbia College, New York.
The Rev. Seth Hart, Rector of St. George's Church, Hempstead, including Christ Chapel, North Hempstead, Long Island.
The Rev. Samuel Haskill, Rector of Christ Church, Rye, Westchester County.
The Rev. Thomas Y. How, D. D., Assistant Rector of Trinity Church, New York.
The Rev. David Huntington, Stamford, Delaware County.
The Rev. Samuel F. Jarvis, Rector of St. James's Church, Hamilton Square, and Minister of St Michael's Church, Bloomingdale, New York.
The Rev. Stephen Jewett, Missionary in Washington County.
The Rev. Evan Malbone Johnson, Minister of St. James's Church, New Town, Long Island.
The Rev. Samuel Johnston, Deacon, Missionary, Genesee and Niagara Counties.
The Rev. Cave Jones, residing in the City of New York.
The Rev. Ravaud Kearney, Minister of St. Paul's Church, East Chester, West Chester County.
The Rev. William B. Lacey, Missionary in Chenango County, and parts adjacent.
The Rev. Thomas Lyell, Rector of Christ Church, New York.
The Rev. Daniel M'Donald, Principal of the Academy, Fairfield, Herkimer County, and officiating in the Church there.
The Rev. John M'Vickar, Rector of St. James's Church, Hyde Park, Dutchess County.
The Rev. James Milnor, Rector of St. George's Church, New York.
The Rev. David Moore, Rector of St. Andrew's Church, including Trinity Chapel, Staten Island.
The Rev. Daniel Nash, Missionary, and Rector of the Churches in Otsego County.
The Rev. Samuel Nicholls, Deacon, Tutor in the Academy, Fairfield, Herkimer County
The Rev. William H. Northrop, Deacon.
The Rev. George W. Norton, Deacon, Ontario County.
The Rev. Benjamin T. Onderdonk, an Assistant Minister of Trinity Church, New York.
The Rev. Henry U. Onderdonk, M. D., Missionary, Canandaigua, Ontario County, and parts adjacent.
The Rev. Henri L. P. F. Peneveyre, Rector of the French Church, Du St. Esprit, New York.
The Rev. Joseph Perry, Rector of St. James' Church, Milton, and Christ Church, Ballston, Saratoga County.
The Rev. William Powell, Minister of St. John's Church, Yonkers, West Chester County.
The Rev. Joseph Prentice, Rector of Trinity Church, Athens, and St. Luke's Church, Catskill, Green County.
The Rev. John Reed, Rector of Christ Church. Poughkeepsie, Dutchess County.

The Rev. Joshua M. Rogers, Missionary at Turin, Lewis County, and parts adjacent.
The Rev. Gilbert H. Sayres, Minister of Grace Church, Jamaica, Long Island.
The Rev. Charles Seabury, Rector of Caroline Church, Brookhaven, and Missionary to Huntington and Islip, Long Island.
The Rev. Hugh Smith, Deacon, officiating in Grace Church, New York.
The Rev. Cyrus Stebbins, Rector of St. George's Church, Schenectady.
The Rev. Petrus S. Ten Broeck, Minister of Trinity Church, Fishkill, and St. Philip's Church, Phillips Town, Dutchess County, and St. Peter's Church, Peekskill, Putnam County.
The Rev. James Thompson, Missionary, Greene and Delaware Counties.
The Rev. F. Vanhorne, residing in Coldenham.
The Rev. George Weller, Missionary, West Chester County.
The Rev. Alanson W. Welton, Missionary, Ontario and adjacent Counties.
The Rev. Eli Wheeler, Rector of St. John's Church, Johnstown, Montgomery County.
The Rev Russel Wheeler, Missionary, Harmony Church, Butternuts; St. Matthew's Church, Unadilla, Otsego County, and parts adjacent.
The Rev. Isaac Wilkins, D. D., Rector of St. Peter's Church, West Chester.
The Rev. Joseph Willard, residing in New York.

NEW JERSEY.

The Right Rev. John Croes, D. D., Bishop, and Rector of Christ Church, New Brunswick.
The Rev. Abraham Beach, D. D., residing near New Brunswick.
The Rev. Charles H. Wharton, D. D., Rector of St. Mary's Church, Burlington.
The Rev. John C. Rudd, Rector of St. John's Church, Elizabeth Town.
The Rev. Simon Wilmer, Rector of Trinity Church, Swedesborough.
The Rev. James Chapman, Rector of St. Peter's Church, Perth Amboy.
The Rev. John Croes, jun., Rector of Christ Church, Shrewsbury.
The Rev. Lewis P. Bayard, Rector of Trinity Church, Newark.
The Rev. George Y. Morehouse, Rector of St. Andrew's Church, Mount Holly.
The Rev. Daniel Higbee, Minister of St. Mary's Church, Colestown; St. John's Church, Salem; and St. George's Church, Penn's Neck.
The Rev. James Montgomery, Deacon, Minister of St. Michael's Church, Trenton.
The Rev. Samuel C. Stratton, Deacon, Missionary.

PENNSYLVANIA.

The Right Rev. William White, D. D., Bishop, senior of the American Church, presiding in the House of Bishops and Rector of Christ Church, St. Peter's, and St. James's, Philadelphia.
The Rev. Robert Blackwell, D. D., residing in Philadelphia.
The Rev. James Abercrombie, D. D., senior Assistant Minister of Christ Church, St. Peter's, and St. James's, Philadelphia.
The Rev. Joseph Pilmore, D. D., Rector of St. Paul's Church, Philadelphia.
The Rev. Frederick Beasley, D. D., Provost of the University of Pennsylvania, Philadelphia.
The Rev. John Campbell, Rector of —— Church, Carlisle.

The Rev. Joseph Turner, residing in Southwark, Philadelphia.
The Rev. Slator Clay, Rector of St. James', Perkiomen, and St. Peter's, Great Valley.
The Rev. Joseph Clarkson, Rector of St. James', Lancaster, St. John's, Pequea, and Bangor Church, Church Town.
The Rev. James Wiltbank, one of the Collegiate Masters of the Latin School in the University of Pennsylvania, Philadelphia.
The Rev. Robert Ayres, residing in Brownsville.
The Rev. Francis Reno, officiating in the Counties of Beaver and Alleghany.
The Rev. Absalom Jones (a colored man), Rector of the African Church of St. Thomas, Philadelphia.
The Rev. John Taylor, residing in Pittsburgh.
The Rev. Levi Bull, Rector of St. Gabriel's, Berks County, and St. Mary's, Chester County.
The Rev. John Armstrong, Rector of St. John's, Yorktown.
The Rev. Jackson Kemper, Assistant Minister of Christ Church, St. Peter's and St. James's, Philadelphia.
The Rev. Richard D. Hall, Rector of St. James the Greater's, Bristol.
The Rev. George Boyd, Rector of St. John's Church, Northern Liberties, Philadelphia.
The Rev. Abiel Carter, Rector of Trinity Church, Pittsburgh.
The Rev. George Sheets, Deacon, Minister of Trinity Church, Oxford, and All Saints, Lower Dublin.
The Rev. Samuel Phinney, officiating at Wilkesbarre, and in the Counties of Bradford and Susquehannah.
The Rev. Jacob Morgan Douglass, Deacon, residing in Philadelphia.
The Rev. Thomas P. May, Deacon, residing in Montgomery County.
The Rev. Charles M. Dupuy, Deacon, residing in Philadelphia.
The Rev. Joseph R. Walker, Deacon, residing in Philadelphia.

DELAWARE.

The Rev. Robert Clay, Rector of Emanuel's Church, Newcastle.
The Rev. William Wickes, Rector of Trinity Church, Wilmington.
The Rev. William Pryce, residing in Wilmington.

MARYLAND.

The Right Rev. James Kemp, D. D., Bishop, and Rector of St. Paul's Parish, including Christ Church, Baltimore.
The Rev. William E. Wyatt, Associate Minister of St. Paul's Parish, Baltimore.
The Rev. John V. Bartow, Rector of Trinity Church, Baltimore.
The Rev. John P. K. Henshaw, Rector of St. Peter's Church, Baltimore.
The Rev. Edmund D. Barry, Principal of an Academy in Baltimore.
The Rev. John Allen, Teacher in Baltimore.
The Rev. William Ninde, Teacher in Baltimore.
The Rev. Joseph Jackson, Rector of St. John's, Washington County.
The Rev. George Williams, Rector of St. Mark's, Frederick.
The Rev. Frederick W. Hatch, Rector of All-Saints, Frederick Town.
The Rev. Alfred Dashiell Deacon, Montgomery County.
The Rev. Matthew Johnson, Rector of St. James's, Baltimore County.
The Rev. Daniel Stephens, Rector of St. George's, Harford.
The Rev. Nathan Wheaton, Deacon.

The Rev. Walter D. Addison, Rector of St. John's, Georgetown, District of Columbia.
The Rev. Ruel Keith, Assistant Minister of St. John's, Georgetown, District of Columbia.
The Rev. William Hawley, Rector of St. John's Church, City of Washington.
The Rev. Andrew C. M'Cormick, Rector of —— Church, City of Washington.
The Rev. William Gibson, Rector of Queen Anne, Prince George's.
The Rev. Ralph Williston, Rector of St. Paul's, Prince George's.
The Rev. Noble Young, Rector of —— Church, Prince George's.
The Rev. John Weems, Rector of Port Tobacco, Charles County.
The Rev. Johu Brady, Rector of William and Mary, St. Mary's County.
The Rev. Neale H. Shaw, Rector of All-Faith, St. Mary's.
The Rev. John Bauzman, Rector of All-Saints, Calvert.
The Rev. Purnell F. Smith, Rector of Christ Church, ——.
The Rev. William Duncan, Rector of All-Hallows, Anne-Arundell.
The Rev. Henry L. Davis, Rector of St. Anne's, Annapolis.
The Rev. William Duke, Residing in Elkton.
The Rev. Joab G. Cooper, Principal of Washington College, Chester Town.
The Rev. George D. S. Handy, residing in Kent County.
The Rev. Samuel H. Turner, Rector of St. Paul's, Kent.
The Rev. William J. Bulkley, Rector of St. Paul's, Queen Anne.
The Rev. John Forman.
The Rev. Thomas Bayne, Rector of St. Peter's, Talbot.
The Rev. William M. Stone, Rector of Stepney, Somerset.
The Rev. Thomas P. Irving, Teacher in Hagers' Town.

VIRGINIA.

The Right Rev. Richard Channing Moore, D. D., Bishop, and Rector of the Monumental Church, City of Richmond.
The Rev. John Buchanan, Rector of Henrico Parish.
The Rev. William H. Hart, Assistant Minister of Henrico Parish.
The Rev. John Dunn, Shelburn Parish, Loudon County.
The Rev. Andrew Syme, Bristol Parish, Dinwiddie.
The Rev. John Woodville, St. Mark's Parish, Culpepper.
The Rev. William H. Wilmer, St. Paul's Church, Alexandria, District of Columbia.
The Rev. Oliver Norris, Christ Church, Alexandria, District of Columbia.
The Rev. William Meade, Frederick Parish, Frederick County.
The Rev. Alexander Balmain, D. D., Frederick Parish, Frederick County.
The Rev. Edward C. M'Guire, Deacon, St. George's Parish, Fredericksburgh.
The Rev. William King, Stanton Parish, Augusta.
The Rev. Alexander Hay, Antrim Parish, Halifax County.
The Rev. Hugh C. Boggs, Berkley Parish, Spotsylvania.
The Rev. John P. Phillips, St. Martin's Parish, Hanover.
The Rev. Thomas Hughs, Residing in Virginia.
The Rev. Samuel Low, Christ Church, Norfolk Borough.
The Rev. Charles Crawford, Amherst County.
The Rev. William Crawford, Louisa County.
The Rev. Armistead Smith, Matthews County.
The Rev. John Ravenscroft, Mecklenburgh County.
The Rev. John L. Bryan, Deacon, Berkley County.

The Rev. William Steele, Prince William.
The Rev. Thomas Horrel, Berkley County.
The Rev. George Lemon, Fauquier County.
The Rev. George Michlejohn, (aged 100) Mecklenburgh.
The Rev. Needler Robinson, Chesterfield County.
The Rev. John Bracken, D. D., Williamsburgh.
The Rev. John Hyde Saunders, Cumberland.
The Rev. John Seward, Lancaster County.
The Rev. Benjamin J. Allen, Deacon, Jefferson County.
The Rev. Robert S. Symes, Eastern Shore.
The Rev. Jacob Keeling, Nansimond.
The Rev. George Halson, residing near Norfolk.

NORTH CAROLINA.

The Right Rev. Richard Channing Moore, D. D., of Virginia, performing Episcopal offices under the 20th Canon of the General Convention, by invitation of the Convention of the Diocese.
The Rev. Bethel Judd, Rector of St. John's Church, Fayetteville.
The Rev. Jehu Curtis Clay, Rector of Christ Church, Newbern.
The Rev. Adam Empie, Rector of St. James's Church, Wilmington.

SOUTH CAROLINA.

The Right Rev. Theodore Dehon, D. D., Bishop, and Rector of St. Michael's Church, Charleston.
The Rev Christopher Edwards Gadsden, D. D., Rector of St. Philip's Church, Charleston.
The Rev. William Percy, D. D., Rector of St. Paul's Church, Charleston.
The Rev. Christian Hankel, Rector of Trinity Church, Columbia, and Professor of Mathematics and Natural Philosophy in South Carolina College.
The Rev. Andrew Fowler, Rector of the Episcopal Church on Edisto Island.
The Rev. John B. Campbell, Rector of St. Helena's Church, Beaufort.
The Rev. Hugh Fraser, Rector of All Saints Parish, Waccamaw.
The Rev. John Jacob Tschudy, Rector of St. John's, Berkeley.
The Rev Charles B. Snowden, Rector of St. Stephen's Parish, and upper St. John's, Berkley.
The Rev. Thomas Frost, Assistant Minister of St. Philip's Church, Charleston.
The Rev. Maurice H. Lance, Rector of Prince George's, Winyah, Georgetown.
The Rev. Philip Matthews, Rector of St. Helana's Church, on the Island of St. Helena.
The Rev. Frederick Dalcho, M. D., Assistant Minister of St. Paul's Church, Charleston.
The Rev. Thomas Gates, D. D., residing in St. George's Parish, Dorchester.
The Rev. Thomas Mills, D. D., residing in the upper part of the State, without a cure.
The Rev. Paul T. Gervais, residing in St. John's Parish, Colleton.
The Rev. Milward Pogson, residing in St. James's Parish, Goose-Creek.
The Rev. Albert Muller, Deacon, Charleston.

The next General Convention will be held in the city of Philadelphia, on the third Tuesday in May, A. D. 1820.

JOURNAL OF THE PROCEEDINGS

OF THE

BISHOPS, CLERGY, AND LAITY

OF THE

Protestant Episcopal Church,

IN

THE UNITED STATES OF AMERICA,

IN

GENERAL CONVENTION.

HELD IN

ST. JAMES'S CHURCH, IN THE CITY OF PHILADELPHIA, FROM THE 16TH TO THE 24TH DAY OF MAY INCLUSIVE, A. D. 1820.

HOUSE OF BISHOPS.

The Right Rev. William White, D. D. of Pennsylvania, presiding Bishop.

The Right Rev. John Henry Hobart, D. D. of New York.

The Right Rev. Alexander Viets Griswold, D. D. of the Eastern Diocese.

The Right Rev. Richard Channing Moore, D. D. of Virginia.

The Right Rev. James Kemp, D. D. of Maryland.

The Right Rev. John Croes, D. D. of New Jersey.

The Right Rev. Nathaniel Bowen, D. D. of South Carolina.

The Right Rev. Thomas C. Brownell, D. D., LL. D. of Connecticut.

CLERICAL AND LAY DEPUTIES.

N. B.—The deputies, whose names are in Italicks, were not present.

CLERICAL DEPUTIES.

MAINE.

Rev. Petrus S. Ten Broeck.

NEW HAMPSHIRE.

Rev. James B. Howe,
Rev. Robert Fowle,
Rev. Charles Burroughs.

MASSACHUSETTS.

Rev. J. S. J. Gardiner, D. D.,
Rev. *Asa Eaton,*
Rev. James Morss,
Rev. Thomas Carlile.

VERMONT.

Rev. Abm. Bronson,
Rev. George Leonard,
Rev. Stephen Beach,
Rev. *Joel Clapp.*

RHODE ISLAND.

Rev. Salmon Wheaton,
Rev. John Laurens Blake.
Rev. Nathan B. Crocker,

CONNECTICUT.

Rev. Ashbel Baldwin,
Rev. Daniel Burhans,
Rev. Harry Croswell,
Rev. Birdsey G. Noble.

NEW YORK.

Rev. Isaac Wilkins,
Rev. Thomas Lyell.
Rev. Davis Butler,
Rev. Benjamin T. Onderdonk.

NEW JERSEY.

Rev. Charles H. Wharton, D. D.,
Rev. John Croes, Jun.,
Rev. John C. Rudd,
Rev. Lewis P. Bayard.

PENNSYLVANIA.

Rev. Levi Bull,
Rev George Boyd,
Rev. Jackson Kemper,
Rev. Bird Wilson.

DELAWARE.

Rev. Richard D. Hall,
Rev. John Foreman.

MARYLAND.

Rev. John P. K. Henshaw,
Rev. William Wickes,
Rev. William E. Wyatt, D. D.,
Rev. Samuel C. Stratton.

VIRGINIA.

Rev. William H. Wilmer, D. D.,
Rev. John S. Ravenscroft,
Rev. William Meade,
Rev. George Lemmon.

NORTH CAROLINA.

Rev. Adam Empie,
Rev. Richard S. Mason,
Rev. John Avery,
Rev. Gregory T. Bedell.

SOUTH CAROLINA.

Rev. John I. Tschudy,
Rev. Andrew Fowler,
Rev. Christopher E. Gadsdon, D. D. *
Rev. John B. Campbell,
Rev. *Maurice H. Lance,*

LAY DEPUTIES.

MAINE.

Robert H. Gardiner, Esq.

NEW HAMPSHIRE.

Nathaniel Adams, Esq.,
Hon. James Sheafe.
Enoch G. Parrot, Esq.,

MASSACHUSETTS.

Col. George Sullivan,
Hon. James Lloyd,
Samuel Hubbard, Esq.,
Dudley Atkins Tyng, Esq.

VERMONT.

Clement Trowbridge, Esq.,
Daniel Henshaw, Esq.,
Col. Josiah Dunham,
Jeremiah Stratton, Esq.

* Appointed agreeably to a regulation of the South Carolina Convention, providing in case of absence in the elected delegation. *Committee of Publication.*

RHODE ISLAND.

Col. Thomas Lloyd Halsey,
Stephen B. Northam, Esq.,
Col. Alexander Jones,
Gen. George D' Wolfe.

CONNECTICUT.

Gen. Mathias Nicoll,
James Lambert,
Richard Adams,
John L. Lewis.

NEW YORK.

Hon. Rufus King,
Hon. Philip S. Van Rensselaer,
Dr. John Onderdonk,
Richard Harrison, Esq.

NEW JERSEY.

William Coxe, Esq.,
Joseph V. Clark, Esq.,
Samuel I. Read, Esq.,
Peter Kean, Esq.,

PENNSYLVANIA.

Samuel Sitgreaves, Esq.,
Thomas McEuen, Esq.,
William Meredith, Esq.,
Walter Kerr.

DELAWARE.

Hon. Kensey Johns,
Thomas Cooper, Esq.,

MARYLAND.

Hon. John C. Herbert,
Tench Tilghman, Esq.,
Francis S. Key, Esq.,
William Donne, Esq.,

VIRGINIA.

Col. Wm. Mayo,
Hon. Charles F. Mercer,
Philip Nelson,
John Nelson, jr.

NORTH CAROLINA.

Duncan Cameron, Esq.,
Josiah Collins, Esq.,
Marsden Campbell,
John Stanley, Esq.

SOUTH CAROLINA.

Col. Lewis Morris,
Major Andrew Hassell,
William Heyward,
Colin Campbell.

Clergy who attended the sittings of the Convention.

MASSACHUSETTS.—The Rev. George T. Chapman.

NEW YORK.—The Rev. Samuel F. Jarvis, D. D., The Rev. James Milnor, D. D., The Rev. Jonathan M. Wainwright, The Rev. Thomas Breintnall.

NEW JERSEY.—The Rev. Abiel Carter, The Rev. Simon Wilmer, The Rev. George H. Woodruffe.

PENNSYLVANIA.—The Rev. Joseph Pilmore, D. D., The Rev. Joseph .rner, The Rev. Frederick Beasley, D. D., The Rev. James Wiltbank, The .ev. Charles M. Dupuy, The Rev. Jacob M. Douglass, The Rev. Wm. Augustus Muhlenberg, The Rev. Samuel C. Brinckle, The Rev. Manning B. Roche, The Rev. John Rodney, The Rev. William Richmond, The Rev. John V. E Thorne, The Rev. Samuel Sitgreaves.

MARYLAND.—The Rev. Joseph R. Walker, The Rev. John Johns, The Rev. Joseph Jackson.

JOURNAL

OF THE PROCEEDINGS OF THE

House of Clerical and Lay Deputies.

PHILADELPHIA, Tuesday, May 16, 1820.

This being the day appointed for the meeting of the General Convention of the Protestant Episcopal Church of the United States of America, several Clerical and Lay Deputies attended in St. James's Church, at 5 o'clock, P. M., and a quorum being present, the Rev. Wm. H. Wilmer, D. D. was requested to take the chair *pro tempore*, and the Secretaries of the house in the last Convention, acted as Secretaries *pro tempore*.

The house then proceeded to read the Testimonials of the Clerical and Lay Deputies, which were severally approved, and the following gentlemen took their seats in the house.

CLERICAL DEPUTIES.

From New Hampshire, Rev. Charles Burroughs. From Massachusetts, Rev. James Morss, Rev. Thomas Carlile. From Rhode Island, Rev. Nathan B. Crocker. From Vermont, Rev. George Leonard. From Connecticut, Rev. Ashbel Baldwin, Rev. Daniel Burhans, Rev. Birdsey G. Noble. From New York, Rev. David Butler, Rev. Thomas Lyell, Rev. Benjamin T. Onderdonk. From New Jersey, Rev. John C. Rudd, Rev. John Croes, jr., Rev. Lewis P. Bayard. From Pennsylvania, Rev. Levi Bull, Rev. Jackson Kemper, Rev. Bird Wilson, Rev. George Boyd. From Delaware, Rev. Richard D. Hall, Rev. John Foreman.

From Maryland, Rev. Wm. E. Wyatt, D. D., Rev. Wm. Wickes, Rev. John P. K. Henshaw, Rev. Samuel C. Stratton. From Virginia, Rev. Wm. H. Wilmer, Rev. George Lemmon, Rev. Wm. Meade, Rev. John S. Ravenscroft. From North Carolina, Rev. Adam Empie, Rev. Richard S. Mason. From South Carolina, Rev. John J. Tschudy.

LAY DEPUTIES.

From Massachusetts, Dudley Atkins Tyng, Esq. From Rhode Island, Col. Thomas Lloyd Halsey, Col. Alexander Jones. From Vermont, Col. Josiah Dunham. From Connecticut, Gen. Matthias Nicoll, Richard Adams, Esq. From New York, Hon. Philip S. Van Rensselaer, Richard Harison, Esq. From New Jersey, Peter Kean, Esq., Joseph V. Clark, Esq. From Pennsylvania, Samuel Sitgreaves, Esq., Thomas M'Euen, Esq., Wm. Meredith, Esq. From Maryland, Tench Tilghman, Esq., Hon. John C. Herbert, Francis S. Key, Esq., William Donne, Esq. From Virginia, Col. Wm. Mayo, Mr. Philip Nelson, Mr. John Nelson. From North Carolina, Duncan Cameron, Esq.

The house proceeded to the election of a President, Secretary and assistant Secretary, when it appeared, that, the Rev. William H. Wilmer, D. D., was chosen president, the Rev. Ashbel Baldwin, Secretary, the Rev. John C. Rudd, assistant Secretary.

On motion, Resolved,—That clergymen of the Protestant Episcopal Church who may be in the city of Philadelphia during the session of this convention, and not members thereof, be admitted to the sittings of this house.

The Rev. Mr. Butler and the Rev. Dr. Wyatt were appointed to inform the House of Bishops, that this house was organized and ready to proceed to business.

The House of Bishops returned, for answer, that they also were organized and ready to proceed to business.

The following message was received from the House of Bishops.

"The House of Bishops propose to the House of Clerical and Lay Deputies, to attend Divine Service to-morrow at 10 o'clock, A. M., and on every subsequent day, during the sitting of the Convention, at nine o'clock, A. M., Sunday excepted."

The Rev. Mr. Kemper, the Rev. Mr. Bull, and Samuel Sitgreaves, Esq. were appointed a Committee to prepare and report rules of order, for the government of this house.

On motion, Resolved,—That this house concur with the House of Bishops in the proposed time of meeting.

The house adjourned until 10 o'clock, A. M., to-morrow.

WEDNESDAY, May 17, 10 o'clock, A. M.

The house attended Divine Service in St. James's Church. Service was performed by the Rev. John S. Ravenscroft, and a sermon preached by the Right Rev. Bishop Moore.

After Divine Service the house met.

The Rev. Dr. Wharton, a Clerical Deputy from New Jersey, The Rev. Salmon Wheaton, a Clerical Deputy from Rhode Island, Hon. Charles F. Mercer, a Lay Deputy from Virginia, and Walter Kerr, Esq., a Lay Deputy from Pennsylvania appeared and took their seats.

On motion, Resolved,—That the names of all the members returned as Deputies to this Convention, be inserted on the Journal designating the attending members.

The Rev. Mr. Meade asked, and obtained leave of absence for the remainder of the day.

The Rev. Mr. Kemper, from the committee appointed to prepare rules of order made report, which after consideration and amendment, were adopted as follows:

1. The morning service of the Church shall be performed every day during the session of the Convention.

2. When the President takes the chair, no member shall continue standing, or shall afterwards stand up, except to address the chair.

3. No member shall absent himself from the service of the house, unless he have leave or be unable to attend.

4. When any member is about to speak or deliver any matter to the house, he shall with due respect, address himself to the President, confining himself strictly to the point in debate.

5. No member shall speak more than twice in the same debate, without leave of the house.

6. While the President is putting any question, the members shall continue in their seats, and shall not hold any private discourse.

7. Every member who shall be in the house when any question is put, shall, on a division, be counted, unless he be personally interested in the discussion.

8. No motion shall be considered as before the house unless seconded, and, when required, reduced to writing.

9. When a motion is under consideration, no other motion shall be made, except to amend, to divide, to commit or postpone it; but a motion to adjourn shall always be in order and shall be decided without debate. A question on amendment shall be decided before the original motion.

10. All Committees shall be appointed by the President, unless otherwise ordered.

11. When the house is about to rise, every member shall keep his seat until the President leaves his chair.

A message was received from the House of Bishops, informing this house, that they had adopted the alteration of the first article of the constitution, proposed at the last General Convention, altering the time of meeting from the third Tuesday in May to the first Tuesday in October.

A certificate from the Secretary of the Convention of the Protestant Episcopal Church in the State of Maine, together with a copy of the Constitution of the Church in that State, was received and read, and application made for admission into union with the General Convention. Whereupon, Resolved,—That this house recognize the Protestant Episcopal Church in Maine as in union with the General Convention.

This resolution, together with the accompanying documents, was sent to the House of Bishops.

The house adjourned.

THURSDAY, May 18, 9 o'clock, A. M.

Divine Service was performed by the Rev. Mr. Butler, and a sermon preached by the Rt. Rev. Bishop Hobart. After Divine Service the house met.

On motion of P. Kean, Esq., Resolved,—That a list of the members of this house be published for the use of the Convention.

A letter was received by the President from the Rev. Levi Bull, stating that circumstances of a domestic nature rendered it necessary for him to return to his family; he therefore resigned his seat in this house.

On motion, Resolved,—That the Right Rev. Bishop Moore be requested to furnish a copy of his sermon, preached at the opening of this Convention, for publication. The Rev. Mr. Kemper was appointed to carry this resolution to the House of Bishops.

A message was received from the House of Bishops, informing this house, that they concurred in the admission of the Church in the State of Maine into union with the General Convention.

The Rev. Petrus S. Ten Broeck, a Clerical Deputy from Maine, and Robert Hallowell Gardiner, a Lay Deputy from the same State, produced testimonials of their appointment which were read and approved, and they took their seats.

On motion, Resolved,—That a Committee consisting of one member from each State represented in this Convention, be appointed to examine the journals of the different State Conventions, Episcopal charges, addresses and pastoral letters which have been, or which may be laid before this house during the present session; to make inquiry into the state of the Church in each Diocese, and into the attention paid to the Canons and rules of the Church; to draw up a view of the state of the Church, and to report the same to this house agreeably to the forty-fifth Canon.

The following gentlemen were appointed to compose said Committee.

From Maine—Rev. Petrus S. Ten Broeck.
From New Hampshire—Rev. Charles Burroughs.
From Massachusetts—Rev. Thomas Carlile.
From Vermont—Rev. George Leonard.
From Connecticut—Rev. Daniel Burhans.
From New York—Rev. Benjamin T. Onderdonk.
From New Jersey—Rev. John C. Rudd.
From Pennsylvania—Rev. Jackson Kemper.
From Delaware—Rev. Richard D. Hall.
From Maryland—Rev. Wm. E. Wyatt, D. D.
From Virginia—Rev. Wm. Meade.
From North Carolina—Rev. Adam Empie.
From South Carolina—Rev. John J. Tschudy.

A Canon respecting that part of the 45th Canon, which requires the reading of the Episcopal addresses on the Journals of the several State Conventions, before this house, was proposed and adopted, and sent to the House of Bishops.

On motion of Francis S. Key, Esq., Resolved,—As the opinion of this house, that the practice of returning thanks for sermons preached before the General Convention, and requesting copies for publication ought to be discontinued.

On motion, Resolved,—That a Lay Deputy from each State be added to the Committee on the state of the Church. Whereupon, the following gentlemen were appointed.

From Maine—Robert H. Gardiner, Esq.
From Massachusetts—Dudley Atkins Tyng, Esq.
From Rhode Island—Col. Thomas L. Halsey.
From Vermont—Col. Josiah Dunham.
From Connecticut—Gen. Matthias Nicholl.
From New York—Richard Harison, Esq.
From New Jersey—Peter Kean, Esq.
From Pennsylvania—Thomas M'Euen, Esq.
From Delaware—Hon. Kensey Johns.
From Maryland—Francis S. Key, Esq.
From Virginia—Col. Wm. Mayo.
From North Carolina—Duncan Cameron, Esq.

The Rev. Mr. Boyd offered for the consideration of the house, a resolution concerning the administration of Baptism, which was ordered to lie on the table.

The Rev. Mr. Kemper proposed a Canon for consideration, relative to candidates for holy orders: ordered to lie on the table.

The Rev. Mr. Boyd offered for consideration, a preamble and resolutions on the subject of a missionary society; ordered to lie on the table.

The Rev. C. E. Gadsden, D. D., a Clerical Deputy from South Carolina, presented the certificate of his appointment and took his seat.

On motion, Resolved,—That the testimonial of the Rev. Dr. Gadsden be referred to a Committee.

The Rev. Mr. Meade, Francis S. Key, Esq., and Richard Harison, Esq. were appointed to compose said Committee.

On motion, Resolved,—That a Committee be appointed to examine the Journals of the last General Convention, and report the unfinished business, if any, to this house. The Rev. Mr. Hall, the Rev. Mr. Wheaton, Hon. C. F. Mercer, and William Meredith, Esq. were appointed to compose said Committee.

A message was received from the House of Bishops informing this house of their concurrence with the resolution requesting a copy of Bishop Moore's sermon, preached at the opening of this Convention, for publication: and that they had also returned their thanks to Bishop Moore, for his sermon.

On motion, Resolved,—That the resolutions and proposed Canons laid on the table, be printed for the use of the house.

The Rev. Mr. Tschudy presented and read a memorial from the Convention of South Carolina, on the subject of a Theological Seminary, which was sent to the House of Bishops.

A message was received from the House of Bishops, communicating a proposition submitted to them, for the publication of certain selections from the Book of Psalms in metre, with their determination thereon; which after being read and considered, was concurred in by this house.

A message was received from the House of Bishops proposing certain instructions to be observed in editions of the Book of Common Prayer, which were read and concurred in by this house.

The House of Bishops informed this house, that they concurred in the adoption of the Canon repealing a part of the forty-fifth Canon.

A message was received from the House of Bishops with a Canon passed by that house, repealing the 1st Canon of 1817.

On motion, Resolved,—That the Canon be referred to a Committee.

The Rev. Mr. Kemper, and the Rev. Mr. Onderdonk were appointed the Committee.

Hon. John C. Herbert proposed for consideration, a Canon relative to applicants for holy orders, which was referred to the same Committee.

The following documents which had been laid before the house in conformity with the forty-fifth Canon, were referred to the Committee on the state of the Church.

From Maine, a copy of the Constitution of the Church in that State, and a Journal of their first Convention.

From New Hampshire, written Journals for 1817, 1818, 1819.

From Massachusetts, printed Journals for 1819, 1820.

From Vermont, written Journals for 1817, 1818, 1819.

From Rhode Island, written Journals for 1818, 1819, 1820.

From Connecticut, printed Journals for 1818, 1819.

From New York, printed Journals and Charges for 1817, 1818, 1819, and an Episcopal address.

From New Jersey, printed Journals for 1817, 1818, 1819, one Charge and a written document on the state of the Church.

From Pennsylvania, printed Journals for 1818, 1819, 1820.

From North Carolina, printed Journals for 1817, 1818, 1819.

From South Carolina, printed Journals for 1818, 1819, 1820.

The house adjourned.

FRIDAY, May 19, 9 o'clock, A. M.

Divine Service was performed by the Rev. Dr. Wyatt, and a sermon preached by the Right Rev. Bishop Kemp.

After Divine Service the house met.

The Rev. Mr. Kemper from the Committee on the Canon sent from the House of Bishops, repealing the first Canon of 1817, reported in favour of concurrence; whereupon, this house concurred in adopting the proposed Canon, and notice of this concurrence was sent to the House of Bishops.

The same Committee reported an amended Canon as a substitute for the one offered yesterday by the Hon. John C. Herbert, which was read.

The Rev. Mr. Hall, from the Committee on the Journal of the last General Convention, reported as unfinished business the resolutions offered by the Hon. Charles F. Mercer, in 1817, which resolutions were read and ordered to lie on the table.

P. Kean, Esq. proposed a Canon providing for the change of the place of meeting of the General Convention in certain cases, which was read and ordered to lie on the table.

The Hon. John C. Herbert asked and obtained leave of absence for the remainder of the day.

P. Kean, Esq. offered the following resolution, which was ordered to lie on the table.

Resolved,—That the meeting of the next General Convention be held at ———.

The Rev. Mr. Kemper called up his resolution on the Theological Seminary, which after considerable discussion, was ordered to lie on the table.

The Rev. Mr. Boyd called up his resolutions on the subject of a Missionary Society, and the following persons were appointed to compose a Committee on the subject. The Rev. Mr. Boyd, the Rev. Mr. Henshaw, Duncan Cameron, Esq., Francis Key, Esq.

Robert H. Gardiner, Esq. proposed a Canon relative to the consecration of Bishops during the recess of the General Convention, as a substitute for the fifth Canon, which was referred to a Committee consisting of the Rev. Mr. Burroughs, Robert H. Gardiner, Esq., and Samuel Sitgreaves, Esq.

The Rev. Mr. Boyd called up his resolution on the subject of Pastoral Letters, which, after considerable debate, was amended by making it a Canon, which was adopted, and sent to the House of Bishops for their concurrence.

The consideration of the Canon offered yesterday by the Rev. Mr. Kemper, was called up and referred to a committee consisting of the Rev. Mr. Noble, the Rev. Dr. Gadsden, and P. Kean, Esq.

A communication was received from the House of Bishops, on the subject of a standard copy of the Bible, which was read and ordered to lie on the table.

The Rev. Mr. Bayard asked and obtained leave of absence for the remainder of the session.

The Bev. Dr. Wharton asked and obtained leave of absence until Monday.

The house adjourned.

SATURDAY, May 20, 9 o'clock, A. M.

Divine Service was performed by the Rev. Mr. Rudd, and a sermon preached by the Right Rev. Bishop Croes.

After Divine Service the house met.

The Hon. James Lloyd, a Lay Deputy from Massachusetts, appeared and took his seat.

A message from the House of Bishops informed this house, that they had concurred in adopting the Canon concerning Pastoral Letters.

The Rev. Mr. Croes offered for consideration a Canon repealing a part of the 35th Canon which was referred to a Committee consisting of the Rev. Mr. Rudd, the Rev. Dr. Wyatt, and the Rev. Mr. Stratton.

The resolution of the House of Bishops adopting the alteration of the first article of the Constitution was taken up, and after discussion was sent back to the House of Bishops with the non-concurrence of this house.

The Rev. Mr. Hall and Col. Dunham asked and obtained leave of absence until Monday.

William Meredith, Esq., from the Committee appointed at the last General Convention on the Theological Seminary, made a report, (*See Appendix*) which was read and referred to a Committee consisting of Duncan Cameron, Esq., Rev. Dr. Gadsden, Hon. James Lloyd, Rev. Mr. Onderdonk, and the Rev. Mr. Morss.

Richard Harison, Esq. offered the following resolution and proposed alteration of the Constitution, which resolution was adopted and sent to the House of Bishops.

Resolved,—that it be made known to the several State Conventions of this Church, that it is proposed to consider at the next General Convention, and if deemed expedient, finally to ratify the following alteration of the first article of the Constitution :—

By striking out so much of the first article as relates to the time of holding the General Convention, and by inserting, after the words "United States of America," in the said article, the words "at such time in every third year, and ;"—and further, by inserting after the word "convention" the following clause :—"and in case there shall be an epidemic disease, or any other good cause to render it necessary to alter the place fixed on for any such meeting of the convention, the presiding bishop shall have it in his power to appoint another convenient place, (as near as may be to the place so fixed on) for the holding of such convention."

The President requested leave of absence from the house until Monday, which was granted, and the Rev. Mr. Burhans was called to the chair, *pro tem.*

The communication from the House of Bishops on the subject of a standard copy of the Bible was taken up, and the resolution of that house concurred in, and notice of concurrence was sent to the House of Bishops.

The following gentlemen were appointed the Commitee of this house pursuant to the resolution.

The Rev. Mr. Wilson, Rev. Dr. Wharton, Rev. Dr. Wyatt, Rev. Mr. Kemper, and Samuel Sitgreaves, Esq.

Peter Kean, Esq. offered the following resolution, which was ordered to lie on the table.

Resolved, if the House of Bishops concur therein, that a committee be appointed to inquire into the expediency and practicability of establishing a college for the education of youth, to be under the care and superintendence of trustees to be appointed by the General Convention, and that the said Committee report to the next General Convention the result of their inquiries, together with a plan for the government of said institution, should they deem its establishment practicable.

The Rev. Mr. Mason proposed several resolutions on the subject of correct editions of the Book of Common Prayer which were ordered to lie on the Table.

Hon. C. F. Mercer asked and obtained leave of absence for the remainder of the session.

The house adjourned until Monday morning 9 o'clock.

MONDAY, May 22, 9 o'clock, A. M.

Divine Service was performed by the Rev. Mr. Tschudy, and a sermon preached by the Right Rev. Bishop Bowen.

After Divine Service the house met.

Mr. James Lambert, a Lay Deputy from Connecticut, and the Hon. Kensey Johns, a Lay Deputy from Delaware, appeared and took their seats.

The rules of order were read.

The Rev. Mr. Noble from the committee on the proposed Canon concerning candidates for Holy Orders made report which was laid on the table.

The Hon. John C. Herbert called up the consideration of the Canon proposed by him, amending the 17th Canon. The proposed Canon was adopted and sent to the House of Bishops.

The Rev. Mr. Boyd called up the consideration of his resolution on the subject of diversity of practice in administering Baptism, which resolution he withdrew and offered the following as a substitute:

Resolved,—That the Right Rev., the House of Bishops be respectfully requested to express to this house their opinion on the diversity of practice which prevails in the administration of baptism, and to suggest the most effectual mode for producing uniformity under the second rubric in the office for the administration of private baptism.

This resolution was referred to the committee on the state of the Church.

An addition to the report of the Committee on the Theological Seminary, appointed at the last General Convention, was received and read, and referred to the Committee of this house on that subject. (*See appendix.*)

The Rev. Mr. Rudd from the Committee on the proposed Canon amending the 35th Canon, made report unfavourable to the adoption of said Canon.

On motion, Resolved,—That the proposed Canon be recommitted, and that two members be added to the Committee. Whereupon, the Rev. Mr. Meade and Samuel Sitgreaves, Esq. were appointed.

A message was received from the House of Bishops proposing an amendment to the Canon passed by this house, amending the 17th Canon, which amendment was concurred in by this house, and notice of concurrence sent to the House of Bishops.

Duncan Cameron, Esq., from the Committee on the subject of the Theological Seminary, made the following report which was read.

The Committee to whom was referred the report from the Trustees of the Theological school, having, according to order, had the same under consideration—report:

That while they lament that the efforts made to establish the school in the city of New York have not been more successful, they are deeply impressed with the conviction that the establishment of an institution for the theological education of candidates for the ministry, is an object of too much importance to the character and interests of the Protestant Episcopal Church in the United States, to be abandoned or delayed.

The Committee are aware that difficulties are inseparably connected with all new undertakings, and that ultimate success can only be expected after long experience. They cannot, however, permit themselves to doubt the practicability of establishing a theological school adequate to the exigencies of the Church, if a simultaneous and zealous effort for that purpose be made by its friends throughout the United States. They anxiously hope such an effort will be made—and confidently believe that the Great Head of the Church will bless the exertions which may be made to prepare and send forth labourers into his vineyard.

The Committee are of opinion, that it is of great importance to the success of the institution, that it should be located in some place where the professors and students can have access to public libraries, enjoy the benefits resulting from literary society, and live comfortably at a moderate expense.

Without detracting from the great advantages which the city of New York affords to students in the various departments of literature and science, the Committee are of opinion that the city of New Haven offers inducements for the establishment of the Theological school in that place (at least for the present, and while its funds are so limited) which ought not to be overlooked or disregarded.

For the purpose of carrying into effect the views of the committee contained in this very brief report, they recommend the adoption of the following resolutions:

Respectfully submitted,

DUNCAN CAMERON, Chairman.

1. Resolved,—That the Theological school instituted at New York, under the authority of the last General Convention of the Protestant Episcopal Church of the United States, be transferred to and located within the city of New Haven in the diocese of Connecticut.

2. Resolved,—That the management of the said school be and is hereby vested in a board of trustees, which shall consist of the Bishops of the several dioceses within the United States, of six clergymen and six laymen, to be appointed by the House of Clerical and Lay Deputies at every meeting of the General Convention, any *seven* of whom shall be competent to form a board for transacting business. They shall have power to collect and manage funds for the benefit of the school; to appoint professors and teachers therein, and prescribe their duties; regulate the admission of students, and prescribe the course of studies to be observed by them; to made such by-laws and regulations as may be necessary for the government of the school; and, generally, to take such measures as they may deem essential to the prosperity of the institution. The

said board of trustees shall have power to fill vacancies which may occur by death, removal or resignation of any clerical or lay member thereof, and it shall be their duty to make a full and detailed report of their proceedings and of the state of the school to the next General Convention.

3. Resolved,—That the Bishops of the several dioceses within the United States, and where there is no bishop, the standing committee of the diocese, be and they are hereby earnestly and respectfully requested to adopt such measures as they may deem most advisable to collect funds in aid of the Theological school, and to cause the same, when collected, to be transmitted to the treasurer of the board of trustees.

A message was received from the House of Bishops with information that they concurred in the resolution of this house on the proposed alteration of the first article of the Constitution.

Robert H. Gardiner, Esq. offered the following resolution which was ordered to lie on the table.

Resolved,—That it be the duty of the Secretary of each General Convention, to cause to be published the sermon preached at the opening thereof.

The consideration of the resolution and proposed alteration of the Constitution offered by the Hon. C. F. Mercer in 1817, was called up and, after considerable debate, was indefinitely postponed.

The house adjourned, to meet at six o'clock this evening.

MONDAY EVENING, 6 o'clock.

The house met.

The Rev. Mr. Burroughs from the Committee on the proposed substitute for the fifth Canon made report favourrable to the adoption of said Canon.

On the question, shall this Canon be adopted, it was decided in the negative.

The consideration of the report of the Committee on the Theological Seminary was called up, read, and discussed for some time, and ordered to lie on the table.

The Committee on the state of the Church made a report which was read and ordered to lie on the table.

The Rev. Mr. Foreman asked and obtained leave of absence for the remainder of the session.

The house adjourned.

TUESDAY, May 23, 9 o'clock, A. M.

Divine Service was performed by the Rev. Mr. Baldwin, and a sermon preached by the Right Rev. Bishop Brownell.

After Divine Service the house met.

The consideration of the report of the Committee on the state of the Church was called up, and after long discussion it was, on motion of the Rev. Mr. Onderdonk,

Resolved,—To strike out the following section and resolution:

"In conclusion, your Committee beg leave to report that they would recommend to this Convention, to call the attention of the clergy to the rubrics and offices of the Church in relation to the holy Sacrament of Baptism. They consider it of the first importance to the character of the Church and to the good education of its youthful members, that pious principles and conduct should be required in those who are received as sponsors in baptism. It must produce consequences highly injurious to the Church, fatal to the welfare of those who are to be nurtured in its bosom, and not less so to those who unadvisedly enter into the most serious engagements in their behalf, to admit into so highly responsible a solemnity those who do not understand and feel the importance of its sanctions, and who do not sincerely mean, with the help of divine grace, faithfully to perform them. This end, and many others deserving consideration, we believe would also be promoted by administering baptism publicly; and, when necessity requires it to be administered in private, by using the form of private baptism and afterwards requiring the infant and its sponsors to be brought into the church, that the congregation may be certified, in the form prescribed, of its admission into the Church, that the sponsors may enter into their obligations in the face of the Church, and that its prayers may be offered up to the Almighty to grant His blessing to the ordinance.

The Committee therefore recommend the following resolution:

Resolved,—That it is the opinion of this General Convention that the ordinance of baptism ought in all possible cases to be administered in public, and that when necessity shall require it to be administered in private, that then the office for private baptism should be used, and that the infant and the sponsors should be afterwards required to appear in Church and conform to the service of the Church in that respect—and that the Right Rev. the Bishops be respectfully requested to call the attention of the clergy to this subject, and to enjoin upon them a particular care in requiring proper qualifications in those who are admitted as sponsors."—

And, to insert the following, as a substitute :

The House of Clerical and Lay Deputies reverting to the notices of private baptism in some of the preceding statements, respectfully request the House of Bishops to insert in the Pastoral Letter solicited by this house, their opinion and advice on the subject of the existing custom of administering private baptism without a great and reasonable cause, and of using in private the public office ; and also on the subject of the proper qualifications of sponsors in baptism.

The report as amended was adopted as follows, and sent to the House of Bishops.

REPORT.

The House of Clerical and Lay Deputies, in compliance with the 45th Canon, have taken a general view of the state of the Church, and offer to the House of Bishops the result of their inquiries, respectfully requesting that venerable body to draw up, and cause to be published, a pastoral letter to the members of the Church.

MAINE.

The Church in the State of Maine, which, for many years, had become greatly depressed and almost extinct, has, within a few years, assumed a more flourishing aspect. It consists of two congregations—the one in Gardiner, the other in Portland. Both of these congregations are supplied with pastors, whose labours have succeeded to the extent of the rational expectations of the friends of the Church. Rev. G. W. Olney, is the Rector of Christ Church, Gardiner; and Rev. P. S. Ten Broeck of St. Paul's Church, Portland.

Agreeably to the recommendation of the Right Rev. Bishop Griswold, a Convention of delegates from those Churches was held in Brunswick, on the 3d day of May, 1820, at which time they acceded to the Constitution of the Protestant Episcopal Church in the United States of America, and elected delegates to the General Convention. They are again annexed to the Eastern Diocese.

NEW HAMPSHIRE.

There are nine Episcopal Churches in this State. St. John's Church in Portsmouth, of which the Rev. Charles Burroughs is

Rector, has eighty families, eighty communicants, and about seventy catechumens; and reports, during the last three years, fifty-three baptisms, twenty-two deaths, and three marriages. Trinity Church in Holderness, of which the Rev. Robert Fowle is Rector, has about thirty families, and reports, during the last three years, twenty-six baptisms, eight marriages, and nineteen deaths. Union Church in Claremont, of which the Rev. James B. Howe has recently been insti. uted Rector, in the place of the Rev. Mr. Barbour who has left the Church, reports ninety-five communicants and seventy catechumens. Major Ashley of that town lately left to the Church a legacy, which will probably yield an annual income of seven hundred dollars. Another Episcopal Society has been formed in the village of Claremont, and they have purchased a meeting-house for a place of worship. This Society is associated with Union Church, and the Rev. J. B. Howe officiates for them every third Sunday. The Episcopal Church in Cornish contains about twenty families. The Rev. George Leonard has been chosen its Rector, and officiates for them every third Sunday. St. Thomas's Church at Concord, was organized in March, 1818, and has thirteen families, and ten communicants. Christ's Church at Bradford, was organized in July, 1817, and contains ten families, and reports thirty-seven baptisms. St. Peter's Church, Drewsville, has been formed three years, has an annual income of one hundred and thirty dollars from Church property, and has ten families, who propose soon to erect a chapel. Christ's Church at Hopkinton, has twenty families. In the vacant Churches of this State, religious services are generally performed by lay readers, and occasionally they have been favoured with the labours of missionaries.

MASSACHUSETTS.

The Church in this State still continues in as flourishing a situation as it was at the time of the meeting of the last General Convention. The Church at Marblehead has been vacated by the removal of the Rev B. B. Smith to the Diocese of Virginia, and this, it is believed, is the only change of importance that has taken place. There is a very general attention paid to the observance of the Canons and Rubrics, and, with but very few exceptions, the established usages of the Church. A large and elegant stone church, of which the Rev. Samuel F. Jarvis, D. D., has been chosen Rector, is now nearly completed in the town of Boston, besides which, a few small congregations have been collected in other towns. Exertions are making to call the attention of the friends of our Church to the subject of missions to such small portions of our communion as are to be found in many parts of the State; a circular letter for this purpose has been published, and it is expected that much good may result from such a measure. On the whole, we regard the situation of the Church in this State as promising.

The Churches in this State, are Trinity Church, Boston, Rev. J. S. J. Gardiner, D. D., Rector; Christ Church, Boston, Rev. Asa Eaton, Rector, which reports, for the last two years, one hundred and twenty-nine baptisms, and two hundred and thirty communicants; St. Peter's Church, Salem, Rev. Thomas Carlile, Rector, reports, for the last three years, twenty-eight baptisms, and consists at present of one hundred families and fifty-two communicants; St. Paul's Church, Newburyport, Rev. James Morss, Rector, reports, for the last two years, forty-six baptisms and eighty-six communicants; St. James's Church, Greenfield, and Trinity Church, Montague, Rev. Petrus Strong, Rector, baptisms for the last year twenty-three, communicants seventy-two; Christ Church, Cambridge; St. Andrew's Church, Hanover, Rev. Calvin Walcott, Rector, reports, for the last year, twenty-five baptisms and forty communicants; the Church at Quincy reports sixteen communicants; Trinity Church, Marshfield; St. Matthew's Church, South Boston; Church at Bridgewater has ten communicants; St. Michael's Church, Marblehead, has twenty-four communicants; St. James's Church, Great Barrington; Church at Lenox; Church at Lanseborough; Church in Dedham, in which the Rev. Chever Fech officiates; and the Churches in Newton and Hoghinton.

VERMONT.

The Church in Vermont appears to be in a prosperous condition; the number of communicants has considerably increased since the last report; three new churches have been erected and consecrated, and a subscription is now filled for building another this season at Windsor. A church is also erecting at Guilford, which last town, we are informed, has almost unanimously attached itself to the doctrines, discipline and worship of the Protestant Episcopal Church. Some new congregations have recently been organized, and all, it is hoped, are, through Divine grace, increasing in piety and in the virtues of the Christian life. Though there have been some acquisitions to the number of the Clergy, there is still a want of the labours of more, and a wide field is open for their active and pious exertions The extensive demesnes of the Church in this State, are not yet secured; but a suit is now pending before the Federal Circuit

Court for their recovery, which, if gained, will place the temporalities of the Church in a respectable condition.

RHODE ISLAND.

The Church in Rhode Island continues in a prosperous and flourishing condition. During the last three years, one new church has been erected; Sunday schools have been established in all the congregations, and the number of communicants has very considerably increased. There is a Church Missionary Society, in and for that State, which promises to be useful. In some of the parishes, at the present time, there is an awakened concern for spiritual things, and a more than usual attention to religious duties. There is also generally a decided and increasing attachment to the peculiarities of our Communion; and it is believed that, in no one of the United States, are the order, worship and rules of the Episcopal Church, better, or more uniformly regarded.

The Churches in this State are: St. Michael's, Bristol, Right Rev. A. V. Griswold, rector, who reports, for the last three years, ninety-two baptisms, and one hundred and sixty-nine communicants. Trinity Church, Newport, Rev. Salmon Wheaton, rector, reports, for the last three years, one hundred and thirteen baptisms, and one hundred and fifty communicants. St. John's Church, Providence, Rev. N. B. Crocker, rector, reports, for the last three years, fifty baptisms, and one hundred and fifty-nine communicants. St. Paul's Church, North Providence, Rev. J. L. Blake, rector, reports, for the last three years, thirty-eight baptisms, and fifty-five communicants. At St. Paul's Church, S. Kingstown, Rev. Mr. Burgh, Deacon, officiates.

CONNECTICUT.

Since the last General Convention, in many respects, no material change has taken place. Of the Clergy, several have removed, and some have been added. The *Notitiæ Parochiales* of the Annual Conventions evince a manifest increase of the Church in the Diocese, many particulars of which are necessarily omitted in consequence of the vacancy of the Episcopate for several years. But it is with no small satisfaction we state the recent consecration of the Right Rev. Thomas C. Brownell, D. D., LL. D., to that sacred office. Under his ministrations, by the Divine blessing, the increase of the Church in piety, numbers, and respectability, is gradually advancing. Since his consecration, a number of Churches have been visited, and the holy rite of Confirmation administered to about four hundred persons.

With regard to the Fund for the support of the Episcopate, it appears, from the report of the treasurer, at the last Convention, that it then amounted to about sixteen thousand dollars; and there is a probability that the diocesan will soon be relieved from all parochial duties.

The churches generally are in good repair, and the congregations remarkable, not only for their regular attendanee, but also for their fervency of devotion.

The Episcopal Academy of the Diocese, at Cheshire, under the superintendence of the Rev. Tillotson Bronson, D. D., Principal, and the Rev. Asa Cornwall, Assistant, is flourishing, and the number of students gradually increasing.

On the whole, the Diocese is, at present, more prosperous and flourishing than at any former period. The greatest harmony prevails among the Clergy and Laity, and all are peculiarly united in their attachment to the Liturgy and distinctive doctrines of the Church.

NEW YORK.

The Diocese of New York consists, at present, of the Bishop, fifty-six presbyters, fifteen deacons, and one hundred and eighteen organized congregations.

Since the last General Convention, the following persons have been admitted, by the Bishop of this Diocese, to the holy order of deacons:—Asahel Davis, Samuel Nichols, William H. Northrop (since deceased), George H. Norton, David Brown, Leveret Bush, Thomas Osborne (since removed to South Carolina), Intrepid Morse (since removed to Ohio), Charles M'Cabe, Alexis P. Proal, George Upfold, M. D., John Grigg, jun., James W. Eastburn (since removed to Virginia and deceased), George B. Andrews (since removed to Connecticut), James I. Bowden (since removed to Maryland), John V. E. Thorn (since removed to Pennsylvania), William Richmond (since removed to Pennsylvania), Deodatus Babcock, William Barlow, William H De Lancey, Frederick T. Tiffany, and Benjamin P. Aydclott, M. D., belonging to this Diocese; and John Toland, of the Island of St. Martin's, West Indies; and, by letters dismissory from the Right Rev., the Bishop of that Diocese, Lemuel Birge, of Rhode Island.—Total 24.

Within the same period, the following deacons have been ordered priests:—the Rev. Joshua M. Rogers, the Rev. Samuel Johnston (since removed to Ohio), the Rev. Ezekiel G. Gear, the Rev. Gregory T. Bedell (since removed to North Carolina), the Rev. Nathaniel F. Bruce, M. D., (since removed to Connecticut), the Rev. Charles W. Hamilton, the Rev. David

Brown, the Rev. George H. Norton, the Rev. Henry Anthon, the Rev. Thomas Breintnall, from Pennsylvania, the Rev. Hugh Smith (since removed to Georgia), the Rev. Lucius Smith, from Connecticut, and the Rev Samuel Nichols, of this Diocese; and the Rev. John Toland, of St. Martin's, W. I.—Total 14.

The following Clergymen have been instituted to the following Rectorships:—the Rev. Evan M. Johnson, to that of St. James's Church, Newtown, Queen's County; the Rev. William B. Lacey, to that of St. Peter's Church, Albany; the Rev. Thomas Breintnall, to that of Zion Church, New York; the Rev. Russell Wheeler, to that of Zion Church, Butternuts, Otsego County; the Rev. David Brown, to that of St. James's Church, Hyde Park, Dutchess County; and the Rev. Gilbert H. Sayres, to that of Grace Church, Jamaica, Queen's County.

In addition to the above, the following Clergymen have taken charge of the parishes annexed to their respective names:—the Rev. Nathaniel Huse, from Connecticut, of St. Paul's Church, Paris, Oneida County; the Rev. Samuel Phinney, from Pennsylvania, of St. Andrew's Church, Coldenham, Orange County; the Rev. John Brown, of St. Thomas's Church, New Windsor, Orange County; the Rev. Charles M'Cabe, deacon, of St. James's Church, Milton, Saratoga County; the Rev. Cyrus Stebbins, of Christ Church Hudson, Columbia County; the Rev. Alexis P. Proal, deacon, of St. John's Church, Johnstown, Montgomery County; the Rev. George Upfold, M. D., Deacon, of Trinity Church, Lansingburg Rensselaer County, and Grace Church, Waterford, Saratoga County; the Rev. David Huntington, of St. Peter's Church, Waterville, and St. John's Church, Delhi, Delaware County; the Rev. Henry M. Shaw, Deacon, from North Carolina, of Trinity Church, Utica, Oneida County; the Rev. Lucius Smith, of St. Peter's Church, Auburn, Cayuga County; the Rev. Ravaud Kearney, of Trinity Church, New Rochelle, West-Chester County; the Rev. Henry U. Onderdonk, of St. Ann's Church, Brooklyn, King's County; the Rev. William Barlow, Deacon, of St. John's Church, Canandaigua, Ontario County; the Rev. Samuel Nichols, of St. Matthew's Church, Bedford, West-Chester County; the Rev. John Grigg, jun., Deacon, of St. John's Church, Phillipsburgh, West-Chester County; the Rev. Jonathan M. Wainwright, from Connecticut, (assistant minister), of Trinity Church, New York; the Rev. William A. Clark, of Christ Church, Balston Spa, Sarato a County; the Rev. George Otis, Deacon, from the Eastern Diocese, of St. Paul's Church, Waddington, St. Lawrence County; and the Rev. Frederick T. Tiffany, Deacon, of Christ Church, Cooperstown, Otsego County.

A number of the Clergy of this Diocese continue to prosecute the arduous and all-important labours of the Missionary Service. Besides older missionaries, whose names appear in the last triennial report, there have been engaged in this service, since the last General Convention, the Rev. Amos Pardee, from Massachusetts, the Rev. George H. Norton, the Rev. Leveret Bush, Deacon, the Rev. Deodatus Babcock, Deacon, and the Rev. Francis H. Cuming, Deacon, from New Jersey.

The following persons, are, at present, candidates for orders in this Diocese:—James P. Cotter, James P. F. Clarke, William B. Thomas, George W. Doane, Moses Burt, G. M. Robison, Eleazar Williams, Ezra B. Kellogg, John Garfield, William Jarvis, William Thompson, Richard Bury, Lawson Carter, Benjamin Dorr, Peter Williams, jun, William L. Johnson, Alonzo Potter.

Since the last General Convention, this Diocese has been deprived by death, of the Rev. Henry Moscrop, the Rev. John Bowden, D. D., the Rev. William H. Northrop, Deacon, the Rev. Theodosius Bartow, and the Rev. Barzillai Bulkley. But a still more afflicting source of the diminution of its Clergy, has been found in the painful necessity of exercising Ecclesiastical discipline, by the suspension from the ministry of the Rev. Timothy Clowes, and the Rev. Nathan Felch; and the degradation of Thomas Y. How, previously suspended under the 2d Canon of the General Convention of 1817.

There have been duly organized in this Diocese, and received into union with its Convention, St. Paul's Church, Redhook, Dutchess County; St. John's Church, Monticello, Sullivan County; St. Paul's Church, Buffalo, Niagara County; St. Thomas's Church, Mamaroneck, West-Chester County; St. Paul's Church, Ticonderoga, Essex County; St. Thomas's Church, New Windsor, Orange County; Zion Church, Sandyhill, Washington County; St. Paul's Church, Turin, Lewis County; St. Michael's Church, Genesee, Ontario County; Zion Church, New York, (the former corporation of this name having, upon the destruction of their house of worship, been legally dissolved;) Grace Church, Norway, Herkimer County; Christ Church, North Hampstead, Queen's County; St. John's Church, Delhi, Delaware County; St. Paul's Church, Waterloo, Seneca County; and St. Peter's Church, Verona, Oneida County.—Total 15.

The following Churches have been consecrated by the Bishop: —St. Paul's Church, Windham, Greene County; Christ Church, Balston Spa, Saratoga County; St. Paul's Church, Turin, Lewis

County; St. Paul's Church, Waddington, St. Lawrence County; Zion Church, Onondaga Westhill, Onondaga County; St. Paul's Church, Richmond, Ontario County; Zion Church, New York, (rebuilt after destruction by fire;) Christ Church, Binghamton, Broome County; Zion Church, Butternuts, Otsego County; St. Paul's Church, Redhook, Dutchess County; St. Philip's Church, New York, (erected for the accommodation of the coloured members of the Church in that city;) St. Peter's Church, Oneida Castle, Oneida County, (the congregation of which is composed of Indians, and in which there is used a translation of our Liturgy in the Mohawk language;) St. Peter's Church, Waterville, Delaware County; St. Paul's Church, Paris, Oneida County; and St. George's Church, Newburgh, Orange County. —Total 15.

The reports of the Missionaries and parochial Clergy, published in the Journals of the last three Conventions, furnish an aggregate of four thousand six hundred and eighty nine baptisms, of which four hundred and nine are specified as cases of adults, and eighty-seven of Indians. The aggregate number of Confirmations is not given in the Journals of 1817 and 18. In 1819 the Bishop reported one thousand four hundred and seventy-four. In that and the previous year, he confirmed one hundred and forty-five Indians. The number of Communicants reported at the last Convention, is four thousand two hundred and thirty-five.

No small share of the prosperity of this Diocese is to be ascribed to Missionary services. The number of labourers at present engaged in them is fifteen. The peculiar situation of the immense portion of the Diocese, formed by the western district of the State, renders these services indispensable, and should excite our brethren in New York to increasing exertions in their support; while the similarity of cases between that section of their State and the new States and Territories of our Union, should command for these services, as intimately connected with the duty of extending Missionary labours to the latter, the approbation of the Church generally.

It is proper that we here notice the efforts made by our brethren of this Diocese, for the religious instruction of the Indians, within the borders of their State. The Oneida tribe have now a handsome and commodious church, and are still enjoying the faithful services of their licensed catechist and lay-reader, Mr. Eleazar Williams, who is himself of Indian extraction, and a candidate for holy orders. He leads their devotions in their church, by the use of a translation of our

Liturgy into the Mohawk language; in which they join with every appearance of devout attention, and with the full effect of proper participation. A young Indian of the Onondaga tribe, son of a chief who was killed in the service of the United States, during the last war, is now making suitable preparation for devoting ardent piety, great zeal, and natural talents of a most respectable order, to the work of the Ministry among his countrymen.

The congregations of this Diocese receive frequent visits from the Bishop. The Clergy are generally distinguished for conscientious observance of the Canons and Rubrics of the Church. The laity, in conjunction with their pastors, have formed numerous associations for distributing the Holy Bible, the book of Common Prayer, and other approved religious books and tracts; for aiding the Ecclesiastical authority in the support of missionaries; and for the interesting and inestimable charity of Sunday-school instruction.

Upon the whole, we have reason to be thankful for the continuance of the Divine blessing to this portion of our Zion, and to hope that it proves, in some good degree, instrumental in that promotion of the glory of God, of the interests of Evangelical piety, and of the eternal welfare of the human race, for which the Church of God was established.

NEW JERSEY.

The state of the Church, in the Diocese of New Jersey, through the Divine goodness, still continues, however slowly, to improve.

Though there has been but one addition to the number of congregations, since the last report (the Church at Paterson), yet there has been an increase of members and of communicants, in several. More Clergymen now belong to the Diocese, and possess cures, than at any former period. The churches, with scarcely an exception, are in excellent repair. One of which, St. Michael's church, at Trenton, has been lately rebuilt, in an elegant style, and others have been improved and repaired. The vacant churches have enjoyed the regular administration of the word and ordinances, more frequently than formerly. They have been annually visited by the Bishop, some of them oftener; several of them by the Rectors in their vicinity; and all of them, by Missionaries. There is, therefore, cause for gratitude to the Divine Head of the Church, that, struggling with difficulties and discouragements, as our section of it has been for many years, we are yet permitted not only to live, but to anticipate, with considerable confidence, a still better state of our ecclesiastical affairs.

Since the preceding General Convention, the Bishop of the Diocese has admitted to priest's orders, the Rev. James Montgomery, formerly a deacon, in the Diocese of Pennsylvania; and to deacons' orders, Samuel Breighton Stratton, (since removed to Maryland,) Francis H. Cuming, (since removed to the Diocese of New York,) George H. Woodruff, and Clarkson Dunn.

Two institutions have taken place within the same time, the Rev. James Montgomery, to the Rectorship of St. Michael's Church, Trenton, (since removed to the Diocese of New York;) and the Rev. Abiel Carter, lately of the Diocese of Pennsylvania, to the same Rectorship.

Two candidates for holy orders have been admitted.

Confirmations have been administered in eight Churches. The number confirmed, was one hundred and fifty-three. The number of baptisms reported since the last General Convention, is four hundred and eighty-two, and the present number of communicants, upwards of eight hundred. The Rubrics and Canons of the Church are generally observed with attention, and the authority of the Church respected.

The Funds of the corporation for the relief of widows and children of clergymen of the Protestant Episcopal Church in this State; of the Episcopal Society for promoting Christian knowledge and piety; and the Fund for supporting Missionaries, have increased considerably since the last report. The permanent Fund of the Episcopal Society has advanced from four hundred and seventy-five to upwards of eight hundred dollars; at the same time, a very considerable number of Bibles, prayer-books and religious tracts have been gratuitously distributed by the Society, among the needy members of the Church, and others.

The number of instituted Rectors in the Diocese, is nine. The whole number of clergymen, fifteen; three more than were reported at the last meeting.

PENNSYLVANIA.

There are, at this time, in the State of Pennsylvania, thirty clergymen of the Episcopal Church; the greater part of whom are engaged in the discharge of parochial duty.

The following persons have been ordained Deacons, in this Diocese, since the last General Convention:—Richard S. Mason, Wm. A. Muhlenberg, Henry R. Judah, Samuel C. Brinckle,

Manning B. Roche, Thomas Breintnall, William Westerman, Joseph Spencer, John Rodney, Bird Wilson, William S. Wilson, Charles G. Snowden, John Johns, Samuel Bacon, Henry Pfeiffer, and Samuel Sitgreaves, jr.

The following Deacons have been ordained Priests:—the Rev. George Sheets, the Rev. Albert A. Muller, of South Carolina, the Rev. Jacob M. Douglass, the Rev. Charles M. Dupuy, the Rev. Thomas P. May, the Rev. Frederick Dalcho, M. D., of South Carolina, the Rev. John V. E. Thorn, the Rev. Bird Wilson, and the Rev. Samuel Bacon.

There are, at present, the following candidates for orders in this Diocese:—Samuel Marks, Charles P. M'Ilvaine, Ephraim Bacon, James Doughen, John P. Bankson, Robert Piggot, Richard H Morgan, Joseph Mason, Peter Van Pelt.

This Diocese has been deprived, by death, of the Rev. Absalom Jones, the Rev. Thomas P. May, and the Rev. John Campbell.

St. Thomas's Church, Whitemarsh, St. Luke's Church, Germantown, and Christ Church, Leacock, Lancaster County, have been consecrated by the Bishop.

New churches are erecting at Lancaster, Easton and Mantua.

Four recently organized parishes have been received into union with the Convention of the Diocese.

The number of baptisms since the last General Convention, has been one thousand six hundred and sixty-eight, and of confirmations, seven hundred and twenty-four. The number of communicants reported to the last Diocesan Convention, is one thousand five hundred.

From the representations of the missionaries who are sent out under the patronage of the Society for the advancement of Christianity in Pennsylvania, the agreeable intelligence is derived, that a degree of religious sensibility is perceptible among the members of our communion generally, and an attachment to the distinctive principles of our Church, which, it is hoped, will, in time, lead to the most beneficial results. Under the influence of this pious zeal, the missionaries who have been sent into the interior parts of the State have been thankfully received and cordially welcomed; and under their labours, congregations have been collected and organized, which will soon be able to erect for themselves places of public worship, and support their pastors.

Societies have been established and respectably supported, for Sunday School instruction, and for distributing the Book of Common Prayer, and religious tracts. The Episcopal fund is rapidly increasing, and the corporation for the relief of widows and orphans of clergymen has an extensive fund which promises to answer the purposes of its establishment.

Upon the whole, it may be remarked, that the Church in Pennsylvania, under the blessing of her Divine Founder and Head, is as rapidly increasing in prosperity as, when all circumstances are considered. we have any reason to expect.

DELAWARE.

The state of affairs and the cause of religion, it is believed, are certainly improving; and it is hoped, the set time to favour this part of our Zion is near at hand. Since the last General Convention, several churches in the State have been repaired, and placed in good order, and have received considerable additions of families and communicants. There are fourteen Churches in this State, and the most of them have regular and stated religious services; and those, which are not thus favoured, are visited occasionally by the clergy of the State. The Church in Wilmington has especially been favoured with God's blessing within two years past, and has arisen from its desolate state. At Newcastle the prospect is brightening. The churches in Kent county are promising. At Middletown, exertions have been made to rescue the fine building the congregation of Ann's possess, from dilapidation; and the labour, bestowed lately upon them, has not been in vain.

The Conventions of late have been more interesting, and are well attended; and the rules of the Church are well observed. The Churches in Sussex county are in an improving State. Some of the congregation have made considerable exertions to repair their places of worship; and their labours have not been in vain.

On the whole, we have great reason to be thankful to the Great Head of the Church, that our prospects in this State justify the hope, that ere long, by the faithful coöperation of the Clergy and Laity, we shall yet see more "refreshing times from the presence of the Lord," and the cause of our Zion in this State arise from the desolations of many generations.

There are, in the State of Deleware, four officiating Clergymen. There are about two hundred communicants. There have been one hundred and fourteen persons confirmed; and one candidate received for holy orders, viz. Mr. Wells Wolfe.

MARYLAND.

It appears from the Journals of Conventions held in this Diocese since the General Convention, that eight hundred and nineteen persons have been confirmed, eight churches have been consecrated, fifteen persons have been admitted to holy orders; eight to the office of deacon, and seven to that of priest; and nineteen clergymen have removed into the diocese, from other states. Several religious societies have been established, and some are already productive of much good. Among these, are the "Prayer Book and Homily society of Maryland," "the Baltimore Female Tract society," (both of which receive some degree of support from persons not residing in that city,) and the Sunday schools attached to the different parishes of the diocese. In several parishes, where the ministry could not be obtained or supported, gentlemen, distinguished by their piety and standing in society, have received from the Bishop the appointment of lay readers; and thus are instrumental in preserving among the members of our Church their attachment to her most devout and excellent services. Though much pressed by the cares of an extensive parish, containing about four hundred families, the Bishop continues to discharge the duties of his office throughout the diocese, and it was remarked in his last statement to the annual Convention, that, with the possible exception of some remote chapels, he had then completed his tour of Episcopal visitation.

The Canons and rubrics of the Church are, it is believed, in most respects generally observed; and upon the whole, we are allowed to cherish the hope that the prosperity of the Protestant Episcopal Church continues to strengthen and increase in Maryland, that her principles are better understood than formerly, that prejudices once entertained against her are removed, that there is an increased attachment to her rites and ordinances, and that true religion is gaining ground in the hearts and lives of her members.

VIRGINIA.

The Almighty continues his gracious smiles to this part of his Church. Since the last General Convention a considerable number of new congregations has been formed, and a large increase of ministers been added. The number of regular congregations is about fifty, and of officiating ministers thirty. The most delightful unity prevails amongst the ministers. A strong attachment binds them and their congregations together. The conduct of communicants is becoming more and more serious and consistent; and very few are now to be found, who bring reproach upon religion and the Church by immoralities, or an attendance upon the vain and sinful amusements of the world. The services of the Church are more punctually and zealously observed, and promise to be esteemed in proportion as they are duly understood. The ordinance of baptism especially, which has hitherto been so neglected, or lightly and profanely performed, begins to excite the more serious attention of the clergy and laity. Whereas the directions of the rubric enjoin the most public and solemn performance of it, where the prayers of the whole congregation may be obtained, it has been too customary, either through a false modesty or irreligious indifference, to prevail upon ministers to disobey the rubric, and let down the ordinance to a mere private ceremony, which has often been accompanied with unbecoming frivolity and mirth.

The impiety of such a proceeding now appears in its true colours; and a reformation has already begun and considerably advanced, which, it is hoped, will be aided and supported by the general voice of the Church.

In this diocese a fund for the Episcopate has been commenced.

The College of William and Mary has made an offer which promises important benefits to students of theology, and has elected a clergyman of our Church a professor therein who will take charge of such students.

A society has been organized to assist indigent young men who are candidates for the ministry, and from which the most beneficial results may be expected.

NORTH CAROLINA.

At a period no more remote than the fall of 1816, the Protestant Episcopal Church in this state, was nearly at the lowest point of depression. There were, indeed, some who felt a lively interest in her welfare and who wept when they remembered Zion. But, like Israel of old, they hung their harps upon the willows in almost hopeless anguish. Even those few houses of God, which had, for some years before, occasionally or statedly resounded with his praise, were closed and deserted; and the pious of our communion, though attached both by education and principle to the Church of their fathers despairing of seeing her ever again arise from the dust, stood ready to abandon her cause, and to unite themselves with any among whom they could enjoy, in any measure, the benefit of divine ordinances. But, blessed be the name of the Lord, the set time for Him to have compassion upon this part of Zion had come. He viewed with an eye of relenting mercy, the desolations with which his justice had visited her sins. The prayers of the faithful were heard by the Great Head of the Church, and the decree was sent forth—Let Jerusalem be rebuilt.

In the spring of 1817, was held the first Protestant Episcopal Convention, ever held in North Carolina. At which were present lay delegates from four different parishes, and three of the Clergy, whom Divine Providence, had, for the time being, brought to that state. Of these, two have since removed, the Rev. Bethel Judd, rector of St. John's Church, Fayetteville, to whom has succeeded the Rev. Gregory T. Bedell; and the Rev. Jehu C. Clay, rector of Christ Church, Newbern, whose place is now supplied by the Rev. Richard S. Mason. Besides these three, the Church in this State is blessed at present, with the labours of four others, the Rev. John Avery, rector of St. Paul's Church, Edenton; the Rev. John Phillips, who is settled in Trinity Church, Tarborough, and performs stated services at various places in its vicinity; the Rev. William Hooper, Professor in the University of North Carolina; and Rev. Thomas Wright, missionary. Mr. Hooper will also act in the capacity of missionary, as far as it may be in his power; and the Rev. John Toland is daily expected who will engage in the same service.

Besides these seven Clergy, there are at present six candidates for holy orders.—William M. Greene, George S. Phillips, Robert Davis, William Lowry, John Davis, and Burton H. Hicocks.

Since the last General Convention, the Right Rev. Richard C. Moore, D. D. has admitted the Rev. Richard S. Mason to the holy order of priesthood; and William Hooper, Thomas Wright, and Henry M. Shaw, to that of Deacons. The last mentioned of these gentlemen, has since removed to the diocese of New York.

The Right Rev. Bishop Moore has also consecrated a new church lately erected in Fayetteville, by the name of St. John's Church; and held confirmation at various places, where were confirmed as follows: Fayetteville, sixty; Newbern, fifty three; Edenton, thirty; Wilmington, one hundred and thirty-eight; amounting in all, to one hundred and eighty-one.

It may tend farther to throw light on the condition and history of the Church in this State to remark, that, a few years ago the number of communicants in all our churches did not exceed fifty; whereas, they amount now to more than three hundred and fifty; that besides the Protestant Episcopal Missionary Society of North Carolina, various charitable and religious societies have been established by the members of our communion; that Bible classes and Sunday Schools are to be found in almost every parish; and that the baptisms reported at the several Diocesan Conventions since the last General Convention, are two hundred and seventy-five; of which, twenty are stated to be the cases of adults.

Since the Church was organized in this State, ten parishes have, at different times been represented in the annual Conventions; and at least six more places will organize Churches as soon as they are visited by the Missionaries that have lately been appointed for that purpose.

We are happy in reporting that, as far as we know and believe, the Clergy in this section of the country strictly observe the Canons and Rubrics of the Church. The case of private baptism forms, it is believed, the only exception; and in that article, even, a reformation has commenced, which, we trust, will ere long become complete and universal.

By the good providence of our God, the Church in this State has obtained help of the Lord at the very time when she seemed most likely to become extinct. Had this help been delayed but a few years longer, death would probably have swept away all those Episcopal predilections which yet exist in every section of the country; and which, by the blessing of Heaven, will become the seminal principles by which the Church, like the fabled phœnix, shall rise from her ashes. Her prospects are every day brightening more and more. Her friends are every where excited to hope and exertion. May their most sanguine hopes soon be realized! may the great Head of the Church prosper the work! and may this section of Zion speedily become the joy of the whole earth.

SOUTH CAROLINA.

The diocese of South Carolina, it appears, has been deeply afflicted since the meeting of the last General Convention. The Clergy and Laity of that Church have not only to deplore the loss of their late diocesan, the Right Rev. Dr. Dehon, the recollection of whose virtues and talents they love to cherish in their hearts; but death hath also deprived them of the Rev. Dr. Percy, late rector of St. Paul's church, Charleston, and of the Rev. Thomas Frost, late assistant minister of St. Philip's church, Charleston. The Episcopal office, however, was not suffered long to remain vacant; but was happily filled by the election of the Rev. Dr. Bowen in February, 1818, who appears, from an address of his clergy, to possess their thorough confidence and affection. A fund for the support of the Bishop was likewise instituted in the same year, which is progressing and promises to effect the important object it contemplated.

The number of Clergymen within the diocese of South Carolina, has evidently increased, and there is yet no visible decline of the zeal of either the Clergy or the Laity. Mr. David I. Campbell, Mr. Francis P. Delavaux, Mr. Henry Gibbes, Mr. John W. Chandler, and Mr. William Wilson, who had been received as candidates for holy orders by Bishop Dehon, were admitted to that of deacons; the four first named in the diocese of South Carolina, and the last in that of Pennsylvania by letters dimissory from the former. Mr. Edward Rutledge, received as a candidate for orders in this diocese, was ordained deacon, by virtue of letters dimissory, in the diocese of Connecticut. The Rev. Frederick Dalcho, the Rev. Albert A. Muller, the Rev. Maurice H. Lance, the Rev. Frances P. Delavaux, the Rev. Thomas Osborne (since removed to the diocese of Ohio,) the Rev. Alston Gibbes, and the Rev. Joseph M. Gilbert have within the same period been ordained priests; the two first at Philadelphia, and the others in South Carolina. Several candidates are now preparing for the ministry in that Diocese, and there is a prospect flattering to the hopes of the friends of the Church, that it will in this Diocese yet effectually be restored from the state to which it had, after the Revolutionary war, been reduced. At present, it appears, there are more of its parishes supplied, than at any intermediate period since the war.

The Protestant Episcopal Society for the advancement of Christianity in South Carolina, which was instituted a few years ago, and has prospered in an unexampled manner, has done much good. This society is, by its constitution, strictly identified with the Church. It devises and executes liberal things. By its funds it has helped to re-establish old parishes, which had fallen into decay. It actually contributes to the support of several ministers.

A society has been also formed, consisting of young men and others, having missions for its object; and it has already been instrumental of good by the employment of the Rev. Mr. Fowler in a quarter of the diocese, which had never been visited by an Episcopal clergyman since the revolution. There is a happy prospect of extending the borders of our Church farther into the interior by the formation, with the help of the Protestant Episcopal society for the advancement of Christianity in South Carolina, of congregations in one or two of the interior districts.

Sunday schools have been established in several parts of the diocese, and have been the occasion of good to many, it is hoped, particularly to the people of colour. They are, however, of too recent a date to enable us to say much about them. Tracts have also been published and distributed by the Protestant Episcopal society for the advancement of Christianity in South Carolina, calculated to excite attention, to instruct the people in practical religion, and to attach them to the doctrine, discipline and liturgy of the Church. Among those tracts is a catechism, edited under the authority and direction of the Bishop and his clergy, which is explanatory of the one in the book of Common Prayer. The people of colour are beginning to be instructed in those doctrines and principles of the Christian religion, which will tend to promote their comfort and well-being here and their everlasting happiness hereafter, with a prospect of success conducive to their improvement and amelioration.

On the whole, the condition of the Church in South Carolina is favourable. The Bishop has visited, since his entering on the duties of the diocese, almost every parish within it. Confirmation is regularly administered. The Rubrics and Canons are conscientiously observed. Both clergy and laity evince a resolution to adhere to the order of the Church and to oppose all innovation.

The number of baptisms, reported to the Diocesan Conventions within the last three years, is eight hundred and thirty-nine; yet that number is defective, as reports do not appear to have been received from all the parishes every year. The number of communicants appears to be one thousand four hundred and fifty-seven, although that too falls a little short of the truth.

OHIO.

By a letter from the Right Rev., the Bishop of this diocese, addressed to the House of Bishops in this Convention and by them transmitted to the House of Clerical and Lay Deputies, it appears that the said Right Reverend Bishop has admitted the Rev. Intrepid Morse, Deacon from New York, to the holy order of priests, and Mr. Benjamin Birge, of Kentucky, to that of Deacon; and has confirmed, since his settlement in his diocesan capacity, two hundred and thirty-four persons.

At Dayton, on the Miami, and in several places in the east, and north-east of the State, new parishes have been formed.

The Clergy of the diocese are six, besides the Bishop.—Philander Chase, Jr., has been admitted a candidate for holy orders.

In laying the preceding statement before the House of Bishops, the House of Clerical and Lay Deputies solicit their counsel and their prayers for the blessing of Almighty God.

In conclusion, the House of Clerical and Lay Deputies, reverting to the notices of pri.ate baptisms in some of the preceding statements, respectfully request the House of Bishops to insert in the pastoral letter solicited by this House, their opinion and advice on the subject of the existing custom of administering private baptism, without great and reasonable cause, and using in private the public office; and also on the subject of the proper qualifications of sponsors in baptism.

Signed by order of the House of Clerical and Lay Deputies.

W. H. WILMER, PRESIDENT.

May, 23, 1820.

The Rev. Mr. Carlile asked and obtained leave of absence for the remainder of the Session.

The house adjourned, to meet at five o'clock this evening.

TUESDAY, 5 o'clock, P. M.

The house met.

The Rev. Gregory T. Bedell, a Clerical Deputy from North Carolina, appeared and took his seat.

The consideration of the report of the Committee on the Theological Seminary was called up, and the report read.

The first resolution proposed by the Committee, as follows, was then reconsidered.

1. Resolved,—That the Theological Seminary instituted at New York, under the authority of the last General Convention of the Protestant Episcopal Church of the United States, be transferred to and located within the city of New Haven in the diocese of Connecticut.

It was proposed to amend the first resolution, by substituting the city of Philadelphia, for the "city of New Haven," which was negatived.

It was then proposed to amend the resolution by striking out the word "New Haven." The question being taken by States it was decided in the negative, as follows.

Maine—Clergy, No; Laity, No.
New Hampshire—Clergy, No; Laity, ——.
Massachusetts—Clergy, No; Laity, No.
Vermont—Clergy, No; Laity, No.
Rhode Island—Clergy, No; Laity, divided.
Connecticut—Clergy, No; Laity, No.
New York—Clergy, Aye; Laity, No.
New Jersey—Clergy, Aye; Laity, Aye.

Pennsylvania—Clergy, No; Laity, No.
Delaware—Clergy, No; Laity, Aye.
Maryland—Clergy, No; Laity, No.
Virginia—Clergy, No; Laity, No.
North Carolina—Clergy, No; Laity, No.
South Carolina—Clergy, No; Laity, ——.
So the question for striking out was lost.
The first resolution was then adopted.

The second resolution offered by the Committee was then taken up and read as follows:

2. Resolved,—That the management of the said seminary be and is hereby vested in a Board of Trustees, which shall consist of the Bishops of the several dioceses within the United States, of twelve Clergymen and twelve Laymen, to be appointed by the House of Clerical and Lay Deputies, at every meeting of the General Convention; any *seven* of whom shall be competent to form a board for transacting business. They shall have power to collect and manage funds for the benefit of the seminary; to appoint professors and teachers therein, and prescribe their duties; regulate the admission of students, and prescribe the course of studies to be observed by them; to make such by-laws and regulations as may be necessary for the government of the seminary; and generally to take such measures as they may deem essential to the prosperity of the institution. The said Board of Trustees shall have power to fill vacancies which may occur by death, removal or resignation of any Clerical and Lay member thereof, and it shall be their duty to make a full and detailed report of their proceedings and of the state of the seminary to the next General Convention.

It was proposed to amend the resolution by inserting after the word "institution" the following which was agreed to by the house: "Provided, that the capital of the sums subscribed and collected in pursuance of this resolution and of the resolutions on this subject passed at the last General Convention, shall be carefully invested in some secure and productive fund, and shall remain inviolate and untouched, except for the pupose of erecting suitable buildings for the accommodation of the seminary; and that the interest only of the said capital shall be employed for the compensation of professors or other current and annual expenditures, except that they may continue and provide for the present professor.

The following amendment was then proposed and negatived: to strike out the words, "at every meeting of the General Convention;"—and insert at the end of the resolution the following: "who may remove the Clerical and Lay Trustees, or any of them, (other than the Bishops) if they think proper so to do, and to elect others in their places."

The following amendment was then proposed: to insert after the words "observed by them," the following, "not inconsistent with the Canons and the course of studies which is or may be established by the House of Bishops."

This amendment was under consideration when a motion was made to adjourn.

Col. Halsey asked and obtained leave of absence for the remainder of the session.

The house adjourned.

WEDNESDAY, May 24, 9 o'clock, A. M.

Divine Service was performed by the Rev. Mr. Morss, and a sermon preached by the Rev. Dr. Wilmer.

After Divine Service the house met.

The Rev. Dr. Wharton, and the Hon. Kensey Johns asked and obtained leave of absence for the remainder of the session.

The amendment of the second resolution on the subject of the Theological Seminary, under consideration when the house adjourned last evening, was called up and agreed to.

The resolution as amended was then adopted.

The third resolution offered by the Committee was read, considered and adopted as follows:

3. Resolved,—That the Bishops of the several dioceses within the United States, and where there is no Bishop, the Standing Committee of the diocese, be and they are hereby earnestly and respectfully requested to adopt such measures as they may deem most advisable to collect funds in aid of the Theological Seminary, and to cause the same when collected to be transmitted to the Treasurer of the Board of Trustees.

The resolutions as amended were then adopted as follows, and sent to the House of Bishops.

1. Resolved,—That the Theological Seminary, instituted at New York, under the authority of the last General Convention of the Protestant Episcopal Church of the United States, be transferred to and located within the city of New Haven in the diocese of Connecticut.

2. Resolved,—That the management of the said seminary be and is hereby vested in a Board of Trustees which shall consist of the Bishops of the several dioceses within the United States, of twelve Clergymen and twelve Laymen to be appointed by the House of Clerical and Lay Deputies, at every meeting of the General Convention; any *seven* of whom shall be competent to form a board for transacting business. They shall have power to collect and manage funds for the benefit of the seminary; to appoint professors and teachers therein, and prescribe their duties; regulate the admission of students, and prescribe the course of studies to be observed by them, not inconsistent with the Canons, and the course of studies which is or may be established by the House of Bishops: to make such by-laws and regulations as may be necessary for the government of the seminary, and generally to take such measures as they may deem essential to the prosperity of the institution; *provided*, that the capital of the sums subscribed and collected in pursuance of these resolutions, and of the resolutions on this subject passed by the last General Convention, shall be carefully invested in some secure and productive fund and shall remain inviolate and untouched, except for the purpose of erecting suitable buildings for the accommodation of the seminary; and that the interest only of the said capital shall be employed for the professors, or other current or annual expenditure, except that they may continue and provide for the present professor.

3. Resolved,—That the Bishops of the several dioceses within the United States, and where there is no Bishop, the Standing Committee of the diocese, be, and they are hereby earnestly and respectfully requested to adopt such measures as they may deem most advisable to collect funds in aid of the Theological Seminary, and to cause the same when collected, to be transmitted to the Treasurer of the Board of Trustees.

The amendment of the seventeenth Canon proposed by the House of Bishops, was taken up, considered and adopted, and notice of concurrence sent to that house.

Samuel Sitgreaves, Esq., from the Committee on the subject of the thirty-fifth Canon reported a Canon, which was adopted and sent to the House of Bishops.

A Canon concerning the consecration of Bishops in the recess of the General Convention and repealing the fifth Canon of 1808 was received from the House of Bishops, and adopted by this house, and notice of concurrence sent to that house.

The Rev. Mr. Boyd from the Committee on the subject of a missionary society, reported in favour of forming such society, and offered a constitution, which was considered and adopted with amendments and sent to the House of Bishops.

A message was received from the House of Bishops informing this house that they concurred in the resolutions on the subject of the Theological Seminary. With this concurrence of the House of Bishops, was a declaration of that house on the subject, which was read.

On motion Resolved,—That a Committee be appointed to nominate Trustees for the Theological Seminary. The Rev. Mr. Morss, the Rev. Mr. Boyd, the Rev. Dr. Gadsden, William Meredith, Esq., and Gen. Matthias Nicoll were appointed to compose said Committee.

The house adjourned until 5 o'clock, P. M.

WEDNESDAY, 5 o'clock, P. M.

The house met.

A message was received from the House of Bishops, accompanied by a Canon, to govern in case of a Clergyman declaring himself no longer a minister of this Church, and repealing the 1st Canon of 1817. This Canon was concurred in by this house, and notice sent to the House of Bishops.

The Rev. Mr. Noble, from the Committee appointed to consider the Canon proposed on the subject of Candidates for holy orders, reported the Canon with amendments, which were considered and adopted; and the Canon as amended was sent to the House of Bishops.

The Rev. Mr. Morss from the Committee appointed to

nominate Trustees for the Theological Seminary made report, and the following gentlemen were appointed Trustees:

Rev. D. Burhans, Rev. H. Croswell, Rev. B. G. Noble, Hon. Jonathan Ingersol, Hon. Sam. Wm. Johnson, Nathan Smith, Esq., Richard Adams, Esq., Connecticut; Rev. Dr. Jarvis, George Sullivan, Esq., David Leas, Esq., Massachusetts; Rev. Nathan B. Crocker, Rhode Island; Rev. J. M. Wainwright, Isaac Lawrence, Esq., New York; Rev. Chas. H. Wharton, D. D., New Jersey; Rev. Jackson Kemper, Rev. George Boyd, William Meredith, Esq., Pennsylvania; Rev. Dr. Wyatt, Francis S. Key, Esq., Maryland; Rev. Dr. Wilmer, Hon. Bushrod Washington, Virginia; Duncan Cameron, Esq., North Carolina; Rev. Dr. Gadsden, William Heyward, Esq., South Carolina.

The resolution offered by Mr. Kean on Friday last, on the subject of the place of meeting of the next General Convention, was called up, and the blank filled with the word Philadelphia, and notice sent to the House of Bishops.

The Rev. Mr. Mason called up the consideration of his resolutions on the subject of the Calendar and improved edition of the Book of Common Prayer. The following substitute, proposed by William Meredith, Esq., was adopted and sent to the House of Bishops.

Resolved,—That it be respectfully requested of the House of Bishops, to take measures for making known any errors or omissions in the octavo edition of the Book of Common Prayer, published by Gaine in 1793, which was established by the forty-third Canon as the standard book, so that they may be avoided or supplied in future editions; and that they be also respectfully requested to correct and supply any errors or omissions in the calendar, and tables prefixed thereto, and to extend the table of the days on which Easter will fall for two cycles of the moon, from the year of our Lord 1823.

A message was received from the House of Bishops, informing this house that they had non-concurred in the adoption of the proposed Canon, entitled "Of the officiating of persons not regularly ordained, and repealing the thirty-fifth Canon." This message was accompanied with the reasons, in writing, of the House of Bishops, which were read.

The following resolution was proposed by the Rev. Mr. Onderdonk, and adopted by the house.

Resolved,—That a Committee of this house be appointed to take into consideration the practicability and expediency of providing a fund to be at the disposal of the General Convention, and that the same Committee be requested (should they deem it expedient) to report to the next General Convention, a plan for raising and maintaining such a fund, and that they be further empowered to collect and hold any monies in trust, for the disposal of the General Convention.

The Rev. Mr. Onderdonk, the Rev. Mr. Kemper, Richard Harrison, Esq., Joshua Jones, Esq., and William Meredith, Esq. were appointed the Committee.

On motion of Samuel Sitgreaves, Esq., Resolved,—That the Rev. Mr. Kemper, the Rev. Mr. Boyd, and Thomas M'Euen, Esq. be a Committee on the part of this house, in conjunction with a Committee to be appointed by the House of Bishops, should that house agree thereto, to make a collection of the Journals of the General Convention, and of the several Diocesan Conventions, and of other important documents, connected with the history of the Church in the United States; and to deposit the same, subject to the disposal of the General Convention, in such hands as may be deemed proper, for the present and until a further order of the Convention.

On motion, Resolved,—That all business before this house not acted upon, be referred to the next General Convention.

A message was received from the House of Bishops, informing that they had concurred in adopting the Constitution of a missionary society, sent by this house, with some amendments, which amendments were agreed to by this house, and the Constitution was adopted. (*See Appendix.*)

A message was received from the House of Bishops, concurring with the resolution of this house on the subject of errors and omissions in the Book of Common Prayer, and informing that they had appointed the Presiding Bishop, with such other persons as he may choose to associate with him, their committee.

The Pastoral Letter from the House of Bishops was received and read.

A message was received from the House of Bishops signifying their concurrence with the resolution of this house, on the subject of collecting Journals and other documents, and informing that they had appointed the Presiding Bishop their Committee.

A message was received from the House of Bishops, proposing an amendment to the resolution of this house fixing the place for the next meeting of the General Convention, by inserting New York instead of Philadelphia; whereupon the following resolution was proposed: Resolved,—That this house concur in adopting the amendment proposed by the House of Bishops. The question being taken by States, was decided in the negative, as follows:

Maine—Clergy, Aye; Laity, Aye.
New Hampshire—Clergy, Aye; Laity, ——
Massachusetts—Clergy, No; Laity, Aye.
Vermont—Clergy, Aye; Laity, ——
Rhode Island—Clergy, No; Laity, No.
Connecticut—Clergy, Aye; Laity, Aye.
New York—Clergy, Aye; Laity, Aye.
New Jersey—Clergy, Aye; Laity, Aye.
Pennsylvania—Clergy, No; Laity, No.
Delaware—Clergy, No; Laity, No.
Maryland—Clergy, No; Laity, No.
Virginia—Clergy, No; Laity, No.
North Carolina—Clergy, Aye; Laity, No.
South Carolina—Clergy, Divided; Laity, ——

So the question for concurring was lost, and notice thereof sent to the House of Bishops, who returned for answer that they had receded from their proposed amendment of the resolution of this house fixing the next meeting of the General Convention at Philadelphia.

The following persons were appointed managers of the Missionary Society:

Rev. Jackson Kemper, Rev. George Boyd, Rev. Wm. Augustus Muhlenberg, Messrs Richard North, C. N. Banker, Stephen North, John Read, John Claxton, Charles Wheeler, Israel Rinsman, Hugh De Haven, jr., and Richard S. Smith, Pennsylvania. Rev. Christopher E. Gadsden, D. D., South Carolina. Rev. Gregory T. Bedell, North Carolina. Rev. Wm. H. Wilmer, D. D., Wm. Meade, Hon. Bushrod Washington, Virginia. Rev. Wm. E. Wyatt,

D. D., Rev. I. K. Henshaw, Maryland. Rev. Richard D. Hall, Delaware. Rev. Abiel Carter, New Jersey. Rev. James Milnor, D. D., New York. Rev. Nathaniel S. Wheaton, Connecticut. Rev. Thos. Carlile, Massachusetts.

The Rev. Mr. Rudd, the Rev. Mr. Kemper, and the Rev. Mr. Boyd were appointed a Committee to superintend the printing of the Journals and the Pastoral Letter, and notice of this appointment was sent to the House of Bishops who returned for answer, that they had appointed the Presiding Bishop, and the Right Rev. Bishop Hobart, a Committee to unite with the Committee of this house.

On motion, Resolved,—That the Committee of this house appointed to superintend the printing of the Journal and Pastoral Letter, be directed to cause to be printed one thousand copies of the Journal of the present Convention, a like number of the Journal of the last Convention, and an equal number of the Pastoral Letter, and also to prepare and report to the next General Convention the Constitution of the Church as it was originally adopted in 1789, and the Canons in the order in which they were adopted, noticing in italics the alterations in, and additions thereto; their report to be accompanied by an index of the principal matters contained in the Constitution and Canons.

On motion, Resolved,—That the thanks of this house be presented to the President, Secretary, and Assistant Secretary for the services rendered by them, respectively, during the present session.

Pursuant to the request of this house, the Right Rev. the members of the House of Bishops attended in the same, for the purpose of closing the session of the Convention by prayer, which was performed by the Right Rev. Bishop White, Presiding Bishop:—after which the house adjourned *Sine Die.*

Signed by order of the House of Clerical and Lay Deputies.

WILLIAM H. WILMER, PRESIDENT.

Attested, ASHBEL BALDWIN, Secretary.

JOURNAL

OF THE

House of Bishops.

PHILADELPHIA, TUESDAY, May 16, 1820.

This day being the day prescribed by the Constitution of the Protestant Episcopal Church in the United States of America for the meeting of the General Convention of the same, and the city of Philadelphia having been appointed by the last Convention as the place of meeting at this time, the Right Rev. William White, D. D. of the diocese of Pennsylvania, the Right Rev. John Henry Hobart, D. D. of the diocese of New York, the Right Rev. Alexander Viets Griswold, D. D. of the Eastern diocese, the Right Rev. James Kemp, D. D. of the diocese of Maryland, the Right Rev. John Croes, D. D. of the diocese of New Jersey, the Right Rev. Nathaniel Bowen, D. D. of the diocese of South Carolina met in the vestry room of St. James's Church, at five o'clock, P. M.

Agreeably to the established rules of order, the Right Rev. Bishop White being senior Bishop took the chair as presiding Bishop in this house.

The Rev. Wm. Augustus Muhlenberg was appointed Secretary to the house.

The Rev. Mr. Butler and Rev. Dr. Wyatt, as a committee from the House of Clerical and Lay Deputies brought a message that their house was organized, and that having chosen the Rev. William H. Wilmer, D. D. President, the Rev. Ashbel Baldwin Secretary, and the Rev. J. C. Rudd, Assistant Secretary, they were ready to proceed to business. The Committee was requested to state to the House of

Clerical and Lay Deputies that the House of Bishops was also ready to proceed to business.

The house proposed to the House of Clerical and Lay Deputies to attend Divine Service to-morrow at 10 o'clock, A. M., and on every subsequent day during the sitting of the Convention, Sunday excepted, at nine o'clock, A. M.

A message was received from the House of Clerical and Lay Deputies stating that they concurred in the above proposal.

Adjourned.

WEDNESDAY, May 17, 10 o'clock, A. M.

The Bishops attended Divine Service in St. James's Church.

Morning prayer was read by the Rev. Mr. Ravenscroft; a sermon on the occasion of the opening of the Convention was preached by the Right Rev. Bishop Moore, and the Holy Communion was administered by the Right Rev. the Presiding Bishop, assisted by other Bishops present.

Divine Service being ended the house met in the vestry room, when the Right Rev. Richard Channing Moore, D. D. of the diocese of Virginia, and the Right Rev. Thomas C. Brownell, D. D., LL. D., of the diocese of Connecticut, took their seats.

The following alteration of the Constitution which was proposed at the last General Convention, and by a resolve thereof was made known to the Convention of every State, agreeably to the eighth article of the Contitution, was adopted, and information sent to the House of Clerical and Lay Deputies.

Resolved,—That it is expedient to alter the first article of the Constitution of this Church, so far as it fixes the time of the meeting of the General Convention thereof, by striking out the words—" third Tuesday in May in the year of our Lord 1808, and on the third Tuesday in May"—and inserting instead thereof the words—*first Tuesday in October, in the year of our Lord*, 1823, *and on the first Tuesday in October, &c.*

Adjourned.

THURSDAY, May 18, 9 o'clock, A. M.

The Bishops attended Divine Service. Morning prayer was read by the Rev. Mr. Butler, and a sermon was preached by the Right Rev. Bishop Hobart. After Divine Service the house met. Present as yesterday.

A message was received from the House of Clerical and Lay Deputies, with sundry documents relative to the Church in Maine, informing this house that they had recognized the Protestant Episcopal Church in the State of Maine as in union with the General Convention.

Whereupon this house informed the House of Clerical and Lay Deputies that they concurred in receiving the Church in Maine into union with the General Convention.

A message was received from the House of Clerical and Lay Deputies stating that they had passed a resolution requesting the Rt. Rev. Bishop Moore to furnish a copy of his sermon delivered at the opening of this Convention. Whereupon,—Resolved,—That this house concur in the same and also return their thanks to Bishop Moore for his sermon. Information of the same was sent to the House of Clerical and Lay Deputies.

There was laid before the house a letter addressed to the Presiding Bishop and to the President of the House of Clerical and Lay Deputies, signed by John Cole, and by Edward J. Cole, residents of Baltimore, requesting the two houses to give their sanction to selections from the book of Psalms in metre, to be used in churches.

Whereupon it was Resolved,—That the house are of opinion that they cannot consider the merits of this selection as a subject of discussion, consistently with the resolve of the two houses in the Convention of 1814, adopted on mature consideration and for weighty reasons, operating against giving a conventional sanction to any publication not issued as of authority in this Church.

Resolved,—That this house propose to the House of Clerical and Lay Deputies the following instructions to be observed in editions of the Book of Common Prayer.

1. That special attention be paid to the title page and table of contents, so that nothing may be omitted or added.

2. That the Book of Common Prayer be distinguished from the Book of Psalms in metre, the Articles of Religion

and sundry offices set forth by this Church, viz.—*The form and manner of making, ordaining, and consecrating Bishops, Priests and Deacons—the form of consecration of a church or chapel. A prayer to be used at the meetings of Convention, An office of institution of ministers into parishes or Churches*—all of which are of equal authority with the Book of Common Prayer; but which, when bound up with it, ought not to appear as parts thereof.

Resolved,—That this house concur with the House of Clerical and Lay Deputies in repealing that part of the forty-fifth Canon which requires the reading of the Episcopal addresses inserted on the Journals of each State or Diocesan Convention in the House of Clerical and Lay Deputies in General Convention.

A message was received from the House of Clerical and Lay Deputies bringing a memorial from the Convention of the Church is South Carolina to the General Convention of the Protestant Episcopal Church in the United States of America, on the subject of the Theological School, which was referred to the Committee on the said school appointed at the last General Convention.

A Canon entitled—*A Canon repealing the first Canon passed in General Convention in the year* 1817 was proposed and adopted, and information was sent to the House of Clerical and Lay Deputies.

Adjourned.

FRIDAY, May 19, 9 o'clock, A. M.

The Bishops attended Divine Service. Morning prayer was read by the Rev. Dr. Wyatt and a sermon preached by the Right Rev. Bishop Kemp.

A message was received from the House of Clerical and Lay Deputies communicating their concurrence in the resolutions passed by this house yesterday—respecting the application of Messrs. J. and E. Cole of Baltimore for a sanction of the Convention to a proposed selection of the Psalms in metre—respecting instructions to be observed in editions of the Book of Common Prayer, and in adopting a Canon repealing the first Canon passed in General Convention of 1817.

A message was received from the House of Clerical and Lay Deputies stating that they had resolved, that the practice of returning thanks for sermons preached before the General Convention and requesting copies for publication ought to be discontinued.

The house adopted the following:

In the Convention of 1817, on the last day of the session, the House of Clerical and Lay Deputies requested the House of Bishops: "to designate and establish some specific edition of the Old and New Testaments, without note or comment, to be considered as the authentic version or standard, by which the genuineness of all the copies of the Holy Scriptures, used by the members of this Church, is to be ascertained; thereby to secure them against perversions, and the people of our Communion from error either in discipline or doctrine."

It was understood, that this call on the Bishops was occasioned by an error in certain editions, in which there was a corrupt rendering of Acts, vi. 3, in contrariety to the original, and tending to sustain a species of ordination unknown in Scripture. It was also understood, that the Bishops were expected to bestow their attention on the subject individually, after the rising of the Convention.

We have accordingly kept it in our minds: and the result of our observation is, that as in England the printing of the Bible is the privilege of persons specially confided in, and acting under the danger of heavy penalty in case of the non-performance of their trust, whether from design or from carelessness, it will be sufficient to enjoin strict conformity to one of these authorized editions. If incorrectness is found in any of them, we believe it to have happened but seldom. In comparing our different experience, we recollected but few instances; and in these instances, there was no injury to the sense.

In recent English publications, an edition by Eyre and Strahan in 1806 and again in 1812, is spoken of as the most perfect extant. We have not seen it, but are of opinion, that on the ground of the correctness of the English editions generally set forth under a patent, and of what is said of this edition in particular, it may be safely trusted to as a standard.

We ought to caution against the confounding of any of the said editions with others from the same country, issued by an evasion of the law. This fraud is practiced by the appending of a few notes in the lower margin, with the intent of their being either retained or cut off at the pleasure of the purchaser. We have seen very corrupt copies of this description, which may be distinguished by attention to the bottoms of the title pages.

In regard to the editions which have been printed within the United States, we have found them generally as correct as could have been expected, considering the great difficulty of avoiding typographical errors, and that the press is without responsibility. We however conceive, that the guarding against errors of any description is an object worthy of the care of the Church.

The House of Bishops are aware that the present communication does not go to the extent of what was contemplated by the last Convention: and therefore they propose the following resolution:

Resolved,—That the House of Clerical and Lay Deputies appoint a Committee of their body, who, together with the presiding Bishop of the House of Bishops and the Bishops of this Church in New York, Maryland and New Jersey, shall in the recess of the Convention take such measures as they may find suitable for the establishment of a standard, according to which all copies of the Scriptures to be recommended to the use of the members of this Church shall be printed.

A message was received from the House of Clerical and Lay Deputies stating that they had passed a Canon entitled *a Canon concerning Pastoral Letters.*

The Canon was agreed to and notice thereof sent to the House of Clerical and Lay Deputies.

Adjourned.

SATURDAY, May 20, 9 o'clock.

The Bishops attended Divine Service. Morning prayer was read by the Rev. Mr. Rudd and a sermon preached by the Right Rev. Bishop Croes. After Divine Service the House met. Present as yesterday.

A Canon was passed, entitled *a Canon in addition to the seventeenth Canon passed in General Convention in* 1808,—and information thereof was sent to the House of Clerical and Lay Deputies.

A message was received from the House of Clerical and Lay Deputies, stating that they had refused to concur in altering the first article of the Constitution.

A message was received from the House of Clerical and Lay Deputies, stating that they had concurred in the resolution to establish a standard Bible, and that they had appointed the Rev. Bird Wilson, Rev. Dr. Wharton, Rev. Dr. Wyatt, Rev. Mr. Kemper, and Samuel Sitgreaves, Esq., a Committee on the part of their House.

A report of the Committee appointed at the last General Convention on the Theological Seminary, with the Treasurer's report and sundry other documents, was read and ordered to lie on the table.

Adjourned.

MONDAY, May 22, 9 o'clock.

The Bishops attended Divine Service. Morning prayer was read by the Rev. Mr. Tsuchdy and a sermon preached by the Right Rev. Bishop Bowen.

After Divine Service the house met. Present as yesterday.

A message was received from the House of Clerical and Lay Deputies with a proposed Canon entitled *a Canon in amendment to the seventeenth Canon.*

The house adopted and sent to House of Clerical and Lay Deputies the above-mentioned Canon with an amendment.

The committee appointed at the last General Convention on the subject of the Theological Seminary made an additional report.

A message was received from the House of Clerical and Lay Deputies with a resolution, that it be made known to the several State Conventions of this Church that it is proposed to consider at the next General Convention, and, if deemed expedient, finally to ratify an alteration of the first article of the Constitution.

Whereupon this house concurred in the resolution and

notice thereof was given to the House of Clerical and Lay Deputies.

A message was received from the House of Clerical and Lay Deputies stating that they had concurred in the amendment of the proposed *Canon amending the seventeenth Canon.*

Adjourned.

TUESDAY, May 23, 9 o'clock.

The Bishops attended Divine Service. Morning prayer was read by the Rev. Mr. Baldwin and a sermon preached by the Right Rev. Bishop Brownell.

After Divine Service the house met. Present as yesterday. The house adopted two Canons—one entitled a *Canon of the consecration of Bishops in the recess of the General Convention*, and another entitled—*a Canon to govern in the case of a minister declaring that he will no longer be a minister of this Church ;* both of which were sent to the House of Clerical and Lay Deputies.

Information was received that the House of Clerical and Lay Deputies had adjourned, to meet again at five o'clock this afternoon.

Whereupon this house adjourned until the same time.

5 o'clock, P. M.

The house met. Present as this morning.

The report of the House of Clerical and Lay Deputies on the state of the Church, sent to this house agreeably to the requisitions of the forty-fifth Canon, was read and committed to the presiding Bishop, with a request that he would draw up the Pastoral Letter of this house contemplated by the said Canon, and requested by the House of Clerical and Lay Deputies.

Adjourned.

WEDNESDAY, May 24, 9 o'clock.

The house met. Present as yesterday. The Right Rev. Bishop Kemp obtained leave of absence for the remainder of the session.

The house attended Divine Service. Morning prayer was read by the Rev. Mr. Morss and a sermon was delivered by the Rev. Dr. Wilmer.

After Divine Service the house assembled in the vestry room.

A message was received from the House of Clerical and Lay Deputies communicating their concurrence in adopting the Canon—*in addition to the seventeenth Canon.*

A message was received from the House of Clerical and Lay Deputies containing resolutions relative to the Theological Seminary; which resolutions were adopted with the following declaration annexed which was sent to the House of Clerical and Lay Deputies.

The House of Bishops inform the House of Clerical and Lay Deputies that in concurring in the resolutions relative to the Theological Seminary, and in its removal from the city of New York, they deem it proper to declare that they do not mean by this concurrence to interfere with any plan now contemplated, or that may hereafter be contemplated, in any Diocese or Dioceses for the establishment of Theological Institutions or professorships; and further they deem it their duty to express the opinion that the various sums subscribed having been thus subscribed under an act of the Convention establishing the Seminary in New York, the subscribers who have not paid are not now bound, except they think proper, to pay their subscriptions, the institution being removed to a different city.

A message was received from the House of Clerical and Lay Deputies with their concurrence in the Canon—*of the consecration of Bishops during the recess of the General Convention.*

Adjourned to meet at five o'clock, P. M.

Five o'clock, P. M.

The house met. Present as this morning.

A message was received from the House of Clerical and Lay Deputies stating that they had concurred in adopting the proposed Canon entitled a Canon *to govern in the case of a clergyman declaring that he will no longer be a minister of this Church.*

The house refused to concur in the Canon—*of the officiat-*

ing of persons not regularly ordained and repealing the thirty-fifth Canon—proposed by the House of Clerical and Lay Deputies, and notice thereof was given to that house with the following statement of their reasons for non-concurrence.

The Bishops have found by experience that such ministers in many instances preaching in our churches and to our congregations, avail themselves of such opportunities to inveigh against the principles of our Communion; and in some instances have endeavoured to obtain a common right with us in our property. It is therefore not from the want of charity to worthy persons dissenting from us, but for the maintaining of such charity, and to avoid collision, that we declare our non-concurrence.

The Bishops further declare their opinion concerning the thirty-fifth Canon, as it now stands, that it does not prohibit the officiating of pious and respectable persons as lay readers in our churches, in cases of necessity or of expediency; nor the lending of any church to any respectable congregation on any occasion of emergency.

A message was received from the House of Clerical and Lay Deputies with a Canon entitled *a Canon, concerning candidates for orders.*

The Canon was adopted and notice given to the House of Clerical and Lay Deputies.

The house concurred in a proposed resolution from the House of Clerical and Lay Deputies relative to the Book of Common Prayer, and the presiding Bishop was requested, with such persons as he may think proper to associate with him, to take order on the subject of that resolution.

The presiding Bishop proposed a pastoral letter to the members of the Protestant Episcopal Church in the United States, to be published agreeably to the provisions of the forty-fifth Canon, which was sent to the House of Clerical and Lay Deputies.

The House concurred in the constitution of a Missionary Society for foreign and domestic missions, proposed by the House of Clerical and Lay Deputies, with amendments, and notice thereof sent to the said house.

The house concurred in a resolution to collect the Journals, &c. proposed by the House of Clerical and Lay Deputies, and appointed the presiding Bishop a Committee for the purpose on the part of this house.

A message was received from the House of Clerical and Lay Deputies with a resolution appointing the city of Philadelphia as the place of meeting for the next General Convention.

The house agreed to the resolution with an amendment naming *New York* instead of Philadelphia.

A message was received from the House of Clerical and Lay Deputies stating that they refused to concur in the proposed amendment; whereupon this house agreed to recede from the same.

A message was received from the House of Clerical and Lay Deputies stating that they had appointed a Committee to superintend the publication of the Journals, whereupon this house appointed the presiding Bishop and Bishop Hobart to act in conjunction with that Committee.

A message was received from the House of Clerical and Lay Deputies stating that they were ready to rise and requesting this house to unite with them in closing the session with prayer.

Resolved,—That this house will attend in the House of Clerical and Lay Deputies for the purpose specified in the above message.

The members of the Convention united in singing the one hundred and thirty-third Psalm, the presiding Bishop offered up several appropriate prayers, and dismissed the Convention with the benediction.

Adjourned *sine die.*

Signed by order of the House of Bishops.

WILLIAM WHITE,

PRESIDING BISHOP.

Attested: WM. AUGUSTUS MUHLENBERG, Secretary.

Canons

PASSED IN GENERAL CONVENTION, 1820.

CANON I.—Repealing a part of the forty-fifth Canon passed in 1808.

That part of the forty-fifth Canon which requires the Episcopal addresses inserted on the Journal of each State or Diocesan Convention, to be read in the House of Clerical and Lay Deputies in General Convention, is hereby repealed.

CANON II.—Repealing the first Canon passed in 1817.

The principal object contemplated by the first Canon passed in General Convention in the year 1817, having been accomplished by the election and consecration of a Bishop for the Diocese of Ohio, the said Canon is hereby repealed.

CANON III.—Concerning Pastoral Letters.

Whereas, there is reason to fear that the Pastoral Letters issued from time to time by the House of Bishops, and addressed to the members of the Episcopal Church, fail of their intended effect for want of sufficient publicity: It is hereby made the duty of every clergyman having a pastoral charge, when any such letter is published, to read the same to his congregation on some occasion of public worship.

CANON IV.—In addition to the seventeenth Canon, passed in 1808.

In the case of a minister of some other denomination of Christians applying for holy orders in this Church, the Standing Committee may receive testimonials of his piety, good morals, and orderly conduct from twelve members of the denomination from which he came; provided the members of the committee have such confidence in the persons thus testifying, as to satisfy them of the correctness of the testimony; and also a testimonial to the same effect from at least one clergyman of the Protestant Episcopal Church.

CANON V.—Amending the seventeenth Canon, passed in 1808.

When any person, not a citizen of the United States, who has officiated as a minister among any other denomination of Christians, shall apply for orders in this Church, the Bishop, to whom application is made, shall require of him, (in addition to the Qualifications made necessary by the seventeenth Canon,) satisfactory evidence that he has resided at least one year in the United States, previous to his application.

CANON VI.—Of the Consecration of Bishops during the recess of the General Convention.

If, during the recess of the General Convention, the Church in any State or Diocess should be desirous of the consecration of a Bishop elect, the standing committee of the Church in such State or Diocese may, by their President or by some person or persons specially appointed, communicate the desire to the standing committees of the Churches in the different States together with copies of the necessary testimonials: and if the major number of the standing committees shall consent to the proposed consecration, the standing committee of the State or Diocese concerned, shall forward the evidence of such consent, together with other testimonials, to the Presiding Bishop of the House of Bishops, who shall communicate the same to all the Bishops of this Church in the United States; and if a majority of the Bishops should consent to the consecration, the Presiding Bishop, with any two Bishops, may proceed to perform the same; or any three Bishops to whom he may communicate the testimonials.

The evidence of the consent of the different Standing Committees shall be in the form prescribed for the House of Clerical and Lay Deputies in General Convention; and without the aforesaid requisites no consecration shall take place during the recess of the General Convention.—But in case the election of a Bishop shall take place within a year before the meeting of the General Convention, all matters relative to the consecration shall be deferred until the said meeting:

The fifth canon is hereby repealed.

CANON VII.—To govern in the case of a minister declaring that he will no longer be a minister of the Church.

If any minister of this Church shall declare to the Bishop of the diocese to which he belongs, or to any Ecclesiastical authority for the trial of clergyman, or, where there is no Bishop, to the Standing Committee, his renunciation of the ministry, and his design not to officiate in future in any of the offices thereof; it shall be the duty of the Bishop, or, where there is no Bishop, of the Standing Committee, to record the declaration so made. And it shall be the duty of the Bishop to admonish, or to suspend him, or to displace him from his grade in the ministry, and to pronounce and record, in the presence of two or three clergyman, that the person, so declaring, has been admonished, or suspended, or displaced from his grade in the ministry in this Church. In any diocese, in which there is no Bishop, the same sentence may be pronounced by the Bishop of any other diocese, invited by the Standing Committee to attend for that purpose. In the case of displacing from the ministry, as above provided for, it shall be the duty of the Bishop to give notice thereof to every Bishop of this Church, and to the Standing Committee in every diocese, wherin there is no Bishop.

The second Canon of 1817 is hereby repealed.

CANON. VIII.—Concerning candidates for orders.

In addition to the testimonials produced by a person wishing to become a candidate for holy orders as prescribed by the seventh canon, he must lay before the Standing Committee a satisfactory diploma, or certificate from the instructors of some approved literary institution, or a certificate from two presbyters appointed by the ecclesiastial authority of the diocese to examine him, of his possessing such academical learning as may enable him to enter advantageously on a course of theology.

When a person applying to be admitted a candidate, wishes the knowledge of the Latin and Greek languages and other branches of learning not strictly ecclesiastical to be dispensed with, the Standing Committee shall not recommend him as a candidate until he has laid before them a testimonial signed by at least two Presbyters of the Church, stating that in their opinion he possesses extraordinary strength of natural understanding, a peculiar aptitude to teach and a large share of prudence.

Done in General Convention, in the city of Philadelphia, in the year of our Lord 1820.

BY ORDER OF THE HOUSE OF BISHOPS.

WILLIAM WHITE,
PRESIDING BISHOP.

Attested: WM. AUGUSTUS MUHLENBERG, Secretary.

BY ORDER OF THE HOUSE OF CLERICAL AND LAY DEPUTIES.

WILLIAM H. WILMER, PRESIDENT.

Attested: ASHBEL BALDWIN, Secretary.

APPENDIX.

NO. I.

Report and Documents on the Theological Seminary.

REPORT.

The Committee on the subject of the Theological school, appointed by General Convention in 1817, report to the General Convention now assembled, as follows:

Before the meeting of the committee, their chairman at the desire of the members individually addressed a letter, dated July 13, 1817, to the Rev. Dr. Bowen, who had been designated by the House of Bishops, to solicit contributions in the States of New York, New Jersey, Pennsylvania and Maryland. This letter detailed the reasons which were supposed to have operated in the founding of the school. At the desire of Dr. Bowen, and with the concurrence of a majority of the members of the committee, another letter dated December 12, 1817, was prepared, with a blank to be filled with the names of any persons whom Dr. Bowen might associate with himself for the accomplishing of the object. These letters as also an extract from an address of Bishop Hobart, to the Convention of the Church in New York, enforcing the importance and necessity of the institution were printed, and copies of them are herewith presented (*See end of the report.*)

On the day on which the first mentioned letter was issued, another in the same words was addressed to the Rev. William H. Wilmer, who has been appointed by the House of Bishops, to collect in the States of Virginia, North and South Carolina, and Georgia. It has been understood that some circumstances occurred which prevented Mr. Wilmer's engaging in this work. But the duties assigned to him were in some measure discharged by the Rev. Dr. Brownell, who collected a considerable sum, principally in the State of South Carolina.

The Rev. Daniel Burhans had been appointed by the House of Bishops to make collections in New Hampshire, Massachusetts, Vermont, Rhode Island and Connecticut: but was prevented by sickness and death in his family. Subsequently there was an appointment of the Rev. Dr. How, and the Rev. Samuel F. Jarvis; and afterwards of the Rev Jonathan M. Wainwright: but unexpected hindrances have prevented success in that section of the union.

After these preliminary arrangements made by the chairman, under the authority of the committee individually, a meeting of the committee was held in the city of Philadelphia, on the 15th and 16th of January 1818, at which were present Bishop White, Bishop Hobart, Bishop Croes, Dr. Wharton, Dr. How, and W. Meredith, Esq. who acted as secretary of the committee. They issued an address to the members of this Church, a printed copy of which is herewith presented. *(See end of the report.)* They also adopted the following resolutions, proposed by Bishop Hobart.

1 Resolved,—That the chairman be requested to address a circular letter to the Bishops and the Standing Committees of the dioceses of New Jersey, Maryland and Virginia, (measures having been taken for the collection of funds in the State of New York,) and to the Standing Committees of the dioceses where there are no Bishops, enclosing several copies of the address before mentioned, requesting them to take effectual measures by the appointment of persons to collect subscriptions and otherwise in their respective dioceses, to provide funds for the institution.

2. That the chairman, as Bishop of this Church in Pennsylvania, be requested, in conjunction with the Standing Committee, and such other persons as he may think proper, to carry into effect in his diocese the provisions of the foregoing resolution.

3. That a circular letter, with copies of the address first mentioned, be transmitted by the chairman to each clergyman of the Church, requesting his co-operation and influence in promoting the object of the address.

4. That the Rev. Dr. How be appointed with the Rev. Mr. Jarvis, to collect subscriptions in the eastern diocese, and to receive instructions on this subject from the Right Rev. Bishop Griswold, generally, and in the town of Boston, from the Rev. Dr. Gardiner, to each of whom the chairman will address a letter requesting his co-operation and influence.

5. That the Bishops who are of this committee, be authorized and requested to make such additional arrangements relative to the appointment of agents and other measures, connected with the collection of monies for the use of the seminary, as they may from time to time think proper.

It was also resolved, that the monies which may be collected be deposited by the sereval persons collecting, in some safe bank in the respective States, to be drawn thence in such way as this committee may hereafter direct;. the choice of the place of deposit to be determined in each case, by the Bishop and Standing Committee of the diocese, and, where there is no Bishop, by the Standing Committee; and that the several collectors be requested to inform the chairman of this Committee, of the amount collected and of the place where it is deposited, and that the Bishops and Standing Committees be requested to report to him the measures which they may have adopted to collect funds for the institution.

And it was further resolved, that the Rev. Jackson Kemper be appointed Secretary to the chairman of this Committee, to assist him in that character in the performance of the several duties stated in these resolutions.

The duties committed to the chairman by these resolves, were performed with the assistance of the Rev. Jackson Kemper, appointed with that view by the Committee; who deem it their duty to state, that on all occasions they received the active cooperation and important aid of their chairman.

Their next meeting was in the city of Philadelphia, on the 7th and 8th of October 1818; at which were present Bishop White, Bishop Hobart, Bishop Croes, Dr. Wharton, and William Meredith, Esq.; at this meeting the following resolutions were adopted; the first resolve being proposed by Bishop White, and the others by Bishop Hobart.

1. Resolved,—That it is expedient to carry into immediate operation, the Theological School of the Protestant Episcopal Church in the United States of America, and that for this purpose, a professorship of biblical learning, comprehending the exposition of the Holy Scriptures, with whatever relates to the evidences of revealed religion and biblical criticism,—a professorship of systematic theology, giving correct views of the doctrines of scripture and of the authorities sustaining them,—a professorship of historick theology, giving correct information of the state of the Church in all ages, and of the Church of England in particular from the reformation, embracing a view of the constitution of the Christian Church, of the orders of the ministry, and of the nature and duty of Christian unity,—a professorship of the ritual of the Church and of pulpit eloquence, comprehending all the points relative to the liturgy, to the correct and devotional performance of the service of the Church, to the composition and delivery of sermons, and to the duties of the clerical office.

2. That as soon as the funds of the institution will admit, these professorships be filled, and the professors detached from all parochial charge, and devoted solely to the objects of the institution.

3. That, when the funds of the institution admit, the Rev. Charles Henry Wharton, D. D., be appointed Professor of systematic theology, and that the Rev. Samuel F. Jarvis be now appointed Professor of biblical learning, and the Rev. Samuel H. Turner, Professor of historic theology; and that these two last-named professors receive for the present, and until they can be detached from parochial cures and devoted solely to the objects of the institution, a salary each of eight hundred dollars per annum.

4. That until the other professorship be filled, and until the professor of systematic theology enter on the duties of his office, the subject of systematic theology be assigned to the professor of historic theology, and that the professor of biblical learning and the professor of historic theology provide by joint arrangement for the object assigned to the professor of the ritual of the Church and of pulpit eloquence.

5. That the professors be regulated in their instructions by the provisions of the Canons, and the course of study set forth by the House of Bishops; that they conduct the students through all the books prescribed in that course, making them thoroughly acquainted with the subjects of which those books respectively treat; that the present professors provide for the daily instruction of the students; and that when the professors are detached from parochial cures, they shall each be daily engaged in instruction; that the students be frequently exercised in the devotional performance of the service of the Church, and in the composition and delivery of sermons; and that particular attention be paid to their progress in the spiritual life, and to their correct views of the nature and responsibility of the duties of the clerical office.

6. That until the further and complete organization of the institution, the Bishops who are members of the committee be charged with making such temporary arrangements as may be necessary.

7. That as soon as the funds will admit, theological scholarships be established for the education of young men of piety and talents, who may be destitute of pecuniary means.

8. That David J. Greene Esq., of the city of New York, be appointed the Treasurer of this institution, with power to collect and receive the monies which may be subscribed or granted

for the benefit thereof, and to place them at interest on good security, in trust, for the use of the institution.

9. That the Bishops composing this committee be authorized and requested to make arrangements for providing funds for the institution, and for this purpose to publish an earnest appeal to the members and friends of the Protestant Episcopal Church, stating the wants of the Church with respect to clergymen, the number of young men of piety and talents desirous of an education for the ministry, but who are destitute of adequate pecuniary resources, and the indispensable necessity of a liberal endowment of the Theological Seminary, to the honour, prosperity, and vital interests of the Church.

The plan contemplated in the above resolutions not succeeding, another meeting of the committee was held in the city of Philadelphia, the 7th of February, 1819, the same members present as at the previous meeting. A letter was laid before the committee, by Bishop Hobart, from C. C. Moore, Esq., of the city of New York, addressed to him, containing an offer of the grant of sixty city lots, provided the buildings of the Theological school should be erected thereon. And the following resolves, proposed by Bishop Hobart, were adopted.

1. Resolved, That the offer of Mr. Moore be accepted, and that the buildings for the use of the Theological Seminary be erected on or near the lots of ground granted by Mr. Moore for the use of the institution

2. That as the funds of the institution do not admit of the adequate support of all the contemplated professors, the subjects assigned to the professors of systematic divinity, and of the ritual of the Church, and of pulpit eloquence, be at present assigned to the professor of biblical learning.

3. That in consideration of the more extensive sphere of duty assigned to the professor of biblical learning, and of his situation as having a family, his salary be fixed at two thousand five hundred dollars per annum, with a house, as soon as one can be erected; and, in the mean time, with an allowance of five hundred dollars per annum in lieu of a house, in the expectation of his applying himself solely to the discharge of the duties of his station,—and that the same consideration not applying to the professor of historic theology, his salary be fixed at one thousand dollars per annum, in the hope that the funds of the institution will speedily admit of a more adequate remuneration of his services, and also of securing to the in titution, the learning and talents of the Rev. Dr. Wharton, the professor of systematic theology, agreeably to the resolution of the 9th of October last.

4. That the Bishops, members of this Committee, who, agreeably to a resolution of the 9th of October last, were charged with making temporary arrangements for the management of the seminary, be further directed to frame and report to this Committee, a plan for the complete organization thereof.

The Committee were induced to make the arrangements, contained in the above resolutions, in the expectation that the prospect of the permanent establishment of the institution, under the professors appointed, if a sufficient support could be provided for them, would operate strongly in aid of the collection of funds for that object. No subsequent arrangements have been made; the Committee being persuaded that some new excitement is necessary in favour of the contemplated institution; and looking forward to the approaching meeting of the General Convention, as affording the only effectual means of awakening the attention of the members and friends of the Protestant Episcopal Church, to an object so essentially connected with its honour and prosperity.

For the state of the funds, the collections made, and the sums subscribed and not paid, we refer to the account of the treasurer and the exhibit annexed. In the State of New York, the sums subscribed which are considerable, being made payable on the condition of the whole sum subscribed, amounting to one hundred thousand dollars, only a small proportion of them have been collected. A bequest of one thousand dollars, of James M'Evers of the city of New York, to Bishop Hobart in trust for a theological school, has been paid by him to the treasurer of this institution. The lots granted by Mr. Moore are at present valuable, and as the city increases, might be made a source of large revenue. The professors have conducted the instructions of the institution, according to the Canons and the course of study prescribed by the House of Bishops.

SIGNED BY ORDER OF THE COMMITTEE:

WILLIAM WHITE, CHAIRMAN.

May 20th, 1820.

Dr. *The Protestant Episcopal Theological Seminary in account with D. J. Greene, Treasurer.* Cr.

Dr.

Date	Particulars	Amount
1818. Dec. 19th.	To paid draft of Rt. Rev. Bishop White, on the Bank of Pennsylvania, in favour of Rev. J. Kemper	28 85
1819. January 5th.	To cost of 4,300 dolls. six per cent. Treasury Note stock of 181–, at 99 1-4 per cent.	4,267 75
February 4th.	To cost of 500 dolls. six per cent. stock of 1813, at 100 1-2 per cent.	502 50
June 15th.	To cost of 1,200 dolls. six per cent. stock of 1812, at 101 per cent.	1,212
1820. January 10th.	To paid Rev. Dr. Jarvis, on account of his salary	1,500
April 5th.	To paid Rev. Mr. Turner	500
April 7th.	To paid Rev. Dr. Jarvis, the balance of the sum of 2,000 dolls. which I was authorized by the Rt. Rev. Bishop White, to pay to him as salary for one year, commencing April 1st, 1819	500
May 11th.	To paid Rev. Mr. Turner, the balance of the sum of 1,000 dolls. which I was authorized by the Rt. Rev. Bishop White to pay him as salary for one year, commencing April 1st, 1819—but which Mr. Turner computes from May 1st, 1819	500
	To balance credited in account,	1 15
		9,012 25

Errors excepted.

D. J. GREENE,
Treasurer.

New York, May 11th, 1820.

Cr.

Date	Particulars		Amount
1818. March 17th.	By Cash of Rt. Rev. Bishop Hobart on account of collections made by the Rev. T. C. Brownell,		4,000
April 7th.	By Cash of Rev. T. C. Brownell, balance of his collections		310
1819. January 9th.	By Cash of M. C. R. Duffie, as the donation of "an unknown friend"		20
January 30th.	By Cash of Rt. Rev. Bishop Bowen, as balance of his collections		474
March 30th.	By Cash of Rt. Rev. Bishop Hobart being collections of Rev. Mr. Wainwright	110	
	Fee to "N. B. and S. H. T."	30	
	22d Bequest of James M'Evers (of New York,)	1,000	
	Interest thereon-	52 50	
		1,192 50	1,192 50
April 12th.	By div. payable April 1st, on 4,800 dolls. six per cent. stock		72
August 23d.	By do July 1st, 6,000 do		90
October 12th.	By do Oct. 1st, 6,000 do		90
1820. January 10th.	By do Jan. 1st, 6,000 do		90
	By proceeds of six per cent. stock sold viz. 500 of 1813, bought Feb. 3d, 1819, 1,200 1812, June 15th, — 1,700 at 102 1-4 per cent.		1,738 25
	By a deposit in the Bank of South Carolina, by Rev. Dr. Gadsden, made in June, 1819		250
April 4th.	By div. payable April 1st, on 4,300 dolls. six per cent. stock		64 50
April 6th.	By proceeds of 600 dolls. of six per cent. stock, of 1812, at 103 1-2 per cent. part of 4,300, bought Jan. 5th, 1819		621
			9,012 25
May 11th.	By balance in Phenix Bank		1 15
	By six per cent. Treasury Note stock of 1812, standing in my name in trust for the Seminary, bearing interest from 1st April		3,700
			3,701 15

Recapitulation.

Collections in Carolina - - - -	4.560 00	
do Connecticut - -	110 00	
do New York - - -	1,576 50	
		6,246 50
Dividends on Stock, - - -		406 50
Gain on purchase of Stock, - - -	32 25	
Loss, - - - - - - - -	14 50	
	17 75	
Gain on sales of Stock, - - - - -	59 25	
		77 00
		6,730 00
Rt. Rev. Bishop White's order, - - -	28 85	
Salaries, - - - - - - - -	3,000	
		3,028 85
		3,701 15

Balance consists of Stock 3,700,—Cash 1 15

Exhibit by the Committee.

In addition to the above, it appears from the books of Dr. Brownell, that of the sums subscribed principally to the south of Maryland, $3,180, remain to be collected. And $15,275 is the amount of the sums subscribed in New York, to be paid on condition that the whole subscription shall reach $100,000.

Documents &c., referred to in the Report.

LETTER TO THE REV. NATHANIEL BOWEN, D. D.,

PHILADELPHIA, July 13, 1817.

REV. AND DEAR SIR,

With this letter, there are sent to you certified copies of extracts from the Journal of the late General Convention, on the subject of a Theological school: And there is subjoined to them a certificate of your appointment to the labour of soliciting donations, in certain specified States, for the accomplishing of that object.

From the circumstance of your being designated to this work by the Bishops of our Church, it ought to be believed that you are competent to the stating of the reasons which have occasioned the contemplated solicitation. Of your sufficiency, no one is better satisfied than the writer of this letter. But, as for some years past the founding of a Theological school has been a subject much discussed in his personal intercourse with his brethren in the Episcopacy, he thinks there may be a use in his stating to you, to be communicated as in your discretion may seem expedient, the important point of view in which, to the best of his recollection and belief, the subject presents itself to their minds, as well as to his own.

He perceives an inducement to this communication, in his being aware, that there are some who, laying due stress on the religious qualifications called for by the ministry, and being laudably desirous of fencing the sanctity of its character in this respect, entertain the opinion, that it requires but a slender furniture of intellectual information.

If this opinion were carried much farther; and if it were contended, concerning the whole Christian world, that it has no need even of elementary instruction, for the benefiting by those holy Scriptures, which themselves testify that they were written for our learning, although extravagant, it would be consistent. On the other hand, if it be confessed that at least some persons must be possessed of what can only be the fruit of study, aided by human art; the only questions which occur, relate to the extent in which literary information is necessary, and to the persons who should be especially looked to for the possessing of it. The result of this train of sentiment must be the conviction, that no branch of learning, which has a tendency to open the sense of Scripture, can be foreign to the clerical department. That especial importance attaches to the languages, in which it has pleased the Holy Spirit to convey to the world the glad tidings of salvation, cannot consistently be denied by any, who know that "faith cometh by hearing, and hearing by the word of God:" by that word, locked up in languages not in common use. It would be easy to show, that the like importance is to be ascribed to history, to chronology, to criticism, and to the knowledge of ancient customs. And there cannot be an exclusion of natural science, so long as this shall be a store-house, from which the infidel draws his weapons, for the assailing of the Christian fortress.

It is known to many, with what dishonest artifice the enemies of our holy religion are continually bringing forward frequently refuted objections, for the deceiving of the ignorant, and the beguiling of the unstable. To whom shall such persons look, for the being confirmed in their most holy faith, if not to those who have consented to be vested with the official character of its defenders?

Besides the shock to be expected from the quarter of infidelity, there is that of the obtrusion of opinions grafted on the word of God, some centuries subsequent to the Christian era; and from which this Church was purged at the time of the reformation. From this cause their arise questions, which respect even the object of divine worship. It is easy to solve them satisfactorily from the word of God, and from the practice of the primitive Church; while, on the other hand, plausible pretensions are set up, which not only ensnare weak minds, but may even be formidable to persons of considerable strength of intellect, if there are wanting the resources for the detecting of traditionary imposture; to which, of course, the Protestant minister of the Gospel is at any time ready to surrender any portion of his flock; if he does not find in his acquirements a counterpoise to the continually existing danger.

Among Protestants also there are opinions, pronounced by our ecclesiastical standards and institutions, to be far wide of "the faith which was once delivered to the saints." On the one hand, there are denials of the divinity and of the atonement of the blessed person, than whom "there is none other name given among men whereby they can be saved," while, on the other, there are attached to those essential truths, dogmas unknown in the Christian Church, until some hundreds of years after its establishment. Further, there is the rejection of the divine designation of an order of men, of whom it is said—"How shall they hear without a preacher; and how shall they preach except they be sent?" And there is a disallowance of those sacraments, one of which is "the washing of regeneration"; and the other is ordained to be "a showing forth of the Lord's death till he come." There are named but few of the errors, which strip Christianity of some of its most endearing properties. For the sustaining of them the stores of literature are ransacked and abused; and they must therefore be met by learning properly applied.

It would be an entire misunderstanding of what has been stated, if it were considered as holding up any measure of theological learning, as what may dispense with the religion of the heart. But it has been found, that where no just censure has lain for deficiency in this respect, persons have been seduced from our pale, through the want of pastoral ability to defend its doctrines and its institutions; while it has also had the effect, through the medium of the lessening of the ministerial character, to detach many from an attendance on divine ordinances, and from whatever constitutes a visible profession of religion. This is the result, not only with men of cultivated understandings, who are likely to be the first to disesteem a pastor far below them in the scale of theological acquirement; but descends to persons of the lowest grade in society, who insensibly receive their impressions of official ability from the higher.

The bishops, in their anxiety for the encouragement of literature, do but endeavour to perpetuate the character of the venerable Church from which their Episcopacy is derived; and of the institutions of which they are not ashamed to wish an imitation in this Church as ability and other circumstances may permit. When, in the sixteenth century, the Church of England disengaged herself from the yoke of a foregin hierarchy, the good would have been evanescent, if, with the regaining of her integrity, she had not cultivated the literary means of defending it in the times to follow. In every succeeding age, and in the present not less than in any other, learned divines of her communion have ranked among the foremost in the defence and in the elucidati n of divine truth; of which their works translated into different languages of Europe, are imperishable evidence. One reason of the glory of the Church of England in this respect, are the endowments which she possesses, for divines who devote themselves to sacred literature, as a field of labour distinct from that of a parochial ministry. For while we consider the latter department, as too important to be superceded by any studies of the closet; yet, where the one may be perused by a few of the clergy, for the better securing of the proficiency of the whole, it is an important gain to the church of Christ; and in part, the ground on which a Theological School is at this time an object of desire.

While we look up with filial reverence to the example of the Church of England, we do not withhold the tribute of praise from those religious communions in the United States, which have been before us in their exertions to secure the literary sufficiency of their future ministers. We honour their conduct in this matter: we propo e the liberality of their respective members, to the emulation of the members of our Church: and we lament the lateness of similar industry and public spirit among ourselves. For this, the only apology must be the destitute condition in which our Churches were left by the war of the revolution; the more immediate measures, necessary for the organizing of our communion, and the demands for the supply of a ministry, accommodated in some instances rather to the necessities of congregations, than to what it were wished to be considered as a standard of sufficiency. Whatever may be the weight of these considerations, it is to be hoped that the time is come, when there may be successfully attempted the long neglected provision; and when a claim may be made, on the ground of the excellency of the institutions of this Church, of its respectability in the eye of the world, and of the wealth of a great proportion of its members.

The preceding sentiments have not been expressed without the being aware, that independently on the establishment of a Theological school, the learning called for by the ministry may be the acquirement of private study; especially when encouraged and aided by parochial clergymen of acknowledged talents and attainments. But, setting aside the danger of being misdirected in the choice of a guide; it must be obvious in this, as in every line of literary pursuit, first, in regard to the teacher, that consummate ability is best acquired by the devoting of all his talents and all his time, to the specific branch for which he has been selected; and further, in regard to the learner, that proficiency is much promoted by an association of kindred minds, in the same honourable search of truth; it being the best mean of excitement of ardour and of the securing of diligence. Although these are considerations which the reason of the thing suggests, and which experience confirms, they ought not to be carried to the extent of shutting the door to the ministry against a sufficiency of information, from whatever source it may have been obtained. Nothing of this sort is contemplated by the proposers of the present design; who, while they advocate what, in their opinion, and in that of the wisest men of various denominations, is the best expedient for the obtaining of a learned ministry, are desirous of resting resort to the school on the talents and the zeal which they expect to be conspicuous in its professors; aud not on an exclusive privilege to be vested in them for ecclesiastical education.

You will consider me, Rev. and dear sir, not as undertaking to display fully the advantages to be expected by our Church from a Theological seminary; but only as suggesting hints, which may be enlarged on by you in conversation, as circumstances may require. Even of going thus far, I should doubt of there being any use, were it not, that I hereby express my own anxious desire, and testify to that of my brethren, the other bishops, for the success of an enterprize, in which we fondly anticipate the supply of a learned and godly ministry to our Church, when there shall be an end of all our cares and labours in her behalf.

With my wishes and prayers for your personal safety and satisfaction in the good work before you, I remain, Rev. and dear Sir,

Your affectionate Friend and Brother,

WILLIAM WHITE,

Bishop of the Prot. Epis. Church in the State of Pennsylvania.

Extracts from the Right Rev. Bishop Hobart's address to the Convention of the State of New York, Oct. 22, 1817.

"In the month of May a meeting of the General Convention of our Church was held in this city, which, from the respectability of its members, and the objects of its counsels, excited great interest. Among the measures there adopted, provision was made for the establishment of a Theological school under the auspices of the General Convention. The clergyman appointed to collect subscriptions in this diocese is pursuing his arduous work with all that zeal which a strong sense of the importance of the object can inspire; and by the documents with which he is furnished, and his own judicious representations, is calling forth the liberality of the community.

"But I think I should fail in my duty, if I neglected to impress on you my brethren, and through you, on the Episcopalians of the diocese, the immense importance of the proposed Theological establishment. There cannot be an object presented to them, which has equal claims on their beneficence.

Without a ministry the Church cannot *exist*; and destitute of a *learned*, as well as a *pious* ministry, she cannot *flourish*. These are axioms, which it would be an insult to the understanding of any person to suppose that he denies or doubts. As a *general* proposition, it is also true, that the ministry will not be distinguished for learning, unless there are public institutions, which, in the professorships attached to them, in the libraries with which they are furnished, and in the association of young men of similar pursuits and views, supply both the most advantageous *means* of theological improvement, and the most powerful *motives* diligently and faithfully to employ these means. A candidate for orders thus situated, directed by able affectionate, and pious professors, having access to richly furnished libraries, associated in the exercises of piety, as well as in his studies with those who are preparing for the exalted office of ministers of Christ and stewards of the mysteries of God, would make much greater and more substantial progress in all the preparatory qualifications for the ministry, than if left to solitary instruction, and solitary study.

"But a still further, and most eminent benefit of the contemplated Theological school, will consist in the pecuniary aids which it will furnish to youths of piety and talents, who are destitute of the funds to procure the necessary education for the ministry. Young men of this description have often furnished the brightest examples of ministerial fidelity, talents, and zeal. Many such, however, are now lost to the church, from the want of funds with which to aid them in procuring the necessary education. There can be no species of benevolence more grateful to the friends of religion, and of the temporal and eternal happiness of mankind, than that which takes a youth of piety and talents, from a state of depression and obscurity, and furnishing him with the means of education and of theological study, prepares him for becoming the respectable and successful herald of the cross of the Redeemer and the dispenser, under God, of spiritual blessings to his fellow men.

" But for all these purposes—for the salaries of professors for procuring libraries, for supporting candidates for the ministry, destitute of pecuniary means, for erecting the requisite buildings, funds are necessary, and *large* funds. This, then, is no ordinary call on the liberality of Episcopalians. It is a call, on the successful issue of which, in procuring *large* contributions, depend, if not the existence, certainly the extension and prosperity of their church. I would respectfully say to you, brethren, especially my brethren of the Laity, and to Episcopalians in general—Look at what is done in this respect, by *other Christian denominations*—professorships handsomely endowed, commodious buildings, extensive libraries, numerous students. They annually send forth ministers disciplined by the exercises of piety, and fitted by the studies of the school for the eloquent and faithful exercise of their functions. Ought we not to be alarmed for the welfare of our own Church, destitute as she is of all public provision for theological education? Benevolent individuals of other denominations freely bestow contributions to this object to the amount of hundreds, and frequently of thousands of dollars. Should we not be excited to at least, equal liberality in the cause of a church which has every possible claim on our affection, and on our zealous exertions? Many Episcopalians in this city, and elsewhere in the state, have already liberally contributed. They will have the prayers and the gratitude of the Church, and affording the most effectual means of perpetuating the blessings of our holy religion, they will have the gratitude of posterity; they will not be forgotton, for this good which they have done, by their God. May their example be emulated by others; may every Episcopalian, when called on for his subscription to the theological school, consider that he is to make his contribution to an object of more importance to the interests of religion and the Church, than any other for which he can be solicited; and which, therefore, demands the largest exercise of beneficence.

PHILADELPHIA, December 12, 1817.

GENTLEMEN,

IT having been represented to me by the members, residing in New York, of the committee appointed by the late General Convention, to carry into effect the resolution of that body, for the institution of a theological seminary, as the wish of Dr. Bowen, who had been appointed to collect subscriptions for the purpose, in the State of New York, that more persons should be authorized to aid in that duty; and as expedient and desirable, in order to the more effectual prosecution of it; and it being also represented, that you are willing to serve the Church in this important matter; viz.

I do accordingly, by the desire, and with the advice and concurrence of a majority of the above mentioned committee, hereby nominate and appoint you to collect subscriptions for the uses of the General Theological Seminary, to be instituted and conducted under the authority of the General Convention of the Protestant Episcopal Church in the United States; requesting you to use your best exertions in this behalf, and to deposit all such sums as you may receive in the hands of David I. Greene, Esq. cashier of the Phœnix Bank in New York, to be by him held, or invested in approved stock, subject to such disposition as may hereafter be made thereof by the authority of the General Convention.

WILLIAM WHITE,

Bishop of the Prot. Epis. Church in the Commonwealth of Pennsylvania, and Chairman of the Theological Committee.

To the Members of the Protestant Episcopal Church in the United States.

The committee of the said Church appointed at the last General Convention on the subject of a Theological Seminary, being now assembled in the city of Philadelphia, address the members of their communion on the important subject: and in the discharge of this duty, they enjoy the advantage of a unanimity of opinion, among themselves, manifested on the first comparison of their respective views of what had been committed to their consideration.

They perceive the importance of carrying the design into effect, at all events; although doubtless, it will be with a degree of usefulness bearing some proportion to the means with which they may be supplied, by the liberality of those who may consent with them in the object of their solicitude. The most essential supply of the exigencies of the church in this institution, will be the appointing of three professors, whose respective services may be applied to so many different subdivisions of theological science. Biblical learning, comprehending the exposition of the Holy Scriptures, with whatever relates to the authenticity of the sacred books, and the correct translation of them—Systematic theology, giving correct views of the doctrines of scripture, with the authorities sustaining them, and what may be called historic theology, giving correct information of the state of the Church in all ages, and of the Church of England in particular, from the period of the reformation. In this subdivision, will be embraced a knowledge of the opinions of the early fathers, of the constitution of the Christian Church and of the various orders of the ministry. It is desirable, that provision may be made for the maintenance of the professors; so as to detach them from all concerns of parochial cure; without which, the design may be carried into operation, but not with equal prospect of benefit to the Church. It is not improbable, that the system may be hereafter improved, by the appointment of additional professors, especially in some of the learned languages; but whose subsistence may not be altogether dependent on their professorships.

The appointment of a professor, whose services shall be devoted to the exerc sing of the students in composition and delivery, will be highly expedient. In the mean time, such important objects are not to be unattended to. But whether they may be the most usefully attached to one of the three professorships defined, or be attended to by each professor, in his sphere, in exercises bottomed on the subjects which will be before him may be left to future deliberation.

The next object of expense occuring to the committee, is the erecting of a building for the di erent lectures, and for a library, the apartment for which may serve as a place of worship for the professors and the students. The committee do not contemplate the appropriation of any part of the funds, to the erection of a building for the residence of the students. The accommodation of the professors with houses, which may constitute a part of their maintenance is however deemed desirable.

But while the committee calculate, that this institution will furnish the means of theological attainments on an extensive scale, to all classes of candidates for orders; they regard as an object of peculiar importance the education for the ministry of young men of piety and talents, who may be destitute of pecuniary resources.

When the General Convention sanctioned the establishment of a Theological Seminary, they commissioned three reverend gentlemen to solicit subscriptions in the different departments of the United States. Two of the reverend gentlemen have been prevented by other occupations from entering on the work: and the only gentleman who undertook it, found his district disproportioned to the fulfilment of the expectations of the Church.

Accordingly the committee have found it necessary to make new arrangements. The persons appointed in consequence of these arrangements, will be furnished with the necessary evidences of their authority.

The committee will finish their present session, without those details of the projected seminary, which, according to a provision of the General Convention, must be submitted to the Bishops of this Church, and obtain the consent of the majority of them before the plan can go into operation. They defer those details until there shall be ascertained the amount of the collections; which must govern, in determining the amount of the expense to be incurred. Those details have been the subject of serious deliberation with the committee; but from their great importance, the committee are desirous of bestowing on them still farther consideration, and they entertain the confident expectation, that the plan, in its principles and details, will be satisfactory to the members of the Church; and agreeable to the views of the General Convention, as expressed in their resolutions on the subject.

The committee ought not to conclude this address, without earnestly entreating every member of their communion, whom providence may have blessed with abundance or with competency, to consider the proposed institution, as of the utmost importance, for the sustaining of its reputation, and for the giving of due effect to the labours of its ministry. They would also earnestly impress the necessity of extraordinary liberality towards an institution, the establishment of which is so fundamentally connected with the interests and the prosperity of the Church.

The committee, although not unaware that there are some, who conceive of the clerical calling, as requiring but a slender furniture of intellectual information, accommodate this address to persons, who know, that for the defending of the Christian fortress against the assaults of infidelity, the ministerial combatant must be possessed of weapons of defence, drawn from the same stores which they abuse, of history, of chronology, of criticism, and of natural science; and that the same preparation is required for the defending of the doctrines of the reformation against traditionary imposture; and for the vindicating of the faith of the earliest and best ages of the Church, against innumerable novelties of modern times.

In all exertions for the purpose which have been disclosed, this Church will be treading in the steps of the mother Church of England; and will be aiming at an imitation of attainments, which have rendered her the most distinguished Church of the reformation. By the act of transmitting to us her episcopacy, she has deposited a trust in the matter in question, and in some degree committed her reputation on the event of a due discharge of it.

Even in the circumstances of a great and increasing measure of literary improvement, in a considerable proportion of the members of this Church, there may be perceived a motive for a pròportionate improvement of the literary qualifications of those who are to officiate among them in the ministry. For it is naturally the effect of the contrary want of qualification, that men of cultivated understanding, exchange their religious connexion for some other, in which they are no longer witnesses of what they consider dishonour done to religion in general, and to the Church in which they were baptized and educated, in particular; or have recourse to the worse retreat of the abandonment of a visible profession, and perhaps to infidelity.

Under the weight of these considerations, the success of the design is now committed to the blessing of God, through the medium of the solicited liberality of those who owe to his bounty whatever they may possess, and are dependent on him for its continuance.

(Signed)

WILLIAM WHITE,
Bishop of the Protestant Episcopal Church in the Commonwealth of Pennsylvania.

JOHN HENRY HOBART,
Bishop of the Protestant Episcopal Church in the State of New York.

JOHN CROES,
Bishop of the Protestant Episcopal Church in the State of New Jersey.

CHARLES HENRY WHARTON,
Rector of St. Mary's Church in Burlington.

W. MEREDITH.

The subscribers, members of the committee, unavoidably prevented from attendance on the framing of the preceding address, approve of, and concur in it.

(Signed)

WILLIAM HARRIS,
President of Columbia College, New York.

CHARLES F. MERCER,
of Virginia.

NO. II.

The committee appointed at the last General Convention, on the subject of a theological school, beg leave to make a further report.

In the caption to the subscription book drawn up by Dr.

Bowen, it is stated that "persons will pay their subscriptions as they shall choose agreeably to the one or other of the following conditions." And one of these conditions is, that "any individual may subscribe on the condition of not being required to pay until one hundred thousand dollars in all shall have been subscribed. This caption, it was thought, gave all the subscribers the option, when called on to pay, of declining unless one hundred thousand dollars had been subscribed. But Dr. Bowen authorizes the committee to state that he considers that no sums of those subscribed at his solicitation are liable to the above condition except those which are stated to be so by a memorandum which the subscribers have annexed to their names on the pages of the book of subscriptions. The sums of this description amount to five thousand five hundred dollars subscribed by eight persons.

It may be proper futher to notice that the Rev. professors of the seminary not wishing that the studies of each year, the recitations of each week, and the proportion of the recitations to be assigned to each of the professors should be surrendered to their direction, applied to the committee for instructions to those purposes. The committee confiding in the sufficiency of the professors were content to leave the arrangements in question to their determination; especially, as they were matters in which experience might dictate alterations from time to time. There was however, an endeavour to obtain a meeting of the committee in October last; which failed on account of the indisposition of some of the members and the necessary engagements of others. A meeting was held in December, but there being a mere quorum, the time being so near this triennial meeting, and the institution not having suffered nor being likely to suffer in the business, no order was taken thereon.

WILLIAM WHITE, *Chairman.*

May 22, 1820.

NO. III.

CONSTITUTION OF THE PROTESTANT EPISCOPAL MISSIONARY SOCIETY IN THE UNITED STATES, FOR FOREIGN AND DOMESTIC MISSIONS.

OF THE NAME AND OFFICERS.

1. This institution shall be designated "The Protestant Episcopal Missionary Society in the United States, for Foreign and

Domestic Missions." Its officers shall consist of a president, vice presidents, two secretaries, and a treasurer, together with such officers as may be deemed necessary.

2. The affairs of this society shall be conducted by a board of twenty four managers, to be appointed by the general convention, twelve of whom shall reside in or near the city of Philadelphia, and six members shall constitute a quorum for the transaction of business.

3 The officers of this society, with the exception of those provided for in this constitution, shall be appointed by the board of managers, and continue in office during the recess of the general convention, or until others are appointed.

4 The presiding bishop of this church shall be the president of this society, and the other bishops, vice presidents, in the order of seniority establi hed in their house.

OF AUXILIARY SOCIETIES.

The board of managers shall take such measures as they may deem proper, to establish auxiliary societies; to secure patronage, and to enlarge the funds of the institution. The bishop of every diocese shall be president of the auxiliary societies, organized in the same.

OF MEMBERS.

1. Every person subscribing annually, the sum of three dollars, shall be a member of this society during the continuance of such subscription.

2. Every person giving a benefaction of fifty dollars or upwards, at one time, shall be considered a patron of this society.

3. The subscription books shall be so arranged, that at the time of subscribing, every person may contribute either to the cause of foreign or domestic missions; and the money shall be appropriated according to the intention of the donor.

4. If any money shall be given to this society by individuals, congregations or other societies, without specifying to what particular object it is to be applied, the board of managers may appropriate it as they shall think best.

OF THE FUNDS.

All benefactions and donations, exceeding the sum of fifty dollars, made to this society if requested by the contributors at the time of subscription or donation, shall be vested in some good and productive stock, and the interest only of such monies shall be appropriated to the objects of the institution.

OF THE DUTIES OF OFFICERS.

1. The board of managers shall have power to make all by-laws necessary for their own regulation, and to appoint from among their number, all such committees, as shall be necessary to transact the various parts of duty assigned them.

2. The treasurer shall keep distinct accounts of the money received by him, whether to be applied to foreign or domestic missionary purposes; and shall be required to render his account at least once in every year, to the board of managers.

3. The board of managers shall make a full report of their proceedings, and of the funds of the society, at every meeting of the General Convention.

4. No missionary of this society shall be employed within the bounds of any organized diocess, except with the consent and approbation, and under the direction of the Bishop; or, if there be no Bishop, the ecclesiastical authority of the same.

CONCLUSION.

It is recomended to every member of this society, to pray to Almighty God for his blessing upon its designs, under the full conviction, that unless " He directs us in all our doings, with his most gracious favour, and furthers us with his continual help," we cannot reasonably hope, either to procure suitable persons to act as missionaries, or expect that their endeavours will be crowned with success.

NO. IV.

Addition to the report on the state of the church, received after the rising of the convention. (*Committee of publication.*)

In the eastern diocese, since the last General Convention, eight hundred and sixty-six persons have been confirmed by the apostolic rite of laying on of hands. Twenty have been admitted as candidates for holy orders; of whom there are ten still remaining on that list. Messrs James B. Howe, George Taft, Allston Gibbs, Calvin Wolcott, George Otis, Joel Clapp Herbert Marshall, Carlton Chase, Patrick H. Folker, Jasper Adams, Addison Searle, Edward Lippit, Rodolphus Dickinson, Isaac Boyle, Marcus A. Perry, and Milton Wilcox have been ordained deacons. The Rev. Stephen Beach, Gideon W. Olney, Chever Felch, George T. Chapman, George Leonard, Benjamin B. Smith, Calvin Wolcott, James B. Howe, George Taft, Patrick H. Folker, and Joel Clapp, deacons, have been admitted to the order of presbyters. The Rev. William Montague, of Massachusetts, and the Rev. James Nichols, of Vermont, having declared their intention no longer to officiate as ministers of this Church, have been suspended from all exercise of the said ministry according to the seventeenth canon of the General Convention, in the year of our Lord 1817. Seven new churches have been erected and consecrated to the worship of Almighty God. Two more, it is expected, will soon be finished.

And a good house already built, has been obtained by a new parish in Claremont, New Hampshire. The Churches have been regularly visited, and are generally in a flourishing state.

List of the Clergy

OF THE

PROTESTANT EPISCOPAL CHURCH

In the United States of America.

EASTERN DIOCESE.

Composed of the States of Maine, New Hampshire, Massachusetts, Vermont, and Rhode Island.

The Right Rev. Alexander Viets Griswold, D. D., Bishop.

MAINE.

The Rev. G. W. Olney, Rector of Christ Church, Gardiner.
The Rev. P. S. Ten Broeck, Rector of St. Paul's Church, Portland.

NEW HAMPSHIRE.

The Rev. Charles Burroughs, Rector of St. John's Church, Portsmouth.
The Rev. Robert Fowle, Rector of Trinity Church, Holderness.
The Rev. James B. Howe, Rector of Union Church, Claremont.
The Rev. Addison Searle, Deacon, officiating in Concord, and Hopkinton.

MASSACHUSETTS.

The Rev. Thomas Carlile, Rector of St. Peter's Church, Salem.
The Rev. Asa Eaton, Rector of Christ Church, Boston, and St. Mary's, Newton.
The Rev. Cheever Felch, Chaplain, United States Navy, officiating in St. Paul's Church, Dedham.
The Rev. John S. J. Gardiner, D. D., Rector of Trinity Church, Boston.
The Rev. Samuel Griswold, Rector of St. James's Church, Great Barrington.
The Rev. Samuel F. Jarvis, D. D., Rector of St. Paul's Church, Boston.
The Rev. James Morss, Rector of St. Paul's Church, Newburyport.
The Rev. Titus Strong, Rector of St. James's Church, Greenfield.
The Rev. Calvin Wolcott, Rector of St. Peters' Church, Hanover, and —— Church, Marshfield.
The Rev. Aaron Humphrey, officiating at Lanesborough.
The Rev. Edward Lippitt, Missionary in Quincy and Bridgewater.
The Rev. Isaac Boyle, Deacon, officiating in Hopkinton.
The Rev. James Bowen, residing in Framingham.

VERMONT.

The Rev. Stephen Beach, Rector of Trinity Church, Fairfield, Grace Church, Sheldon, and Union Church, St. Albans.
The Rev. Abraham Bronson, Rector of —— Church, Manchester, and —— Church, Arlington.
The Rev. Carlton Chase, Deacon, officiating in Immanuel Church, Bellows' Falls.
The Rev. Joel Clapp, Rector of —— Church, Shelburne.
The Rev. George Leonard, Rector of St. Paul's Church, Windsor.

RHODE ISLAND.

The Right Rev. Alexander V. Griswold, D.D., Rector of St. Michael's Church, Bristol.
The Rev, Jasper Adams, Deacon, Professor of Mathematics and Natural Philosophy, in Brown University, Providence.
The Rev. John Laurens Blake, Rector of St. Paul's Church, North Providence.
The Rev. Nathan Bourne Crocker, Rector of St. John's Church, Providence.
The Rev. Lemuel Burge, Deacon, officiating in St. Paul's Church, North Kingston, and St. Paul's Church, South Kingston.
The Rev. G. Taft, Assistant Minister in Bristol.
The Rev. Salmon Wheaton, Rector of Trinity Church, Newport.

CONNECTICUT.

The Right Rev. Thomas C. Brownell, D. D. LL. D., Bishop, and Rector of Christ Church, Hartford.
The Rev. John Tyler, Rector of Christ Church, Norwich.
The Rev. Philo Shelton, Rector of Trinity Church, Fairfield, St. John's, Bridgeport.
The Rev. William Smith, D. D., residing at Norwalk.
The Rev. Ashbel Baldwin, Rector of Christ Church, Stratford.
The Rev. Tillotson Brownson, D.D., Principal of the Episcopal Academy, Cheshire.
The Rev. Reuben Ives, Rector of St. Peter's Church, Cheshire, and St. Andrews, Meriden.
The Rev. Truman Marsh, Rector of the Associated Churches in Litchfield.
The Rev. Jonathan Judd, Rector of St. John's Church, Stamford and the Church in Horseneck.
The Rev. Daniel Burhans, Rector of Trinity Church, Newtown.
The Rev. Menzies Rayner, Rector of St. Paul's and St. Peter's Churches, Huntington.
The Rev. Calvin White, residing in Derby.
The Rev. Asa Cornwall, Assistant in the Episcopal Academy, Cheshire.
The Rev. Joseph Perry, Minister of the Churches in East Haven and West Haven.
The Rev. Benjamin Benham, Rector of the Churches in New Milford, Brookfield and Bridgewater.
The Rev. David Baldwin, Rector of Christ Church in Guilford, St. John's, North Guilford, and Union Church, North Killingworth.
The Rev. Joseph D. Welton, residing at Waterbury.
The Rev. Birdsey G. Noble, Rector of Christ Church, Middletown.

The Rev. Bethel Judd, Minister of the Church in New London.
The Rev. Isaac Jones, Assistant Minister in the Associated Churches, Litchfield.
The Rev. Jasper D. Jones, residing in Cheshire.
The Rev. Sturgis Gilbert, Rector of the Churches in Woodbury and Roxbury.
The Rev. Reuben Sherwood, Rector of St. Paul's Church, Norwalk.
The Rev. Charles Smith, Rector of St. Matthew's Church, Wilton.
The Rev. Harry Croswell, Rector of Trinity Church, New Haven.
The Rev. Alpheus Gear, Rector of St. John's Church, Waterbury.
The Rev. Rodney Rossiter, Rector of St. Peter's and St. Matthew's Church, Plymouth.
The Rev. Smith Miles, Rector of the Church in Chatham.
The Rev. Solomon Blakeley, officiating in the Churches at East Haddam, Middle Haddam, and Pettipauge.
The Rev. Chauncey Prindle, officiating in the Church in Woodbridge.
The Rev. Peter G. Clark, Assistant Minister, Norwich.
The Rev. Nathan B. Burgis, officiating Minister of the Church in Glastenbury.
The Rev. George S. White, residing at Brooklyn.
The Rev. George B. Andrews, officiating Minister at Kent, Sharon, and New Preston.
The Rev. Nathaniel S. Wheaton, Assistant Minister, Hartford.
The Rev. Origen P. Holcomb, officiating in the Churches of Branford and North Branford.
The Rev. David Belden, residing in Wilton.
The Rev. Nathaniel F. Bruce, M. D., residing at Hartford.
The Rev. Samuel H. Turner, Professor of Historic Theology in the Theological Seminary of the Protestant Episcopal Church in the United States, New Haven.

NEW YORK.

The Right Rev. John Henry Hobart, D. D., Bishop, and Rector of Trinity Church, including St. Pauls and St. John's Chapels, New York.
The Rev. Henry Anthon, Minister of St. Paul's Church, Redhook, Dutchess County.
The Rev. Benjamin P. Aydelott, Deacon, residing in New York.
The Rev. Deodatus Babcock, Deacon, officiating in St. Paul's Church, Buffalo, Niagara County.
The Rev. Amos G. Baldwin, officiating in Ogdensburg, St. Lawrence County.
The Rev. William Barlow, Deacon, Minister of St. John's Church, Canandaigua, Ontario County.
The Rev. William Berrian, an Assistant Minister of Trinity Church, New York.
The Rev. Thomas Breintnall, Rector of Zion Church, New York.
The Rev. David Brown. Rector of St. James's Church, Hyde Park, Dutchess County.
The Rev. John Brown, Rector of St. Thomas's Church, New Windsor, and Minister of St. George's Church, Newburgh, Orange County.
The Rev. Nathaniel F. Bruce, M. D., residing in Catskill, Greene County.
The Rev. Barzillai Bulkley, Rector of St. George's Church, Flushing, Long Island.

The Rev. Leveret Bush, Deacon, Missionary at Oxford, Chenango County, and parts adjacent.
The Rev. David Butler, Rector of St. Paul's Church, Troy, Rensselaer County.
The Rev. Orin Clark, Rector of Trinity Church, Geneva, Ontario County.
The Rev. William A. Clark, Minister of Christ Church, Balston Spa, Saratoga County.
The Rev. James P. Cotter, Deacon, Assistant Instructor in the Academy at Jamaica, Queens County.
The Rev. William Creighton, Rector of St. Mark's Church, New York.
The Rev. Francis H. Cuming, Deacon, Missionary at Binghamton, Broome County, and parts adjacent.
The Rev. Asahel Davis, Deacon, residing in Albany.
The Rev. H. De Lancey, Deacon, officiating in Grace Church, New York.
The Rev. Henry J. Feltus, Rector of St. Stephen's Church, New York.
The Rev. Samuel Fuller, Missionary in Albany and Green Counties.
The Rev. Ezekiel G. Gear, Missionary in Onondaga County, and Counties adjacent.
The Rev. John Grigg, jun., Deacon, Minister of St. John's Church, Philipsburg.
The Rev. Charles W. Hamilton, Missionary in Washington County, and parts adjacent.
The Rev. William Hammel, residing in New York.
The Rev. William Harris, D. D., President of Columbia College, New York.
The Rev. Seth Hart, Rector of St. George's Church, Hempstead, Long Island.
The Rev. Samuel Haskell, Rector of Christ Church, Rye, Westchester County.
The Rev. David Huntington, Rector of St. John's Church, Delhi, and Minister of St. Peter's Church, Waterville, Delaware County.
The Rev. Nathaniel Huse, Minister of St. Paul's Church, Paris, Oneida County.
The Rev. Stephen Jewett, Missionary in Washington County.
The Rev. Evan Malbone Johnson, Rector of St. James's Church, New Town, Long Island.
The Rev. Cave Jones, residing in New York.
The Rev. Ravaud Kearney, Minister of St. Paul's Church, Eastchester, and Trinity Church, New Rochelle, Westchester County.
The Rev. William B. Lacey, Rector of St. Peter's Church, Albany.
The Rev. James Keeler, Deacon, Minister of St. Matthews Church, Unadilla, Otsego County.
The Rev. Thomas Lyell, Rector of Christ Church, New York.
The Rev. Charles M'Cabe, Deacon, officiating in St. James's Church, Milton, Saratoga County.
The Rev. Daniel M'Donald, Minister of Trinity Church, and Principal of the Academy, Fairfield, Herkimer County.
The Rev. John M'Vickar, Professor of Rhetoric and Moral Philosophy in Columbia College, New York.
The Rev. James Milnor, D. D., Rector of St. George's Church, New York.
The Rev. David Moore, Rector of St. Andrew's Church, including Trinity Chapel, Staten Island.
The Rev. Daniel Nash, Missionary in Otsego and Chenango Counties.
The Rev. Samuel Nicholls, Minister of St. Matthew's Church, Bedford and North Castle, Westchester County.

The Rev. George H. Norton, Missionary in Seneca and Ontario Counties.
The Rev. Benjamin T. Onderdonk, an Assistant Minister of Trinity Church, New York.
The Rev. Henry U. Onderdonk, M. D., Minister of St. Ann's Church, Brooklyn, Long Island.
The Rev. George Otis, Deacon, Waddington and Madrid, St. Lawrence County.
The Rev. Amos Pardee, Missionary at Manlius, Onondago County, and parts adjacent.
The Rev. Henri L. P. F. Peneveyre, Rector of St. Esprit, New York.
The Rev. Samuel Phinney, Minister of St. Andrew's Church, Coldenham, Orange County.
The Rev. William Powell, residing at Bloomingdale, New York.
The Rev. Joseph Prentiss, Rector of Trinity Church, Athens, and St. Luke's Church, Catskill, Greene County.
The Rev. Alexis P. Proal, Deacon, Minister of St. John's Church, Johnstown, Montgomery County.
The Rev. William Richmond, Deacon, Minister of St. Michael's and St. James's Churches, New York.
The Rev. John Reed, Rector of Christ Church. Poughkeepsie, Dutchess County.
The Rev. Joshua M. Rogers, Missionary at Turin, Lewis County, and parts adjacent.
The Rev. Gilbert H. Sayres, Rector of Grace Church, Jamaica, Long Island.
The Rev. Charles Seabury, Rector of Caroline Church, Setauket, and Missionary to Huntington and Islip, Long Island.
The Rev. Henry M. Shaw, Deacon, Minister of Trinity Church, Utica, Oneida County.
The Rev. Lucius Smith, Minister of St. Peter's Church, Auburn, Cayuga County.
The Rev. Cyrus Stebbins, Minister of Christ Church, Hudson, Columbia County.
The Rev. James Thompson, Missionary in Greene and Delaware Counties.
The Rev. Frederick F. Tiffany, Deacon, Cooperstown, Otsego County.
The Rev. John V. E. Thorne, Minister of St. George's Church, Flushing, Queens County.
The Rev. George Upfold, M. D., Deacon, Minister of Trinity Church, Lansingburgh, Rensselaer County, and Grace Church, Waterford, Saratoga County.
The Rev. Frederick Vanhorne, residing at Coldenham, Orange County.
The Rev. Jonathan M. Wainwright, an Assistant Minister of Trinity Church, New York.
The Rev. Alanson W. Welton, Missionary, in Ontario and adjacent Counties.
The Rev. Eli Wheeler, Minister of Christ Church, North Hempstead, Long Island.
The Rev. Russel Wheeler, Rector of Zion Church, Butternuts; and Missionary in other parts of Otsego County.
The Rev. Isaac Wilkins, D. D., Rector of St. Peter's Church, West Chester.
The Rev. Samuel Nicholls, Deacon, residing in Connecticut, officiates every second Sunday in St. Matthew's Church, Bedford, Westchester County.
Mr. Eleazar Williams, a young man of Indian extraction, a candidate for

Holy Orders, is licensed by the Bishop as a lay reader and a catechist, to officiate in the Mohawk language, in St. Peter's Church, Oneida Castle, Oneida County, the congregation of which is composed of Indians; and employed by the Committee for propagating the Gospel in the State of New York in those capacities, and likewise as a schoolmaster among the Indians.

Peter Williams, jun., a coloured man, a candidate for Orders, is licensed by the Bishop as a lay reader and catechist, to officiate, when no clergyman is present, in St. Philip's Church, New York, the congregation of which is composed of coloured members of the Protestant Episcopal Church.

NEW JERSEY.

The Right Rev. John Croes, D. D., Bishop, and Rector of Christ Church, New Brunswick.
The Rev. Abraham Beach, D. D., residing near New Brunswick.
The Rev. Charles H. Wharton, D. D., Rector of St. Mary's Church, Burlington.
The Rev. John C. Rudd, Rector of St. John's Church, Elizabeth Town.
The Rev. Simon Wilmer, Rector of Trinity Church, Swedesborough.
The Rev. James Chapman, Rector of St. Peter's Church, Perth Amboy.
The Rev. John Croes, jun., Rector of Christ Church, Shrewsbury, and Christ Church, Middletown.
The Rev. Lewis P. Bayard, Rector of Trinity Church, Newark.
The Rev. George Y. Morehouse, Rector of St. Andrew's Church, Mount Holly.
The Rev. Abiel Carter, Rector of St. Michael's Church, Trenton.
The Rev. Richard F. Cadle, Deacon, Minister of St. John's Church, Salem, and St. George's Church, Pennsneck.
The Rev. Daniel Higbee, residing at Morestown.
The Rev. Augustus Fitch, Deacon, residing at Bellville.
The Rev. George H. Woodruff, Deacon, lately a Missionary, residing at Trenton.
The Rev. Clarkson Dunn, Deacon, a Missionary to the vacant Churches.

PENNSYLVANIA.

The Right Rev. William White, D. D., Bishop, senior of the American Church, presiding in the House of Bishops and Rector of Christ Church, St. Peter's, and St. James's, Philadelphia.
The Rev. James Abercrombie, D. D., senior Assistant Minister of Christ Church, St. Peter's, and St. James's, Philadelphia.
The Rev. Robert Ayres, residing in Brownsville.
The Rev. Frederick Beasley, D. D., Provost of the University of Pennsylvania, Philadelphia.
She Rev. Robert Blackwell, D. D., residing in Philadelphia.
The Rev. George Boyd, Rector of St. John's Church, Northern Liberties, Philadelphia.
The Rev. Samuel C. Brinckle, Deacon, Minister of St. David's Church, Radnor.
The Rev. Levi Bull, Rector of St. Gabriel's Church, Berk's County, St. Mary's, Chester County, and Bangor Church, Churchtown.
The Rev. Slator Clay, Rector of St. James', Perkiomen, and St. Peter's, Great Valley.

The Rev Joseph Clarkson, Rector of St. James', Lancaster, and St. John's, Pequea.

The Rev. Jacob Morgan Douglass, Rector of St. Paul's, Chester, St. Martin's, Marcus Hook, and St. John's, Concord.

The Rev. Charles M. Dupuy, Rector of St. Luke's Church, Germantown.

The Rev. Jackson Kemper, Assistant Minister of Christ Church, St. Peter's and St. James's, Philadelphia.

The Rev. James Montgomery, residing near Philadelphia.

The Rev. William Augustus Muhlenberg, Deacon, Assistant Minister to the Rector of Christ Church, St. Peter's, and St. James's, Philadelphia.

The Rev. Joseph Pilmore, D. D., Rector of St. Paul's Church, Philadelphia.

The Rev. Elijah G. Plumb, Missionary in Northumberland County.

The Rev. Francis Reno, officiating in the Counties of Beaver and Alleghany.

The Rev. Manning B. Roche, Deacon, Missionary in Southwark and Mantua.

The Rev. John Rodney, Deacon, Minister of Trinity Church, Easton.

The Rev. Charles G. Snowden, Minister at Huntingdon and adjacent parts, Huntingdon County.

The Rev. George Sheets, Rector of Trinity Church, Oxford, and All Saints, Lower Dublin.

The Rev. John Taylor, residing in Pittsburgh.

The Rev. Joseph Turner, residing in Southwark, Philadelphia.

The Rev. Bird Wilson, Rector of St. John's Church, Norristown, and St. Thomas's, Whitemarsh.

The Rev. James Wiltbank, Master of the Grammar School in the University of Pennsylvania, Philadelphia.

The Rev. Samuel Sitgreaves, Deacon, residing at Easton.

The Rev. Samuel Bacon, now in Africa, agent of the American Colonization Soctety.

Mr. John P. Bankson, a candidate for orders, is employed by the Episcopal Missionary Society of Philadelphia, as a catechist in Africa, in connection with the American Colonization Society.

DELAWARE.

The Rev. Robert Clay, Rector of Emmanuel's Church, Newcastle, and St. James's Church, ———.

The Rev. John Foreman, Deacon, Minister of St. Peter's, Lewes, St. Paul's, Georgetown, Christ, Laurel, ——— Church, Little Hill, St. George's, Indian River, and Prince George's, Dagsborough, Sussex County.

The Rev. Richard D. Hall, Rector of Trinity Church, Wilmington.

The Rev. Joseph Spencer, Deacon, Minister of Christ Church, Dover, and Christ Church, Milford, Kent County, and St. Matthew's Church, Cedar Creek, Sussex County.

MARYLAND.

The Right Rev. James Kemp, D. D., Bishop, and Rector of St. Paul's Parish, including Christ Church, Baltimore.

The Rev. Walter D. Addison, Rector of St. John's Church, Georgetown, District of Columbia.

The Rev. Ethan Allen, Deacon, Minister of St, John's, Prince George's.

The Rev. John Allen, Teacher in Baltimore.
The Rev. John Armstrong, St. Peter's, Montgomery, and Zion, Frederick.
The Rev. William Armstrong, Deacon.
The Rev. Charles C. Austin, Deacon.
The Rev. Edmund D. Barry, D. D., Principal of an Academy in Baltimore.
The Rev. John V. Bartow, Rector of Trinity Church, Baltimore.
The Rev. John P. Bausman, Christ Church, Calvert.
The Rev. Thomas Bayne, Rector of St. Peter's, Talbot.
The Rev. James J. Bowden, Deacon, Trinity Parish, Charles County.
The Rev. John Brady, Rector of William and Mary, and St. Andrew's, St. Mary's County.
The Rev. William J. Bulkley, Rector of St. Paul's, Queen Anne.
The Rev, Jehu C. Clay, St. John's, Washington.
The Rev. Henry L. Davis, D. D. Rector of St. Anne's, Annapolis.
The Rev. William Duke, Residing in Elkton.
The Rev. Henry Pfeiffer, Deacon, Missionary.
The Rev. William L. Gibson.
The Rev. Levin J. Gillis, Deacon, Queen Anne's Parish, Prince George's County.
The Rev. George D. S. Handy, residing in Kent County.
The Rev. William Hawley, Rector of St. John's Church, City of Washington.
The Rev. John P. K. Henshaw, Rector of St. Peter's Church, Baltimore.
The Rev. Thomas Horrell, St. James's Parish, Anne-Arundel.
The Rev. Reuben Hubbard, St. Michael's, Talbot.
The Rev. Joseph Jackson, Rector of St. Thomas's Parish, Baltimore County.
The Rev. John Johns, Fredericktown.
The Rev. Matthew Johnson, Rector of All Saints, Calvert.
The Rev. John R. Keech, Deacon, St. John's, and St. James's, Baltimore County.
The Rev. Ruel Keith, Christ Church, Georgetown, District of Columbia.
The Rev. Joseph Lanston, Deacon.
The Rev. Charles Mann, Rector of William and Mary Parish, Charles County.
The Rev. Andrew C. M'Cormick, Rector of —— Church, City of Washington.
The Rev. William Ninde, Rector of St. Stephen's, Cecil, and Shrewsbury, Kent.
The Rev. Thomas Reid.
The Rev. Neale H. Shaw, Rector of King and Queen, and All-Faith, St. Mary's.
The Rev. Purnell F. Smith, Rector of All-Hallows and Worcester, Worcester County.
The Rev. Daniel Stephens, Rector of Havre de Grace, and St. George's, Hartford.
The Rev. William M. Stone, Rector of Stepney, Somerset.
The Rev. Samuel C. Stratton, Coventry, Somerset.
The Rev. Joseph R. Walker, Rector of —— Church, Chester, and St. Paul's, Kent.
The Rev. John Weems, Rector of Port Tobacco, Charles County.
The Rev. George Weller, Rector of Great Choptank and Dorchester, Dorset County.
The Rev. William Westerman, Rector of St. Mark's, Frederick County.

The Rev. William Wickes, Somerset, Somerset.
The Rev. Ralph Williston, Rector of St. Paul's, Prince George's.
The Rev. William E. Wyatt, D. D., Associate Minister of St. Paul's Parish, Baltimore.
The Rev. Noble Young, Rector of —— Church, Prince George's.

VIRGINIA.

The Right Rev. Richard Channing Moore, D. D., Bishop, and Rector of the Monumental Church, Richmond.
The Rev. Benjamin Allen, St. Andrew's Parish, Jefferson County.
The Rev. Thomas G. Allen, Dumfries Church, Dettingen Parish, Prince William.
The Rev. Joseph R. Andrus, St. Paul's Church, King George County.
The Rev. Alexander Balmain, D. D., Frederick Parish, Winchester County.
The Rev. Hugh C. Boggs, Berkley Parish, Spotsylvania.
The Rev. John L. Bryan, Christ Church, Norborne Parish, Berkley County.
The Rev. John Buchanan, D. D., Rector of Henrico Parish.
The Rev. Charles Crawford, Louisa County.
The Rev. John Dunn, Shelburn Parish, Loudoun County.
The Rev. George Halson, residing near Norfolk.
The Rev. William H. Hart, Assistant Minister of Henrico Parish.
The Rev. Frederick W. Hatch.
The Rev. Alexander Hay, Antrim Parish, Halifax County.
The Rev. William King, Augusta Parish, Staunton.
The Rev. George Lemmon, Hamilton and Leeds Parishes, Fauquier.
The Rev. Samuel Low, Christ Church, Norfolk Borough.
The Rev. Enoch M. Low, Norborne Parish, Berkeley.
The Rev. Edward C M'Guire, St. George's Parish, Fredericksburgh.
The Rev. Herbert Marshall, Minister of Hungar's Parish, Northampton.
The Rev. William Meade, Frederick Parish, Frederick County.
The Rev. Oliver Norris, Christ Church, Alexandriá, District of Columbia.
The Rev. John Ravenscroft, St. James's Parish, Mecklenburgh County.
The Rev. Benjamin B. Smith, officiating in St. George's Parish, Accomack.
The Rev. William Steele, Dettingen and Leed's Parishes, Prince William.
The Rev. Andrew Syme, Bristol Parish, Dinwiddie.
The Rev. William H. Wilmer, D.D., St. Paul's Church, Alexandria, District of Columbia.
The Rev. John Woodville, St. Mark's Parish, Culpepper.
The Rev. Samuel Wydown, St. Martin's Parish, Hanover County.

NORTH CAROLINA.

The Right Rev. Richard Channing Moore, D. D., of Virginia, performing Episcopal offices under the 20th Canon of the General Convention, by invitation of the Convention of the Diocese.
The Rev. John Avery, Rector of St. Paul's Church, Edenton.
The Rev. Gregory T. Bedell, Rector of St. John's Church, Fayetteville.
The Rev. Adam Empie, Rector of St. James's Church, Wilmington.
The Rev. Richard S. Mason, Minister of Christ Church, Newbern.
The Rev. John Phillips, Rector of Trinity Church, Tarborough.
The Rev. Thomas Wright, Deacon, Missionary.
The Rev. William Hooper, Professor in the University of North Carolina.

SOUTH CAROLINA.

The Right Rev. Nathaniel Bowen, D. D., Bishop, and Rector of St. Michael's Church, Charleston.
The Rev Christopher E. Gadsden, D. D., Rector of St. Philip's Church, Charleston.
The Rev. John Barnwell Campbell, Rector of St. Helena Church, Beaufort.
The Rev. John I. Tschudy, Rector of St. John's Parish, Berkeley.
The Rev. Christian Hanckel, Rector of Trinity Church, Columbia.
The Rev. Paul Trapier Gervais, residing in Charleston.
The Rev. Maurice H. Lance, Rector of Prince George's, Winyah, Georgetown.
The Rev. Milward Pogson, Rector of St. James's Church, Goose-Creek.
The Rev. Frederick Dalcho, M. D., Assistant Minister of St. Michael's Church, Charleston.
The Rev. Thomas Gates, D. D., residing in St. George's, Dorchester.
The Rev. Thomas Mills, D. D.
The Rev. Philip Matthews, Rector of St. Helena Church, St. Helena Island.
The Rev. Andrew Fowler, A. M., Missionary at Chatham, and the parts adjacent.
The Rev. Albert A. Muller, A. M., Rector of Christ Church Parish, and Minister of Grace Church, Sullivan's Island.
The Rev. Charles B. Snowden, A. B.
The Rev. Francis P. De Lavaux, Rector of St. Matthew's Parish.
The Rev. Parker Adams, Rector of Claremont Church, Stateburg.
The Rev. Robert S. Symes, officiating at St. Paul's Church, Charleston.
The Rev. Allston Gibbs, Assistant Minister of St. Philip's Church, Charleston.
The Rev. Henry Gibbes, Deacon, All Saints Parish, Waccamaw.
The Rev. John W. Chandler, Deacon, St. Mark's Parish.
The Rev. Joseph M. Gilbert, Rector of the Church on Edisto Island.
The Rev. Hugh Fraser, residing in All-Saints Parish.
The Rev. David I. Campbell, Deacon, St. Stephen's Parish.
The Rev. William S. Wilson, Deacon, St. John's, Colleton.
The Rev. Patrick H. Folker, Charleston.
The Rev. Edward Rutledge, A. M., Deacon, St. Thomas's Parish.

OHIO.

The Right Rev. Philander Chase, D. D., Bishop, and Rector of St. John's Church, Worthington.
The Rev. Samuel Johnston, Minister of Christ Church, Cincinnati.
The Rev. James Kilbourn, Deacon, officiating in St. John's Church, Worthington.
The Rev. Intrepid Morse, Minister of St. James's Church, Zanesville, and the congregations in its vicinity.
The Rev. Roger Searle, at St. James's Church, Boardman.
The Rev. Joseph Willard, residing in Marietta.
The Rev. Thomas Osborne, Professor in the College at Cincinnati.

N. B. No lists were received from Maryland and Virginia. The names, &c., for those States are taken, with a few alterations, from Sword's Almanack for 1820.—*Committee of Publication.*

CERTIFICATES OF CONSECRATION.

Know all men by these presents, that we, William White, D. D., Bishop of the Protestant Episcopal Church in the State of Pennsylvania, Presiding Bishop; John Henry Hobart, D. D., Bishop of the Protestant Episcopal Church in the State of New York; James Kemp, D. D., Bishop of the Protestant Episcopal Church in the State of Maryland; John Croes, D. D., Bishop of the Protestant Episcopal Church in the State of New Jersey, under the protection of Almighty God, in Christ Church, in the city of Philadelphia, on Thursday the eighth day of October, in the year of our Lord one thousand eight hundred and eighteen, did then and there rightly and canonically consecrate our beloved in Christ, NATHANIEL BOWEN, D. D., Rector of St. Michael's Church in the city of Charleston, of whose sufficiency in good learning, soundness in the faith, and purity of manners we were fully ascertained, into the office of Bishop of the Protestant Episcopal Church in the State of South Carolina, to which he hath been elected by the Convention of said State.

Given in the city of Philadelphia, this eighth day of October, in the year of our Lord one thousand eight hundred and eighteen.

WILLIAM WHITE, (L. S.)
JOHN HENRY HOBART, (L. S.)
JAMES KEMP, (L. S.)
JOHN CROES. (L. S.)

Know all men by these presents, that we, William White, D. D., Bishop of the Protestant Episcopal Church in the State of Pennsylvania, Presiding Bishop; John Henry Hobart, D. D., Bishop of the Protestant Episcopal Church in the State of New York; James Kemp, D. D., Bishop of the Protestant Episcopal Church in the State of Maryland; John Croes, D. D., Bishop of the Protestant Episcopal Church in the State of New Jersey; under the protection of Almighty God, in St. James's Church in the city of Philadelphia, on Thursday the eleventh day of February, in the year of our Lord one thousand eight hundred and nineteen, did then and there rightly and canonically consecrate our beloved in Christ, PHILANDER CHASE, D. D., Rector of St. John's Church in the town of Worthington, in the State of Ohio, of whose sufficiency in good learning, soundness in the faith, and purity of manners we were fully ascertained, into the office of Bishop of the Protestant Episcopal Church in the State of Ohio, to which he hath been elected by the Convention of said State.

Given in the city of Philadelphia, this eleventh day of February, in the year of our Lord one thousand eight hundred and nineteen.

WILLIAM WHITE, (L. S.)
JOHN HENRY HOBART, (L. S.)
JAMES KEMP, (L. S.)
JOHN CROES. (L. S.)

Know all men by these presents, that we, William White, D. D., Bishop of the Protestant Episcopal Church in the State of Pennsylvania, Presiding Bishop; John Henry Hobart, D. D., Bishop of the Protestant Episcopal Church in the State of New York; Alexander Viets Griswold, Bishop of the Protestant Episcopal Church in the Eastern Diocese; under the protection of Almighty God, in Trinity Church in the city of New Haven, on Wednesday, the twenty-seventh day of October, in the year of our Lord one thousand eight hundred and nineteen, did then and there rightly and canonically consecrate our beloved in Christ, THOMAS C. BROWNELL, D. D., LL. D., Assistant Minister of Trinity Church, New York, of whose sufficiency in good learning, soundness in the faith, and purity of manners we were fully ascertained, into the office of Bishop of the Protestant Episcopal Church in the State of Connecticut, to which he hath been elected by the Convention of said State.

Given in the city of New Haven, this twenty-seventh day of October, in the year of our Lord, one thousand eight hundred and nineteen.

WILLIAM WHITE, (L. S.)
JOHN HENRY HOBART, (L. S.)
ALEXANDER VIETS GRISWOLD. (L. S.)

JOURNAL OF THE PROCEEDINGS

OF THE

BISHOPS, CLERGY, AND LAITY

OF THE

Protestant Episcopal Church,

IN

THE UNITED STATES OF AMERICA,

IN A

SPECIAL GENERAL CONVENTION.

HELD IN

ST. PETER'S CHURCH, IN THE CITY OF PHILADELPHIA, FROM THE 30TH DAY OF OCTOBER, TO THE 3D OF NOVEMBER, INCLUSIVE, A. D. 1821.

LIST OF MEMBERS PRESENT.

HOUSE OF BISHOPS.

The Right Rev. William White, D. D. of Pennsylvania, presiding Bishop.

The Right Rev. John Henry Hobart, D. D. of New York.

The Right Rev. Alexander Viets Griswold, D. D. of the Eastern Diocese.

The Right Rev. James Kemp, D. D. of Maryland.

The Right Rev. John Croes, D. D. of New Jersey.

The Right Rev. Thomas C. Brownell, D. D., LL. D. of Connecticut.

HOUSE OF CLERICAL AND LAY DEPUTIES.

CLERICAL DEPUTIES.

MASSACHUSETTS.

Rev. Samuel F. Jarvis, D. D., Rev. Thomas Carlile.

RHODE ISLAND.

Rev. Salmon Wheaton, Rev. Nathan B. Crocker.

CONNECTICUT.

Rev. Daniel Burhans, Rev. Ashbel Baldwin, Rev. Birdsey G. Noble, Rev. Harry Croswell.

NEW YORK.

Rev. David Butler, Rev. Thomas Lyell. Rev. Benjamin T. Onderdonk, Rev. Orin Clark.

NEW JERSEY.

Rev. Charles H. Wharton, D. D., Rev. John C. Rudd, Rev. John Croes, Jun., Rev. Abiel Carter.

PENNSYLVANIA.

Rev. Frederic Beasley, D. D., Rev. Bird Wilson, D. D., Rev. Jackson Kemper, Rev. George Boyd.

DELAWARE.

Rev. Richard D. Hall.

MARYLAND.

Rev. William E. Wyatt, D. D., Rev. John P. K. Henshaw.

VIRGINIA.

Rev. William H. Wilmer, D. D., Rev. Simon Wilmer.
Rev. William Meade,

NORTH CAROLINA.

Rev. Richard S. Mason, Rev. Gregory T. Bedell.

SOUTH CAROLINA.

Rev. Christopher E. Gadsden, D. D., Rev. Christian Hanckell,
Rev. John I. Tschudy, Rev. Maurice H. Lance.

LAY DEPUTIES.

RHODE ISLAND.

Col. Alexander Jones, Jeremiah Lippitt, Esq.
Stephen T. Northam, Esq.,

CONNECTICUT.

Hon. Sam. Wm. Johnson, Nathan Smith, Esq.

NEW YORK.

Richard Harison, Esq., John Wells, Esq.
Hon. Morris S. Miller,

NEW JERSEY.

Peter Kean, Esq., Daniel Garritson, Esq.
Joseph V. Clark, Esq.,

PENNSYLVANIA.

William Meredith, Esq., Walter Kerr, Esq.,
Thomas M'Euen, Esq., Levi Pauling, Esq.

DELAWARE.

George Read, Esq., John Cummins, Esq.

MARYLAND.

Hon. John C. Herbert, Tench Tilghman, Esq.

VIRGINIA.

Col. Wm. Mayo, Philip Nelson, Esq.,
Edmund I. Lee, Esq.

NORTH CAROLINA.

Duncan Cameron, Esq., Josiah Collins, Esq.

SOUTH CAROLINA.

Wm. Heyward, Esq., Lewis L. Gibbes, Esq.,
Col. Lewis Morris.

Clergy who attended the sittings of the Convention.

New York.—Rev. James Milnor, D. D., Rev. Henry U. Onderdonk, M. D., Rev. Jonathan M. Wainwright, Rev. Wm. Richmond, Rev. Lawson Carter, Rev. James Cotter.

New Jersey.—Rev. J. M. Douglass, Rev. R. F. Cadle.

Pennsylvania.—Rev. Robert Blackwell, D. D., Rev. Joseph Pilmore, D. D., Rev. Joseph Hutchins, D. D., Rev. James Abercrombie, D. D., Rev. James Wiltbank, Rev. Benjamin Allen, Rev. Charles M. Dupuy, Rev. Manning B. Roche, Rev. Samuel Sitgreaves, jr., Rev. Peter Van. Pelt, jr.

Maryland.—Rev. Wm. Hawley.

John Read, Esq., Isaac Lawrence, Esq., Trustees of the Theological Seminary.

Gulian C. Verplank, Esq., Manager of the New York Education Society.

JOURNAL

OF THE PROCEEDINGS OF THE

House of Clerical and Lay Deputies.

PHILADELPHIA, TUESDAY, Oct. 30, 1821.

Pursuant to notice from the presiding Bishop, calling a special General Convention of the Protestant Episcopal Church of the United States of America, agreeably to the provisions of the 42nd Canon, several Clerical and Lay Deputies attended in St. Peter's Church at 12 o'clock, and a quorum being present, the Rev. Wm. H. Wilmer, D. D., was requested to take the chair pro tempore, and the Rev. J. C. Rudd was requested to act as Secretary pro tempore.

The house then proceeded to read the testimonials of the Clerical and Lay Deputies, which were severally approved, and the following gentlemen took their seats in the house.

CLERICAL DEPUTIES.

From Massachusetts, Rev. Sam. F. Jarvis, D. D., Rev. Thos. Carlile. From Rhode Island, Rev. Salmon Wheaton, Rev. Nathan B. Crocker. From Connecticut, Rev. Daniel Burhans, Rev. Ashbel Baldwin, Rev. Birdsey G. Noble. From New York, Rev. David Butler, Rev. Thomas Lyell, Rev. Benj. T. Onderdonk, Rev. Orin Clark. From New Jersey, Rev. Chas. H. Wharton, D. D., Rev. John C. Rudd, Rev. John Croes, Jr., Rev. Abiel Carter. From Maryland, Rev. Wm. E. Wyatt, D. D., Rev. John P. K. Henshaw.

From Virginia, Rev. Wm. H. Wilmer, D. D., Rev. Wm. Meade, Rev. Simon Wilmer. From North Carolina, Rev. Richard S. Mason, Rev. Gregory T. Bedell. From South Carolina, Rev. Chris. E. Gadsden, D. D., Rev. John J. Tschudy, Rev. Christian Hanckell, Rev. Maurice H. Lance.

LAY DEPUTIES.

From Rhode Island, Col. Alexander Jones, Stephen T. Northam, Esq., Jeremiah Lippitt, Esq. From Connecticut, Hon. Sam. Wm. Johnson, Nathan Smith, Esq. From New York, Richard Harison, Esq., Hon. Morris S. Miller, John Wells, Esq. From New Jersey, Peter Kean, Esq., Joseph V. Clark, Esq., Daniel Garritson, Esq. From Maryland, Hon. John C. Herbert. From Virginia, Col. Wm. Mayo, Mr. Philip Nelson, Edmond I. Lee, Esq. From North Carolina, Duncan Cameron, Esq., Joshua Collins, Esq. From South Carolina, William Heyward, Esq., Lewis L. Gibbes, Esq.

The house proceeded to the election of a president, secretary and assistant secretary, when it appeared that the Rev. William H. Wilmer, D. D., was chosen president, the Rev. Ashbel Baldwin, secretary, and the Rev. J. C. Rudd, assistant secretary.

The Rev. Dr. Wharton was appointed to inform the House of Bishops that this house was organized, and ready to proceed to business.

The House of Bishops returned for answer, that they also were organized, and ready to proceed to business.

On motion, the rules of order adopted by the last General Convention, were adopted as the rules of this convention.

The house adjourned until 10 o'clock, A. M., to-morrow.

WEDNESDAY, Oct. 31, 10 o'clock, A. M.

The house attended Divine Service in St. Peter's church. Service was performed by the Rev. Dr. Wyatt, and a sermon preached by the Right Rev. Bishop Kemp.

After Divine Service the house met.

The minutes of yesterday were read and approved.

The Clerical and Lay Deputies from Pennsylvania, presented the certificate of their appointment, and the following gentlemen took their seats, viz.

Rev. Frederic Beasley, D. D., Rev. Bird Wilson, D. D., Rev. Jackson Kemper, Rev. George Boyd, William Meredith, Thomas M'Euen, Walter Kerr, Levi Paulding, Esqrs.

Col. Lewis Morris, a Lay deputy from South Carolina, the Rev. H. Croswell, a Clerical deputy from Connecticut, the Rev. Richard D. Hall, a Clerical deputy from Delaware, George Read and John Cummins, Esqrs., Lay deputies from Delaware, and Tench Tilghman, Esq., a Lay deputy from Maryland, appeared and took their seats.

On motion, resolved, that clergymen of the Protestant Episcopal Church, the trustees of the Theological Seminary, and the managers of the New York Education Society, who may be in the city of Philadelphia, during the session of this Convention, and not members thereof, be admitted to the sittings of this house.

On motion, resolved, that the seat on the right of the chair be reserved for the use of the right Rev. the Bishops, whenever they may choose to attend the sittings of this house. This resolution was sent to the house of Bishops, who presented their thanks to this house for their attention.

The report of the trustees of the Theological Seminary was read. (*See Appendix, No.* 1.)

A message was received from the House of Bishops, relative to the call of this special Convention, and accompanied by certain documents relating to the same subject, which were read. (*See Appendix, No.* 1.)

On motion, resolved, that the papers received from the House of Bishops relative to the Theological Seminary, and the report of the Trustees of the seminary, be referred to a committee of seven on the part of this house, and that the House of Bishops be respectfully requested to appoint such number of their own body as they may think proper, to be, with the members appointed on the part of this house, a joint committee on the said papers and the matters therein contained.

The following gentlemen were appointed the committee. Duncan Cameron, Esq., Richard Harris, Esq., Col. Alexander Jones, Rev. Daniel Burhans, Rev. David Butler, Rev. Dr. Wharton, Rev. Dr. Gadsden. This resolution was sent to the House of Bishops.

A message was received from the House of Bishops, informing this house of their concurrence with the resolution, proposing a joint committee, and that the Right Rev. Bishops Hobart and Kemp had been appointed on the part of their house.

A message was received from the House of Bishops, with a report of the presiding Bishop on the subject of a standard copy of the book of Common Prayer, which was ordered to lie on the table, and the house adjourned until 6 o'clock this evening.

WEDNESDAY EVENING, 6 o'clock.

The house met.

The report of the presiding Bishop on the subject of a standard copy of the book of Common Prayer, was read, and referred to a select committee, consisting of Peter Kean, Esq., Rev. R. S. Mason, and William Meredith, Esq. (*See Appendix, No.* 2.)

The house adjourned until one o'clock, P. M. to-morrow.

THURSDAY, Nov. 1, 1 o'clock, P. M.

This being thanksgiving day, the members attended Divine Service in the different churches.

The house met.

The minutes of yesterday were read and approved.

The report of the managers of the Missionary Society was presented, and read. (*See Appendix, No.* 3.)

On motion of the Rev. Simon Wilmer, it was referred to a committee.

The Rev. Mr. Boyd, Rev. Dr. Jarvis, and Rev. Simon Wilmer, were appointed the committee.

On motion, resolved, that when this house adjourn, it will adjourn until to-morrow, 10 o'clock, A. M., and that this resolution be communicated to the House of Bishops.

A communication was received from the House of Bishops, on the subject of the last rubric in the communion service, which was laid upon the table, and the house adjourned.

FRIDAY, Nov. 2, 10 o'clock, A. M.

Morning prayers were read by the Rev. Mr. Mason. After Divine Service, the house met.

The minutes of yesterday were read and approved.

The Rev. Mr. Boyd, from the Committee on the report of the board of managers of the Missionary Society, made report, and offered as an amendment the following, as a fifth article under the first head of the constitution.

"The president and vice presidents of this society shall be ex-officio members of the board of managers, and when present shall preside at its meetings."

This amendment was adopted and sent to the House of Bishops.

Duncan Cameron, Esq., from the Committee on the Theological Seminary, made the following report, which was read.

The Committee to whom was referred the communications relative to the General Theological Seminary, having had the same under consideration, report the following constitution for the General Theological Seminary of the Protestant Episcopal Church in the United States of America.

Submitted.

DUNCAN CAMERON,

Chairman of the Committee of the House of Clerical and Lay Deputies.

CONSTITUTION OF THE GENERAL THEOLOGICAL SEMINARY OF THE PROTESTANT EPISCOPAL CHURCH IN THE UNITED STATES OF AMERICA.

I. The Theological Seminary of the Protestant Episcopal Church in the United States of America, shall be permanently established in the state of New York. The trustees of the said Seminary shall have power, from time to time, to establish one or more branch schools in the state of New York, or elsewhere, to be under the superintendence and control of the said trustees.

II. The management of the said Seminary shall be vested in a board of trustees, who shall have power to constitute professorships, and to appoint the professors, and to prescribe the course of study in the respective schools, and to make rules and regulations and statutes for the government thereof; and generally to take such measures as they may deem necessary to its prosperity; provided, that such rules and regulations, and course of study, and measures be not repugnant to the constitution and Canons of the Church, and to the course of study for candidates for orders which is or may be established by the House of Bishops.—The Bishops in their individual and collective capacity, shall be visiters of the Seminary, and shall see that the course of instruction and discipline be conducted agreeably to the foregoing provision.—The trustees shall make report to every general Convention of their proceedings, and of the state of the Seminary.

III. The board of trustees shall be permanently constituted, as follows:—The Bishops of the Church shall be ex-officio members of the board. Every diocese shall be entitled to one trustee, and one additional trustee for every eight clergymen in the same; and to one additional trustee for every two thousand dollars of monies in any way given or contributed in the same to the funds of the Seminary, until the sum amounts to 10,000 dollars; and one additional trustee for every 10,000 dollars of contributions and donations, as aforesaid, exceeding that sum. The trustees shall be resident in the dioceses for which they are appointed. They shall be nominated by the diocesan Conventions respectively, to every stated general Convention, who may confirm or reject such nominations. The senior Bishop present shall preside at every meeting of the board of trustees; and whenever demanded by a majority of the Bishops present, or a majority of the Clerical and Lay trustees present, the concurrence of a majority of the Bishops present, and a majority of Clerical and Lay Trustees present, shall be necessary to any act of the board. Eleven trustees shall constitute a quorum. The trustees shall continue in office until their successors are appointed. In the interval between the stated meetings of the general Convention, the board shall have power to supply all vacancies, from the dioceses respectively in which they may have occurred.

IV. For the present, and until the next stated general Convention, the board of trustees shall consist of the Bishops of the Church, and of the 24 trustees of the general Theological Seminary, heretofore established by the General Convention, and of fourteen trustees chosen by the managers of the Protestant Episcopal Theological Education Society in the State of New York. These trustees shall exercise the powers of the permanent board, as detailed in the foregoing article, and agreeably to the provisions thereof.

The board of trustees shall always meet in the diocese where the Seminary is established, at such stated periods as they may determine; and special meetings may be called by the Bishop of the said diocese, and shall be called by him at the requisition of a majority of the Bishops.

V. The professors of the General Theological Seminary heretofore established by the General Convention, and the professors in the Theological Seminary in the diocess of New York shall be professors in the General Theological Seminary hereby established in that diocese.

The board of trustees shall have power to remove professors and other officers; but no professor shall be removed from office, except at a special meeting of the board called to consider the same; nor unless notice of an intended motion for such removal, and of the grounds thereof shall have been given at a previous meeting of the board. The nomination of professors shall be made at one meeting of the board of trustees, and acted upon at a subsequent meeting; due notice being given of the object of the said meeting to every member of the board.

VI. The funds and other property and claims to funds or property of the General Theological Seminary, heretofore established by the General Convention, shall be vested in and transferred to the General Seminary hereby established, as soon as an act of the board of managers of the Protestant Episcopal Theological Education Society, in the state of New York, shall vest in and transfer to the same Seminary, all their funds, and other property and claims to funds and property—and all engagements and responsibilities entered into or assumed by either of the said institutions, for the purpose of their foundation, consistent with the other provisions of this constitution, shall be considered as binding upon the General Seminary, so established within the state of New York.

VII. This constitution shall be unalterable, except by a concurrent vote of the board of trustees, and of the General Convention.

The house proceeded to the consideration of the proposed constitution, which passed a first and second reading.

A message was received from the House of Bishops, informing this house that they had unanimously adopted the constitution of the General Theological Seminary of the Protestant Episcopal Church in the United States of America, as reported by the committee to whom were referred all papers relative to the subject.

The further consideration ot the subject was postponed until evening.

The communication from the House of Bishops on the subject of the last rubric in the communion service, was read and returned to that house. (*See Appendix, No.* 4.)

A message was received from the House of Bishops, informing this house that they had disagreed to the proposed amendment of the constitution of the Missionary Society, and proposing a substitute for the present constitution.

The house adjourned until 6 o'clock, P. M.

FRIDAY EVENING, 6 o'clock.

The house met.

On motion, resolved, that with the consent of the House of Bishops, the next Convention shall meet on the day and at the place appointed, at the hour of 10, A. M., in order to attend the services usually performed at the opening of the Convention.

The house resumed the consideration of the constitution of the General Theological Seminary, which was read a third time, and adopted as reported by the committee, and notice sent to the House of Bishops.

Mr. Meredith, from the committee on the subject of a standard copy of the book of Common Prayer, reported the following resolution, which was adopted and sent to the House of Bishops.

Resolved, by the House of Clerical and Lay Deputies, the House of Bishops concurring, that a joint committee of one or more Bishops to be appointed by the House of Bishops, and of three members of the House of Clerical and Lay Deputies to be appointed by the house last mentioned, be authorized during the recess of the General Convention, to superintend the printing of the Book of Common Prayer, correcting and supplying any errors and omissions in the edition heretofore established as the standard Book, and introducing a table of the days on which Easter will fall for 38 years, being the time of two cycles of the moon, as reported by the presiding Bishop to this convention; and that in the choice of an edition for this purpose, the said committee for the sake of the greater accuracy, give a preference to one to be printed from stereotype plates, and authenticate the same by their certificate.

The committee also proposed a Canon, "providing for a

new and more complete and correct standard of the Book of Common Prayer," which was adopted and sent to the House of Bishops. (*See Appendix, No.* 6.)

Mr. Meredith, Rev. Dr. Beasley, and Rev. Dr. Wilson were appointed the committee on the part of this house, for superintending the printing of a standard copy of the Book of Common Prayer—Notice of this appointment was sent to the House of Bishops.

The Rev. Mr. Onderdonk, from the committee appointed by the last General Convention to consider the practicability of providing a fund to be at the disposal of the General Convention, reported a canon, which was ordered to lie on the table.

A message was received from the House of Bishops, concurring in the resolution adopted by this house relative to the convention attending service on the first day of the session.

A message was received from the House of Bishops, informing this house, that they had concurred in the resolution and Canon relative to a standard Book of Common Prayer, and that they had appointed the presiding Bishop the committee on the part of their house

The message from the House of Bishops, with the proposed substitute for the present constitution of the Missionary Society was read, and referred to a committee consisting of the Rev. Mr. Henshaw, Rev. Mr. Boyd, and Rev. Mr. Kemper.

On motion, resolved, that when this house adjourn, it will adjourn until 9 o'clock, A. M., to-morrow.

The Rev. Dr. Wharton, Rev. Mr. Burhans, Mr. Smith, Mr. Cummins, and Mr. Garrison asked and obtained leave of absence for the remainder of the session.

The house adjourned.

SATURDAY, Nov. 3, 9 o'clock, A. M.

Morning prayers were read by the Rev. Mr. Carlile.

After Divine Service the house met.

The minutes of yesterday were read and approved.

The Rev. Mr. Henshaw, from the committee on the proposed substitute for the present constitution of the Missionary Society, reported the substitute sent from the House of Bishops, with some amendments, which were considered, and the constitution as amended was sent to the House of Bishops.

The Rev. Mr. Rudd, and the Rev. Mr. Kemper, were appointed a committee to superintend the printing of the Journals, and notice of this appointment was sent to the House of Bishops, who returned for answer that they had appointed the presiding Bishop, to unite with the committee of this house, and that they had resolved that 1200 copies of the Journal should be printed and distributed in the several dioceses, according to the number of Churches in each.

In this resolution the house concurred, and notice of concurrence was sent to the House of Bishops.

A message was received from the House of Bishops, proposing further amendments to the constitution of the Missionary Society, which are concurred in by this house, and notice of concurrence sent to the House of Bishops, and the constitution as amended was finally adopted. (*See Appendix, No.* 5.)

The house proceeded to the choice of 24 directors and 2 secretaries of the Missionary Society.

Mr. Meredith and Mr. Tilghman were appointed tellers.

The election having been made, notice thereof was sent to the House of Bishops, who returned for answer that they had concurred in the election made by this house, and the following persons were declared duly chosen, by the concurrent vote of both houses.

Pennsylvania—Rev. Jackson Kemper, Rev. James Montgomery, Rev. Benjamin Allen, Messrs. Richard North, Richard Dale, Thomas Hale, John Claxton, Charles Wheeler, Israel Kinsman, Hugh de Haven, jr. and James Nixon.

Delaware—Rev. Richard D. Hall.

Maryland—Rev. Dr. Wyatt, Rev. J. P. K. Henshaw.

Virginia—Rev. Dr. Wilmer, Rev. Wm. Meade.

North Carolina—Rev. G. T. Bedell.

South Carolina—Rev. Christian Hanckell, Lewis L. Gibbes.

New Jersey—Rev. Abiel Carter.

New York—Rev. Dr. Milnor, Rev. B. T. Onderdonk.

Rhode Island—Rev. Salmon Wheaton.

Massachusetts—Rev. Thomas Carlile.

Secretaries—Rev. George Boyd, Samuel J. Robbins.

On motion, resolved, that the thanks of this house be presented to the President and Secretaries for the services rendered by them respectively, during the present session.

The House of Bishops informed this house that they were ready to rise, and proposed closing the session by prayer. This house informed the House of Bishops that they were ready to unite in the proposed devotions. The House of Bishops then attended in this house, and prayer was performed by the presiding Bishop, after which he addressed the Convention in the following words:

BRETHREN OF THIS CONVENTION,

I take the liberty of giving vent to the feeling which possesses me, at the conclusion of our session.

I have attended all the meetings of the General Conventions, from the beginning of our organization. On some of those occasions, we assembled with apprehensions in the minds of many judicious men who had the interests of the Church at heart, that the deliberations would be disturbed by angry passions, and end in disunion. In every instance, the reverse was the issue, which led me to hope, that there was in this matter a verifying of the promise of the great Head of the Church, of being with her to the end of the world.

The reason of this call of your attention to the fact stated, is the harmony with which we are concluding the present session; after having met with diversity of sentiment on some important points; on which, in consequence of mutual concession, and the merging of local attachments in the great object of general good, we are now separating with comfirmed zeal for the great cause in which we are engaged; to be followed, it is to be hoped, by renewed endeavors for its advancement, each of us in his proper sphere.

With this prospect before me, I invite you to lift your hearts and your voices, in singing to the praise and glory of God, a psalm appropriate to the occasion.*

* The address of the presiding bishop was inserted in the Journal by request of the House of Clerical and Lay Deputies.

COMMITTEE FOR PUBLICATION.

The members of both houses then united in singing the 133d pslam—after which the benediction was pronounced, and the house adjourned, sine die.

Signed by order of the House of Clerical and Lay Deputies.

WILLIAM H. WILMER,
PRESIDENT.

ATTESTED, ASHBEL BALDWIN, SECRETARY.

JOURNAL

OF THE

House of Bishops.

TUESDAY, Oct. 30, 1821.

This being the day appointed for a special convention of the Protestant Episcopal Church, the Rt. Rev. Wm. White, D. D., Bishop of the Protestant Episcopal Church in the state of Pennsylvania, the Rt. Rev. John Henry Hobart, D. D., Bishop of the Protestant Episcopal Church in the state of New York, the Rt. Rev. Alexander V. Griswold, D. D., Bishop of the Eastern Diocess, the Rt. Rev. John Croes, D. D., Bishop of the Protestant Episcopal Church in the state of New Jersey, and the Rt. Rev. Thomas C. Brownell, D. D., LL. D., Bishop of the Protestant Episcopal Church in the state of Connecticut, assembled in the vestry room of St. Peter's Church, in the city of Philadelphia.

The Rev. Wm. Augustus Muhlenberg was chosen secretary to the house.

A message was received from the House of Clerical and Lay Deputies, that they were organized and ready to proceed to business, whereupon this house returned for answer that they were also ready to proceed to business, and had agreed to attend Divine Service every day during the session.

Adjourned.

WEDNESDAY, Oct. 31.

The bishops attended Divine Service. Prayers were read by the Rev. Dr. Wyatt, and a sermon was delivered by the Rt. Rev. bishop Kemp. The holy communion was administered by the Rt. Rev. the presiding bishop, assisted by the other bishops present.

The house met. Present as yesterday. The Rt. Rev. bishop Kemp of Maryland, appeared and took his seat.

The minutes of yesterday were read and approved.

The presiding bishop stated to the house that in consequence of the request of the major number of the bishops, grounded on an application made to them by the trustees of the Theological Seminary, herewith presented, (*See Appendix, No.* 1.) and agreeably to authority vested in him, he had called this special convention. The bishops who made the request were, bishops Griswold, Moore, Kemp, Bowen, and Brownell. The statement was communicated to the House of Clerical and Lay Deputies.

A message was received from the House of Clerical and Lay Deputies, that they had provided seats for the Rt. Rev. the bishops, whenever they might please to attend in the same. The house returned their thanks.

The presiding bishop made a report "on certain matters referred to him by the last General Convention, to take order." (*See Appendix, No.* 2.) Whereupon the house adopted the proposal in the said report with regard to a standard book —and appointed the presiding bishop on the part of this house, a committee to carry the same into effect. Notice thereof was given to the House of Clerical and Lay Deputies.

The report of the trustees of the Theological Seminary was read. (*See Appendix, No.* 1.)

A message was received from the House of Clerical and Lay Deputies, that they had adopted a resolution to refer all papers relative to the General Theological Seminary to a committee of seven members; whereupon this house concurred in the resolution, and appointed bishops Hobart and Kemp to act on the part of this house with the aforesaid committee.

Adjourned to meet at 7 P. M.

7 P. M. The house met, and adjourned.

THURSDAY, Nov. 1st.

This being Thanksgiving day, the bishops attended Divine Service in the several churches.

The house met. Present as yesterday.

The minutes of yesterday were read and approved.

The presiding bishop made a communication relative to the Missionary Society. (*See Appendix, No.* 3.)

The house adopted an opinion on the use of part of the communion service, which was sent to the House of Clerical and Lay Deputies. (*See Appendix, No.* 4.)

A message was received from the House of Clerical and Lay Deputies, that they had adjourned until to-morrow morning at 10 o'clock; whereupon this house adjourned to the same hour.

FRIDAY, November 2nd.

The bishops attended Divine Service. The house met—present as yesterday. The minutes of the preceding meeting were read and approved.

The report of the committee, to whom were referred all papers relative to the Theological Seminary, was read; whereupon the house unanimously resolved to adopt the constitution of the General Theological Seminary of the Protestant Episcopal Church in the United States of America, as reported by the committee—and gave notice thereof to the House of Clerical and Lay Deputies.

The report of the managers of the General Missionary Society was read. (*See Appendix, No.* 3.)

A message was received from the House of Clerical and Lay Deputies, with an alteration of the constitution of the General Missionary Society; whereupon this house disagreed to the proposed alteration, and adopted a substitute for the present constitution, and sent it to the House of Clerical and Lay Deputies.

Adjourned to 6 o'clock P. M.

6 P. M.

The house met. Present as this morning.

A resolution was received from the House of Clerical and Lay Deputies, that the convention would hereafter commence business on the first day of the session, which was concurred in and returned.

The house adopted a resolution and a Canon respecting a

standard book, received from the House of Clerical and Lay Deputies, and appointed the presiding bishop on the part of this house, a committee to carry the resolution into effect. (*See Appendix*, No. 6.)

Adjourned to 9 A. M. to morrow.

SATURDAY, November 3d.

The bishops attended Divine Service. The house met—present as yesterday The minutes of the preceding meeting were read and approved.

The house returned thanks to the Rt. Reverend Bishop Kemp for his discourse, delivered at the opening of the convention, and requested a copy of the same for publication.

The constitution for the Domestic and Foreign Missionary Society of the Protestant Episcopal Church in the United States of America, after undergoing amendments proposed by the House of Clerical and Lay Deputies, was finally adopted. (*See Appendix*, No. 5.)

Resolved, that 1200 copies of the Journal of this Convention be printed and distributed in the different diocesses, according to the number of churches in each—and that the presiding bishop be a committee on the part of this house, to carry the resolution into effect.

The House of Clerical and Lay Deputies sent the names of certain persons chosen directors and officers of the Missionary Society, which this house concurred in by ballot.

"Resolved, that the thanks of the house be given to the secretary for the attention and ability with which he has discharged the duties of his office."

The convention being ready to rise, the house adjourned to the House of Clerical and Lay Deputies. The presiding bishop, after reading several appropriate prayers from the liturgy, addressed the members of the convention, and invited them to join in singing the 133d Psalm—after which the convention adjourned, sine die.

WM. WHITE,

PRESIDING BISHOP.

WM. AUGUSTUS MUHLENBERG, Secretary.

APPENDIX.

NO. 1.

Report of the Trustees of the Theological Seminary.

The committee appointed by the board of trustees of the Theological Seminary, to prepare a " Report of the proceedings of the Board, and of the State of the Seminary," and lay the same before the General Convention, beg leave respectfulyl to offer the following statement:

The board of trustees met at New Haven on the 13th day of July, 1820, and pursuant to the powers vested in them by the General Convention, proceeded to form a plan for the organization of the Seminary. A copy of this plan is herewith presented to the Convention,

On the 7th of September, 1820, the seminary was publicly opened, with, an inaugural discourse by the Rev. professor Turner. Ten students presented themselves at the opening of the institution, and four others joined it in the course of the first session. Two of these were obliged to retire before the close of the session, on account of ill health, and another obtained leave of absence, and has not since returned.

During the second session, which terminated in July last, there was an accession of seven new students, though one of the former number was obliged to leave the institution early in the session, on account of ill health. Since the close of the session, two of the students who had spent a year in the institution, and had been for two years previous engaged in their theological studies, have been admitted to the holy order of deacons.

During the present session, which commenced in September, seven new students have entered the seminary;—so that, at present, the institution numbers twenty-two pupils. The following is an alphabetical list of the names of all who have entered the institution, and of the dioceses from which they came.

From Connecticut, David Botsford.* From New Hampshire, Franceway R. Cossit.† From New York, Augustus L.

* Admitted to Orders.
† Had leave of absence, and has not returned.

Converse. From New Jersey, Robert Croes. From Vermont, Palmer Dyer. From New York, Manton Eastburn. From Connecticut, John M. Garfeild,‡ Bennet Glover,* Richard Haughton,§ Lemuel Hull, Edward Ives, William Jarvis. From New York, Wm. L. Johnson, Saml. R. Johnson, Isaac Low. From Pennsylvania, Henry M. Mason, Samuel Marks, Matthew Matthews. From Virginia, Sylvester Nash. From Connecticut, Seth B. Paddock. From Massachusetts, William Potter. From S. Carolina, Francis Rutledge.§ From Connecticut, William Shelton. From Maryland, Frederick Schroeder. From S. Carolina, Martin Snell, Edward Thomas. From Pennsylvauia, Peter Van Pelt, Jr.§ From New York, J. Lawrence Yuonnet.

The course of studies pursued by the students has been conformable to that prescribed by the house of Bishops. The progress which they have made in this course, will be seen by the following extracts from the reports of the professor.

"During the first session," he says, "the pupils of the institution have pursued the following course of studies:—The criticism of the Greek and Hebrew texts, comprehending accounts of the most important versions and editions of the Bible, together with discussions on the vowel points, targums, talmuds &c—All those parts of Jewish antiquities which tend to illustrate the Pentateuch—The Pentateuch itself which has been carefully read in the Septuagint version, and compared with the Hebrew text; the variations having been, in general, pointed out, and where it was found practicable, accounted for. Besides various commentators and critics, the works of *Marsh, Prideaux, Gray* and *Jennings* have been used as text books. In addition to these studies, some of the pupils have read *Pearson on the Creed.* Their wish to pursue systematic thelogy, at this time, acceded to, from the consideration that they had been pursuing studies in divinity, between one and two years before they entered the seminary."

At the close of the second session, the professor reports as follows:—"The historical books of the Old Testament, from Joshua to Esther inclusive, have been examined, and the more important difficulties carefully considered. The canonical authority of the different works has been investigated, *Gray's Key* having been used as a text book; the imperfections of which I have attempted to supply by a reference to other authorities, and principally to the very valuable work of Carpzov.

‡ Not a regular student, being engaged in teaching a school,
§ Left the institution on account of ill health.

When the students had advanced to the period where Prideaux commences his useful connection, this work was used, and the first part of it has been studied by them with attention. Thus the history has been brought down to the time of Simon the Just, when according to the Jews the canon of the Old Testament was completely settled. The chief points of difference between Prideaux in his account of the Assyrian empire, and others who prefer the authority of Herodotus to that of Ctesias, and particularly between him and Dr. Hales, have been made known to the students. Some notice, although not very considerable, has also been taken of the book of Job, and of the Psalms. In the New Testament, the four gospels, in Greek, have been the subject of study—Greisbach's edition having been used as the text, and Schleusner principally as the lexicographer. Besides the commentators recommended in the prescribed course, other critics have been used, among whom Middleton, whose work on the article corrects so ably many of the errors of Wakefield, holds a conspicuous rank. The first three Evangelists were reviewed, and St. John's gospel read in archbishop Newcome's Greek Harmony. The authority of each gospel has been examined, and particular attention has been paid to certain parts, the authenticity of which has by some been doubted on insufficient grounds The work of Dr. Campbell has been used by the pupils, and his first six dissertations have been made the subject of study and recitation."

The professor continues—and the observation applies equally to the preceding, and to the present session—"It has been my endeavor to accompany the exercises with such remarks as appeared beneficial, and once a week a written lecture, on some subject connected with the course of studies, has been delivered."

It may be proper to add, that all the students have attended the instructions of the Rt. Rev. Bishop Brownell, one day in each week, in the department of pulpit eloquence, and the composition of sermons, and that he has given these instructions gratuitously.

At the close of each session, public examinations have been held, in the presence of the trustees and the clergy. On these occasions the students have acquitted themselves in such a manner as to meet the approbation of the board of trustees, who have also expressed their sense of the ability, fidelity and zeal of the Rev. Professor.

At the annual meeting of the trustees, held at New Haven, the 24th of July last, the necessity of an additional professor became so apparent, that the board were induced to take measures to effect so desirable an object. They accordingly resolved to open a subscription, by which each subscriber should become responsible for $50 per annum, for the term of three years, for the purpose of supporting a professor of systematic theology. The salary was to be fixed at $1000 a year; and if more than that sum should be subscribed, the surplus was to be devoted towards the support of the present professor. Thirteen subscriptions were immediately obtained from the persons present; and the trustees were so fully confident that the requisite sum would be made up, that they appointed the Rev. Bird Wilson to the professorship. As this gentleman has not yet accepted the appointment, the matter rests till his determination shall be communicated to the board of trustees.

From the approbation with which this plan of support has been received, there is but little doubt that a sum can be obtained in this way, equal to the temporary support of two professors; while the money obtained in other ways, may be expected to accumulate to such a fund, before the temporary support shall fail, as to render it no longer necessary.

Immediately on the organization of the seminary, it became a primary object of the board of trustees, to make arrangements for obtaining the requisite funds for its support and endowment. This must. of necessity, be a gradual and progressive work. The resolutions passed by the board on this subject, may be seen in the appendix to the" Plan of the Seminary," page 20. Some progress has already been made towards carrying this object into effect; enough, indeed, to show that the seminary meets the general approbation of the Church, and will receive a liberal patronage; and to warrant the trustees in saying, that if the objects of the General Convention in the establishment of it, should by any means be defeated, it will not be from any impracticability of obtaining the necessary funds for its support.

At the period, however, when the measures in progress for obtaining subscriptions, were, by the arrangements made, to have become general throughout the union, the legacy of the late Mr. Sherred, for the advancement of theological learning, became known to the public. This circumstance has had the effect of suspending all further efforts till the intention of the General Convention in relation to it, shall be expressed. What has already been done in the several dioceses, may be estimated from the following view.

SOUTH CAROLINA.

This diocess took an early interest in the cause of a general Theological Seminary, and gave a proof of that interest in the liberal subscriptions obtained there, in the year 1818. The sum of $1675, of this subscription, remained due when the institution was removed from New York to New Haven. This sum, (with the exception of $25,) the agent there informs the trustees will be collected without difficulty. Two hundred and ten dollars has already been added by new subscribers, and of the whole sum, $710 has already been collected and forwarded to the treasurer. The ladies of South Carolina have also raised a further sum of $2000, for the purpose of founding a *scholarship*, to take the name of the late bishop of that diocess.

The friends of the institution have thought it best to defer any further, or general effort, to obtain subcriptions till the ensuing winter.

NORTH CAROLINA.

North Carolina, which has but within a few years assumed the rank of a diocess, has manifested a distinguished zeal and liberality in the cause of the seminary. Nearly $10,000 has already been subscribed in this diocess, towards the endowment of a professorship. The subscriptions are payable in five annual instalments, commencing the first of May last, with the condition that till the whole sum is subscribed, the interest of the monies in the hands of the trustees of the fund shall be devoted to the support of necessitous students in the seminary. The principal agent in procuring these subscriptions assures the board of trustees, that he has the fullest confidence that the remainder of the sum necessary to constitute the professorship, will be subscribed within a reasonable period.

VIRGINIA.

In the year 1818 there were subscriptions obtained in this diocess, for the general seminary, to the amount of more than $1400; about 1200 of which remained unpaid when the institution was transferred to New Haven. During the last winter an agent was appointed to visit this state, for the purpose of collecting these subscriptions, and soliciting further patronage, but the depression of the times deterred him from prosecuting his object. He collected little more than $100 of the former subscriptions, and obtained other subscriptions to the amount of about $300, cheifly in the District of Columbia.

MARYLAND.

A public meeting of the Episcopalians was called at Baltimore, in this diocess, in January last, by the trustees residing there. The bishop presided, and warmly recommended the seminary to the patronage of his diocess. The subject was taken up with much zeal, and a board of agents was appointed from among the most respectable citizens. But before the time appointed for commencing the subscriptions, the bequest of the late Mr. Sherred became known, and it was determined to postpone the collections to the present autumn. The liberal spirit with which the subject has been met in this diocess, affords a pledge that whenever the subscription books shall be opened there, no reasonable expectations of the church will be disappointed.

PENNSYLVANIA.

A meeting of the friends of the seminary has also taken place at Philadelphia, previous to the meeting at Baltimore, on the call of the bishop and other trustees residing in Pennsylvania. A board of agents was appointed, which was subsequently divided into four committees, for the purpose of soliciting subscriptions. Only one of these committees has yet acted to any extent: the others thought it expedient to defer acting till the present autumn. The sum actually obtained by this board is understood to be about 1260 dollars. The ladies of Philadelphia took an early interest in the prosperity of the seminary, and originated a subscription for the purpose of founding a *scholarship*, to take the name of the present venerable bishop of the diocess. More than $1800 were raised and invested for this object some months ago, and it is understood that nearly the whole amount is now raised.

NEW JERSEY.

No efforts have yet been made to obtain subscriptions in this diocess. One gentleman has manifested his good will towards the seminary by a donation of $20, and another has contributed ten dollars.

NEW YORK.

A board of agents has been constitutnd in this diocess, but owing to peculiar circumstances, they have not yet thought it expedient to make any considerable effort to obtain subscriptions. For themselves, they have subscribed with great liberality, and they have collected a few subscriptions from their friends—chiefly among those who had subscribed while the institution was at New York. In this way, upwards of $3,200 have been obtained, exclusive of 1175 dollars subscribed out of the city; the greater part of which has been paid directly to the treasurer. Several gentlemen in this diocess have contributed liberally towards the establishment of a theological library; and the value of the books transmitted from the city of New York, cannot be estimated at less than $3,000.

CONNECTICUT.

Arrangements have been commenced in this diocess to endow a professorship, to take the name of the first bishop of the diocess. Agents were appointed to collect subscriptions for this object, during the last winter, but owing to the indisposition of one of them, and sickness in the family of another, the business was delayed till spring. When this period arrived, the fact of Mr. Sherred's bequest became public, and it was thought propper under such circumstances, to defer collections till the intention of the General Convention should be declared. One gentleman had subscribed $1000 towards the professorship, and aided in obtaining about 700 dollars more in his immediate vicinity. Four other gentlemen had tendered 500 dollars each. From the knowledge which the committee possess, they feel confident in assuring the convention that if the institution should remain where it now is, the sum necessary to constitute the professorship will be made up in this diocess, within a reasonable period.

MASSACHUSETTS.

An agent was appointed to visit Boston during the last spring, who obtained subscriptions there to the amount of 1815 dollars —1715 dollars of which have been paid. Besides this sum, a generous individual made a proffer of 1500 dollars—the interest to be paid semi-annually, till the donation shall be paid into the hands of the treasurer. Another individual has promised a donation of 1000 dollars. The agent being unable to prolong his stay in Boston, the business was undertaken by a committee there, but from which no report has yet been received.

No application has yet been made for subscriptions in the other parts of the eastern diocess, though assurances of patronage have been given, whenever the effort shall be made.

RECAPITULATION.

Diocesses.	*Sums promised, or subscribed since the removal.*
South Carolina, ...	$ 3,810.
North Carolina, (about) . . .	10,000.
Virginia, (about)	400.
Maryland and Delaware, no application.	

Pennsylvania, ...	3,060.
New York, ...	4,375.
New Jersey, no application. . . .	30.
Connecticut, ...	3,700.
Massachusetts, ...	4,315.
Vermont, New Hampshire, Rhode Island, and Maine, no application.	———
	29,690.
Value of the library, say	4,000.
Funds when removed, ...	3,700.
	37,390.

Only a small proportion of the above funds has yet come into the hands of the treasurer. A part has been invested by agents abroad—some remains in the hands of agents; and there must be a trifling deduction for the expenses of agents. It results, therefore, that the convention must seek for a just estimate of the funds of the institution in the foregoing statement at large, and not in the account of the treasurer. The following report of his receipts and expenditures was presented to the board of trustees, at their annual meeting in July last.

"A summary statement of the receipts and expenditures of the treasurer of the Episcopal Theological Seminary, from Sept. 8, 1820, to July 26, 1821.

Amount received applicable to current expenses; consisting of sundry subscriptions, interest and dividends on stock, ...	$2435.15
Amount received on account of Massachusetts Professorship, ...	800.00
Do. Do. Do. Seabury Professorship,	110.00
	$3345.15

DISBURSEMENTS—VIZ.

Paid Rev. Dr. Jarvis balance of salary, . . .	1000.00
Professer Turner on account of salary, .	900.00
Sundry bills for rent of rooms, furniture, stationery, printing, &c	351.74
For ten shares Eagle Bank, ...	1000.00
Balance in treasury, ...	93.41
	$3345.15

Of the aforesaid balance there is applicable to

current expenses,	83.41
Seabury Professorship,	10.00
	$93.41

Of the aforesaid 10 shares in Eagle Bank,

8 belong to the Massachusetts Professorship,	800.00
1 Seabury Professorship,	100.00
1 General Fund,	100.00
	$1000.00

New Haven, July 26, 1821.

(Signed,) CHARLES DENNISON, *Treasurer*."

No express provision was made by the last convention for the formation of a Theological library, but the trustees are happy to report that a valuable foundation has already been laid for one, which it is hoped may soon be commensurate with the wants of the institution. This has been chiefly effected by the liberality of a few individuals. A few books, for which there was a pressing necessity, have been purchased from the donation of a gentleman, who directed that it might be subject to such an expenditure. The library of the institution consists, at present, of more than 900 volumes—upwards of 300 of which are folios, and many of the books extremely rare and valuable. This is exclusive of a valuable collection of theological books, deposited for the use of the students, by a gentleman of Connecticut.

The legislature of Connecticut has passed an act, upon the petition of the trustees of the seminary, by which the institution is incorporated within that state, upon the same principles on which it was established by the convention, and with leave to hold funds to the amount of 200,000 dollars.

In concluding this report, the committee beg leave to express their hopes that the course which has been pursued by the board of trustees may meet the approbation of the convention, and that the progress and present state of the seminary may not be thought to have come short of the expectations which were entertained at the time of its establishment at New Haven.

BY THE COMMITTEE,

THOMAS C. BROWNELL, CHAIRMAN,

HARRY CROSWELL, Secretary.

Circular to the Bishops requesting a call of a Special Meeting of the General Convention.

New Haven, May 25th, 1821.

Right Reverend Sir,

Mr. Jacob Sherred, late of the city of New York, died in March 1821, leaving by his will, dated the 28th of January 1820, to his executors, the Rev. John Cornelison, George Arcularius, and Jacob Lorillard, the residuum of his estate, after the payment of certain legacies, in trust for purposes which will appear from the following extract:

"Item,—I give and bequeath unto my sister Elizabeth, the sum of ten thousand dollars of lawful money aforesaid, and in case my sister Elizabeth should not be living at my decease, then I give and bequeath the aforesaid legacy or sum of ten thousand dollars to the children or child of my said sister Elizabeth, living at my decease if any there shall be; to be equally divided among them, share and share alike, if more than one, and if but one child of my said sister Elizabeth shall be living at my decease, then the whole of the said legacy or sum of ten thousand dollars, to go to such child, to whom I give and bequeath the same accordingly. But insomuch as I am ignorant whether my said sister Elizabeth is now living, and whether she hath, or hath not, left any children or child now living, not having heard from or of her in many years, and being ignorant of her place of residence, *my will is that unless the said legacy shall be claimed of my said Executors, by the said legatee or legatees, within the period or space of five years from and next immediately after my decease, the said legacy shall lapse,* and I do hereby absolutely revoke the same; and *the said sum of ten thousand dollars, together with any accumulation thereof as hereinafter mentioned, shall be subject to the residuary bequest hereinafter by me made.* And I do hereby order and direct my said executors, as soon as conveniently may be after my decease, to place at interest in there own name upon real security, or invest in the purchase of six per cent. or other public stocks of the United States, or of the state of New York, or the stock or stocks of banking or other incorporated companies, at their discretion, the aforesaid sum of ten thousand dollars, if the same shall not then yet be claimed by the aforesaid legatee or legatees, and in like manner, from time to time to invest or place at interest in like stock or securites, the interest or dividends of such stock or securites, in or upon which the said capital sum shall be so invested, until the said legacy shall be claimed by the said legatee or legatees as aforesaid, or until the expiration of the said period of five years from and next immediately after my decease as aforesaid, whichever shall first happen, so as to produce as great an accumulation of capital, as reasonably may be in the nature of compound interest, and if the said legacy shall be claimed by the said legatee or legatees within the said period of five years as aforesaid, then the same, together with such accumulation thereof shall be paid or transferred to such legatee or legatees as aforesaid, and if the same shall not be claimed, by the said legatee or legatees within such period as aforesaid, then *the same, together with such accumulation thereof shall sink into and become part of my residuary estate, and shall go and be applied, according to the disposition hereinafter by me made of the same.* And as to all the rest, residue and remainder of my personal estate and effects, not otherwise disposed of by this my will, I give and bequeath the same, and every part thereof unto my said executors, their executors administrators and assigns, upon the trusts, and for the intents and purposes herein after expressed and declared of and concerning the same; that is to say, upon trust that they do and shall place the same to interest upon real security, or invest the same in the purchase of six per cent. or other public stock of the United States or of the state of New York, or in the stock or stocks of banking or other incorporated companies at their discretion, and that they do and shall in like manner from time to time invest or place at interest in like stocks or securities, the interests or dividends arising thereon, so as to produce as great an accumulation of capital, as reasonably may be in the nature of compound interest *until there shall be established within the state of New York, under the direction, or by the authority of the General Convention of the Protestant Episcopal Church in the United States of America, or of the Convention of the Protestant Episcopal Church in the state of New York, a college, academy, school or seminary, for the education of young men designed for holy orders in the Protestant Episcopal Church in the United States of America,* and upon such college, academy, school or seminary being so established then upon further trust, that they do and shall pay or transfer all such stock or securities to the trustees, directors or managers, for the time being of such college, academy, school or seminary, or their treasurer or other officer thereto authorized for the use and purposes of such college, academy, school or seminary, and for which the receipt of any three or more of such trustees, directors, or managers as my said executors shall in their discretion deem it expedient to require, or of such treasurer or other officer thereto authorized, shall be a sufficient discharge to my executors. Provided always, and my will is, and I do hereby declare that it shall and may be lawful to and for my said executors from time to time at their discretion, to call in the amount of, and to sell and transfer all or any such stocks or securities wherein or upon which the before mentioned legacies or bequests any or either of them shall be placed out or invested in pursuance of this my will or any part thereof respectively and again to place at interest or invest the same in other securities or stocks, as aforesaid, to vary, alter or transpose all or any such stocks or securities when, where and so often as it shall by them be deemed expedient so to do. And that they or any of them shall not be answerable or accountable for the insufficiency or deficiency of any such stocks or securities."

The amount of this residuary bequest, exclusive of the ten thousand dollars which may at the expiration of five years lapse and become a further endowment, is estimated at not less than seventy thousand dollars.

As soon as the conditions of this will were made known, the trustees of the General Theological Seminary resident in New York, in connexion with the agents appointed in that city for the purpose of obtaining subscriptions to the funds of the institution, deemed it their duty to take immediate measures to ascertain whether it was the intention of the testator to endow the institution with which they were connected. They accordingly sent exemplifications of the will to gentlemen learned in the law in various parts of the United States, requesting them to give their opinions on the matters at issue. A request was also made to the bishop of Connecticut by the three Trustees, that he would summon a special meeting of the board for the purpose of receiving and comparing such opinions and taking such proper measures, as were or might be suggested by the same, in order to secure the bequest to the General Seminary. The Trustees have accordingly met, and have received the opinions, some written and some verbal, of many of the most distinguished jurists in the United States.

The two questions which are chiefly to be considered, are, First, whether a Seminary to be established within the state of New York, by the General Convention, will be entitled to the bequest, *in preference* to a Seminary established by the Convention of the state of New York; and if so, Secondly, what measures the General Convention ought to adopt to secure the bequest to its own Seminary.

Two constructions of the will are contended for. One is that the testator intended his bounty for a Seminary to be established within the state of New York, by the authority and under the direction of the General Convention; and that *in default* of that Convention to establish and assume the direction of such a seminary, then that it should go to a Seminary there to be established, by the authority and under the direction of the Convention of the state of New York. The other construction is that the testator intended the bequest for the Seminary which should be *first established* within the state of New York by the authority and under the direction of either Convention, whichever it might be that should first make the establishment.

The most obvious reasons assigned for the first construction are that the General Convention is first named, and may therefore reasonably be presumed to have been first and principally in the mind of the testator. The General Convention is the superior body, whose duty it is to prescribe the course of education and the qualifications of candidates for holy orders, and may well be supposed to have possessed the greatest share of the testator's confidence. A donation in trust to the superior body is more likely to be in accordance with the views and considerations which commonly influence donors than one to the inferior body. Any other construction leaves the testator's intention entirely doubtful on this point, and it is not probable that he named the two bodies, one of which was to establish and superintend the charity without intending a preference of one over the other.

On the other hand, it is contended, that the naming of the General Convention first does not denote a preference, because where two objects are mentioned for which there is no common term, one must necessarily be named before the other. The language also of the will is that the executors are to retain the fund in their hands and to reinvest the interest, etc., "*until* there shall be established under the authority of the General Convention, *or* of the State Convention, a College or Seminary, etc., and *upon* such College or Seminary being established, *then* to pay over to its Trustees." The literal meaning, it is contended, of such language is, that whichever Convention should first establish a seminary conformable to the description in the will, acquires a right to the legacy which cannot be taken away by the subsequent establishment of another. To this it is replied that from the very terms of the bequest it evidently appears that the Testator was in no hurry to establish a Seminary, since he speaks not only of an accumulation of interest, while the property continues in the hands of the executors, but also of an accumulation in the rate of compound interest, which implies its continuance in their hands at least two years after it is vested in the manner required by the testator. And further it cannot reasonably be supposed that one who was so well known to love the prosperity and peace of the Church meant to hold out his bequest as an invitation to the two Conventions to run a race, or enter into any contest, for the priority.

If a Seminary established by the General Convention within the state of New York be in equity entitled to the bequest, the second question which remains to be considered respects the measures to be adopted in order to secure it; Whether it be necessary or expedient to call a special meeting of the General Convention as soon as may conveniently be done.

As to the necessity of this measure, there is some diversity of opinion, among those who advocate the rights of the General Convention. Some are of opinion that the right will not lapse, unless the Convention at their next regular triennial meeting, should neglect to act upon the bequest; others on the contrary, think that the Convention is bound to assemble as soon as can conveniently be done.

But though there is a diversity of opinion as to the necessity of the measure of calling a special meeting of the General Convention, with regard to its expediency there seems to be little or no doubt. Some express themselves in stronger language than others; but most, if not all agree that a special meeting should immediately be called, and a Theological Seminary established under its direction and authority within the state of New York. This opinion has been greatly strengthened in the view of the Trustees, by the consideration that the interests of the present General Seminary, as well as those of all other parties concerned, require as speedy a decision of the question as possible. The exertions which have hitherto been made with considerable success for increasing the funds of the Institution are now paralyzed, and must continue to be so, till it is known what course the General Convention will pursue. The Trustees therefore have felt it to be their duty, a duty which they owe to the Seminary of which they are the guardians, a duty which they owe to their Brethren, to the Convention, and to the Church at large, to suggest the propriety of calling a special meeting of the General Convention in the manner prescribed by the 42d Canon, and as soon as can conveniently be done. In consequence of this conviction they have passed the following resolution, which they have directed us to transmit to you, with the present circular.

"Resolved,—That in the opinion of the Board of Trustees it

is expedient that a special meeting of the General Convention be called for the purpose of ascertaining whether any, and what measures shall be taken in relation to the bequest of the late Jacob Sherred, Esq."

T. C. BROWNELL,
CHAIRMAN.

HARRY CROSWELL, Secretary.

*** It being the opinion of Counsel that the requisition of the several Bishops for the call of a special meeting of the General Convention should be uniform and should state the special object of such meeting, and that they should be preserved in the archives of the General Convention, therefore

Resolved,—That the following form of a requisition be respectfully proposed to each of said Bishops as that which may be proper to send for the aforesaid purpose.

[DATE]

To the Rt. Rev. William White, D. D., presiding Bishop of the Protestant Episcopal Church of the United States,

RT. REVEREND SIR,

In consequence of a communication received by me from the Board of Trustees of the Theological Seminary of our Church, agreed to at a meeting of that body held at New Haven on the 24th and 25th days of May last, I have deemed it proper to request that a special meeting of the General Convention of the Protestant Episcopal Church in the United States may be called agreeably to the Forty-Second Canon of said Ch rch; and that such special meeting be held at Philadelphia, at as early a period as may be practicable, for the purpose of taking into consideration the last Will and Testament of Jacob Sherred, Esq., and determining whether any, and what measures should be taken for the purpose of obtaining the legacy bequeathed by him for the purpose of educating Candidates for Holy Orders in said Church.

NO. II.

THE REPORT OF THE PRESIDING BISHOP, ON CERTAIN MATTERS REFERED TO HIM BY THE LAST GENERAL CONVENTION, TO TAKE ORDER.

The house of clerical and lay deputies of the last General Convention, having requested of the house of Bishops "to take measures for making known any errors or omissions in the octavo edition of the Book of Common Prayer, published by Hugh Gaine, in 1793, which was established by the 43d Canon as the standard book, so that they may be avoided or supplied in future editions; and that they be also respectfully requested to correct and supply any errors or omissions in the calendar and tables prefixed thereto, and to extend the Table of the days on which Easter will fall for two cycles of the moon from the year of our Lord 1823 [erroneously in the printed journal 1813.]"

And the house of Bishops having requested the presiding Bishop, with such persons as he may think proper to associate with him, to take order on the said subject;

The presiding Bishop respectfully reports to the house of Bishops, as follows:

1st. He has carefully prepared and appends to this report a table for finding Easter extended through two cycles of the moon, from 1824 to 1861 inclusive.

2d. In the 3d paragraph of the first of the tables for finding the holidays, to "1799," he has inserted 1899, omitting "and also the number 1." Consequently the 4th paragraph has been omitted.

3d. In the table of fasts," he has changed "the season of lent" to "the forty days of lent." The corrected error was not begun in Gaine's book, but may be found in that published by Hall & Sellers, in 1790, under the direction of a committee of the convention of 1789. In the proposed book, published by them, it was agreeable to the English editions. The error must have been an oversight of the committee, and makes an inconsistency of the table of fasts with that of feasts: the latter comprehending the Sundays in lent, agreeably to the practice of the Christian Church in all ages.

4th. It was stated to the reporter by a member of the late and of the present convention [Wm. Meredith, Esq.] that in all our Prayer Books there was the omission of a note found in the English books, underneath the months of March and April, in the calendar, intended to show the use of the golden numbers, in a column attached to the said months only. On investigating the subject, we found that the note was wanting in Prayer Books edited before the adoption of the Gregorian style in 1751, but was found in all the succeeding editions consulted. From these circumstances it seems probable, that in making out the calendar for the American Church, there was taken a book prior to the said date. The column, with the golden numbers, may have been called for at the crisis of the change of style; but, as it is insufficient for the finding of Easter, from its not showing how the golden numbers are to be found; and as this, with the whole process for the finding of the said festival, is provided for by a table appropriated to that object; it was thought proper to omit the column and the figures included in it.

5th. In ascertaining errors in Mr. Hugh Gaine's book of 1793, your reporter has been kindly assisted by Mr. Wm. Hall, who printed the proposed book in 1785 & 6. He has furnished the list of errors appended to this report, besides noting various places, in which the sense may suffer from the want of stops, or from their being injudiciously placed.

6th. In addition to sundry errors in editions proposed to be made according to H. Gaine's book, some of the editions have framed the tables of contents, according to their respective judgments, and not according to the standard, which ends with "The Psalter, or Psalms of David," not including the metre Psalms. It must be evident, that the comprehending of any document under the same cover with the Book of Common Prayer, does not constitute it a part thereof, although set forth under the same authority. As much misunderstanding and inconvenience may arise from the misnomers stated, the matter is noticed, with the hope of its being a caution against the like mistake in future.

7th. In consequence of information received of several editions now proceeding from presses, it has been thought proper to communicate to the printers what the reporter has done, under the authority given to him to take order.

He concludes with submitting to the house the propriety of establishing a standard book, to supercede that of H. Gaine, of which the known copies are very few. In the event of such a measure, he proposes to the house, that an edition be taken from the stereotype plates, belonging to the Common Prayer Book Society of Pennsylvania. A committee to be appointed by both houses, to act during the recess, for the accomplishing of this object.

WM. WHITE, Pres. Bp.

A TABLE

Of the Days on which Easter will fall for 38 years, being the Time of two Cycles of the Moon.

Year of our Lord.	Golden Number.	Epact	Sunday Letter.	Easter Day.
1824	1	0	DC	April 18
5	2	11	B	3
6	3	22	A	March 26
7	4	3	G	April 15
8	5	14	FE	6
9	6	25	D	19
30	7	6	C	11
1	8	17	B	3
2	9	28	AG	22
3	10	9	F	7
4	11	20	E	March 30
5	12	1	D	April 19
6	13	12	CB	3
7	14	23	A	March 26
8	15	4	G	April 15
9	16	15	F	March 31
40	17	26	ED	April 19
1	18	7	C	11
2	19	18	B	March 27
3	1	0	A	16
4	2	11	GF	April 7
5	3	22	E	March 23
6	4	3	D	April 12
7	5	14	C	4
8	6	25	BA	23
9	7	6	G	8
50	8	17	F	March 31
1	9	28	E	April 20
2	10	9	DC	11
3	11	20	B	March 27
4	12	1	A	April 16
5	13	12	G	8
6	14	23	FE	March 23
7	15	4	D	April 12
8	16	15	C	4
9	17	26	B	24
60	18	7	AG	8
1	19	18	F	March 31

CORRECTIONS OF H. GAINE'S BOOK.

Contents, 2d column, last line, for instrustion—instruction.

Prayers, &c., Prayer in Time of Dearth and Famine, after "behold," for "We"—"we."

Collects, &c., 1st in Advent, for "ought"—"aught."

Wednesday before Easter 7th column, 5th and 4th line from bottom, for "ye"—"you."

Thursday before Easter, for "to day"—"to-day."

Tuesday in Easter week, for "witensses"—"witnesses."

4th Sunday of Easter, Gospel, line 3, for "him"—"me."

St. John the Evangelist, Epistle, line 21, for "by"—"be."

St. John Baptist, Epistle, line 3, before "loved"—"have."

Psalm 18. 10, for "road"—"rode."
" 33. 8, for "goldly"—"godly."
" 44. 1, for " ast"—"cast."
" 45. 17, for "in stead"—"instead."
" 47. 5, before "let"—"yea."
" 74. 16, for "rocks"—"rock."
" 78. 15, for "day time"—"daytime."
" 78. 71, for "choose"—"chose."
" 90. 5, for "a sleep"—"asleep."
" 144. 4, for "nought"—"naught."
" 147. 14, before "flour"—"the."

NO. III.

The presiding Bishop reports to the House of Bishops, in reference to the society for foreign and domestic missions, instituted at the last General Convention, that owing, as he supposes, to the state in which the business of that body was concluded, neither were the intended managers constitutionally chosen, nor had any bishop a right to a seat or a vote at their board: although doubtless, the contrary was supposed to have been provided for by the Convention generally.

The intended managers perceived these defects, and have not carried the design into effect. They have reported their proceedings to the house of clerical and lay deputies; and the presiding Bishop judges it to be sufficient to refer this house to their report.

To the house of clerical and lay deputies, of the General Convention, of the Protestant Episcopal Church, in the United States of America.

THE MANAGERS OF THE MISSIONARY SOCIETY

RESPECTFULLY REPORT,

That soon after the adjournment of the last General Convention, they proceeded to organize themselves, as a board for the transaction of business. At this time it was discovered with regret, that although the constitution, intended for the government of the Missionary Society, provided, that the presiding Bishop of the Church should be its president, and the other Bishops vice presidents, in the order of seniority, yet no provision had been made, by which the Bishops were authorized, either to sit, or vote, with the board of managers. This circumstance could only be regarded as an oversight, unintended on the part of the house of clerical and lay deputies, and overlooked by the House of Bishops, when the constitution was before them, and received their approbation. The embarrassment of the managers in relation to this subject, was much relieved, when it was ascertained, that the presiding Bishop, viewed the subject in the same light, and that he was willing to sit with the board, and preside at its meetings.

Among the first acts of the managers, after they began to execute the highly responsible trust reposed in them, was to announce the formation of the society, to those institutions in England, belonging to our own Church, which are employed in different ways in promoting the interest of the Redeemer's kingdom. Letters were written to the secretaries of the three following societies. "The Society for propagating the Gospel in foreign parts." "The Society for promoting Christian knowledge." "And the Church Missionary Society." Answers have been received, from the Rev. Anthony Hamilton, secretary of the Society for propagating the Gospel in foreign parts, and from the Rev. Josiah Pratt, secretary of the Church Missionary Society. Both of the Rev. Gentlemen, in behalf of the societies which they represent, express great satisfaction in the establishment of a society, for missionary purposes in the American branch of the Episcopal Church. Accompanying the letter of the Rev. Mr. Hamilton, the six last reports of the society, of which he is the secretary, were received. And at different times, several packages, have come to hand, from the

Church Missionary Society, containing their reports, Missionary Registers, and other publications calculated to give information upon the subject of Missions. In one of these parcels were contained several complete sets of the Reports of the Society, and of the Missionary Register, from the commencement of its publication, intended for the use of the Bishops in the United States, which have been forwarded to them accordingly. It will no doubt be gratifying to the Convention, as it was to the managers to learn, that the last mentioned society, as an evidence of its good wishes, for our success, has voted an appropriation of two hundred pounds sterling (supposing the society here to be in operation)which awaits the order of those, who may be authorized to receive it. As these letters may be interesting to the Convention, they are herewith submitted.

At an early period, the managers appointed a committee, to devise a plan by which, the designs of the convention, might most effectually be attained. After due deliberation upon the subject, it was thought advisable to prepare an address, to the members of the Church, informing them of the measures, which had been adopted; urging by suitable considerations the important duty of sending the gospel to the destitute, and requesting their co-operation, by the formation of auxiliary societies and associations. Such an address was prepared, and printed in one or two periodical publications, when it was discovered, that by reason of an informality in the mode of our appointment, we had been acting without authority. The informality referred to, will be perceived, upon refering to the Journal of the last Convention.

When this circumstance was known, the managers were at a loss, to determine whether, they should continue to act, under an informal appointment, or suspend all further proceedings—To pursue the one course might subject them to censure, to adopt the other, seemed like abandoning an object, in which they believed, the members of the Church felt much interested. At this time letters were written, to the Rt. Rev. the Bishops, requesting their opinion upon the subject. Answers were received from all except the Bishop of New York. Some of them were decidedly in favour of our proceeding, while a majority thought it in-expedient; this decided the matter, and all thought of continuing to act as a board, under the authority of the Convention, was given up.

Under the circumstances above described, the managers would probably have stayed all further proceedings, had not an idea been suggested, which appeared to promise a happier result—It was thought that if the members of the board would consent to form themselves, into an association and could obtain the sanction of the Bishops, they might at least make some preparation for their more efficient action, at a future day. Letters were accordingly written to the absent members of the board, all of whom except judge Washington, readily consented to the proposition, and he requested that if the unanimous consent of the board of managers, was deemed essential, that his might be considered as given. Nothing now seemed wanting but the approbation of the Rt. Rev. the Bishops, to the proposed plan. They were written to with a view of obtaining it, but in this the managers were not successful. From this time the board have not met, until within a few days, when they were called together, to prepare this their report, all of which is respectfully submitted to the house of clerical and lay deputies, in Convention assembled.

JOHN READ, PRESIDENT.

R. S. SMITH, Secretary.
Philadelphia, October 30th 1821.

TO THE REV. GEORGE BOYD.

Church Missionary House.
London, Sept. 21st 1820.

DEAR SIR,

I feel much satisfaction in acknowledging your letter of the 9th ultimo, and a copy of the Journal of the General Convention of the American Church.

"Our committee cordially rejoice in the formation of the Protestant Episcopal Society in the United States for Domestic and foreign Missions." They accept with pleasure your invitation to carry on a correspondence and interchange of publications with you. Feeling as we do the extent and arduousness of the work in which we are engaged, to extend the blessings of the Gospel to a world that lieth in error and in sin, we hail with gratitude every auxiliary which comes forward to take part in it. It is, however, with peculiar feelings of satisfaction that we witness the Protestant Episcopal Church in the United States embodying itself into a society, for the purpose of concentrating its strength and rendering its exertions more efficient in this Holy Cause. Though we wish well to the labours of other bodies of Christians to extend the Redeemer's Kingdom; yet, as Episcopalians, we especially rejoice in the prospect of seeing the Churches gathered from among the Heathen settled on those foundations, which, we are persuaded, are at once more scriptural and better suited to promote the best interests of mankind.

In testimony of our disposition to impart to your Society all the missionary information in our power, we are preparing a package of our publications for your use. One parcel is addressed to each of the Bishops, which the committee request their acceptance of; and the remainder we place at the disposal of the Managers of the Society to be made use of in such manner as they deem most subservient to its interests.

Copies of a work containing a summary view of the Society for the propagation of the Gospel in foreign parts are also sent; as it supplies most conclusive and eloquent arguments in behalf of missions, from authorities which members of an Episcopal Church will be likely to respect. It was compiled by me, chiefly from documents in the library of our own Society; and we were glad of the opportunity of putting forth a work which might serve the Society in its collections throughout the Kingdom, and at the same time testify our respect and regard to the elder body among us.

We have received the Episcopal Magazine of the United States from January to April inclusive, and shall be thankful for the numbers in continuation.

A single pamphlet forwarded through the post office, so done up that the parcel is open at the ends, will not be subjected to the full postage. I mention this circumstance, as we have been subject to very heavy charges at the post office, in consequence of our friends in America not being aware of it.

I remain, Dear Sir,
with much respect,
ever faithfully yours,
JOSIAH PRATT.

P. S. I should have stated above, that any number of the "Quarterly papers" may be obtained of Mr. Seeley, No 169 Fleet Street, should you wish for more than we have forwarded to you. I would just add, that when your Society comes into active operation, you will, probably, find it advantageous yourselves to prepare and put forth some such paper.

Rev. Sir,

I am instructed by the Society for the propagation of the Gospel in foreign parts to acknowledge the receipt of your letter announcing the foundation of the Protestant Episcopal Missionary Society in the United States.—The board are anxious to express their earnest wishes for the success of your Society in their laudable endeavours; and to invite further communications as opportunities may present themselves. They beg you to accept for the use of the Protestant Episcopal Missionary Society in the United States copies of their six last reports, with an assurance of the satisfaction they have derived from your important communication.

I am Rev. Sir,
Your obedient servant
Anthony Hamilton,
Secretary of the Society, P. G. F.
No 42 Castle Street, Leicester Square.
November 23d 1820.

To the Rev. George Boyd.

Church Missionary House,
London, July 10th, 1821.

Dear Sir,

Bishop Griswold having suggested to me in a letter under date of the 16th November last, but which did not reach me till 12th ultimo, that the Protestant Episcopal Missionary Society in the United States for foreign and domestic missions, is desirous to avail itself of the offer, conveyed in a letter of mine to the Bishop under date of July 31st, 1817, to afford pecuniary aid to such an Institution on its formation, the Bishop's letter was laid before our committee yesterday; and they came to a unanimous resolution to grant £ 200 sterling to the Institution for its establishment.

You will, therefore, have the kindness to inform the Directors of the Society that that sum awaits their appropriation, at such period and in such manner as they may deem expedient.

I have much pleasure in making this communication, and in assuring you of the cordial satisfaction felt by our committee in thus co-operating with their Episcopal Brethren in the United States, in promoting the extension of the Redeemer's Kingdom among the Heathen.

We hope you receive our registers and other publications regularly. They are forwarded monthly to your address, through Messrs. Morrall and Watson, Liverpool.

We shall at all times be glad to hear of the plans and operations of your Society.

I remain, Dear Sir,
faithfully yours,
JOSIAH PRATT.

NO. IV.

CONCERNING THE LAST RUBRIC IN THE COMMUNION SERVICE.

The House of Bishops being informed of what they consider as a great misunderstanding, in various places, of the rubric at the end of the communion service, think it their duty to declare their sense of the same, and to communicate it to the House of Clerical and Lay Deputies.

In the Common Prayer Book of the church of England, the words in the parenthesis are—"if there be no communion." In the review of 1789, it was put—"if there be no sermon or communion"—and this has been interpreted to mean, that if there be a sermon, what has been called the ante-communion service is to be omitted—Against this construction the Bishops object as follows—

1st. The construction rests on inference; deduced in contrariety to the positive direction—"Then shall follow the sermon." Had an exception been intended, it would doubtless have been expressed positively, as in other rubrics. Further; the rubric in question prescribes, that "when there is a communion, the minister shall return to the Lord's table:" which presumes him to have been there before, in the ante-communion service, unless in the permitted alternative of some other place.

2d. The argument on the other side proves too much, and therefore nothing. It is said of those who urge it, that they conceive themselves bound to use the whole service on a communion day: whereas it should be dispensed with, on the same principle on which it is supposed to be superseded by the sermon. On the other hand, if there being either a sermon or the communion should be thought to warrant the omission; can it be, that the convention designed to leave in the book the ante-communion service, with all the collects, the gospels, and the epistles attached to them, to be little more than a dead letter; never to be used, except on the few occasions, when the said service is unconnected with either of the said provisions? For, it is not required to be used, either with the morning or with the evening prayer.

3d. There is a rubric, prescribing the place in the service, at which notice shall be given of holidays, &c. Can it be supposed, that a provision of this sort, was intended to be done away, not professedly, but indirectly? and that even there should be no provision for notifying the communion?

4th. It is understood, that the morning prayer, and the administration, of the communion were designed to be distinct services, to be used at different times of the day. Probably, at the time of the reformation, the practice was generally conformable to the provision; and it is said to prevail at present in some places in England. Now, although there is probably no church in the United States of which the same can be affirmed; yet, why raise a bar against so reasonable and so godly a practice? an effort for which, would reduce the whole to the sermon; except, when the communion were to be administered: and then, there would be the latter part of the service only.

5th. The construction casts a blemish on the observance of every festival of our church. To speak in particular of Easter Sunday, Whitsunday, and Christmas day: can it be supposed, that the convention intended to abrogate the reading of the portions of scripture, the most pertinent of any in the Bible? or that the members of the body were so careless, as not to perceive the effect of the word introduced by them into the parenthesis? Neither of these was the case; although they had not the sagacity to foresee the use which would be made of their superaddition: a use, which may be applied hereafter to the abandoning of the observance of those festivals. For why should the church retain them, after dispensing with whatever is attached to them in the respective services. The remark applies equally to the two days of fasting or abstinence—Good Friday and Ash Wednesday. It is here supposed, that on the former, there are the service and sermons in all our churches furnished with the ministry. But according to the opposite opinion, the sermon dispenses with the recital of the consummation of our Saviour's sufferings, and not only on Good Friday, but on every day of passion week, if there be sermons. Could this have been intended?

6th. There is the magnitude of the change thus made in the liturgy, without the subjecting of the resulting consequences to the consideration of any General Convention: for this is here affirmed, without the apprehension of contradiction from any of the surviving members. The most obvious of the consequences, and such as could not have escaped the notice of the least attentive, were, the dispensing with the reading of the Ten Commandments; the weekly return of which may well be thought to have a beneficial effect on morals; and the deranging of a selection of passages of scripture, always supposed to have been made with great judgment, and suited to the different seasons of the year. They were of like uses in the church, before the prevalence of the corruptions of the Papacy; have withstood, in some measure, its systematic hostility to a general knowledge of the scriptures; and, probably, have prevented a greater enormity of unevangelical error, than what we now find: for although the selections were in Latin, they were at least instructive to the many who understood the language, at a time when even among that description of people, the possession of a Bible was rare. To the present day, they are held in high esteem, not only by our parent church, but by the Lutheran churches of Sweden, of Denmark, of sundry German principalities, and of this country. In some of the European States, the subject of the sermon is expected to be taken from the epistle, or from the gospel for the Sunday. There seems no reasonable objection, in any future review of the Liturgy, to the making of some abbreviation, suited to the joining of services designed to be distinct; but there may be doubted the expediency of making so great an inroad as that projected on the service now in question.

7th. The ante-communion service continued to be used as before, by the clergy who were present in the convention, in which it is now imagined to have been dispensed with. It is confidently believed that there was not an exception of an individual; although, on the other side, the major number must be supposed to have been desirous of the innovation. In the interpretation of a law, immediate practice under it has heen held to be a good expositor: especially when, as in the present case, a contrary sense had not been heard of for a long course of years.

The question may occur—why did the convention introduce the words, "Sermon or," into the parenthesis? It was to reconcile the other rubric referred to, with frequent and allowable practice. The said rubric says—"then shall follow the sermon" Perhaps, when the service was compiled there was a sermon on every saint's day, as well as on every principal festival. In modern usage, it has been otherwise: which made it convenient to provide for the minister's proceeding to the blessing. The parenthesis means, that although there be no sermon, or although there be no communion, the minister shall act as directed by the rubric.

The bishops therefore deem it their duty to express the decided opinion, that the rubrics of the communion service as well as other general considerations enjoin the use of that part which precedes the sermon, on all occasions of sermon or communion, as well as on those festivals and fasts, when neither sermon nor communion occurs.

NO. V.

The Constitution of the Domestic and Foreign Missionary Society of the Protestant Episcopal Church, in the United States of America.

ART. I.

This institution shall be denominated the *Domestic and Foreign Missionary Society of the Protestant Episcopal Church, in the United States of America.*

ART. II.

It shall be composed of the Bishops of the Protestant Episcopal Church, and of the members of the House of Clerical and Lay Deputies of the General Convention of said Church, for the time being; and of such other persons, as shall contribute, by subscription, three dollars, or more, annually to the objects of the institution, during the continuance of such contributions; and of such as shall contribute at once thirty dollars, which contribution shall constitute them members for life.

Members who pay fifty dollars, on subscribing, shall be denominated patrons of the society.

It shall be the privilege of the subscribers, to designate, on their subscriptions, to which of the objects, domestic or foreign, they desire their contributions to be applied. If no specification be made, the board of directors, may apply them to either, or both, at their discretion.

ART. III.

The society shall meet triennially, at the place, in which the General Convention, shall hold its session. The time of meeting shall be on the first day of the session, at five o'clock, P. M.

A sermon shall be preached, and a collection made in aid of the funds of the society, at such time, during the session of the Convention, as may be determined at the annual meeting; the preacher to be appointed by the House of Bishops.

Art. IV.

The presiding Bishop of this church ahall be president of the society; the other Bishops, according to seniority, vice presidents. There shall be two secretaries, and twenty-four directors, who shall be chosen, by ballot, at each meeting.

Art. V.

The directors, together with the president, and vice presidents, and patrons of the society—who shall, ex officio, be directors—shall compose a body to be denominated the Board of Directors of the Domestic and Foreign Missionary Society of the Protestant Episcopal Church, in the United States of America. They shall meet annually in the city of Philadelphia, except in the year of the meeting of the General Convention, when they shall assemble at the place of the meeting thereof. *Nine* members of the board of directors shall be necessary to constitute a quorum to do business.

The meetings of the board of directors shall always be opened with using a form of prayer to be set forth by the House of Bishops for that purpose, or one or more suitable prayers selected from the liturgy.

Art. VI.

At the annual meetings, all missionary stations, appointments of missionaries, and appropriations of money, and all by-laws necessary for their own government, and for conducting the affairs of the missions, shall be made; provided, that all appointments of missionaries shall be with the approbation of the Bishops present. Special meetings may be called by the president, or by one of the vice presidents, as often as may be necessary to carry into effect, the resolutions adopted at the annual meetings of the board; at which special meetings, *seven* members, including the president or one of the vice presidents, shall be a quorum to transact business.

The board of directors, whether at their annual or special meetings, may appoint such committees as may be necessary or useful.

Art. VII.

There shall be annually appointed a treasurer and two members of the society, who together shall be termed trustees of the permanent fund.

The treasurer shall receive all contributions which shall be made to the society, and enter them in detail, distinguishing between what may be contributed for domestic, and what for foreign purposes, if any such distinction should be made; and present a statement of his accounts annually, or oftener, if required, to the board of directors. He shall not pay monies unless on an order from the board, signed by the president, or in his absence, by the senior vice president, who may attend the meeting, when such order is given.

Twenty per cent of all monies, which shall be contributed, to carry into effect the objects of the institution, shall be vested by the trustees, in their own name, as officers of the society, in some safe and productive stock, to constitute a permanent fund. The residue of the contributions, with the interest arising from the permanent fund, shall be appropriated to the objects, for which the society was formed.

Art. VIII.

The board of directors, at their annual meetings, shall take such measures as they may deem proper, to establish auxiliary societies in any diocess, with the advice and consent of the Bishop of the same; to secure patronage, and to enlarge the funds of the institution. The Bishop of every diocess shall be president of the auxiliary societies organized within it.

Art. IX.

In any diocess where there is a Bishop or an ecclesiastical body duly constituted under the authority of the convention of the same for missionary purposes, aid may be given in money; but the appointment of the missionary shall rest with the Bishop or ecclesiastical body aforesaid. He shall act under their direction; and shall render to them a report of his proceedings, copies of which shall be forwarded to this society.

Art. X.

The board of directors shall, at every meeting of the society, present a detailed report of their proceedings; which if approved and adopted by the society, shall, on the next day, be presented by their president, to the General Convention, as the report of the society.

ART. XI.

The present convention shall elect, by ballot, the twenty-four directors and two secretaries, provided for, by the 4th article, to act till the first stated meeting of the society; and the first meeting of the board of directors shall take place at Philadelphia, on the third Wednesday in November instant.

ART. XII.

It is recommended to every member of this society, to pray to Almighty God, for his blessing upon its designs under the full conviction, that unless he direct us in all our doings, with his most gracious favor, and further us, with his continual help, we cannot reasonably hope, either to procure suitable persons to act as missionaries, or expect that their endeavors will be successful.

NO. VI

Canon

PASSED IN GENERAL CONVENTION, in 1821.

PROVIDING FOR A NEW, MORE COMPLETE AND CORRECT STANDARD OF THE BOOK OF COMMON PRAYER.

The edition of the Book of Common Prayer to be chosen by the committee appointed by this Convention, and authenticated by their certificate shall, after the publication thereof, be taken and received as the standard with which all new editions are thereafter to be compared, for the purpose of correction, agreeably to the xliii canon—and so much of the said canon as establishes another standard of the Book of Common Prayer, shall thereafter be and remain repealed.

Done in General Convention, in the city of Philadelphia, in the year of our Lord, 1821.

BY ORDER OF THE HOUSE OF BISHOPS:

WILLIAM WHITE,
PRESIDING BISHOP.

Attested: WM. AUGUSTUS MUHLENBERG, Secretary.

BY ORDER OF THE HOUSE OF CLERICAL AND LAY DEPUTIES.

WM. H. WILMER, PRESIDENT.

Attested: ASHBEL BALDWIN, Secretary.